# GENESIS
# OF A
# MUSIC

Danlee Mitch

HARRY PARTCH PLAYING THE CLOUD-CHAMBER BOWLS

# GENESIS OF A MUSIC

AN ACCOUNT OF A CREATIVE WORK,
ITS ROOTS AND ITS FULFILLMENTS

## HARRY PARTCH

*Second Edition*

A DACAPO PAPERBACK

Library of Congress Cataloging in Publication Data

Partch, Harry, 1901-1974.
   Genesis of a music.

   (A Da Capo paperback)
   "This Da Capo Press paperback edition . . . is an
unabridged republication of the second enlarged
edition published by Da Capo Press in New York in
1974."
   "Bibliography on Harry Partch": p.
   Bibliography: p.
   1. Vocal music—History and criticism.
2. Musical intervals and scales. 3. Musical
instruments. 4. Musical temperament. I. Title.
[ML1400.P3   1979        780'.92'4        79-12690
ISBN 0-306-80106-X pbk.

Published by Da Capo Press, Inc.
A Subsidiary of Plenum Publishing Corporation
233 Spring Street, New York, N.Y. 10013

Manufactured in the United States of America

# PREFACE TO THE SECOND EDITION

SLIGHTLY more than twenty-five years ago, in the spring of 1947, I put the final word to the final draft of *Genesis of a Music*. However, during the intervening years I have produced the major portion of my works in both music and theater, quintupling—probably—my output of 1930–1947. In that time I have also built or adapted twenty-two medium to very large new instruments, and many smaller ones; only six large instruments were depicted and explained in the 1947 work.

This second edition contains limited new material. A new preface and new Chapters 12 and 13 on instruments and notation are obviously necessary; an added Chapter 14 provides the background for six major works. As addenda there are listings of music, performances, phonograph records, films, notes on major theater works, a bibliography, and a chronology of the building of my instruments.

In the earlier preface one paragraph calls for clarification, and in Chapter 1 an idea needs explanation and omissions need to be recognized. The paragraph, the first full one on page *xviii*, has given me considerable torment. It says, briefly, that with modern technology—records—the composer might consider his work as a painter thinks of his, and that his paints and brushes (instruments and notation) may be discarded. They are no longer important.

I had no real passion for that notion then and I have none for it now. I have long believed in the Corporeal, especially in my large theater works, where the musicians in a very real sense are also actors. Why, then, did I write such words? Very realistically, I did so because of the infinite difficulty in mounting a large theater work, or any large work. Forty-five to fifty years ago, I had not heard one ensemble play the music that I had written for it, and in a kind of desperation I determined to write nothing that I could not project as actual sound. Even so, the long years of waiting until productions were possible seemed endless—seventeen in the case of *Oedipus*, beginning when I visited W. B. Yeats in Dublin in 1934, to show him my musical outline for his version of the ancient drama, and ending finally with rehearsals at Mills College in 1951.

Because of my dedication to all that goes into theater—lights, costumes, dance, movement, the physical excitement of seeing the instruments played—records have been a rather sad compromise. Still, I must stand by

that earlier preface, because the likelihood of solving the total theater problem seems today, if anything, even more distant.

The concepts of One Voice and the Corporeal (pages 7–8) have bewil-
dered not a few persons who have witnessed my large works and have found
that they cannot progress logically from the One Voice to the theatrical
spectacle.

Personally, this is not a problem. Greek drama took its original form
from religious festivals; the chorus, for example, was an ingredient, but
it took its spirit from the epic chant, or from any chant that told a story—
one voice and one instrument. Homer was reputedly a wandering singer
of stories. Some years ago I heard a man from the Balkans, in person, in
epic chant, playing a one-stringed instrument and singing stories—a direct
descendant of Homer.

I myself sang and played one instrument, often entirely alone, for some
sixteen years (1930–1947): Li Po poems, Biblical passages, hitchhiker inscriptions, and the transcontinental freight-train trip, *U.S. Highball.* Yet
the step from those somewhat less than epic presentations to the profound
Sophocles drama, *Oedipus,* was to me most logical.

In discussing the idea of a Corporeal music in Chapters 1 and 2, the
verbal concepts of several contemporary composers were examined. I realize
now that this survey was not adequate to the facts. I had largely turned my
back on anything European or European-influenced, of a contemporary
nature, and since one man cannot know of every creative effort that is happening everywhere, I prefer to leave the chapter untouched. An attempted
rectification could easily permit further omissions.

The Harmonic Canon bridge described and illustrated in Chapter 6 of
the first edition has been reluctantly abandoned in all Harmonic Canons
since the original. Its great virtue lay in the maintenance of all strings at a
constant height above the soundboard. Its fault lay in the dampening of
resonance, due to the grooves in the soundboard. I feel certain that a refinement of this idea, in imagination and construction, could preserve the virtue
and eliminate the fault.

\*      \*      \*      \*      \*

A chronology of the book itself: Before I was twenty, I had tentatively
rejected both the intonational system of modern Europe and its concert
system, although I did not realize either the ultimate scope or the conse-

quences of that rejection. In 1919, as I recall, I had virtually given up on both music schools and private teachers, and had begun to ransack public libraries, doing suggested exercises and writing music free from the infantilisms and inanities of professors as I had experienced them.

When I was twenty-one I finally found, in a library, the key for which I had been searching, the Helmholtz-Ellis work, *On the Sensations of Tone.* Under this new impetus, doubts and ideas achieved some small resolution, and I began to take wing. About 1925 I wrote a string quartet in Just Intonation and compiled a set of Just-Intonation resources soon afterward. The first draft of my book, later called *Genesis of a Music,* was written around 1927.

Further drafts piled up for the next twenty years. The second, in 1930, resulted in the first review of my work, in the New Orleans *Times-Picayune* (where I was a proofreader), in December of that year. A third followed in 1934 as the result of research at the British Museum, a fourth in 1940, at the height of what for me was the Great Depression, a fifth under a Guggenheim Fellowship in 1944, in preparation for submission to the University of Wisconsin Press, a sixth the next year under guidance of the Press, and the seventh—and finally accepted—version in 1947.

A well-known person of the nineteenth century, writing at the age of forty, remarked (in effect) that he would like to be listened to, but hoped that his readers would discount him if he were still writing at ages when the fire of youth is diminished. Now, decades after publication of the first edition, I can concur with him to a degree. If, at the present juncture, I were to see first publication of this book, I can surely say that my exposition would be different. I would indeed like to make a few changes, but I subscribe wholly to every dominant theme that I expressed in 1947. Therefore let me reassure those who prefer no diminution of "fire" that the book is an exact reprint except for the sections indicated.

\*     \*     \*     \*     \*

The earlier preface was in no way autobiographical. A few brief summaries of my life have appeared, mostly as the result of interviews, and I recall—in both interviews and personal contacts—the question, repeated literally hundreds of times, how did you ever get started?

A preface is very much like a summation (I have never known of a preface being written *before* the writing of the book it finally prefaced)—

a summation by an attorney with a client (the book) under possible sentence of death. In his summation, the attorney is allowed rather more latitude than in the examination of witnesses, which constitutes the body of his efforts. A preface is also conceived as a direct statement by author to reader, and I hope that my present readers will abide me while I offer a brief autobiography, because this is the only way I can even begin to explain how I *ever got started*. I do not claim that it presents a tough life, an exciting one (except within myself), or even a particularly unusual one. But since my musical work has been virtually my whole life, it might not be inappropriate to consider my life as a prelude to *Genesis*. These recollections are based on facts as I know them from experience, and from surmises, again from experience.

Recently, a reviewer looked over the list of my "musical influences" as I had stated them for a program—Christian hymns, Chinese lullabyes, Yaqui Indian ritual, Congo puberty ritual, Cantonese music hall, and Okies in California vineyards, among others, and remarked, as I recall, that these seemed *improbable* or *whimsical*. Yet I can document them, at least in part. My parents received the "call" (as those with missionary zeal referred to the experience) some time in the 1880's and were sent to China. Before 1900 both began to have doubts, which very soon ended in resignations. The crisis came during the Boxer Rebellion, and I was born in Oakland in the middle of 1901 soon after they returned. Because of my mother's health we moved, about two years later, to southeastern Arizona.

My father's apostasy took the direction of agnosticism, secularism, atheism—he had many of the writings of Robert Ingersoll about. But my mother could not go that route, and she took up, at various times prior to her death in 1920, Unity, Mary Baker Eddy, New Thought. For my part, I can say only that subjects of intense concern to my parents were not necessarily of intense concern to me. The reading material—Robert Ingersoll, Mary Baker Eddy, *et al.*—simply did not stack up, in excitement, beside the wild immoralities of Greek mythology, or, in adventure, with the *Anabasis* of Xenophon. In our library there were more books in Chinese, accordion folded, with ivory thongs, illustrated by gory colored lithographs of the beheading of missionaries, than there were books in English.

Hymns, with voices and an old reed organ, and Chinese tunes, sung by my mother, were a part of that Arizona experience. Into my twenties I could still sing one or two Chinese songs (in Chinese, of course), and

Chinese was occasionally spoken in our home—always when we had Mandarin-speaking visitors.

Yaqui Indians, very timid and aloof, were all about us in the declining years of the Old West. (I recall watching through a telescope "bad men" holed up in some nearby rocks, and I fear that my five-year-old sympathies were all for the hunted.) Later, when I heard the Yaqui Spring Ritual on a record, the sounds seemed amazingly familiar to me.

I began to hear music on Edison cylinder records when I was ten, but I can't recall exactly what. Later, when I knew, I reacted to certain small shafts of intense life—Hebrew chants, Chinese theater, and Congo ritual—with a kind of intimate passion. My painter friend Gordon Onslow-Ford speaks of the "delight in recognizing something never seen [heard] before," and what might be called a wide-consciousness intuition could account for some of my early beliefs or imaginings as to what I actually heard.

The small child feels that he is the center of the world, in both his joys and his disasters. It is redundant to say *the world he knows*. There is no other. And every lonely child builds worlds of his own, both with objects and in fantasy, a dozen a year, or even a dozen a day.

> Can this world
> From of old
> Always have been so sad,
> Or did it become so for the sake
> Of me alone?*

And the quality would be unchanged if other words were substituted: *Always have been so happy for the sake of me alone*.

Living just outside the tiny railroad town of Benson, Arizona, about three hundred population and with eleven saloons for transient railroaders along its board walks, we were very dependent upon mail-order articles, even including canned foods. Among items ordered were a variety of musical instruments. I recall a cello, a violin, a mandolin, a guitar, a cornet, and numerous harmonicas. These were not just passing fancies. My older sister learned to play the violin very well, and my older brother the mandolin. But I do not think that any of my family devoured as avidly as I did the *idea* of music.

*Arthur Waley. *Japanese Poetry, the 'Uta.'* Lund Humphries & Co., Ltd., London, 1946. Quoted by permission.

At that time my father was employed in the immigration service and was transferred rather frequently in the Arizona-New Mexico area, always to some railroad junction near the Mexican border. He understood Mandarin, as the immigration officials knew, of course. They may not have known that the Cantonese-speaking Chinese, who constituted the bulk of the illegal immigrants, were as incomprehensible to Mandarin speakers as Manx-speaking Gaels would be to Melanesian Islanders.

When I was fourteen, in Albuquerque, I began seriously to write music, at the same time delivering drugs on my bicycle everywhere in town (including the wide-open red-light district), hopping bells in the local Harvey House, and playing piano—including *Hearts and Flowers*—in a movie house. (One did not have to be very good in the small town that Albuquerque then was.) Interspersed at this time are recollections of my mother visiting jails, complaining loudly about their condition, and occasionally bringing a prostitute home to spend the night. (My father would bring hobos home also, but he insisted that they work. I do not recall that my mother ever demanded that the prostitutes work.)

The only other notable event within this purview was a kind of adolescent auto-da-fé—the burning of fourteen years of my music in a big iron stove—a confession, to myself, that in pursuing the respectable, the widely accepted, I had not been faithful. I say adolescent, even though I was twenty-eight at the time, because the act involved many adolescent dreams, and because I had written a large part of the music as an adolescent. The works burned were a symphonic poem, a quartet, an unfinished piano concerto, and numerous short pieces and songs. The time-span between my initial divergent gropings (mostly theoretical) to the resolution of the fire was about ten years—ten years in which I began to evolve my own direction, in reaching for a supernal freedom, while at the same time enduring a kind of anguish in abandoning all that I had struggled to learn of the old ways *(and not so old!).*

Adlai Stevenson remarked that much of life is a conspiracy against freedom. I wanted to be free, and in the tiny vortex of my being I found freedom. I can still relive the great surge of exhilaration that uplifted me on that occasion. But it is a curious fact that I destroyed nothing truly valuable to me. As late as 1960 I was still pulling out bits of ideas from that pot-bellied stove, ideas stored away in memory—that mysterious structure of cells and spirit.

Finally, to bring at least a semicolon to the personal story, when I saw, in the late twenties, that it was necessary to devise instruments of my own, I did not find it a fearful step. Until his death in 1919, my father had always maintained a small woodshop; I was familiar with common tools.

\* \* \* \* \*

I am not trying to institute a movement in any crypto-religious sense. If I were, *idea* would soon turn into something called *form*, and the world is already plagued with its ephemera. Nor is the much revered master-disciple relationship very promising, either historically or by observed example.

Originality cannot be a goal. It is simply inevitable. The truly path-breaking step can never be predicted, and certainly not by the person who makes it at the time he makes it. He clears as he goes, evolves his own techniques, devises his own tools, ignores where he must. And his path cannot be retraced, because each of us is an original being.

In the fragile moment of achievement the conditioned attitude evaporates, showing perhaps that there is, in total experience, a deep and abiding tie with peoples and animals and things removed in time and space. The adventurer will undoubtedly experience ridicule, but he is inured to danger; he was not born in the woods to get scared by an owl. To the extent that he is obliged to fly in the face of honored usages he begins to acquire, after decades of weathering, the strange patina of the recidivist, the unregenerate criminal. And envy of the criminal, which borders on a secret American nostalgia, lies—very logically—in the fact that crime is one area where individuality is taken for granted. Wrote William Bolitho: "All the poets are on one side, and all the laws on the other."

Once I had found a direction that carried an inherently compelling force, in almost total disregard for current "laws," and once I had articulated that force, in words, the actual doing became dominant, and theory was often tedious, even unimportant. When the index of doing went up, the index of theory went down, even though I look upon much of this book as a naked searching for the truth—sworn to on the Bible, on the blood of a cock, or on nothing.

Simple truth, offered through words and other symbols, is not to be confused with analysis, which may progress through various stages and end in apotheosis. The explanation *can* become the central fact, substituting for the fact and finally outliving the fact. Witness Aristotle's exposition of Greek music, still extant, while the art is long gone. Examples abound, even in contemporary endeavors. We forget the work, essentially, yet strain for an academic *explanation* of the work.

Creatively, the virtue of music schools, as presently constituted, can lie only in the possible rebellion against them. A foundation official has stated: "Under present conditions the best service you can perform for the potential artist is to throw him out." If the drive of the creative student is strong he will not have to be thrown out, because he will not be there.

Rules and standards become meaningless once the simple truth is faced. Let us give to nuts and bolts the standardization of thread that we have come to expect, but let us give to music—magic, to man—magic.

My peaks of wrath and nadirs of depression, through some four decades, were akin to the fulminations and despair of the Hebrew prophets, and for exactly the same reasons: the endowed priests of the temples sanctifying form without content, ritual without value. Hollow magic.

Indeed we have magic—pre-packaged. Not only do we find ourselves with ever more imaginative devices servicing consistently trivial distractions, but in art the searching man must humble himself before banks of highly technical equipment, and cater to those technicians and administrators who have been chosen to preside. We have usurpation by an academically incestuous elite, and the rebellion against this sort of thing constitutes a thoroughly moral stand. How can it be misunderstood?

Oliver Evans, the poet: "It is not that we are misunderstood, but that we are understood too well."

Having been *understood too well,* it is very natural that we want to go away—run away! Arthur Carson, who was about seventeen when I knew him in 1952, carries the idea to its ultimate:

> Go away run away
> Over the cloud
> And over the cliff.
> And jump into the mouth of god
> And be tasted
> And the whole thing is over
> When you flip through the air.*

*Unpublished. Quoted by permission of the author.

Time, in the moment of that *flip through the air,* is capricious to say the least—taking care of all, both the meaningful and the meaningless. Many works and ideas valuable to me, from decades to thousands of years old, have largely been ignored in my lifetime. Nevertheless, considering only what we know, the historical record that Time has spared, the material available to inspire spiritual resuscitation is truly awesome.

There is also the area that we do not know. I care even more for the divination of an ancient spirit of which I *know* nothing. To encompass—at least intuitively—thousands of years of man's sensitivity to his world is to rise above the merely encyclopedic.

During the years that have brought me past the end of my seventh decade I have witnessed at least three series of revolving Ixion-wheels, of major fashions in music: the influence of Sibelius in my teens and twenties, of Paris-trained composers in my twenties and thirties, of the twelve-tone row in my thirties and forties. And I am witnessing at present the incubation of an electronic-music establishment.

One can be eminently creative in any medium, of course, but the more I see of fashions the more I discern, with infinite clarity, another path—that of Man, the bright adventurer, the magic-maker. When I feel optimistic, it holds brilliant promise, like an Arizona morning before dawn, with its cardboard stage set and dark eastern silhouette in honor of the sun's holy rising.

On the wall of the projection room of a company specializing in children's films are inscriptions of appreciation. One of these touched me in an extraordinary way. Along with the *thank you* were the following words, painted, illuminated, by the child-author:

> *Once upon a time*
> *There was a little boy*
> *And he went outside.*

*Encinitas, California*                                               H. P.
*June, 1969–April, 1972*

Acknowledgements: If I were to offer a list of the persons who have aided me—financially, morally, musically—during the past twenty-five years, it would be of an absurd length, and I regret the presumptuous sound that this statement might seem to carry. These persons know who they are. They also know that I offer, in return, as always before, faith, respect, love.

—H. P.

# Author's Preface

PERHAPS the most hallowed of traditions among artists of creative vigor is this: traditions in the creative arts are per se suspect. For they exist on the patrimony of standardization, which means degeneration. They dominate because they are to the interest of some group that has the power to perpetuate them, and they cease to dominate when some equally powerful group undertakes to bend them to a new pattern. It is not difficult for the alert student to acquire the traditional techniques. Under the pressures of study these are unconsciously and all too easily absorbed. The extent to which an individual can resist being blindly led by tradition is a good measure of his vitality.

Traditions remain undisturbed when we say: let us improve ourselves; let us become better pianists, teachers, conductors, better composers. They remain undisturbed when we say: let us increase the knowledge and appreciation of "good" music. Traditions remain undisturbed, uninvestigated, and therefore a culture of music based upon such palpably noble precepts is already senile.

The quality of vitality that makes any culture significant involves something else, the presence of which constantly undermines tradition; it is found in the perceptive freshness of the Tang Dynasty poets, the bold curiosity of the Renaissance Florentines. In large measure it is compounded of investigation, investigation, investigation. In poetry and in many other forms of creative expression investigation may take an entirely intellectual and metaphysical path, but in music, because of the very nature of the art, it must also take a *physical* path. A phalanx of good pianists, good teachers, good composers, and "good" music no more creates a spirit of investigation and a vital age in music than good grades in school create a spirit of investigation and a body of thinking citizens. To promote a youthful vitality in music we must have students who will question every idea and related physical object that they encounter. They must question the corpus of knowledge, traditions, and usages that give us a piano, for example—the very fact of a piano; they must question the tones of its keys, question the music on its rack, and, above all, they must question, constantly and eternally, what might be called the philosophies behind device, the philosophies that are really responsible for these things.

Good grades in school are the result of a less commendable ability, and no aspect of the musical scene could be more depressing than the prospect that those with the ability to get good grades in school, to copy others, to absorb and apply traditions with facility, shall hold the fort of "good" music.

Music, "good" or not "good," has only two ingredients that might be called God-given: the capacity of a body to vibrate and produce sound and the mechanism of the human ear that registers it. These two ingredients can be studied and analyzed, but they cannot be changed; they are the comparative constants. All else in the art of music, which may also be studied and analyzed, was created by man or is implicit in human acts and is therefore subject to the fiercest scrutiny—and ultimately to approval, indifference, or contempt. In other words, all else is subject to change.

Implicit in the man-made part of the musical art are (1) an attitude toward one's fellow man and all his works; (2) a source scale and (3) a theory for its use; (4) more than occasionally a vocal design; (5) a complexity of organized tones which we call a composition; (6) a musical instrument or instruments; (7) a powerful emotional reaction to the composition.

These disparate ingredients, which operate through various degrees of the conscious and premeditated and the unconscious and spontaneous, are listed above at random and for three reasons: (1) because twenty-four years of work in this musical field gives me no answer to the question of priority as regards chicken versus egg; (2) because, therefore, any rational sequence would require defense; and (3) because at this point of discussion sequence is unimportant and defense impertinent.

The creative individual, in developing the man-made ingredients and in examining the God-given, finds the way to a special kind of truth. This truth is the product of each new day, of each complex organism, its singular environment, experience, and emotional needs. It is the realization of the *daimon*.

Musical creators have been, and are, the exponents and the victims of system, philosophy, and attitude, determined for them by textbooks and classrooms, and by the atmosphere in which they grow; in short, by their milieu. Consequently the later history of Western music is of *one* system, *one* philosophy, *one* attitude, and it is characterized by successive bodies of practitioners made up of multitudes of innocent believers and sprinklings of individualists who are frequently unequal to the struggle—the struggle of fundamental dissent with the musical practicalities.

The canons of music do not comprise a *corpus juris*, common or codified, and the prevailing attitude is a symptom, a danger signal, of possible decay that no person imbued with a spirit of investigation can perceive without misgivings. Investigators and experimenters are at least as reverent toward our European heritage as the average music lover—probably more so, because they are acolytes of the creative spirit that has produced such phenomena as the past three hundred years of Western music. But it is a dynamic reverence.

In a healthy culture differing musical philosophies would be coexistent, not mutually exclusive; and they would build from Archean granite, and not, as our one musical system of today builds, from the frame of an inherited keyboard, and from the inherited forms and instruments of Europe's eighteenth century. And yet anyone who even toys with the idea of looking beyond these legacies for materials and insight is generally considered foolhardy if not actually a publicity-seeking mountebank. The door to further musical investigation and insight has been slammed shut by the inelastic and doctrinaire quality of our one system and its esthetic forms.

Under the circumstances it is not incumbent upon a composer to justify his investigation, his search. The burden of explanation for dissatisfaction rests elsewhere. It belongs to those who accept the forms of a past day without scrutinizing them in the light of new and ever-changing technological and sociological situations, in the light of the interests that stand to profit by the status quo, and in the light of their own individualities, this time and this place.

This time and this place offer today's composer an inestimable advantage over the composer of even a hundred years ago; for the agent that is able to free music from the incubus of an external body of interpreters is now actually with us. Having entered the age of musical recordings—and recordings constantly improving in fidelity—we have only to grasp the opportunity for a truly individualistic and creative music. Never before in the history of the art has the composer been able to hope for a situation at all similar to that of the visual artist, who paints a picture only once. Until recently the composer has had to gear his creative faculties to the traditions, comprehension, and practice of the only body capable of giving his work life—the body of interpretive musicians who alone had it in their power to paint and repaint his picture.

That time is past. The creative musician can now play his music for a record—once—and with a good performance and a good recording be content to end the effort right there. The record requires no body of interpretive musicians to perpetuate it; hence it need not be of great concern to the composer that his theories are not widely understood, that his notation is a cryptogram to everyone but himself and his little group, that he has built instruments which perhaps may never be touched again. These were only his tools—his paints and brushes—and there the picture is, on the record. It might please his ego if he thought others would use his tools, but —fundamentally—what matter?

Twenty-four years ago, when I first began groping for answers to problems of intonation, I was a composer. I am still a composer, and my every musical act has been geared to that premise. Not a ratio of vibrational lengths has been put on paper nor one piece of wood glued to another which did not have as its ultimate objective the creation of music.

The music which is the result of this groping has been in the process of composition for seventeen years, and virtually every presentation of it has prompted numerous questions about its acoustical basis, its sociological postulates, its historic antecedents, and its compositional mechanics, the sum total of which cannot be treated adequately in less than a volume such as this.

The work is not offered as a basis for a substitute tyranny, the grooving of music and musical theory into another set of conventions. What I do hope for is to stimulate creative work by example, to encourage investigation of basic factors, and to leave all others to individual if not idiosyncratic choice. To influence, yes; to limit, no.

This is not to say that my attitude toward this work is objective. Objectivity would imply a lack of passion and a complete disinterest, which, if it is not an anomaly in any human being, is at least an anomaly in a composer faced with the subject of music. However I may have weighed the virtues and the shortcomings of the formulas and theories I propound, I expect— and welcome—just as intense a scrutiny of them as I have endeavored to project upon the work of some of my musical predecessors and contemporaries.

Since 1928, when a first draft of Monophonic principles was completed, the work has undergone many evolutions. In its original form it was compounded of a measure of experimentation on violins and violas and an even larger measure of intuition. In time greater knowledge of similar work by others led to several revisions in which history and the comparative aspects were stressed, although the basic principles remained unchanged. Now I have concluded, as with theses propped by the Bible, that any musical attitude can be justified by historical precedent, and that an individual experience in a given medium is by far the best substantiation conceivable. Consequently, what the book contains of history and comparative analyses is presented to clarify the bases of present-day practice and of possible expansion in the future, and not as a basic factor in the evolution of this theory and its application, except in the most general sense. The basic factors are still: experience, intuition.

The word Monophony applies to both music and intonation, for reasons that will become evident in due course. For purposes of presentation the subject matter falls naturally into two divisions: (1) music and the attitude it embodies, a vocal design, and to some extent possible emotional reactions, discussed principally in Part I; (2) scale, theory, and instruments built specifically for the scale and theory, comprising the subject of intonation, discussed in Parts II and III. Part IV is a brief presentation of historic and proposed intonations.

At the same time that I acknowledge my great indebtedness to many workers in music, especially workers in intonation, I should make it clear that I do not intend this book for musicologists, nor even for musicians in the ordinary sense. It is addressed to those who are searching for more than intellectual openings into the mysteries of music and intonation. I have written it for those with a musically creative attitude: (1) for composers; (2) for those who expect to compose; (3) for anyone, even without a knowledge of ordinary musical theory, who has this creative attitude.

Although translations into conventional musical terms are frequent throughout the work, such translations are in no way necessary to the statement of principles or to the development of the ideas and arguments presented, and they may therefore be ignored.

H.P.

*Madison, Wisconsin*
*April, 1947*

# Table of Contents

## PART FOUR

## Intonations: Historic, Implied, Proposed

# List of Illustrations

## Numbered Diagrams

## *Photographs*

# PART I
## Corporeal versus Abstract Music

# CHAPTER ONE

# From Emperor Chun to the Vacant Lot

## *Apologia*

IT WOULD seem axiomatic that any music, whether it is that of a well-known writer of symphonies or that of an anonymous folk singer, reveals the philosophic attitude of its creator. It also seems self-evident that if his attitude is vigorous and individualistic, his practical requirements are not necessarily satisfied by the traditions he was born to; they may even require direct antitheses. Simple repetition does not, and cannot, fulfill the creative urges of such a person. He is living *his*, a new, life, and though he is a generated bundle of physical and mental similarities to millions of other entities, he is still a new being. Neither physically nor mentally is he a simple repetition.[1]

As a student, he may be well aware of the historic turning points of his art, but his creative processes do not evolve from a historical or intellectual gambit and end with an intellectual checkmate, for the sake of scholastic controversy. His variation or his direct *volte-face* is arrived at by way of cumulative experience and groping, and the satisfaction is that of a creative experience, not of comparative situations. Nevertheless, he begins to develop a judicial attitude toward the things he was born to—to praise and to criticize. And judgment is immanent in his creative process, whether it is written, spoken, or only thought out in his mind.

When this man cannot modify the ways that have been bequeathed to him so that they will serve his philosophic concepts, he has only one sure recourse; intuition, an awareness that gains its strength and direction from the specific knowledge, whimsey, motives, predilections, and so forth, that are his sum of ingredients. And when he resorts to words to plot his course—

[1]In Oswald Spengler's words, "practical requirements, so called, are merely the mask of a profound inward compulsion." The thinker, he writes, "has no choice; he thinks as he has to think. Truth . . . is to him the picture of the world which was born at his birth. It is himself over again . . . because truth and his life are identical." *The Decline of the West* (translated by Charles Francis Atkinson), xiii, 242 (quoted by permission of Alfred A. Knopf, Inc.). It might be added

the way of his intuition—he eventually finds that his exposition is compounded of his judgments—praise and criticism, a good measure of supporting argument, and at least a few ventures into the history of mankind and of his art. I speak from my own mental experiences in breaking with the accepted ways. Mine is a procedure more of antithesis than of simple modification, and the statement of this fact is essential as a groundwork for the pages that follow. Further, it is chronologically correct. The break came first, by intuition; the justification came second, by critical and historical analysis.

Sometime between 1923 and 1928 I finally became so dissatisfied with the body of knowledge and usages as ordinarily imparted in the teaching of music that I refused to accept, or develop my own work on the basis of, any part of it. With respect to current usage this refusal was a rebellion; from the standpoint of my creative work it was the beginning of a new philosophy of music, intuitively arrived at. Just how old this "new" philosophy actually is has since been a continual revelation to me.

The reasons for my dissatisfaction—mostly inchoate at the time—are revealed hereafter in connection with specific topics. At this point I may merely mention how profoundly annoyed I became over the widespread emphasis on skills at an instrument, emphasis on the "technique" of playing and composing music, both by authors of books and by teachers. All too rarely did I find consideration of intrinsic content by either author or teacher. Various degrees of intrinsic content were simply accepted, having long ago been determined for us. If a product was "polished," either in performance or in "technique" of composition, *ipso facto* it was "good." If an instrumentalist could manipulate the black and white digitals or other paraphernalia more dexterously than most instrumentalists he was *ipso facto* an "artist." And if he could "interpret" something written several centuries ago in a way to please the cognoscenti he was *ipso facto* a "great artist" and became the recipient, at every turn, of expressions of homage.

To any serious creative person this is a fundamentally unwholesome situation. Not only has a re-examination of intrinsic value been rare, but never in my entire musical experience—with the single exception of my

that the truth of the "world which was born at his birth" is a dynamic value, because he is a dynamic value, that the world as "himself over again" does not mean everything in it over again, and that simple repetition, even within his own work, may be convenient and profitable—it may mean shoes for the baby, but divorced from the baby it is hardly truth, nor is it even momentarily exhilarating.

introduction to the writings of Spengler—have I encountered any discussion of the basic philosophic attitudes, or values, or approaches of the music under consideration. Music is not causally related to historic movements, except by means of isolated sentimental legends—how Chopin's Revolutionary Etude was composed, for instance. One is told, when he points this out, that we are living in an "age of specialization." What can the history of mankind or his religions and social mores and philosophies have to do with music in an age of uncorrelated vacuums?

An intellectually weary observer might say that a creative person always reacts negatively—that is, rebelliously—when he discovers that he is not constitutionally fitted for "success" in the patterns of human endeavor that he was born to. The professional "adjuster" of personalities would of course discover in his "subject" those faculties that might fit into the patterns, and try to develop these. The "subject" is good at numbers, therefore he might possibly find his niche as a bookkeeper, for example. Even though the "adjuster" could personally do very little about it, the whole situation would seem more healthy if, once in a while, he would question whether the entire profession of bookkeeping might not represent maladjustment. Since a given personality never lives in duplicate—one following the course of "adjustment" and the other (the "twin") following his intuition—we can only conjecture how great a loss the world may have suffered because of these individual "adjustments." It may be providential that there are persons who do not take readily to dragooning, or to filling this bill of "success." Occasionally some individual has enough persistence or strength of impact to force re-examination upon a culture.

Some seventeen years ago I abandoned the traditional scale, instruments, and forms in toto (I had begun to abandon them as early as 1923), and struck out on my own. I came to the realization that the spoken word was the distinctive expression my constitutional makeup was best fitted for, and that I needed other scales and other instruments. This was the positive result of self-examination—call it intuitive, for it was not the result of any intellectual desire to pick up lost or obscure historical threads. For better or for worse, it was an emotional decision. After all, like other American musicians of my day, I was trained to regard Abstraction and all its appurtenances as noble. Like others of similar training I had a vague knowledge that previous cultures had accepted something like this idea of spoken words in music, but I too was encompassed by the popular assumption that the *present*, in relation to the past, means *progress*. It involved no small inner struggle to emerge from that spell, to discover that present "progress" clothed a skeleton of bondage to a specific and limited past, and to emerge from mental turmoil to a realization that what was called progress was not necessarily progress to me, however sincerely it might be accepted as such by many, perhaps even a great majority.

Having decided to follow my own intuitive path I began to write music on the basis of harmonized spoken words, for new instruments and in new scales, and to play it in various parts of the country. I set lyrics by the eighth-century Chinese Li Po, intoning the words and accompanying myself on my Adapted Viola, scenes from Shakespeare, Biblical psalms; later, drawing on my experiences as a wanderer, I wrote music exploiting the speech of itinerants (*Bitter Music*), hitchhiker inscriptions copied from a highway railing (*Barstow*), a cross-country trip (*U. S. Highball*), and newsboy cries (*San Francisco*), generally using an ensemble of my own instruments.

This autobiographical introduction to the exposition of Abstract and Corporeal music, as the terms are used here, will help to explain my interpretations, to give my readers a focus on the points of similarity and difference in the history of music, and to provide a grasp of the conscious and unconscious fulfillments represented by movements and individuals.

The examination of even a small part of the world's music and what it means to various peoples and to various creative persons is in some ways rather like a plunge into dominant night. It is a plunge into a realm of the comparatively measureless. Not until we reach the musical equinox do we find the comparatively measurable, the dominant day of precise aural quantities which can be noted in fairly precise aural reactions—ratios, consonances, dissonances. In the dominance of night is a more ineffable value, in which the seen and the heard are out of perspective, distorted by untold ages of prejudice, elusive and illusory, and consequently of less ultimate concern than those qualities that can be discerned through the intuitive faculties.

This ineffable value is related less to fact than to effect; but the mechanical means for producing known or conjectured effects can be examined, notwithstanding the non-universality of the effects of music, which is too patent to be labored.

It is a comparatively simple matter to limn the whole panorama of music, the waxing and waning of one type of music shadowed against another in the same process, of the academic versus the ecclesiastical versus folk versus popular, which at one moment in history and in a given spot are virtually synonymous, at another quite irreconcilable. But beyond an analysis of circumstances and mechanics are questions that can be little more than skirted: what is it that makes Beethoven what he is to some, and the *Red River Valley* what it is, apart from geography, to others? What was the music of vanished civilizations like in terms of actual reactions?

It is quite impossible for us Westerners to imagine what ancient Greek music was really like, even after we know the salient facts about it. The Greeks could not use phrases that would convey absolute meaning to us. And we do not know and can never know the exact nature of the spirit with which they met a mordant human artifice or creation of their own milieu.

Even when we hear a highly developed exotic music and know the facts regarding it, such as the classic Chinese drama as interpreted by Mei Lan-fang, who toured the United States some years ago, many of us cannot meet it on a common level of spirit. True, Americans especially are capable of a wide range of response. Somewhere along the American line a composer, whatever opposition and indifference he meets, will find mountain people to like him if he writes mountain music, valley people to like him if he writes "valid" music, sinophiles to like him if he writes "Chinese" music, and someone to "understand" him if he goes off the deep end to write something that no one understands. But this is not the whole story.

## One Voice

Throughout history the Monophonic concept has been consistently manifested through one medium: the individual's spoken words, which are more certainly the juice of a given identity than anything else in the tonal world. Of all the tonal ingredients a creative man can put into his music, his voice is at once the most dramatically potent and the most intimate. *His* voice does not necessarily mean his own voice and it certainly does not mean the specialized idiosyncrasy known as "serious" singing. It means his conception as expressed by the human voice and it means *one* voice. The instant when other voices are added to that one voice is an instant of metamorphosis. Thereafter *his* identity is not that of the inner self alone but the identity of a group. The drama and the intimacy of the individual are superseded by a different esthetic or sociological quality.

The origin of music in speech intonation among the early peoples to whom we ascribe civilizations—the Greeks and the Chinese particularly—seems pretty well established. The theories that have been advanced for an Abstract origin or an ecstatic, percussive, dance-inspired origin for music, among primitive tribes of a later day, are not especially pertinent to this essay.[2] Here it seems wiser to center our attention on the early enlightened peoples.

## From Epic Chant to Symphony

From Terpander, about 700 B.C., to the nineteenth-century Beethoven, the more approved and more serious types of European music may be indexed according to the extent to which they preserved the vitality of words or, conversely, the extent to which they were "independent" of words.

For the essentially vocal and verbal music of the individual—a Monophonic concept—the word Corporeal may be used, since it is a music that is vital to a time and place, a here and now. The epic chant is an example, but the term could be applied with equal propriety to almost any of the important ancient and near-ancient cultures—the Chinese, Greek, Arabian, Indian, in all of which music was physically allied with poetry or the dance. Corporeal music is emotionally "tactile." It does not grow from the root of "pure form." It cannot be characterized as either mental or spiritual.

The word Abstract, on the other hand, may be used to denote a mass expression, in its highest application, the spirits of all united into one and transported into a realm of unreality, neither here nor now, but transcending both. The symphony is an example. Abstract music grows from the root of non-verbal "form," how "pure" being a matter of individual opinion. It may be characterized as either mental or spiritual. It is always "instrumental," even when it involves the singing of words, because the emotion of an individual conveyed through vitally rendered words would instantly end the characteristic domination of non-verbal "form."

Thus the mere presence of words in music is not in itself the criterion of its classification. The chants of the Roman church, early in its history, were actually in a language that none but the learned clergy understood,

[2]Jules Combarieu, one-time professor of music history at the Collège de France and a lover of Germanic music, is pleased to find a common origin for Abstraction and the more benighted expressions: "The musical metaphysics of the Germans and primitive magic are one and the same thing." *Music—Its Laws and Evolution*, 95.

though some of them were sung with the natural rhythm and inflections of the Latin words. An important distinction, then, as regards the Corporeal and the Abstract, is between an individual's vocalized words, intended to convey meaning, and musicalized words that convey no meaning, whether rendered by an individual or a group, because they are beyond the hearers' understanding, because they have been ritualized, or because of other evolvements of rendition.

The peoples of history have radicated their instinctive Corporeal attitudes in many variations of musical utterance, in:

Stories sung or chanted, including much folk music.

Poems recited or intoned, including some folk music and some, but not all, popular music.

Dramas, such as the early seventeenth-century Florentine music-dramas, for example.

Music intended specifically for dances which tell a story or describe a situation; both ancient and modern.

The tendency toward an Abstract character, on the other hand, is evident in such musical forms as:

Songs with words that are intended not to convey meaning but simply to set the mood of the music.

Songs or dramas with words that do not convey meaning because of the style of composition or manner of rendition; most modern operas come under this head.

All purely instrumental music, whether programmed or not, though programmed music often tends toward the Corporeal.

## Plato the Reactionary

In ancient times the voice of authority was directed more often toward preserving the Corporeal standard in a given culture than toward investigating deviations from it. A paternal dictum of Emperor Chun about 2300 B.C., for instance, emphasizes the importance that was attached to word value in music:

Teach the children of the great that through thy care they may become just, mild and wise; firm without severity; upholding the dignity and pride of their station without vanity or assumption. Express these doctrines in poems, that they may be sung to appropriate melodies accompanied by the music of instruments.

*Let the music follow the sense of the words* [*italics mine—H.P.*]; let it be simple and ingenuous, for vain, empty and effeminate music is to be condemned. Music is the expression of the soul's emotion; if the soul of the musician be virtuous, his music will be full of nobility and will unite the souls of men with the spirits of heaven.[3]

Some nineteen centuries later Plato insisted repeatedly, in various phraseology, that rhythm and harmony are regulated by the words and not the words by them, which sounds very much like the retort of a gentleman of tradition to some young maverick who was already breaking the rules.

For the Greeks the noblest purpose of music was to enhance drama. Dramatists were frequently the composers of the music for their words. This music took the form of recitative in some of the dialogue, accompanied note for note by aulos or kithara or both. In this economy of accompaniment the words were perfectly understood by the audience. There were also lyrical passages and, at critical dramatic points, floods of music, by chorus, actors, and instruments. Consequently the modern scholar reading ancient drama gains only a fraction of the total result. As one modern writer puts it, "to the Greeks the words are but part of a complex art form that weaves poetry, music, acting, and the dance into a profound and moving unity."[4]

Aristotle, like Plato, was obviously annoyed with the direction that musical practice was taking, which was, palpably, toward the word-independent Abstractions of the "concert stage" and away from the classic word-dominated form. He insisted that "the right measure will be attained if students stop short of the arts which are practiced in professional contests, and do not seek to acquire those fantastic marvels of execution which are now the fashion in such contests, and from these have passed into education."[5]

In the *Problems*, attributed in part to Aristotle, is further evidence of the place of music in classical Greece. In a remark on "recitation," which probably applied to declamation on precise tones, the author asks: "Why does recitation with a musical accompaniment have a tragic effect when introduced into singing? Is it owing to the resulting contrast? For the contrast gives an expression of feeling and implies extremity of calamity or grief, whereas uniformity is less mournful."[6] In this context "uniformity" obviously means unaccompanied recitation.

[3]Krehbiel, "Chinese Music," in *Century Magazine*, 41 (N.S., 19): 453.
[4]Durant, *Life of Greece*, 379–380.
[5]*Politica*, translated by Benjamin Jowett (*The Works of Aristotle*, Ross ed.), Book VIII, 1341a.
[6]*Problemata*, translated by E. S. Forster (*The Works of Aristotle*, Ross ed.), Book XIX, 917b-918a, quoted by permission of Oxford University Press.

Plato further confirms the existence of a trend toward the Abstract, however incipient, when he speaks of the "complexity, and variation of notes, when the strings give one sound and the poet or composer of the melody gives another,—also when they make concords and harmonies in which lesser and greater intervals, slow and quick, or high and low notes [tones] are combined—or, again, when they make complex variations of rhythms, which they adapt to the notes [tones] of the lyre."[7] All of this, perhaps needless to remark, the chronic "aginner" Plato opposes, but it shows a trend toward a harmonic music heard for the sheer joy of harmony —an Abstract conception.[8]

Through his denunciations of the musical innovators Plato reveals the approved classical manner. He calls to account the poets who

make still further havoc by separating the rhythm and the figure of the dance from the melody, setting bare words to metre, and also separating the rhythm from the words, using the lyre or the flute alone. For when there are no words, it is very difficult to recognize the meaning of the harmony and rhythm, or to see that any worthy object is imitated by them. And we must acknowledge that all this sort of thing, which aims only at swiftness and smoothness and a brutish noise, and uses the flute and the lyre not as the mere accompaniments of the dance and song, is exceedingly coarse and tasteless.[9]

Implying that innovations were threatening, Plato undertakes to interpret Homer:

. . . when anyone says that mankind most regard: "The newest song which the singers have," they will be afraid that he may be praising, not new songs, but a new kind of song; and this ought not to be praised, or conceived to be the meaning of the poet; for any musical innovation is full of danger to the whole State, and ought to be prohibited.[10]

Finally, in an entertaining bit of dialectic, Plato has Glaucon asking, "Then we shall not maintain artificers of lyres with three corners and complex scales, or the makers of any other many-stringed curiously harmonized instruments?" To which Socrates promptly answers, "Certainly not."[11]

These views of the Greek philosophers may seem amusing in the light of later historical developments. For it is the departures from the standard they sought to entrench, and the innovators so unqualifiedly denounced by

---

[7] *Laws* (Jowett ed.), 5:195.

[8] Someone has made the pertinent remark that we are not very bright if we assume that the Greek musician immediately damped each string of the lyre before plucking another. Neither are we very bright, it might be added, if we assume that through several centuries he resisted the temptation to pluck two or more strings simultaneously.

[9] *The Dialogues of Plato* (B. Jowett, ed.), 5:49.   [10] *Republic* (Jowett ed.), 3:112.   [11] *Ibid.*, 85.

them, that are today (aside from the "artificers of lyres and complex scales") the established and accepted standards, and the pillars of Abstract, rhythmic, and harmonic music, in professional, educational, and artistic life. Today the classical standards of ancient Greek days have only an occasional unheralded and unexpounded existence in folk and popular music.

We can engender some understanding of the disapproved deviations from Greek standards because they approach our own standards, but it is infinitely more difficult, if not impossible, to imagine the classical word-dominated form. And we are hardly helped by the composers who have interpreted the nine or ten extant fragments of ancient Greek music as modern songs with accompaniments by modern instruments.

Since Greek accent marks expressed rise and fall in pitch, it is fairly safe to assume that the ancient speech had a tonal character, though it differed in essential qualities from that most famous of tonal languages, the Chinese. Also, because of the Greek preoccupation with words in music, and the concern many Greek writers show for sliding tones in their general classifications, it may be assumed further that these tonal characteristics were incorporated in their music.[12]

## Oriental Excursus

Japanese drama was originally an offshoot of the Chinese, although it subsequently developed a highly individual and independent existence. Noh ("accomplishment," the drama of accomplished grace), which stemmed, in the fourteenth century, from the Japanese social-religious culture, was an amalgam and refinement of epic recital (corresponding to the Greek epic chant), the dance, and the popular sports, juggling and comedy. Noh developed from and into many forms, the vocal and bodily mechanics of which consisted of dancing, reciting, chanting, and outright singing. Obviously, then, music occupied approximately the same place among the Japanese of this period as it had in ancient Greece two thousand years before. It was the expression of a fundamentally similar concept of musical values.[13]

---

[12]Johnson, *Musical Pitch*, 20–25; Davy, *Letters*, 2:316. George Herzog writes that "the element which is strong in 'tone-languages,' intrudes upon the music of the peoples speaking such languages. . . . Owing to our notion of the essentially abstract quality of music, to our ideals of 'absolute music' and *l'art pour l'art*, we are all too apt to look upon music as a development of its own, a realm apart." "Speech-Melody and Primitive Music," in *Musical Quarterly*, 20:452–466.

[13]Lombard, *Japanese Drama*, 18, 33, 72, 74, 87, 90, 161, 184, 293, and *passim*.

Noh eventually brought Kabuki, a revolt against Noh's growing eso-
tericism and a re-establishment of Noh's original ideals, a movement that
is somewhat comparable to the Tuscan or Florentine re-establishment of
the Greek ideals at about the same time, around 1600. Kabuki, introduced
by a beautiful young dancer and an acolyte Buddhist who gave up pros-
pects of priesthood to write her music,[14] is sufficiently modern, at least in its
developed forms, to remain a vital art in Japan today, and to make phonograph records occasionally available.

The effects of such records on Westerners who have no knowledge of
the Japanese language and little knowledge of Japanese history and culture are quite divergent, but there are some who are deeply affected by the
drama, and many who agree that it creates an emotional tension quite
unlike anything ever produced by Western music. A working knowledge
of the language employed—Chinese, Japanese, or Greek—is almost a pre-
requisite to a full appreciation of any such music, for without it precise criteria for its rhythm and overall sound are lacking. But even without that
knowledge some Westerners find meaning for themselves in its emotional
and dramatic projection.

The Greeks and the Chinese, the first peoples known to have perceived
the science of intonation, conceived of music itself in parallel situations,
especially in the drama. This is no mere coincidence, any more than are
other similarities in the cultural development of peoples widely separated
in time and space. All are "but evidence of the essential oneness of human
nature in its reaction to similar conditions, whether in India, Greece or
Japan."[15]

The Chinese, like the Greeks, felt no hesitation in setting spoken words
to music, or in writing on their pictures, or in putting vivid paint on their
sculpture. Their minds never posed questions about the propriety of such
associations. For them the idea of "purity" and "independence" in music
and art simply did not exist.

Present-day Cantonese music-theater, which one can hear in San Francisco and New York if he can succeed in filtering the continuous percussion
from his senses, is certainly a far cry from the classic Chinese type, yet even
here there is frequent and illuminating evidence that the audience understands the words, despite the percussion and the tiresome cracking of pea-
nut shells. No vowel sounds are sustained over three or four ordinary

[14]*Ibid.*, 288.      [15]*Ibid.*, 17.

measures or even half that much, to say nothing of vowels brooding like a
nemesis over three or four measures of slow music, as in the current Western
manner of rendition. To an Occidental the words seem to flow exactly as
they do in Chinese speech, the only element of variation being the stylized
falsetto.

The intense mood created in Japanese and Chinese drama with a single
instrument and voice should deter us from feeling sorry for the Greeks
because they developed no symphony orchestra, but used only a lyre or
kithara or, occasionally, a reed pipe. It is also worth remembering as an experience in heard Corporeal music, not merely in conjectured Corporeal
music. It is indispensable for contrast in evaluating what happened after
Greece on the European scene. This development—Christian hymnology.

## *Not "Out of the Parchment"*

Early in the second century the Church incorporated in its service the
practice of antiphony—the singing of alternate verses by men and boys.
This pattern, derived from Jewish and Syrian cultures, had been introduced
into the West from Antioch and was essentially anti-Greek.[16] As such it
was apparently offensive to the Greek-indoctrinated Romans, for in that
same century a provincial official complained to the emperor that the chief
"fault" of the Christians was that they were "accustomed to meet before
daylight on a certain day and sing among themselves alternately—*secum
invicem*—a hymn to Christ as God."[17]

What the Romans considered a fault the now-Christianized Greeks
still tried to correct. Though antiphony also found its way into Athens,
here it was forced into the traditional Greek manner—that is, speaking on
tones rather than actual singing.[18] It is not easy to depart from centuries of
practice.

Antiphonal singing brought an entirely different spirit into music. It
became a thing of dolorous chants in extreme *sostenuto*—without spontaneity—and ceased to be Corporeal in any sense. The hymn, a generic term
that can be applied to all theistic adoration in music, was the inevitable

---

[16]The Christian practice of antiphony should not be confused with the Greek idea of *anti-
phonia*, which was simply a parallel vocal or instrumental part in the 2/1, or "octave." Indeed
the Greeks had hymns, and of course the strict religious devotees of the gods—who undoubtedly
caroled hymns on attenuated vowels (Henderson, *Forerunners of Italian Opera*, 1)—were very
numerous, which need not detract in the least from the more perceptive Greek expressions.

[17]Hawkins, *History of the Science and Practice of Music*, 1:106; Hope, *Medieval Music*, 42.

[18]Hope, *Medieval Music*, 44.

musical vehicle to express the introspection and "faith" of the first converts, the zealots. And the hymn, like the philosophies that mother it, is a mass expression beyond the boundaries of the individual and the Corporeal, beyond this time and place (with ineludible exceptions), and it is not particularly important that the words be understood; they assert a pre-known transcendent belief, and they have no story to tell.[19]

Add to this the fact that Latin, the language of the developing ritual, though it disappeared as a living tongue, continued to be the language of that ritual, and the result is foregone. It seems probable that even before Latin disappeared Greek was sometimes used in the Roman churches, the powers of the Church apparently not being in the least concerned with the communicative power of words.[20] The laity was neither expected nor encouraged to understand the words of the chant, even if the manner of singing in sustained and ornamented tones had permitted them to do so.

By a canon of the decade 360–70 "the people" were forbidden to "sing out of the parchment" because their uncultivated voices "destroyed the harmony,"[21] and since the service from which they were barred as participants was in Greek or Latin it became quite beyond their comprehension as time went on. The listener perforce came to think of music itself as conveying meaning. Plato's complaint that "harmony" had no "meaning" without words implied understood words, and the evolution from sung words that conveyed no meaning—except in a general mood-like way—to an Abstract music entirely without words was easy and inevitable.

Whether one interprets history in such a way as to ascribe the "independence" of music to the beginning of the Christian era or to a later time, there is no question but that, very close to the beginning, it became a new art. It became a language in itself. The insistence with which this simulation was carried on is manifest in the "motives," "subjects," "phrases," "questions," "responses," and "periods" of our musical forms, all entirely apart from the circumstance that sung words might be involved.[22]

[19]In this regard, Berlioz quotes the comment of Lesueur, one of his early teachers: "It is one of the gravest errors to see a remnant of Grecian music in the plain chant, which is a monstrous tradition of the barbarous hymns the druids used to howl round the statue of Odin while offering up their horrible sacrifices." Berlioz, *Letters*, 367.

[20]Henderson, *Forerunners of Italian Opera*, 5.

[21]Hawkins, *History of the Science and Practice of Music*, 1:106.

[22]Jules Combarieu (see note 2, page 8 above), who calls the setting of words to music a "commonplace and low task," nevertheless devotes an entire chapter to showing how music *is* a language, and declares that music (Abstract, of course) has "collected, accentuated and idealized all the emotional accompaniment of articulated and logical speech." And he adds that the

The fact is that the ancient spirit was gone. And it was gone because the ancient, lovely, and fearless attitude toward the human body was gone. Musical "morals" denied the human body—through the one agent of the body that they could control: words from the vocal organ— because the "mother morals" denied it and have succeeded in nursing this denial, yea these many centuries. D. H. Lawrence advises us never to forget that "modern morality has its roots in hatred, a deep, evil hate of the instinctive, intuitional, procreative body."[23] How could the "morality" of music conceive anything different, anything different at all, than occasionally a bastard exception?

This fundamental ingredient—the "morality" which denied the human body—is entirely missed by both Spengler and that group of music historians who trace the decline and disappearance of the "Appollonian" music, or the "Oriental," modal, vocal, and monodic (in the ancient sense) music in Europe sometime between the tenth and sixteenth centuries, and the emergence of a "Faustian" or "European," harmonic, polyphonic, instrumental and Abstract, and "independent" music at the same time.[24] These reiterated teachings stop short of the actualities and are palpably misleading, for the attributes they impute to the early music of the Church are merely the superficial cloakings of a spirit that underwent a complete metamorphosis at the beginning of the Christian era, when the seeds were sown which soon choked out the Corporeal attitudes and, in music, the vitality of words.

The ancient pagans told stories in their language, accompanied by music. They gave dramas, accompanied by music. If the words were not

"elements of musical language [*Abstract again*] are co-ordinated in a way analogous to the logic of the ordinary verbal thought." *Music—Its Laws and Evolution*, 94, 164–175, 239. A "commonplace" and "low" coordination would naturally be assumed.

[23]*Phoenix*, 558.

[24]The effect of Spengler's *Decline of the West* in forcing us into a more sober contemplation of the cultural forces about us is surely salutary. But in his musical allusions Spengler has touched only a fraction of the total spirit. He comes from a time and a tradition that accepts *a priori* music as a "wordless art" and a "cathedral of voices" and the greatness of the eighteenth-century Germanic expression of that concept; his idea of Faustian is Germanic, and—what is more—art-conscious Germanic. The English folk song, or the Tennessee mountain song, telling its story to music, is quite as much a part of Western ("Faustian") culture as the Art of the Fugue or a Mozart sonata, and I venture to suggest that the singer of it would hold little mystery for the body-conscious, present-conscious Greek, or vice versa. The possible coexistence in the same culture of a "here-and-now" attitude with a "becoming" attitude he fails to consider. Yet the total of mankind's music is full of the evidence, and so also are single artists and thinkers embodiments of such coexistence, William Blake for example. The musical aspect of Spengler's thesis, largely because of the wealth of possible data omitted, narrows down to an expression of musical academism. The body of folk song has a quality and a history less affected by the ups and downs

understood, the music had no power to excite. The later Christians, after the establishment of the pagan-adapted philosophy, heard no stories but praises to the only God, which they knew were praises to the only God, but which they heard in a "timeless" language they did not understand, and so required no alert and intuitive attentiveness on their part—only simple passivity.

Passivity implies mental relaxation, and devious have been the innuendos regarding what goes on in people's minds in this state. Thus Virgil Thomson insists "that persons in a concert hall who are doing their own private business, whether that business is looking impressively social or thinking about love or laying plans for tomorrow, are not necessarily receiving any musical communication, though sometimes they may be doing that too."[25] After nearly two thousand years of enforced passive listening in "serious" music, many modern composers are endeavoring to make audiences "think." In view of history, Abstraction hardly seems the most efficient fillip.

To point out that not only the Japanese drama but also the type of early ecclesiastical chant which contains a residual pattern of pagan practice sometimes exercises a powerful effect, even though neither language is understood, is not to say that the two have anything fundamental in common. For the Japanese was expected to be understood during a large part of the performance; the Latin was not. The ecclesiastical, whatever its Abstract musical value in today's terms, had and has almost no significance as a Corporeal expression. It was a forced miscegenation of the Abstract with the Greek musical creed.

Thus after the beginning of the Christian era the music that had been inspired by a non-European philosophy (Christianity) in a non-European place of origin (the Near East) developed via the Roman Church into a form of declaration that ultimately, in eighteenth-century Germany, became a mass expression in "pure form," transcending language and space

of cultures than the conscious art forms, and projects a philosophic concept that, to say the least, is different from the music that the individual Spengler admires. The stories of the men here outlined, who in a very real way sought reinvigoration from this more constant mother-body of music, he passes over. Much else that Spengler states is actually beyond his knowledge or too close for perspective—that music was the "art that failed" in Greece, and that "music after Wagner . . . is impotence and falsehood," for example. This last, and also the assertion that today we are "playing a tedious game with dead forms to keep up the illusion of a living art," might suggest Spengler as a refugee from an American music school. *Decline of the West*, 207, 210, 219, 223, 225, 227, 230, 245, 250, 259, 293.

[25]*The State of Music* (copyright by Virgil Thomson, 1939), 199–200; quoted by permission of William Morrow and Company, Inc.

and the human body—the souls of all participants united in the Abstract, neither here nor now but timelessly.[26] On the other hand, the musical idea that had been cultivated into flower by the European Greeks was buried in the ashes of Rome.

## One Church, One Music

Out of those ashes rose no phoenix, but an agent called the Bishop of Rome. Through his efforts even vestigial remnants of the Greek idea were ruthlessly uprooted. At Milan the ancient Greek practice of a note to a syllable prevailed through several centuries, whereas at Rome "a string of notes was sung to a syllable," with the "unfortunate" singer "toying" with such ornaments as long as his breath would hold out. Such lack of "oneness" in the ritual could not be tolerated, and the spiritual Bishop of Rome badly needed a physical arm to effect the desired oneness. In the eighth century there appeared in Rome for the bishop's blessing just such an arm—Charlemagne. The Greek musical predilections of Milan immediately presented a challenge to the zealous Charlemagne, and soon thereafter the hot flame of his new Christianity and a huge bonfire in the middle of the city devoured the Greek-inspired chant and hymn books. After this the Roman, or Gregorian, use was undisputed in Italy.[27]

The following "tall" story, of Italian origin, is quite revealing as to the character of this music:

Gregory the Great, to stimulate his devotion, used to visit the graves of the departed. Whilst so engaged, he once saw one of the tombs uplifted, and the head of a long-buried man appear, with his pale tongue thrust out, as if in agony. The saint, nothing daunted, accosted the spectre, and was informed that he was the Emperor

---

[26]Corroboration, both of this consummation in modern Germany and the fact that to the modern scholarly mind *music* and *Abstraction* are synonymous is found in surprising places. *Time Magazine* for January 7, 1946, quoted the novelist Thomas Mann as declaring: "The relation of the German to the world is abstract and mystical, that is, musical."

Combarieu, the Frenchman who looks enviously at the German aptitude for Abstract expression, explains that "a long heredity has formed him [the composer] for the game of abstractions. Unknown to himself, he profits by the special education which theologians and philosophers have conferred on the human mind from very remote ages. If, in addition, he belongs to a race which seems to have, as innate gifts, the taste for abstruse speculations, the aptitude for searching analysis, a leaning to reverie—if, finally, he have that spark of talent which we cannot explain—those forms of composition which his predecessors have rendered supple and polished in so many ways become familiar to him. . . . The fugues of the *Clavecin bien tempéré* and the six Brandenburg Concertos of J. S. Bach may be cited as the finest specimens of the power of abstraction arrived at by a composer." *Music—Its Laws and Evolution*, 86. This and other passages from the book are quoted by permission of D. Appleton–Century Company, Inc.

[27]Hope, *Medieval Music*, 93, 94; Combarieu, *Music—Its Laws and Evolution*, 188.

Trajan, condemned to suffer forever for his idolatry. Pitying so illustrious a sufferer, the saint resolved to importune the Divine Mercy for him, and succeeded so well that the Almighty at length set the Emperor free and admitted him into Paradise. But, as the course of Divine justice had been interrupted, He resolved to inflict some bodily suffering upon the saint, and accordingly ordained that Gregory should be afflicted with pain in the abdomen—*dolore intestinale*—except at such times as he should be occupied in saying Mass. Gregory then bethought himself of some way of avoiding his malady by prolonging the service of the Mass to the utmost extent, and so he instituted the chant called after him Gregorian, which was at first more prolix and dreary than it has since become. Some thought this rather hard of the saint, because this style of the chant, though it would relieve him of his pains, would be very apt to give *others* the pain in the abdomen from its length and dreariness.

And Gregory himself seems not to have been too happy over his alleged handiwork, since, in a synod of 595, he wrote of "the priests, each cultivating his organ to attain an edifying voice, (thus) irritating God."[28]

It would appear that Gregory's annoyance was entirely on the score of vocal vanity, not of word integrity. This was natural, for the ascendancy of words in music had already ended. Words, those constituent units of idea which are by nature the antithesis of what is called absolute, were forced by precept to assume the cloak of the absolute! Doubtless some realistically minded man asked: "What were the words of the music? What did they say? What meaning did they carry that is of value to me?" But there was no answer, because one realistic minded man among so many dark-age minds was relegated to limbo.

That man might also have wondered at the inordinate sustaining of the vowel of a syllable in certain words. A word has four properties: (1) a rhythm (that is, its natural pattern of dynamics, and a reasonable length of time for its speaking to cover); (2) phonics; (3) an intrinsic meaning; and (4) drama (the obligation along with its fellow words to hold the interest). Our realistically minded man might have drawn four conclusions: to the extent that the vowel of a syllable is inordinately sustained (1) its rhythm is damaged; (2) its phonics is distorted; (3) its meaning is dissipated; and (4) its drama is demoralized. In fact, it would seem to him that after the words had been accepted as an inspiration they were dismissed without a thought.

The severity of the whole Christian *démarche*, cutting off the people and the language of the people from a music appropriate to their daily emotions,

[28]Hope, *Medieval Music*, 9–10, 52–53.

their place, and their time, had its inevitable reaction in the pleasant and romantic art of the troubadours, trouvères, minnesingers, and meister-singers, of the eleventh to sixteenth centuries. The musical consummation of this era: a wedding of instinctive desire to instinctive expression without benefit of clergy.

Here was a rebirth of the spirit of Greek epic chant, though it never gained the high repute it had in ancient Greece; the approved music with any continuity was still and only the ecclesiastical. Though verses and music have come down to us, we can recapture neither language nor manner, and consequently there is little to be said outside the realm of conjecture and but one point to be made here on the minstrel art.

The point is that minstrel poet and minstrel composer and minstrel performer were generally one and the same. It must occur to many persons with poetic instincts that because this is no longer true today, we may have lost an important value. We do not exclaim, upon seeing a poem printed in a magazine, "But what's this doing *here?* where's the music? and the voice?" Print is a poem's sarcophagus, voice its living, though fleeting, soul.

## The Florentine Intuition

The capitulation of the city of Constantine the Great to the Turks in 1453 is credited by history with having many far-reaching effects—on music no less than on the voyages of Columbus. In view of the static condition of music in Constantinople in the centuries immediately preceding this event it is hard to understand how the scholarly Byzantine refugees who poured into Italy could have been such agents of ferment as to produce the phenomenon of Florence, a few decades before 1600.[29]

The mere contact with Greek creed and dogma is alleged to have been responsible in some way for releasing the ancient latent paganism of the democratic, restless, radical, and inquisitive people of Tuscany. Actually, in this renascence of earlier Greek values, the Tuscans were only reclaiming the purer Hellenic spirit of which they were a wayward segment long before the Roman impositions. As the historian Naumann says, expressing the Christian viewpoint: "The art of the Hellenes, which the Renaissance

---

[29]Henderson says that it should be "particularly noted" that the three Greek scholars primarily responsible for Florence's fever over all things Greek left Constantinople before the city's fall in 1453. *Forerunners of Italian Opera*, 69n. It might also be noted that Constantinople had been threatened or had been actually under siege by the Turks since 1422, and that the three Greeks were probably more moved by prudence than by love of travel in Italy.

sought to revive, was not the art of a people who had had the fear of God before their eyes and the thought of a future state before their minds, but of one steeped in heathen tradition and given up to the enjoyment of worldly pleasures."[30]

Reviewing the long history of liturgical drama and "Sacred Representations" in Italy before the year 1600, W. J. Henderson declares that modern opera is a child of the Roman Catholic Church.[31] We might also say that resentment is a child of a good solid fist on the jaw. The first "operas" in the Florence of about 1600, which in expressed theory have so little in common with opera as currently practised, were a reaction, a rebellion, an insurgence, written by composers who happened also to be scholars and aristocrats. In general terms the movement was the scholars' counterpart of the troubadours' reaction to the dry theology and restrictive bans of the Church, but specifically it was a reaction against word distortion in the florid secular polyphony and word distortion in the restrictive liturgical polyphony.

This, being a negative explanation of an essentially creative idea, is somewhat misleading, as anyone who has searched for the truth will agree. It is both easier and generally more effective to explain creative reforms in relation to known practices. Not all the theories of the Florentine coterie were products of rejection. They worked in the field of secular drama, and Italy's first secular drama with a secular subject had already been produced at Mantua before 1483, nearly a century previous to the Florentine insurgence. This was Poliziano's *Favola di Orfeo*, the ancient myth so favored by composers from Poliziano to Gluck that this period in the history of music might be called the "Era of Orfeo." Only the lyrics of Poliziano's work remain; the music is lost.[32] It is thus impossible to say whether or not Poliziano supplied the whole suggestion for the Florentine adventure, but it was definitely Vicenzo Galilei (died *c*. 1600), lutenist, mathematician, and— most important to the modern world—father of the famous Galileo, who first broke the trail.

Those who may have wondered how pregnant or sterile for the creation of significant art the house of the dilettante actually is, whether dedicated to a "future state" or to "worldly pleasures," must be reminded of the house

---

[30]Emil Naumann, *History of Music*, translated by F. Praeger, 1:517; quoted by permission of Cassell and Company, Ltd.

[31]Henderson, *Forerunners of Italian Opera*, 1.    [32]*Ibid.*, 52, 68, 98, 99.

of Count Bardi in Florence, in the last decades of the sixteenth century. Among the circle of accomplished men—composers, poets, actors—who met in this house of dilettantism was Galilei. Blazing the way toward a reproduction of the tonal effect of ancient drama, Galilei wrote and sang—or intoned—a dramatic *scena* from Dante's *Purgatorio* to the accompaniment of a single instrument, playing the viola as he intoned. The manuscript of this *scena* is also lost, but it is recorded that the presentation was eminently successful and that Galilei was inspired to write a second monody—the *Lamentations of Jeremiah*—for the same combination of voice and viola.[33]

Similar efforts followed Galilei's success in fairly quick succession. Giulio Caccini (*c.* 1558–1615) declared that the "wise and noble personages" with whom he associated in Florence "determined me to place no value upon that music which makes it impossible to understand the words."[34] And a preface to one of the works that became the prototypes of modern opera, the *Euridice* of Jacopo Peri (1561–1633), another of the group, states that he "applied himself to an investigation of that species of musical imitation which would the readiest lend itself to the theatric exhibitions," and "directed his researches to discover the methods of the ancient Greeks on similar occasions. He carefully remarked what Italian words were, and what were not capable of intonation; and was very exact in minuting down the several modes of pronunciation, and the proper accents to express grief, joy, and all the other affections of the human mind, with a view to make the bass move in proper time, now with more energy, now with less, according to the nature of each."[35]

Here, at long last, was a highly conceived attempt to transfer the spirit of the Corporeal music of ancient Greece to a time and place characteristic of Western Europe; here, finally, was a musical phoenix rising from the ashes of ancient Rome! Others of the little group of Florentines pursued the same idea, the best known of whom is Claudio Monteverdi (1567–1643).

Let no one be misled by the term "prototype" or by the words "dialogue" and "recitative" as applied to these early Florentine operas. What-

---

[33]Naumann, *History of Music*, 1:518, 523.

[34]Henderson, *Forerunners of Italian Opera*, 222. In view of Caccini's observation that he learned more from the "camerata," the circle of cultivated men about Count Bardi, than he had learned in thirty years in the schools of counterpoint (*ibid.*), one wonders whether the quality of music schools has varied much in three hundred years.

[35]Hawkins, *History of the Science and Practice of Music*, 2:524.

ever the manner of performance in their day—whether or not it fulfilled satisfactorily the composers' ideal of word vitality in music—we can be certain that the ideal will not be fulfilled in a modern revival. In this present day Peri and Monteverdi are predefeated; the ideal of the prototype is not that of modern rendition, and the modern manner of "declamation" is no more than vocalistic *bravura*. "What a fine instrument you have!" is a common compliment to the opera singer, and a perpetual reminder that the human voice is just another instrument, designed, in the modern mind, for pure beauty of tone and skillful *leggiero* and *fioriture*, and quite divorced from the civilized organic necessity of its evolution, namely: words. Equally non-perspicacious is that other common remark of Anglo-Saxons, "But I don't want to hear opera in English—if I understand the words it spoils the music!" which is nothing if not a frank admission that opera—to be acceptable—has got to be Abstract—without finitude or ubiety except in the most unreal sense. The exact source of this treachery to words will soon be revealed.

It is something of a final indictment that we are content to present, and to sit for two and three hours listening to, drama in a language we do not understand. Of course, we go to the drama to listen to its music, which to us carries meaning, perhaps all we desire. It does not seem to occur to us, at least not forcibly enough to alter our conduct, that the words are redundant, and that we are therefore two times twice hypocrites. From the double standpoint of actors and auditors we present a spectacle of coordinate and coexistent affectations. As actors we pretend to present drama in words and music when in reality we are presenting it in music only, and, by implication, that the words are understood when we know they are not, regardless of our familiarity with the language. As auditors we pretend to be listening to drama in words and music and by implication that we hear understandable words.

When the music of the drama is so surpassingly Abstract that we are gladly called hypocrites to listen to it, the situation that our operatic self-analysis has revealed is perhaps less reprehensible, but to say that this thing was sired by the Florentine Corporealists is to insult them.

It did not need the malediction of Nietzsche to relegate Florentine Corporealism to a bastardly existence: the Italian imitators had accomplished this by negation, and Bach *et al.* by Abstractional affirmation, some two hundred years before Nietzsche published *The Birth of Tragedy*.

Nietzsche, a master of word impact, could only gaze in awe at the Abstractional music impact of Beethoven. By nature searching, he openly envied that which he could only imitate, felt scornful of that which he tossed about with polemical abandon. Words were a matter of mastery and contempt, pure music of envy and fascination; thus: "It was the demand of thoroughly unmusical hearers that before everything else the words must be understood, so that according to them a rebirth of music is to be expected only when *some mode of singing*[36] has been discovered in which text-word lords over counterpoint like master over servant." Again, referring to the Florentine pathfinders: "The man incapable of art creates for himself *a kind of art*[36] precisely because he is the inartistic man as such."[37]

The penetrating Nietzsche is not to be dismissed merely on grounds of obsessive aspiration. The phrases "some mode of singing" in "a kind of art," are the giveaway, for they sound like a primal confession of inexperience. Nietzsche calls his own attitude toward a coupling of music and dramatic tragedy "prophetic," and, implying some kind of ultimate discernment, the "strangest possible kind of 'objectivity'."[38]

In word-idea the Nietzsche ability to engrave images was almost boundless, but in music—and despite his preoccupation with himself as "prophet"—the critical faculties were obviously trained on what the ear heard, and the ear heard Bach and Beethoven in unexampled reproduction.[39] What did the ear hear in the "path" of the Florentine Corporealists?—the Italian negation of "opera," undoubted calumnies on Gluck, and the bane of Bayreuth. Indeed must Nietzsche wish to believe that "Music is the essential idea of the world, drama . . . but the reflection of this idea, a detached adumbration of it."[40] Who ("inartistic" or otherwise) wouldn't?

## Paris—the Egg Hatches

Florentine music-drama became a contagion in Italy. But, in Henderson's words, "The reform of the Florentine coterie conquered Italy for less

---

[36]Italics mine.—H.P.

[37]*Ecce Homo and the Birth of Tragedy*, translated by Clifton P. Fadiman (Modern Library edition), 297; quoted by permission of Random House, Inc.

[38]*Ibid.*, 71.

[39]An observation of Helmut Rehder's is applicable here, though he is not speaking specifically of music: "German idealism had taught the concept of the absolute. By inclination and education Nietzsche was steeped in the absolute, and it appeared natural to him to regulate his life according to it." *Nietzsche and His Place in German Literature*, 5.

[40]Nietzsche, *Birth of Tragedy*, 317.

than fifty years."[41] The combination of the scale-tossing Italian composer with the liquid Italian larynx and the Galilei-Peri-Caccini-Monteverdi idea constituted a richer and a freer field for the polyphonic virtuosi who were rife in the Italy of about 1600 and who quickly reverted to a more spectacular form of the older degeneracy. The virtue of Florence became the vice of Italy.

The Florentine purpose? Ah, but why mention this, when the singer is so beautiful, her voice so limpid, and (through her) the composer (any one of several dozen) so famous?

Heinrich Schütz (1585–1672), sometimes called the "father of German music," reacted to this Italian scene precisely as his countryman Martin Luther had reacted to the lush ritual of the Roman Church a century before—reform! Schütz reapplied the Florentine idea to his music, most or all of which was a blend of the religious, the dramatic, and the polyphonic. For his *Seven Words from the Cross*, according to *Grove's Dictionary*, Schütz hit upon the idea of giving the words of a single character to a single voice, "for the sake of dramatic consistency."[42] (What monuments of ineluctable logic the human mind is capable of arriving at!) But Schütz was no Luther, for the idea took no root in Germany; indeed, two more centuries were to pass before the Germanic culture produced an exponent of any musical idea apart from "independence" and Abstraction.

If the Florentine intuition developed continuity anywhere in the Western world, that place was Paris. A vagrant ovum, fertilized in ancient Greece, in embryo on the Bosporus, laid on the Arno, finally hatched on the Seine.[43] The men who worked on some facet of the Florentine idea over a period of several centuries and gave it this continuity in Paris were not all Frenchmen, but they were part, and to some degree the result, of the ferment of Paris, and offered their works initially or entirely in the Paris arena. This continuity begins with the Italian-born Jean Baptiste Lully (1632–1687) and continues through three centuries to the near-contemporary Satie, Debussy, and Ravel and the contemporary Honegger and Milhaud.

[41]Henderson goes on to say, "The return to showy productions . . . was swift, and the student of operatic art can today discern with facility that the invention of the Florentines was soon reduced to the state of a thread to bind together episodes of pictorial and vocal display." *Forerunners of Italian Opera*, 212.

[42]*Grove's Dictionary*, 4:641.

[43]Indicating the possibility of a more direct route from Greece to France, Combarieu tells us that "In the sixteenth century some composers, such as Claude de Jeune and Mauduit, imitat-

Other Italians there were, both before and after Lully, who worked in the Florentine mold for the Paris Opera, but it was Lully who set the tone. So great was his zeal for natural accents that the time signatures of his recitatives change at almost every bar.[44] In fact, the more natural manner of recitatives became so normal to the Parisian audience that a visit of an Italian opera company in the year 1752, along with dazzling vocalistic mountain-scaling and dulcet *bel canto*, brought a storm of protest and controversy.[45] Into this melée Jean Jacques Rousseau (1712–1778) dropped his pro-Italian *Letter on French Music* and into it also the defenders of the French style tossed Jean Philippe Rameau (1683–1764). A skirmish became a war.

The French-speaking, Swiss-born Rousseau championed the Italian-born Italian style, whereas the French-speaking, French-born Rameau was persuaded to champion the Italian-born French style. Rousseau called the French language impossible for recitative and French singing a "prolonged barking." For this heresy against the French integrity of words the artists of the Opera touched a match to an effigy of Rousseau, and Rameau philosophized thus: "If I were twenty years younger I would go to Italy, and take Pergolesi [*one of Rousseau's idols*] for my model, abandon something of my harmony and devote myself to attaining truth of declamation."[46]

For both participants and onlookers the quarrel was the excuse for streams of wit and sarcasm, not all of it perceptive. For we have good reason to believe that nearly all concerned—possibly excepting Rousseau—missed entirely the most amusing angle, namely that the singer employed by either "school" was, and into eternity would be, a "singer"; that whatever the source of the recitative—the Rousseauists or the Rameauists—and however the singer chewed it, it invariably came out "singing."

ing the eccentricities of certain poets of that period, bethought themselves of writing melodies in the fashion of antiquity, by measuring French words into shorts and longs, like the Sapphic and Alcaic Odes of Horace." *Music–Its Laws and Evolution*, 313.

[44]Scholes, *Oxford Companion*, 783.

[45]Berlioz had his own theory for the state of opera in opera's private back yard: "As the Italian public has also the habit of talking during performances as loudly as we talk at the Bourse, the singers have been led little by little, as well as the composers, to seek after every means of concentrating upon themselves the attention of that public which pretends to like *its* music. They consequently aim at sonority above everything; to obtain it, they have suppressed the use of *delicate shades* . . . of the *lower notes* of the scale in all voices; they no longer admit any but the high notes." *Letters*, 384–385.

[46]*Grove's Dictionary*, 4:321, 452.

Clearly indicating that the gap between French theory and French practice in the recitative was pretty wide, Rousseau prophesied that one day some French composer would realize a "recitative appropriate to the simplicity and clarity of our language," that this recitative would "proceed by very small intervals," that it would have "few sustained notes [tones]," and that it would be "nothing that resembles song."[47]

Whether the next notable participant in this continuing Franco-Italian controversy, the Bavarian Christoph von Gluck (1714–1787), provided the fulfillment of Rousseau's prophecy is for Frenchmen to decide. Some are of the opinion that this event was not realized until the *Pelléas and Mélisande* of Debussy, a century and a half later. Gluck, who wrote for the Paris Opera, carried on his own private war with the Italianists; like Berlioz after him, he "blasphemed" their "gods."[48] The very title of one of Gluck's barrages in this war, *Essay on the Revolutions of Music*, is indicative of its temperature. Wrote Gluck:

I resolved to avoid all those abuses which had crept into Italian opera through the mistaken vanity of singers and the unwise compliance of composers . . . and which had rendered it wearisome and ridiculous. . . . I endeavored to reduce music to its proper function . . . without interrupting the action, or weakening it by superfluous ornament. . . . I have therefore been careful never to interrupt a singer in the heat of a dialogue . . . either for the purpose of displaying the flexibility of his voice on some favorable vowel [!], or that the orchestra might give him time to take breath before a long-sustained note [tone] . . . there was no rule which I did not consider myself bound to sacrifice for the sake of effect.[49]

Let us not be rash in concluding, when we hear modern revivals of Schütz and Gluck, that reform comes cheap to these composers. For one thing, the works rampant on the stage of their day, which aroused their righteous instincts, have long since passed from opera repertory, and, for another, let this fact be contemplated: syllables from Monteverdi, Schütz, Gluck, Mozart, Weber, Wagner, Verdi, Puccini, Moussorgsky, Wolf, Debussy, and Ravel, are expelled from the gullet in exactly the same vocalistic manner by almost any "serious" singer, and the Italian, French, German, or Russian of their origin makes less than an iota of difference. If this seems a cruel concentration of onus it will be relieved; the middle initial of all musicians—all of us—is *C*, for "Culpable."

[47]Lockspeiser, *Debussy*, 201.    [48]Berlioz, *Letters*, 5.

[49]*Grove's Dictionary of Music and Musicians*, 2:401; quoted by permission of The Macmillan Company.

## Berlioz the Unbelieving

In the century following Gluck on the Paris scene, many other composers preserved the continuity of music-drama. Two of these are the Belgian, André Grétry (1741–1813), and the Frenchman, Hector Berlioz (1803–1869). The fifty works which Grétry wrote for the Paris Opera-Comique, according to Scholes, "charmed by their melody and by their faithful expression of the accent and sense of the words."[50]

Jacques Barzun, who has brought a wealth of critical insight and historical background to the Wagnerian ideas and their precursors, writes that "Grétry, whose own works are not without charm or power, simply and lucidly put forth the same arguments [as Gluck] for the use of musical art as the underscoring of speech." Showing something of the eventual result of this development, through the further agent of Berlioz, Barzun goes on to say that "seventy-five years after rationalism, in the middle of a century which first gave him all its resources of invention and achievement, another was to attempt the same project in the name of Germanism, irrationalism, and realism combined. Wagner sums up and re-embodies, without truly resembling, the school of Romanticism."[51]

Berlioz, unlike Gluck and Grétry, had no *idée fixe* in his musical bag. His drama-hungry imagination encompassed all known and many hitherto unknown devices, explored what were in his day bizarre theatric and musical effects. His restless and impatient attitude toward hand-me-down authority brought from Mendelssohn the comment that Berlioz "believed in neither God nor Bach" (with notable sequence in these names!), and from Berlioz himself its exclamation point: "The expressive accent of a musical work is not enhanced in any way by its being embodied in a perpetual canon."[52]

With perhaps more than the usual complex of human inconsistencies, predilections, and prejudices, Berlioz conceived of orchestras and choruses measured in hundreds, with multiple brass bands in flank,[53] and thought of Oriental music as "a grotesque noise, analogous to that which children

---

[50]Scholes, *Oxford Companion*, 384.

[51]*Darwin, Marx, Wagner*, 280, 281–282; quoted by permission of Little, Brown & Company and the Atlantic Monthly Press.

[52]Berlioz, *Memoirs*, 103, 156.

[53]Said Prince Metternich: "Are you not the man, monsieur, who composes music for five hundred performers?" Said Berlioz: "Not always, monseigneur; I sometimes write for four hundred and fifty." Story by Berlioz in *Letters*, 13.

make when at play,"[54] but these can be taken in stride in view of the many pages of high zest for his subject and wealth of perceptions.

Remarking on the degeneration of opera, Berlioz gives as one cause "the preponderance that has grown up of the execution over the composition, of the larynx over the brain, of matter over mind, and, at last, too often the cowardly submission of genius to nonsense." This nineteenth-century echo of Aristotle is matched by the Plato-like statement: "Dramatic musical composition is a double art; it results from the association and intimate union of poetry and music."[55]

Just what this meant to Berlioz is less clear than his attitude on the practical result of the "intimate union." We should have singers for operas, he says in effect; we *do* have—operas for singers. The pernicious necessity of writing a role to the taste of a certain virtuosity gives the composer little choice, for the six styles of singing he will encounter (given in an invidious vein) are (1) the innocently silly; (2) the pretentiously silly; (3) the culpable; (4) the vicious; (5) the criminal; and (6) the rascally; he mentions no others. For salt in this tasty brew he adds: "the art of singing has become the art of screaming."[56]

Berlioz' writing is tortured with accounts of his efforts, mostly frustrated, to get certain qualities and effects out of his performers. When the director of the Opera requested him to turn the spoken dialogues of Weber's *Der Freischütz* into recitatives, he tried diligently to preserve the natural tempo of speech, but "could never make the actors abandon their slow, heavy and emphatic way of singing recitative." Despite his dreams of vast performing bodies he decries the tendency to over-orchestrate passages with voice, "exciting singers to wrestle violently with the orchestra in the emission of tone."[57]

One of the obvious solutions to opera's troubles, he believed, is an intimate theater: "I am sure that the musical fluid (I beg leave to thus designate the unknown cause of musical emotion) is without force, warmth or vitality at a certain distance from its point of departure. We *hear*, but we do not *vibrate*. Now, we *must vibrate* ourselves with the instruments and voices, and be made to vibrate by them in order to have true musical sensations." Again, pleading for an intimate music: "What pleasure could we take in the conversation of the wittiest people in the world, if we were obliged to carry it on at a distance of thirty paces? Sound beyond a certain

[54]Berlioz, *Letters*, 370.    [55]*Ibid.*, 378, 383.    [56]*Ibid.*, 376, 377.    [57]*Ibid.*, 388, 396.

distance, although we may still hear it, is like a flame that we see, but the warmth of which we do not feel."[58]

Berlioz was a free intellectual agent, an antagonist of any idea as a tyrannical principle, both in theory and work, but by the criterion of his own recitatives he follows in the Florentine trail. Taken as a whole, his life is a plexus of paradoxes; from the point of any one perfervid moment he is thoroughly consistent. His plea is always for understanding of the creative urge, and for the cooperation to feed and sustain it that can only come from understanding. Iteration and reiteration of this theme, in high-spirited, bitter, melancholy, witty prose, brought a whimsical view of himself as a Hamlet, not mad all the time, for "he is but mad north-north-west; when the wind is southerly, he knows a hawk from a hand-saw well enough."[59]

## *"Sprechgesang" in Bayreuth*

Richard Wagner (1813–1883) continues the line of auspicious figures who nominally or actually believed in preserving those characteristics of a word in music which make it vital, its natural spoken inflections, accents, and rhythm—in short, its inherent drama. "In the later works," says *Grove's Dictionary*, "the vocal melody often springs direct from the words . . . in some cases indeed it is but an intensified version of the actual sounds of the German language."[60]

In a measure of lip service to the word-ideal Wagner himself discourses through numerous excursions in periphrasis on the right method for setting words to music. In one place he figuratively bangs his fist on the table, and shouts through the italics, blackface type, indentations, capitalization, and various other artifices of typographical pantomime: "I declare aloud that the error in the art-genre of Opera consists herein: that a Means of expression (Music) has been made the end, while the End of expression (the Drama) has been made a means."[61] This is extraordinarily lucid for its author, and anyone who has innocently encountered the Wagner prose must respond with an audible "Amen" to Barzun's succinct characterization of Wagner's writings as "the incorruptible witness

[58]*Ibid.*, 379, 384.
[59]*Ibid.*, 402.
[60]*Grove's Dictionary of Music and Musicians*, 5:605; quoted by permission of The Macmillan Company.
[61]Wagner, *Prose Works*, 21:7.

of his obliquity."[62] In another sentence, remarkable only for its all-encompassing scope, Wagner states flatly: "We have had to recognize Speech itself as the indispensable basis of a perfect Artistic Expression."[63]

The distribution of power between words and music was by no means constant with the protagonist of Bayreuth, at least theoretically. But it is always an unequal struggle, despite the speech-music theory, despite the fact that one of a group of French admirers, whom Barzun singles out, "could point to the realism of having 96 per cent of the music [in *Die Meistersinger*] a mere notation of normal speech inflections."[64]

Why Wagner's players in their roles do not give the effect of the "German language," as *Grove's Dictionary* implies they do, whatever the qualification "intensified" may mean, and why his "means" does overwhelm his "aim," despite his prolix discourses, is a subject for further discussion in regard to singers. It is sufficient here to note that Wagner defeated himself (in the light of the Corporeal) by prescribing a full symphony orchestra—the right bower of the Abstract concept—as an accompaniment to the subtle drama of spoken—that is, musically declaimed—words, a situation which goes the limit in human contradictions.[65]

## St. Petersburg's Non Credo

In his expressed ideals Modest Petrovich Moussorgsky (1839–1881) is part of the taproot of the Corporeal spirit, whatever the current mode of rendition makes of his music. The harrying opposition of those to whom Abstract beauty is or should be *de rigueur* provoked in Moussorgsky a rather indefensible deprecation of the idea of sheer beauty, but one also in which his Corporeal banner is clearly displayed: "The artistic presentment of beauty alone, to use the word in its material sense, is sheer childishness, only fit for the babes and sucklings of art. To trace the finer characteristics of human nature and of the mass of mankind, resolutely to penetrate into

[62]Barzun, *Darwin, Marx, Wagner,* 307.
[63]Wagner, *Prose Works,* 2:357.
[64]Barzun, *Darwin, Marx, Wagner,* 319.
[65]On this point Barzun writes that the vocal parts "must resemble declamation rather than singing . . . For this reason also they sing alone, and since their single voices might find a full orchestral commentary difficult to overcome, the orchestra is divided, and one half of it concealed in a pit beneath the stage. Where this arrangement is carried out, as at Bayreuth, the proper balance is said to be achieved—at the expense of instrumental sound. Elsewhere the unequal contest goes on between the solitary philosophic voice and the brass-reinforced orchestra —often at the expense of the singer." *Ibid.,* 284–285; quoted by permission of Little, Brown & Company and the Atlantic Monthly Press.

these unexplored regions and to conquer them—that is the mission of the genuine artist."[66]

In the mid-nineteenth century Russians had, in "serious" music, only the choice of Germanic classicism or Italian opera. In the opinion of the "Powerful Coterie" the nation was ripe for some music of its own and opera on a better dramatic basis than the vocal *tours de force* of Patti and Masini. The "Powerful Coterie" (Balakirev, Borodin, Rimsky-Korsakov, Moussorgsky) was a nineteenth-century St. Petersburg version of sixteenth-century Florence's Galilei, Caccini, Peri, Monteverdi, *et al.*, composers drawn together by devotion to a common ideal—in this case the musical potential of Russia and, with Moussorgsky particularly, the potential of Russians, from lowliest to Czar.

The first tentative antecedent in Russia of Moussorgsky's "mad idea" was Alexander Dargomizhky (1813–1869), on the fringe of the "Coterie." Dargomizhky wrote an opera, *The Stone Guest*, for which his generating Corporeal declaration was simply: "I insist that the note shall be the direct expression of the word." Moussorgsky also stressed this theme: "Whenever I hear people speaking, no matter who it is or what they say, my brain immediately sets to work to translate what I have heard into music"; and again, "In my 'opera dialogue' I endeavor, as far as possible, to show up very clearly the slight changes in intonation that occur in the course of conversation apparently for the most trivial reasons and in the least important words."[67] (The phrase "slight changes in intonation" causes one to speculate on what Moussorgsky might have done in a more sensitive system of music, that is, one which offered smaller intervals than are available in the twelve-tone "octave.")

While working on his second completed opera, *Khovanstchina*, Moussorgsky wrote: "I am now deep in the study of human speech; I have come to recognize the melodic element in ordinary speech and have succeeded in turning recitative into melody. I might call it 'melody justified by the meaning'." In a "confession of faith" he asserts that only the great reformers have given laws to music, that these laws are continually subject to alteration, that it is his task "to reproduce not only the voice of emotion, but, more especially, the varying modulations of human speech." Virtually single-handed, Moussorgsky was trying to fill a vacuum which he alone

---

[66]Oskar v. Riesemann, *Moussorgsky* (Tudor), 104; all passages from this book are quoted by permission of Alfred A. Knopf, Inc.
[67]*Ibid.*, 162, 171, 172, 176.

could discern. In admiring Russian "Corporealism" in the visual art of his day, Moussorgsky asks: "why, in spite of their excellent qualities, is no such life to be found in the latest musical compositions? Why, when listening to them, is one so uncertain of their meaning?" which inevitably recalls Plato and his question about the "meaning" of music without words. The biographer Riesemann says of Moussorgsky: "He is never quite at home in the forms of instrumental music; his creative fancy can function with perfect freedom only when the sung word provides firm ground for the imaginative faculty to work upon."[68]

Words can be sung and sung and sung, fortunately for individuality in musical expression but unfortunately for Moussorgsky in an age of Abstraction, since "Moussorgsky's artistic career coincided with an age that neither saw nor wished to see beauty in what actually exists—its endeavor was to fashion beauty according to abstract laws."[69]

The seeming or elliptical assumption that the present age of "serious" music has improved in liberality, and now appreciates beauty fashioned in the Corporeal spirit, is wholly false. To find true Corporeality in manner of presentation it is necessary to go to the folk and popular singers, for it is present-day fact that few if any of the singers and masters of the concert ever escape their bondage to pure tone and vocal amplitude in the rendition of the word-loving, sensitive, subtle, and natural Moussorgsky.

Russia seems quite content to have only one really bad Corporeal boy to remember, but the spirit was infectious elsewhere (as it has been ever since Emperor Chun), and quickly touched another Slav, the Bohemian Leoš Janáček (1854–1928). Janáček's chief work, called at various times *Her Stepmother* and *Jenufa*, and widely performed in Europe after World War I, brought this comment from one reviewer: "It is perhaps the most intensely national of all operas. Its vocal music gives living expression to the intrinsic nature of peasant song and speech. As in Moussorgsky's operas, the music that carries the dialogue is entirely in speech-rhythm and includes no songs or other formal pieces."[70]

The Moussorgsky fever also touched Paris (which, had it not been Paris, might have been immune after two centuries of fever in its own right), but first, and en route from Bohemia: Vienna interlude.

[68]*Ibid.*, 108, 142, 221, 266.
[69]*Ibid.*, 100.
[70]W. McNaught, *Modern Music and Musicians*, 180; quoted by permission of Novello and Company, Ltd.

## Corporealism in Vienna (and Boston)

In the year 1860, in the old Austro-Hungarian Empire, two men were born who instinctively groped beyond the Abstractive attitudes of their time in their intuitive reach for the Corporeal. One of these, Hugo Wolf (1860–1903), dedicated his creative powers almost exclusively to bringing words into a rational equipoise with their harmonization. The other, Gustav Mahler (1860–1911), realized a Corporeal perception in a single composition, late in his life. The very word *Corporeal* appears in an anecdote written by a contemporary regarding Wolf's power in the reciting of poetry, and with startling effect: "Never in my life have I heard such reading. . . . I can only say this: when he spoke the words, they assumed a prodigious truth, they became corporeal things . . . Then, wandering about Europe, I heard nothing of him for some time, until his Goethe songs appeared. These struck into the very depths of me; and then I suddenly remembered. Yes, it was the same! The same man as in those nights."

This faculty for putting himself—his Corporeal self—into his music, Wolf acquired "from no teacher," says the biographer Ernest Newman. "It was clearly congenital in him." Like Moussorgsky, Wolf embodied a deep and broad sympathy for humanity, and also like Moussorgsky, "his music needed . . . constant fertilisation of the actual word if it was to bear its richest fruit."[71]

It is sometimes said of Wolf's songs that they are not merely correct declamation, which is of course true, since anyone who sees clearly beyond his formal vehicle puts a viable something into his work that cannot be formulated. But it does not follow that because Wolf is not *merely* correct declamation that the declamatory element may be submerged or ignored. Indeed, it is conceivable that that viable ingredient may only be released through the mechanism its creator stipulated, namely—declamation.

Neither Wolf nor Mahler expounded the mechanics of his approach to creative music, but unlike the story of Hugo Wolf the story of Gustav Mahler holds a contradiction—in fact, a double contradiction. Mahler spent most of his life with his fingers in the presentation of opera, in which work he was a fervent disciple of Wagner. Nevertheless, all his creative music was written in the traditional Abstract forms. The double contradiction appears in the fact that in one of his works, *The Song of the Earth,*

[71]*Hugo Wolf* (John Lane Company), 25, 26, 223; quoted by permission of Alfred A. Knopf, Inc.

for two solo voices (not simultaneous), he achieves a notable Corporeal effect, and this without resort to drama, story, or the true and tried emphasis on the integrity of spoken words.

"One of his key ideas," writes Ernst Křenek, "was the complete integration of drama and music, the dream of all truly theatrical composers since Monteverdi." Showing at least a nodding acquaintance with logic, Mahler, as director of the Royal Opera in Budapest, insisted that all the words of "drama" be sung in the language understood by his audience—that is, Hungarian.[72]

Despite this understanding and persistence, Mahler's love-hate attitude toward the text for his *Song of the Earth* invariably forced the words (which presumably inspired him) into traditional melodic and harmonic molds, to be rendered by the academic singer. By the criteria of both the score and the manner of rendition, he need not have stretched a long arm for the lyrics of ancient China to complement his intense personal message. The words might just as well have depicted an Eskimo cleaning fish by the light of the aurora borealis, or—nothing. Deprived of their subtle but very real integrity by Mahler's individuality and academic (to some degree Wagnerian) vehicles, the Chinese element is, from one standpoint, a tenuous, extrinsic, even ridiculous, reach for universality; from another, and measured by results achieved, it is a cause for gratitude.

Mahler does achieve a glimpse into universality, but not by such externals; he achieves it by an extraordinary revelation of himself as a living human spirit, and this he must have felt in at least a subconscious way, for the composition is prophetic.

*The Song of the Earth* confines its vitally human element to solo voice, and it is a Monophonic concept; that this concept is achieved despite the limitations of conventional methods makes it perhaps an even greater attainment. Bruno Walter declares that every note Mahler writes "speaks only of himself; every word he sets to music, though it may have been written thousands of years ago, expresses but himself. *Das Lied von der Erde* is the most personal utterance in Mahler's creative work and perhaps in music."[73]

[72]Ernst Křenek in Walter, *Gustav Mahler*, 180. The mere substitution of languages in recitative is far from an adequate solution of this difficulty. That it is quite impossible to put one language into the spoken tonal frame of another language was understood perfectly far back in the seventeenth century, by Heinrich Schütz, who in 1627 virtually rewrote Peri's *Daphne* for presentation in a German translation. *Grove's Dictionary*, 4:634.

[73]Walter, *Gustav Mahler*, 124.

The universal insistence among Mahler exegetes that *The Song of the Earth* is of the same stuff as his last symphonies is misleading. It is not. It is not concert music; the symphonies are. It is actually antithetical. Like Berlioz, Mahler indulged in huge conceptions for the Abstract, but also like Berlioz he was capable of the intensely personal.

Though *The Song of the Earth* requires a symphonic body for performance—and here is a prime paradox—it belongs in the home, in an intimate group, where the voices are not lost in vibrations-philharmonia, where inhibited strangers do not sit stiffly in flank, before and behind. And the final evidence of this antithesis is demonstrated in the periodic discomfiture of the Boston critics, who in the execution of their duties perforce report on their "feelings" at the occasional public exhibition of Mahler—the individual, Corporeal Mahler—musically naked.

It must be said that Corporeality is present beneath the Abstract habiliments of many other compositions. Douglas Moore's unaccompanied song *Come Away Death*, truly a Monophonic concept even though its words are not treated as spoken words, is an example. The singing of Elsie Houston is another, and the works of Frédéric Chopin might be said to approach the concept, through the sublimation of the piano as the One Voice.

Superficially, these judgments are suspect, but actually they betoken a healthy procedure—to admit, maintain, and proclaim that no preconceived end result can be achieved through formula, any formula, that is unvivified by the systole and diastole of spontaneity, purpose, thought, emotion, or whatever the symbol of the ingredient which has significance for some section of humanity. The formula for Corporealizing music through preserving the vitality of spoken words is actually as much a cliché as the sonata, and is lacking in imaginative, emotional anima unless the composer himself releases it.

## Back to Paris

On the subject of "Opera" in general and Claude Debussy (1862–1918) in particular an isolated sentence from the *Oxford Companion to Music* reads: "The *Pelléas and Mélisande* of Debussy (1902) stands alone in the whole opera repertory as the most determined and consistent attempt ever made to apply the foundation principles of the Florentine initiators of opera."[74] In his *Apologia*, where he discusses the principles upon which *Pelléas et*

[74]Scholes, *Oxford Companion*, 637.

*Mélisande* is based, Debussy expresses a desire to dispense with "parasitic musical phrases." He continues: "Melody is, if I may say so, almost anti-lyric, and powerless to express the constant change of emotion and life.[75] Melody is suitable only for the *chanson*, which confirms a fixed sentiment. I have never been willing that my music should hinder, through technical exigencies, the change of sentiment and passion felt by my characters. It is effaced as soon as it is necessary that these should have perfect liberty in their gestures or in their cries, in their joy and in their sorrow."[76]

Debussy was somewhat influenced by both Wagner and Moussorgsky at various times, though he was critical of both. But it would be frivolous not to assume the further influence of the centuries-old tradition in the French recitative. Still, by his own "apology" he seems to be only indirectly preoccupied with the vitality of words. In his concern for each ephemeral emotion he must have had a Moussorgskian ideal, or do the lines quoted above indicate that he is content to allow each such emotion to be interpreted by the music and then to present the music, in lieu of vital words, as the fact of emotion? Without a more definitive explanation it is difficult to say, but it hardly seems likely, nor does it seem likely that Debussy will get any more "*decibel canto*" subtracted from the performances of his opera than the conductors and performers choose to subtract. Mary Garden, in the role of Mélisande, apparently chose to subtract a good deal, if the Abstractionists' wails over her "mediocre voice" are an index. (Let us kneel before the God of Art, and murmur, "Please, Sir, grant us more mediocre voices!") What a commentary upon the parlous degeneracy of music-drama that Debussy's expressed theory—which is essentially a statement on words and music as they should not be united—is generally considered to constitute a radical departure in opera theory, even from Wagner!

At least two other composers in the Paris of this period left their Corporeal marks in the French tradition: Erik Satie (1866–1925), and Maurice Ravel (1875–1937). Of *Socrate*, Satie's setting of the dialogues of Plato, one commentator writes that "the vocal line represents the rise and fall and the inflections of the voice of a person reading aloud, lightly supported by a deliberately exiguous accompaniment . . . by its very sobriety and restraint

---

[75]Debussy obviously uses the word melody in the sense of discrete sustained tones; a succession of gliding spoken tones can also be a melody.

[76]Lawrence Gilman, *Debussy's Pelléas et Mélisande*, 51; quoted by permission of G. Schirmer, Inc.

the music throws into admirable relief the beauty of the text, and is truly Greek in its avoidance of exaggeration. The death of Socrates, for example, is a model of the narrative style in music." "His music has line . . . and the enormous merit of condensation. It is devoid of trappings and useless decoration, and when it has no more to say it stops." Another critic declares that the works of Satie "are as simple, as straightforward, as devastating as the remarks of a child."[77]

Ravel's principal Corporeal contribution is the melodrama in farcical vein, *L'Heure Espagnol*. A hearing of this one-act play on records leads to two conclusions: first, it needs no "apology"—except perhaps that the orchestra is sometimes too heavy for the subtlety of implied inflections; second, East and West cannot be as far apart as has been imagined, for the addition of a few Cantonese "clangs" and a peanut-eating audience would make *L'Heure Espagnol* and the Canton Music Hall sisters under the skin.

Many of the lines in Ravel's farce are frankly sung, but the difference between these and the spoken harmonizations is always distinct, a fact the more notable because the harmonic oneness of either sung words and music or spoken words and music is never obscure. It is this oneness which is absent in free or semi-free declamation to music, a device used by too many composers from Beethoven and Weber to Honegger, Milhaud, Schönberg, Berg, and Copland for elaboration in the precise limits of this review.

## *Voice in the Wilderness*

It is an act of revolution when the educated musician wearies of Music's pampered doctrines and shoves them into the dogmahouse, even temporarily, but when the inquisitive man of literature ventures on the precincts of music he is obliged to cope with none of its encumbrances and therefore with none of the censure occasioned by "revolt."

William Butler Yeats (1865–1939) was neither a musician nor a composer, but he was a poet who had great respect for the inherent musical beauty of spoken words, unburdened by symphony orchestras and the Abstract beauty of sustained "word" tones. Speaking of drama's needs generally and of the Dublin Abbey Theater in particular he writes:

[77]Rollo H. Myers, *Modern Music, Its Aims and Tendencies*, 41, 80 (quoted by permission of Kegan Paul, Trench, Trübner and Company, Ltd.); Thomson, *Musical Scene*, 119.

We require a method of setting to music that will make it possible to sing or to speak to notes a poem like Rosetti's translation of "The Ballad of Dead Ladies" in such a fashion that no word shall have an intonation or accentuation it could not have in passionate speech. An English musical paper said the other day, in commenting on something I had written, "Owing to musical necessities, vowels must be lengthened in singing to an extent which in speech would be ludicrous if not absolutely impossible." I have but one art, that of speech, and my feeling for music dissociated from speech is very slight, and listening as I do to the words with the better part of my attention, there is no modern song sung in the modern way that is not to my taste "ludicrous" and "impossible." I hear with older ears than the musician, and the songs of country people and of sailors delight me. I wonder why the musician is not content to set to music some arrangement of meaningless liquid vowels, and thereby to make his song like that of the birds; but I do not judge his art for any purpose but my own. It is worthless for my purpose certainly, and it is one of the causes that are bringing about in modern countries a degradation of language. I have to find men with more music than I have, who will develop to a finer subtilty the singing of the cottage and the forecastle, and develop it more on the side of speech than that of music, until it has become intellectual and nervous enough to be the vehicle of a Shelley or a Keats. For some purposes it will be necessary to divine the lineaments of a still older art, and re-create the regulated declamations that died out when music fell into its earliest elaborations.[78]

Some of these phrases—"the lineaments of a still older art," and "I hear with older ears than the musician"—ring in the mind long after the printed words have receded. It is not remarkable that a man of literature with an eager and anxious temperament should one day explode over the much-marvelled artifices in the modern degeneration of words in music, or, the art of song.

Edmund Dulac and others undertook to carry out some part of Yeats's musical ideas in their settings of certain of the poetical plays which Yeats based on Irish legend, using zither, harp, flute, drum, and gong. But although the scores show syllables allotted exact tones, in the actual rendition the spoken tones and the music were generally not integrated, except by accident.[79]

Provoked by the allegation in the English musical paper Yeats mentions—"owing to musical necessities"— a rude voice might retort, "*What*

[78]*Plays and Controversies*, 183–185; passages from this book are quoted by permission of Macmillan and Company, Ltd.

[79]Yeats and Dulac both informed me (1934–35) that these experiments were not satisfactory. I gathered that a complete understanding as to purpose, as between poet and composers and executants, was lacking; also, it was evident that the *sine qua non* of any such effort—persistence in the face of apparent failure—was not a party to the adventure.

musical necessities?" and Yeats replies in a footnote: ". . . the local time-table, or, so much suet and so many raisins, and so much spice and so much sugar, and whether it is to be put in a quick or a slow oven, would run very nicely with a little management."[80]

It is significant that some composers and some dramatists feel the need of each other's art, but they are rare and far between, and do not fortuitously coincide. Had Moussorgsky's name been Dennis or Yeats's name been Igor, and had they encountered each other in the same decades of vitality, Yeats's ideal might have been spared the complete frustration of its Dublin fate.

## The Schönberg Adventure

Perhaps the one contemporary composer whose work—aside from one or two notable exceptions—represents better than any other the apotheosis of Abstraction and John Sebastian Bach is Arnold Schönberg (b. 1874). One of the notable exceptions is *Pierrot Lunaire*, composed in 1912, and this is an exception indeed. The mechanics of its execution are explained by the composer in his preface to the work:

The melody indicated for the speaking voice by notes (apart from a few specially indicated exceptions) is not meant to be sung. The reciter has the task of transforming this melody, always with a due regard to the prescribed intervals, into a speaking melody. That is accomplished in the following way:

1. The rhythm must be kept absolutely strict, as if the reciter were singing; that is to say, with no more freedom than he would allow himself if he were just singing the melody.

2. To emphasize fully the contrast between the sung note [tone] and the spoken note [tone] whereas the sung note [tone] *preserves* the pitch, the spoken note [tone] gives it at first, but abandons it either by rising or by falling immediately after. The reciter must take the greatest care not to fall into a singsong form of speaking voice; such is absolutely not intended. On the contrary, the difference between ordinary speech and a manner of speech that may be embodied in musical form, is to be clearly maintained. But, again, it must not be reminiscent of song.[81]

The execution of *Pierrot Lunaire*, under Schönberg's direction, shows these glides to be vastly but effectively exaggerated, and to do no harm to the drama, or melodrama, of the piece, but rather to enhance it. Further, the words are heard as spoken words. But the contrast of the innate drama

[80]Yeats, *Plays and Controversies*, 184n.
[81]Egon Wellesz, *Arnold Schönberg*, 139; passages from this book are quoted by permission of E. P. Dutton & Co., Inc.

of *Pierrot Lunaire*—this single composition—with the consistent Abstractional distortion of word forms in other of Schönberg's compositions, and with the sheer Abstractionism of most of his instrumental works, leads to the conclusion that its composer must consider *Pierrot* as a whimsical adventure.

The musical philosophy of this composition is not developed in later works, although in his setting of Byron's *Ode to Napoleon Bonaparte*, written in 1942, thirty years after *Pierrot*, it is repeated, after a fashion, in that the *Ode* is scored for "Recitation, Piano, and String Orchestra." But recitation to music, even when it is rhythmically integrated as skillfully as in the *Ode*, cannot be a high form of the Corporeal ideal because of the inharmonic relation between instruments and voice. Consequently any consideration of recitation to music—the art of the *diseur* or *diseuse*—even in as exciting a form as that produced by the Sitwell-Walton combination,[82] has been omitted here, although it is certainly Corporeal music. There are times when an acute organ of hearing in a *diseur* will bring an unconscious harmonic integration, and this is certainly true in the frequent harmonic oneness of Sitwell's voice with Walton's music, although the amount of "unconsciousness" involved might be open to question.

Egon Wellesz, pupil and biographer of Schönberg, obscures the real saliency of *Pierrot* when he writes: "I am to some extent distrustful of people who know only *Pierrot Lunaire*, and admire Schönberg on the strength of this one work, without troubling to know his other compositions. Such an admiration seeks out from the treasures of a composer of genius the particular work that may have a certain effect on even an unpracticed hearer, without considering that *Pierrot Lunaire* represents only a single link in a chain of which all the other links are of equal value."[83] Wellesz fails to suggest how significant may be that "certain effect on even an unpracticed hearer."

## The Vacant Lot

A casual examination of the contemporary American lot for composers with Corporeal attitudes involves an occupational hazard. To begin with, the presence or lack of Corporeality as here defined is one man's opinion;

---

[82]Two records (four sides—recording by Decca) of Edith Sitwell's poems, music by William Walton; title: *Facade–Melodrama for Voice and Chamber Orchestra*, recited by Edith Sitwell and Constant Lambert.

[83]Wellesz, *Arnold Schönberg*, 7.

secondly and admittedly, Corporeality is realizable without harmonized spoken words; and, thirdly, most present-day composers don't like Corporeality and don't pretend to.

At the risk of inviting criticism for being discovered, or not discovered, or misinterpreted, two of our contemporaries are isolated. In discussing opera Virgil Thomson aims at its crux:

You cannot write an opera, as you can a song, by making up a tune and then fitting words to it. You have to start from a text and stick to it. You must scan it correctly and set it to tunes convincingly. In the more vigorous operatic epochs singers even articulate it comprehensibly. Speech so scanned and set, if intoned with clear articulation, is both easier to understand and more expressive than speech that is not intoned; and it can be heard farther.

All the rest of an opera is just the icing on the cake . . . You can add ballets, earthquakes, trained seals, trapeze acts, and an orchestra of a hundred and fifty musicians with sirens and cowbells. . . . It has no limits about vocal or instrumental style. It is stylistically the freest of all the musical forms and the most varied. It can stand any amount of interpolated numbers, musical, scenic, or acrobatic. [But] . . . Let us repeat it over and over. Basic opera is nothing more or less than an intoned play. Start from there, as the opera did and as every reformer of the opera has to, and you will arrive at complete musical theater. Start from anywhere else, and you arrive at incomplete musical forms and at very uninteresting theater.[84]

Marc Blitzstein is another who attacks the subject of words in music squarely:

The setting of English words is a large field, full of traditions, all of them bad. In so-called "serious" music, there are the execrable formulas of wind pronounced "wined," all *a's* broad, and all *r's* rolled ("—Ond the mon took the maiden's hond, ond verrrry verrrry merrrry were they!"), and of the distortion of words and meaning to fit musical phrase. In "popular music," where these things are managed much better indeed, there are other tedious and worn-out tricks . . . There is a school which asks for singing while singing, and speaking while speaking. This sounds very pure, and very sound: but when it is a question of theatre, it simply will not do.

Blitzstein is here not speaking of opera, an impending tackle which he skirts with a single hip-swinging phrase—"an enormous mess and tangle of a subject."[85]

Living performances of experimental musical theater, by these and many other Americans, and by Europeans of the past fifty years, are

[84]*The State of Music* (copyright by Virgil Thomson, 1939), 193–195; quoted by permission of William Morrow and Company, Inc.

[85]Marc Blitzstein, "Music in the Theatre," in John Gassner and Philip Barber, *Producing*

denied to anyone who does not spend the greater part of his life in or near New York, Paris, or Vienna, and even records and scores, which elide every visual quality of the theater, are seldom available—a tyranny of off-center centralization. The answer that these works would have been presented to a three-thousand-mile radius of nonresidents if they had been "successful" is hardly satisfactory.

Perhaps a national psychosis is too great a challenge to one generation of mortal men. Yet it does no harm to point out a native ability which prevails against all erotic instincts to make the daily erasure of even the freshest of bodily odors a national rage, an attitude which also waves aside the best efforts of the American music-theater mind because one circumscribed audience does not exercise itself into a dithyramb of approval.

Indeed and alas! a music-drama vacant lot.

## "Independence" Born of Aspiration

Why is it that lyrics and drama in association with music so continually edge toward Abstraction, toward concert music, toward the "star" system of virtuosi, that philosophic men of musical bent from Emperor Chun and Plato to the Vacant Lot must continually endeavor to rein them? Does the sum-total arbiter of values really prefer these qualities in lyrics and drama? Or is there a universal tendency to adulterated Corporealism (or, simply, adulteration) after an initial enunciation and demonstration of high principles? To attribute the situation to human vanity may be an oversimplification, yet it is basic. The goods-on-the-counter of the musical philosopher —if he has the strength to inject an agent of ferment—is philosophical integrity of idea. The goods-on-the-counter of the prima donna—if she can crash the Metropolitan—is generally altitudinous vocalisms on trapeze. The referee in this battle of mutually exclusive purposes—if he can resolve his chronic confusion long enough to know it—is the personification of ultimate value to our society.

Both classicists and romanticists lived in a twilight zone of conscious belief in the "immaculate conception" of music—in the "architectonics" of musical form—and an unconscious fascination for its opposite.[86] A very

---

the Play, together with the New Scene Technician's Handbook, 470, 473, 475; quoted by permission of The Dryden Press, Inc.

[86]Says the critic Ernest Newman: "The general habit of composers is to ignore everything in the words that will interfere with their developing their melody on its own lines. There is not a song-writer of genius, from Schubert to Brahms, in whose work examples of this sacrifice of the

few from both schools consciously accepted the opposite, with by no means a delivery of equal results. A few, such as Berlioz and Mahler, and perhaps still others, did not accept, yet occasionally delivered a Corporeal product.

The Abstractive trend frequently stems more from internal desire than from external influence, man being a many-sided creature. The inherent tendency to expand physically, to elaborate, to aspire, leads complex identities, again Berlioz and Mahler as examples, into using bodies of performers so huge as to shorten their lives by exasperation. That this can lead only to a super-concert music, and Abstraction, is obvious. Such means preclude the drama that an intense individual can embody. I have seen my own work, in evolving (progressing is not necessarily the word) from one performer to five performers, take on the character of Abstraction from the sheer inertia of numbers!

Still another agent for a type of Abstraction is the vicarious glow to be gained from having written works for a special talent, a special voice, a special virtuoso. The mind says to the voice: "I'll give you the vehicle for your 'instrument' if you'll give me glory." It's strictly *quid pro quo*. Not idea, but physical individual "talent" dominates the chemistry. Sometimes the composer is himself the performer; he has goods on two counters, very often in competition with each other in his soul.

Spontaneity of execution is the essence of music vitally connected to the human body, through the mouth, the ears, and the emotions. Spontaneity does not necessarily imply any inconstancy of execution; it is almost always present when a piece of music is performed, with almost no deviations, as it was conceived, and the same every time. That this ideal is possible only with a very few performers is very evident, and that it is actually on the threshold of a new age as a result of greater (electronic) tonal means requiring only one or a very few performers is also very evident. Let some seventh son of a seventh son say that it will one day cross the threshold![87]

poet to the musician cannot be plucked by the handful." *Hugo Wolf* (John Lane Company), 157 (quoted by permission of Alfred A. Knopf, Inc.). Yet the fact that these composers "of genius" were drawn to words at all is evidence of the unconscious fascination true Corporeality held for them.

[87]Until the electronics engineer has been educated into becoming a good husband, the carrying of his bride Music over the threshold augurs no good. The affianced has a body of well-tested and exciting dynamics, but the suitor-engineer, with an obsession for maintaining "level" in his nervous fingers, twirls them into electromagnetic oblivion in the flick of an eyelash. Perhaps some of the old lady's habits do need changing, but not by a nascent, dial-twirling, prospective young husband who gives no notice.

The men who have formed the subject matter of this critique were chosen because they have accomplished, or because they have stated or implied theories for accomplishing, a music vitally connected to the human body. Emphasis has been on statements rather than music for very good reasons. Although neither words nor musical notation is absolute, notation is far less absolute than words, and singers are inclined to attack any notes put before them in conformity with their "voice training," even when specific instructions come from the rumble seat.[88]

## Notes on Notes

Let us examine some of the scores of these men, however, in the light of their own hypotheses. All were consciously trying to bring to music a quality of musical speech, in greater or lesser measure—a quality which contributes to a product arbitrarily described herein as Corporeality. They might, and sometimes did, achieve Corporeality without too much actual incorporation of dominant speech qualities, but it is nevertheless profitable to look in their work for such devices as did, or did not, promote these qualities.

One of the salient characteristics of spoken words—perhaps the most salient—is the tonal glide. Indicated glides in the scores of these men are few. Throughout operatic performance, however (and all composers are aware of this fact), singers—and the most famous especially—*do* glide, for dramatic effect, particularly in attack and release. This is a practice which very few composers—Schönberg is a notable exception—have chosen to rationalize and to notate.[89]

Monteverdi, at the fountainhead of the idea, is perhaps the most disappointing. The last two syllables of nearly all Monteverdi's recitative phrase-endings are sustained beyond the speed of syllable movement in the major part of the phrases, and the recitatives are thick with syllables

---

[88]An example is the *parlando, senza espressione* notation given by Mahler for the voice in the last movement of his *Song of the Earth;* this instruction is corroborated, a few bars later, with *sempre parlando*. In the whole history of the performance of this composition these instructions by the composer were probably never followed, and they certainly are not today. Still, it must be stated that neither Mahler's notation nor his orchestration at the point in question is calculated to effect a true *parlando* (the affirmation-intoxication-negation of Wagner in miniature!).

[89]The difficulty of notating a vocal line that preserves the integrity of spoken words is not a small one, but neither is it insurmountable (see chapter on Notation), and the compensations are large. Few orthodox musicians would call such vocal lines "musical," and Combarieu declares that the songs of birds are not "musical" either, because they are "very difficult to take down in notation." See his *Music—Its Laws and Evolution*, 155. Will some divine power please

elongated to suit the Monteverdi melodic sense; in both cases a capitulation of words to preconceptions of musical form. Gluck, on the other hand, consistently preserves more natural spoken rhythms in his recitatives. Like Monteverdi, Schütz, and even Berlioz and Moussorgsky, Gluck liberally mixes the siblings Phonic—Mono, Poly, Homo. Further, the definite contrast between the singing of words—in the polyphonic and homophonic forms—and the speaking of words on tones, a contrast implicit in the works of all these men, can be extremely gratifying. In actual rendition it is almost never achieved.

Chorus was generally stipulated. At its best, whatever its value as Abstract esthesia (or anesthesia), the chorus has only the dramatic value of contrast; by the criterion of inherent dramatic value, with its words having the double noose of musical form and unison voices tightened around their necks, it becomes ridiculous. Even a mob is made up of individuals, and mobs speak in unison only for "art." The chorus will cease to be ridiculous only when its sociological function is transformed or simplified: when it sings in meaningless syllables or short reiterated phrases, or interjects comments in one- or two-syllable words, and abandons the effort to convey one message by the words of many.

It has taken the ancient frustrations of the Negro people to bring innate warmth and humanity to this institution dedicated to the gregarious opening of the mouth to say words in time. And at least half of this result is attributable to the lack of interest in written notation, which whites and pseudo-whites, impregnated with rules as they are, cannot engender short of revolution.[90]

Many of our music-drama reformers became intoxicated with the power of their accompanying orchestras—Wagner, for example, who thus lost control of his pet and painfully evolved thesis. From the standpoint of tonal amplitude his right-hand orchestra knew not what his left-hand music-drama was doing, nor cared. It is therefore fitting irony that Wagner is becoming less and less known for his music-dramas, except in a mythical way, and more for blocks of Abstract symphonic music bodily subtracted from his music-dramas; for such he has become a standard part of academic education.

create a "musical" bird to sing the Air for G String in exact Equal Temperament for M. Combarieu?

[90]Other exceptions or near-exceptions might be pointed out: the "harp-singers" of the South, for example, but here again the effects spring from innate desire, not musical education.

The most characteristic musical feature of Debussy's one opera is reminiscent of neither Moussorgsky nor Wagner, his immediate predecessors, nor of Gluck. This feature, sustained phrase-endings, is an echo of Monteverdi, whether conscious or not. As an occasional device toward greater musicality it is charming, even delicious, but its consistent use destroys word-meaning, and device becomes vice. His greatest climax (like some of Wagner's greatest) is entirely on sustained tones, which is opera, not drama.

Moussorgsky, using a rule that might be called "word integrity," seems to come closest to a true Corporeality, from the test of both score and available rendition. The necessity of basing one's judgment on the understanding of performers and the quality of the performance—which, when a large company is involved, is unpredictable—of course makes this only a tentative and possibly ephemeral opinion. The composer is seldom able to write down exactly what he wants, or fails to do so because he is harassed by the immensity of his job—or because he knows jolly well he'll be glad to take anything in the way of a performance that he can get. A final obstacle to definitive judgment is the fact that the great majority of composers played—in performance and on records—find it mortally difficult to articulate a complaint over the way their life works are treated—or mistreated!

The constellation of men here presented were examined mostly from the touchstone of the requirements they placed upon themselves. How well they entertained or do entertain their audiences is alien territory.

CHAPTER TWO

# American Musical Tendencies

THE FUNDAMENTAL stimuli that are the reasons for the music of these United States are intriguing to ponder. First, does Abstraction continue to guide us in the uniting of words and music? Have the Germanic traditions in the Abstract, enhanced in coming to us by way of the well-known English devotion to them, taken full possession of our educational and creative endeavors in music? Is there any evidence of a drift away from the general assumption that music, to merit comparison with the "best," *must* be Abstract? Does popular music, either in tendencies or intrinsic characteristics, offer any hope of relief from the iniquities in the usages of "serious" music? Can our American leanings in the "big business" of the concert system come to any good end? Finally, will the American genius for perverting a spark of individual imagination into a commodity for nationwide distribution permit us—ever—to hope for a significant evolution in American music? These questions suggest a few of the drives; there are others.

## From Dawn to Sonata

The reverberation of words in music has come down through the ages, and the reverberation—truth compels us to add—is in inverse proportion to word integrity. Composers, since the sun-up of history, have been fascinated by words. They have taken proprietary possession of them, and in recent centuries· have spirited them to an ambivalent hideout called "musical form." Other composers and philosophers have used every instrument of argument and demonstration at their command to succor the "victim."

Both kidnappers and rescuers did, can, and do commit humdrum musical trivialities; tonal tedium waves the flag of no one idea. But only the rescuers argue. Argument—aside from an occasional potshot—is abjured by the great majority, the practitioners of "independent" music, who might or might not have involved themselves with kidnapped words. Being the faction *de jure* and having been the faction *de jure* for at least a thousand years, this is natural. There is perhaps nothing that will instill confidence so thoroughly as being "right" for a thousand years.

At its farcical worst the attitude of this great majority—wandering the gamut of Abstraction from variations to sonata—has a dead-end, holier-than-thou nuance of "immaculate conception," but even at its best it suggests an antithesis, a polarity of two ideations. These music-philosophy concepts—the ages-old Greek sublimation of a thoroughly "maculate" conception and the (probably equally ancient but conveniently designated) Anno Domini negation of immediate values in transcendent "purity"—are and will undoubtedly remain contradictory to a fare-ye-well.

The "pure" counterpart of this situation in painting incites D. H. Lawrence to a violent protest which, although one might wish that it could be made with some mellowing reservation, still needs to be said. "Oh, purify yourselves, ye who would know the esthetic ecstasy," he calls in mockery. "Purify yourselves of all base hankerings for a tale that is told, and of all low lust for likenesses. Purify yourselves, and know the one supreme way, the way of Significant Form. I am the revelation and the way! I am Significant Form, and my unutterable name is Reality. Lo, I am Form and I am Pure, behold, I am Pure Form. I am the revelation of Spiritual Life, moving behind the veil." The jeer in Biblical tone ends with the straight statement: "I find myself equally mystified by the cant phrase Significant Form and Pure Form. They are as mysterious to me as the Cross and the Blood of the Lamb."[1]

Eighteenth-century classicism, compounded of the spirit of Abstract esthesia in the early ecclesiastical music and the mechanics of Corporealism in the popular forms—the innovations of discant, rounds, *faux bourdon*, dances[2]—produced an abundance of Abstractionist technicians in the execution of "form": conductors, instrumentalists, singers. Consequently those composers whose individualities fitted the bill of Abstract goods—like Bach, who enhaloed all he touched, from jigs to masses, with the poly-

---

[1]*Phoenix: The Posthumous Papers of D. H. Lawrence*, 565–566, 567; all passages from this book are quoted by permission of The Viking Press, Inc.

[2]Compare H. G. Farmer: "The minstrels were not only the real disseminators but the innovators. Indeed, how could music have made the progress that we see in the early MiddleAges had the church and written music been the only means? . . . The minstrel was not bound by conventional *usus* like the church singer." *Historical Facts for the Arabian Musical Influence*, 160; quoted by permission of William Reeves, Ltd.

phonic nimbus of the Abstract—got assurance of authentic reproduction and posterity for their music from the Abstractionist technicians, whereas those composers who did not fit this particular bill, like Moussorgsky, got—Abstractionist technicians!

This is not to suggest that anyone is proposing an ecumenical prohibition of the Abstract. There is nothing wrong with Abstract music as such, but it deserves a better fate than to serve as the testament of the scribes and the pharisees, the press-badge of gratuitous "emcees" at circumcision, the squire of the musicians' union, and an article of merchandise for the minions of the subscription series and for those other more obscure "lovers of music" whose "loving" ears are tuned in only on the cash register.

In view of this situation, which has been general for some little time, it is not congenital pessimism which has prompted the repeated assertions of defeat for the Corporeal spirit in music; it is simply knowledge of the "technical" situation.

## Composers on the Prowl

Who are the traitors—willful or otherwise—to words in music-drama on the contemporary scene? First, the conductors (with possible exceptions), who yield to the temptation to look important and provocative; second, the stars (exceptions improbable), who yield to the temptation to look and sound important and provocative; third, the composers (statement as to possible exceptions reserved), who yield to the desperate temptation to allow the conductors and the stars to look and sound important and provocative so that by hook or crook some pitiful vagrant ray from the glory of the conductors and the stars will vicariously glow upon them and make them seem a bit more important and provocative than they feel.

Certainly composers have a right to use words—or any other available materials—in any way that the total result justifies, in good or bad prosody. To some composers and singers, particularly in popular and folk fields, each word is in itself a not-to-be-denied ingredient. To other composers and singers songs are primarily melodies, musical forms, and tonal structures, in which the words fix the general mood, but beyond that serve merely as types of embouchures, to give consonant impulse and vowel quality to each chord progression.

Given the second hypothesis and—corollarily—given a song (or an opera) that tends to fulfill that hypothesis, remarks on prosodiacal or non-prosodiacal results are fruitless and irrelevant because other, more Abstract, considerations become esthetically predominant. But that does not alter the fact that an Abstract music-drama is Corporeal hypocrisy.

"When Dargomizhky says that he insists on the note directly expressing the word, what does he mean?" asks Jacques Barzun. "And when Moussorgsky speaks of turning recitative into melody, again what does he mean? If there is an *ex*pression, a *trans*lation of words *into* music, we certainly leave words behind and enter a new realm of discourse, the language of music; and if that is so, what is to stop us from committing all the delightful abominations that you stigmatize as Abstract?"[3]

The question might be put thus: exactly how *ex* should the *ex*pression of words be in music? And the answer might be given: as *ex* as the result justifies, which of course authorizes anything. Of the composers mentioned in the first chapter, Mahler, we might say, is on the extreme right, because his music with words is completely *ex*; his words do not arrest our attention as words; they are left completely behind. The vowels of his words, in sustained form, arrest our attention, but this is something else—something we are more likely to call conventional melodic form. A duplication of conceivable speech, on the other hand, harmonized in a musical setting, may be said to represent the extreme left; words are not left behind at all but remain in the foreground of consciousness. Moussorgsky, then, is fairly left of center (whatever his formula may have been for turning "recitative into melody"), because the words of his recitatives are frequently *ex* only to the extent that they control and consequently harmonize with the musical structure; they do arrest us as words, almost as much as they would if spoken dramatically in a play without music.

Certainly nothing should stop us from going as stark *ex* as our tastes and instincts dictate, especially to the end of "delightful abominations!" The crucial question is whether this *ex*-directed process—however devious or naive—should usurp all our schools of singing and composition, and turn them into a horse with blinders on. On such issue a good guess could be made regarding the position of Jacques Barzun.[4]

The desideratum for which I am pleading is a congenial milieu for the music of creators who do not fit into the Abstractionist framework of "serious" music, composers who want their words to sound not like mellif-

[3]Letter to the author, 1945.
[4]See *Teacher in America*, 115–125, and *passim*.

luous melody but like words, and their vowels to have only their natural brief span of enunciation. For them the Abstractionist technicians are not to be trusted.

## A Bottle of Cosmic Vintage

From one standpoint the twentieth century is a fair historic duplicate of the eleventh. At that time the standard and approved ecclesiastical expression failed to satisfy an earthly this-time-and-this-place musical hunger; result: the troubadours. Today, and especially in America, the approved Abstraction is a full musical fare for only a small percentage of our people, and the resulting hunger is satisfied by anything that breaks the formal barriers in the direction of Corporeality—hillbilly, cowboy, and popular music, which, whatever its deficiencies, owes nothing to sciolist and academic Europeanisms.

The devitalized tricks of "serious" singing, if they belong anywhere, certainly do not belong here, and they are nationally resented, consciously or otherwise. Examples are (1) the ubiquitous rolled *r's*, an articulation common in European tongues but alien to America; (2) precise attack and precise release (like the tones of an organ), as opposed to the gliding tones so characteristic of American speech, the *portamento* of "faulty attack" and "faulty release"; and (3) the affected stylization of "refined" English. Many of our folk and popular singers unconsciously tend to preserve word form and drama. Frequently their manner is simple. Frequently they "explode" consonants, and sustain such consonants as *l*, *m*, *n*, and *z* rather than the vowels preceding them.[5] Frequently they break a word off short of its notated time and let it fall or rise in a gliding inflection regardless of the notation. Frequently they personify a directness of word appeal, characteristic of this age and this land, and characterized by suggestions of actual times, actual localities, actual identities, and actual human situations, all of which is the very antithesis of the Abstract concept.

By mere control of the lips, mouth, tongue, palate, glottis, and diaphragm under emotional stimulus, the human voice is ready to express all the feelings and attitudes which the cumulative centuries have symbolized in words and poured into the dictionary—from joyful spite to tragic ecstasy, from ecstatic melancholy to hedonic fatuity, from furtive beatitude

---

[5]Ogden asserts that the vowel sounds in speech are normally ten times the duration of consonants (*Hearing*, 221). Most composers and singers seem to feel that 10,000 to 1 is also a good ratio!

to boisterous grotesquerie, from portentous lechery to obdurate athanasia—prescience, felicity, urbanity, hauteur, surfeit, magniloquence, enravishment, execration, abnegation, anguish, riot, debauch, hope, joy, death, grief, effluent life, and a lot more.

This bottle of cosmic vintage is the endowment of all of us. Do the freedom-fearing music schools of Europe and America train singers to give us even a little draught of these vocal potentialities? They concoct one special brand of their own, put it in an atomizer in the singers' throats, and send it in a sweet sickening stream over the proscenium and the kilocycles; it anoints the hair, it titillates the brows, it mizzles on the temples, and this wretchedest of intellectual infamies in the name of music—mark the term!—is called "musical tone."

## One Music—One Appetite

Couple these shortcomings of "serious" music with the austerity of the concert hall—rampant formality, huge impersonal assemblies with closely placed, hard, stiff-backed seats, black and white "tails," brisk robots on stage. Time was—in another and Continental age—when means were provided for drinking at concerts, and even in this country some of the small opera houses of early days had drinking tables at the rear of the orchestra or in the mezzanine—congenial to potable offerings in the love of music, and in fairly intimate surroundings.

Can we take no pride in a human gathering of smaller proportions than would fill a stadium? And will someone tell us the name of the presumptuous god who ordained that the respective appetites of spirit and flesh must remain forever strangers? And if there is none such, will the Arbiters of Pure Beauty please close their eyes on this sordid world and then inform us what is wrong with having tables strewn with glasses of beer and chocolate malteds along with music, at least in some situation more intimate than the concert hall?[6]

Except for the brief release of a ten-minute intermission, to allow Abstractionism's communicants the "smoke" of self-fortification for the remainder of something that frequently takes on the character of an

---

[6]Back in the early twenties, long before Hollywood Bowl became a cemented, be-shelled, be-uniform-ushered stadium, a few of us would take sandwiches and bottles of pop high up on the hillside there, and consume them quite without regard to whether we liked or did not like the music being played. That is a singular memory. Never since has the idea of the symphony orchestra seemed so painless in contemplation.

"ordeal by Abstract beauty," the Masters of the Concert arrest all the simple, uncomplicated, uncontroversial appetites of the flesh, slap them into jail, and hold them incommunicado for the duration—of the concert.[7] See, in the obscure background, the ancient ghost in its ecclesiastical habit? For they shall not "sing out of the parchment," nor shall they contribute anything except their stiff and reverent presence!

Considering the widespread vegetation of such and similar traditions, perhaps it becomes apparent why our bars are filled with rebelling youngsters, groping among bar entertainers for a better value. And the guess might be hazarded that the crux of rebellion isn't the Abstract fare quite so much as the cold punctilio of its dishing. Again—a vacuum, which is filled by the first thing that comes along, in this case the bar.

Contemporary visual art, and attitudes toward it, which arouse explosive resentment in D. H. Lawrence, in many ways parallel this situation in "serious" music. In viewing paintings, he maintains, we "are only undergoing cerebral excitation. . . . The deeper responses, down in the intuitive and instinctive body, are not touched. They cannot be, because they are dead. A dead intuitive body stands there and gazes at the corpse of beauty: and usually it is completely and honestly bored."

And intuition died, declares Lawrence, because "Man came to have his own body in horror." We are afraid of the "procreative body" and its "warm flow of intuitional awareness," and fear is "poison to the human psyche." "We don't live in the flesh. Our instincts and intuitions are dead, we live wound round with the winding sheet of abstraction." Our youngsters who look forward to creative careers are "totally enclosed in pale-blue glass bottles of insulated inexperience"; in speaking to one of them Lawrence felt that he was "like my grandfather."

Finally: "The history of our era is the nauseating and repulsive history of the crucifixion of the procreative body for the glorification of the spirit, the mental consciousness. Plato was an arch-priest of this crucifixion. . . . in the eighteenth century it became a corpse, a corpse with an abnormally active mind: and today it stinketh."[8]

<hr />

[7]Contrast the deportment of an audience of Greeks at their ancient music-dramas: "It is a lively audience, not less or more mannerly than such assemblages in other lands. It eats nuts and fruit and drinks wine as it listens; Aristotle proposes to measure the failure of a play by the amount of food eaten during the presentation." Durant, *Life of Greece*, 381. Presumably, much food consumed would indicate failure.

[8]*Phoenix*, 552, 554, 556, 569, 570, 584.

Music's "winding sheet of abstraction" is the always predictable audience in the concert hall, but the musical counterpart of Lawrence's "corpse with an abnormally active mind" is less distinct. Music seems to have several corpses, and not all of them stink, at least not of death. The corpse of one Corporeal music, for example, involves more than the appetite for music and recognizes the fact. Generally speaking, it is the Corporeal bastard in the bar.

## Into the Skyliner Age

Both the musical idea of Abstraction and the temperament which genuinely prefers it find themselves in sterile company. Abstraction continues to be the music of the "great interpreters," the papistical, while Corporeality continues to be the music of the "great unwashed," a poor specimen of Corporeality for the most part, it must be said, because the scribes are not prophets—they have lost touch with the people and have given them nothing better, or, if they are prophets, they're automatically convicted.

I am trying to hope that we are not entering an era where the only men of significance in music will be those facile at quoting Bach and Beethoven, Brahms and Tschaikowsky. It is something of an understatement to call this a conceivable situation, and it is also an understatement to say that it would show some similarity to the quoting of Plato and Aristotle, Ptolemy and Boethius, by the scholarly little men of some ten centuries ago. If we are entering such an age it is already dead, and I can think of no epitaph more fitting than this: "They did not like modern music." It was the tendency ten centuries ago, also, to reject "modern," or individual, thinkers, but to the everlasting credit of the little "interpreters" who lived in the dark ages let it be said that they did not engage press agents to label them as "great artists."

What of the immediate future? The consistent development of our present musical attitudes would seem to call for even larger masses of performers, even greater volume, greater speed in tones tumbling over themselves on instruments, and away from the individual and the individual's subtlety. One American musician has been heard to remark that the only way music will achieve validity in comparison with a modern super-fortress or skyliner is by parallelism in volume!—thousand-piece orchestras and—if this isn't a worthy analogue—electronic amplification of thousand-piece orchestras!—"swiftness, smoothness, and a brutish noise"![9] (Perhaps those pathologic aural masochists who might survive the apocalyptic concert by a thousand-piece, electronically amplified symphony would require oxygen equipment for their revival, and psychiatric attention to prepare them for the next apocalypse, materials and activities which would assist in rounding out the technical praxis of our new age.)

Nor does the dawning day of skyliners throw any rosy glow on music envisioned as a perpetuation of the *status quo ante*. Virgil Thomson gives a pithy picture: "The symphony orchestras are the king-pin of the international music-industry. Their limited repertory is a part of their standardization. The Appreciation-racket is a cog in their publicity machine."[10]

We might, perhaps, congratulate ourselves that we are not likely to develop music-minded Platos and Aristotles to condemn us as "dangerous to the state" because of our musical acts and views, that we are not likely to exile modern Timotheuses for introducing a few new scale tones (or are we?), and that we do not use or misuse "semitones" by Chinese-fashioned edicts. But this is a superficial view. On second thought we must wonder why men of the Plato-Aristotle-Ptolemy-Zarlino-Mersenne-General Thompson breadth of interest take no part in musical discussions (aside from the "appreciation" and "I-love-music" attitudes), why there is so much unanimity on the content of music at the same time that battles rage over its commas and exclamation marks—that is to say, its "interpretation"; why there are so few "searchers" in music as compared with the social and natural sciences, and even with literature; in fine, why

---

[9]Carlos Chavez, symphony conductor and composer, in plotting a direction, writes: "Nothing prevents us from making a whole new adjustment, in which—if the orchestra has new and greater capacities—the volume of air vibrated shall be greater and the music entirely new. . . . With the electric apparatus of sound production we shall be able to perform music adequate to the enormous theaters of our epoch and to places in the open air . . . The collaboration of engineers and musicians should produce, in a few years, a material appropriate and practical for huge electric musical performances." *Toward a New Music*, 177–178 (quoted by permission of W. W. Norton & Company, Inc.: copyright 1937 by the publishers). I have great sympathy for Chavez' general position, yet this is an instance of a mature and influential pressure toward ostentatious negation of the individual. Here Chavez' otherwise perceptive thinking is caught in the grandiose, sticky web of the symphony. The implication that only great vibrations are appropriate to the "open air" is a *non sequitur*. What of the intimate patio? and what of the ancient Greek theater?

[10]*The State of Music* (copyright by Virgil Thomson, 1939), 128; quoted by permission of William Morrow and Company, Inc.

music is such a dead issue. At least a part of the failure of the men of music is the failure of the intern who is unable to recognize death. The pressing need is for a realignment of music with rationality—with something for a realistic, philosophic, or scientific bent to operate upon, and therefore with something other than a mandarin tradition in theory, and something other than a body of musical criticism dedicated to the cerements of the musical corpus—Aristotle's "fantastic marvels of execution" and Plato's "swiftness, smoothness, and a brutish noise."

It has long been evident—ever since Plato and Aristotle at least—that the ability to manage the fingers expertly and swiftly on a musical instrument implies just that. "Interpretation," set up as a value, is a red herring. The possession of swift and expert fingers does not imply profundity, nor perception—even musical perception—and it is about as unrelated to qualities that make human character valuable as any ability can be. A case might even be made out to show that such qualities are insidiously and progressively debased in most of those who happen to have this so-called musical gift by the fanaticism with which they protect the physical investment. It is not necessary to go to Aristotle for corroboration, but the question that Aristotle points up is still open in these big-business days of concert darlings. The question: whether swift fingers induce inanity, and therefore are not worth the risk, or whether swift fingers simply, and almost invariably, give way to inanity in every rest of more than one fast beat.

The situation in music is actually only one of the more obvious aspects of a general paralysis of individuality. Lawrence shows it in visual art. What is the situation from the more fundamental—the sociological—viewpoint? It begins in the cradle. The late Scudder Mekeel, who was in the forefront of the battle to free the American personality from the tyranny of race prejudice, asserts that "by the very way in which we train our children, we make certain that they can never really carry individualism very far, or take full advantage of being themselves. This is the crux of our particular system of social control."[11]

Where is the "Bill of Rights"—in the age of skyliners and electronically amplified symphony orchestras—to forestall destruction of individuality in the individual? Is our "particular system" of musical control any less rigorous?

[11] "Race Relations," in *Mental Hygiene*, 29: 185.

## Ennui over the Waves

It has been said that because today more people hear Beethoven in twenty-four hours (on the radio) than heard him in his whole lifetime the people have music. Momentarily disregarding the question of the quality of emanations from the radio we can say: yes, and a citizen doubtless sees more policemen now in twenty-four hours than Beethoven saw in his whole lifetime. The people hear more music, and *ipso facto* they are more musical? The people have more law, and *ipso facto* they are more lawful?

The analogue is not so absurd. If we are to make of this age one that is at all comparable to that of ancient Greece or the Italian Renaissance it will be through a surge of real individuality, stimulating ideas, and a resolution to execute them faithfully. Hearing more music—ninety-nine per cent of which is not Beethoven but the equivalent of radio vibrations of frankfurters—accomplishes just one thing: ennui in the ear-drum.

Beethoven is a value that may be expected to persist because he has had value for generations of human beings. The point is not the value of Beethoven, but whether in our schools of serious music we shall confine ourselves to finer and still finer degrees of perfection in the "interpretation" of past treasures, whether we shall go on devouring or unconsciously absorbing vibrating frankfurters to that point of melomaniacal satiety at which our appetite vanishes, or whether some few of us will chuck the music school, turn off the radio, and go into the kitchen and cook ourselves a nourishing meal. We want good music—ah, yes!—with two strikes in the music schools and all but two or three of the 1600 kilocycles on the broadcast band already against it!

That ninety-nine per cent which—a thousand to one—will be heard at a given moment on the radio, is not Beethoven but an industrialized development of something which small groups of musically leaderless people spontaneously cooked up a few generations ago, and which—without the familiar American knack for "giving the people what they want"[12]—might have evolved into a charming, colloquial, and provincial particle of American culture.

Radio's use of Abstract music, conceived with all the "independent" intentions in the world, as background and "incidental" music in a thorough-

[12]A knack which Thomson calls "the outrageous designs of finance-capital on consumers' taste." *State of Music*, 250.

ly dependent application, and the purists' protests against this use, is but
further evidence of a widespread unconscious reaction against Abstraction.
It almost seems that the curve, which began with a Corporeal genesis in the
West, then saw the Corporeal mechanics used to establish an Abstract
musical philosophy, is now beginning to come full circle with an application
of the Abstract mechanics to a Corporeal musical idea. But the circle will
not be complete until the Corporeal idea is accepted consciously, along
with conscious efforts to make it a significant declaration.

That intermittent extraneity which the radio and movies call "incidental" is of course not a significant declaration. But even the worst of it,
even that which is obviously born of outside pressure and inward weariness,
suffers not so much because of bad intrinsic quality as because of the
subservient, scene-changing, punctuating role it is cast in. It is no integral
part of the moment's drama; with tiresome repetition of device it "pre-
pares" the moment, or "comments" on it, or connects it to another, or it is
obliged to accompany a weak moment to save the situation from sheer
cliché.

The "singing commercial," however obnoxious its sentiment or the
product it sells, is meticulously prepared; it suffers from lack of imagination
less often, and in mechanics of presentation it has much more to offer. If,
from a musical standpoint, a better solution for "incidental" music were instituted, many times more work would be required on each program, and
therefore so much could not be programmed so often to "entertain" so
many, the oft-repeated alibi for democratic mediocrity. The time is rapidly
coming when we must either decide to do something about this "incidental"
situation which, along with the juke box and other influences, is turning us
into a nation of amusiacs, or admit, frankly, that our kind of democracy
means selling music short.

Thus does the "universal language" at least fail to become any more
universal; thus does present-day serious music remain in the hermitage of
false eclecticism. The average American who chances to hear a record or a
radio offering of Chinese music promptly walks down the street giving what
he considers a perfect imitation of Chinese speech—the music doesn't touch
him, except ludicrously; the Oriental-educated Chinese who listens to a
European symphony concert says with utmost politeness: "It's very nice,
but why do they keep repeating the same piece?"—it doesn't touch him;
the exponent of jive who happens to hear one of the poignant, melancholy

songs from the Near Orient says quickly: "Let's dig 'im a hole so he can die quick!"—needless to say, the music doesn't touch him. Examples could be continued for a complete turn of the clock. Where is the precious seed of universality in all this?[13]

## *"Corporeal" Genes in Our Seed?*

To explain the psychological reactions to various types of music is not my purpose here, but one observation is perhaps pertinent. It is surely significant that education and conditioning so often fail to explain a music and the reactions to it adequately, and that some other, generally ignored, agent must also be operative. There is also immanent human desire, or there would never have been the phenomenon of the Florentines, and Moussorgsky, and those others who have intuitively resisted the vogues of their day and created music outside their own, or anyone's, education and conditioning. And such an inborn desire in individuals and in whole peoples, when it breaks through the fences of consciousness despite the lack of enlightened leadership and despite steam-pressure exploitation of mediocrity, can give us at least a general faith in the future.

One little story and one small example of such intuitive entry into the world outside of knowledge is suggested by part of the subtitle of the present book: "The Relation of Its Music to Historic and Contemporary Trends." The question immediately asserts itself: what conceivable connection is there between the Monophonic concept in "Its Music" and the Monophonic concept in intonation, outlined in the balance of this volume? The answer is simple: the connection lies in the fact of their union, a union conceived without previous knowledge of the long and coexistent presence— one of the longest associations in the history of music—of ratio-idea and music-enhanced word-vitality in the same culture, the Greek.

I developed the intonational system first, without any extensive knowledge of the history of acoustical-musical theory, and when I determined the reason for, and the form of, its music—that is, the essential truth and comparative significance of musically spoken words—I was as ignorant of Spengler and his "Faustian-Appollonian" interpretation of music history, of

---

[13]In a world populated by xeno-melophobics one or all of four reactions follow the impact of a new music, or of an old or exotic music brought to light, in the following order of probability: (1) it's monotonous; (2) it's melancholy; (3) what does it mean? (4) why play it? Berlioz offers at least partial corroboration: any new work, "according to the critics, is *invariably tiresome*." Berlioz' italics; *Letters*, 382.

the Tuscan dramatic flash of 1600, of Richard Wagner's dramatic thesis, as any human being can be. Perhaps my readers will understand something of the shock I got when—after several years of fashioning a special viola, and of writing and intoning vital-word music and accompanying myself on the new instrument, much of the time without assistance—I read of Vicenzo Galilei, who—three hundred and fifty years before—had written and intoned a dramatic *scena*, reviving an idea in music that had been dormant for at least a thousand years, and accompanying himself on a viola! and to have on this and other occasions the whole vast panorama of the association of vital words and music spread before me.

It is comforting to find a modicum of history pillared beneath, although the strength of intuition and of immanent desire which is the point of this little account was capable of sustaining itself without history—and this in a musical day characterized by practices and listening habits which in every salient respect were antithetical to it.

Perhaps these facts in themselves explain why Monophony, or its creative products, are not exactly parallel to any other theories or practices—Ptolemaic, Zarlinean, Florentine, Wagnerian, or Spenglerian.

A few random characteristics and thought processes of this intuition, which became guides for an individual expression: it is frankly and extremely Corporeal. It is intimate; one voice and one instrument is the ideal; a few more are admissible, but nothing approaching a mass of participants, either of voices or instruments, which inevitably produces the mass in spirit, or Abstraction. It must be intimate to escape dependence on the Abstractionist technicians, who would not understand it, like it, or play it; it must be intimate to provide an affirmative and individual relief from the pretentious values and fallacious standardizations of the concert hall, from the impersonal ubiquity of the radio (which could be very personal), and from the mass and unthinking reactions to mass inculcations.

The ideal for this music I first expressed many years ago: "to disclose a manner of impressing the intangible beauty of tone into the vital power of the spoken word, without impairing either." This did not, and does not, mean that I believe in a rigid contract between tone and word for all other composers. If Monophony as an intonational system is to have any value or any influence, temporary or more enduring, and if the Monophonic concept in music is to become any stimulus, neither system nor music can be limited one to the other, and it is more salutary if both are admittedly open to variation, correction, or adaptation, if they find response. If they do not, words are not important.

## The Enchanted Land

At this point questions loom on every side. What is the connection, if any, between a blind love of tradition in music and personality paralysis? What is the connection, if any, between the tendency toward exploitation and a widespread taste for the banal-mediocre? between social-political illiberalism and a widespread taste for the banal-mediocre?

One experience is not much, but when it operates without advance reputation it invites honesty—it combats no fear of *ex cathedra* or *ex neighbor* opinion. (There can be no fear of *ex cathedra* opinion when the subject is *extra cathedra*.) When a subject is unknown to everyone, and everyone realizes that it is, no one is under any pressure to say anything except what he really thinks.

Honesty on one subject has a way of horning honesty on other subjects into open air, and of stimulating opinions and attitudes of a general nature. The suggestion is consequently made, on the foundation of experience, that the interconnections aforementioned do exist—and significantly.

The courses corrective? They are at least two. Perhaps it is possible to teach a man how to find both his superior self and his child-creative self under be-medaled diploma wrappings, but the psychologist James H. Leuba has different ideas: "To seek to mold character by proposing ideals, imparting knowledge, providing rewards and punishment, is often an appalling waste of effort." And he suggests that the time may not be far distant "when years of labored and unreliable efforts by the direct method [*indicated above*] will be replaced by a vastly shorter and more reliable indirect method [*acting upon the body*]."[14]

Whether it is achieved through biochemical action on the body or through bio-spiritual action on the mind, there is—veritably—a universality which is ultimately attainable without reducing the entire world to the minus centigrade of the average swing band. In the world of perception beyond knowledge—here is the enchanted land! But perception cannot be manifested without opportunity: the opportunity to hear, to create, and to be heard. And opportunity simply does not appear where there is little sensitivity in powerful places, and where seemingly endless frankfurters vibrate

[14]*God or Man?* 92, 94.

through the brain accompanied only by the drone bass of a profit motive. It is the people interested in music who confer on individuals the privilege of becoming powers in music. Consequently it is up to us to see that more of the powers in music are leaders also.

Without aspiring to those ambitious ideas expressed by the fashionable words "timeless" and "immortal," we can do much to exert an influence worthy of our obligation to help point a way, and we need not be too despondent. There is a German proverb which denies the proverbial impertinence of proverbs when it says, literally: "What is not can yet become."

Music itself does not emerge from the dimensions of ambient night. The shadows of music are bred in deceit—half enticing, half forbidding, with myriad degrees of light-dark infusion—true interpretation with misinterpretation. Perhaps the passage of this discussion to the smallest units of aural reaction is not an emergence into brilliant sunlight, but it is at least an emergence in which interpretation can be more finely delineated, and misinterpretation within the determined confines countered with greater certitude.

# PART II

## An Introduction to Intonation

# CHAPTER THREE

# Definitions Pertaining to Intonation

## *To Clear the Atmosphere*

THE DEFINITIONS in this chapter, which are given as an aid in studying the Monophonic ideas on intonation and to establish a degree of tonicity for the statement of those ideas, may be examined cursorily at first and without undue concern if a given definition is not fully grasped at once. Each idea will be carefully scrutinized in the course of the work; wherever the reader encounters an unusual term he may refer back to these definitions if the specific meaning is obscure.

A writer on theory must make a rough guess as to how much knowledge of the subject is possessed by the majority of those he hopes to interest, and he starts from this guess. If the guess is wrong, if an interested reader finds that the starting point is beyond his understanding, he has only to skip the definitions, referring to them later as questions arise which they may elucidate, and perhaps again after finishing the balance of the work.

Whatever rewards the reader gains may entail great labor, and the course taken to them may try his patience, but if he has seized the initiative in wondering about the problems of intonation and has come this far he has done his part; the rest is up to the book.

From here to the end of the volume ratios appear frequently. In the original manuscript the two numbers of each ratio were shown one above the other, and this form is significant to the exposition in certain cases, the "over" number and the "under" number frequently having connotations of a very specific nature, as will be seen. The exigencies of typesetting, however, made it difficult to preserve this form where ratios occur in the text. Both numbers of a ratio appear in the same line; therefore, the number preceding the diagonal will be considered "over" and the number following the diagonal will be considered "under." In the diagrams the two numbers are always shown one above the other, so that the "over" and "under" connotations, if applicable, are obvious.

**1/1:** Monophony; the unison; unity; the Prime Unity; the generating concept from which the expanded system of music here presented takes its name (see Monophony).[1]

**2/1:** the "octave"; this symbol is used throughout without translation into conventional nomenclature (see Octave).

**3/2:** the just "perfect fifth."

**4/3:** the just "perfect fourth."

**5/4:** the just "major third."

**6/5:** the just "minor third."

**7/6:** the septimal "minor third."

**5/3:** the just "major sixth."

**8/5:** the just "minor sixth."

**12/7:** the septimal "major sixth."

**9/8:** the large just "whole tone," or "major second."

**10/9:** the small just "whole tone," or "major second." This ratio and the ratio above are confounded in tempered theory.

**8/7:** the septimal "major second."

**16/9:** the small just "minor seventh."

**9/5:** the large just "minor seventh." This ratio and the ratio above are confounded in tempered theory.

**7/4:** the septimal "minor seventh."

**16/15:** the large just "semitone," or "minor second."

---

[1]Anyone who has fought his way through either present-day musical nomenclature or the Minoan labyrinth of Greek nomenclature must find it refreshing to have anything as simple and rational as ratios to represent musical materials. The irrationality of the current variety is of course widely acknowledged, but on the whole the Greek nomenclature is probably worse; their musical philosophers alone saved the Greeks from music-theory obliquity. One name—Dorian, for example—could and still can mean many things, according to the time B.C. or A.D. that is implied, and according to which theorist—ancient, medieval, or modern—was or is speaking. It could mean a sequence of intervals (but not always the same sequence), an absolute pitch (but just what pitch no one is perfectly sure), a range of pitch, and a style of composition. Consequently the handicap of Greek names, even in outlining the history of music theory, has been fairly consistently avoided in this volume. Unequivocal, but still quite dispensable, are the Greek- and Latin-derived names for ratios that theorists used throughout the Middle Ages, the most common of which were:

Diapason, octave, duple interval—2/1.        Diatessaron, sesquitertian interval—4/3.
Diapente, sesquialterate interval—3/2.        Sesquioctavan interval—9/8.

Two other obscurely derivative terms are frequently found in ancient and medieval theories and even in modern works; these are "superparticular"—a ratio in which the first number contains the second with one aliquot part over, such as 5/4, 6/5; and "superpartient"—a ratio in which the first contains the second with more than one aliquot part over, such as 5/3, 7/4. A large number of subclassifications involving terms derived from these two terms are occasionally encountered.

**25/24:** the small just "semitone," or "minor second." This ratio and the ratio above are confounded in tempered theory.

**15/8:** the small just "major seventh."

**48/25:** the large just "major seventh." This ratio and the ratio above are confounded in tempered theory.

**45/32** and **64/45:** generally considered to be the just "tritones."

**7/5** and **10/7:** the septimal "tritones."

**1/1–392:** the "G" which is in the scale of "A" at about 440 cycles; 1/1–392 is simply a starting point for pitch measurement, above and below, such as "middle C."

**7-White–5-Black:** a term used to denote the key or digital pattern of all present-day popular keyboard instruments.

**Arithmetical Proportion:** an ancient principle of scale structure by which a sounding body is divided into a number of exactly equal parts, and a scale constructed from the resulting relationships, or ratios; this does not produce equal scale steps. The Arithmetical Proportion has been seized upon by some theorists as the ancient substantiation of "minor tonality," since, starting with the one part that gives the highest tone, it results in a series of tones the exact reverse of a fundamental and its series of partials, down to an arbitrary low tone determined by the number óf equal parts used (see page 174). The Arithmetical Proportion may be considered as a demonstration of Utonality ("minor tonality").

**Beats:** a phenomenon of alternate strengthening and lessening of tone produced by a very narrow interval in a simultaneous sounding, or by out-of-tuneness in the simultaneous sounding of an interval intended as a small-number proportion; as a very narrow interval approaches unison, or as an out-of-tune interval approaches a small-number proportion the beats become slower (see page 138).

**Cents:** a system devised by Alexander J. Ellis for quickly determining the width of a musical interval; a cent is the hundredth part of one of the twelve equal intervals between degrees in a 2/1 of Equal Temperament; therefore, 1200 cents to the 2/1 (see the next chapter).

**Chromelodeon:** one of the Monophonic instruments; the one more frequently used to date (1947) is a six–2/1 harmonium from which the old reeds were removed and into which reeds of the forty-three-degree Monophonic scale were placed, in sequence, so that the new 2/1 covers a much wider keyboard extent—three and a half octaves (see page 207).

**Comma:** either 531 441/524 288, the Pythagorean comma, or 81/80, the comma of Didymus (sometimes also called the "syntonic" comma).

**Complement:** that ratio which, added to another ratio (multiplied), makes 2/1; for example, 4/3 is the complement of 3/2: $4/3 \times 3/2 = 2/1$ (see the next chapter); in conventional terms, the "inversion" of an interval —a "perfect fourth" is the inversion of a "perfect fifth."

**Cycles:** the number of vibrations per second which a tone makes; the pitch of a tone; the word "cycle" to describe one of the Pythagorean successions of 3/2's is always used in quotation marks (see Pythagorean).

**Difference Tone:** a phenomenon which results from the sounding of two simultaneous tones—for example, tones of 300 and 200 cycles sounded together give a difference tone of 100 cycles (see pages 386–387).

**Equal Temperament:** twelve-tone Equal Temperament; any other equal temperament is not capitalized and is qualified by its number of degrees; for example, "nineteen-tone equal temperament." Any temperament, equal or otherwise (the various meantone temperaments), involves a varying degree of flatting or sharping of the acoustically correct ratios so that any tone of the temperament can serve in several senses—for example, "C" as the first step in the scale on "C," as the second step in the scale on "B" or "Bb," as the third step in the scale on "A" or "Ab," etc.—and still convey the "impression" of correct intonation (see Chapter 17).

**Fundamental;** *see* Unity.

**Geometric Proportion,** *see* Harmonical Proportion.

**Harmonic:** same as Partial, which see.

**Harmonic Canon:** not capitalized, harmonic canon refers to the monochord (see Chapter 6); Harmonic Canon refers to an instrument built at the University of Wisconsin for studying scales (see page 235).

**Harmonic Content:** practically synonymous with quality of tone; the term used to indicate that characteristic of a musical tone which is determined by the distribution and comparative energy of its partials, or harmonics; the *klang*.

**Harmonical Proportion:** that monochord procedure by which intervals are determined by the relation of the whole string to the half, the half to the third, the third to the fourth, the fourth to the fifth, and the fifth to the sixth, or 2 to 3, 3 to 4, 4 to 5, 5 to 6, etc. It is possible to determine the tones corresponding to the overtone series by this procedure, and in this sense the lower "overtones" delineate Otonality ("major tonality"; see page 89).

**Identity:** one of the correlatives, "major" or "minor," in a tonality; one of the odd-number ingredients, one or several or all of which act as a pole of tonality: 1–3–5–7–9–11 in this theory. This term is not to be confused with the ingredients of Harmonic Content, or with Partial.

**Interval:** a pitch relation between two musical sounds, a ratio. Interval, ratio, tone, are virtually synonymous in this exposition; a ratio is at one and the same time the representative of a tone and of an interval, and a tone always implies a ratio, or interval.

**Just Intonation:** a system in which interval- and scale-building is based on the criterion of the ear and consequently a system and procedure limited to small-number ratios; the initial interval in Just Intonation is 2/1, and stemming from this are the wealth of musical intervals inherent in small-number tonal relationships. Just Intonation is the generic term describing this procedure; Monophony (which see) is a specific system.

**Key:** used only to denote the key or lever of a keyboard; in the sense of tonality, "key" is always used in quotation marks.

**Monophony:** an organization of musical materials based upon the faculty of the human ear to perceive all intervals and to deduce all principles of musical relationship as an expansion from unity, as 1 is to 1, or—as it is expressed in this work—1/1. In this sense of growth from unity Monophony is a development of the theories deduced by Pythagoras of Samos on his monochord, in the sixth century B. C.; beginning with the whole string of the monochord, or 1, Pythagoras divided the string into two parts and produced the interval 2/1, then into three parts and four parts, producing the intervals 3/2 and 4/3. In another sense Monophony may be regarded as an organization deducible from the sounding of one tone, or the sounding of 1, or 1/1; in this sense it is an evolved expression of the phenomenon of the overtone series, first perceived by Marin Mersenne, French monk of the seventeenth century; this interpretation, however, involves a certain equivocation with the analyzed phenomenon of sound, that is, with the *klang*, with the components of a tone.

**Note:** a blob of ink on a sheet of paper which is the symbol of a tone; the widely current practice of using the word note to indicate a musical sound, or pitch, is not followed in this work.

**Numerary Nexus:** the number common to all identities in the ratios of one tonality—the common anchor; the characteristic of a series of ratios that determines them as a tonality. In the 8/5 Otonality the Numerary Nexus is 5, as seen in the sequence of the six Odentities: 8/5–1/1(5/5)–6/5–7/5–9/5–11/10(5); in the 5/4 Utonality the Numerary Nexus is also 5, as seen in the sequence of the six Udentities: 5/4–1/1(5/5)–5/3–10(5)/7–10(5)/9–20(5)/11.

**Octave:** a keyboard distance, but not an interval, or pitch distance; the physical distance of the twelfth key from any given key in the 7-White–5-Black keyboard, about seven inches; the word is of course a misnomer in this sense, but it is already a misnomer on the piano keyboard, and because no other term is so easily understood it is used to designate this keyboard distance on the Chromelodeon.

**Odentity:** one of the Otonality correlatives, limited to 1–3–5–7–9–11 in this work; for example, "the 9 Odentity of 8/5 unity is 9/5."

**Otonality:** a tonality expressed by the over numbers of ratios having a Numerary Nexus; in conventional musical theory, "major tonality."

**Overtone:** same as Partial, which see.

**Partial:** one of the series of tones present in almost any musical sound; the quality or timbre of a tone depends upon the comparative energy of the various constituents of the series. An overtone, or partial, is an ingredient implicit in the phenomenon of sound, and is never spoken of in this book in a looser connotation; the identities of a tonality can of course be deliberately placed to simulate the series of partials, but in this sense they are not partials.

**Polypythagorean:** an adjective used here to describe the genesis of multi-tone scales achieved by superimposing likenesses of Equal Temperament fractional parts of a semitone above the original, thereby obtaining so-called quartertones, and sixth tones, and other irrational divisions of the 2/1 (see Pythagorean).

**Prime Unity:** 1/1, the first tone of a Monophonic system of music; the word unity implies a generative tone, either at top or bottom of its generated sequence; it does not imply "root," and it does not necessarily imply a bass locus.

**Ptolemaic Sequence:** the sequence of intervals rationalized by Ptolemy, second-century Alexandrian, and called by him the Intense Diatonic; as used herein it denotes the modern diatonic or seven-tone "major" scale in

Just Intonation, whether or not the conventional "keynote" is used; the simplicity of the degree-relationships is of course unaffected by different starting points. The Ptolemaic Sequence is significant in that it expresses this scale in the simplest possible terms—that is, in ratios of the smallest numbers permissible to the esthetic purpose; the sequence of intervals between degrees of the scale (using the modern starting point) is always:

| *Do* | *Re* | *Mi* | *Fa* | *Sol* | *La* | *Si* | *Do* |
|------|------|------|------|-------|------|------|------|
| 9/8 | 10/9 | 16/15 | 9/8 | 10/9 | 9/8 | 16/15 | |

**Pythagorean:** an adjective describing the construction of a scale or musical system by successions of 3/2's (just "perfect fifths"); such systems are generally based on "cycles"—the end of the "cycle" being the point at which one of the 3/2's falls in the vicinity of a certain number of 2/1's above or below the starting tone; the loosely termed "circle of fifths" of current musical theory is a tempered expression of Pythagoreanism. Pythagoras is credited with discovery of the twelve-tone "cycle" in the West (see Chapter 16).

**Ratio**[2]: a relationship, or interval, expressing the vibrations per second, or cycles, of the two tones concerned, generally in the lowest possible terms; of the two ways of considering a ratio—up or down from a constant—the current musical practice of conceiving intervals upward is followed in this exposition, except where the reverse is specifically indicated (see the next chapter); a ratio represents a tone and an interval at one and the same time; in its capacity as the symbol of a tone it is the over number that is nominally representative (in the upward manner), but since the over number exists only in relation to the under number, the ratio acquits its second function, as representative of an interval; conventional musical example: 3/2 represents "D" in the "key of G"—upward from "G"; it is thus simultaneously a representative of a tone and an implicit relationship to a "keynote"—or unity.

**Ratios of 1:** 1/1, 2/1 (compare these and the following, through the "Ratios of 9," with the ratios listed at the beginning of this chapter).

**Ratios of 3:** those ratios with identities no larger than 3, in which 3 is present: 3/2, 4/3.

**Ratios of 5:** those ratios with identities no larger than 5, in which 5 is present: 5/4, 8/5, 5/3, 6/5.

---

[2] Euclid's definition: "Ratio is a mutual relation of two magnitudes of the same kind to one another in respect of quantity." Johnson, *Musical Pitch*, 40.

**Ratios of 7:** those ratios with identities no larger than 7, in which 7 is present: 7/4, 8/7, 7/6, 12/7, 7/5, 10/7.

**Ratios of 9:** those ratios with identities no larger than 9, in which 9 is present: 9/8, 16/9, 9/5, 10/9, 9/7, 14/9.

**Ratios of 11:** those ratios with identities no larger than 11, in which 11 is present: 11/8, 16/11, 11/6, 12/11, 11/10, 20/11, 11/7, 14/11, 11/9, 18/11.

**Ratios of 13:** those ratios with identities no larger than 13, in which 13 is present: 13/8, 16/13, 13/12, 24/13, 13/10, 20/13, 13/7, 14/13, 13/9, 18/13, 13/11, 22/13.

**Semitone:** one of the twelve equal intervals which constitute the 2/1 in Equal Temperament; in this theory the semitone has no significance beyond its convenience as the equivalent of 100 cents (see Cents) and as a reference measure for indicating the approximate width of very small intervals by an easily understood concept—for example, "one-fiftieth of a semitone."

**Temperament,** or **Tempered Scale:** the word temperament originally meant simply a system of tuning, any system, but in modern usage it applies specifically to a system which deliberately robs its intervals of their purity in order to implement the idea of every-tone-in-several-senses (see Equal Temperament).

**Tonality:** a psychological phenomenon having as its chief characteristic a tonal polarity around a 1 Identity; the sounding of various of the identities—either Odentities or Udentities—with a Numerary Nexus will create this polarity, and the smaller the odd-number identities played the stronger the polarity. Acoustically, the identities of a tonality represent the maximal consonance of any given number of stipulated identities because of the Numerary Nexus: the tones of the triad 8/7–10/7–12/7—with the Numerary Nexus 7—are in the relation 8:10:12, or 4:5:6 (Identities 1–5–3), and create a polarity around 8/7, the 1 Odentity. This is the maximal consonance that three different tonal identities in music can attain. Were the triad 10/7–12/7–7/7(1/1) chosen, with the relation between tones of 5:6:7 (Identities 5–3–7), the polarity around 8/7 would still be created, though it would not be as strong (see page 160 and all of Chapter 11).

**Tonality Diamond:** an arbitrary arrangement of the Monophonic ratios designed to constitute *prima facie* proof of the at least dual identity of each ratio, and consequently of the capacity of a Monophonic system of

Just Intonation for providing tones which may be taken in more than one sense each (see pages 110 and 159).

**Tone:** the regular vibration of a sounding body that registers itself in the brain via the air and ear, and generally an implied ratio, of almost any extent; the word is not used in this exposition in the sense of a "step," or a "whole tone," except in quotation marks, and the word semitone (which see) is used only in the explanation of cents (which see), and in translation of ratios; that short-cut to new resources called the quartertone is discussed only in the analysis of its acoustic validity (see page 428). The implications in the use of "tone" as an *ex cathedra* measure for musical materials are basically fallacious and offer a good example of the limitations mothered by equivocal nomenclature.

**Twelve-tone Equal Temperament,** *see* Equal Temperament.

**Udentity:** one of the Utonality correlatives, limited to 1–3–5–7–9–11 in this work; example: "the 5 Udentity of 7/4 unity is 7/5."

**Undertone:** not used in this exposition except in connection with other theories; the ever-recurrent controversy over the merits of undertones as the spring source of "minor" tonality is irrelevant to the Utonality postulate (see page 89); the term "undertone series" implies a series the exact reverse of the overtone series, but neither overtones nor undertones are predicated as determinants of Monophony's tonalities; these are implicit in small-number ratios.

**Unity:** the generating tone of any tonality, the 1 Identity; in the Tonality Diamond (which see) the unity is always represented by a ratio having 1, 2, 4, 8, or 16 as one of its numbers (in the Primary Tonalities—see Chapter 8). The word fundamental applies to the generating tone of a series of partials, or harmonics, and in this sense it is also represented by 1; however, there is no confusion in the text as between the two ideas—the fundamental of a series of partials is always so qualified, whereas the word unity is applied to the ratio of the generating tone of a musical tonality.

**Utonality:** one of those tonalities expressed by the under numbers of ratios having a Numerary Nexus—in current musical theory, "minor" tonality.

# CHAPTER FOUR

# The Language of Ratios

## Frequencies as Ratios

OF THE MANY characteristics of a musical tone the most important for musical science is the number of pulsations it creates, in a given length of time, in the air in which it is heard. We call these pulsations vibrations, and when we use the sixtieth part of a minute as our measure of time, it is now customary to call them cycles. The number of cycles—per second—determines the pitch of the tone.[1]

A system of music is an organization of relationships of pitches, or tones, to one another, and these relationships are inevitably the relationship of numbers. Tone is number, and since a tone in music is always heard in relation to one or several other tones—actually heard or implied—we have at least *two* numbers to deal with: the number of the tone under consideration and the number of the tone heard or implied in relation to the first tone. Hence, the ratio.[2]

It is well to plunge at once into ratio nomenclature and to disregard the more familiar "A–B–C" terminology by which the ratios in our conventional scales are expressed. The advantages of doing so, in opening new tonal vistas, in getting to the analyzable root of music and the core of the universe of tone, are inestimable. If time is taken out to translate each ratio into what is assumed to be a synonymous word value, these vistas are dimmed or lost altogether, and the values, which are not synonyms, are nevertheless convicted of fraud by alleged synonyms. After hearing a "major third" on the organ or piano or some other instrument with tempered intonation, this interval becomes fixed in the mind as a pretty poor consonance, at least by some comparisons. A certain modern composer, one

---

[1] The use of the word cycles prevents any confusion as between vibrations in whole and halves of vibrations, the latter being the French manner of indicating frequencies.

[2] In Euclid's words, "all things which consist of parts numerical, when compared together, are subject to the ratios of number; so that musical sounds or notes [tones] compared together, must consequently be in some numerical ratio to each other." Davy, *Letters*, 2:265.

of numerous possible examples, convicts his "thirds" of inexactitude—that is, of not being exact widths—for no real reason except his confounding of just intervals and tempered intervals[3] (see page 153).

If ratios seem a new language, let it be said that it is in actual fact a language so old that its beginnings as an expression of the essential nature of musical sound can only be conjectured. In learning any new language, results are more immediate if a total plunge is made, so that the new medium surrounds and permeates the thinking; and it is no more time-consuming and tedious than translation, which frequently cannot be exact in any case.

Before proceeding to a study of the Monophonic intervals, experimental instruments will be described on which each ratio can be computed and its tones tested. For the present, what is required is a facility in thinking with this precise article—this *sine qua non* of musical structure—and for such facile thinking it is necessary to have a thorough understanding of its nature and functions.

The handling and consideration of tones is, by virtue of their vibrations, an exact mathematical process. If a tone makes 200 cycles, the 2/1 ("octave") above it makes 400 cycles, a doubling of 200, or 200 more cycles. This additional 200 cycles is not, however, constant for the 2/1 measure, since 200 cycles added to 400 do not give the 2/1 ("octave") above 400 cycles. To get the 2/1 above 400 we multiply by 2 and, conversely, to get the 2/1 below 400 we divide by 2. The cycles, or frequencies, of two tones constitute a ratio, and it has long been established that two pairs of tones with the same ratio—200 cycles to 400 cycles and 400 cycles to 800 cycles, for example, both 2/1's—are accepted by the ear as identical musical relationships.

This 2 to 1 relationship is a constant one. Musicians frequently wonder why they cannot add the ratio of one interval to another to get the correct result, just as they add a "perfect fifth" and a "perfect fourth" to get an "octave" at the piano. But the fact is that Nature does not offer one tone and its doubling (200 to 400) as a given quality of relationship, and the same quality of relationship in two tones which are not a ratio of doubling (200 to 600, for example).[4]

[3]Hindemith, *Craft of Musical Composition*, 1:78.
[4]With cents, explained at the end of this chapter, it is possible to add and subtract quantities which represent ratios.

The 2 to 1 relationship, based on the factor of 2, applies only to progression in pitch by 2/1's. There is of course much more to the calculation of musical intervals than successive 2/1's. But if the factor of 2 applies to the 2/1, then certain decrements of the factor of 2 must apply to intervals narrowing downward from a 2/1, or—increments of the factor of 2 starting from 1. In a Just Intonation the computations are very simple, since each small-number ratio is itself a particular measure of the factor of 2. The interval 300/200, or 3/2 (just "perfect fifth"), for example, an interval narrower than a 2/1, represents a certain measure of the factor of 2, and the ratio 250/200, or 5/4 (just "major third"), an even smaller measure. Obviously, then, if it is impossible to add frequencies by some constant— 200 cycles, for example, which was suggested above—to get a series of 2/1's, it is also impossible to add frequencies by constants to get any series of intervals smaller than 2/1. Positively, if a sequence of 2/1's is determined by the factor of 2, by multiplication, then any sequence of intervals narrower than 2/1 is determined by their respective proportions of the factor of 2—by multiplication. Therefore, when any two ratios—two intervals—are to be added, *multiply* their ratios.

The handling of small-number ratios, representing the intervals to which the ear is most responsive, involves nothing more than simple multiplication and division of improper fractions. Only when the expedient of temperament is introduced do the computations become at all complicated, when logarithms are employed to produce deliberately chosen irrational percentages of the factor of 2 (see page 101).

Conceive of a sequence of five intervals, somewhat at random in pitch, having a lower constant of 1200 cycles, the five ratios being: 2400/1200, 1800/1200, 1600/1200, 1500/1200, 2000/1200. In their lowest terms these ratios are: 2/1, 3/2, 4/3, 5/4, 5/3. This same series of relationships could just as well be considered with an upper constant of, say, 2400 cycles; the ratios would then be 2400/1200, 2400/1600, 2400/1800, 2400/1920, 2400/1440, which, reduced to the lowest possible terms are, again: 2/1, 3/2, 4/3, 5/4, 5/3. Thus a musical ratio represents the relationship between cycles; reduced to its lowest terms it is an abstract quantity applicable to any range of pitch in the total musical scale, and in this form its primacy— that is, its first rank in the significant resources of music—is the more manifest, as will be shown in the next chapter.

Since, in the concept of the interval 2/1 (the "octave"), the lower number is exactly half the upper number, any ratio in which the lower number is less than half the upper, such as 5/2, represents an interval wider than a 2/1; and one in which the lower number exceeds half the upper, such as 3/2, represents an interval smaller, or narrower, than a 2/1. Consequently, when an interval is wider than a 2/1, the upper number may be halved or the lower number doubled to bring it within a 2/1. The ratio 16/5 is brought within a 2/1 by writing it 8/5, and the ratio 5/2 is brought within a 2/1 by writing it 5/4. Nearly all ratios in this exposition are expressed in the less than 2/1 form.

A system of music is determined for one 2/1; the system is then duplicated in every other 2/1, above or below, that is employed. Consequently, symbols—ratios in this exposition—are used to denote the degrees of one 2/1, and the symbols are repeated in every 2/1 of the musical gamut. Musicians are accustomed to this idea; the "octave" above or below a given "A" is still "A." The situation here is identical; a 2/1 above or below any given 9/8 is still 9/8. Only the physicists who are not practising musicians will find this objectionable, since, acoustically, a 2/1 below a given 9/8 should be expressed 9/16, and a 2/1 above 9/8 should be expressed 9/4. But such a procedure would mean that every one of the approximately seven 2/1's of the common musical gamut would have a set of symbols of its own, and when forty-three degrees—ratios—in a single 2/1 are involved the number of total symbols would be unwieldy. The relative positions of two or more 2/1's, when tables or diagrams or examples involve ratios both up and down from a given 1/1, are indicated in this exposition by "Lower 2/1," "Higher 2/1," "Third 2/1," and "Fourth 2/1," etc.

It is common practice musically to consider ratios (intervals) as being built upwards (with the larger numbers above) from a lower constant, and this practice is followed throughout this book except when the reverse is specifically indicated. Such ratio symbolism is just one of several possibilities, and is a matter of arbitrary choice; the reverse form in practical application is synonymous, and in order that this fact may not be obscured the reverse will be indicated from time to time.

## Monochord Procedures

Suppose we have a metal string stretched across two bridges, and make a mark on the wood beneath that divides the string in half, then a mark that indicates a third of the string, and finally a mark that divides the third in half, or into sixths of the whole string, as shown in Diagram 1. Suppose the whole string makes 100 cycles when in vibration; if a third bridge is placed at the halfway mark, either half of the string would then give tones of 200 cycles, and if the bridge is placed at the one-third mark and only one-third of the string set in vibration the resulting tone would make 300 cycles. Thus the relationship of the half to the whole is 200 to 100, or 2/1; and the

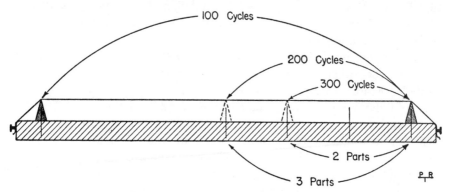

DIAGRAM 1.—THE RELATIONSHIP OF CYCLES TO PARTS OF STRING

relationship of the third part to the half is 300 to 200, or 3/2. Each of these ratios represents both a given tone and an interval between two tones. The ratio 3/2, via the agent 3, represents the higher tone of that relationship; at the same time it represents the interval from 3 to 2, or 3/2. For lack of a better term this concept might be called "*upward* ratio thinking" from a *lower* constant, the number 2, in 3/2 (200 cycles), representing the constant.

Now, without regard to cycles, let us think in terms of parts of a string length, the ancient monochord procedure. If one-half the string represents three equal parts (each a sixth of the whole string) one-third of the string represents two equal parts. When sounded, one-third represents 2 parts and one-half represents 3 parts, or the ratio 2/3. The ratio 2/3, via the agent 3, represents the lower tone, while at the same time it represents the interval from 2 to 3, or 2/3, exactly the same interval as 3/2. We thus see that the numbers of vibration are inversely proportional to the string lengths (see page 99 for reservations regarding this generalization). And the mental process of considering ratios as parts of a sounding body, rather than as vibrations, or cycles, as here presented, is essentially "*downward* ratio thinking" from an *upper* constant, the number 2 in 2/3—representing the upper tone of the relationship—being the constant.

These very elementary examples are essential to a thorough understanding of the Monophonic procedure, where the under number of a ratio is arbitrarily chosen to represent 1/1, unity, or the Prime Unity, and is always the lower of the two ratio tones, heard or implied. In the ratios 5/4, 4/3, 3/2, 8/5 the under numbers 4, 3, 2, and 5 represent the constant 1/1, and 5/4 represents a single tone upward from 1/1 (and an implied interval to 1/1), 4/3 represents a single tone upward from 1/1 (and an implied interval to 1/1), 3/2 represents a single tone upward from 1/1 (and an implied interval to 1/1), and 8/5 represents a single tone upward from 1/1 (and an implied interval to 1/1).

Expressed in the "downward thinking" manner, as parts of string lengths, these ratios would be 4/5, 3/4, 2/3, 5/8; and 4, 3, 2, and 5—this time the over numbers and the higher tones, heard or implied, of each ratio—would again represent 1/1. And each ratio would represent a single tone, but *downward* instead of upward from 1/1, and an implied interval to 1/1. Below is a schema of these examples:

$$\frac{5}{4} \quad \frac{4}{3} \quad \frac{3}{2} \quad \frac{8}{5} \quad \text{(higher tones of intervals upward from 1/1)}$$
$$\overline{4} \quad \overline{3} \quad \overline{2} \quad \overline{5} = 1/1, \text{ the Prime Unity}$$
$$\overline{5} \quad \overline{4} \quad \overline{3} \quad \overline{8} \quad \text{(lower tones of intervals downward from 1/1)}$$

The scale of four tones is designed to be identical in the two processes; the upper scale ascends from 5 to 8 (from left to right); the lower scale ascends only if read in reverse, from 8 to 5 (right to left). To achieve exactly the same *pitches* in both scales, without regard to synonymous interval values, the lower scale would be written: 5/8, 2/3, 3/4, 4/5.

## "Thinking" in Ratios

Upon further investigation of the nature of ratios we find that each has its complement within the 2/1, and if the ratio is composed of small numbers its complementary ratio is also composed of small numbers.

In the ratio 3/2, 2 represents 1/1, the lower limit of the 2/1. The tone at the upper limit of the 2/1 may be represented by 4 (a doubling of 2); hence the interval from the 3 of 3/2 to this upper limit of the 2/1 is the interval from 3 to 4, or 4/3, which is therefore the complement of 3/2 within the 2/1; the two intervals might be expressed thus: 2:3:4. In the ratio 5/4, 4 represents 1/1; the 2/1 above 4 is 8; the complement of 5/4, therefore, is the interval from 5 to 8, or 8/5, and the two intervals might be expressed, 4:5:8. In the ratio 6/5, 5 represents 1/1; the 2/1 above 5 is 10, and the complement of 6/5 is therefore the interval from 6 to 10, or 10/6, or, in its lowest terms, 5/3; the two intervals might be shown in this form, 5:6:10.

To find the sum of two intervals multiply the two ratios. The sum of 5/4 and 6/5, for example, $5/4 \times 6/5 = 30/20$, which, reduced to its lowest terms, is 3/2 (a "major third" and a "minor third" make a "perfect fifth"). To find the interval between two tones invert the smaller or narrower ratio and multiply. For example, to find the interval between 3/2 and 4/3 invert the smaller, 4/3, and use it as a multiplier: $3/2 \times 3/4 = 9/8$, which is therefore the interval representing the tonal distance between the 4 of 4/3 and the 3 of 3/2. (The difference between a "perfect fourth" and a "perfect fifth" is a "major second.")

To find a given interval above a given tone is of course simply a matter of multiplying the two ratios involved; to find the same interval distance downward from the same tone, the procedure is inversion and multiplication. For example, a 6/5 above 3/2 is arrived at thus: $3/2 \times 6/5 = 9/5$; and a 6/5 below 3/2 thus: $3/2 \times 5/6 = 5/4$.

## Where Do Ratios Fall on the Piano?

It is inadvisable to think of these ratios in terms of piano keys except with the most precise reservations. To do so without reservations is a triple abuse—of the ratios, of the piano, and of oneself. One can go crazy trying to reconcile irreconcilables, but given an appreciation of the essentiality of ratios in understanding musical resources some knowledge of the piano's discrepancies may prove enlightening.

If in the teaching of simple arithmetic the number 1 was called Sun, 2 called Moon, 3 called Jupiter, and 4 called Venus, and if this procedure were carried to the point where the teachers themselves no longer knew that Sun = 1, Moon = 2, Jupiter = 3, and Venus = 4, and forced upon students the euphemistic proposition that Moon + Moon = Venus, because they had learned it that way, we would have in simple arithmetic a fairly exact parallel to the "Tonic–Supertonic–Mediant" or the "C–D–E" nomenclature in the teaching of the science of musical vibrations. And the idea that Moon + Moon = Venus could accurately represent $2 + 2 = 4$ is no more awkward, to put it charitably, than the idea that the ascending musical intervals "C-F+F-C=C-C" can accurately represent $4/3 \times 3/2 = 2/1$.

In resorting to the piano two procedures are possible. First, one can adopt the negative procedure of regarding ratios as altered piano tones. One would say that 16/9, for example, is "F" one twenty-fifth of an equal semitone flat in the "key of G." On the other hand, it is quite as possible to think of the piano tones as altered ratios. This is the constructive approach, and the more fruitful one, since it predicates an understanding of the function and indispensability of ratios. In accordance with this procedure one would say that "F" in the "key of G" is 16/9 plus one twenty-fifth of an equal semitone. If translation into conventional values seems desirable in the pursuit of the Monophonic theory, the second is certainly the procedure recommended. Following the explanation of cents a table of piano discrepancies with the nearest small-number ratios will be given.

## Ellis' Measure of Cents

One more step in the simple mechanics of dealing with ratios must be presented in preparation for the exposition of the Monophonic concepts and principles, namely, the measure of musical intervals established by Alexander J. Ellis in an appendix to his translation of Helmholtz's *On the Sensations of Tone*.[5] This measure is the cent, the hundredth part of an equal semitone—1200 to the 2/1. Cents provide a logarithmic device which enables the theorist to add and subtract numbers representing the respective magnitudes of the various ratios, which he cannot do with the ratios themselves. They give the adventurer his longitude and latitude and thus establish his whereabouts in that vast, barely explored sea which lies from the number 1 to the faraway shores of the number 2. The ratios on previous and subsequent pages, then, are the familiar or exotic islands that lie within the boundaries of this little-known sea.

If "G" is the starting point, the intervals of the piano keyboard contain cents as shown in Diagram 2. The tempered "major third," "G to B," contains 400 cents. The true "major third," 5/4, contains only a trifle over 386 cents. The difference, nearly 14 cents, is approximately one-seventh of 100. Therefore "B" in the "key of G," which is 14 cents sharper than 5/4, may be expressed as 5/4 plus 14 cents, or approximately one-seventh of a semitone.

[5]Pages 446–451.

The tempered "minor third," "G to B♭," contains 300 cents, whereas the true "minor third," 6/5, has nearly 316. The difference, a trifle less than 16 cents, is approximately one-sixth of 100. Therefore "B♭" in the "key

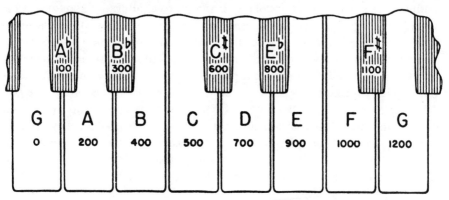

DIAGRAM 2.—CENTS ON THE PIANO KEYBOARD

of G," which is 16 cents flatter than 6/5, may be stated as 6/5 minus 16 cents, or approximately one-sixth of a semitone.

Below are translations of all so-called diatonic intervals to the nearest small-number ratios, the discrepancies being expressed in approximate plus or minus number of cents:

| INTERVAL | RATIO | INTERVAL | RATIO |
|---|---|---|---|
| "G" | 1/1 (the unison) | "G to C♯" | 7/5 plus 17.5 cents, *or* 10/7 minus 17.5 cents |
| "G to A♭" | 16/15 minus 12 cents | "G to D" | 3/2 minus 2 cents |
| "G to A" | 9/8 minus 4 cents, *or* 10/9 plus 18 cents | "G to E♭" | 8/5 minus 14 cents |
| "G to B♭" | 6/5 minus 16 cents, *or* 7/6 plus 33 cents | "G to E" | 5/3 plus 16 cents, *or* 12/7 minus 33 cents |
| "G to B" | 5/4 plus 14 cents | "G to F" | 16/9 plus 4 cents, *or* 9/5 minus 18 cents |
| "G to C" | 4/3 plus 2 cents | "G to F♯" | 15/8 plus 12 cents |

This table represents, of course, the falsities that are found not only in the "key of G" but in any "key" of Equal Temperament. If the "key of C" is chosen, "C to D♭"—the smallest interval—is 16/15 minus 12 cents, etc.

For finding the number of cents in a given ratio Ellis provides a simple arithmetical method—not adequate for investigation of a many-toned scale—and also methods by logarithms that give results up to three decimal places. For present purposes computations to a tenth of a cent are generally sufficient. All the Monophonic ratios in this exposition, and many others besides, are given in cents to one decimal point, either in the text or in the table of Appendix I. Knowledge as to computation of cents is important only to that adventurous soul who wishes to organize a scale or system beyond the ratios expounded in this volume. For this purpose a table of five-place logarithms, obtainable at almost any bookstore, and the library loan of Helmholtz's *On the Sensations of Tone* are the essentials. On pages 448–449 Ellis explains his procedure for obtaining results to a tenth of a cent, by example, and on pages 450–451 he supplies tables to be used in conjunction with the table of five-place logarithms. Ratios and cents are the two instruments by which the investigator examines and organizes his theoretical musical resources.

For purposes of an immediate paper comparison of ratios in Just Intonation the logarithm is no better than the ratio, and is therefore used in this work only in computing cents and in examination of the numerous temperaments. For exactitude we have the ratio itself: for the purpose of establishing whereabouts by *prima facie* comparison we have cents.

# CHAPTER FIVE

# Basic Monophonic Concepts

## *The Inner Ear: Music's Middleman*

A TONE, IN MUSIC, is not a hermit, divorced from the society of its fellows. It is always a relation to another tone, heard or implied. In other words, it is a musical interval, the relation between two tones. This relation is continually mutable, to be sure, but it never ceases to exist.

Why is it a relation? Because the tiny bony snail inside the human head, with its tiny longitudinal partition, with some twenty-three thousand fibers stretching across it, and with at least twelve times twenty-three thousand tiny hair cilia to pick up the smallest displacement of the air and send that sensation via nerve conduits to the brain, makes it a relation.[1] The acuity of this organ of hearing is relatively much greater than that of the human organ of vision,[2] for with those musical intervals which the ear hears with maximal perception it performs lightning-like computations; it can determine almost immediately, exactly or approximately, the relationship in vibrations per second, or cycles, of two tones sounded simultaneously; it can say instantly whether the two tones are in the correct ratio (in tune) or not in the correct ratio (out of tune).

The ear informs us that tones which are in small-number proportion, say in the relation of 2 to 1, are strong, clear, powerful, consonant. Perhaps these are not the adjectives another person would choose,[3] but whatever adjectives are used to describe the sensation, we know that it is different from the sensation created by a large-number proportion of, say, 23 to 20, which to the ear may be strident, confused, discordant; and the ear does not inform us what the relationship of these tones is, in vibrations per second, or cycles, except in comparison with what it can bring judgment to—that is,

---

[1]Fletcher, *Speech and Hearing*, 115, 125.     [2]Lloyd, *Music and Sound*, xii.

[3]And perhaps the word consonance is ambiguous in modern thought, as Max F. Meyer contends (*Mechanics of the Inner Ear*, 99n), yet it indicates a difference between the aural sensation of 2/1 and 21/10, for example, a difference that few ears could not appreciate if given a chance. A Funk and Wagnalls definition—"agreement, as of sounds; accord; concord"—certainly does

small-number proportions. Consequently, these statements can be conclusively made: the ear consciously or unconsciously classifies intervals according to their comparative consonance or comparative dissonance; this faculty in turn stems directly from the comparative smallness or comparative largeness of the numbers of the vibrational ratio; and the faculty of the ear to bring definitive judgment to comparative consonance decreases as the numbers of the vibrational ratio increase.

However elementary and uncontroversial these generalizations, they are highly important as a basis for the four fundamental concepts of the intonational aspect of Monophony. These follow in logical order, though not necessarily in the order of their potential significance.

## The Four Concepts

1. *The scale of musical intervals begins with absolute consonance (1 to 1), and gradually progresses into an infinitude of dissonance, the consonance of the intervals decreasing as the odd numbers of their ratios increase.*

Beginning with 1/1, the scale continues with 2/1, 3/2, 4/3, 5/4, 5/3, 6/5, 7/6, 7/5, 7/4, 8/7 (all expressed within the 2/1), etc., etc., into progressively larger numbers. This is not a scale in the conventional sense, but a scale of musical values, or grades. Beginning with absolute consonance, it very quickly becomes dissonant—so dissonant that the ear can make few distinctions as between comparative dissonances.

That the inception of this scale was a significant insight is abundantly supported by the fact that the first three of its ratios are the most important scale degrees in nearly every musical system worthy of the name that the world has ever known. Both cumulative experience and historical musical systems confirm its extension.

Long experience in tuning reeds on the Chromelodeon convinces me that it is preferable to ignore partials as a source of musical materials. The ear is not impressed by partials as such. The faculty—the prime faculty—of the ear is the perception of small-number intervals, 2/1, 3/2, 4/3, etc., etc., and the ear cares not a whit whether these intervals are in or out of the overtone series.

nothing to relieve the ambiguity. In the interest of economy, however, it is better to retain the old word, since it is not prejudiced, than to complicate matters with a new one. To make a negative observation, the adjective "pleasant" as applied to consonance is misleading. Positively, the word consonance will have a meaning for the reader before he completes this book.

2. The next concept involves the major postulate of the present exposition: that *every ratio of a Monophonic system is at least a dual identity.* Every ratio implies two relationships; one is expressed by an *over* number which in its odd-number form represents a vibrational identity in a tonality; the other relationship is expressed by an *under* number, which in its odd-number form represents a vibrational identity in another tonality.

Whatever their expression in the ratio, these identities are all considered as odd numbers.[4] It is one of the amazing phenomena of acoustics that the 2/1 of a tone, the doubling of its cycles, gives a tone which we know instantly to be different from the first, but one so like the first that we deny it a separate identity. It is another tone, and yet it is not. The conclusion is that doubling of cycles, while it produces another tone, does not change its identity.[5] The practical effect on ratios of this psychological fact is to make each even number the identity of the odd number achieved by the divisor 2.

In the ratio 3/2, 3 indicates that the ratio is a potential 3 Identity (or Odentity, since it is the over number) in some tonality, and the 2 indicates that the ratio is at the same time a potential 1 Identity (or Udentity, since it is an under number) in another tonality (2 is simply the doubling of 1, and 1, of course, indicates a unity). In every case these odd-number identities are of a vibrational genesis. The 3 Identity in 3/2, for example, represents the tone achieved by 3 vibrations in relation to 2 vibrations. It will be shown below that the over odd numbers of ratios with a Numerary Nexus represent what is commonly called "major" tonality, and that the under odd numbers of ratios with a Numerary Nexus represent what is commonly called "minor" tonality.

These correlated hypotheses will be amply demonstrated in due course. Here Concept Two may be stated: *Over-number tonality, or Otonality ("major"), is an immutable faculty of ratios, which in turn represent an immutable faculty of the human ear.*

In a sense, tone is the pattern of Otonality. The harmonic content of a given tone—that mixture of partials which gives it its quality—is simply some sequence of small whole-number vibrations in relation to 1, the funda-

---

[4]The term "prime numbers" has been avoided because the multiple 9 also assists in the delineation of tonality (see Chapter 8).

[5]Combarieu writes: "The notion of the octave may practically have been drawn from the fact which is at the basis of all society: the psychological difference between man and woman." *Music—Its Laws and Evolution,* 112. This is simply an observation that men's voices sing a 2/1 lower than women's voices. Would M. Combarieu like to suggest some extra sexes to sing apart by other intervals than the "octave"?

mental. That is to say, 2, 3, 4, 5, 6, 7, 8, 9, 10, 11, may be the partials which give a tone its quality as well as the sequence of upper numbers of the ratios that give a tonality its quality. But despite the similarity of pattern, a fundamental and its partials is a different concept from the identities of a tonality. The first is a scientific phenomenon implicit in musical sound; the second is a psychological phenomenon implicit in musical ratios. Here it may be said in passing that the possibility of altering the quality of tonality, as the electronics expert alters the quality of a tone, by introducing, removing, amplifying, or weakening one partial or another, introduces a new musical prospect (see page 123).

The historic Harmonical Proportion is associated with Otonality, since its principle of successive fractional proportions can be employed for the attainment of Otonality: the string is divided into successive parts of 1/2, 1/3, 1/4, 1/5, 1/6, 1/7, 1/8, etc., and the resulting proportions create the "major chord" (and a good deal more) and correspond to a series of partials. The first advocate of the Harmonical Proportion was Pythagoras of Samos, who, if we may believe what was written about him, carried the banner of the Proportion like a cross to the infidels (see page 363).

3. *Under-number Tonality, or Utonality ("minor"), is the immutable faculty of ratios, which in turn represent an immutable faculty of the human ear.*

We may say that tone is, in a sense, the pattern of Utonality as well as of Otonality. The Utonality pattern might be arrayed as the exact reverse of the pattern of a tone and its series of partials. But this would have no particular significance; whether the so-called undertone series is a possibility outside ingeniously contrived paraphernalia, what the "root" (unity) of the "minor" triad is, and whether the difference tones produced by the triad equivocate its consonance are all considerations that have no bearing on the concept stated above. The important fact is the immanence of Utonality in ratios, that Utonality can create an aural sensation quite as definite as the visual sensation of a new moon. The casual hearer of the one and the casual observer of the other are moved only by effect, and that effect is in no way changed by the name given to it. The one significant aspect of Utonality is that willy-nilly it is coexistent with Otonality in a Monophonic system of Just Intonation.

It has been obvious for many hundred years—to all who have taken the trouble to listen and analyze—that Utonality coexists with Otonality in truly tuned "diatonic" scales; yet even now it is common to accord "major" high honor, but to trifle with "minor," to doubt, frown upon, and reject it, and finally to relegate it to a dubious and bastard origin. Paul Hindemith, for example, calls it a "clouding" of "major," and Hauptmann calls it a "falsehood of the major."[6] The coexistence of elements so obviously equal in importance as the over and under numbers of a series of ratios is no trifling characteristic of musical resource; it is a concept that has all the substance of a cornerstone, difference tones notwithstanding (see page 162).

The historic Arithmetical Proportion, the division of a string into a given number of exactly equal parts (not equal intervals), is the ancient source of Utonality, thus corresponding to Utonality as the ancient Harmonical Proportion does to Otonality. The Arithmetical Proportion gives intervals the exact reverse of the series produced by the Harmonical Proportion (or of a series of partials), from the highest, $1/1$, to whatever low tone is chosen (dependent on the number of equal parts; see page 174).

4. The fourth concept presupposes a rather extensive knowledge of the history of musical intervals. With this knowledge the concept is fairly obvious, but without it there is a wide gap between statement and evidence. This gap will be filled, however, in the course of the exposition.

Theorized scale intervals, implying successive tones, have run the gamut from 1 to three-digit and even four-digit numbers in the history of music, but the story of consonance—that is, the story of man's acceptance of simultaneous sounds as consonances—has been much less adventurous. Even now, in our Western "golden age of music," we imply and comprehend, as a people, no odd number higher than 5 as a consonance, or—even if we accept certain claims regarding the so-called dominant seventh chord and the diminished triad (see page 124)—at least no higher than 7.

Surveying in retrospect the conjectured millenniums that have carried us from 3 to 5, and actually living a part of the hundreds of years of movement from 5 to 7 (it was three hundred years ago that Marin Mersenne called 7 consonant[7] and less than a decade ago that Paul Hindemith called Mersenne's consonance "chaos"[8]), standing here uncertainly *vis-a-vis* 7 and contemplating the serried "infinity" of 9, 11, and 13 in the decades or centuries or millenniums ahead, we may well pause to ponder the inscrutability of man and his apparently lethargic cochlea.

---

[6]Hindemith, *Craft of Musical Composition*, 1:78; Combarieu, *Music—Its Laws and Evolution*, 128.
[7]Shirlaw, *Theory of Harmony*, 32.     [8]Hindemith, *Craft of Musical Composition*, 1:38.

In the face of such lethargy it requires both temerity and good luck to announce with impunity that Monophony extends its boundaries of consonance through the number 11. Yet the fact is that it does so; and, lest the charge be made that Monophony is too futuric to be of contemporary value, it can be demonstrated that man has already responded to prodding, and this in the infinitesimal span of a single lifetime. That is to say, human ears have reacted to consonances of 11 in a manner to make us wonder why they have had to wait so long. Furthermore, in the tuning of the Chromclodeon it was possible to put most of the ratios of 11 in perfect tune simply by eliminating beats or by establishing the correct wave period by ear (see page 139). This is ample evidence that the capacity of the ear is far greater than history reveals or the current art of music acknowledges.

It is probable that as early as the beginning of recorded history the natures of 2/1, 3/2, and 4/3—the odd-number identities of 1 and 3—had already been divined, since we know that mathematics was a highly developed science in the ancient cultures of Egypt and China. Whether in such ancient cultures these intervals were ever related to what we know as consonance can only be conjectured. The first historical statement interpreted as defining intervals in terms of their consonance was made by the father of geometry, Euclid, who ascribed this quality to 2/1, 3/2, and 4/3. Thus all ratios of 3 or under were called consonant at least as early as the fourth century B.C.[9]

The four ratios of 5, namely 5/4, 8/5, 6/5, and 5/3, were recognized as scale degrees by Archytas in the fourth century B.C. and by subsequent Alexandrians,[10] but some sixteen hundred years passed before they were recognized as "imperfect consonances" by Odington,[11] and three hundred more years before Zarlino, in the sixteenth century, accorded them complete recognition along with a perceptive analysis. Just a century after Zarlino, Mersenne introduced a ratio of 7 as a consonance for the first time in history[12]; though all the intervals of 7 (7/4, 8/7, 7/6, 12/7, 7/5, 10/7) had been given by Ptolemy in his reorganization of the Greek modes in the second century, they were never called consonant.[13]

[9]Helmholtz, *Sensations of Tone*, 226.

[10]Hawkins, *History of the Science and Practice of Music*, 1:32. Archytas used 5/4 in his explanation of the Greek enharmonic genus—the other three ratios of 5 were implied, as a "square" of this scale shows (see page 171).

[11]Hughes,"Theoretical Writers on Music," in *Oxford History of Music*, Introductory Volume,129.

[12]Shirlaw, *Theory of Harmony*, 32, 39.

[13]Hawkins, *History of the Science and Practice of Music*, 1:32.

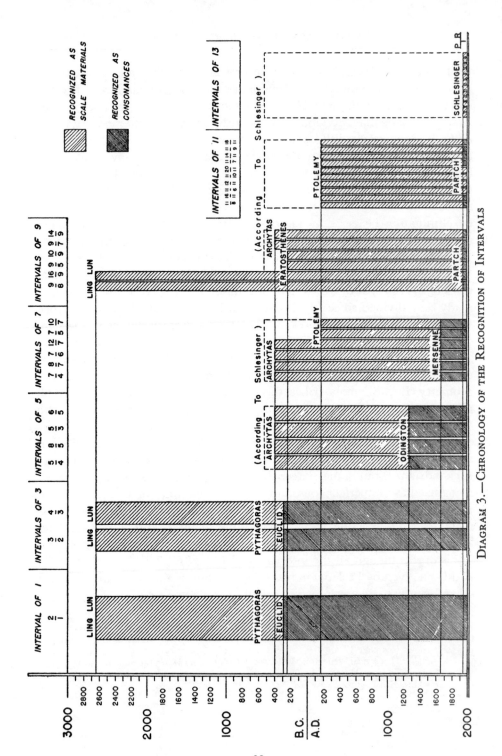

DIAGRAM 3.—CHRONOLOGY OF THE RECOGNITION OF INTERVALS

Tartini, another century later (eighteenth), accepted and reinforced 7's claim to consonance, both in his theories and in actual playing of the violin.[14] In the three centuries since Mersenne at least seven important theorists have opposed its inclusion in the arcanum of consonance and at least as many more have approved it.[15] The number 7 is not represented in our current theory and seldom in our current practice, and the issue is still sky-high.

The number 9, though not a prime, is nevertheless an identity in music, simply because it is an odd number—not a multiple of 2; it is the only identity in this category that comes within the limit arbitrarily imposed for this theory. The number 15 is in the same category, but for the purpose of delineating tonality it is outside our arbitrary limit.

The ratios of 9 include two with numbers that are multiples of 3 or less: 9/8 and 16/9. These are a special case, as will be seen later; along with the ratios of 1 and 3 they were theorized in ancient China, allegedly in the twenty-seventh century B.C., as scale degrees of the pentatonic, though never called consonant.[16]

The other ratios of 9, namely 9/5, 10/9, 9/7, and 14/9, are given as scale degrees in Monophony, and all ratios of 9 are considered comparative consonances, depending on range of pitch, on the extended or close form of the interval (9/4, for example, as against 9/8), and on the quality of the instrument (see page 153). The same observations hold for the ratios of 11, all of which are found in the Monophonic fabric: 11/8, 16/11, 11/6, 12/11, 11/10, 20/11, 11/7, 14/11, 11/9, 18/11.

The ratios of 13 are given in Kathleen Schlesinger's explanation of the ancient Greek harmoniai (see Chapter 18), and isolated ratios with even larger prime numbers are found in the scales compiled by Ptolemy. Miss Schlesinger makes no claim for the consonance of 13, which is of course a comparative matter anyway. The Monophonic fabric, being predicated on a limit of 11, for the reasons discussed in Chapter 8, does not encompass the ratios of 13.

In referring these data to the diagram or dramatization of the history of consonance (Diagram 3), the reader will doubtless find many points

[14]Perrett, *Questions of Musical Theory*, 91.

[15]*Pro*: Mersenne, Tartini, Euler, Fétis, Serre, Hauptmann, Ellis, Perrett, Meyer; *Contra*: Zarlino, Descartes, Rameau, Helmholtz, Öttingen, Riemann, Brown.

[16]Richard, "Chinese Music," in *East of Asia Magazine*, 1:307 (December, 1902).

obscure—exposition in relation to diagram or vice versa—until he has finished Chapter 15, on the history of intonation, and Chapter 18, on contemporary Just Intonations. Concept Four may be summarized as follows:

*In terms of consonance man's use of musical materials has followed the scale of musical intervals expressed as Concept One; from the earliest times it has progressed from the unison in the direction of the great infinitude of dissonance.*

# CHAPTER SIX

# Instruments for Demonstration

## The Empirical Method

IT MAY BE said once again that this volume was written for those who are searching for more than intellectual openings to musical investigation; indeed, only the conviction that there are such has made its preparation seem worth while. And the first act in proving that one's purpose is to excite *musical* brain action, as well as the usual kind, is the preparation of an experimental instrument.

The impulse to the growth and evolution of music is generated by the human ear, not by the piano keyboard, without which the harmony classes of this day and age would be inoperative. And the missing element which the human ear wants and needs most is a musical instrument capable of expressing an infinite range of ideas and of infinite mutability, so that ideas can first be tested, then proved or corrected.

In suggesting directions for experimental instruments the more important historic intervals are specified first. Over these there can be no controversy, and it should be refreshing to the student actually to hear scales which theorists have been discussing and frequently quarreling over for at least two thousand years, many of which they probably never really heard. In the following chapters application of the forty-three Monophonic intervals is specified and, finally, various modern or new-old schemes, which are analyzed in the light of the Monophonic concepts, a procedure which cannot be omitted with any conscience.

After initial demonstrations of intervals on immediately adaptable instruments the next step should be instruments of greater musicality. The avenues for intonational intrigue and the opportunities for exploration are exciting in prospect, appalling in number, and unpredictable in direction.

## The Academic Impasse

The late Dayton C. Miller, path-finding acoustician with poetic instincts, has these apposite words to add on the role science might play:

The science of sound should be of inestimable benefit in the design and construction of musical instruments, and yet with the exception of the important but small work of Boehm in connection with the flute, science has not been extensively employed in the design of any instrument. This can hardly be due to the impossibility of such application, but rather to the fact that musical instruments have been mechanically developed from the vague ideas of the artist as to the conditions to be fulfilled. When the artist, the artisan, and the scientist shall all work together in unity of purposes and resources, then unsuspected developments and perfections will be realized. . . . The artistic world has rather disdainfully held aloof from systematic knowledge and quantitative and formulated information; this is true even of musicians whose art is largely intellectual in its appeal. The student of music is rarely given instruction in those scientific principles of music which are established. Years are spent in slavish practice in the effort to imitate a teacher, and the mental faculties are driven to exhaustion in learning dogmatic rules and facts. . . . Experience indicates that a month devoted to a study of the science of scales and chords and of melody and harmony, will advance the pupil more than a year spent in the study of harmony as ordinarily presented.[1]

Unfortunately it is not only the artistic world that is guilty of disdain. Science also has been reluctant to undertake the thankless groundwork essential to the improvement of musical instruments except where commercial exploitation looms in the background. In general, science has also refused to focus its illumination on the deficiencies of current musical theory, treading with feet of absorbent cotton when it skirts the sacred dogma of the art of music, if not actually discouraging reformatory or tangential endeavors. Almost any book by an acoustician that one happens to pick up contains the implication, if not the positive assertion, that it is futile and irreverent to look for anything better than the present Equal Temperament. In his general attitude Miller is one of the refreshing exceptions.

Some seventy-five years ago Colin Brown, in a lecture at Anderson's College, Glasgow, anticipated Miller's remarks in discussing the study of music theory: "From the earliest times, crude, imperfect, and erroneous hypotheses, misnamed theories, have been often assumed, and facts of all kinds have been taken for granted or sought out, and made to fit them. The result has been disastrous to Musical Science. It has long been neglected, and all but unknown as a popular study. In no school or college in our country has it been distinctively taught as a branch of education.

[1] *The Science of Musical Sounds*, 263–265; quoted by permission of The Macmillan Company.

Theory and Art engross universal attention; while Science, which takes precedence of them both, is overlooked and forgotten."[2]

In attempting to correct an illogical situation a man tends to become an extremist, and very often he deliberately exaggerates illogicality in the belief that arguing past the mark will improve the chances that those he wants to influence will come closer to the mark. But actually the question of which "takes precedence"—theory, art, or science—is beside the point, and until the educational formula is corrected the pioneering composer must determine to develop in himself whatever faculty is required, to make himself into a scientist, an artisan, a historian, a creator of music.

Since Brown and Miller cried in the academic wilderness the picture has changed little if any, else we would find fewer complainers in our own day. Not all these get into print; one that does is Jacques Barzun, who finds that "of all the unmusical people in the world, so many have become instructors in counterpoint and heads of conservatories that they must permit the physicist to play with his tuning forks and the historian with his special kind of notes. . . . Their attention is focused on rules and numbers, and has not been drawn to the meaning of what they work with."[3]

## *Ratios, the Unchanging Value, on a Harmonic Canon*

In any art the creator must have more than mere desire; he must have tools. And it seems to be the curse of music that it requires more tools and more years for acquiring knowledge and instruments and facility than any other. Just what technical and intellectual qualifications the creator must have before beginning work is moot. One thing is certain, however: chord structure, chord sequence, form, and the other subject matter of instruction in composition changes from generation to generation and differs from type to type and from individual to individual. There is just one element in all the study of music which does not change: the ratio. And the reason the ratio does not change is simply and wholly because physiologically the ear does not change except over a period of thousands or millions of years.

Several types of experimental instruments may be built or adapted, without excessive work or expense, for the purpose of establishing the var-

[2]*Music in Common Things*, 3, 5.

[3]*Teacher in America*, 118 (quoted by permission of Little, Brown & Company and the Atlantic Monthly Press). It seems pertinent to observe that Barzun uses the word "numbers" in a generic, not the specific Monophonic, sense.

ious quantities of this unchanging value. One of the easiest, but hardly the most efficient even when carefully constructed, is the monochord, the Greek *kanon*, the root of our word canon, the law, or the giver of laws.[4] The monochord—harmonic canon—is simply a sound-box which is wholly enclosed except for apertures on the sides to permit escape of the amplified sounds. One or more strings[5] (guitar strings or piano wire) are stretched over the box from nut to bridge. A movable bridge, which cuts off any desired string proportion, is then supplied (see the photographs following page 236).

Piano or zither tuning pins—both of which may be obtained at piano supply houses—or even guitar or mandolin tuning gears may be used in one end, and dowels or screws around which to fasten the strings in the other; the end piece in which the tuning pins are placed should be of some kind of hardwood, and the top (or belly), back, and sides of a thin, soft wood; spruce and redwood both have good resonance. For turning the zither pins a tap wrench, obtainable for a few cents at a hardware store or at any large five-and-ten, serves very well. The pitch of the open strings should be approximately that for which the strings were originally intended; for example, the third string of a guitar should be tuned to a 2/1 below 1/1–392 ("G" below "middle C"), and the distance on the harmonic canon—or "polychord"—from bridge to nut should be approximately the same as it is on the ordinary guitar, about 25 inches.

The most critical feature of a harmonic canon is the movable bridge. For accurate results it should be no higher, above the belly of the instrument, than nut and permanent bridge, since a high bridge increases both the tension and the length of the string. I have experimented with bridges just high enough to give a good tone, using guitar first strings, and the results varied greatly from theory. However, a first experimental harmonic canon need not be nearly as elaborate as those pictured herein (Chapter 12), since four strings and their appurtenances, and six pieces of wood (aside from the movable bridges) for the soundbox are the only essentials. A harmonic canon is a simple and direct way of beginning an investigation into tonal resources, and Ellis has shown that the variation from intervals which would be implied by the axiom of frequencies inversely proportional to string lengths, under fairly good conditions,[6] are

---

[4] "As the monochord is very liable to error," writes Ellis, the Greek deductions regarding harmonic law "were happy generalisations from necessarily imperfect experiments." Ellis in Helmholtz, *Sensations of Tone*, 15n.

[5] Harmonic canon is a preferable term for the instrument, since a single string ("mono" chord) is insufficient for proper experimentation.

generally not as great as the maximum deviations from just intervals implicit in twelve-tone Equal Temperament. But it must be kept in mind that results on a harmonic canon are almost always approximations.

## On the Cello

The cello has several features to recommend it as an experimental instrument aside from its well-known musicality. With the bow, sustained tones in double stops are possible; the eyes are normally close to the fingerboard in playing; there is plenty of room for small-interval marks on the long fingerboard; and pinheads or brads or other indicators are easily hammered into holes in the fingerboard which have been prepared' with an awl.[7] Instead of inserting pinheads or brads immediately, however, it is perhaps a good plan to wrap a thickness of heavy paper around the fingerboard and paste it securely; marks on this will be substituted for pinheads, and in this way the investigator can experiment until he is sure what he wants. Also, a bridge lower than that ordinarily used, to decrease the extra tension on the strings when high stops are made, is advisable.

The main disadvantages of the cello are in part the same as those of the harmonic canon. Non-uniformity in strings and in bowing technique, increase of tension in stopping, inexact stopping, and the almost unconscious use of vibrato, etc., are factors not conducive to a really adequate intonational investigation. But with all its faults, the experimental cello nevertheless represents an immediately feasible beginning, the end result of which might be unpredictably fruitful.

## On the Harmonium

A third possibility is the harmonium, or reed organ, which in another American age reposed in the parlor of nearly every home. Even now an

---

[6] That frequencies are inversely proportional to string lengths is strictly true only under perfect conditions. Ellis says that if a "heavy string of uniform density, perfect elasticity, of no thickness, but capable of bearing a considerable strain, could have its vibrating length determined with perfect accuracy—none of which conditions can be more than roughly fulfilled"—then would the pitch numbers of its parts be "inversely proportional to their lengths." Alexander J. Ellis in Helmholtz, *On the Sensations of Tone*, 441; quoted by permission of Longmans, Green and Company, Ltd.

[7] Such an act represents the final degree of unspeakable effrontery to the average cellist. It "disfigures" his instrument, and, what is worse, it seems to insult his musicianship. The creative artisans who wandered off the beaten paths to evolve the viol family were obviously not activated by such an exaggerated respect for the things they were born to.

occasional harmonium is seen in the second-hand stores if not in a neighbor's basement or attic. The harmonium lacks the mutability of the harmonic canon and the musicality of the cello, but it does have the capacity to present consonances with at least temporary accuracy, and it is a comfort to anyone who has studied the piano even casually to have the familiar keyboard under his fingers. Several sets of reeds—four or five—are really necessary for any extensive investigation; these can be obtained either from a reed organ company or a reed organ repair man.

Reeds are tuned by scratching the base of the vibrating flange to flatten, and by scratching the tip of the flange to sharpen. This may be done with a small file or other sharp instrument. Some sort of simple harmonic canon (or the experimental cello) is a great aid in tuning; an approximation of the tone desired can be found on the harmonic canon, and then be refined to exactitude by sounding it with the reed of a small-number relationship and continuing the scratching process until beats are eliminated and the correct proportion of the fundamental sounds attained (see page 139 for the Chromelodeon tuning guide).

Doubtless other instruments or contrivances for experimenting with ratios will suggest themselves to the experimenter. Pipes are possible but not easy, and are never advisable without monitoring by a more dependable tonal medium.[8] The "laws" governing the behavior of a column of air in a flute or reed-blown pipe are intricate and capricious in the extreme. Dayton C. Miller observes that "one cannot even approximately calculate the length of a flute tube which will sound a given note [tone]; one cannot by theoretical calculation locate any finger hole on a flute tube which will produce a given tone."[9]

## Four-Part Design for Measuring Ratios

A stretched string is a thing of beauty, and the laws governing its performance are comparatively simple. For the benefit of those wishing to peer into the musical forgotten or unknown via the harmonic canon or the cello, parts of string lengths to be measured off from the nut for one 2/1 (the interval 2/1 will of course be found by measuring off half the string

---

[8]Richard Stein, Saxon theorist, constructed a clarinet in "quartertones" about 1906. Overmyer, "Quarter-Tones—and Less," in *American Mercury*, 12:207.

[9]*Anecdotal History of the Science of Sound*, 43; quoted by permission of The Macmillan Company.

#### STRING ONE: JUST INTONATION OF THIRTEEN DEGREES
(more will be given in Chapters 7 and 8)

| Ratio...... | 1/1 | 16/15 | 10/9 | 9/8 | 6/5 | 5/4 | 4/3 | 3/2 | 8/5 | 5/3 | 16/9 | 9/5 | 15/8 | 2/1 |
|---|---|---|---|---|---|---|---|---|---|---|---|---|---|---|
| Part to be measured off | 0 | 1/16 | 1/10 | 1/9 | 1/6 | 1/5 | 1/4 | 1/3 | 3/8 | 2/5 | 7/16 | 4/9 | 7/15 | 1/2 |

#### STRING TWO: TWELVE-TONE EQUAL TEMPERAMENT*

| Ratio....... | 1/1 | 196/185 | 55/49 | 44/37 | 63/50 | 578/433 | 99/70 | 433/289 | 100/63 |
|---|---|---|---|---|---|---|---|---|---|
| Part to be measured off | 0 | 11/196 | 6/55 | 7/44 | 13/63 | 145/578 | 29/99 | 144/433 | 37/100 |

| Ratio....... | 37/22 | 98/55 | 185/98 | 2/1 |
|---|---|---|---|---|
| Part to be measured off | 15/37 | 43/98 | 87/185 | 1/2 |

#### STRING THREE: PYTHAGOREAN HEPTATONIC (LYDIAN)

| Ratio....... | 1/1 | 9/8 | 81/64 | 4/3 | 3/2 | 27/16 | 243/128 | 2/1 |
|---|---|---|---|---|---|---|---|---|
| Part to be measured off. | 0 | 1/9 | 17/81 | 1/4 | 1/3 | 11/27 | 115/243 | 1/2 |

#### STRING FOUR: MIXOLYDIAN HARMONIA (DIATONIC) ACCORDING TO SCHLESINGER†

| Schlesinger ratio‡..... | 14/14 | 13/14 | 12/14 | 11/14 | 10/14 | 9/14 | 8/14 | 7/14 |
|---|---|---|---|---|---|---|---|---|
| Monophonic ratio..... | 1/1 | 14/13 | 7/6 | 14/11 | 7/5 | 14/9 | 7/4 | 2/1 |
| Part to be measured off | 0 | 1/14 | 1/7 | 3/14 | 2/7 | 5/14 | 3/7 | 1/2 |

---

*The double equivocation involved in stipulating temperament on a vibrating string—the inherent falsities of the string and the constitutional falsities of Equal Temperament—must be remembered. If the conditions surrounding the stopping of a string were perfect, these ratios would not be adequate for perfect Equal Temperament; they would have to be determined by logarithms. The ratios above are taken in part from Ellis' tables (Ellis in Helmholtz, *Sensations of Tone*, 453–456); in certain cases I substituted other ratios for those Ellis stipulates because they have smaller numbers and achieve equally close results, or because they achieve closer results without a great increase in the size of the numbers. See Appendix I for the ratios that come closest to hundreds of cents—100, 200, 300, etc. The above ratios are all within about a tenth of a cent of perfect twelve-tone Equal Temperament.

In determining the ratios of this scale by seven-place logarithms, the first degree is the twelfth root of 2, $\sqrt[12]{2}$, or 2 to the one-twelfth power, $2^{1/12}$. The whole scale might then be expressed: $1-2^{1/12}-2^{2/12}-2^{3/12}-2^{4/12}-2^{5/12}-2^{6/12}-2^{7/12}-2^{8/12}-2^{9/12}-2^{10/12}-2^{11/12}-2^{12/12}$ (2). The log. of 2 (.3010300) is divided by 12, and this quotient is successively multiplied by 2, 3, 4, 5, 6, 7, 8, 9, 10, and 11. The corresponding antilogarithms of these results, multiplied by 100,000, over 100,000, which represents 1, give the ratios. The seventh degree, $2^{6/12}$, is of course determined by the square root of 2, and gives the so-called tritone, the exact half of the 2/1. The ratios of the "equal semitone" are, with progressive accuracy: 18/17, 89/84, 196/185 (see Appendix I.)

Percy C. Buck gives an admirably concise explanation of the mathematical process in, and the geometrical nature of, Equal Temperament: "When the number 1 has been twelve times multiplied by the twelfth root of 2, the result is 2; when the number 2 has been so multiplied twelve times it becomes 4; the number 4 so multiplied becomes 8; and the numbers reached after each process of twelve multiplications form the Geometrical Progression 1, 2, 4, 8, 16, etc., etc." *Acoustics for Musicians*, 88; quoted by permission of Oxford University Press.

†*The Greek Aulos*, 12.

‡The Schlesinger ratios are based on parts of string lengths, explained in Chapter 4.

length) are given on the opposite page, for various scales, and the methodology established.[10]

To stimulate the comparative faculties, it is advisable to give the harmonic canon four strings and to mark each string of either this instrument
or the cello with a different system of intonation, perhaps as follows: the
first string in Just Intonation; the second in Equal Temperament; the
third in a Pythagorean heptatonic scale, and the fourth in the Arithmetical
Proportion for one of the ancient Greek harmoniai in the diatonic genus,
as given by Kathleen Schlesinger. For a true comparison all four open
strings should be of the same pitch, perhaps four first strings (guitar or
cello). A more thorough investigation would require that all four strings
(those for the cello in the usual tuning, 4/3–1/1–3/2–9/8: "C–G–D–A"[11])
follow a single plan, with a separate paper covering for the cello fingerboard for each of the four systems.

To the extent that this chapter fails as a stimulus to action it becomes
an amphigory. The little four-part design on the opposite page, a specific
plan of initial action, is intended as an implement to assist the lovers of
music theory in making the modern *corpus* of their art a little less *delicti*.

The significance of all these ratios will become clear in the development
of the Monophonic argument and with further knowledge of the history of
intonation. For the present, isolated situations will be pointed out.

Note the 5/4 (just "major third") as compared with the Pythagorean
81/64, and the fourth mark from the nut under Equal Temperament
(which would give the "major third")—also other comparative degrees.[12]

[10]In the *Harvard Dictionary of Music*, page 361, is a sentence which reads: "Logarithmic frequencies are particularly important—in fact, indispensable—in all calculations concerning tempered intervals or microtonic intervals (exotic scales)." The ratios of frequencies, computed
logarithmically, are a great convenience in calculating equal and meantone temperaments, and
the logarithmic device of cents holds many shortcuts in analyzing any scale, but logarithmic
computations to determine the ratios of frequencies of the degrees of any just scale—"microtonic"
or "diatonic," exotic or familiar—are, to say the least, uncalled for. The ratio of each degree *is*
the ratio of its frequencies.

[11]If the open "G" string is called 1/1–98, then the ratios of this tuning would be correctly
expressed: 2/3–1/1–3/2–9/4. The ratios in the text above follow the plan of preserving the same
symbols in every 2/1 of a musical gamut, explained on page 79.

[12]In analyzing these few just ratios the very ingenious device of a "musical slide rule,"
suggested by Llewellyn S. Lloyd (*A Musical Slide Rule*) might profitably be examined. On two
slips of cardboard, found in the cover pocket of his book, Lloyd marks the points of just and
tempered scales on an equal graph—that is, any 3/2 (or "perfect fifth") interval, for example,
is shown as a constant paper distance; both slips are similarly marked, on the whole. When
another tonality than that chosen as 1/1 (or "keynote") is desired, the second of the cardboard
slips is moved up to any desired point against the edge of the first, showing immediately whether

Note also various pentatonic scales: 1/1–9/8–5/4–3/2–5/3–2/1 and 1/1–9/8–4/3–3/2–16/9–2/1 in the justly intoned scale, and 1/1–9/8–4/3–3/2–27/16–2/1 in the Pythagorean (also present in the just scale, with the same sequence of intervals between degrees, but starting on another degree). The ratio 7/4 in the Mixolydian, according to Schlesinger, is *Mese*, the tonal center of the scale in the most ancient Greek theory, which, in conjunction with the number of equal divisions of the whole string, determined the scale's *ethos* (see Chapter 18).

## Arithmetic and Geometric Divisions

The terms *arithmetic* and *geometric* are frequently used by music theorists in discussing proportions of a string, but they are seldom explained as they pertain to the actual proportioning of a sounding body. It might be a good idea to begin an explanation with a small interval on the harmonic canon, or cello, say the ratio 9/8. This interval is found at one-ninth of the string length from the nut. If this distance from the nut is divided in half, that half nearer the nut will give the interval 17/16 and the other half the interval 18/17. Multiplying both numbers of 9/8 by 2, and inserting the sequential odd number between them, all three intervals—9/8, 17/16, 18/17—can be shown: 16:17:18. This is an *arithmetic* division of the interval 9/8. In the ordinary demands of string proportioning it always gives comparatively small-number ratios.

All other successive-number ratios can of course be divided arithmetically in the same way: 2/1 is divided 2:3:4 (a "fourth" and a "fifth" make an "octave"); 3/2 is divided 4:5:6 (a "minor third" and a "major third" make a "perfect fifth"); and 4/3 is divided 6:7:8 (no translation possible), and so on.

We find that this procedure gives us a *visual* division of the difference in string lengths between the sounding bodies 9 and 8, into two equal parts, but it obviously does not give us an *aural* division into two equal parts (17/16 is wider than 18/17). To effect an "equal temperament" of two intervals within 9/8 we have, for the practical purpose of measuring off a string length, recourse to the ninth proposition in the sixth book of

the triad tones of the new tonality, or "keynote," or any of the tones of the new "diatonic" scale, are available in the original series of just degrees. Lloyd's observations apply only partially when the just ratios specified above are expanded into the full forty-three-degree Monophonic scale, but the "musical slide rule" is not difficult to make, and one might also mark it for the full Monophonic scale.

Euclid's *Elements*, the "ninth of the sixth," well known to those sixteenth-century theorists concerned with the problem of temperament.

It is easy enough with a small celluloid right angle on which millimeters are marked to adapt the "ninth of the sixth" to this particular problem on the harmonic canon. If the string is 700 mm. long, one-ninth of it (the stop for the ratio 9/8) will be 77.8 mm. Draw a line of this length on a sheet of paper. Now subtract 77.8 mm. from the original string length, 700, and mark off another 9/8 ratio—that is, mark off one-ninth of 622.2 mm., or

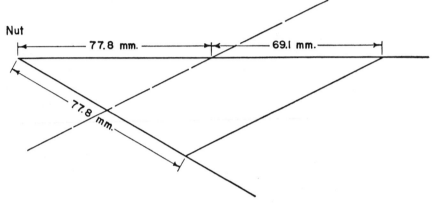

Nut

|← —— 77.8 mm. —— →|←— 69.1 mm. —→|

77.8 mm.

DIAGRAM 4.—ADAPTATION OF EUCLID'S "NINTH OF THE SIXTH"

69.1 mm.—and extend the line to this point. We now have, marked on a piece of paper, a hypothetical string with two successive 9/8 intervals. The second of these two intervals is *visually* shorter than the first, but we know that *aurally* they are equal, because they are both 9/8's.

Now draw a second line, from the point where the hypothetical string crosses the nut, in any acute angle, and also mark off on the second line 77.8 mm., the first 9/8 distance, from the nut point. Connect the ends of the two lines of the angle, making a triangle. Finally, draw a line parallel to this third line through the point of 77.8 mm. on the first line (broken line in Diagram 5). The point where this parallel line crosses the second line will be a division of the ratio 9/8 of the hypothetical string portion 77.8 mm. into two equal parts *aurally*, that is, a division of the subjective *sound* into two equal parts. This is a *geometric* division.

The mathematician has logarithmic ways of finding such geometric proportions and ascertaining the nearest ratio for them that are intellectually more exciting for him, but for the practical purpose of giving the reader a glimpse into some of the intonational lucubrations of the pure theorist the solution adapted from Euclid is quite adequate. And since any tempered interval possesses immanent inaccuracy, there is no particular gain in accurately working out its inaccuracy to the point of anguish. In this volume such divisions into equal aural parts as the above are presented only for the value of contrast.

I strongly suspect that men of scientific and mathematical bent show a partiality to temperaments because these offer them teasers for their arithmetical intellects. Just Intonation is too laughably simple. It takes them back to the seventh grade. The particular problem of Just Intonation is not calculation but application. Application is a problem of physical device, and physical device has an emotional connotation; more often it is not intellectually and mathematically intriguing. Colin Brown's ingenious application of Just Intonation is extremely intriguing, however (see Chapter 18).

As applied to incipient systems of music *arithmetic* and *geometric* (the geometric is more frequently called the Harmonical Proportion) concern a whole string length, or other sounding body, and have already been discussed (see page 175 for a diagram of the Arithmetical Proportion).

# PART III

## The Resources of Monophony

CHAPTER SEVEN

# Analysis of the 5 Limit

## *The Athletic Ear*

BY NO MEANS consistently in the passage of time, but nevertheless with certainty of direction, the world has advanced its harmonic thinking through a limit of vibrational relationships expressible by the number 5. Practice and theory are in happy agreement through this point, but beyond this point they part, at least occasionally. Practice, in *a cappella* singing, for example, reveals proved advances beyond the 5 limit, whereas theory, in dealing with musical resources and in the building of instruments of fixed intonation, studiously excludes any higher prime number.

The following discussion treats of the intervals implied, though not always heard, in modern harmonic usage. By "implied" we mean that the ear jumps the distance between what it actually hears and what it wants to hear. Whether the ear enjoys its jumps and through frequent exercise and a naturally happy disposition becomes athletic and actually prefers jumping is a hotly debated point. My own conviction is that the capacity of the ear would be better realized if it were allowed a few respites—if "consonances" were actually consonances, and not quasi-consonances.

The seven 5-limit ratios which are implied in Equal Temperament are shown below, first in their natural sequence of pitch, later as identities in tonalities. Intervals between degrees are shown in smaller type, and this plan for presenting scales and chords will be followed throughout the book.

| Cents....... | 0 | 315.6 | 386.3 | 498.0 | 702.0 | 813.7 | |
|---|---|---|---|---|---|---|---|
| Degrees ....1/1 | | 6/5 | 5/4 | 4/3 | 3/2 | 8/5 | |
| | 6/5 | 25/24 | 16/15 | 9/8 | 16/15 | 25/24 |
| Cents........ | 315.6 | 70.7 | 111.7 | 203.9 | 111.7 | 70.7 |

| Cents.......884.4 | 1200 |
|---|---|
| Degrees..... 5/3 | 2/1 |
| 6/5 | |
| Cents........ 315.6 | |

*109*

Assuming that we are building a true or just scale on "G," the above scale may be translated: "G———Bb–B–C–D–Eb–E———G." This is obviously not an evenly spaced scale; the comparatively wide intervals from 1/1 to 6/5, 4/3 to 3/2, and 5/3 to 2/1 will be filled after presentation of the tonality potentialities of ratios within the 5 limit.

## Coexistence of "Major" and "Minor"

For this purpose the Incipient Tonality Diamond, depicted in Diagram 6, is the most graphic method. Each succession of ratios between solid lines is a triad—the 1, 5, and 3 Odentities of an Otonality, given within a 2/1. Each succession of ratios between dotted lines is also a triad—the 1, 5, and 3 Udentities of a Utonality, given within a 2/1. It is thus evident that in tuning all intervals of the 5 limit correctly on 1/1 ("G"), we have not only a true triad on 1/1 but, willy-nilly, five other true triads—that is, a total of three true Otonality triads and three true Utonality triads.

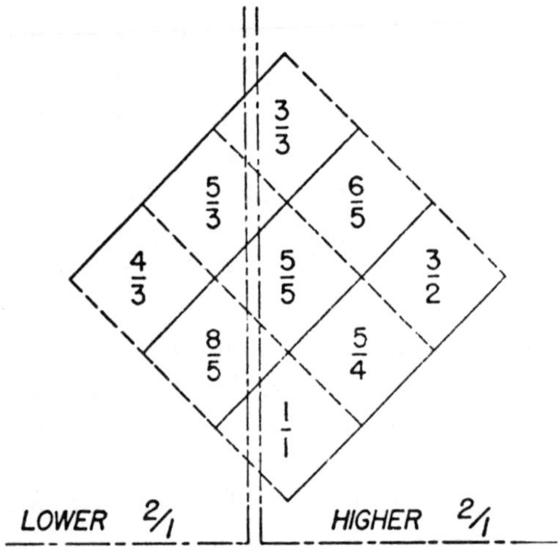

DIAGRAM 5.—THE INCIPIENT TONALITY DIAMOND

Moreover, the character of each ratio begins to reveal itself fully. We see that 1, or any number found in the geometrical succession of doublings based on 1 (2, 4, 8), is part of a ratio which is per se a unity, that 3 or a doubling of 3 is part of a ratio which is per se that identity of tonality, that 5 is part of a ratio which is per se that identity of tonality. If these numbers are the over numbers, the ratios of which they are a part are Odentities of an Otonality, with an under Numerary Nexus. If they are the under numbers, the ratios of which they are a part are Udentities of a Utonality, with an over Numerary Nexus.

The Otonality on 1/1 shows the Odentities 1, 5, 3, above, and has the Numerary Nexus 1 (2 and 4 are doublings based on 1 and have no identity apart from 1; see page 88); the Otonality on 8/5 shows the Odentities

1, 5, 3, above (8 is in the sequence of doublings based on 1, and 6 is the doubling of 3), and has the Numerary Nexus 5; the Otonality on 4/3 shows the Odentities 1, 5, 3, above (4 is in the sequence of doublings based on 1), and has the Numerary Nexus 3. The Utonality under 1/1 shows the Udentities 1, 5, 3, below, and has the Numerary Nexus 1 (4 and 8 are doublings based on 1); the Utonality under 5/4 shows the Udentities 1, 5, 3, below (4 is in the sequence of doublings on 1), and has the Numerary Nexus 5; the Utonality under 3/2 shows the Udentities 1, 5, 3, below (2 is the doubling of 1), and has the Numerary Nexus 3 (6 is the doubling of 3).

The Numerary Nexus of Otonalities is thus the under series of numbers, and the Numerary Nexus of Utonalities is the over series of numbers. The single color used to designate the Numerary Nexus of a given tonality, in the color analogy explained in Chapter 12, assists in the identification of tonality on the Chromelodeon.

The phenomenon of tonality is primarily established by the triad— Otonality or Utonality—with the identities as shown in the Diamond: 1-5-3. Because each line of ratios has a Numerary Nexus the identities are in the relation 4:5:6 (ascending) for Otonalities and in the relation 1/4:1/5: 1/6 for Utonalities. If we stipulate three different identities for a chord these three give the maximal consonance, and this fact is indubitably related to the psychological phenomenon of tonality, with the impression of tonal polarity it establishes around the 1 Identity, or unity.

As relationships to the sound vibration expressed by the number 1, the Incipient Tonality Diamond is more readily comprehended if the ratios in the "lower 2/1" (Diagram 5) are expressed in the correct acoustic manner: as 4/5, instead of 8/5; 2/3, instead of 4/3, etc. Thus, downward from 1/1 (in 1/1 Utonality), the 5 Udentity has four-fifths (4/5) of the vibrations of 1, and the 3 Udentity has two-thirds (2/3) of the vibrations of 1; whereas upward from 1/1 (in 1/1 Otonality), the 5 Odentity has five-fourths (5/4) of the vibrations of 1, and the 3 Odentity has three-halves (3/2) of the vibrations of 1.

## "Minor" Tonality and Its Questioned "Root"

In the matter of Otonality ("major") this Incipient Tonality Diamond holds nothing unfamiliar to the music student, since 3 always represents the so-called dominant degree of the scale, and 5 always represents the so-called mediant degree of the scale. In Utonality ("minor") the conception is somewhat different, since the series of identities descends in pitch from its unity, though the practical results are exactly the same; the unity is here the "fifth of the chord." The long controversy (see Chapter 15) as to the correct location of the "root" of the "minor" triad is rhetoric, so far as creative music goes, since the composer needs no greater authority than his fancy to put the "root" wherever he wants to put it. In the final chord of a cadence it is quite natural to put the 3 Udentity ("root") at the bottom, since the natural position of the unity in the Tonality Diamond is at the top.

The reverse view of Utonality might be compared to a map that is drawn so that the compass direction south points to the top of the page, north to the bottom. This view of a map, "upside down" according to present practice, would show all the land configurations reversed but it would not change the features of geography in the least. Nor does looking at Utonality in a descending manner change the character of Utonality in the least. In maps it is merely a matter of custom to make the top north; in musical theory it is essential that the custom of building the correlative identities of Utonality upward be reversed—for the numbers of the ratios and their naturally descending inclination cannot be denied.

## Blank Walls of Nomenclature

Regardless of whether the nomenclature of current musical theory is adequate for current practice, it has two prejudicial aspects: first, it divorces the facts of the science of sound from the practice of the art of music—a bit of supreme irony; and, second, it is incapable of the elasticity which would permit its continued use in any theoretical *démarche* or expansion such as Monophony. The superficiality of its terms is manifest: "minor," for example, does not in itself convey anything of fundamental significance. Hence the necessity, in this exposition, of a complete reorganization of nomenclature.

Further, there is an especial pitfall in the ordinary terms "third of the chord" and "fifth of the chord," since in Otonality, as here analyzed, the "third of the chord" is the 5 Odentity, and the "fifth of the chord" is the 3 Odentity; "third" is 5 and "fifth" is 3. The term "of the chord" will consequently be avoided as much as possible.

## Dual Identities

To return to the Incipient Tonality Diamond, it is evident that each ratio is *prima facie* revelation of its potentiality. We see, immediately, that 5/3 is capable of being the 5 Odentity ("mediant") in an Otonality, and that, at the same time, it is capable of being the 3 Udentity ("root") in a Utonality. We see immediately that 3/2 is capable of being the 3 Odentity ("dominant") in an Otonality, and that, at the same time, it is capable of being the unity ("dominant"), or 1 (2 is the doubling of 1), in a Utonality. Thus every ratio may be taken in at least two senses, and one ratio, the Prime Unity, may be taken in six senses, since it is represented three times in the Incipient Tonality Diamond, and each ratio has two numbers.

This faculty of a tone—of serving in more than one sense—is considered essential to modulation by most composers. After seventeen years of composing in this particular system I disagree at least partially. However, making an *a priori* grant of the essentiality of the faculty, we see that in a Monophonic just scale of merely seven degrees we already have a total of eighteen senses (six ratios of two senses each, and one ratio of six senses).

In Equal Temperament there are twelve tones, any one of which may be taken in twelve senses—given a lenient disposition toward the twelve-tone scale (see page 163; also Chapter 17), which makes a grand total of 144 senses. The fact that these senses are frequently not as sensible to the ear as they are intended to be will be discussed in another connection. Suffice it to stress the fact that the eighteen senses of our incipient scale of seven degrees within the 5 limit *are* the senses intended.

This extended analysis of the Incipient Tonality Diamond is basic to a thorough understanding of the intricate and subtle tonality relationships of the Monophonic system, with its hexad basis of tonality—that is, through the number 11, which will be presented in the next chapter. Intricacy and subtlety are inherent in a musical system of numbers, even within a 5 limit, and because of the nature of the human animal they become a delight to both his mind and his ear.

## Multiple-Number Ratios

As is seen in the seven-degree 5-limit scale above, there are three comparatively wide gaps, two of 315.6 cents each and one of 203.9 cents. By subdividing these lacunae it is possible not only to increase the degrees of the scale but to increase the number of tonalities, and since it is not possible to do so with the ratios having numbers limited to 5 or under, multiple-number ratios of 5 or under are appropriated.

The question as to whether the ear prefers a ratio composed of multiples of small prime numbers to a ratio of approximately the same width which involves smaller numbers but a larger prime number is one that cannot be answered categorically; each instance is a different problem. The fairly close intervals 9/8 (203.9 cents) and 8/7 (231.2 cents) are an example. Considered only as melodic relationships to 1/1, the ear might generally prefer 9/8, in which both numbers are multiples of 3 or less, to 8/7, a ratio with smaller numbers but involving a prime number higher than 3. There are, however, many instances in which a composer will prefer 8/7 for melodic or tonality considerations; the ear by no means always prefers the multiple-number ratio (see below).

However, to complete closely related triads we will keep the scale within the 5 limit for the present. Six new ratios, composed of numbers which are multiples of 5 or under, are added in two of the wide gaps, those at the beginning and end of the scale given above, thus increasing the number of degrees to thirteen:

| Cents....... | 0 | 111.7 | 182.4 | 203.9 | 315.6 | 386.3 |
|---|---|---|---|---|---|---|
| | | (new) | (new) | (new) | | |
| Degrees.....| 1/1 | 16/15 | 10/9 | 9/8 | 6/5 | 5/4 |
| | 16/15 | 25/24 | 81/80 | 16/15 | 25/24 | 16/15 |
| Cents........ | 111.7 | 70.7 | 21.5 | 111.7 | 70.5 | 111.7 |

| Cents ......| 498.0 | 702.0 | 813.7 | 884.4 | 996.1 | 1017.6 |
|---|---|---|---|---|---|---|
| | | | | | (new) | (new) |
| Degrees..... | 4/3 | 3/2 | 8/5 | 5/3 | 16/9 | 9/5 |
| | 9/8 | 16/15 | 25/24 | 16/15 | 81/80 | 25/24 |
| Cents........ | 203.9 | 111.7 | 70.7 | 111.7 | 21.5 | 70.7 |

| Cents....... | 1088.3 | 1200 |
|---|---|---|
| | (new) | |
| Degrees..... | 15/8 | 2/1 |
| | 16/15 | |
| Cents........ | 111.7 | |

To put it in another way, each of these multiple-number ratios is the result of two ratios within the 5 limit: 8/5 × 4/3 = 32/15, which, reduced within a 2/1, is 16/15; 5/3 × 4/3 = 20/9, which, reduced, is 10/9; 3/2 × 3/2

=9/4, reduced, 9/8; $4/3 \times 4/3 = 16/9$; $3/2 \times 6/5 = 18/10$, in reduced terms, 9/5; and $3/2 \times 5/4 = 15/8$.

Symmetry is inherent in a Monophonic scale. It is not planned; it is inevitable. Starting from 1/1 upward and from 2/1 downward there is the same sequence of intervals between degrees to 4/3 and 3/2 respectively, which are separated by the exactly central 9/8. It follows that each ratio has its complement ("inversion") at the corresponding point from the opposite end of the scale: $16/15 \times 15/8 = 2/1$; $10/9 \times 9/5 = 2/1$; $9/8 \times 16/9 = 2/1$; $6/5 \times 5/3 = 2/1$; $5/4 \times 8/5 = 2/1$; and $4/3 \times 3/2 = 2/1$.

The wide gap between 4/3 and 3/2 will not be subdivided now. The ratio generally used in translating Equal Temperament into terms of Just Intonation is 45/32, thus:

$$\begin{matrix} 4/3 & 45/32 & 3/2, \\ 135/128 & 16/15 & \end{matrix}$$

which gives the so-called tritone (the sum of three "tones"—200 cents + 200 cents + 200 cents—a compounding of fallacious nomenclature). Although this ratio is composed of numbers which are multiples of 5 or under, they are excessively large for a 5-limit scale, and are sufficient justification, either in this form or as the tempered "tritone," for the epithet "diabolic," which has been used to characterize the interval. This is a case where, because of the largeness of the numbers, none but a temperament-perverted ear could possibly prefer 45/32 to a small-number interval of about the same width.

In the Pythagorean ratio 81/64 both numbers are multiples of 3 or under, yet because of their excessive largeness the ear certainly prefers 5/4 for this approximate degree, even though it involves a prime number higher than 3. In the case of the 45/32 "tritone" our theorists have gone around their elbows to reach their thumbs, which could have been reached simply and directly and non-"diabolically" via the number 7. However, since 7 is outside the province of this phase of the discussion, the lacuna 4/3–3/2 will be abeyed, temporarily.

The nature of multiple-number ratios is to be considered later from two aspects—from the standpoint of their incidence in the hypothetical Perpetual Tonal Descent and Ascent (next chapter), and also from the aspect of graphs of their harmonic curves (see Chapter 9). For the present it will be sufficient to ascertain what these ratios (and a thirteen-degree scale) have accomplished in increasing the number of tonalities beyond the six of the Incipient Tonality Diamond.

## Secondary Tonalities in a 5 Limit

Because they involve multiple-number ratios the eight new tonalities (four Otonalities and four Utonalities) within the 5 limit will temporarily be called secondary—they will not necessarily be secondary in an 11-limit system.

| OTONALITIES (upward) | | | UTONALITIES (downward) | | |
|---|---|---|---|---|---|
| 1 Odentity (Unity) | 5 Odentity | 3 Odentity | 1 Udentity (Unity) | 5 Udentity | 3 Udentity |
| 3/2 | 15/8 | 9/8 | 4/3 | 16/15 | 16/9 |
| 6/5 | 3/2 | 9/5 | 5/3 | 4/3 | 10/9 |
| 16/9 | 10/9 | 4/3 | 9/8 | 9/5 | 3/2 |
| 16/15 | 4/3 | 8/5 | 15/8 | 3/2 | 5/4 |
| | 5/4 | 6/5 | | 5/4 | 6/5 |

The previous assertion that a ratio is *prima facie* revelation of its potentiality still holds in these secondary tonalities, once the unity is ascertained, although a bit more mental effort is involved. In the secondary Otonality on 3/2 we know that 3 represents the 1 Odentity or unity of an Otonality (since the over number represents an Odentity in an Otonality); the 5 Odentity must therefore be 3 × 5, or 15, and the 3 Odentity must be 3 × 3, or 9. The Numerary Nexus of this Otonality is 1 (2 and 8 are in the sequence of doublings).

In the Otonality on 6/5 the triad reveals itself better if it is written 6/5–30/20–18/10, multiplying the middle ratio by 10/10 and the third ratio by 2/2. We know that the 6 in 6/5 represents the 1 Odentity or unity, that 6 × 5, or 30, is the 5 Odentity, and that 6 × 3, or 18, is the 3 Odentity. The Numerary Nexus of this tonality is 5 (20 and 10 are in the sequence of doublings on 5).

In the Utonality under 15/8 the triad is better revealed if written 15/8–60/40–30/24, multiplying the middle ratio by 20/20 and the third ratio by 6/6. We know that 8 represents the 1 Udentity or unity of a Utonality (since the under numbers represent Udentities in Utonality); that 8 × 5, or 40, is the 5 Udentity, and 8 × 3, or 24, is the 3 Udentity. The Numerary Nexus is 15 (30 and 60 are doublings based on 15). All the other secondary tonalities can of course be clarified similarly. The intervals between identities is always 5/4–6/5, upward for Otonalities, downward for Utonalities, and this sequence can be tested; for example, the 16/15 Otonality: a 5/4 upward from 16/15—16/15 × 5/4 = 4/3; and a 6/5 upward from 4/3—4/3 × 6/5 = 8/5. In the 15/8 Utonality: a 5/4 downward from 15/8—15/8 × 4/5 = 3/2, and a 6/5 downward from 3/2—3/2 × 5/6 = 5/4.

Two further secondary triads would become available if 25/24 were inserted between 1/1 and 16/15, and its complement, 48/25, inserted between 15/8 and 1/1, both ratios having numbers which are multiples of 5 or under. However, these two ratios were not included in the larger Monophonic fabric and consequently will not be considered here.

## Summation of the 5-Limit Resources

In recapitulation: a scale of thirteen degrees tuned correctly on 1/1 ("G" in this theory—it could be any pitch) gives fourteen tonalities, seven Otonalities and seven Utonalities, each with identities complete through the predetermined limit, that is, 5.

As for the senses in which the thirteen degrees may be taken, 1/1, 3/2, and 4/3 may each be taken in six; 6/5, 5/3, 5/4, and 8/5 may each be taken in three; and the other six ratios may each be taken in two, making a total of forty-two senses.

To be sure, this does not begin to compare in mobility, granting the hypothesis regarding the desirability of many senses, with the 144 senses (assuming the "chromatic" maximum) of Equal Temperament; yet it shows far greater capacity than most theorists accord to so meager a Monophonic system, and, more important, the procedure as a whole points the way to continued investigation and experiment.

Furthermore, within the circumscribed resources of a 5 limit, tonality is restricted to the triad, the basis of present-day tonality. Variety in the quality of tonality calls for extension of the triad basis with its single 1-5-3 quality (or—with "inversions"—three variants of the same quality). Although it has been stressed that partials in certain arrangements and energies, which impart quality to a single musical sound, are a different concept from the series of identities of a tonality, we can learn how to impart quality from this phenomenon, and with the introduction of all identities through 11, in the next chapters, variety of quality is offered in almost bewildering abundance.

The expansion of man's consciousness of musical materials is evident in two facts: first, the 3 limit for intervals of the most perfect consonance; second, the 5 limit for intervals of the simplest "diatonic" scales, in the process of evolution since Pythagoras (discussed at some length in Chapter 10).

A formula is thus manifest which, along with harmonic, psycho-physiological, and historical considerations, becomes the justification for the extension of the limit to 11.

# CHAPTER EIGHT

# Application of the 11 Limit

## *The Problem of 7*

THE MUSICAL realization of Europe's eighteenth and nineteenth centuries was preceded, and in some measure at least indirectly prepared, by a succession of learned men, some of whom were perceptive and daring: Odington, Vicentino, Zarlino, Salinas, Galilei, Mersenne, Descartes, Rameau, Tartini, and others. These were mostly theorists, to be sure, but nevertheless aggressive participants in the musical thinking of their day. Among them there was no agreement that a 5 limit should prevail, but because it was expedient in the building and tuning of fretted and keyboard instruments and because its demands on notation were less complex, and for no other primary reasons, it did prevail in practical music. By the time the value of the harmonies that 7 involves had been theoretically recognized the patterns of both instruments and notation, with their 5 limit, had fixed themselves too definitely in the education and theoretical thinking of the army of musicians to be dislodged.

In another way the men whose work is widely recognized as the heart of the "Western Golden Age of music"—Bach, Mozart, Haydn, Beethoven, and many more—were also daring men, who simply appropriated as a medium of expression whatever was at hand, which happened to be instruments and notation based on the 5 limit.

In the wake of the golden-age masters came a second series of men whom we cannot call daring. These were the devoted admirers of the masters, who implemented their admiration with textbooks in which works of the masters were analyzed in the most scholarly fashion and rules laid down stemming from such analyses, who noted, in countless pages, each and every exception to these rules as found in the works of the masters, and who fervently devoted themselves to tying music to the age of the masters—and incidentally to the number 5—for ever and ever and ever and ever.

This is the setting and a part of the *dramatis personae* of the struggle between entrenched theory and the golden-age music on the one hand, and investigative theory and unconscious desire on the other, over the 5 limitation. From the standpoint of academic theory, the gate to 7 was slammed shut two hundred to three hundred years ago by a corpus of significant music which apparently confined its harmonic structure to less. But if the paint on the "forbidden" sign and the catches on the gate were ever very effective, they are now seemingly in need of attention, because Hindemith goes to some pains, in recent writings, to refurbish the sign and to hammer a few more nails into the rickety proscription.[1]

And even though rickety, because of inertia, the theoretical proscription still holds, despite the fact that 7, 9, and 11 were propounded as components of current scales in ancient Greek music,[2] despite the fact that 7 was called consonant and demonstrated to be consonant by Mersenne in the middle of the seventeenth century,[3] and thereafter by Tartini, Euler, Serre, Perrett,[4] and despite the fact that the comparative consonance of the ratios 7/4, 7/5, and 7/6 and of the triad 7:9:11 is at least tentatively acknowledged in hearing after hearing.

The reasons are two and easy: lethargy and the piano, the latter being incapable of the 7 and 11 ratios, though 7 is sometimes vaguely implied. In the face of something that amounts to a collective exasperation over the problem of 7 it may seem little short of absurd to appropriate all the ratios through the number 11. But the reasons for so doing are basic and ample, and—of supreme significance—experience with the sounds themselves is a final and decisive testimonial to the reasons.

Instruments designed to solve the problem of expansion are suggested in other parts of this work (see Chapters 6 and 12). At this point the reasons for the Monophonic stand at the number 11 will be discussed, with the tacit admission throughout that an 11 limit is wholly arbitrary, and without any implication of finality. These reasons fall into three categories—psychological, harmonic, historic.

## Why the Break to *11?*—the Psychological Reason

In the break to 11 a more expanded scale is inevitable, and in the theory here presented the number of degrees is tentatively tied to the number of fixed tones on the Chromelodeon—forty-three to the 2/1.

---

[1]*Craft of Musical Composition,* 1:38.                    [3]Shirlaw, *Theory of Harmony,* 32.
[2]Hawkins, *History of the Science and Practice of Music,* 1:32. [4]Perrett, *Questions of Musical Theory,* 40.

The common reaction to this disclosure is: can the human ear perceive so many degrees in the 2/1? The unequivocal answer is: it can, and frequently a good many more, depending largely on the range of pitch in which a test is made. It is not necessary to cite the experiments of scientists to corroborate this assertion, since seventeen years of playing music in a forty-three-tone scale and of slow playing of the scale for the most exacting scrutiny, in the full glare of a line-up, have repeatedly corroborated its perceptibility.[5]

The smallest interval in the Monophonic fabric measures 14.4 cents. Were this interval to be duplicated throughout the 2/1 in equal steps the result would be a scale of eighty-three tones to the 2/1 with 4.8 cents as a remainder. Consequently, if every degree of the forty-three-tone Monophonic scale is heard clearly, the implication is that eighty-three degrees would also be heard clearly, and this potential in the average devotee of music has been amply demonstrated; the persons I have encountered who are unable to hear this particular interval of 14.4 cents can be numbered on one hand.

The test has always been made in a median register, and inasmuch as the ability to perceive gradations of pitch diminishes at the acute and grave ends of the auditory sensation area, there might be legitimate skepticism of the Monophonic fabric in these outer ranges; but since by far the greater proportion of sounds heard in any music are in the median register, the doubt is a somewhat academic one. Furthermore, music is not a fantasy of chromaticism. A scale is a source of materials, from which chords and melodies are drawn, and in which the scale as a scale appears only occasionally if at all.

Several psychologists have made a point of differentiating between two allied abilities, which for musical practice seem to boil down to (1) the ability to perceive differences in pitch and (2) the ability to perceive differences in width of interval. Gilbert J. Rich concludes from his experiments that the first is about six times as acute as the second. At the range of pitch of about 275 cycles, for example, he finds that the ear perceives differences in pitch of about one cycle, but that it requires an addition of

[5]Both Seashore and Fletcher give graphs showing average pitch discrimination. For the range of pitch from approximately the second to the third "C's" above "middle C" Seashore gives an average maximum of about three hundred "just-noticeable differences," with a given intensity and timbre. This ability varies with individuals and decreases markedly in the lower ranges of pitch. *Psychology of Music*, 60. Fletcher's graph shows similar conclusions. *Speech and Hearing*, 152.

six cycles to hear a difference in width of interval.[6] The experiment was conducted with pairs of successive tones, not simultaneous soundings, and apart from data of a melodic nature that may have been obtained it is hard to perceive any significance in the experiment, or to perceive, for musical as opposed to putative psychological purposes, any difference between the abilities in regard to pitch and width of interval unless the subject of consonance-dissonance is also introduced (see page 415 for a more definitive discussion).

"The employment of small intervals is therefore limited [because of Rich's experiment]," writes the psychologist Ogden, "for although the smallest interval used in our music is considerably larger than a bare difference of volume [interval width], it would be impossible to use intervals much smaller [than the semitone] without approaching the region of liminal uncertainty."[7] In view of my experience in presenting the music of Monophony I am compelled to say that this statement and the many others which resemble it are made on the basis of an error and a lack; the error: wrong or insufficient experimental direction; the lack: absence of, or an absence of an interest in, actual music which proves the contrary.

Ogden himself tends to agree. "Let us not be dogmatic," he writes, for "if the threshold for volume difference [interval perception] were lowered, there would be an increase in the range of permissible intervals, and we are in no position to deny this accomplishment to the musicians of certain Oriental peoples."[8]

The intonational thesis of Monophony is fourfold: first, the expression of true or just intervals in an expansion from unity; second, augmentation of the chromatic potential; third, expansion of tonality; fourth, attainment of variety in the quality of tonality. Regarded in this light, the forty-three degrees as a tonal succession need no justification beyond the statement that each separate degree is easily perceived in the common registers of music.

---

[6]"Study of Tonal Attributes," in *American Journal of Psychology*, 30:145–150. Pronouncements of this sort which have been tossed into the musical pond by high academic authority have caused ripples of repetition for many years. Carl E. Seashore does not repeat without an investigation of his own, but he is accepted as an authority and is quoted by writers who do not investigate. He tells us that the twelve tones of our present scale are the smallest that the "unselected average" can enjoy. *Psychology of Music*, 127–128. At the risk of seeming querulous I ask, is this not similar to the familiar excuse for bad movies and mediocre radio programs?

[7]Robert Morris Ogden, *Hearing*, 123; this and the subsequent quotation from Ogden are quoted by permission of Harcourt, Brace and Company, Inc.

[8]*Ibid.*, 199.

*What's the matter with 13?*—The stimulation which the break to 11 causes will undoubtedly provoke the question: why not include 13, and what would be the effect of this inclusion?

The ratios within the 11 limit total twenty-nine, and wide gaps are divided by fourteen multiple-number ratios according to the pattern of successive intervals established by those within the 11 limit. The additional ratios of 13 would number twelve, and additional multiple-number ratios geared to the new pattern might number six, making sixty-one tones to the 2/1. From a scale standpoint this is not objectionable, and from a harmonic standpoint it is far from objectionable. Also, from a historic standpoint it would render practicable all the diatonic harmoniai of the ancient Greek aulos, as expounded by Kathleen Schlesinger (see Chapter 18).

The reasons why Monophony proceeds to the limit of 11 are basic and quite specific, as will be seen, but the reason for resting at the limit of 11 is a purely personal and arbitrary one. When a hungry man has a large table of aromatic and unusual viands spread before him he is unlikely to go tramping along the seashore and in the woods for still other exotic fare. And however skeptical he is of the many warnings regarding the unwholesomeness of his fare—like the "poison" of the "love-apple" tomato of a comparatively few generations ago—he has no desire to provoke further alarums.

## The Harmonic Reason

From a harmonic standpoint the expansion of Identities 1–3–5 through 7–9–11 provides a new and highly intriguing triad, and immediately makes possible a wide variety in quality. The six identities of a single Otonality or a single Utonality may be combined into twenty different triads, into fifteen different quadrads, and into six different quintads, and if various "inversions" and extended forms of the possible chords are considered, the total is multiplied several fold. They are given below, expressed in identity terms:

### The twenty triads

| | | | |
|---|---|---|---|
| 1–3–5 | 1–5–9 | 3–5–7 | 3–9–11 |
| 1–3–7 | 1–5–11 | 3–5–9 | 5–7–9 |
| 1–3–9 | 1–7–9 | 3–5–11 | 5–7–11 |
| 1–3–11 | 1–7–11 | 3–7–9 | 5–9–11 |
| 1–5–7 | 1–9–11 | 3–7–11 | 7–9–11 |

### The fifteen quadrads

| | | | |
|---|---|---|---|
| 1–3–5–7 | 1–3–7–11 | 1–5–9–11 | 3–5–9–11 |
| 1–3–5–9 | 1–3–9–11 | 1–7–9–11 | 3–7–9–11 |
| 1–3–5–11 | 1–5–7–9 | 3–5–7–9 | 5–7–9–11 |
| 1–3–7–9 | 1–5–7–11 | 3–5–7–11 | |

### The six quintads

| | |
|---|---|
| 1–3–5–7–9 | 1–3–7–9–11 |
| 1–3–5–7–11 | 1–5–7–9–11 |
| 1–3–5–9–11 | 3–5–7–9–11 |

On the basis of numerous tests there can be little doubt that the number 7 is implied—though very badly implied—throughout today's musical thinking. The ratios 6/5 and 5/4 are implied in all our triads, and the ear—though it prefers fact to implication—quickly realizes the implication, despite the fact that these intervals are one-sixth and one-seventh of a semitone out of tune, respectively, in Equal Temperament. Likewise, but to a lesser degree, the ear tends to realize the implication of 4:5:6:7 (in Monophonic ratios 1/1–5/4–3/2–7/4) in the "dominant seventh" chord, even though the 7 ingredient is a third of a semitone too sharp in Equal Temperament. This explanation of the chord—positing the consonant 7 Odentity and avoiding the dissonant 9/5 (1/1–5/4–3/2–9/5—the best such chord possible in a 5-limit theory)—has been advanced by a long line of important men in science and theory, beginning at least as early as Euler (eighteenth century). Also, the ear tends to recognize the "diminished triad" as 5:6:7 (in Monophonic ratios 1/1[5/5]–6/5–7/5, or 5/4–3/2[6/4]–7/4) even though the 7 ingredient is again too sharp in Equal Temperament, this time a sixth of a semitone.[9]

*Inconsistencies in the 5-limit thinking.*—In the "pure scale era" of sixteenth-century Italy the "diminished triad" was frankly called consonant by theorists.[10] To anyone who has taken the trouble to make the tests it is in-

[9]Theorists have tried hard to find the "diminished seventh" quadrad in the series of partials. This chord is a "diminished triad" with a "minor third" added. What kind of a "minor third" to add, however, is a problem. The ratios must have a Numerary Nexus if the quadrad is to have maximum consonance, but if the next interval in the series of partials, 8/7, is added, so that the chord is 5:6:7:8 (1/1 [5/5]–6/5–7/5–8/5), it loses its characteristic musical quality. To preserve a Numerary Nexus, Ellis postulates his "septendecimal harmony," 10:12:14:17 (1/1–6/5–7/5–17/10, or 5/4–3/2–7/4–17/16). Ellis in Helmholtz, *Sensations of Tone*, 346n, 464, 469. The two highest tones in the quadrad are in the ratio 17/14 (falling between 6/5 and 11/9 in the Monophonic fabric; see below). Ellis writes, "The chord 10:12:14:17 . . . is a comparatively smooth discord superior to the tempered form." For the most part this superiority is of course due to the initial 5:6:7.

[10]Lloyd, *Music and Sound*, 65.

conceivable that a human ear could react to the Pythagorean 1/1–32/27–
1024/729 (the third ratio a Pythagorean "minor third" added to a Pythagorean "minor third"—32/27 × 32/27), or to 1/1–6/5–36/25 (the
third ratio a 6/5 × 6/5), or to 1/1–6/5–45/32 as consonant. The ear could
jump the distance between what it heard and what it wanted to hear, or—
at least a part of the time—voices and viols intoned unconsciously the consonance 5:6:7 and the ear found it infinitely pleasing. Hence the label.

The tendency of the ear to try very hard to hear what it knows it does
not hear will be discussed at length later. It is palpably not a constructive
argument for Equal Temperament; it is quite negative—an eagerly appropriated balm for the sins of commission (or of omission, depending on
the viewpoint).

*Inconsistencies in the 3-limit thinking.*—Going backward chronologically, an
exactly parallel situation to this implication-plus-prohibition of 7 prevailed
in the Middle Ages with respect to 5. The Pythagorean scale of 1/1–9/8–
81/64–4/3–3/2–27/16–243/128–2/1, giving the highly equivocal 81/64
(21.5 cents high) instead of 5/4, and 27/16 (also 21.5 cents high) instead of
5/3, was generally theorized as the basis of music.[11] These ratios were postulated because theorists were afraid of the number 5, preferring the 81/64
and 27/16 derivatives of the number 3 thought process. Yet there is not a
musician, having been conditioned to the idea of more acoustic "thirds"
and "sixths," who would not admit that what the ear tried to assume in the
above medieval scale—if the ear ever actually heard it—was 5/4 and 5/3
instead of 81/64 and 27/16.

The same lethargy now prevails respecting the number 7, which offers
no dissonant ingredient in either the "dominant seventh" chord or the
"diminished triad," but only further consonance, and all because 7 lies outside the 5 limit of our mental cage. We grow to love our chains, which is
always human but only occasionally sufferable, since the results are only
occasionally rational.

To chain oneself, as a creator—to impose limitations within which to
work—is a legitimate exercise of personal freedom; to be forced to endure
such limitations because of a conspiracy of factors quite beyond the ordinary creator's control is a musical horse of another color.

*Only one further step to 11.*—In the so-called chord of the ninth the Identity

[11]Hawkins, *History of the Science and Practice of Music*, 1:400n. As early as 1482 Ramis de
Pareja pointed out the discrepancy between Pythagorean theory and actual practice. Schlesinger, "Greek Foundations of Theory," in *Musical Standard*, 27:177.

9 is implied very well in current music, since this particular 9 (9/8 and 16/9), as represented on the piano and in tempered scale theory, is only 3.9 cents too sharp or flat. But the other ratios of 9 are badly represented; those involving the number 7, for example, are 35.1 cents false, an out-of-tuneness quite sufficient to destroy their subtlety.

If we agree that 7 and 9 are already implied to an incipient degree in present-day music, and that in practice—as opposed to theory—7 and 9 are already at least partially accepted, there is just one further step in Monophony—to the number 11—and not three further steps. The musician will undoubtedly ask: if we concede that the "seventh of the chord" sometimes implies the Identity 7, and the "ninth of the chord" sometimes implies the Identity 9, why cannot the "eleventh of the chord" imply the Identity 11? The answer is that in Equal Temperament the ear does not realize the implication, and if the ear does not realize an implication, it does not exist.

Repeated tests have confirmed this assertion. The 7 implied by Equal Temperament in the chord 5:6:7 is 17.5 cents false, and the 9 implied in the chord 4:5:6:7:9 is only 3.9 cents false, whereas the 11 implied in the chord 4:5:6:7:9:11, or in any part of the chord, is 48.7 cents false. Moreover, the 7 and 9 Identities are much stronger than 11. Since the importance of an identity in tonality decreases as its number increases (see Chapter 11), 11 is the weakest of the six identities of Monophony; hence the necessity for exact intonation. The bruited argument that the larger the prime number involved in the ratio of an interval the greater our license in playing the interval out of tune can lead only to music-theory idiocy. If it is not the final straw—to break the camel's tympanum—it is at least turning him into an amusiacal ninny.

Although Arnold Schönberg has called "F♯" the 11 Identity in the "key of C," quite without reservation,[12] the fact is that the 11 Identity is virtually a "quartertone"—48.7 cents—below "F♯" in the "key of C." It seems obvious, even when the effort is not as conscious as Schönberg's, that in this modern day *we are trying to express harmonies of 7, 9, and 11 in a system— instruments and notation—designed for those of 3 and 5 only.*

## The Historical Reason

Perhaps it is significant, perhaps not, in discussing the historical aspect of the stand at 11, that in the theoretical exposition of Ptolemy, Alexan-

[12]"Problems of Harmony," in *Modern Music*, 11:170.

drian scientist of the second century, the ratios within the 11 limit are either given or implied, as a body. "Implied," in the sense intended here, does not signify any sort of temperament; it signifies a realization of all intervals between degrees (see page 172). These scales were either Ptolemy's own, or versions by Archytas, Eratosthenes, or Didymus, explaining the diatonic, chromatic, and enharmonic genera in terms of monochord ratios. Although prime numbers larger than 11 appear, they do not appear nor are implied as a body; that is, not all possible ratios within a limit higher than 11 are given or implied.

In Ptolemy's scales there is enough evidence to warrant the conclusion that his procedure was generally governed by the principle of appropriating the smallest-number ratios permissible to the purpose of the scale in question. In this light it is quite natural that he should have used all the ratios of the 11 limit as a body.

## *Orientation of Ratios in the 11 Limit*

The ratios of the 11 limit, totaling twenty-nine, are given below, with the intervals between degrees and the number of cents in each degree and each interval between degrees:

| Cents....... | 0 | 150.6 | 165.0 | 182.4 | 203.9 | 231.2 |
|---|---|---|---|---|---|---|
| Degrees.....1/1 | | 12/11 | 11/10 | 10/9 | 9/8 | 8/7 |
| | 12/11 | 121/120 | 100/99 | 81/80 | 64/63 | 49/48 |
| Cents........ | 150.6 | 14.4 | 17.4 | 21.5 | 27.3 | 35.7 |

| Cents.......266.9 | 315.6 | 347.4 | 386.3 | 417.5 | 435.1 |
|---|---|---|---|---|---|
| Degrees..... 7/6 | 6/5 | 11/9 | 5/4 | 14/11 | 9/7 |
| 36/35 | 55/54 | 45/44 | 56/55 | 99/98 | 28/27 |
| Cents........ 48.7 | 31.8 | 38.9 | 31.2 | 17.6 | 63.0 |

| Cents.......498.0 | 551.3 | 582.5 | 617.5 | 648.7 | 702.0 |
|---|---|---|---|---|---|
| Degrees..... 4/3 | 11/8 | 7/5 | 10/7 | 16/11 | 3/2 |
| 33/32 | 56/55 | 50/49 | 56/55 | 33/32 | 28/27 |
| Cents........ 53.2 | 31.2 | 35.0 | 31.2 | 53.2 | 63.0 |

| Cents.......764.9 | 782.5 | 813.7 | 852.6 | 884.4 | 933.1 |
|---|---|---|---|---|---|
| Degrees..... 14/9 | 11/7 | 8/5 | 18/11 | 5/3 | 12/7 |
| 99/98 | 56/55 | 45/44 | 55/54 | 36/35 | 49/48 |
| Cents........ 17.6 | 31.2 | 38.9 | 31.8 | 48.7 | 35.7 |

| Cents.......968.8 | 996.1 | 1017.6 | 1035.0 | 1049.4 | 1200 |
|---|---|---|---|---|---|
| Degrees..... 7/4 | 16/9 | 9/5 | 20/11 | 11/6 | 2/1 |
| 64/63 | 81/80 | 100/99 | 121/120 | 12/11 | |
| Cents........ 27.3 | 21.5 | 17.4 | 14.4 | 150.6 | |

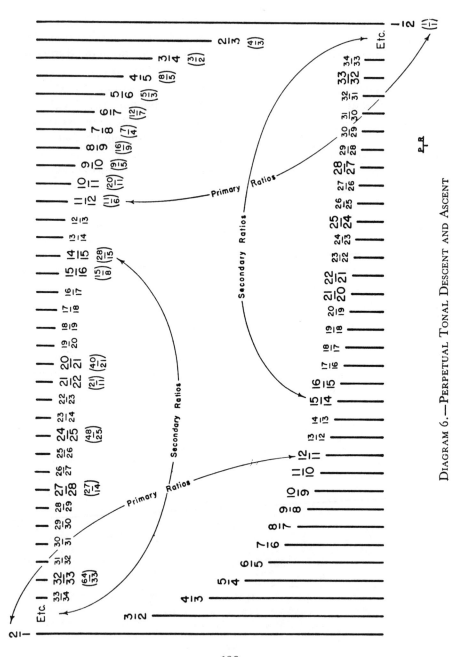

DIAGRAM 6.—PERPETUAL TONAL DESCENT AND ASCENT

The exact center of the above sequence is the 50/49 ratio between 7/5 and 10/7, the only place where this ratio appears, and the complement of each interval is in the corresponding position in the other half of the scale.

In the previous chapter the wide intervals on either side of 1/1 in the 5-generated scale—1/1 to 6/5 and 5/3 to 2/1—were divided by ratios each of which is the result of two ratios within the 5 limit. In exactly the same way as in the 5-generated scale the wide 1/1 to 12/11 and 11/6 to 2/1 intervals in the new Monophonic scale are divided, that is, by multiple-number ratios based on the 11 limit; or, to put it in another way, by the result of two ratios within the 11 limit.

There are two facts to remember in subdividing these ratios: first, successive-number ratios are appropriated simply because they are the ratios of the smallest numbers available for the purpose; and, second, the successive-number ratios to be chosen must also be multiple-number ratios based upon the prescribed limit of 11. These, coupled with the primary ratios within 11, contribute to the further increase of new tonalities (see Chapter 10).

In a scale fabric where a given identity number is chosen as a limit, and every ratio smaller than a 2/1 within it included, which is the method of Monophony, the successive tones necessarily bear to each other successive-number ratios: note the ratios between degrees of the scale given above.

## Perpetual Tonal Descent and Ascent

For the purpose of considering which successive-number ratios to use as degrees a hypothetical Perpetual Tonal Descent and a hypothetical Perpetual Tonal Ascent are graphed. The ratios within the 11 limit and ratios both numbers of which are multiples of 11 or under are distinguished by their large size in the accompanying diagram. In theory, the Perpetual Tonal Descent involves every successive-number ratio to the narrowest interval the imposed limit allows—121/120 in the scale above, which is found in two places. Diagram 7 shows only the beginning of the descent (and ascent). The descent begins with 2/1, and is followed by a scale on downward in pitch, 3/2, 4/3, 5/4, 6/5, 7/6, 8/7, 9/8, 10/9, 11/10, 12/11, and so on, in theory *ad infinitum*. Very soon—somewhere between 9/8 and 16/15—the ear fails to appreciate these successive-number intervals as such (see the next chapter).

Consider each line of the diagram as part of a hypothetical string; consider the bottom of the diagram as the nut, over which each string passes; consider the lines marked 2/1 and 1/2 as exactly half the string lengths, the second halves extending beyond the diagram, at the top. The point where each string in the descent *ends*, within the diagram, is the point at which it would be stopped to obtain the inscribed ratio, which is expressed in the usual manner—a vibrational relationship to a lower constant.

The Perpetual Tonal Ascent to the 2/1 is the perfect reflection of the descent to the unity. Its reverse character is seen better if its ratios are considered as parts of string lengths to an upper constant. In this sense the over and smaller number of each ratio represents the constant—the half of the string not shown, above the diagram, expressed in theoretical parts of its length—1, 2, 3, 4, 5, 6, etc., progressively, whereas the under and larger number is the representative of the tone—always one more part (and this one part only is shown in the diagram) than is contained in the constant. The point where each line of the ascent *begins*, within the diagram, is the point where it would be stopped to obtain the inscribed ratio. The ratios of the ascent in parentheses are in the usual vibrational-ratio symbolism, and are synonymous with the string-part ratios under which they occur. The ratios of the ascent could also be considered as vibrations related to an upper constant 1 (the half of the string not shown representing 1) without losing their successive-number form—as one-half of the vibrations made by 1, two-thirds of the vibrations of 1, three-fourths of the vibrations of 1, four-fifths of the vibrations of 1, etc., etc.

Given the form generally used in this volume, however, the ascent loses its successive-number ratio character but becomes Monophonically more recognizable, and each ratio is instantly seen as the complement of its corresponding ratio in the descent: 1/2 becomes 1/1 (total interval eclipse, the complement of 2/1); 2/3 becomes 4/3, the complement of 3/2, the second integral of the descent; 3/4 becomes 3/2, the complement of 4/3, third integral of the descent, and so on. The complements are generally as consonant or dissonant as their descending counterparts. Zarlino attributed a superior degree of consonance to a ratio of successive numbers, considering 8/5 and 5/3 as "composite" intervals ($4/3 \times 6/5 = 8/5$ and $4/3 \times 5/4 = 5/3$) and less consonant than the intervals found consecutively in the succession 1–2–3–4–5–6.[13]

[13]Shirlaw, *Theory of Harmony*, 41.

Like the descent, the ascent is the simplest means of access or egress and, with the descent, subdivides the inordinately wide gaps 1/1 to 12/11 and 11/6 to 2/1 in the twenty-nine-degree scale given above. No other ratios in the same range have comparable potentialities.

## *Placing of the Multiple-Number Ratios*

The ratios available to us—successive-number and multiple-number ratios based on an 11 limit—to subdivide the gap 1/1 to 12/11 are, from widest to narrowest: 15/14, 16/15, 21/20, 22/21, 25/24, 28/27, 33/32, 36/35, 45/44, 49/48, 50/49, 55/54, 56/55, 64/63, 81/80, etc. Any one of these is the result of two intervals within the 11 limit; for example, 3/2 × 11/8 = 33/16, or 33/32.

The complements of these intervals, which are available to divide the interval 11/6 to 2/1, are, from narrowest to widest: 28/15, 15/8, 40/21, 21/11, 48/25, 27/14, 64/33, 35/18, 88/45, 96/49, 49/25, 108/55, 55/28, 63/32, 160/81, etc. Given in parts-of-string or fractional-parts-of-1 ratio symbolism they would be: 14/15, 15/16, 20/21, 21/22, 24/25, 27/28, 32/33, 35/36, 44/45, 48/49, 49/50, 54/55, 55/56, 63/64, 80/81, etc. Each of these ratios is also the result of two ratios of the 11 limit; for example, 4/3 × 16/11 = 64/33, or 32/33.

The two gaps should contain degrees spaced approximately as they are spaced in the sequence of the twenty-nine ratios shown previously, in which the smallest interval between degrees is 14.4 cents and the largest exactly 63 cents. Eight, four in each 12/11 gap, would seem to accomplish this. The eight below were chosen from the possible thirty because they are important identities of the secondary tonalities (see Chapter 10):

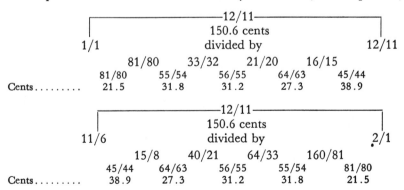

Six other intervals in the sequence of twenty-nine ratios of the 11 limit, although narrower than the two 12/11's, require subdivision to produce a somewhat even scale; these are:

| | 1. 7/6 | 6/5 | 2. 9/7 | 4/3 | 3. 4/3 | 11/8 |
|---|---|---|---|---|---|---|
| | | 36/35 | | 28/27 | | 33/32 |
| Cents......... | | 48.7 | | 63.0 | | 53.2 |

| | 4. 16/11 | 3/2 | 5. 3/2 | 14/9 | 6. 5/3 | 12/7 |
|---|---|---|---|---|---|---|
| | | 33/32 | | 28/27 | | 36/35 |
| Cents......... | | 53.2 | | 63.0 | | 48.7 |

The widest, 28/27, is four and one-half times as wide as the narrowest interval between degrees, 121/120, in the 11-limit scale. Each of the six is therefore divided, as before, by a ratio which is the sum of two intervals of the 11 limit, and the six new ratios are also identities in the secondary tonalities:

| | 1. 7/6 | 32/37 | 6/5 | 2. 9/7 | 21/16 | 4/3 |
|---|---|---|---|---|---|---|
| | | 64/63 | 81/80 | | 49/48 | 64/63 |
| Cents......... | | 27.3 | 21.5 | | 35.7 | 27.3 |

| | 3. 4/3 | 27/20 | 11/8 | 4. 16/11 | 40/27 | 3/2 |
|---|---|---|---|---|---|---|
| | | 81/80 | 55/54 | | 55/54 | 81/80 |
| Cents......... | | 21.5 | 31.8 | | 31.8 | 21.5 |

| | 5. 3/2 | 32/21 | 14/9 | 6. 5/3 | 27/16 | 12/7 |
|---|---|---|---|---|---|---|
| | | 64/63 | 49/48 | | 81/80 | 64/63 |
| Cents......... | | 27.3 | 35.7 | | 21.5 | 27.3 |

## Six Different "Tritones"

In the thirteen-degree 5-limit scale expounded in the previous chapter, only one wide interval was left after the division of the two gaps at either end: the 9/8 between 4/3 and 3/2. In the process of explaining the twelve-tone scale in terms of Just Intonation theorists introduced the large-number ratio 45/32 as the division of this interval, "C♯" in the "key of G," between "C" and "D"; examine this same 4/3 to 3/2 interval and its division in the complete scale of forty-three degrees:

| | | | —9/8— | | | | |
|---|---|---|---|---|---|---|---|
| | | | 203.9 cents | | | | |
| 4/3 | | | divided by | | | | 3/2 |
| | 27/20 | 11/8 | 7/5 | 10/7 | 16/11 | 40/27 | |
| | 81/80 | 55/54 | 56/55 | 50/49 | 56/55 | 55/54 | 81/80 |
| Cents.... | 21.5 | 31.8 | 31.2 | 35.0 | 31.2 | 31.8 | 21.5 |

## The Forty-Three-Tone Scale

Diagram 7 graphs the sequence of steps of the Monophonic fabric against a scale tempered to exactly twelve equal steps; the ratios that correspond most closely to the common chromatic scale (excepting "C♯") are shown in a larger size. Below is given the sequence of fabric degrees, showing the number of cents in each degree and in each interval between degrees, as usual:

| Cents | 0 | 21.5 | 53.2 | 84.5 | 111.7 | 150.6 |
|---|---|---|---|---|---|---|
| Degrees | 1/1 | 81/80 | 33/32 | 21/20 | 16/15 | 12/11 |
| | 81/80 | 55/54 | 56/55 | 64/63 | 45/44 | 121/120 |
| Cents | 21.5 | 31.8 | 31.2 | 27.3 | 38.9 | 14.4 |

| Cents | 165.0 | 182.4 | 203.9 | 231.2 | 266.9 | 294.1 |
|---|---|---|---|---|---|---|
| Degrees | 11/10 | 10/9 | 9/8 | 8/7 | 7/6 | 32/27 |
| | 100/99 | 81/80 | 64/63 | 49/48 | 64/63 | 81/80 |
| Cents | 17.4 | 21.5 | 27.3 | 35.7 | 27.3 | 21.5 |

| Cents | 315.6 | 347.4 | 386.3 | 417.5 | 435.1 | 470.8 |
|---|---|---|---|---|---|---|
| Degrees | 6/5 | 11/9 | 5/4 | 14/11 | 9/7 | 21/16 |
| | 55/54 | 45/44 | 56/55 | 99/98 | 49/48 | 64/63 |
| Cents | 31.8 | 38.9 | 31.2 | 17.6 | 35.7 | 27.3 |

| Cents | 498.0 | 519.5 | 551.3 | 582.5 | 617.5 | 648.7 |
|---|---|---|---|---|---|---|
| Degrees | 4/3 | 27/20 | 11/8 | 7/5 | 10/7 | 16/11 |
| | 81/80 | 55/54 | 56/55 | 50/49 | 56/55 | 55/54 |
| Cents | 21.5 | 31.8 | 31.2 | 35.0 | 31.2 | 31.8 |

| Cents | 680.5 | 702.0 | 729.2 | 764.9 | 782.5 | 813.7 |
|---|---|---|---|---|---|---|
| Degrees | 40/27 | 3/2 | 32/21 | 14/9 | 11/7 | 8/5 |
| | 81/80 | 64/63 | 49/48 | 99/98 | 56/55 | 45/44 |
| Cents | 21.5 | 27.3 | 35.7 | 17.6 | 31.2 | 38.9 |

| Cents | 852.6 | 884.4 | 905.9 | 933.1 | 968.8 | 996.1 |
|---|---|---|---|---|---|---|
| Degrees | 18/11 | 5/3 | 27/16 | 12/7 | 7/4 | 16/9 |
| | 55/54 | 81/80 | 64/63 | 49/48 | 64/63 | 81/80 |
| Cents | 31.8 | 21.5 | 27.3 | 35.7 | 27.3 | 21.5 |

| Cents | 1017.6 | 1035.0 | 1049.4 | 1088.3 | 1115.5 |
|---|---|---|---|---|---|
| Degrees | 9/5 | 20/11 | 11/6 | 15/8 | 40/21 |
| | 100/99 | 121/120 | 45/44 | 64/63 | 56/55 |
| Cents | 17.4 | 14.4 | 38.9 | 27.3 | 31.2 |

| Cents | 1146.8 | 1178.5 | 1200 |
|---|---|---|---|
| Degrees | 64/33 | 160/81 | 2/1 |
| | 55/54 | 81/80 | |
| Cents | 31.8 | 21.5 | |

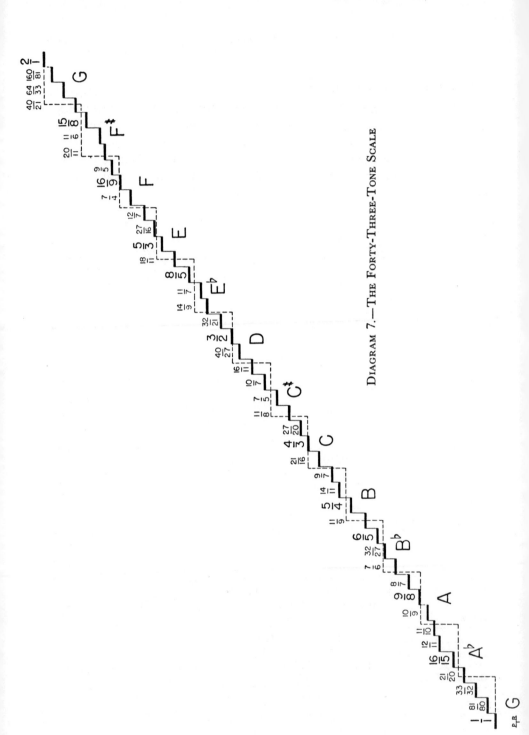

DIAGRAM 7.—THE FORTY-THREE-TONE SCALE

The inevitable symmetry of the structure is apparent, just as it was apparent in the degrees of the 5-limit scale (previous chapter). Each ratio has its complement in the other half of the scale, and there is the same sequence of intervals between degrees, starting from 1/1 and 2/1, and proceeding to 7/5 and 10/7, respectively. Also, each interval between degrees is a successive-number ratio.

As will be seen either from the sequence of unequal quantities of cents or from the unequal steps more graphically presented in the diagram, successive degrees cannot be equal in a Monophonic Just Intonation. No interval between degrees is equal to the following interval; and no multiple of an interval will go into another interval in such a way as to form a "cycle" or "circle"; and there is no extensive "column," to use the Ellis terminology, in a Monophonic system of Just Intonation.

## The Facts about Intervals on the Piano

The following examples are for the benefit of students of "harmony" as it is ordinarily taught: we say that the "octave" contains six "whole tones," four "minor thirds," and three "major thirds," and that twelve "perfect fifths" equal seven "octaves." The facts are that no acoustically true interval will go a certain number of times into a 2/1 without a varying remainder, and that no acoustically true interval to an $n$th power will go into 2/1 to an $n$th power without a varying remainder. To be more specific: the theoretic "major whole tone" to the sixth power $—(9/8)^6—$does not equal 2/1, but an interval 23.5 cents wider than 2/1; the just "minor third" to the fourth power $—(6/5)^4—$does not equal 2/1, but an interval 62.6 cents wider than 2/1; the just "major third" to the third power$—(5/4)^3—$does not equal 2/1, but falls 41.0 cents short of 2/1, and, finally, the really perfect "perfect fifth" to the twelfth power$—(3/2)^{12}—$the "cycle" or "circle of fifths"$—$does not equal seven "octaves," or 2/1 to the seventh power$—(2/1)^7—$but is 23.5 cents wider than $(2/1)^7$. In Equal Temperament, then, to achieve its twelve equal degrees, each 3/2 is robbed of one-twelfth of 23.5 cents, or nearly 2 cents, and the result is the ratio 149831/100000 for the tempered "perfect fifth." Now, 149831/100000 to the twelfth power$—(149831/100000)^{12}—$does equal $(2/1)^7$, at least for the practical purposes of the piano.[14] In other words, twelve quasi-"perfect fifths" do

[14]The approximation 149831/100000 is 2 to the 7/12 power, and is found by means of seven-place logarithms (see page 101).

fit perfectly, for practical purposes, into seven "octaves," and this is the only perfect thing about the "solution." And the ramification of evil complications in this one little act of perverting nature is actually endless.

## More Ratios for the Experimental Instrument

The cello fingerboard or the harmonic canon with computed stops may now be marked for thirty more intervals, and the ratios learned in relation to the thirteen that are well known. The proportions to be measured from the nut are always found by subtracting the under number from the over number, using this difference as the numerator, and the over number as the denominator, of the proportion to be measured off. Example: the scale degree 14/11 is found by measuring 3/14 of the string length from the nut.

*Reminder:* These proportions are for a string tuned 1/1. For a string tuned to another ratio, each ratio desired as a stop must first be computed in relation to the open string; the result of this computation is then the basis of the proportion to be measured off for the desired stop. For example, if a string is tuned 3/2 and the desired stop is 14/9, the relation between these two is 28/27, which indicates that the stop 14/9 is available at 1/28 of the open 3/2 string.

## Transposition and/or Good Acoustic Means

Composers have long been accustomed to a system that permits exactly parallel motion by a distance of any one of the tempered intervals removed. This is not a capacity of Monophony except, under some circumstances, by the most consonant intervals, 4/3 and 3/2. It is not possible to transpose a highly intricate composition in Monophony from one tonality to another and at the same time preserve the fidelity of each of the original chord relationships—unless, of course, the composer brings a piano attitude to his work and accepts with complacence the sixth-of-a-semitone maximum falsity of tempered intervals. With this attitude any one of Monophony's forty-three degrees might be used as a "keynote," and the ensuing triads would generally not be as false as they are on the piano. Given this much laxity Monophony is capable of anything.

It is quite conceivable that an instrument could be built that would be capable of an automatic change of pitch throughout its entire range, up or down by any reasonable interval, and if Just Intonation can surmount the many hazards and problems of initial tonal application, notation, and comprehension, the problem of transposition may be considered minor, one for which a solution will inevitably be found. Transposition and parallelism are devices which have brought a false simplicity to the mental processes of music, for which both mind and ear are paying dearly. We can be certain that if good and significant music is born in Just Intonation, for justly intoned instruments, and if this music is heard and approved, both the instruments and their acoustic conception will be eagerly sought and studied, and their values recognized. And the instruments will be snatched, at least temporarily, from the fate which is the ever-present dread of the musical pioneer — the jaws of the room marked "Rare Instrument Collection."[15] Good artistic results will be conveyed through good acoustic means, as they are not now. Few persons will know or care what the means is, what its nature is, or how it came into being, but the rewards to some individual John Doe's ear will be great.

[15]I can only partially sympathize with the curator's attitude toward rare and unique instruments. Paintings and sculpture and many other museum objects are fulfilling their purpose in being looked at. Whether or not the dead can experience frustration, I for one feel an intense frustration for those artisans who created instruments to *sound*, when I see the results of their labor placarded with the injunction "Do Not Touch" or displayed in locked glass cases.

# CHAPTER NINE

# The One-Footed Bride

## *The Fact of Consonance*

ACCORDING to Galileo, "agreeable consonances are pairs of tones which strike the ear with a certain regularity; this regularity consists in the fact that the pulses delivered by the two tones, in the same interval of time, shall be commensurable in number, so as not to keep the eardrum in perpetual torment, bending in two different directions in order to yield to the ever-discordant impulses."[1] The fairly "perpetual" torment which is our heritage in Equal Temperament has long obscured this aural axiom.

Here we shall examine something of the nature of the more important musical intervals, and the procedure by which each of the Monophonic scale degrees is tuned on the Chromelodeon with no other aid than the ability of the ear to distinguish pulsations "commensurable in number" and those which bend its tympanum "in two different directions." The conclusions reached lead, at the close of the chapter, to a rough graph of comparative consonance which I term the One-Footed Bride.

## *The Chromelodeon's Proof*

After the initial pitch (1/1–392) has been established on the Chromelodeon by means of a tuning fork, a procedure is charted by which every interval can be tested in its relation to certain key ratios, and also, as a check, to various others. To illustrate the actual mechanics of tuning, assume that the interval intended as 3/2 is slightly out of tune, so that beats are heard, perhaps two or three per second between the second partial of "3" and the third partial of "2," both of which should be 6 (to find the first common partial multiply the two numbers of a ratio). If the interval is only very slightly out of tune it is almost impossible for the ear to determine whether it is too wide or too narrow. Consequently a test is made; the higher reed is scratched at its base to flat its tone. If, after replacing and

---

[1] Dayton C. Miller, *Anecdotal History of the Science of Sound*, 11; quoted by permission of The Macmillan Company.

testing the reed, the beats are faster, we know that it was a mistake to flat it, that it was flat to begin with. Hence we scratch the reed at its tip, testing continually, until the beats disappear entirely—that is, until the two pulsations are "commensurable in number." On the harmonium type of instrument, in which the feet control the amount of air pressure in the bellows, the reeds may be in tune at one pressure and at a lesser or greater pressure be very slightly out of tune (slow beats in higher partials, which are likely to reappear even though the generator tones may seem to be in perfect tune); the reeds should be tuned at an average bellows pressure. Despite this failing, efficient, pedal-operated bellows are generally superior, in a musical sense, to an electric motor hook-up, since the feet control the volume somewhat as a violinist controls volume with his bow.

Experience in tuning the Chromelodeon has proved conclusively that not only the ratios of 3 and 5, but also the intervals of 7, 9, and 11 are tunable by eliminating beats.[2] The proof of this experience lies in the subtle series of relationships in the Monophonic fabric, for a ratio has not merely a single small-number easy-to-tune relationship, but several, which provide checks for every result. The initial procedure is as follows:

CHROMELODEON TUNING GUIDE

| Interval Relationship (Upward) | 3/2 | 4/3 | 5/4 | 6/5 | 8/5 | 5/3 | 8/7 | 7/4 | 11/8 | 16/11 |
|---|---|---|---|---|---|---|---|---|---|---|
| From 1/1 get | 3/2 | 4/3 | 5/4 | 6/5 | 8/5 | 5/3 | 8/7 | 7/4 | 11/8 | 16/11 |
| From 3/2 get | 9/8 | | 15/8 | 9/5 | | | | | | |
| From 4/3 get | | 16/9 | | | 16/15 | 10/9 | | | | |
| From 9/8 get | 27/16 | | | 27/20 | | | | | | |
| From 16/9 get | | 32/27 | | | | 40/27 | | | | |
| From 27/16 get | | | | | 81/80 | | | | | |
| From 32/27 get | | | | | | 160/81 | | | | |
| From 8/7 get | 12/7 | 32/21 | 10/7 | | | 40/21 | | | | |
| From 7/4 get | 21/16 | 7/6 | | | 21/20 | 7/5 | | | | |
| From 12/7 get | 9/7 | | | | | | | | | |
| From 7/6 get | | 14/9 | | | | | | | | |
| From 11/8 get | 33/32 | 11/6 | | | 11/10 | | 11/7 | | | |
| From 16/11 get | 12/11 | 64/33 | 20/11 | | | | | 14/11 | | |
| From 11/6 get | | 11/9 | | | | | | | | |
| From 12/11 get | 18/11 | | | | | | | | | |

[2]Ogden declares that there is no "fusion" (no consonance, that is) in ratios with numbers over 7. But he immediately amends this by saying that ratios with larger numbers "manifest

The given tone is 1/1–392. Every ratio appearing in the column at the left is seen first in one of the horizontal lines of ratios above. Thus, in considering "From 3/2 get" 3/2 appears first as a 3/2 above 1/1 in the line immediately above; in considering "From 12/7 get," 12/7 appears first as a 3/2 above 8/7 in the line "From 8/7 get," etc.

The first step is to tune 3/2 to 1/1–392; then 9/8, 15/8, and 9/5 are tuned to 3/2, and the relationships of these ratios above 3/2 are shown in their respective columns in the top line of ratios. Next 4/3 is tuned to 1/1, and, in turn, 16/9, 16/15, and 10/9 are tuned to 4/3, the relationships of these ratios to 4/3 being shown in their respective columns in the top line of ratios. Continuing, 9/8 (which was tuned to 3/2) becomes the tone to which two more ratios are tuned, and so on. The ratios 11/8 and 16/11 are left until last. They are the least easy to tune, but by this time the ear's sensitivity is whetted to a hyper-sharpness, and although the ear's mind is surely a bit weary after tuning the 122 reeds generally found in a harmonium, it is moved to an elementary observation: How easy it is to tune *in tune!*

In the matter of checks, 7/4, for example, which is originally tuned in relation to 1/1, can be checked against 3/2 (in the easy-to-hear 7/6 interval), and against 5/4 (in the easy-to-hear 7/5 interval). There are several for each newly tuned ratio, and these are conclusive checks.[3] A further, less conclusive, but good overall check consists in sounding each two consecutive degrees to determine in a comparative way the frequency of the *wah-wah*, or beats, each pair creates. Because the forty-three degrees are fairly close it is sometimes possible actually to count the *wahs*, especially in the lower register. The test is of course only comparative: the *wah-wah* in the interval 56/55 (between 5/4 and 14/11) will obviously be much faster than the *wah-wah* in the successive interval 99/98 (between 14/11 and 9/7). However, the *wah-wah* a 2/1 higher should be exactly twice as frequent, and the *wah-wah* a 2/1 lower exactly half as frequent.

## The Sine Curve of One Tone

In view of the startling fact that a forty-three-tone just scale through the 11 limit can be tuned by ear, the nature of the aural effect which makes

varying degrees of failure" to "fuse." *Hearing*, 125–126. A "varying degree of failure" not only indicates an open mind on Ogden's part but a verging of some of these intervals on "success."

[3]Consult the Tonality Diamond, page 159, and the table of secondary tonalities, page 161, for the complete checks.

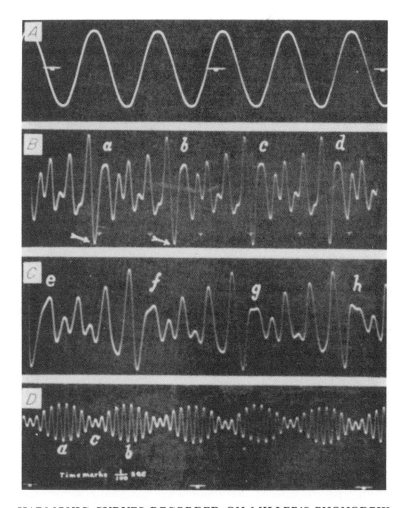

HARMONIC CURVES RECORDED ON MILLER'S PHONODEIK

Reproduced from Dayton C. Miller's *Sound Waves: Their Shape and Speed*
(1937) facing page 52, by permission of The Macmillan Company

possible this process—the nature of Galileo's pulsations "commensurable in number"—demands examination, and for this purpose the best possible method is the graph which mathematicians call the sine curve, or simple harmonic curve.

This graph, which becomes an oscillogram in a series of curves and which is described in numerous books on acoustics, is a line profile of a transverse wave which represents the displacement of air caused by a musical sound. The displacement is by condensation and rarefaction,[4] and the sine curve in the oscillogram is a graphic representation of this action; it is the symbol of a function. In a pure tone, without harmonic content, typical of a tuning fork or electronic oscillation, the oscillogram is a simple series of pendular loops, of crests and troughs, shown in the sketch below.[5] In a

really musical tone, however, with a rich harmonic content, it is a highly jagged line, but one in which the mean of the various joggles is still somewhat similar to the simple harmonic curve. For our purposes here, and despite the fact that the Chromelodeon tone has a very rich harmonic content, a simple curve is quite satisfactory, since it demonstrates the principles involved without preliminary complications. Further, the important "phase" principle is the same in either the simple or the jagged profile.

## The Sine Curve of Two Tones

When two different tones are sounded together their vibrations exist simultaneously in the same air, and they produce a single harmonic curve which is quite different from the harmonic curve of either when sounded separately. This composite curve is the algebraic sum of the two curves of the individual tones,[6] or, in language less mathematical and precise, the mean of the two curves. However, for the purpose of briefly illustrating the phase principle, the following curves are shown as though the two tones were given separately: when two tones of the same pitch are in like phase

[4]Miller, *Science of Musical Sounds*, 16.
[5]See the photographs of several of Miller's **Phonodeik** records of sine curves facing page 140.
[6]Miller, *Science of Musical Sounds*, 60.

their curves—one solid, one dotted—may be described in a rough sketch such as this:

and they strengthen each other; when the two are in opposite phase, their curves may be described thus:

and they tend to dampen or cancel out each other. When the two tones are not the same pitch, but are in the relation 3/2, for example, like and opposite phase still operate; the two tones are in like phase every three waves of the upper tone to every two waves of the lower tone.

More frequently than not the like and opposite phases of two tones do not exactly coincide, but are slightly "askew," with one delayed in time relation to the other. Fortunately for music, however, this fact has no bearing on comparative consonance.[7] Two tones which are consonant when they have like phases that exactly coincide are just as consonant in a "different" phase, since their vibrational ratio is unchanged, and the wave period which the simultaneous sounding of the two tones creates in the air is of exactly the same frequency regardless of phase difference.

### Significance of Wave Period to the Consonance Idea

Wave period may be defined as the wave pattern between like phase and like phase, or from maximum to maximum, in acoustic parlance; it is the exact repetition of this wave period which makes the wave train—and musical sounds—a periodic phenomenon. In the records from Miller's Phonodeik, depicted opposite page 140, the distances from *a* to *b* in Curves *B* and *D* are wave periods. It will be seen that comparative frequency of period in any given range of pitch has a prime bearing on the comparative consonance of intervals. When the high frequency of period is destroyed by a deviation from a small- to a large-number ratio not only the generator

[7]Meyer, *Mechanics of the Inner Ear*, 47.

tones are thrown out of distinguishable proportion but the two series of tones which they generate are also thrown out of proportion; where partials of one had coincided with partials of the other in the small-number proportion, in the deviation or large-number proportion these "unisons" are out of tune, and consequently create beats.

## The Euler and Helmholtz Theories

Hermann Helmholtz (1821–1894) seized upon this characteristic of large-number proportions as the explanation of dissonance, and tended to ascribe comparative consonance to those intervals which generated the fewest beating partials. This was a conscious effort by Helmholtz to put consonance and dissonance on a physiological basis rather than the psychological basis on which Euler had left it the century before.[8] The Euler explanation, founded on the idea of a conscious feeling for orderly as opposed to disorderly relations of tone, had its source, like Galileo's explanation, in the commensurability of numbers, which is of course synonymous with the ancient Greek deductions embodied in small-number proportions. In criticizing Euler's theories Helmholtz writes: "A man that has never made physical experiments has never in the whole course of his life had the slightest opportunity of knowing anything about pitch numbers or their ratios. And almost every one who delights in music remains in this state of ignorance from birth to death."[9] This is very much like saying that people do not know that two heard tones are in the relation 3/2 and implying that consequently there must be some reason besides the 3/2 relation why they recognize it as a consonance.

Both musical theorists and acousticians are cognizant of the light that Helmholtz projected on the subject of acoustics, and no practical musician and tuner will belittle the significance of beating partials; yet the fact is that after Helmholtz's day consonance and dissonance were expressible in exactly the same terms as they were before—namely, small-number proportions = comparative consonance.

## The Post-Helmholtz Theories

Karl Stumpf (1848–1936), psychologist and theorist, was the first to show the inadequacy of the Helmholtzian theories, and by the very simple

[8]Helmholtz, *Sensations of Tone*, 194, 231.
[9]*Ibid.*, 231; quoted by permission of Longmans, Green and Company, Ltd.

process of demonstrating that, whereas Helmholtz had ascribed consonance to the relative absence of beating partials, it is quite possible to produce pairs of dissonant sinusoidal tones by the baker's dozen that have nary a partial—beating, bleating, or even fleeting. In trying to resolve the controversy that ensued Stumpf suggested that comparative "fusion"—found when two tones approach the sensation of a single tone—is the criterion of consonance. "Fusion," he said, is an "immanent relation," giving rise to a uniformity that in itself cannot be further analyzed. By way of elaboration he suggests that "the mechanism of synergy, connate with the individual, may have been acquired in the course of generations, and perhaps the influences under which it took shape may have been in part mental influences. Impressions that affect the sense organ, together with relative frequency, might gradually set up a disposition to conscious fusion."[10]

This rather involved language leads to the observation that the disposition toward "conscious fusion" in the association of tones is very debatable. It is perhaps "conscious" with tuners but is certainly "unconscious" to an appalling degree with most musicians. At any rate, "fusion," conscious or unconscious, means: small-number proportions = comparative consonance.

The psychologist Theodor Lipps (1851–1914) advanced the theory that the human ear unconsciously experiences either a "micro-rhythmic sensation" of a simple sort—which is consonance—or a "micro-rhythmic sensation" of a complex sort and lacking a high degree of "fusion"—which is dissonance.[11] But whatever the type of "micro-rhythmic sensation" postulated by Lipps, in simpler language it becomes the usual equation: small-number proportions = comparative consonance.

The music psychologist Felix E. Krueger (b. 1874), like Helmholtz, undertook to relate the question of consonance and dissonance to physiology and to the effects of difference tones in the various intervals.[12] Granted that combinational tones—difference and possibly summation—are an ingredient that enhance or diminish consonance in a given situation, for gen-

[10]Moore, "Genetic Aspect of Consonance and Dissonance," in *Psychological Monographs*, vol. 17, no. 2, pp. 6–7, 12, 14; Ogden, *Hearing*, 135.

[11]Moore, *op. cit.*, 7. Ogden remarks that Lipps's "hypothesis amounts to little more than the tautology that simple ratios of vibration fuse because they are simple, while complex ratios fail to fuse because they are complex." *Hearing*, 134. And Meyer says that Lipps derived "by purely linguistic operations *the laws of tone relationship from the laws of rhythm*." "Unscientific Methods in Musical Esthetics," in *Journal of Philosophy, Psychology, and Scientific Methods*, 1:710.

[12]Moore, "Genetic Aspect of Consonance and Dissonance," in *Psychological Monographs*, vol. 17, no. 2, p. 9. Ogden, *Hearing*, 130–133.

eral as opposed to specific determinations on this question we are left, when Krueger has finished, with the familiar proposition: small-number proportions = comparative consonance.

Henry T. Moore, to conclude the list of fairly modern conso-disso disputants, published a work in 1914 in which he outlines a genetic, or evolutionary, theory regarding the acceptance of consonance. The Moore theory might be called the "Progress of Consonance," since it starts with the idea of a "dissonant octave" on a nascent ear, and ends with tentative and partial acceptance of a consonant "minor seventh" on a comparatively sophisticated ear.[13] At first glance this thesis tends to support the history of consonance given here under Concepts (Chapter 5), but whereas Moore postulates a development in the sensory capacity of the individual ear, perhaps even in the course of a single experiment, I wish to suggest that for millenniums the ear has been capable of much more than has been required of it; the history of intonation is a witness for this stand (see Chapters 15 and 18).

Writes Moore: "A certain initial disposition to synthesis is predetermined for a given interval by the simplicity of its numerical ratio,"[14] which is to say, of course, that small-number proportions = comparative consonance.

## *The Older Theories Stand Up*

We are grateful—we must be—for a spirit of investigation, and the efforts of men of learning and curiosity to answer some of the unplumbed phenomena of experience, but our gratitude need not cancel our right to wonder at their results when their ridicule of the "number mysticism" of our less "scientific" predecessors, and their experiments and their footnotes, leave us with exactly the same sum and substance as was given us many ages ago, the "number mysticism" of Pythagoras, Ptolemy, Zarlino, Galileo, Keppler, Euler, *et* multitudinous *al.*

To the musical creator whose life is primarily geared to hearing, and only incidentally to literary and laboratory postulates, the number-inci-

---

[13]Moore, *op. cit.*, 21, 39, 57–58. Ogden corroborates Moore: "A ready ability to perceive and set aside the structural uniformities of the more common intervals would leave the mind free, as it were, to discover any uncommon components, whether tonal, vocal, or noisy, which might chance to be present in the sound complex." *Hearing*, 142; quoted by permission of Harcourt, Brace and Company, Inc.

[14]Moore, *op. cit.*, 19.

dence or "commensurability" in the vibrations of two generator tones is of fundamental significance. In a small-number ratio such as 8/5 (813.7 cents) the frequency is high, since the two tones 8 and 5 are in like phase at every eighth loop of the higher tone; in such a ratio as 77/48 (818.2 cents, present in the Monophonic fabric from 9/7 upward to 33/32) the frequency is low, since the two tones are in like phase only at every seventy-seventh loop of the higher tone. On the Chromelodeon the move from the long wave period of 77/48 to the short wave period of 8/5 is actually a resolution into consonance.[15]

## Dayton C. Miller's Demonstrations

Several acoustical laboratory instruments have been devised to graph and record the harmonic curves of tones, one of which is Dayton C. Miller's Phonodeik, described in his *Sound Waves: Their Shape and Speed*. The same volume contains a plate showing four highly interesting Phonodeik records, which are reproduced above, facing page 140. Miller's own explanation of these particular records is as follows:

Curve A, is a record from a Koenig tuning fork with a resonance box, giving the tone middle C of frequency 256 vibrations per second. It represents the simplest pure tone, produced by a simple harmonic vibration. Curve B represents the sound from four forks giving the tones of the common chord, *do, mi, sol, do,* tuned in pure intonation, having 256, 320, 384, and 512 vibrations per second, respectively.[16] The ratios of these frequencies are as 4:5:6:8; that is, the tones are harmonics of a fundamental of frequency 64. The wave form is exactly periodic, repeating itself every 64th of a second. This period is indicated by arrows marked on the record. Curve C is the record from four forks tuned to the equally-tempered tones of the common chord, having 256, 322.6, 383.6, and 512 vibrations per second, respectively. The ratios of these frequencies are as 400:504:599:800. The combination of these incommensurable frequencies results in a non-periodic curve, with a progressive change in the wave form. The exactness of tuning in Curve B is shown by the constancy of a particular phase relation of higher partials as at *a, b, c,* and *d.* The "out-of-tuneness" of the tones producing Curve C is evident by the progressive change in the relative phases of the partials as indicated at *e, f, g,* and *h.*

[15]Seashore says simply: "Consonance depends fundamentally upon the degree of coincidence of sound waves." Yet he is inclined to test consonance only on the basis of the conventional intervals expressed in the usual just terms, that is, within the 5 limit. He ignores the ratios of 7. The "degree of coincidence of sound waves" in 10/7, which he does not use, is obviously far greater than in the ratio 36/25 (6/5 × 6/5), which he does use. *Psychology of Music*, 126–130. The ratio 36/25 is 13.8 cents higher, or wider, than 10/7.

[16]In Monophonic terms: 1/1–5/4–3/2–2/1.

When two simple tones are sounding simultaneously, in general, beats are produced, equal in number to the difference of the frequencies. Curve D, Plate I, is the wave form resulting from the combination of the tones from two tuning forks having frequencies of C = 2048 and D = 2304, respectively, the ratio of the frequencies being 8:9. If the two waves are in like phase at a certain instant, their resultant effect is a wave of large amplitude as at *a*, signifying a loud sound. This condition is repeated at regular intervals along the wave train, as at *b*, which is exactly eight waves of one tone and nine waves of the other from *a*. A point *c*, midway between *a* and *b*, is four waves of one tone and four and one-half waves of the other from *a*, and the two waves neutralize each other, resulting in a minimum of sound. The waxing and waning of sound in this manner, as the result of the combination of two simple tones, constitutes the phenomenon of beats. The number of beats per second is equal to the difference of the frequencies of the generating tones.[17]

## *Their Significance for the Perception of Intervals*

From a Monophonic standpoint the records show much more than Miller has indicated. We are not here considering the complex waves that result from the sounding of more than two tones, but Curves B and C illustrate how consonance is related to frequency of wave period. Curve B, a profile of the "common chord" in Just Intonation, shows a trifle more than four wave periods in the portion of its train depicted. Curve C, a profile of the same chord at the same approximate pitches, but in Equal Temperament, shows not a single wave period; that is, the wave form does not return, in this given line, to a point where it starts to repeat itself, a situation which acousticians, perhaps too charitably, call a "non-periodic curve." The high frequency of wave period in Curve B, as compared with the very low frequency of wave period in Curve C (exactly how low may be determined from the frequencies of pitch which Miller gives), clearly indicates the superior consonance of Curve B.

Even more illuminating is Curve D, which shows the high frequency of wave period in the small-number ratio 9/8, which Miller cites as a demonstration of beats. From this actual profile of a sounded 9/8 one may imagine or deliberately construct curves for pure tones in other small-number ratios, which will become natural steps to an understanding of the "tunability" of Monophony's forty-three degrees to the 2/1. When these degrees are slightly out of tune they are rendered in tune by ear, and the question naturally arises: what is the appearance of the harmonic curve in

[17]*Sound Waves: Their Shape and Speed*, chapter 2 and pp. 51–52; quoted by permission of The Macmillan Company.

a deviation from a small-number ratio; for example, what would be the appearance of the ratio 91/80 (one of the numerous large-number approximations of the interval 9/8) if the lower tone were exactly the pitch of the 8 of 9/8 but the upper tone very slightly higher than the 9 of 9/8? The obvious answer is that such a harmonic curve would require 91 waves and 80 waves to complete a single wave period, instead of the 9 waves and 8 waves in Miller's Curve D. This example is cited only as an illustration, not with the idea of suggesting that the ear can always appreciate this difference between an outright dissonance and an interval that borders on dissonance (see below).

However, all the small-number Monophonic degrees might be slightly out of tune by an infinitude of large-number ratios; in the place of 2/1 we might have 199/100, 200/99, 200/97, etc.; instead of 3/2 we might have 31/20, 220/147, 2560/1701, 121/81, etc.; instead of 5/4 we might have 49/40, 96/77, 56/45, 99/80, 1120/891, etc.; instead of 7/5 we might have 141/100, 139/100, 88/63, 108/77, etc., all of which destroy the simple relationship, in the order given above, of two waves to one wave from like phase to like phase, three waves to two waves, five waves to four waves, and seven waves to five waves, relationships which make for high frequency of wave period in pure tones, fewer beating partials in rich tones, and corresponding consonance. Nearly all the above deviations are obtainable on the Chromelodeon, ready for comparison.

## *Where Does the Ear Give Up?*

Max F. Meyer is the author of a pertinent study dealing with the nervous stimulations received by the brain as the result of musically excited rhythmic movements within the inner ear. Among the intervals he uses as examples is the ratio 25/24 (between 5/4 and 6/5, among other places), for which he has constructed a compound curve. This is similar to the actual curve for 9/8 photographed by Miller except that it shows, of course, 25 waves of the higher tone against 24 waves of the lower from maximum to maximum. In this simultaneous sounding of 25 and 24 Meyer declines "to express a definite opinion as to what we actually hear." He adds, "Let the reader who wants to know this find it out by an experiment of his own."[18]

Such experiments are easy to make on the Chromelodeon, and one conclusion stands out against all others: the ear (or this ear) cannot pos-

[18]*Mechanics of the Inner Ear*, 50, 54.

sibly hear 24 to 25 as such, even though the two tones definitely preserve their individual integrity (the question Meyer raises), for if one is slightly out of tune, so that the ratio is, let us say, 24.1 to 25, the beats will simply be a trifle slower. Yet in a median register on the Chromelodeon both 9/8 and 10/9 are clearly heard, by tuning them to eliminate beats and by the establishment of high frequency of wave period in 8 to 9 and 9 to 10. Almost anyone can distinguish and tune 6/5, which is the only 5-limit ratio in this particular range of ratios. Consequently, at some point, to be determined by the individual, in the narrowing of intervals between the wide 6/5 and the narrow 16/15 or 25/24, and at the corresponding point in the approach to 2/1 (and, incidentally, at some prime number larger than 11 in the wider intervals), the ear refuses to distinguish between rational and irrational numbers.

Perrett claims that the ear can hear the exact ratio 8/7 in higher registers (see below), and the Chromelodeon offers corroboration. However, for the purpose of tuning the Chromelodeon the question is academic: Monophony does not require the hearing of an 8/7 for its tuning.[19] But the matter is important for its bearing on the psychologic perceptions of, and capacity for, relative consonance.

## *Enigma of the Multiple-Number Ratio*

One perplexing problem remains to be touched upon, namely the strength of a multiple-number ratio as compared with a ratio of approximately the same width involving prime numbers or a prime number, the foremost example of which is 9/8 as compared with 8/7. Just why the ear hears 9/8 with speedier conviction than it hears 8/7, either consecutively or simultaneously sounded, can only be conjectured at present. To be sure, 9/8 is the difference between two of the strongest consonances, 3/2 and 4/3, but further, the wave period, from maximum to maximum, has an added regularity in 9/8 — three 3's of the 9 and four 2's of the 8—a frequency of period in air-particle displacement much greater in each of the tones of 9/8. The explanation that suggests itself is that some of this strength is carried over into the simultaneous sounding. With 8/7, it is a clear case of eight waves against seven waves; because of the involvement of the prime number 7, there is no added regularity.

[19]Although an 8/7 tuning is stipulated in the Chromelodeon Tuning Guide for two ratios, this is only to preserve a consistent upward representation of relationships. In actual tuning, the 2/1 above the tone to which a reed is to be tuned may be employed instead, and the interval becomes 7/4.

## Conclusions Regarding Consonance

These observations and excursions tend to bring into focus some of the phenomena encountered in tuning the small-number ratios of the Monophonic fabric, and suggest at least two tentative conclusions:

1. In any given range of pitch the comparative consonance of an interval is determined by the relative frequency of the wave period in the sounding of the interval. The more frequent the period the more consonant is the interval; the more infrequent the period the more dissonant is the interval. Note the high frequency of period in the interval 2/1 (every two waves of the upper tone), and the diminishing frequency of period in the intervals 3/2, 5/4, 7/5, and 9/8: the smaller the numbers of a ratio the more consonant the interval, a principle stated in Chapter 5, and as ancient as almost any precept of man.

2. Each consonance or comparative consonance is a little sun in its universe, around which dissonant satellites cluster. This concept is often expressed for 2/1, but in tuning the Chromelodeon it becomes evident that it applies also, though in a rapidly diminishing area, and with decreasing force, to the less consonant intervals. It also becomes evident, in examining the Monophonic fabric, and with experience in tuning, that the satellite areas diminish in approximately inverse proportion to the increase in the odd numbers of the ratios, a premise which will be cited again in the discussion of the elements of resolution (Chapter 11).

## Obfuscation in the Moderns

Now let us listen to several men of science and one modern composer who have interpreted certain experiments in a manner which obscures some of the manifestations mentioned above. Llewellyn S. Lloyd's experiment, designed to enhance an understanding of beats, begins with the word "Suppose" and two pure-tone generators, one a lower constant, the other rising from unison. Proceeding, Lloyd declares that, starting with the departure from unison, the beats become continually faster until they are no longer perceptible as beats, after which the simultaneity of the tones becomes less unpleasant until, at the "minor third," it is actually "pleasant."[20]

If the rising tone is a sliding, siren-like agent, any observation of results is practically valueless for a science of music which is based on precise ratios. If the rising tone is tuned to whole-number cycles, observations are

[20]*Music and Sound*, 41–42.

again valueless, since more often than not the all-important small-number ratios fall in the decimal points of cycles. Whatever the method, the experiments of this sort that were examined ignore virtually all the points of diminished dissonance at the small-number ratios—12/11, 11/10, 10/9, 9/8, 8/7, and 7/6, and, instead, describe a streamlined whisk from the eclipse 1/1 to the consonance 6/5 (the familiar 5 limit), and with all the blinds drawn en route. Lloyd remarks elsewhere: "The niceties of 'intonation' have an arithmetical fascination which must be resisted."[21] It is regrettable that he himself resists such niceties in the experiment mentioned above.

In Sir James Jeans's similar experiment tuning forks are used, one with a lower constant of 261 cycles, and others set exactly at higher cycles—262, 264, 266, etc. Jeans declares: "It is found to be a quite general law that two tones sound well together when the ratio of their frequencies can be expressed by the use of small numbers, and the smaller the numbers the better is the consonance."[22] Yet with this fundamental truth in mind the tuning forks in question were used only at exact cycles, which in his experiment did not, in any case, coincide with the small-number ratios the principle of which Jeans cites—in this particular case 12/11, 11/10, 10/9, 9/8, 8/7, and 7/6, nor even with 6/5 and 11/9, which were elided. The only experiment of this kind which could have value for a systemic music is one that would provide tones giving each small-number interval exactly, and also a small deviation from such interval, for example, 11/10 and 111/100. The Chromelodeon comes close to this ideal, but it is never possible to know the exact ratio of deviation when an interval is out of tune.

Jeans's observation that the ratio 320/261, one of the relationships of his fork vibrations, is still "unpleasant,"[23] in the progress from 1/1 to 5/4, is the more remarkable in view of his stated axiom of consonance. Whether or not "unpleasant" is the proper word, it is certain that an irreducible ratio involving numbers in the hundreds calls for some distinctive label!

Of similar experiments made by other psychologists or acousticians, that by Helmholtz seems to be the most perceptive, since his chart shows dips toward diminished dissonance for both the ratios 7/6 and 7/5, though it is not easy to imagine less desirable instruments for this particular purpose than those Helmholtz used—violins, which tend to obscure the proportions of any consonance.[24]

---

[21]*Ibid.*, 150.                              [23]*Ibid.*, 50.
[22]*Science and Music*, 49–50, 154.            [24]*Sensations of Tone.* 192–193.

Paul Hindemith, in his explanation of the "minor" triad as a "cloud-ing " of the "major" triad, states the following "results" from an experiment on a violin played in double stops. Starting at the narrowest point at which two tones could be considered a "third," then gradually widening the interval, Hindemith declares that it is impossible to say at what exact point "minor" is reached, and at what exact point "major" is reached.[25] Questions of tonality are beside the point here, and Hindemith's observation is mentioned only because it is similar to some of those cited above in qualitative misconception. In the first place, the continual change of phase of the two tones in double stopping on the violin[26] causes a beating or undulating effect that tends to defeat positive observation. In the second place, to view the world continually through equally tempered clouds is very likely to convince us that some of its wonders look "cloudy." (Incidentally, Helmholtz's observations and chart, mentioned above, with exact dips toward consonance at 6/5 and 5/4, flatly contradict Hindemith.)

## *The Variability of Consonance*

Up to this point all observations on relative consonance have implied intervals in a median register and within a 2/1. I strongly contend that for general determinations of musical theory it is the ratio itself in any given register which is of prime significance, and that sundry other matters— some of which are touched on below—depend upon esthetic considerations of the moment. That relative consonance depends to a certain extent on register, on the harmonic content of the tones in question, and on close or extended form of the interval, is well known among composers. For example, a 5/4 ratio represented by 50 cycles against 40 cycles (in the first 2/1 of the piano) is much less consonant than one represented by 500 cycles against 400 cycles (in the 2/1 above 1/1–392). Also, a 5/4 interval sounded by two bassoons (which have a rich harmonic content) is less consonant than the same tones by French horns (which have a purer, more mellow, quality). And, finally, a 5/4 which is comparatively dissonant in a low register will become more consonant when the upper tone is raised a 2/1, to 10/4 (or 5/2).

Perrett's observations that if 8/7 is taken above "middle C" it is consonant, and that the triad 6:7:8, or 1/1–7/6–4/3, is "sensitive to the

---

[25]*Craft of Musical Composition*, 1:78.
[26]Helmholtz, *op. cit.*, 208.

slightest mistuning,"[27] have a very gracious ring. In the case of either a low 8/7 or a low 5/4 the comparative dissonance is of course fostered by the low frequency of wave period in the simultaneous soundings. And if this low frequency of period of the generating tones is attended by two series of partials inevitably dissonant if they rise high enough, the result is even more dissonant. So far as can be ascertained, the enhancement of consonance that results when an interval is changed from the close to the extended form (for example, from 16/15 to 32/15, by simply raising the upper tone a 2/1) results from a doubling of frequency of the wave period. Whatever the reason, it is generally true, throughout the musical register, that consonance can be enhanced in this manner if consonance is the desideratum of the moment.

With modern composers consonance is more frequently than otherwise not the desideratum, and with some it is religiously avoided. In fact, after listening to the works of many modern composers one can imagine *alter-ego* gremlins loitering about them whenever they sit down to the piano and whispering impishly, "Careful! Don't let them catch you with your consonances down!"[28]

But whether they are consophiles or consophobes, they are justified in objecting to the common acoustical terms "pleasant" for consonance and "unpleasant" for dissonance, terms which are indefinite if not actually misleading.[29] Both can be powerful, both can be provocative, and both can become obnoxious if overdone.

## 340 Interval Values within the 2/1

If the impression has been given that the Monophonic fabric is an unending succession of sunny consonances, revelation of the 340 different intervals between degrees within a 2/1 will dispel this. Monophony is a musical system which, like music itself, is a play of comparative consonance

[27]*Questions of Musical Theory*, 92, 94.

[28]Persons who think of the twelve-tone scale as a synonym for "atonality" and have merely *heard* of someone who writes music in a forty-three-tone scale, knowing nothing of his preoccupation with true consonance as opposed to true dissonance, immediately formulate a little equation in their minds, to wit: *twelve is to forty-three as atonality is to unendurable.*

[29]Nor are the terms of the psychologists very clarifying. The criteria, and associated terms, for consonance encountered in their writings include: mechanism of synergy, micro-rhythmic sensation, conscious fusion, fusion, smoothness, purity, blending, fractionation. So many terms confuse the issue. The word consonance evolved as it did to express the idea that it does express, and—even though it is one of a homonym—spelled in this way it expresses nothing else.

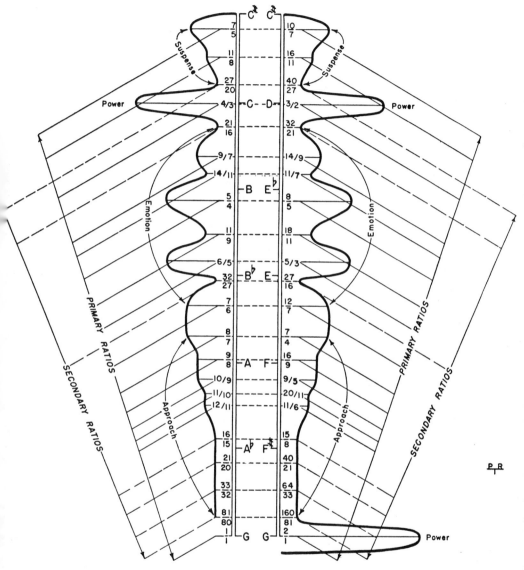

DIAGRAM 8.—THE ONE-FOOTED BRIDE: A GRAPH OF COMPARATIVE CONSONANCE

155

against comparative dissonance. Dissonant intervals outnumber consonant intervals in any musical system, but because they are outside the ear's ability to measure quickly with mathematical exactitude they are the lesser subject of examination.

If every possible interval within the forty-three degrees were a distinctive one, there would be $42 \times 43$, or 1,806 different intervals within a 2/1. However, many of the interval distances are duplicated, so that the total is reduced to 340—all listed in Appendix I. Though the degrees of the fabric involve only ratios based on the 11 limit, or small-number multiple-number ratios based on the 11 limit, the intervals between degrees involve many large-number multiples of 11 or under, all of which are highly dissonant. Tables have been prepared to show the numerous situations in which the 340 different interval values within a 2/1 may be found. These have not been included, since they would be very space-consuming, and since any given interval can always be easily ascertained, once ratios are understood, and its exact value in cents obtained from the table of Appendix I. This value may then be compared with the known and heard values of the Monophonic ratios, which are of course included in the 340. Appendix I actually contains 399 intervals, since the twelve ratios of 13, which must be added to play the ancient Greek harmoniai according to Kathleen Schlesinger, and various historic ratios, are also listed.

## Explication of the One-Footed Bride

The arbitrarily named categories into which intervals will now be grouped, according to psychological (or whimsical) reactions, could of course include all the 340 intervals contained in the Monophonic fabric, but the resulting diagram would be awkwardly large, and the idea of classification can be established as well with the forty-three intervals.

In present musical theory there is to be found the beginning of a classification which is fair so far as it goes. The strongest consonances are "perfect"; all other intervals are "major" or "minor" except the "tritone," which is "augmented" or "diminished."

In this exposition 2/1, 3/2, and 4/3 (ratios of the 3 limit) are the *Intervals of Power*. Those ratios that lie between 4/3 and 3/2 ("tritone" intervals)— 27/20, 11/8, 7/5, 10/7, 16/11, 40/27—are the *Intervals of Suspense*. The ratios between 21/16 and 7/6, at the threshold of the descent to 1/1, and those between 32/21 and 12/7, at the threshold of the ascent to 2/1, are the

*Emotional Intervals.* The ratios starting with 8/7 and descending to 1/1, and those starting with 7/4 and ascending to 2/1, are the *Intervals of Approach.*

For music students the Intervals of Power are the "perfect" intervals; the Intervals of Suspense are an expansion and acoustic rationalization of the "tritone"; the Emotional Intervals are an expansion and acoustic rationalization of "thirds" and "sixths"; and the Intervals of Approach are acoustic intervals which are varying amounts of "seconds" ("whole tone" and "semitone") and "sevenths" ("major" and "minor").

If, starting with 7/5 at the top left and 10/7 at the top right, the Monophonic ratios are placed in columns, descending in pitch on the left, and ascending in pitch on the right, each ratio will be exactly opposite its complement. And if, in addition, a heavy line is drawn, toward the outer edges of the page for the more consonant intervals and toward the ratios themselves for the more dissonant intervals (in other words, a graph of consonance for each column of ratios), the result will be as depicted in Diagram 8, those ratios on the right ascending to the supreme consonance 2/1, and those on the left descending to the absolute eclipse of interval distance 1/1 (which is partly why the One-Footed Bride is so called).

It is fairly foolish to undertake to pin consonance to a graph less general than this unless it is predicated on specific range, specific quality of tone, specific relevance of combinational tones, and specific assurance that these qualitative and quantitative factors are invariable. Short of a lifetime of laboratory work which the composer cannot undertake, the general is the only practicable approach.

The One-Footed Bride depicts the more important classifications and analyses thus far presented (exclusive of tonality): the fabric on an equal graph, its relation to twelve-tone Equal Temperament, the twenty-nine primary intervals, the fourteen secondary intervals, the graph of comparative consonance, and the psychological classification.

# CHAPTER TEN

# The Twenty-eight Tonalities

## *Demonstrations of the Tonality Diamond*

THE MAJOR contribution of Monophony as an intonational system is its realization of a subtle and acoustically precise interrelation of tonalities, all stemming or expanding from unity, 1/1. This interrelation is not capable of manifold modulations to "dominants" or to any of the other common scale degrees; it is not capable of parallel transpositions of intricate musical structures; it does not present any tone as any specific tonality identity. Conversely, it is capable of both ordinary and hitherto unheard modulations to the natural limits imposed by Just Intonation and the arbitrary limit of 11; it is capable of an expanded sense of tonality, from Identities 1–3–5 to Identities 1–3–5–7–9–11; it is capable of great variety in that expanded sense (see page 123); it does offer twenty-eight possible tonalities, more than are inherent in Equal Temperament, and therefore a greater total of tonality identities, or assumable senses, than does Equal Temperament.

Few composers will regard the total virtues of Equal Temperament and those of Monophony as equal in value. Whichever of the two sets is accepted as superior, it can be stated unequivocally that they cannot coexist in the same musical system, given the present ideas behind musical instruments or the present conception of musical values, and that—short of a mechanical revolution in the construction of instruments and a psychic evolution in musical conceptions—they will not coexist in the same musical system in the future. Such xenogamy is conceivable but not yet practical.

The Incipient Tonality Diamond within the 5 limit (page 110) is now expanded to include all the primary ratios based on the 11 limit, each series being expressed within a 2/1, upward in pitch for Otonalities, downward in pitch for Utonalities. See Diagram 9, the Expanded Tonality Diamond. As in the smaller diamond, Otonalities appear between solid lines from left to right, and Utonalities between dotted lines from right to left.

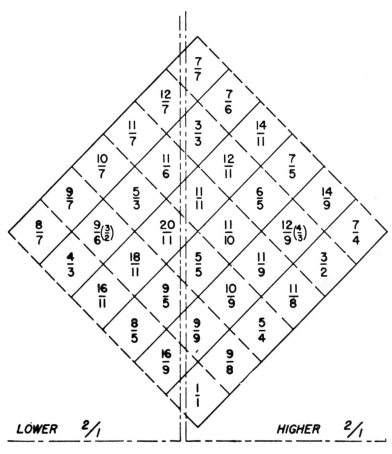

DIAGRAM 9.—THE EXPANDED TONALITY DIAMOND

To cite two examples of increased resources: the ratios of the 8/5 Otonality are 8/5 (unity), 9/5, 5/5(1/1), 11/10, 6/5, 7/5. The tonality's Numerary Nexus is 5, and the Odentities are 1(8), 9, 5, 11, 3(6), 7. The ratios of the 5/4 Utonality are 5/4 (unity), 10/9, 5/5(1/1), 20/11, 5/3, 10/7. The Numerary Nexus 5 lies above Udentities 1(4), 9, 5, 11, 3, 7.

As in all other Monophonic tonalities, the unities of the new Otonalities—8/7, 16/9, 16/11—are revealed by a 2, 4, 8, or 16 as the over number, and the unities of the new Utonalities—7/4, 9/8, 11/8—by a 2, 4, 8, or 16 as the under number. The 16/11 Otonality, for example, is composed of 16/11, 18/11, 20/11, 11/11(1/1), 12/11, 14/11, showing the Odentities 1(16), 9(18), 5(20), 11, 3(12), 7(14), over the Numerary Nexus 11. The 9/8 Utonality has 9/8, 9/9(1/1), 9/5, 18/11, 9/6(3/2), 9/7, showing the Udentities 1(8), 9, 5, 11, 3(6), 7, under the Numerary Nexus 9.

Each line of six ratios is a condensed representation of tonality ingredients; these ingredients hold the potentiality of the maximal consonance that can be achieved by the Identities 1–3–5–7–9–11. If the orthodox manner of building a chord in "thirds" is followed, the identities are in this order: 1–5–3–7–9–11. The fact of tonality is the fact of maximal consonance for a stipulated number of different identities. As explained in Chapter 7, the constituents—the various identities—of a tonality have a Numerary Nexus, and therefore the identities in the 11 limit, following the orthodox structure in "thirds," are in the relation 4:5:6:7:9:11 (ascending) for Otonalities and in the relation 1/4:1/5:1/6:1/7:1/9:1/11 (descending) for Utonalities. The least consonant relationships are those showing the largest numbers: 9:11, 7:11, and 7:9; and the most consonant those showing the smallest numbers: 4:5, 4:6(2:3), and 5:6. If we stipulate six tones in a chord, of differing identities, these six are the most consonant possible, and they do create the psychological phenomenon of finality in a single tone or chord— around the 1 Identity, or unity.

## Tonalities outside the Diamond

The sixteen Secondary Tonalities are so called because some of their identities are represented by multiple-number ratios of the 11 limit, and they have the common characteristic that none involves 1/1 as an identity. Two of the Secondary Tonalities, 3/2–O and 4/3–U (those given in the diamond are 3/2–U and 4/3–O), are complete through their 11 Identities. Four, 6/5–O and 5/3–U, and 32/21–O and 21/16–U, are complete through

9; six, 16/15–O, 15/8–U, 32/27–O, 27/16–U, 9/5–O, and 10/9–U, have the 9 Identities, but 7 is missing in all. The remaining four of the secondary tonalities, 7/5–O, 10/7–U, 27/20–O, and 40/27–U, are represented only by triads; that is, they are complete only through the 5 Identities.

### THE SIXTEEN SECONDARY TONALITIES

#### Otonalities (Upward)

| Unity | 5 Odentity | 3 Odentity | 7 Odentity | 9 Odentity | 11 Odentity |
|-------|-----------|-----------|-----------|-----------|------------|
| 3/2 | 15/8 | 9/8 | 21/16 | 27/16 | 33/32 |
| 6/5 | 3/2 | 9/5 | 21/20 | 27/20 | ——— |
| 9/5 | 9/8 | 27/20 | ——— | 81/80 | ——— |
| 16/15 | 4/3 | 8/5 | ——— | 6/5 | ——— |
| 32/21 | 40/21 | 8/7 | 4/3 | 12/7 | ——— |
| 32/27 | 40/27 | 16/9 | ——— | 4/3 | ——— |
| 7/5 | 7/4 | 21/20 | ——— | ——— | ——— |
| 27/20 | 27/16 | 81/80 | ——— | ——— | ——— |

#### Utonalities (Downward)

| Unity | 5 Udentity | 3 Udentity | 7 Udentity | 9 Udentity | 11 Udentity |
|-------|-----------|-----------|-----------|-----------|------------|
| 4/3 | 16/15 | 16/9 | 32/21 | 32/27 | 64/33 |
| 5/3 | 4/3 | 10/9 | 40/21 | 40/27 | ——— |
| 10/9 | 16/9 | 40/27 | ——— | 160/81 | ——— |
| 15/8 | 3/2 | 5/4 | ——— | 5/3 | ——— |
| 21/16 | 21/20 | 7/4 | 3/2 | 7/6 | ——— |
| 27/16 | 27/20 | 9/8 | ——— | 3/2 | ——— |
| 10/7 | 8/7 | 40/21 | ——— | ——— | ——— |
| 40/27 | 32/27 | 160/81 | ——— | ——— | ——— |

## The Question of Extraneous Phenomena

To catalog the effects of minor tonal phenomena upon Monophony's listed resources would expand this volume to encyclopedic size. An outline of the project—and I use the word advisedly—would mean an examination of the effects upon each of the 340 Monophonic intervals, and upon every triad, every quadrad, every hexad, and upon every "inversion" of every triad, quadrad, and hexad, of the following factors: (1) the harmonic content, or quality, of each musical tone in an interval or chord, and its potential for dissonance, in every musical register; (2) combinational tones, difference and summation,[1] of the first order and of the second order, for

---

[1]Perrett calls this Helmholtz's "hypothetical summation tone." *Questions of Musical Theory*, 85.

every type of musical tone in an interval or chord and in every musical register, and their potential for dissonance.

Partials and difference tones have existed either objectively or in the ear of man ever since man developed an ear, long before he first analyzed them. For thousands of years he has heard them, or heard their effect, and has acted or reacted according to each situation. He can still do so. These phenomena are acoustical manifestations to be considered by the composer in each individual situation.

A considerable period spent in composing Monophonic music, for as many as five instruments and voices in one composition, has failed to uncover a single situation in which the Monophonic principles regarding consonance were seriously jeopardized by dissonance-inducing difference tones and beating partials. Monophony is not merely a product of the physics laboratory. In a historical sense it is a renascence and expansion of the monochord values of Pythagoras, Euclid, and Ptolemy.

Whenever an old acoustical manifestation has been newly discerned—partials by Mersenne, difference tones by Sorge and Tartini, summation tones by Helmholtz—one or more musical theorists have promptly appropriated the newly analyzed manifestation for current musical custom. However oblique the new analysis, our theorists invariably apply it to the everyday twelve-tone scale of the piano, and in recent decades, with the development of electrical instruments, they have been busily wiring the equally tempered halo for fluorescent lighting. The result of these attempted rationalizations is uniformly barren—all the subtleties of the manifestations and much, if not all, of their significance are lost. Both partials and difference tones are exhibits in point.

These are cases, first, of failing to see the forest for the trees, and second, of proceeding to cut down the trees and set them up again as equi-distant telephone poles.

## The Question of Multiple Senses

However controversial the significance of partials and difference tones to music theory in general, the fact of the twenty-eight tonalities in Monophony, as shown in the Expanded Tonality Diamond and the table of Secondary Tonalities, plus the fact of the multitude of senses of tonality identities they reveal, is incontrovertible, once the forty-three Monophonic ratios are set up.

The current belief that tonality relationships ("key" relationships) are strongest where there are common tones, and its corollary, that modulation is only possible—or at least more convincing—through common tones, were mentioned in Chapter 7. Debatable as these beliefs are (see the next chapter), the multiplicity of senses (that is, the interrelated common tones) of the Monophonic fabric is nevertheless examined, since it is significant as an index of tonality potentialities.

Perrett harmonizes on the assumption that the postulate of common tones for modulation does not hold for chords related by the number 7, since 7 is implicit in chords. Musical composition on the basis of this principle would mean the end of the common-tone requirement; if the harmonic content of a tone is the criterion, much more than 7 is implicit in chords. In diminishing degree 9 and 11 are also implicit, but with a total of 140 senses for the forty-three Monophonic degrees it is hardly necessary to invoke this procedure. Anyway, the composer will modulate as he chooses, common tones or no.

Appendix II includes a table showing the capacity of each ratio of the Monophonic fabric to serve as identities; it may be summarized as follows:

1/1 may be taken in . . . . . . . . . . . . . . . . . . . . . . . . . . . . . . . . . . . 12 senses
3/2 and 4/3 may each be taken in . . . . . . . . . . . . . . . . . . . . . . 9 senses
16/9 and 9/8 may each be taken in . . . . . . . . . . . . . . . . . . . . . 5 senses
5/3, 6/5, 9/5, 10/9, 8/7, 7/4, 27/20, and 40/27 may each be
    taken in . . . . . . . . . . . . . . . . . . . . . . . . . . . . . . . . . . . . . . . . 4 senses
Ten of the remaining thirty ratios may each be taken in . . . . . 3 senses
Eighteen of the remaining twenty ratios may each be taken in . . 2 senses
64/33 and 33/32 are each limited to . . . . . . . . . . . . . . . . . . . . . 1 sense

From the standpoint of minimum mental effort it would be ideal if any conceivable tone could be taken in any conceivable sense, but this is possible neither in temperament nor in any other practical system yet invented. With any leavening of acoustic conscience it is impossible on the piano, for example, to take "F♯" as the eleventh partial in the "key of C," despite Arnold Schönberg's oblique derivation of the twelve-tone chromatic scale (see page 418).

In earlier stages of European music any one of the twelve scale tones could be taken in no more than four senses, as "root," "third," "fifth," or "seventh of the chord"—making a total of forty-eight senses. With the introduction of "ninth," "eleventh," and "thirteenth of the chord" the total reaches eighty-four senses, and with Schönberg's chromatic and Hindemith's chromatic and Cowell's "clusters" the number of possibly conceivable senses can best be expressed, and most concisely, by $12 \times 12 = 144$. And this is the maximum, since the relation of any one degree to every other possible degree is taken into account.[2]

In comparing this total of 144 senses with the 140 senses of Monophony it must be remembered that a large proportion of the former are, to the ear, incredible; that is, expressed in temperament they are so far removed from what they purport to be that the ear refuses to make the suppositions necessary to an acceptance of them as comparative consonances. Were the fathers of the 144 senses simply to accept the available relationships as dissonant ingredients which they happened to like and therefore appropriated, there would be no question regarding the suppositional capacity of the ear.

## *The Ptolemaic Sequence*

Comparative intonations and comparative implied intonations, such as the twelve-tone chromatic, are discussed in Part IV. At this point, to clear the twenty-eight tonalities from the boards, four types of historic scales, all of which date directly or indirectly from several centuries B.C., will be examined. These four types are (1) the Ptolemaic Sequence; (2) the Pythagorean; (3) sundry other historic scales, mostly Ptolemaic; and (4) the tempered. By a curious acoustic accident or impish fate these four types are all represented in the forty-three Monophonic ratios. Hundreds of other scales, historic and simply novel, are of course possible in the Monophonic fabric. They will not be pursued in the present volume, but will be left to the individual investigator and composer who is intrigued by Monophony's resources.

The succession of scale tones here called the Ptolemaic Sequence is only

---

[2]The act of using a tone in a second sense—"A♭" in the "key of A♭ major," for example, and then as "G♯" in the "key of E major"—is called "enharmony," and is widely discussed by modern theorists as one of the greatest if not the greatest boon of Equal Temperament. The idea that Just Intonation prevents such a psychologic mutation in tonality is a fallacy which is completely exposed by the table of senses given above. In the matter of tonality potential Just Intonation, if intelligently applied to instruments, neither releases nor inhibits a composer any more than Equal Temperament releases or inhibits him. The question of "freedom" is therefore extraneous to the subject of intonation. In any case, if the composer using the forty-three-degree scale were as acoustically lenient as the composers using Equal Temperament he would have "enharmony" to choke a horse—$43 \times 43$, or 1,849 senses at his command!

PTOLEMAIC SEQUENCE IN PRIMARY OTONALITIES (ascending)

*Scale Degrees*

| 1 | 2 | 3 | 4 | 5 | 6 | 7 | 8 |
|---|---|---|---|---|---|---|---|
| 1/1 | 9/8 | 5/4 | 4/3 | 3/2 | 5/3 | 15/8 | 2/1 |
| 4/3 | 3/2 | 5/3 | 16/9 | 1/1 | 10/9 | 5/4 | 4/3 |
| 8/5 | 9/5 | 1/1 | 16/15 | 6/5 | 4/3 | 3/2 | 8/5 |
| 8/7 | 9/7 | 10/7 | 32/21 | 12/7 | 40/21 | 12/11 | 8/7[3] |
| 16/9 | 1/1 | 10/9 | 32/27 | 4/3 | 40/27 | 5/3 | 16/9 |
| 16/11 | 18/11 | 20/11 | 64/33 | 12/11 | 11/9 | 11/8 | 16/11[4] |

PTOLEMAIC SEQUENCE IN SECONDARY OTONALITIES (ascending)

| 3/2 | 27/16 | 15/8 | 1/1 | 9/8 | 5/4 | 10/7 | 3/2[5] |
|---|---|---|---|---|---|---|---|
| 6/5 | 27/20 | 3/2 | 8/5 | 9/5 | 1/1 | 9/8 | 6/5 |
| 9/5 | 81/80 | 9/8 | 6/5 | 27/20 | 3/2 | 27/16 | 9/5 |
| 16/15 | 6/5 | 4/3 | 7/5 | 8/5 | 16/9 | 1/1 | 16/15[6] |
| 32/21 | 12/7 | 40/21 | 81/80 | 8/7 | 14/11 | 10/7 | 32/21[7] |
| 32/27 | 4/3 | 40/27 | 11/7 | 16/9 | 160/81 | 10/9 | 32/27[8] |
| 7/5 | 14/9 | 7/4 | 15/8 | 21/20 | 7/6 | 21/16 | 7/5[9] |
| 27/20 | 3/2 | 27/16 | 9/5 | 81/80 | 9/8 | 9/7 | 27/20[10] |

[3]The correct Ptolemaic ratio for the seventh degree would be 15/14, which is not one of the forty-three Chromelodeon ratios; 16/15 might be used, but the "half step" to 8/7 would then contain 119.4 cents, which is very large. The use of 12/11 results in a "half step" of 80.5 cents (22/21), and a preceding "whole step" of 235.1 cents (63/55).

[4]The correct Ptolemaic ratio for the sixth degree would be 40/33 and for the seventh degree 15/11, neither of which occurs in the Chromelodeon scale. The use of 11/9 and 11/8 for the sixth and seventh degrees makes the sequence:

| | 12/11 | | 11/9 | | 11/8 | | 16/11, |
|---|---|---|---|---|---|---|---|
| | 196.8 cents | | 203.9 cents | | 97.3 cents | | |

which is virtually an equally tempered tetrachord. For perfect tempering the intervals would of course be 200–200–100 cents.

[5]The high seventh degree, 10/7, results in a final "half step" of 84.5 cents (21/20) and a preceding "whole step" of 231.2 cents (8/7); the correct Ptolemaic seventh degree would be 45/32.

[6]The low fourth degree, 7/5, makes a 21/16 ratio with its unity, 16/15, instead of the correct 4/3, the "perfect fourth"; it also makes a small "half step" of 84.5 cents (21/20) and a following "whole step" of 231.2 cents (8/7). The correct fourth degree would be 64/45.

[7]The fourth degree, 81/80, is 5.7 cents too low, and the sixth degree, 14/11, exactly 4 cents too high, the latter variation being virtually identical to the discrepancy between the true "major whole step" (203.9 cents) and the tempered "whole step" (200 cents). The correct fourth and sixth degrees would be 64/63 and 80/63.

[8]The fourth degree, 11/7, is 9.7 cents too low, making what amounts to an equally tempered "half step" of exactly 102 cents. The correct fourth degree would be 128/81.

[9]The first two intervals between degrees of the Ptolemaic Sequence, 9/8 and 10/9, are here reversed, and the fourth degree, which should be 28/15, is wide.

[10]The first two intervals, 9/8 and 10/9, are again reversed, and the seventh degree, which should be 81/64, is wide, giving a high "leading tone" 84.5 cents (21/20) from the unity, 27/20.

### Ptolemaic Sequence in Primary Utonalities (descending)

*Scale Degrees*

| 1 | 2 | 3 | 4 | 5 | 6 | 7 | 8 |
|---|---|---|---|---|---|---|---|
| 2/1 | 16/9 | 8/5 | 3/2 | 4/3 | 6/5 | 16/15 | 1/1 |
| 3/2 | 4/3 | 6/5 | 9/8 | 1/1 | 9/5 | 8/5 | 3/2 |
| 5/4 | 10/9 | 1/1 | 15/8 | 5/3 | 3/2 | 4/3 | 5/4 |
| 7/4 | 14/9 | 7/5 | 21/16 | 7/6 | 21/20 | 11/6 | 7/4[11] |
| 9/8 | 1/1 | 9/5 | 27/16 | 3/2 | 27/20 | 6/5 | 9/8 |
| 11/8 | 11/9 | 11/10 | 33/32 | 11/6 | 18/11 | 16/11 | 11/8[12] |

### Ptolemaic Sequence in Secondary Utonalities (descending)

| 4/3 | 32/27 | 16/15 | 1/1 | 16/9 | 8/5 | 7/5 | 4/3[13] |
|---|---|---|---|---|---|---|---|
| 5/3 | 40/27 | 4/3 | 5/4 | 10/9 | 1/1 | 16/9 | 5/3 |
| 10/9 | 160/81 | 16/9 | 5/3 | 40/27 | 4/3 | 32/27 | 10/9 |
| 15/8 | 5/3 | 3/2 | 10/7 | 5/4 | 9/8 | 1/1 | 15/8[14] |
| 21/16 | 7/6 | 21/20 | 160/81 | 7/4 | 11/7 | 7/5 | 21/16[15] |
| 27/16 | 3/2 | 27/20 | 14/11 | 9/8 | 81/80 | 9/5 | 27/16[16] |
| 10/7 | 9/7 | 8/7 | 16/15 | 40/21 | 12/7 | 32/21 | 10/7[17] |
| 40/27 | 4/3 | 32/27 | 10/9 | 160/81 | 16/9 | 14/9 | 40/27[18] |

[11]As in the 8/7 Otonality scale the seventh degree is not correct for the prescribed sequence; it should be 28/15. With 11/6 the final "half step" is 80.5 cents (22/21) and the preceding "whole step" 235.1 cents (63/55).

[12]As with the 16/11 Otonality scale the sixth and seventh degrees are not the prescribed ones, these being 33/20 and 22/15. With 18/11 and 16/11 the second tetrachord is virtually tempered.

[13]The seventh degree, 7/5, is 27.3 cents too low; the correct ratio would be 64/45. Compare with the 3/2 Otonality scale.

[14]The fourth degree, 10/7, is 27.3 cents too high; the correct ratio would be 45/32. Compare with the 16/15 Otonality scale.

[15]The fourth degree, 160/81, is 5.7 cents too high, and the sixth step, 11/7, exactly 4 cents too low; the correct ratios would be 63/32 and 63/40. Compare with the 32/21 Otonality scale.

[16]The fourth degree, 14/11, is 9.7 cents too high; the correct ratio would be 81/64. Compare with the 32/27 Otonality scale.

[17]The first two intervals between degrees, 9/8 and 10/9, are here reversed, and the fourth degree, which should be 15/14, is wide.

[18]The first two intervals are again reversed, and the seventh degree, which should be 128/81, is wide, giving a low approaching tone just 84.5 cents above the unity, 40/27.

one of the many ancient Greek scales to which Ptolemy gave ratios. Because its degrees are represented by the smallest-number ratios compatible with the tonal intent that created the scale (all within the 5 limit), and because the successive intervals between degrees are small multiple-number ratios (within the 5 limit), this scale, named by Ptolemy the Intense Diatonic, is one of the world's fundamentally beautiful tonal sequences. It is the scale of widest distribution and widest popularity in the West, a pre-eminence it has held for several hundred years at least. In one of its present-day prostituted forms it is any "major" scale on the piano.

The Utonality Ptolemaic Sequence is represented here as the exact reverse of the Otonality sequence; in this way the same succession of intervals between degrees can be shown in the two scales: Otonalities read upward in pitch and the triad represented by Odentities 1–5–3 is of course also upward (first, third, and fifth degrees); Utonalities read downward, and the triad represented by Udentities 1–5–3 is also downward, with 1 as the highest tone (first, third, and fifth degrees from the left). In this form the Utonality scale agrees with the ancient Dorian mode, although in the early days of Greek theory Pythagorean intonation, or an Arithmetical Proportion genesis (according to Schlesinger—see page 447), was imputed to it. The exact Ptolemaic Sequence is possible in eight of the Primary Tonalities and four of the Secondary Tonalities of Monophony, and is available with a one- or a two-degree deviation in all the other sixteen tonalities. In the tabulations on the two preceding pages the usual procedure of giving intervals between degrees is omitted. Deviations from the correct sequence, given below, are indicated in footnotes.

| | 9/8 | 10/9 | 16/15 | 9/8 | 10/9 | 9/8 | 16/15 |
|---|---|---|---|---|---|---|---|
| Cents......... | 203.9 | 182.4 | 111.7 | 203.9 | 182.4 | 203.9 | 111.7 |

## Pythagorean Scales

The intonation that has come to be known as Pythagorean—the second type of historic scale to be considered here—had its origin in sounding-body proportions based on a 3 limit on the part of Pythagoras. From all accounts the number 3 was the embodiment of perfection and the limit of perfection, and became an occult symbol for universal analogies. Since 3/2 and its complement 4/3 do not comprise with 1/1 and 2/1 a very resourceful scale, recourse was had to the multiplication of 3/2 intervals (or 4/3 intervals) to explain the other scale degrees of the ancient Greek heptatonic.

Reading downward in pitch the eight-string lyre tuned in the Dorian mode could be expressed thus[19]:

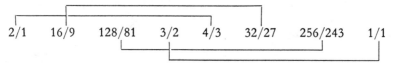

2/1    16/9    128/81    3/2    4/3    32/27    256/243    1/1

and could easily be tuned by 3/2's or 4/3's, since it is a succession of six 3/2's (downward—each ratio expressed within its 2/1) : 3/2, 1/1, 4/3, 16/9, 32/27, 128/81, 256/243.[20]

So far as we know this was the first scale in the West which was expressed in numbers at all, and it is thus significant as a recorded divination of the science of music, even though it is expressed badly. What actual application it had in ancient Greek musical practice is moot, but after the time of Ptolemy and Boethius and throughout the Middle Ages it was presumed to be the basic tuning. That this virtually unsingable scale should have been expounded in an essentially vocal age is an anomaly to be touched upon later.

Two Pythagorean (sometimes called "ditonal") heptatonic scales are found in the Monophonic fabric; also three rather extensive sequences of 3/2's—one of six 3/2's and two of five 3/2's each, although no "cycles" are present (see Chapter 15). The sequence of six 3/2's are (upward): 32/27–16/9–4/3–1/1–3/2–9/8–27/16; and the two sequences of five 3/2's are (upward): 160/81–40/27–10/9–5/3–5/4–15/8 and 16/15–8/5–6/5–9/5–27/20–81/80.

From the first series two heptatonic scales are available (and many others, starting on higher or lower scale degrees), one of which is given as it would correspond to the Ptolemaic Sequence upward (Lydian) and one as it would thus correspond downward (Dorian). The successive intervals between degrees are of only two widths, 9/8 (203.9 cents) and 256/243 (90.2 cents).

Lydian (ascending):

| 16/9 | 1/1 | 9/8 | | 32/27 | 4/3 | 3/2 | 27/16 | | 16/9 |
|------|-----|-----|------|-------|-----|-----|-------|------|------|
| | 9/8 | 9/8 | 256/243 | 9/8 | 9/8 | 9/8 | | 256/243 | |

---

[19]Hawkins, *History of the Science and Practice of Music*, 1:14.

[20]This sequence, and those following, adheres to the procedure of using one symbol for a particular relationship regardless of its place in the range of pitch (see Chapter 4). The acoustically correct form would be: 3/2–1/1–2/3–4/9–8/27–16/81–32/243.

Dorian (descending):

9/8   1/1   16/9        27/16   3/2   4/3   32/27        9/8
   9/8     9/8    256/243      9/8     9/8    9/8     256/243

## *The Ancient Greek Genera*

The Ptolemaic scales, which form the greater part of the third type of historic scale, are found in the *Harmonics* of Ptolemy, second-century Alexandrian. Ptolemy is by no means a comprehensive repository of ancient musical learning, but he gives us clues to ancient practice and he offers many scales in precise ratios.

These are of three types (the genera): enharmonic, chromatic, diatonic. Each has characteristically a width of one interval in the tetrachord (a scale

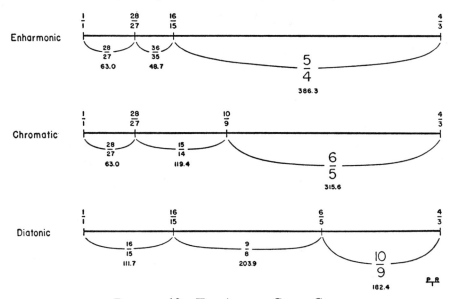

DIAGRAM 10.—THE ANCIENT GREEK GENERA

of four tones—two disjunct tetrachords making the heptatonic scale): (1) a 5/4 or approximately that in the enharmonic; (2) a 6/5, approximately, in the chromatic, and (3) a 10/9, approximately, in the diatonic, with the second degree of the tetrachord fluctuating,[21] as shown in Diagram

[21]Hawkins, *History of the Science and Practice of Music,* 1:34.

10 (assuming a Dorian tetrachord and the stops as each would be made on a string, the open string representing 1/1).

The version of the enharmonic according to Archytas (fourth century B. C.), as given by Ptolemy, is found in the Monophonic fabric starting on 3/2 (downward):

$$
\begin{array}{ccccccc}
3/2 & & 6/5 & & 7/6 & & 9/8 \\
 & 5/4 & & 36/35 & & 28/27 &
\end{array}
$$

and if we attach the same tetrachord disjunctly, a 9/8 interval below the 9/8 shown above:

$$
\begin{array}{ccccccccc}
(9/8) & & 1/1 & & 8/5 & & 14/9 & & 3/2 \\
 & 9/8 & & 5/4 & & 36/35 & & 28/27 &
\end{array}
$$

we have a complete or octachord scale in the enharmonic genus. Tonalities represented in the scale are 3/2 Utonality, by Udentities 1–5–3, and 8/5 Otonality, by Odentities 1–5–3.

The above is an enharmonic of the Dorian type; a Lydian type in this genus can be found starting on 4/3 (upward), and with implications of 4/3 Otonality and 5/4 Utonality:

$$
\begin{array}{ccccccccccccccc}
4/3 & & 5/3 & & 12/7 & & 16/9 & & 1/1 & & 5/4 & & 9/7 & & 4/3 \\
 & 5/4 & & 36/35 & & 28/27 & & 9/8 & & 5/4 & & 36/35 & & 28/27 &
\end{array}
$$

By giving the Dorian type downward and the Lydian type upward, the procedure followed previously, it is possible to show the same sequence of intervals between scale degrees; note the two above. The version by Archytas is the only enharmonic given by Ptolemy which is exactly duplicable in the Monophonic fabric, but so long as the characteristic 5/4 is retained (which gives the scale tonalities), many can be found—for instance, on 5/3 (Dorian, descending). This is one of the enharmonics expounded by Perrett and ascribed by him to Tartini,[22] other ratios being used here, but with the same sequence of intervals between degrees:

$$
\begin{array}{ccccccccccccccc}
5/3 & & 4/3 & & 21/16 & & 5/4 & & 10/9 & & 16/9 & & 7/4 & & 5/3 \\
 & 5/4 & & 64/63 & & 21/20 & & 9/8 & & 5/4 & & 64/63 & & 21/20 &
\end{array}
$$

## Harmonization of the Enharmonic

Perrett harmonizes this scale by going far outside the scale degrees but using the simple progressions "tonic-dominant-subdominant-dominant-

[22]*Questions of Musical Theory*, 40.

tonic,"[23] employing the starting tone 5/3 as a 5 Odentity in 4/3 Otonality ("tonic"), 5/4 as a 5 Odentity and 7/4 as a 7 Odentity in 1/1 Otonality ("dominant"), and 16/9 as the 1 Odentity, 4/3 as the 3 Odentity, and 10/9 as the 5 Odentity in 16/9 Otonality ("subdominant"), and introducing enough new tones to give 1-3-5-7 Odentities in both "dominant" and "subdominant," as follows:

| Tonalities | 4/3–0 | 1/1–0 | 16/9–0 | | | 1/1–0 | 4/3–0 |
| --- | --- | --- | --- | --- | --- | --- | --- |
| Highest 2/1 | | | | 10/9 | | | |
| | 5/3 | 7/4 | 16/9 | 16/9 | 16/9 | 7/4 | 5/3 |
| Fourth 2/1 | 4/3 | 3/2 | 14/9 | | 14/9 | 3/2 | 4/3 |
| | 1/1 | 5/4 | 4/3 | 4/3 | 4/3 | 5/4 | 1/1 |
| Third 2/1 | | | | | | | |
| Second 2/1 | 4/3 | 1/1 | | 16/9 | | 1/1 | 4/3 |
| Lowest 2/1 | | | 16/9 | | 16/9 | | |

It would seem equally interesting to use 5/3 as a 1 Udentity, since it is the starting point of the scale in question, in the Utonality triad 5/3–4/3–10/9, all of which tones appear as scale degrees, or even to use it as a 3 Udentity in the triad 5/4–1/1–5/3—introducing a new tone, 1/1. It would be a challenging test in harmonization to limit materials entirely to scale degrees, however.

## The Enharmonic Wars

Two other versions of the enharmonic as given by Ptolemy are scales of the famous Arithmetical Proportion: that of Eratosthenes, stipulating a division of the monochord into forty equal divisions (theoretically), and that of Didymus, stipulating a division into thirty-two equal parts[24] (neither of these divisions has any bearing on Equal Temperament). The Eratosthenes and Didymus chromatics are not possible in the Monophonic fabric, but are discussed in connection with Schlesinger's interpretation of the ancient harmoniai (Chapter 18).

Throughout the Middle Ages, and even in ancient Greece itself, a controversy over the merits of the enharmonic waxed continually. Plato, one of the first combatants in what might be called the Enharmonic Wars, speaks contemptuously of the theorists who "put their ears alongside of the strings" and strain themselves to distinguish the "least interval."[25] And

[23]*Ibid.*, 26.    [24]Hawkins, *op. cit.*, 1:32.    [25]*Republic*, 234.

although this paper conflagration continued through more than two millenniums, and into the recent nineteenth century in Riemann, it is improbable that more than a few of the vehement participants had ever heard the enharmonic, at least outside the unmusical monochord. Vicentino (*c.* 1550) was an exception (see page 377).

Had any number of the enharmaniacs undertaken the task of really hearing this maligned scale the war would doubtless have ended forthwith. Hawkins, who published his unique and valuable history (also much maligned) in the year of the Declaration of Independence and who may or may not have heard the scale, writes that the intervals of the enharmonic "are to a modern ear so abhorrent as not to be borne without pain and aversion,"[26] and many historians imply strongly that the scale was never anything more than a theory. In answer to those who have relegated this beautiful succession of tones to apocryphy Perrett declares that the Greek notation was actually invented for it, which is hardly indicative of a mere existence in theory.[27] On the Chromelodeon the scale is a good voucher of its one-time existence, hardly constituting a cause for pain and belligerence, and leaving far more persons charmed than indifferent.

## Monophonic Ratios in Ancient Theory

It is historically significant to observe that a square of two disjunct enharmonic tetrachords of Archytas, showing the relation of every degree of the scale to every other degree (the relations that would occur in practical music), and a square of Archytas' Diatonic (see below) reveal that all the ratios of 5, four of the ratios of 7, and two ratios of 9 aside from the multiple-number ratios 9/8 and 16/9, had been impliedly recognized by the fourth century B.C. (read upward in pitch from the ratios in the column at the left to the ratios in the horizontal line at the top—example: from 16/15 upward to 4/3 is the interval 5/4):

| 1/1 | 28/27 | 16/15 | 4/3 | 3/2 | 14/9 | 8/5 |
|------|--------|--------|-------|-------|--------|--------|
| 28/27 | | 36/35 | 9/7 | 81/56 | 3/2 | 54/35 |
| 16/15 | 35/18 | | 5/4 | 45/32 | 35/24 | 3/2 |
| 4/3 | 14/9 | 8/5 | | 9/8 | 7/6 | 6/5 |
| 3/2 | 112/81 | 64/45 | 16/9 | | 28/27 | 16/15 |
| 14/9 | 4/3 | 48/35 | 12/7 | 27/14 | | 36/35 |
| 8/5 | 35/27 | 4/3 | 5/3 | 15/8 | 35/18 | |

[26]Hawkins, *op. cit.*, 1:411.    [27]*Questions of Musical Theory*, 39.

The 6/5 interval that generally characterizes the chromatic genus is
evident in two of the following three scales according to Ptolemy[28] (in the
Ptolemy Intense it is 7/6). Note the tonalities revealed by their 1–5–3, or
triad, Identities:

Didymus Chromatic (downward):

 2/1    5/3     8/5      3/2     4/3    10/9     16/15      1/1
    6/5    25/24   16/15    9/8    6/5    25/24      16/15

Ptolemy Soft Chromatic (downward):

 27/20   9/8    21/20     81/80    9/5   3/2     7/5      27/20
    6/5    15/14    28/27      9/8    6/5    15/14    28/27

Ptolemy Intense Chromatic (downward):

 7/4   3/2     11/8     21/16    7/6   1/1     11/6      7/4
    7/6    12/11    22/21      9/8    7/6    12/11    22/21

These, available in the Monophonic fabric, are Dorian type scales;
Lydian types may be found by substituting the complement of each ratio
for the same scale degree, and the scale will ascend. Example, Ptolemy
Intense Chromatic:

 8/7   4/3     16/11    32/21    12/7   1/1     12/11     8/7
    7/6    12/11    22/21      9/8    7/6    12/11    22/21

Squares of the Ptolemy Soft and Ptolemy Intense Chromatics, along
with the square of Archytas' Enharmonic, reveal theoretical acceptance
as early as the second century of all the relationships here expounded as
ratios within the 11 limit, with two exceptions—20/11 and 11/10—which
will be found in the square of the Ptolemy Equable Diatonic, one of the
scales given below. The chromatic genus of Eratosthenes, in an arithmetical
division of the monochord, now into twenty equal parts, involves the prime
number 19. But it also introduces to music theory the ratio 10/9, the small
"whole tone," and impliedly the complement, 9/5. This scale is not possible in the Monophonic fabric because of the prime numbers higher than
11 which it involves.

Versions of the diatonic genus given by Ptolemy[29] (excluding the Intense, which is called the Ptolemaic Sequence in the present work and has
already been examined), include the following, given in Monophonic ratios:

[28]Hawkins, *op. cit.*, 1:32.
[29]*Ibid.*

Archytas and/or Ptolemy Middle Soft Diatonic (downward);

3/2    4/3    7/6        9/8    1/1    16/9    14/9        3/2
   9/8    8/7    28/27    9/8    9/8    8/7    28/27

Ptolemy Soft Diatonic (downward):

4/3    7/6    21/20        1/1    16/9    14/9    7/5        4/3
  8/7    10/9    21/20    9/8    8/7    10/9    21/20

Ptolemy Equable Diatonic (downward):

2/1    9/5    18/11        3/2    4/3    6/5    12/11        1/1
 10/9    11/10    12/11    9/8    10/9    11/10    12/11

That these Ptolemaic scales, with all their intonational subtlety intact, are quite capable of harmonic music is evident in the many tonalities and fragments of tonalities which inhere in each heptatonic sequence. The possibilities for compositional materials in these few scales alone are vast, in interplay of both tonalities and melodic subtleties, and in flux, from one type and genus to another.

The square of Ptolemy's Equable Diatonic reveals the implication of the remaining two Monophonic ratios based on the 11 limit—11/10 and 20/11. The corroboration of history is not necessary to Monophony; it can stand on the principles stated. But if history is a comfort, here is a little history for our souls—not so much as to prevent us from remembering, with humility, that history is ready to comfort all comers, but enough to delight us in seeing eye-to-eye with one small part of the past.

## The Arithmetical Proportion

Ptolemy's Equable Diatonic tetrachord is also a child of the Arithmetical Proportion, and all of the division which the tetrachord implies is possible in Monophonic ratios. To demonstrate this genesis the duplication of the tetrachord—added by disjunction to complete the heptatonic scale—will be omitted, and our string will be divided into twelve equal parts, following Ptolemy's procedure.[30] The "twelve" is determined by the first interval of the tetrachord from the lowest tone, 12/11 (as twelve parts are to eleven parts—ergo, there cannot be less than twelve). When stopped, the first of the twelve parts, starting from the bridge of the monochord, will make a tone of one vibration (or 1/1). Stopping the string at two parts will

[30]Perrett, *Questions of Musical Theory*, 75.

create a tone of 1/2 vibration (still 1/1), at three parts a tone of 1/3 vibration (expressed 4/3 in order to preserve the same symbols in each 2/1 —4 is the same identity as 1), and—going continually downward in pitch— at four parts a tone of 1/4 vibration (1/1), at five parts a tone of 1/5 vibration (8/5), and so on. In Diagram 11 are shown the successive stops of a single string, each successive length separately, with the Monophonic

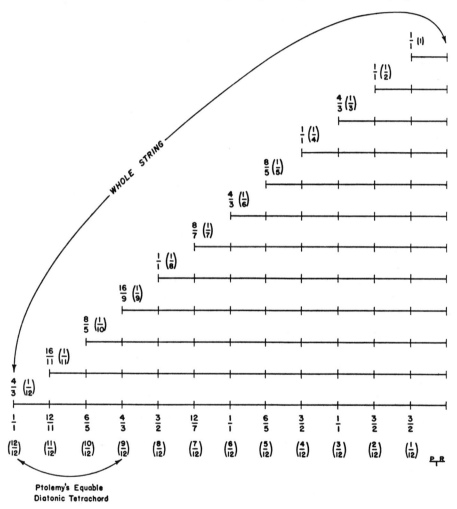

Ptolemy's Equable
Diatonic Tetrachord

DIAGRAM 11.—THE ARITHMETICAL PROPORTION IN TWELVE PARTS

ratios at the left end of each. Ptolemy's ratios (a Monophonic interpretation) are shown in the next to the bottom line, and Ptolemy's ratios in unreduced parts of string lengths are expressed in parentheses in the bottom line. The difference between the Monophonic and Ptolemaic symbols lies in the different concepts of 1/1: the first part, next to the bridge, is 1/1 in Monophonic symbols, whereas Ptolemy calls the whole string of twelve parts 1/1; the acoustical results are identical. The range of pitch, from the tone of the whole string to the tone of one part of it, is exactly three 2/1's and a 3/2.

This is just one example of the Arithmetical Proportion, and tonally a very delightful one. The equal divisions can be of any number which gives desired results, starting always from 1, the segment nearest the bridge. Schlesinger ties the entire system of ancient harmoniai to this principle (see Chapter 18).

## Ptolemy on Trial

Ptolemy is not always crystal clear to the modern researcher, and it may be questioned whether he was always crystal clear to himself. Yet an examination of many of his ratio scales discloses a certain principle: that every musical resource be expressed in the simplest terms permissible to the purpose behind it. There is no preoccupation in Ptolemy with necklaces of 3/2's for the throat of music, a lack which is highly gratifying. There is preoccupation, quite frequently, with the smallest-number ratio that is compatible, in a given situation, with the corresponding esthetic desire.

The education of the historian Burney evidently engendered no sympathy for the Greek predilection for aural subtleties, harmonic proportion, mathematical formula. Prefacing his remarks on Ptolemy with the label of a "bold and original thinker," he lashes out against Ptolemy's Pythagorean yen for analogies:

He passes suddenly from accurate reasoning and demonstration, to dreams, analogies, and all the fanciful resemblances to the Pythagorean and Platonic schools: discovers Music in the human soul, and the celestial motions: compares the rational, irascible, and concupiscent parts of the soul, to the eighth, fifth, and fourth; makes the sciences and the virtues, some Diatonic, some Chromatic, and some Enharmonic: turns the Zodiac into a Lyre, making the equinoctial the keynote of the Dorian mode: sends the Mixolydian to Greenland, and the Hypodorian to the Hottentots!

He seems to have been possessed with an unbounded rage for constructing new scales, and correcting those of former times. He gives us no less than eight different forms of the diatonic scale . . . Most of these scales seem but to differ in deformity, according to our present ideas of harmony and temperament. Indeed there is only one of them which modern ears could suffer . . .

As Burney continues, his wrath increases: "Scarce any rule seems to have been observed, but that of keeping the . . . boundaries of the Tetrachords unmoved from their just ratio of 4/3.[31] The ancient theorists revenged themselves, however, for this confinement by every kind of license in the disposition of the two remaining sounds." The historian then reminds us of the "four kinds of tones, and eleven semitones" which the ancients used, alleges that, "of these fifteen different ratios, eleven are impracticable in Harmony, and rejected by theory, and by the ear," and, finally, fortifies himself with a shot from something labeled "Rousseau" which says, in effect: "It is a waste of one's own time and an abuse of the reader's to drag him through all these divisions."[32]

We can only conjecture whether historians of a future age—when violins and pianos are faded from the ken of man—will still follow the benighted practice of condemning whatever they do not understand, or whether, having got as barren as Burney, things may begin to get better.

## *Other Historic Scales*

The pentatonic scale used by Olympos, Phrygian flutist and lyre player of the sixth century B.C. whom Plutarch called the father of Greek music, is not at all the usual one. Below is one version of his scale[33] (descending):

$$9/8 \quad 1/1 \quad 8/5 \quad 3/2 \quad 6/5 \quad 9/8$$
$$9/8 \quad 5/4 \quad 16/15 \quad 5/4 \quad 16/15$$

This scale is also found on the other side of the world, in one of the tunings of the koto given by the Institute of Music at Tokio,[34] but starting

---

[31]And Schlesinger strongly implies here and there throughout various of her works (see below, page 346) that Ptolemy erred in doing just this, or that he failed at least partly because of this to perceive the true ancient harmonic theory.

[32]Charles Burney, *A General History of Music*, 1:355–356, 357; quoted by permission of Harcourt, Brace and Company, Inc.

[33]Perrett, *Questions of Musical Theory*, 45. Perrett gives this scale on a different starting tone, but the sequence of intervals is exactly the same.

[34]Ellis, "Musical Scales of Various Nations," in *Journal of the Society of Arts*, 33:521, 522. Results of actual tests show wide variations from this scale, however. These, and other tests of actual instruments from many nations by Ellis and his colleague Hipkins took Ellis over the deep

on 1/1 instead of 9/8. It is also available in other places in the Monophonic fabric, for example, on 3/2 (descending):

$$3/2 \quad 4/3 \quad 16/15 \quad \quad 1/1 \quad 8/5 \quad \quad 3/2$$
$$9/8 \quad 5/4 \quad \quad 16/15 \quad 5/4 \quad 16/15$$

Schlesinger gives a version of the famous hexatonic scale of Terpander,
Greek poet and lyrist of the sixth century B.C., which is usually explained
as the Dorian mode with the omission of the sixth degree, ascending.
Schlesinger's version, however, appropriates the Arithmetical Proportion
explained above in connection with Ptolemy's Equable Diatonic.[35] This
scale (descending):

$$2/1 \quad \quad 11/6 \quad 11/7 \quad 11/8 \quad 11/9 \quad 11/10 \quad \quad 1/1$$
$$12/11 \quad 7/6 \quad 8/7 \quad 9/8 \quad 10/9 \quad 11/10$$

is simply the Monophonic Utonality 11/8 through its 11 Udentity (see
Tonality Diamond, in the first part of this chapter).

One final historic scale, a beautiful Chinese sequence from a sculptured
bronze kin (the "scholar's lute") which dates from before the third century B.C.[36] (ascending):

$$1/1 \quad 8/7 \quad \quad 6/5 \quad \quad 5/4 \quad \quad 4/3 \quad 3/2 \quad 5/3 \quad 2/1$$
$$8/7 \quad 21/20 \quad 25/24 \quad 16/15 \quad 9/8 \quad 10/9 \quad 6/5$$

## *Incidence of Tempered Scales—an Inexorable Accident*

The fourth type of historic scale to be considered, the tempered, is
represented in the Monophonic fabric by three sets of eight ratios each
that approximate "whole" and "half steps" of twelve-tone temperament.
This convenient and immediate measure for acoustical contrast may be
credited to the inexorable accident that produced an incidence of quasi-
tempered scales in a Monophonic Just system conceived with all the good
intentions in the world.

Exact temperament would of course imply 100 cents for a "half step"
between degrees and 200 cents for a "whole step." The first two sets of
ratios are the best tempered, since the greatest variation from the correct

end of acoustical disillusion. Scales, said he, are "very diverse, very artificial, and very capricious." *Ibid.*, 526.

[35] *The Greek Aulos*, 24.

[36] Hornbostel, "Musikalische Tonsysteme," in *Handbuch der Physik*, 8:436. This scale is especially interesting as an indication that the Chinese were less bound to Pythagoreanism than the
Chinese theorists known to Westerners at first led us to believe (see Chapters 14 and 15). The

Equal Temperament is 3.9 cents.[37] In the first set two "major" scales are available starting on 40/21 (omitting the "tritone," 27/20) and on 10/7 (omitting the "minor seventh," 14/11). A "natural minor" starts on 8/5 (omitting 27/20). The first four tones of the third set are exactly as given in the 11/8 Utonality scale of the Ptolemaic Sequence in lieu of the correct ratios.

| Ratios......40/21 | | 16/15 | | 6/5 | | 14/11 | | 27/20 | | 10/7 | | 8/5 |
|---|---|---|---|---|---|---|---|---|---|---|---|---|
| Cents in "Steps" | 196.2 | | 203.9 | | 101.9 | | 102.0 | | 97.9 | | 196.2 | |

| Ratios...... | 9/5 | | 40/21 |
|---|---|---|---|
| Cents in "Steps" | 203.9 | 97.9 | |

| Ratios......21/20 | | 10/9 | | 5/4 | | 7/5 | | 40/27 | | 11/7 | | 5/3 |
|---|---|---|---|---|---|---|---|---|---|---|---|---|
| Cents in "Steps" | 97.9 | | 203.9 | | 196.2 | | 97.9 | | 102.0 | | 101.9 | | 203.9 |

| Ratios......15/8 | | 21/20 |
|---|---|---|
| Cents in "Steps" | 196.2 | |

| Ratios......11/8 | | 16/11 | | 18/11 | | 11/6 | | 64/33 | | 33/32 | | 12/11 |
|---|---|---|---|---|---|---|---|---|---|---|---|---|
| Cents in "Steps" | 97.3 | | 203.9 | | 196.8 | | 97.3 | | 106.6 | | 97.3 | |

| Ratios...... | 11/9 | | 11/8 |
|---|---|---|---|
| Cents in "Steps" | 196.8 | 203.9 | |

The third set is particularly interesting because it affords triads composed of the 1–5–3 Identities, in which the 5 Identity is either just or is the "5 Identity" as given by the piano, starting from the same unities, or "roots." Since the 5 Identity is the greatest sufferer in temperament—if we ignore 7—being invariably at least 13.7 cents false, and since the representative of the 5 Identity is only 0.7 of a cent from exact temperament in the list above, the opportunities for comparison are very nearly perfect. The 3 Identity, which in temperament is flatted 1.955 cents,[38] is here just in either triad.[39]

acceptance of the four ratios of 5 and of at least one of the ratios of 7 (others can be implied) is indicated at about the same time as they were being similarly rationalized in ancient Greece.

[37]Incidentally, Ellis discovered a deviation as large as 11 cents from exact temperament in pianos tuned by Broadwoods' (London) best piano-tuners. Most of the deviations, however, were only 1 to 3 cents. Ellis in Helmholtz, *Sensations of Tone*, 485.

[38]The ratio 3/2 (just "perfect fifth") contains 701.955 cents, which is here expressed in accordance with the procedure of giving values in tenths of cents only, as 702.0 cents. For the account of an experiment in hearing an interval that is virtually identical with the interval of 1.955 cents see page 434.

[39]Discrepancies of a tenth of a cent will appear in additions and subtractions of the cents quantities on page 180. Such discrepancies, in diminishing amounts, would appear no matter to what length the decimal places were carried, since cents are a logarithmic measure, and are approximations for all intervals except the 2/1, which is the basic interval of measurement.

### THE OTONALITY TRIAD ON 16/11 (upward)

| *Just Intonation* | | | *With Tempered 5 Odentity* | | |
|---|---|---|---|---|---|
| 1 Odentity | 5 Odentity | 3 Odentity | 1 Odentity | 5 Odentity | 3 Odentity |
| ┌──702.0 cents──┐ | | | ┌──702.0 cents──┐ | | |
| 16/11 | 20/11 | 12/11 | 16/11 | 11/6 | 12/11 |
| 648.7 cents | 1035.0 cents | 150.6 cents | 648.7 cents | 1049.4 cents | 150.6 cents |
| | 386.3 cents | 315.6 cents | | 400.7 cents | 301.2 cents |

### THE UTONALITY TRIAD UNDER 11/8 (downward)

| *Just Intonation* | | | *With Tempered 5 Udentity* | | |
|---|---|---|---|---|---|
| 1 Udentity | 5 Udentity | 3 Udentity | 1 Udentity | 5 Udentity | 3 Udentity |
| ┌──702.0 cents──┐ | | | ┌──702.0 cents──┐ | | |
| 11/8 | 11/10 | 11/6 | 11/8 | 12/11 | 11/6 |
| 551.3 cents | 165.0 cents | 1049.4 cents | 551.3 cents | 150.6 cents | 1049.4 cents |
| | 386.3 cents | 315.6 cents | | 400.7 cents | 301.2 cents |

After hearing an absolutely true triad one feels that the tempered triad throws its weight around in a strangely uneasy fashion, which is not at all remarkable, for what it wants to do more than anything else is to go off and sit down somewhere—it actually requires resolution! Thus has the composition of music for the tempered scale become one long harried and constipated epic, a veritable and futile pilgrimage in search of that never-never spot—a place to sit!

# CHAPTER ELEVEN

# The Question of Resolution

## *The Basis of Resolution*

MODULATION, which has become the *sine qua non* of music in the West, is the term used to denote a move from the psychological effect of magnetism in one series of pitches related to each other by the smallest numbers to another or parallel effect of magnetism and series of pitches. Such a series of pitches has already been characterized as a series of identities with a Numerary Nexus, and as one which represents the maximal consonance of stipulated identities. Not all the identities within a prescribed limit, such as the 11 of Monophony, need be heard; two, or even one—if that one is a 1 or 3 Identity, are sometimes sufficient to create the tonal magnetism.

Modulation is the move from the "feeling" of one tonality to the "feeling" of another.[1] In such a move the moment of resolution into the second tonality is, in its small way, intriguing and exciting, and an examination of it results in a series of observations which help to disclose the comparative power of one resolution against another. Such reflections are not scientific, and certainly not metaphysical, yet they possess elements of both: they are, essentially, the result of experience with true intervals plus deduction.

I do not apologize for being the primary source of the reactions which have led to these deductions. However limited and unrepresentative a man's experience in his chosen field, it is nevertheless his first duty, I am convinced, to analyze his own reactions, notwithstanding the fact that this is not the accepted procedure for psychological investigation. The effect of the musical materials here expounded upon others hardly seems as pertinent as their effect upon the man who thinks they are worth expounding, especially since the field—though occasionally charted—is virtually deserted.

---

[1] Meyer calls modulation "the multiplication of all the number symbols of the diatonic scale by any one of these symbols or by any product of them." *Musician's Arithmetic*, 83. This may be an admirable definition from the standpoint of current musical methodology, but it is so precise as to be short of the truth in Monophony.

Succinctly, a tonal attraction involves three factors: first, perfection; second, departure, or an imperfection which is strong in relation to a desired perfection; third, the perfection implied by the second factor, whether the original perfection or another one.

The identities of a tonality, which draw the tonal vibrations down or up to themselves, represent the temporary perfection; they are magnets, or—as it were—primary planets. Those ratios clustering around each magnet for the brief moment of the prevailing tonality are temporarily magnetized tones, or secondary planets in the orbits of the temporary primary planets, and tend merely to enhance the perfection of the magnets.[2] The urge for resolution inherent in an arrangement of temporarily magnetized tones is an artificial one, since it is arbitrarily set up to produce a specific psychological result. The following observations are therefore not necessarily self-evident, but might be called deductions (which are to be taken in their cumulative import) regarding an artifice which is significant in our musical culture.

*Observation One.*—The extent and intensity of the influence that a magnet exerts is in inverse proportion to its ratio to 1. As a basis of computation all satellites, or temporarily magnetized tones, are primarily under the influence of attraction to the unity, which is the sun in its cosmos, its field being the tonal distance between it and its next higher and lower likenesses, or 1 to 2 and 1 to 1/2.[3] This means simply that the extent and intensity of the influence of 7, for example, are just a seventh of those of 1. However, this observation is to be taken in conjunction with the following:

*Observation Two.*—The intensity of the urge for resolution is in direct proportion to the proximity of the temporarily magnetized tone to the magnet. This simply says that it is harder to deny the urge of those magnetized tones closest to a magnet, and it implies that a magnetic field is of equal intensity on either side of a magnet. There is undoubtedly a point, in the case of a magnetized tone extremely close to a magnet, where the

---

[2]Bingham says that "every melodic interval trends toward one of the tones of the tonic chord of the tonality which it arouses. The law [of melodic progression] is based upon the tendency of every interval, yes, of even a single musical sound, to establish a tonality attitude." "Studies in Melody," in *Psychological Review Monographs*, vol. 12, no. 3, p. 38.

[3]Theoretically, just half the distance from 1 to 2, and from 1 to 1/2—that is, half the extent of the 2/1 above 1 and half the extent of the 2/1 below 1—would represent the field of attraction of 1. But because the various expressions of the Identity 1—1/2, 1, 2, 4, 8, etc.—are so alike in their psychological effect, a resolution to 1/1 from a ratio beyond the half, rather than to 2/1 or 1/2—to which it is closer—, is not necessarily resented. However, the attraction to 1/1 decreases markedly in the close approach to 2/1 (or to 1/2): see Observation Two.

two would be so compounded that the urge would be dampened or lost, but such intervals do not exist in Monophony.

*Observation Three.*—The intensity of the urge for resolution in a satellite, or magnetized tone, is in direct proportion to the smallness of the numbers of its ratio to the unity of the desired perfection. For example, if $1/1$ is considered the Otonality unity of the desired perfection, the urge for resolution in a satellite related to it by the ratio $4/3$ is stronger than one related to it by the ratio $5/3$, if the two situations where these ratios might be involved could ever be exactly parallel. Neither these situations nor any two situations in the psychological phenomenon of resolution are ever exactly parallel, since $4/3$ is affected by its proximity (in the ratio $16/15$) to a strong magnet (the identity in $5/4$ relation to the unity), whereas $5/3$ is affected by a greater proximity (in the ratio $21/20$) to a weaker magnet (the identity in $7/4$ relation to its unity) or by a much lesser proximity (in the ratio $10/9$) to a stronger magnet (the identity in $3/2$ relation to its unity).

## Methods of Establishment and Departure

The establishment of tonality is achieved primarily through the 1–3–5 Identities and in diminishing degree through the 7–9–11 Identities. But it is also achieved in other ways; according to Meyer, through a "variety of conditions"—reiteration, emphasis, a drone bass, etc.[4] The departure from this tonality is also accomplished in a variety of ways, but primarily by introduction of some of the identities of another tonality, which in relation to the previously established tonality represents imperfection, and the smaller the numbers of the ratio of the imperfection to the projected or final tonality (the desired perfection) the stronger and more conspicuous is the imperfection, and the stronger and more conspicuous the demand for resolution to the projected tonality.[5]

## Applying the Factors of Resolution

The understanding of tonal urges demands a cumulative judgment; that is to say, in any given instance judgment must be tempered by the

[4] *Musician's Arithmetic*, 51.

[5] "Subjectively," writes Bingham, "a tonality is a set of expectations" ("Studies in Melody," in *Psychological Review Monographs*, vol. 12, no. 3, p. 37)—which it is sometimes pleasurable to find unfulfilled, he might have added.

factors of all three observations. According to Observation One the 3 Identity is a third as strong as the unity, the 5 Identity a fifth as strong, and so on, but the matter of the tonal distance over which magnetism is exerted—in regard to Observation Two—can be disposed of less easily.

The precise method of determining this extent would involve finding the cube root of 2 (since 2/1 is the field of attraction of the unity) for the field of attraction of the 3 Identity, the fifth root of 2 for the field of attraction of the 5 Identity, and so forth. A simpler procedure, however, produces the same results. A third of 1200 cents (the 2/1 field of attraction), or 400 cents, is the field of 3; a fifth of 1200, or 240 cents, is the field of 5; a seventh of 1200, or 171+ cents, is the field of 7; a ninth of 1200, or 133+ cents, is the field of 9, and an eleventh of 1200, or 109+ cents, is the field of 11.

For the 3 Identity, then, the total of 400 cents is divided to put 200 on each side, or about a 9/8 ratio (203.9 cents) above and a 9/8 ratio below 3. By this process we find that the interval 15/14 (119.4 cents) above and below the 5 Identity comprises its field, and so forth. Below is given the number of Monophonic fabric degrees, above and below, which are in the particular field of attraction of each identity:

For the 3 Identity—about six Monophonic degrees above and below.
For the 5 Identity—about four Monophonic degrees above and below.
For the 7 Identity—about three Monophonic degrees above and below.
For the 9 Identity—about two Monophonic degrees above and below.
For the 11 Identity—about one Monophonic degree above and below.

The greatest of the seeming equivocations in these fields is the submergence of the 11 Identity in the field of the 3 Identity. However, the 3 Identity, as well as all others, is in the field of attraction of 1, but this fact does not destroy its magnetic influence. The inclusion of 11 in the Monophonic hexad (1–3–5–7–9–11) introduces a new character with a minimum of dissonance, and, skillfully handled, adds richness to a resolution in either the resolving chord or the final chord (see below), if richness is the momentary desideratum.

It is never necessary to compute the arcs of magnetic fields for each identity of a tonality, nor is it even advisable to try to remember the comparative latitudes except in a general way, since experience soon teaches what is effective and what is not, and interpretations precisely stated too often act as blocks to further investigation. It is only necessary to remember the decreasing power and increasing subtlety of resolutions to the less familiar identities—7, 9, and 11—if there is any intention of preserving their quality as identities.

It is frequently stated that the higher the numbers of a ratio the less obligatory is it that the ratio be given correctly, the more susceptible is the ratio to temperament, and the more willing the ear to compensate for the inaccuracy, and this is of course the justification for the egregious corruption of 5/4 and 6/5 and their complements in Equal Temperament.

This is a half-truth, one that is incapable of any verbal characterization that does not employ the word negative or the conception of negativism; it illustrates a type of thinking that is perhaps the most basic of all our intonational limitations. The higher the numbers of a ratio the more subtle its effect, and the more scrupulously should we try to forestall its dissipation in the stronger ratios surrounding it. So far as Monophony is concerned the question is academic, since all its identities are implicit in the ratios themselves and are therefore theoretically correct. The problem of making them practically correct introduces the subject of instruments, which is the burden of the next chapter.

These observations on modulation in general and resolution in particular are made in a spirit of investigation; they are tentative gropings in a virtually unexamined realm. Above all, they are not rules, to be consulted prior to action.[6] But as tentative gropings let us pursue them to their source; let us, that is, examine a few of the musical situations that led to their enunciation.

## Examples in Monophonic Ratios

The application of these observations to the common resolution of "dominant seventh" to "tonic" indicates that the powerful effect of this tonal flux is more than a conditioned reflex. The "dominant seventh," first used by the Frenchman Jean Mouton (1475–1522)[7] and first used

---

[6] Compare with the observations of Meyer, who discusses propinquity (Observation Two) as the chief element in the "affinity" of one tone to another, but also mentions "smallness of ratio term." *Musician's Arithmetic*, 128. Also compare Lipps's "law of the number 2" (more frequently called the "law of the tonic") and the principle that the simpler the ratios the closer the melodic "relationship." Bingham, "Studies in Melody," in *Psychological Review Monographs*, vol. 12, no. 3, p. 11.

[7] Hope, *Medieval Music*, 138.

effectively by Monteverdi about a century later, has become the most-used resolving chord in harmonic music. If the 1/1 Otonality is assumed to be the desired perfection, the smallest-number ratio in relation to the unity is 3/2 ("dominant"). An Otonality is then built on 3/2 (Identities 1–5–3–7–1), which resolves to 1/1 Otonality (Identities 1–1–1–5–3), and the result is the common "V$_7$–I."

|        | Resolving Chord: 3/2 Otonality | Resolving Distance | Final Chord: 1/1 Otonality |        |
|--------|--------------------------------|--------------------|----------------------------|--------|
| Higher | 3/2..............0...............3/2 | | | |
| 2/1    | 21/16............21/20..............5/4 | | | Higher |
|        | 9/8..............9/8..............1/1 | | | 2/1 |
| Lower  | 15/8............16/15..............1/1 | | | |
| 2/1    | 3/2..............3/2..............1/1 | | | Lower 2/1 |

The lowest tone, 3/2, the unity of the resolving chord, goes to 1/1, the unity of the final chord (3/2 is in the field of attraction of 1/1), and the resolution is of course quite powerful, even without harmonic support and notwithstanding that the tone 3/2 travels the entire interval distance 3/2 for resolution. This power is attributable to the small number 3 in relation to the final 1 (Observations One and Three). The 15/8 (5 Odentity of the resolving chord) also resolves to the unity of the final chord, but is less powerful, as is manifest when it is sung or played without harmonic support (Observations One and Three). The 9/8 (3 Odentity of the resolving chord) is a stronger identity than 15/8 (the 5 Odentity), but it travels a greater interval distance to reach 1/1 of the final chord, so that the degree of power is about the same as 15/8 to 2/1 (Observations One, Two, and Three). The 7 Odentity of the resolving chord (21/16), moving to the 5 Odentity of the final chord, is undoubtedly the least powerful of the four resolutions considered thus far, as will be appreciated if heard without harmonic support. The comparative weakness of this resolution is attributable to the involvement of the prime number 7, even though it has the smallest interval distance to travel for resolution, 21/20 (Observations One, Two, and Three). The higher 3/2—1 Odentity or unity—of the resolving chord is the same tone as, and is tied to, the 3 Odentity of the final chord.

The above example hardly seems to corroborate Observation Two, regarding the greater intensity of an urge when the magnetized identity is very close, but it is corroborated, very definitely, by the resolution shown below in Diagram 12, which is a very powerful one on the Chromelodeon:

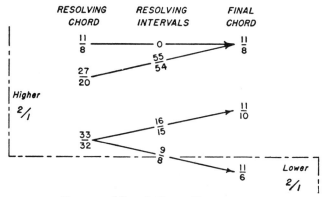

DIAGRAM 12.—A CLOSE RESOLUTION

The resolving chord is little more than a suggestion of tonality, but if 33/32 is considered the 3 Odentity of an 11/8 Otonality, moving to the 3 Udentity of 11/8 Utonality, Observation Three applies to that extent. However, most of the power of the resolution seems to spring from the closeness of the two lowest ratios to the 3–5–1 Udentities of the final chord (11/8 Utonality). The narrow 55/54 (31.8 cents) resolution from 27/20 to 11/8 is particularly striking (Observation Two).

Another resolution that travels narrow resolving distances, as shown below, is that from 3/2–O to 1/1–O. The profusion of identities brings a richness to the resolution that is quite effective on the Chromelodeon; the resolving chord contains an entire hexad (1–5–3–7–9–11, from the bottom up), and the final chord a quintad (3–1–9–5–7–1, from the bottom up, with the unity doubled):

| | Resolving Chord: 3/2 Otonality | Resolving Distance | Final Chord: 1/1 Otonality | |
|---|---|---|---|---|
| Highest 2/1 | 33/32............ | .33/32............... | ...1/1 | Highest 2/1 |
| Middle 2/1 | 27/16............. 21/16............. 9/8................ | .28/27............. .21/20............. .0................ | ...7/4 ...5/4 ...9/8 | Middle 2/1 |
| Lowest 2/1 | 15/8............. | .16/15............. | ...1/1 | |
| | 3/2. ............ | .0................ | ...3/2 | Lowest 2/1 |

Both Observations Two and Three apply here, and with approximately equal force. From resolving chord to final chord, and from the bottom up, 1 moves to 3 (same tone), 5 to 1, 3 to 9 (same tone), 7 to 5, 9 to 7, and 11 to 1.

The so-called plagal cadence, from 4/3 Otonality to 1/1 Otonality, for example, is also interesting in the light of these observations on resolution, as are the Utonality counterparts, or reverse forms, of these resolutions. The Utonality equivalent of 3/2–O to 1/1–O (the resolution diagrammed above) is 4/3–U to 1/1–U, and the reverse of 4/3–O to 1/1–O (the "plagal" cadence) is 3/2–U to 1/1–U.

It is quite true that in sustained tones dissonant or equivocal difference tones may tend to muddy these corresponding Utonality chords, yet on the Chromelodeon the effect of the reverse, the resolution 4/3 Utonality to 1/1 Utonality, for example, is peculiarly gratifying and quite as powerful as the corresponding Otonality resolution. It may be had by substituting the complement of each ratio for each chordal ingredient, and reversing the order of each column from bottom to top, so that there is an entire hexad (11–9–7–3–5–1, from bottom up) for the resolving chord, and a quintad (1–7–5–9–1–3, from bottom up) for the final chord:

|  | Resolving Chord: 4/3 Utonality | Resolving Distance | Final Chord: 1/1 Utonality |  |
|---|---|---|---|---|
| Highest | 4/3............ | ....0........... | ...4/3 | Highest |
| 2/1 | 16/15.......... | ..16/15......... | ...1/1 | 2/1 |
|  | 16/9........... | ....0........... | ...16/9 |  |
| Middle | 32/21......... | ...21/20........ | ...8/5 | Middle |
| 2/1 | 32/27......... | ...28/27........ | ...8/7 | 2/1 |
| Lowest 2/1 | 64/33......... | ..33/32......... | ..1/1 |  |

From resolving chord to final chord, and from bottom up, 11 moves to 1, 9 to 7, 7 to 5, 3 to 9 (same tone), 5 to 1, and 1 to 3 (same tone). All moves are by narrow, or very narrow, intervals.

## Tonality Flux

The potentialities of tonality interplay in the Monophonic fabric are too vast for more than isolated instancing. Most of the above examples were advisedly chosen for their aspects of coincidence with present-day musical theory; the combination of two unfamiliar ideas: unusual symbols

—ratios—and unusual chord relationships is a difficult problem in comprehension, but let the reader take comfort, for it is no easy problem in presentation! On the assumption that graphic delineation may aid comprehension, the interlocking of two pairs of chords is shown in Diagrams 14 and 14. The 1–5–3 triads of 8/7 Otonality and 7/4 Utonality are

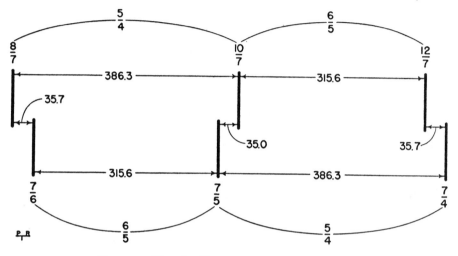

DIAGRAM 13.—AN EXAMPLE OF TONALITY FLUX

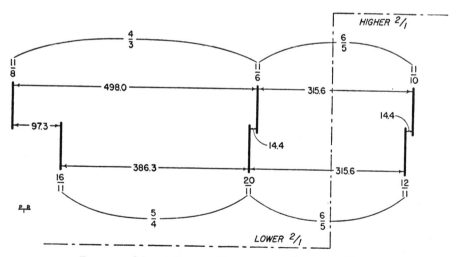

DIAGRAM 14.—A SECOND EXAMPLE OF TONALITY FLUX

measured off on an equal graph in Diagram 13, and the 5–3–1 triad of 11/8 Utonality and the 1–5–3 triad of 16/11 Otonality in Diagram 14.

Subtleties of tonality relationships are thus revealed, even in the commonplace triads, which are quite impossible of execution on Equal Temperament instruments and, worse, are quite impossible of conception in Equal Temperament theory. It is only necessary to mention that such subtleties may be multiplied many times, with consideration of the 7–9–11 Identities and the manifoldly related twenty-eight tonalities.

## An Experiment with a Negative Purpose

In the Science Building of the South Kensington Museum, London, is a small pipe organ which was designed, according to the builder, to prove that Just Intonation prevents even "the simplest modulation." This belief is obscurely tied to another equally benighted persuasion in general musical thinking, that melodic subtleties are impractical and ineffective in any harmonic music, just or otherwise.

The organ mentioned was in a glass case when I saw it, and the builder was not present to demonstrate it, but his thesis was effectively disproved, at least in part, by Colin Brown's harmonium (see pages 440–443), and is being disproved by Perrett and by the music of Monophony. As for the second contention, that in a chordal music subtle melodies are futile, there is only one effectual disproof: significant music.

## Fox-Strangways on the Subject

A few years ago a letter from A. H. Fox-Strangways, founder and first editor of the English quarterly *Music and Letters*, came to me through an intermediary. Fox-Strangways has been an active critic and a forceful intellectual participant in every recent movement or significant discussion looking toward the expansion of musical resources, and the letter I hold is very excellent from several standpoints. It embraces, succinctly and clearly, a good many of the beliefs and prejudices of the average well-educated musician in regard to modulation, melodic subtleties in harmonic music, and any tampering with Equal Temperament theory. Not every creative theorist has his opposition directed into a nutshell, and since the points made by Fox-Strangways must be answered, it is obviously desirable to reproduce his letter virtually in full.[8] The letter was in answer to an

[8]Permission kindly granted by Fox-Strangways in a message dated June 6, 1945.

article on Monophony sent to Fox-Strangways through the aforesaid inter-mediary. This highly chivalrous message, and gracious, considering that it betokened a rejected manuscript, follows:

June 8, 1934.

Dear Sir:

I'm afraid I can make no use of this, for the following reason.

There are many ways of securing just intonation—it depends on (1) what accuracy (2) what practicability you want. This seems to be a good way as far as I understand it.

But the unfortunate thing is that we *don't want* just intonation: it would stop off the simplest modulation—e.g.

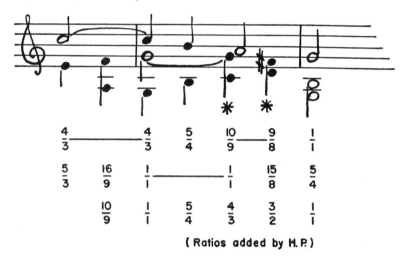

( Ratios added by H. P. )

In the chords * * , A is taken as 80/48 [10/9] and left as 81/48 [9/8] of C. If you have two A's to represent this then there is no modulation—i.e., the *power of taking a note in two senses.*

To go back from Equal Temperament on keyed instruments is to scrap the music of two centuries. We may have entered on an evil course—it has ruined singing, for instance—but we shall have to go on with it—probably in Yasser's direction [see page 304], though I can't at present see how the difficulties are to be got over. What your man says about Indian and Arab scales is true, but irrelevant: they were for melody, and we want harmony. The Indians are "up against it," too: they have imported the harmonium, the issue of which is inevitably European harmony, though they don't know it. A 25-note harmonium [it is actually 23 tones to the 2/1—see page 268] has been invented for them, so that they can play their rāgs, but they won't use it—too difficult, too expensive— they are settling down complacently on the 12-note scale, and contenting themselves with the dozen or so rāgs it will play, and scrapping the many scores of them they used to sing. A few of them hope for a great Preservation Trust? but the old rāgs are rapidly disappearing as Sanskrit is—too difficult, and we're too busy. It's all very sad.

Again, music is not made by acoustic specialists but by musical geniuses, who— Elgar, for instance—"don't know what the supertonic is" and persist in "taking their music from the air," i.e., from what they manage to *think* out of any rotten old fiddle or trombone they may happen to possess: and they accept any kind of temperament that gives scope for *modulation*, which is vital to thinking. Your man will probably say he *can* modulate. So he can; but at an expense of "grey matter" that the ordinary practitioner is not going to contemplate. . . .

There—I've no time, though there's lots more "to it"—sorry.

Yours very truly,

(Signed)  A. H. Fox-Strangways.

## Getting Down to Cases

The accuracy of Just Intonation has not proved "practicable" for a single reason: the lack of significant music for instruments conceived for Just Intonation and incapable of anything else. In Equal Temperament we have achieved a fine balance between a scale as painless as possible and one which can produce the *Well-Tempered Clavichord*. Equal Temperament has proved "practicable" simply because the music written for its instruments is significant.

The modulation in question has been played on the Chromelodeon for many musicians, including a graduate class at the Eastman School of Music in Rochester, New York, and at a lecture at the University of Wisconsin, in three ways: sustaining the 10/9 through the third and fourth beats, sustaining the 9/8 through the third and fourth beats, playing the 10/9 on the third beat and 9/8 on the fourth (which is necessary if both chords are in just tuning). My own reaction is that the difference in quality of the resolving chords is obvious, and that this has little or no bearing on the achievement of the modulation, which is successful in all three instances. The three types were not announced to my hearers, and no one suggested that there was no modulation in any case.[9] The great capacity of Monophony for taking a tone in two or more senses has been amply discussed (see Chapter 8).

[9]After the playing of this modulation at the University of Wisconsin one man correctly stated—from the audience—the nature of the chords in the three renditions. This man was an

To assume that our present musical heritage will be scrapped because a few persons choose to express themselves in their own way and on their own instruments is somewhat over-flattering. It is also evidence of the unconscious but acute sense of interdependence—of what amounts to helplessness—of all elements of the musical structure. When the musician meets a maverick in the field of theory he says (consciously or unconsciously) to himself: "That man menaces my position in society, my job, my art." Not so the artist in paint. He sees no dark cloud of revolution in every dissent; two artists can work with exactly opposite attitudes and utterly different materials without feeling personally menaced by each other. Those who would observe that the artist in a visual medium requires no "interpreter" for the preservation of his work will be answered: with the approach of perfection in reproduction techniques the composer who, with a small ensemble, plays his own work, will require no "interpreter" either.

The contention that harmonic music with melodic subtleties is impractical and ineffective is answered in the two progressions diagrammed above, which have been used in the music of Monophony. Meyer suggests that some Westerner "might get up courage enough to make *an attempt* at harmony and, if successful, *perhaps prove thereby* the presence of some 'tonality' in some exotic music."[10]

Finally, Fox-Strangways has got his roles mixed. It is he who is the "acoustic specialist," one who is convinced of the "evil course" of the accepted musical order and who imprisons himself in pessimism over its "very sad" world-wide effects, and nevertheless defends it. It is the author of the article who is the "ordinary practitioner" for whom Fox-Strangways offers to speak. Incidentally, it is far too generally assumed that "geniuses" do not or will not bother to attain precision in materials and thinking habits. Further, I am a bit nonplussed at the accusation of a relative absence of "grey matter" in my scale, but quite optimistic over the prospect of new exoticisms—in Louisiana, Wisconsin, and California, to pick a few random spots from the map—regardless of what India and Arabia do.

amateur violinist who had heard neither me nor my music before. Several others told me afterward that they had also correctly guessed the modulations. I also asked the specific question: "Was the modulation accomplished? If not, in which playing was it not accomplished?" No one was at all sure that the modulation had not been accomplished in all three instances. I afterwards explained, of course, that any hesitation whatever invalidates the theory that Just Intonation "stops off" modulation.

[10]*Musician's Arithmetic*, 118.

Equal Temperament is a current habit, as is also the scope for modulation which it allows. Composers can "think" only in Equal Temperament for just one reason: because it is all they have got to think in. Music systems are made valid—and workable—by significant music, as these pages have so frequently sought to remind us. But to produce significant music in Just Intonation we must have instruments, and instruments are no small problem. The chapter which follows is an account of one effort which is perhaps the beginning—perhaps a continuation of the beginning made by General Perronet Thompson, Colin Brown, Wilfrid Perrett, Kathleen Schlesinger[11] —of an answer.

[11]See Chapters 15 and 18 for an examination of other instruments in Just Intonation.

*Danlee Mitchell*

ASSORTED INSTRUMENTS
*Center:* HARMONIC CANON III
*Clockwise from left:* HARMONIC CANON I, NEW KITHARA I,
QUADRANGULARIS REVERSUM, MBIRA BASS DYAD

CHROMELODEON I

ZYMO-XYL

*Danlee Mitchell*

SCENE FROM *DELUSION OF THE FURY*

*Ted Tourtelot*

# CHAPTER TWELVE

# String and Voice Instruments and Their Notations

In the first edition the subjects of instruments and notation were treated separately. However, for the large majority of the many new instruments presented here, the notations very logically take their forms from the structures of the instruments, from the particular placement of strings or blocks. Therefore, it is far more efficient to discuss the forms, the intonations, and the notations more or less simultaneously.

In the summer of 1957 I prepared a small booklet with photographs of the instruments I was using at that time. This was designed to accompany the two-record set of *The Bewitched* which I had just brought out under my own label, GATE 5. The first two paragraphs of that booklet introduce this chapter:

It is inherent in the being of the creative art worker to know and understand the materials he needs, and to create them where they do not exist, to the best of his ability. In music, this characteristic must go far beyond the mere competence to compose and analyze a score. It *is* more difficult for the composer to create the colors of needed sound than it is for the painter to create the colors of needed light, but it is no less important that he find it possible to do so. The usual musical traditions are against him in the effort; in our time they are recognizable as traditions only when they have reached the comfortable plateau of academic security. But the rebelliously creative act is also a tradition, and if our art of music is to be anything more than a shadow of its past, the traditions in question must periodically shake off dormant habits and excite themselves into palpable growth.

If one must have the solid feeling of historical respectability beneath him in order to function, our world provides it in myriad variety, beyond the immediate locale, before the immediate past. He does not need to become an archeologist to realize that there is hardly an exotic line he could write, a variant article he could create, or a singular idea he could brew, that would not be felicitous in some tradition, at some point on the globe, at some conjectured time in the cultured past. My instruments belong to many traditions, especially including the present ones: affirmation of parentage provides the primary substance of rebellion.

During the eleven-year period ending in 1962, I trained six large ensembles, with some six months of rehearsals preceding each performance or series of performances. The experience led to many gratifying, and a few troubling, conclusions.

Musicians, who are generally awkward with common tools, nevertheless expect faultless perfection in their instruments. These are mechanical contrivances, however, and it would be salutary if musicians developed the elementary skills needed to maintain them. In particular, the elementary skill of tuning is of supreme importance to musicianship, and a deeper understanding would certainly ensue were it developed.

The attitude of the musician on stage—what I refer to as attitudinal technique—is also relevant. *At no time* are the players of my instruments to be unaware that they are on stage, *in the act.* There can be no humdrum playing of notes in the belief that because the musicians are "good," their performance is *ipso facto* "masterly." When a player fails to take full advantage of his role in a visual or acting sense, he is muffing his part—in my terms—as thoroughly as if he bungled every note in the score.

But before the instruments can sound competently in playing, and thus allow the players to *act* their parts competently, they must be in tip-top condition, and this involves a day-to-day and year-to-year obligation. The instruments do not maintain themselves, especially under the wear and tear and sometimes violent treatment (which I myself stipulate) of daily playing. And not a small part of the element of good condition is the visual; the instruments must be kept *looking well*, since they are almost always on stage as part of the set.

My work takes its character from the instruments I have built, played competently, and from my ideas and attitudes. The clarinets, cellos, and basses for which I occasionally ask can never take over this responsibility, however brilliantly they are played. The plucked strings in general represent the soul of my work and percussion the bodily structure, although percussion with a great variety of timbres and in fine tunings approaches what might be called lyrical percussion, and is certainly not without *soul*. Techniques for the plucked strings are often unusual, but not percussion techniques, or very rarely.

## Notation—On the Horns of Dilemma

In grappling with notation, the composer-pioneer is constantly on the horns of dilemma, a situation that becomes so thoroughly normal to him that when an integrated and rational solution seems to present itself, he is more than likely to remain incredulously perched—and with good reason. In a sense, a notation is the least of a music's ingredients, one that might be supplied on little more than a moment's notice. To provide a notation is a matter of paper and pencil and a good night's sleep; but to evolve a theory, to develop instruments based upon it, and to write and present music conceived therefrom is easily the matter of a lifetime.

An integrated notation involves much more than merely inventing it; that would be easy, but to make it immediately comprehensible and translatable into physical acts is another thing. The status of my notation after four decades of composing for my particular instruments remains unresolved—it is not integrated notation. However anomalous this may sound, it is not unnatural. The first inclination is to sweep the boards clean and to start anew, and this procedure is practicable so long as the composer depends solely upon himself for rendition of his music. That momentous time of departure from self-sufficiency into the complexities of ensemble work brings a totally different situation; from that time on the composer is quite effectively skewered by the education and conditioning of those whose assistance he seeks.

It is seldom possible both to find a group of persons *en rapport* and to reeducate them, which in any case requires a great deal of time. A start must be made by offering music that will stimulate the evolution of both intonation and ideas in general. Without such music, problems in theory could be solved on paper, and even in instruments, into time eternal without producing any noticeable evolution; the proof lies in the unique and "original" instruments in the museums of Europe. Stimulation will result only from a corpus of significant music, an emotionally dynamic music, which will win response from persons who don't give a tinker's damn that $3/2$ is $1/50$ of an equal semitone wider than the vibrational ratio they hear.

The composer who is moved to contribute to this stimulation bends every effort to get his music heard; and to get it heard (if he employs more than his own talents in rendition), he must write his music in such a way that it will not require years to connect fingers or lips or larynx to its execution. Here, however, the horns begin to hurt, because the hodgepodge of lines, numbers, and notes which results from this necessity is no sesame to an understanding of the fabric of theory which the composer has laboriously built up.

Nevertheless, music is composed on the basis of instruments, and instruments are individual. What is rational and well-integrated for one is quite the opposite for another. Symbols should represent, for the player, physical acts upon the strings, levers, wood blocks, or whatever vibratory bodies he has before him, but they do not represent such acts very well unless the peculiarities of string patterns, or of lever or block patterns, are taken into account as the basis for the figuration of the symbols. Results are more immediate and more rational when there is a separate notation for each type of instrument, based entirely upon its individuality, and, in addition, a common-denominator notation based upon ratios or clearly implying ratios. And students of the instruments would know both notations—the one for playing the music of a particular instrument, the other for studying and analyzing the total result.

This idea operates in my notation at least partially at present. A few of the parts are written in ratios, and those that are not so written are immediately translatable into ratios by the assiduous student. More will be said on the general subject of notation toward the end of this chapter.

## The Adapted Viola

The cello has already been cited as one of the most easily adapted instruments (page 99). The Adapted Viola is somewhat similar; its quality is more like that of the viola, but its range is deeper—between the cello and the viola. It has an average-size viola soundbox but a fingerboard about six inches longer than that of the average viola (see photograph). It has cello tuning pegs and cello strings—except the first string, which is a double-length violin first or second, or a monofilament nylon guitar string. The total length is 32 inches, and the string length from bridge to nut is 20 inches.[1]

---

[1] I made the fingerboard from a discarded cello fingerboard, and it was attached to a lengthened neck by a New Orleans violin-maker, Edwin Bentin, in 1930.

ADAPTED VIOLA

The lowest string of the Adapted Viola is 1/1–98 cycles (two 2/1's below 1/1–392),[2] approximately a 3/2 above the lowest cello string, and a 4/3 below the lowest viola string. The four strings are tuned in successive 3/2's as usual—1/1–3/2–9/8–27/16—a 2/1 below the violin tuning. (If the lowest string is considered as the generator the ratios are 1/1–3/2–9/4–27/8.) As shown in the illustration, the instrument is held between the knees in playing, to permit more accurate stopping.

There are twenty-nine stops in each 2/1, as seen in Diagram 15, and these are computed and marked, with lines and bradheads, for two and a half 2/1's on each string. The brads, which are hammered in at the sides of the strings rather than under them, do not interfere with playing in any way.

Ratios other than the twenty-nine marked are stopped comparatively; for example 9/8, which is not marked, is a trifle less than half the distance between 10/9 and 8/7, which are marked. The bridge is flattened on the side of the higher range, lowering the 9/8 string so that triads may be played (bowing three strings at once), but a wooden tooth can be inserted to raise the 9/8 string to normal position.

Considerable experience in marking cello fingerboards for the ratios desired convinces me that making marks while carefully listening to the ratios on one of the Chromelodeons is more practical than the mathematical approach. Different strings vary considerably in accretion of tone, and the difference between wound strings and monofilament strings is sometimes distressing. It is

[2] The expression 1/1–392 is used as a kind of "A"–440 (it is approximately the "G" below that "A") and is in italics in the following scheme:

1/1–1568 ................... third above
1/1–784 ................... second above
*1/1–392* ....... *the "G" above "middle C"*
1/1–196 ................... first below
1/1–98 ................... second below
1/1–49 ................... third below

This scheme is important both for understanding the viola notation and for understanding the tuning instructions in the prefaces to my later theater works.

nevertheless desirable to check the mark made by a *heard* tone with that made by computation. If the desired ratio on the 1/1 string is 16/11, the point at which it is obtained is 5/16 of the string length from the nut. Stops for the other strings involve a preliminary computation. If the desired ratio is 3/2 on the 9/8 string, the interval between 3/2 and 9/8 must first be known. 3/2 x 8/9 = 4/3, and the part of the string length to be measured off is therefore 1/4 from the nut.

Fingerboards may be marked in many ways. For the most effective method I have discovered is the use of a color analogy employing small blocks of colored lacquer under each string for each of the desired ratios. When such fingerboards have been used, intonation has generally been excellent; when they have been discarded, intonation has deteriorated immediately. It is rather sad, but I fear that most cellists would rather commit an indecent act than allow another cellist to catch them with a colored fingerboard.

In a sense, there has been a flat denial in the West for many centuries of the intrinsic spiritual character of both bowed strings and the human voice. Both have been forced, through intense discipline, to try to perform like pipe organs—in precise, discrete steps. Press a key—there is a tone; lift the finger—the tone ends. Yet these tonal means are entitled to their individualities, and it defeats the inner strength of both when the individuals concerned are forced into the molds of crypto-organists.

My own playing of the Adapted Viola depends very much on what I call a *one-finger* technique; it is much closer to the spirit of Indian vina playing than it is to the pipe organ. Inherent in this technique is the

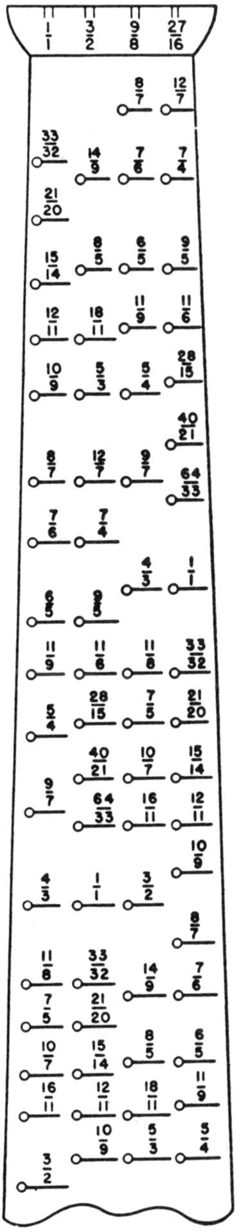

DIAGRAM 15—PORTION OF FINGERBOARD

potential of a fine art, and even when *glides* are not specifically indicated in a score, they become necessary and inevitable once the concept is understood.

The finger may start slowly on its move, increase speed, and hit the next ratio exactly. It may move very fast from the first ratio, and then move slowly and insinuatingly into the next—so slowly, sometimes, that one is not sure as to the point where rest has been achieved. Or, all this may be reversed. What the bow is doing meanwhile, in its capacity of providing an infinitude of nuance, is supremely important.

The only notation that has proven satisfactory for the Adapted Viola has been the straight ratio, which, after decades of use, I find easy to project upon the fingerboard. The following example, using a line from a Li Po poem,[3] provides some indication of the range of pitch. A large *1* indicates the first 2/1 of the instrument; a large *2* the second 2/1, a large *3* the third 2/1.

## Color Analogy for Current Instruments

In three large theater works I have used a number of current instruments.[4] In *Oedipus*, cello, string bass, and clarinet; in *The Bewitched*, cello, piccolo,

---

[3] Shigeyoshi Obata, *The Works of Li Po, the Chinese Poet* (copyright 1922), 117; used by permission of E.P. Dutton and Company.

[4] Certain works of mine will be referred to occasionally in the following pages. Those with longer titles will be abbreviated as follows:

Except for *Daphne*, these and other works are discussed at some length in Chapter 14.

clarinet, bass clarinet; in *Revelation*, cello, string bass, and a small brass band. It is out of the question to ask a large ensemble playing these instruments to become proficient in ratios, but a means of communication must be found, and a color analogy has been used. That outlined in the introductory pages to *Revelation* is the most rational because it is based entirely upon the number of cents in a ratio. Here it is, in essence:

No color ............ one of the twelve semitones, approximately
Blue ........................................ slightly flat
Violet ....................................... more flat
Orange ...................................... slightly sharp
Red ......................................... more sharp

In both full scores and parts, note heads are ringed with the appropriate colors. This is of course very imprecise, but players with good ears can and do make adjustments when hearing the full ensemble, and especially when hearing the precisely tuned Chromelodeons.

## *The Adapted Guitars*

Considerable confusion has resulted from the use of Roman numerals to differentiate my guitars. I purchased my original guitar in 1934 and spent several years (1934–1942) in the effort to evolve effective frets in Just Intonation. The usual low, wire-type frets were not very satisfactory, and I eventually fitted high, stainless-steel frets into slots in a brass plate, which was then screwed onto the neck. Both *Barstow* and *U.S. Highball* were originally written for this guitar, and I played it in performing these pieces for some two years.

In 1945 I developed another guitar which had a smooth and narrowed fingerboard with small and large pinheads, and small brass rivets, embedded in it and polished down to the fingerboard level. Electronic amplification compensated for the reduced tone caused by stopping with fingers.

Both of these guitars were tuned in three pairs of 2/1's, the lower tone of the middle pair being 1/1–98, the pitch of the lowest string on the Adapted Viola. The pairs:

```
                    ┌───5/4──┐  ┌──5/4───┐
(lowest tone) 8/5    8/5   1/1    1/1   5/4    5/4  (highest tone)
                    └───5/4──┘  └──5/4───┘
```

ADAPTED GUITARS I AND II

The three lowest strings and the three highest strings (a 2/1 above) are separated by successive 5/4's. Partly because of this pairing of strings, the instrument is played more like a mandolin than a guitar, but its low range of pitch and 2/1 pairs contribute to a result that is unlike either.

Having transferred my allegiance and the identical tuning to this second guitar, I called it Guitar I. However, in 1952, I removed the high frets from the original guitar and played it with a plastic rod (like a steel in a steel guitar) weighted with lead so that less pressure was required. The six strings of the 1952 reconception have always been tuned to unisons or 2/1's, in pairs: 1/1–98 and 1/1–196. At present—the tuning for *Delusion*—only the string nearest the player is 1/1–98; the other five are 1/1–196.

This reconceived guitar (the instrument on the left in the photograph) has been used in the *Dances, Oedipus, Revelation*, and, most recently, in *Delusion*. It is generally played with a pick. In order to distinguish it from the second Guitar I (1945), it was at first labeled Guitar III. Now, however, it is again Guitar I, since I abandoned the second Guitar I in 1956, believing that the Harmonic Canons (see below) were both more musical and more versatile. This is true, but still they do not take the place of that Guitar.

Adapted Guitar II (the instrument to the right in the photograph), built at the University of Wisconsin in 1945, has always been Guitar II. It has been prominent in the *Intrusions*, the *Dances*, the choruses of *Oedipus*, and in *Revelation* and *Delusion*.

It is a Hawaiian-type guitar—that is, one with a high nut which allows a lead-weighted plastic rod to be pressed down upon the strings to make stops. (Incidentally, the obnoxity of this tonal manipulation to some musicianly ears is due, I am convinced, more to the sugary and pseudo-South Seas music given to the instrument than to any ugliness or sentimentalism in the gliding sound as such.) Four strings are added, making ten in all, and are tuned beginning with a low 4/3—a 3/2 below 1/1–98—the same tone as the lowest cello string. In the rest of the tuning there is a choice between Otonality or Utonality, and the change can be made in about five seconds. Tuning of the two highest strings is varied; one of the Utonality tunings is as follows:

| 4/3 | 16/9 | 4/3 | 16/9 | 16/15 | 4/3 | 32/21 | 16/9 | 15/8 | 64/33 |
|-----|------|-----|------|-------|-----|-------|------|------|-------|
| └─lowest 2/1─┘ | | └─second 2/1─┘ | | └─────────── highest 2/1 ───────────┘ | | | | | |

It is evident that this is 4/3 Utonality (see table of Secondary Tonalities, page 161) except for the ratio 15/8, which has the value of a passing tone in the arpeggio. The identities are, from lowest to highest: 1–3–1–3–5–1–7–3–0–11, with 0 representing the non-identity 15/8. The two open strings 16/15 and 32/21 pass under wing nuts in the tuning head and are screwed down to increase the tension a determined amount—16/15 becomes 10/9 and 32/21 becomes 14/9; if, in this case, the 64/33 string is tuned up to 2/1, the result is 16/9 Otonality, as follows:

| 4/3 | 16/9 | 4/3 | 16/9 | 10/9 | 4/3 | 14/9 | 16/9 | 15/8 | 2/1 |
|---|---|---|---|---|---|---|---|---|---|
| └lowest 2/1┘ | | └second 2/1┘ | | └————————highest 2/1————————┘ | | | | | |

The identities are 3–1–3–1–5–3–7–1–0–9, with 0 again representing 15/8.

Twenty-two stops to produce higher Utonalities and twenty-two stops to produce Otonalities are marked on the fingerboard by triangles, the base of each triangle representing the stopping point. The triangles are colored to correspond with the Chromelodeon color analogy (see below, page 214). Tonalities other than those indicated are of course determined comparatively. (A few of the secondary tonalities are indicated by black triangles.) A narrow piece of thin wood is attached to the side of the fingerboard and shows ratios— in a melodic sense—for the highest 16/9 string (third highest in pitch).

The strings are mostly guitar and tenor-guitar, the exception being a mando-cello string for the lowest 4/3. The instrument rests on the player's lap and is generally played with fingers rather than with a pick.

Notation: Guitar I (current) has blocks of color straight across the fingerboard, with the colors following the color analogy for current instruments. In this graphic notation, either bass or treble clef may be used. Another notation used for Guitar I—preferable when single-string playing is more important than full strokes—involves only the spaces—four within the staff plus those above and below, to represent the six strings. In both notations, color and/or ratios (beneath the note or notes) may or must be used.

For Guitar II, where single strings or precise duads or triads are very important, the six spaces of the staff plus pairs of ledger lines above and beneath the staff represent the ten strings:

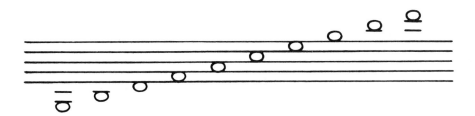

Ratios, indicating either the stop for a single tone, or, in the case of a tonality, a whole chord, are shown atop or below the notes.

## *Chromelodeon I*

There is again some slight confusion to contend with in the use of roman numerals to differentiate between Chromelodeons, but in this case it concerns only Chromelodeon II. Chromelodeon I has always been Chromelodeon I. It was originally a harmonium with a keyboard range of six 2/1's and with two sets of reeds.

My first adaptation of this sort was of an old melodeon loaned to me for the purpose of experiment—hence the name, a melodeon that approaches closer to the chromatic maximum of all "colors," or gradations, of tone ("Panchromelodeon"). Soon afterward, in 1942, I adapted one of the more usual five-2/1 harmoniums, and used it for three years. Chromelodeon I, with a six-octave extent—the word octave signifying a keyboard distance—was adapted at the University of Wisconsin in 1945. Only one feature was added later.

The process of adaptation for Chromelodeon I was as follows: first, the six 2/1's of reeds, seventy-three in each cell-board, or a total of 146 reeds, were removed. In the first cell-board, 73 new reeds tuned to successive ratios of the original 43-degree Monophonic system were inserted, from the 7/4 below 1/1–196 to the 11/8 above 1/1–392, inclusive. This provides a range of a 2/1 and an 11/7, or a 22/7.

Most reed organs have a system of stops which divides the keyboard between the "E" and "F" below "middle C." Treble stops operate from "F"

CHROMELODEON I

up and bass stops from "E" down. New reeds tuned to Monophonic ratios were also inserted in the second cell-board, with those in the upper section (from the lever "F" up) a 2/1 above the reeds in the first cell-board and those in the lower section (from the lever "E" down) a 2/1 below the reeds in the first cell-board. When the stops governing the second cell-board are pulled, the tones of the first cell-board are thus reinforced either a 2/1 above or a 2/1 below, which gives a total range, though not continuous, of about three and a half 2/1's.

The keyboard is not changed in any way, but the Monophonic 2/1 occupies the distance from the lowest "D" to the second highest "A," some three and a half keyboard octaves. The octave of the piano is thus generally a 6/5 on Chromelodeon I, an interval about a fourth as large as the 2/1. The keyboard distances of all other intervals are proportionately wider. The playing of a 1–5–3 triad is possible only with two hands. The "octave" coupler (making it possible by depressing one lever to sound the "octave" above it at the same time), which is found on all harmoniums, operates on Chromelodeon I also, but with very different results: the "octave" is now merely an octave, and sounds a 6/5 (or thereabouts), not an "octave"; in other words, Chromelodeon I couples in "minor thirds."

Although the dislocation of tone and the magnification of what is really a comparatively small tonal gamut at first produces a psychological shock in musicians trained on the piano keyboard, the adjustment is quickly made; the two dissimilar tonal systems take their appropriate niches in the brain cells and are not confused.

The feature added since 1945 is the separate sub-bass keyboard, above the regular keyboard and far to the left (see photograph). This was originally a separate keyboard on the old Chromelodeon II, and when, for practical reasons, I had to abandon that instrument, I saved this portion (all the reeds, in fact) and in 1949 attached it to Chromelodeon I. The large size of these reeds and the increased vacuum power they need for strong vibration led me to rebuild the bellows in 1963, using heavier bellows springs and increasing the size by about fifty per cent.

Each of the sub-bass reeds is tuned to one of the 1 Odentities or 1 or 3 Udentities in the Monophonic system of tonalities. The lowest 4/3 is about 33 cycles (lowest "C" on the piano) and the highest 4/3 about 66 cycles.

| ┌─────────Lower 2/1─────────┐ | | | | | | | ┌─────────Higher 2/1─────────┐ | | | | |
|---|---|---|---|---|---|---|---|---|---|---|---|---|
| *1* | *2* | *3* | *4* | *5* | *6* | *7* | *8* | *9* | *10* | *11* | *12* | *13* |
| 4/3 | 16/11 | 3/2 | 8/5 | 5/3 | 16/9 | 11/6 | 1/1 | 16/15 | 8/7 | 7/6 | 5/4 | 4/3 |
| 1–O | 1–O | 1–O | 1–O | 3–U | 1–O | 3–U | 1–O | 1–O | 1–O | 3–U | 3–U | |
| 3–O | | 1–U | | | 3–U | | 3–O | | | | | |
| 1–U | | 3–U | | | | | 1–U | | | | | |
| | | | | | | | 3–U | | | | | |

The symbols under each ratio indicate its partial potentiality; for example, 3/2 may be a 1 Odentity (of 3/2–O), a 1 Udentity (of 3/2–U), and a 3 Udentity (of 9/8–U). (For the complete table of senses in which each ratio may be taken, see Appendix II.) Since in the descending order of the Utonalities, the 3 Udentity is more naturally below the unity, and since it is the only very strong identity below the unity, this representative of each Utonality was chosen for the sub-bass reeds where it was feasible to do so.

A very valuable adjunct of nearly all harmoniums are the knee swells. In *U.S. Highball*, the pulsing, rhythmic use of the right swell helps materially in pushing that freight train to Chicago. The musicality, versatility, and potentialities of these old-fashioned harmoniums are constantly amazing. I would not trade my two Chromelodeons for any electric organs that I have ever heard.

## New Chromelodeon II

This instrument was obtained through friends in far northern California in 1950. It is unique in my experience in that it has a full piano keyboard—88 keys or levers—although it was always a reed organ, never a piano. It has two banks of reed cells in front, except in the very low bass, and a single row of cells in back—a total of 244 reeds compared to Chromelodeon I's 159 (with the sub-bass).

There is of course an optimum-size hole under each reed, opening into the vacuum chamber, for air to be sucked through most efficiently for the particular reed—large for large reeds, much smaller for very small reeds. However, the latitude within which reeds will sound, even when put into cells two 2/1's higher or lower, is rather considerable. In this respect the reed organ is much more adaptable for experimental purposes than the piano, with its rigid steel harp; if this were not true, the reed organ would be hopeless for my purposes.

CHROMELODEON II

In working with Chromelodeon I while composing *Oedipus*, I experimented with two sets of reeds, one being tuned to small-number relationships with the second. Thus, when both stops were opened there was a series of duads. This was so successful that when I built New Chromelodeon II, which has three sets in the higher register, reeds were switched around so that a triad was heard under each key (actually a duad, with one voice reinforced a 2/1 above) with the three stops open. Now, all the unusual Chromelodeon tunings—for *Oedipus, Revelation, Delusion*—are concentrated in New Chromelodeon II.

Adaptation of the instrument was completed in 1959. It has five usable stops: *Z-A-left-12-X-A-right*. Unlike Chromelodeon I, the playing of successively higher keys does not necessarily sound successively higher tones. With all the stops, there is some jumping about, and in the *X* stop, very much jumping—all for conceptual reasons.

The higher of the two banks of reeds in front remains a twelve-tone scale (the *12* stop), but tuned in one of several possible Just Intonations. It extends from the second "F" below "middle C" to the third "F" above. The approximate pitches of the twenty highest reeds of this stop are shown on a staff, below, with the ratios and the names of levers underneath (the 11/6—eighth reed from the top—is the highest pitch on the instrument, approaching 1/1–3136):

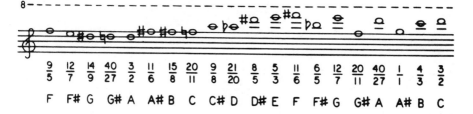

| $\frac{9}{5}$ | $\frac{12}{7}$ | $\frac{14}{9}$ | $\frac{40}{27}$ | $\frac{3}{2}$ | $\frac{11}{6}$ | $\frac{15}{8}$ | $\frac{20}{11}$ | $\frac{9}{8}$ | $\frac{21}{20}$ | $\frac{8}{5}$ | $\frac{5}{3}$ | $\frac{11}{6}$ | $\frac{6}{5}$ | $\frac{12}{7}$ | $\frac{20}{11}$ | $\frac{40}{27}$ | $\frac{1}{1}$ | $\frac{4}{3}$ | $\frac{3}{2}$ |
|---|---|---|---|---|---|---|---|---|---|---|---|---|---|---|---|---|---|---|---|
| F | F# | G | G# | A | A# | B | C | C# | D | D# | E | F | F# | G | G# | A | A# | B | C |

The *A-left* reeds are consistently a 2/1 above the *Z* reeds, up to the bass-treble break ("E"-"F" below "middle C"). Notable dislocation: the third lowest key, 40/21, is below 1/1–49, the lowest key. Another: the second "C" up from the bass end is 5/3, a full 6/5 below the next white key up, 1/1.

The *X* reeds are consistently a 2/1 above the *A-right* reeds, starting with the second "F" above "middle C" and continuing to the highest tone. Notable dislocation: the highest "E" in the treble is 5/3 (*X* and *A-R*), and is approximately a semitone below the highest key, "C", or 9/5. The twenty-four reeds of the $X$ set, beginning with the "F" below "middle C", are tuned to these approximate pitches, with ratios and levers indicated below:

| $\frac{12}{11}$ | $\frac{8}{7}$ | $\frac{9}{8}$ | $\frac{14}{9}$ | $\frac{9}{5}$ | $\frac{11}{10}$ | $\frac{7}{6}$ | $\frac{5}{4}$ | $\frac{4}{3}$ | $\frac{32}{27}$ | $\frac{5}{4}$ | $\frac{40}{21}$ | $\frac{10}{9}$ | $\frac{11}{8}$ | $\frac{1}{1}$ | $\frac{14}{11}$ | $\frac{10}{7}$ | $\frac{27}{20}$ | $\frac{3}{2}$ | $\frac{7}{5}$ | $\frac{16}{15}$ | $\frac{6}{5}$ | $\frac{18}{11}$ | $\frac{11}{7}$ |
|---|---|---|---|---|---|---|---|---|---|---|---|---|---|---|---|---|---|---|---|---|---|---|---|
| F | F# | G | G# | A | A# | B | C | C# | D | D# | E | F | F# | G | G# | A | A# | B | C | C# | D | D# | E |

## TUNING OF NEW CHROMELODEON II

The complete tuning is from low to high; as before, the alphabetical symbols are simply the names of keys, or levers.

| | | | | | | | | | | | | |
|---|---|---|---|---|---|---|---|---|---|---|---|---|
| Z | 1/1–49 | 9/8 | 40/21 | 5/4 | 4/3 | 16/11 | 3/2 | 8/5 | 7/4 | 16/9 | 9/5 | 20/11 | 11/6 |
| A-L | 1/1–98 | 9/8 | 40/21 | 5/4 | 4/3 | 16/11 | 3/2 | 8/5 | 7/4 | 16/9 | 9/5 | 20/11 | 11/6 |

| A | A# | B | C | C# | D | D# | E | F | F# | G | G# | A |

| 12 | | | | | | | | | 16/9 | 40/21 | 1/1–98 | 16/15 |
|---|---|---|---|---|---|---|---|---|---|---|---|---|
| Z | 15/8 | 40/21 | 5/3 | 160/81 | 1/1–98 | 81/80 | 33/32 | 21/20 | 16/15 | 12/11 | 11/10 |
| A-L | 15/8 | 40/21 | 5/3 | 160/81 | 1/1–196 | 81/80 | 33/32 | 21/20 | 16/15 | 12/11 | 11/10 |

| A# | B | C | C# | D | D# | E | F | F# | G | G# |

| 12 | 10/9 | 6/5 | 5/4 | 4/3 | 10/7 | 3/2 | 8/5 | 5/3 | 12 | 16/9 | 40/21 | 1/1–196 | 16/15 |
|---|---|---|---|---|---|---|---|---|---|---|---|---|---|
| Z | 10/9 | 9/8 | 8/7 | 7/6 | 32/27 | 6/5 | 11/9 | 5/4 | A-R | 14/11 | 9/7 | 21/16 | 4/3 |
| A-L | 10/9 | 9/8 | 8/7 | 7/6 | 32/27 | 6/5 | 11/9 | 5/4 | X | 12/11 | 8/7 | 9/8 | 14/9 |

| A | A# | B | C | C# | D | D# | E | F | F# | G | G# |

| 12 | 10/9 | 6/5 | 5/4 | 4/3 | 10/7 | 3/2 | 8/5 | 5/3 | 16/9 | 40/21 | 1/1–392 | 16/15 |
|---|---|---|---|---|---|---|---|---|---|---|---|---|
| A-R | 27/20 | 11/8 | 7/5 | 10/7 | 16/11 | 40/27 | 3/2 | 32/21 | 14/9 | 11/7 | 8/5 | 18/11 |
| X | 9/5 | 11/10 | 7/6 | 5/4 | 4/3 | 32/27 | 5/4 | 40/21 | 10/9 | 11/8 | 1/1–784 | 14/11 |

| A | A# | B | C | C# | D | D# | E | F | F# | G | G# |

| 12 | 10/9 | 6/5 | 5/4 | 4/3 | 10/7 | 3/2 | 8/5 | 5/3 | 16/9 | 40/21 | 1/1–784 | 16/15 | 10/9 |
|---|---|---|---|---|---|---|---|---|---|---|---|---|---|
| A-R | 5/3 | 27/16 | 12/7 | 7/4 | 16/9 | 9/5 | 20/11 | 11/6 | 15/8 | 40/21 | 64/33 | 160/81 | 1/1–392 |
| X | 10/7 | 27/20 | 3/2 | 7/5 | 16/15 | 6/5 | 18/11 | 11/7 | 15/8 | 40/21 | 64/33 | 160/81 | 1/1–784 |

| A | A# | B | C | C# | D | D# | E | F | F# | G | G# | A |

| 12 | 6/5 | 5/4 | 4/3 | 10/7 | 3/2 | 8/5 | 5/3 | 9/5 | 12/7 | 14/9 | 40/27 | 3/2 | 11/6 |
|---|---|---|---|---|---|---|---|---|---|---|---|---|---|
| A-R | 81/80 | 33/32 | 21/20 | 16/15 | 12/11 | 11/10 | 10/9 | 9/8 | 8/7 | 7/6 | 32/27 | 6/5 | 11/9 |
| X | 81/80 | 33/32 | 21/20 | 16/15 | 12/11 | 11/10 | 10/9 | 9/8 | 8/7 | 7/6 | 32/27 | 6/5 | 11/9 |

| A#. | B | C | C# | D | D# | E | F | F# | G | G# | A | A# |

| 12 | 15/8 | 20/11 | 9/8 | 21/20 | 8/5 | 5/3 | 11/6 | 6/5 | 12/7 | 20/11 | 40/27 | 1/1–1568 | 4/3 | 3/2 |
|----|------|-------|-----|-------|-----|-----|------|-----|------|-------|-------|----------|-----|-----|
| A-R | 5/4 | 14/11 | 9/7 | 21/16 | 4/3 | 5/3 | 11/8 | 7/5 | 10/7 | 16/11 | 40/27 | 3/2 | 8/5 | 9/5 |
| X | 5/4 | 14/11 | 9/7 | 21/16 | 4/3 | 5/3 | 11/8 | 7/5 | 10/7 | 16/11 | 40/27 | 3/2 | 8/5 | 9/5 |
| | B | C | C# | D | D# | E | F | F# | G | G# | A | A# | B | C |

## The Chromelodeon Color Analogy

To enable the player to know the ratio which each key represents, and to broaden understanding, a purely arbitrary color scheme is used. As seen in the photographs, it is applied in bands of colors (the scheme was previously used on the Ptolemy—see below, page 219). It has no relation to the recurrent efforts of sundry theorists to draw parallels between the perception of light waves (color) and sound vibrations (tone). Each identity is accorded a color corresponding to the spectrum, but with indigo omitted (it could be included in Schlesinger's schema for the seven identities, involving 13; see Chapter 18), as follows:

| | | | | |
|---|---|---|---|---|
| 1 | red | | 7 | green |
| 3 | orange | | 9 | blue |
| 5 | yellow | | 11 | violet |

The colors are lacquer. The appropriate ratios are painted on the colors with dark blue lacquer, and the whole is covered with a clear plastic varnish for protection. Each key representing one of the twenty-nine primary ratios shows at least two colors in two-color blocks, one beneath the other; the key for the ratio 1/1 shows all six colors on the over half and all six on the under half, since the ratio is present in the twelve Primary Tonalities, and the keys for 3/2 and 4/3 show four each—two colors in each half, since each of these ratios is present in four Primary Tonalities (see the Tonality Diamond on page 110).

Red always indicates a unity; on the over half it indicates the unity of an Otonality and on the under half the unity of Utonality. Orange reveals the 3 Odentity when it is on the over half and the 3 Udentity when on the under half; and so on. A complete tonality can be traced by the color of the Numerary Nexus; for example, all keys with violet in the under halves are Odentities of one Otonality (16/11), and the red, orange, yellow, green, blue, and violet in the over halves show the Odentity of each; similarly, all keys with a green Numerary Nexus in the over halves are Udentities of one Utonality (7/4), and the red, orange, yellow, green, blue, and violet in the under halves show the Udentity of each; and so on. The secondary ratios are distinguished only by a solid color—light blue.

In the pursuit of Abstraction in music every accessory to it has become severe: the black and white keys of the piano, the black and white notation (quite unlike the notation of the Middle Ages), the black and white "tails" of the concert platform. It is as though the men of music were afraid that any loosening of the full-dress G-String might shake their art from its presumption of "independence." The gowns of the ladies-of-the-concert are indeed and of course an exception (a ludicrous but sex-blessed and therefore usual inconsistency), but the general attitude is calculated to produce nothing if not an incontinent reaction.

The painted naked chests of the musicians on stage during the second half of *Delusion*, performed recently, were far less an "incontinent" reaction than a carrying out of what was *right* for this work. To attain significance, a dynamic music theory must be concerned with the broad latitudes of the philosophy of music, and the matter of musicians' garb is not unrelated. Black and white habiliments, Abstraction, the prevalence of Abstractionist technicians, the concert system, the "grand" pretense of musicians, irrationality in music theory, non-precision in musical thinking generally, and virtually universal adulation of the musically factitious, are intra-corroborative symptoms; they are all parts of a picture of practice which offers precisely one conclusion—ritual sans redemptive value.

## Chromelodeon Notation

The solution could hardly be more simple. The keyboard player has the usual keyboard—7-white-5-Black—under his hands; therefore, he plays what is written. When the player sees an "F♯," in the lower part of the treble clef, for example, he plays it automatically. However, he will not *hear* "F♯," but rather a low "E♭" (11/7). At first the sounds are strange, but, as suggested above, the player's eyes and fingers are too well correlated to let that strangeness disturb him once the new psychological process has begun. In this we find proof that the automatic acceptance of a certain note distance as an exact intonational quantity is not very deep-seated in the trained musician—a stimulating discovery to anyone interested in advancing the cause of new instruments.

The familiar notation is a track over which to run a newly conceived train. The designers of new trains—engines and coaches—might wish they had rails closer together or farther apart, or a track of an entirely different nature, but the wish is futile because the new trains, if they are to run in the service of public transportation, must use the system of tracks available. Chromelodeons I and II are new trains offering different values on the same old track—a track which they cannot escape using, at least for the present.

## Old Chromoledeon II

This instrument lasted only about three years (1946–1949). It worked, but it did not have the facile rebound of keys or levers that is necessary in a keyboard instrument intended for an intense compositional purpose. At the time I endeavored to transform it (the University of Wisconsin, 1946), I could only guess at the skills needed—I had no special equipment and lacked the money to hire help even were it available. (In the heyday of reed organs there was a body of technicians with the skills, the knowledge of woods, and the special equipment called for in manufacturing and reconstructing good reed organs. Such technicians, I fear, have all but vanished.) In the circumstances, the instrument was abandoned—but not because it was a poor idea; I thought it a good idea then and I still think so. Therefore, the instrument is outlined here and the original diagram reproduced.

The many impossible stretches on Chromelodeon I in the common harmonic intervals—2/1, 3/2, 4/3—influence the composer toward linear or voice-leading types of music. This is far from a bad influence, but the keyboard distances are *limitations* which were partially eliminated here because the keyboard had more keys to the "octave" within the same octave distance.

Old Chromelodeon II was originally a chapel organ with approximately two and a half sets of reeds in a keyboard range of five 2/1's, and with a set of thirteen sub-bass reeds (those now attached to Chromelodeon I). As shown in Diagram 16, there were four planes of keys: the usual whites, the usual blacks, a higher plane of red keys, seven to the octave, and, finally, a sub-plane of yellow keys partially cut into the whites in series of twos and threes, with three pairs and two triplets occurring in the five-octave extent.

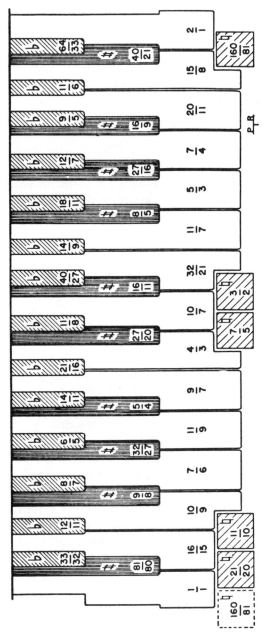

DIAGRAM 16.—A SECTION OF THE KEYBOARD OF OLD CHROMELODEON II

The stops could be pulled to give a continuous scale from the 10/9 below 1/1–196 to the 11/7 above 1/1–392, a compass of approximately two and a half 2/1's. The stop system, dividing the keyboard between treble and bass, provided tones two 2/1's above the upper part of this scale and one 2/1 below the lower part. This gave a compass from the 10/9 below 1/1–98 to the 11/7 above 1/1–1568, or approximately five and a half 2/1's, with one gap between the highest reed of the upper treble cell-boards and lowest reed of the lower treble cell-boards—an interval somewhat larger than a "perfect fifth," or from about the second "E*b*" above "middle C" to the second "B*b*" above.

There were 22 keys in the octave distance, or 44 keys (two octaves) to the 2/1. A chromatic scale—in the right hand—fit the hand very well, the thumb falling on all yellows and some whites, the second finger on blacks and whites, the third on blacks and reds, and the fourth on reds only; for example, a scale from 1/1 to 10/7, "D" to "D" in the right hand:

| Fingering | 2 | 3 | 4 | 1 | 2 | 4 | 1 | 2 | 3 | 4 |
|---|---|---|---|---|---|---|---|---|---|---|
| Keys | 1/1 | 81/80 | 33/32 | 21/20 | 16/15 | 12/11 | 11/10 | 10/9 | 9/8 | 8/7 |

| 1 | 2 | 3 | 1 | 2 | 3 | 1 | 3 | 1 | 2 | 3 | 1 | 2 |
|---|---|---|---|---|---|---|---|---|---|---|---|---|
| 7/6 | 32/27 | 6/5 | 11/9 | 5/4 | 14/11 | 9/7 | 21/16 | 4/3 | 27/20 | 11/8 | 7/5 | 10/7 |

A 4/3 stretch (about an octave) was always possible for one hand, and a 3/2 stretch (generally about one white key wider than an octave) was possible for a broad hand. Another advantage that musicians might appreciate—suggesting that I am after all not so recklessly fast and loose with our sacred cows—was that the lever corresponding to "middle C" on the piano here played very close to the same pitch, the 4/3 below 1/1–392, and every alternate "C" played a tone of that series of likenesses, one or more 2/1's above or below the middle 4/3. In other words, two octaves represented a 2/1 throughout the keyboard; and within successive 2/1's, *each ratio was on the corresponding lever regardless of its position in pitch*, an advantage which Chromelodeon I does not possess, its 2/1 not coming out evenly with the octaves. Thus, on Old Chromelodeon II, 32/21 and 16/15 were always on "E"; 1/1 and 10/7 always on "D"; 5/4 and 16/9 always on "A#"; 12/11 and 14/9 always on "F*b*."

The greatest advantage of Old Chromelodeon II for a practical music, aside from its easy fingering and possibly intrinsic musicality, was in the matter of notation. The seventeenth-century Clavicymbalum Universale, as described by Praetorius,[5] was perhaps very similar except for the yellow sub-keys. It had nineteen keys to the 2/1 designed to distinguish between "sharps" and "flats" in Meantone Temperament. Although the difference between the "sharp of one tone and the flat of the next" grew up with Meantone and loses all meaning in Monophony, the distinction may nevertheless be used to great advantage in notating Monophony's music.

The Clavicymbalum Universale had the conventional seven white keys, but the five blacks were doubled and, in addition, there were single black keys between "E" and "F" and between "B" and "C," examples of the "subsemi-tonia" somewhat contemptuously referred to by medieval theorists.[6] In the Monophonic adaptation to notation, then, all black keys on Old Chromelodeon II were "sharps," all red keys were "flats," and all yellow sub-keys were "naturals."

## A Previous Experiment—the Ptolemy

More than ten years before I adapted Old Chromelodeon II, I had helped to build a new reed organ with a kind of typewriter keyboard—five rows of keys fitting the five fingers and a partial sub-row at the bottom—and with a chordal adjunct similar to the Tonality Diamond (page 110). It was named in honor of the second-century Alexandrian scientist, Ptolemy, because he used or implied the ratios of the 11 limit in the scales he expounded (see Chapter Ten). As with Old Chromelodeon II, the Ptolemy failed as a musical instrument because of the lack of skills, equipment, and money. In retrospect, moreover, I cannot consider that it was practical as an instrument from the standpoint of either fingering or notation. Although diagrams and a

---

[5] Helmholtz, *Sensations of Tone*, 320.

[6] A conjectured diagram of the Clavicymbalum Universale is provided in Yasser, *Theory of Evolving Tonality*, 284.

photograph were included in the earlier edition, it does not seem fruitful to repeat them here.[7]

## Kithara I

This Kithara, built originally in 1938, went through major redesigns and rebuildings for more than twenty years. It will be explained here in its present design, established in 1959. In range, it is an alto Kithara, while Kithara II is a bass Kithara.

In overall shape, this instrument is very much like the ancient kithara (frequently depicted on vases), but there are some notable deviations. The tops of the two arms and the bottom are open, as in the ancient instrument, but the top part of the hollow base, between the two arms, is also open, allowing the strings to fasten below bridges attached to soundboards inside of this base, rather than passing over a bridge outside the instrument.[8]

In all three Kitharas, seventy-two strings are grouped in twelve series of sixes, with each series running across the instrument from front to back. Some of the hexads represent the 1–3–5–7–9–11 Identities of one of the Primary Tonalities, although never in that order—and, indeed, 11 is entirely missing from Kithara I. The strings on Kithara I are either guitar or tenor-guitar.

The hexads are numbered 1 to 12 on the sloping ledge at the top of the hollow base on the playing side. (These numbers play an important role in notation—see below, page 230.) Four of the hexads—1–6–7–12—have Pyrex glass tubes or rods between strings and soundboards—tubes 5/8 inch in outside diameter on 1 and 12, 1/2 inch on 6 and 7. These act as movable bridges, and produce either sliding sounds or the intonation of any higher tone or tonality desired. Ascending ratios, computed on the basis of the 1 Identity

---

[7] An article I wrote describing the Ptolemy, and including a photograph, appeared in *Musical Opinion* (London), June, 1935.

[8] Dimensions: Kithara I, including the added base and the feet (with casters) which support it, totals about 71 inches in height. The instrument proper is 46 1/4 inches high and 43 inches wide at its broadest point; it is 8 3/4 inches deep at the bottom and 4 inches deep at the tips of the hollow arms. The added resonator beneath the instrument proper is 21 1/2 inches high, 43 inches wide at the bottom, and 9 3/4 inches deep.

KITHARA I

KITHARA I (PLAYING AREA)

string in each of these four hexads, are painted in white or colored lacquers along each vertical edge on both sides of the instrument, since it is sometimes played from the opposite side. The eight other hexads are always used *open* (in a guitar sense); the four with rods are *open* when the rods are at the top (as in the photograph).

Much of the time, and especially in ascending chordal strokes away from himself, the player uses a plectrum (generally on the index finger) which is inserted into a section of pressed-paper or plastic tubing at right angles to the length of the finger; he uses the ball of the middle finger in descending chordal strokes toward himself. When the left hand is concerned with rod control, the right hand plays strings, and vice versa. When gliding or sliding sounds are indicated, it is of utmost importance that the rod *begin its move immediately.* Otherwise the beautiful strength of the gliding resonance is lost. The BMI seen in my scores means: *begin move immediately.* It is also important for the Kitharist to develop callouses, especially on the middle fingers of both hands. The tone created by a calloused finger is strong and resonant; that produced by soft, pink skin is timid, trivial.

The instrument is in two major parts firmly bolted together: the instrument proper, with 1/4-inch redwood ply skins, and the additional resonator, of 3/4-inch fir plywood stained to resemble redwood. Thin, vertical-grain redwood soundboards extend inside the ply skins from the top of the hollow base of the instrument proper to the floor of the added base, or resonator, and are firmly glued to the sides and floor.

The tuning given in the first edition has not been used since 1952. The close bass intervals of that tuning often produced a muddy effect, and in all later tunings the bass tones have been spread considerably. In the reconstruction of 1959, the string lengths were shortened, thus helping to produce the alto register.

The lowest tone, in Hexads 7 and 8, is 1/1–98; the highest, in Hexad 12, is the 6/5 above 1/1–392.

As indicated in the tuning chart, the third and fourth strings of Hexad 3 are the same pitch, 16/9, and the fourth and fifth strings of both Hexads 5 and 6 are the same, 20/11 and 7/4. It will also be noted, through comparison with

TUNING OF KITHARA I

| | 1 | 2 | 3 | 4 | 5 | 6 | 7 | 8 | 9 | 10 | 11 | 12 |
|---|---|---|---|---|---|---|---|---|---|---|---|---|
| **Highest 2/1** | 8/7 | | 8/7 | | | 7/6 | 7/6 | | | | 7/6 | 6/5 |
| | | 11/10 | 10/9 | | | | | | 33/32 | | 9/8 | |
| | | | | | | | | | 1/1 | 1/1 | 1/1 | |
| | | | | | 15/8 | | | | | | | |
| | | | 16/9 | | 20/11 | 7/4 | | | | | | |
| | | | 16/9 | 9/5 | 20/11 | 7/4 | | | | | | |
| **Middle 2/1** | 12/7 | | | | | | 5/3 | | | 5/3 | | 12/7 |
| | | 11/7 | | 3/2 | | | 3/2 | 8/5 | 8/5 | | 3/2 | 3/2 |
| | 10/7 | 11/8 | 4/3 | | 16/11 | 7/5 | | | | | | |
| | 9/7 | 11/10 | | | | 7/6 | | 8/7 | 6/5 | 10/9 | | 6/5 |
| | 1/1 | | | 1/1 | | | | 1/1 | | 1/1 | 1/1 | 1/1 |
| | 12/7 | 11/6 | | 9/5 | | | | | | | | 12/7 |
| **Lowest 2/1** | | | | 3/2 | | | 5/3 | 8/5 | 8/5 | 5/3 | 3/2 | |
| | | 11/8 | 4/3 | | 16/11 | | 4/3 | 4/3 | | 10/7 | | |
| | | | | 9/7 | | 7/6 | | | 6/5 | | | |
| | | | | | 12/11 | | 1/1 | 1/1 | | | | |
| **Hexads** | 1 | 2 | 3 | 4 | 5 | 6 | 7 | 8 | 9 | 10 | 11 | 12 |
| **Tonalities** | 8/7– O | 11/8– U | 16/9– O | 9/8– U | 16/11– O | 7/4– U | 4/3– O | 1/1– U | 8/5– O | 5/4– U | 1/1– O | 3/2– U |

the Tonality Diamond (page 110), that Identities 7, 9, and 11 are missing in Hexads 3, 5, 6, and 9; that Identities 5, 7, and 11 are missing in Hexad 11; that Identities 9 and 11 are missing in Hexads 2, 8, and 12; that Identities 1 and 11 are missing in Hexads 4 and 10; and that Identity 11 is missing in Hexad 1. Moreover, Hexads 3, 5, 9, and 11 reveal their highest tones as inharmonic (somewhat like the high tones of Adapted Guitar II)—as close intervals beyond harmonic tones. The only explanation for these chords is that they fill a particular musical requirement.


## New Kithara I

There are at least five good reasons for duplicating an instrument, or for seeming to "duplicate" it:

1. These instruments are very mortal. They are fragile. Unlike the piano, not one has two hundred years of manufacturing know-how behind it. A truck carrying the instruments could overturn in a storm or go up in flames; and it would be comforting to have a few replacements left behind. I have been ex-

NEW KITHARA I (PLAYING SIDE)

traordinarily lucky in fulfilling my commitments so far. Nothing of the sort has happened, even transporting instruments several hundred to a thousand miles, with only one or two days leeway, before going on stage with a dramatic. work or some kind of show.

2. It is always my purpose, in building a duplication, to make a better instrument, one more playable, more resonant—to *correct* obvious mistakes of past years. This is particularly so with New Kithara I. The instrument uses exactly the same tuning as the original Kithara I.

3. A different idea or attitude about the musical purpose of an instrument: thus, while Harmonic Canon II (see below) was built for a sitting player, Harmonic Canon III is for a standing player, thereby making percussion techniques on the strings more effective. (Nevertheless, Harmonic Canons II and III are always interchangeable.)

4. A different concept in regard to tuning: although Harmonic Canon I and New Harmonic Canon I (see below) are interchangeable, they are not immediately so. It would take at least a couple of hours to remove and replace bridges, remove and replace strings, and then tune all eighty-eight strings correctly. (Still, both Harmonic Canon I's follow the same concept; therefore, the roman numeral is not changed.)

5. A different acoustical motivation: Boo I (see Chapter 13) has sections of bamboo that are all closed at one end, while Boo II has sections open at both ends, resulting in a different impact on the ear, just as one pipe organ stop sounds different from another. However, for all practical purposes in my music, Boos I and II are interchangeable.

In the case of New Kithara I, completed at Encinitas in 1972,[9] the first two reasons apply. It is not a new concept and the roman numeral is not changed. But it is an infinitely improved instrument, with much greater resonance, especially in Hexads 2 through 11. It corrects fundamental mistakes made as early as 1938 (see Appendix VI).

Unlike old Kithara I, the resonators for Hexads 2 through 11 go straight to the bottom board at the floor (see photograph), and the soundboards are not cluttered with fixtures to hold the ends of the strings. In this case bronze wires (they are not sympathetic strings), attached at the bottoms of the soundboards,

---

[9] During the past two years I have been assisted by James W. Aitkenhead in building New Kithara I (1972), New Harmonic Canon I (1971), and the percussion instruments (Chapter 13) Boo II (1972) and Mbira Bass Dyad (1972), as well as in replacing the blocks on the Bass Marimba and the Quadrangularis Reversum (both 1971).

are looped with the lower ends of the strings just below the playing area, thus allowing the soundboards to vibrate freely.[10]

## Kithara II

When Kithara I was restrung and retuned in 1952 in order to spread the hexads over a wider range of pitch, I realized that I was not getting the kind of bass resonance that I needed. To correct this fault I built Kithara II in Sausalito in 1954 and transferred to it the new 1952 tuning of Kithara I.

The instrument consists essentially of six large resonators (see photograph)—the two outside arms and the four between—all held in place by 1/4-inch redwood ply skins. The bridges attach to two soundboards of 1/4-inch Sitka spruce on each resonator; all soundboards are at least five feet in length and are firmly stationed on the floor of the instrument. The front and back sides of the resonators are 3/4-inch redwood. Because of this Kithara's height, the player must stand on a riser, and this functions as an added resonator, open at both ends, and with an opening into the instrument proper (not seen in the photograph).[11]

Pyrex rods are used on four hexads—1, 2, 11, and 12. Eight strips of wood, four on each side of these hexads, show the ratios available for higher chords and tones, with each ratio computed on the basis of the 1 Identity of

---

[10] Dimensions: New Kithara I is 76 inches high from the floor to the top of the music rack, including the casters. The width, or breadth, across the front of the instrument is 48 inches at the bottom, 48 inches at the center (just below the playing area), and 43 1/2 inches at the top (measured to the tips of the outside arms). The stabilizers at both ends of the base are 22 inches deep. Of the five resonators beneath the playing area, the four outer ones are 9 1/4 inches deep at the bottom and 7 1/4 inches deep at the top; the central resonator measures the same as the other four at these points and is 4 3/4 inches deep at its top. There is not a single right angle in the entire instrument proper except in the aluminum L's which tie the outside arms together near the top.

[11] Dimensions: The total height of Kithara II is 81 inches, not counting the music rack or the additional walnut triangles which hold the tuning gears. The width at the bottom is 55 inches, and this tapers to 38 inches at the tips of the two outside resonators. The length of the wooden pieces (across the breadth of the instrument at the top) which hold the walnut triangles within the aluminum L's is 40 3/4 inches. The depth of the instrument, including the 1/4-inch skins, is 7 3/4 inches throughout. The added base, to which the instrument is firmly bolted, is 16 3/4 inches high, 51 1/2 inches across, and 24 inches deep. A detached riser, similar to the first, is available for the opposite side of Kithara II, since it is sometimes played from that side, particularly in *The Bewitched* and *Daphne*. The tops of both risers are covered with a reddish linoleum.

KITHARA II

## TUNING OF KITHARA II

| | | 1 | 2 | 3 | 4 | 5 | 6 | 7 | 8 | 9 | 10 | 11 | 12 |
|---|---|---|---|---|---|---|---|---|---|---|---|---|---|
| Highest 2/1 | | | 11/7 | | | 20/11 | 7/4 | 5/3 | 8/5 | | | | |
| | | 10/7 | 11/8 | | | | 7/5 | | 16/11 | | 10/7 | 11/8 | 3/2 |
| | | 9/7 | | 11/9 | 9/7 | 14/11 | 7/6 | 7/6 | 8/7 | 6/5 | | 5/4 | 6/5 |
| | | | 11/10 | 10/9 | | | | | | 11/10 | | 9/8 | |
| | | 1/1 | | 1/1 | | 1/1 | | | | 1/1 | 1/1 | | 1/1 |
| | | 12/7 | | | 9/5 | | | 11/6 | 16/9 | 9/5 | 20/11 | | 12/7 |
| Middle 2/1 | | | 11/7 | 14/9 | 18/11 | 18/11 | 14/9 | | | | 5/3 | | |
| | | 10/7 | | | 3/2 | | | 3/2 | | 7/5 | | 3/2 | 3/2 |
| | | 8/7 | | | 9/8 | 12/11 | | | | | | 5/4 | 6/5 |
| | | | | | | | 1/1 | 1/1 | 1/1 | | | 1/1 | |
| Lowest 2/1 | | | 11/6 | 16/9 | | | | | | | | | |
| | | | | | 3/2 | | | | | 8/5 | 5/3 | 3/2 | |
| | | | 11/8 | 4/3 | | 16/11 | 7/5 | 4/3 | 4/3 | | | | |
| Hexads | | 1 | 2 | 3 | 4 | 5 | 6 | 7 | 8 | 9 | 10 | 11 | 12 |
| Tonalities | | 8/7– O | 11/8– U | 16/9– O | 9/8– U | 16/11– O | 7/4– U | 4/3– O | 1/1– U | 8/5– O | 5/3– U | 1/1– O | 3/2– U |

each hexad. Except in *Revelation*, when three to five of the strings of each of these four hexads were made unisons, the tuning has remained unchanged for all its music.

The lowest tones are the three 4/3's, a 4/3 above 1/1–49 (about 65 cycles, the lowest cello tone). The six lowest strings are mando-cello fourths; the others are either guitar or tenor-guitar strings.

Comparing the hexads with the Tonality Diamond (page 110), we find that the 7 Identity is missing in Hexad 11, the 9 Identity in 4 and 10, the 11 Identity in 1 and 6, and Identities 9 and 11 in 2 and 12. However, five hexads—3, 5, 7, 8, and 9—show all six identities, 1–3–5–7–9–11.

All the large instruments are invariably on stage during a performance, and the players standing on risers are likely to be very conspicuous, These, more than others, must be actors, and footwork—especially on this large Kithara and on the Bass Marimba—must be graceful and agile, since hands must move with lightning speed. For a downward glide of the Pyrex rod, the Kitharist may want to move downward himself in order to see exactly what he is doing. If so, it is very important that he does not bend at the waist, like an amateur California prune picker, but that he keep the trunk vertical while doing a knee bend. This movement is athletic, graceful, a kind of functional dance.

## Kithara Notation

The notation for the Kitharas might be called a number-correlation system at least partially divorced from ratios. If the instruments were cut through horizontally, the strings would give the appearance of seventy-two dots in twelve series of six each, thus:

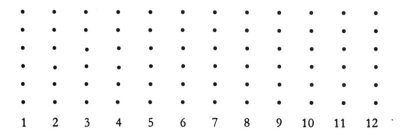

If we then set this pattern of dots on an ordinary five-line staff without clef or "key signature," it would appear as below—an example of a distinctive notation demanded by the individuality of the instrument.

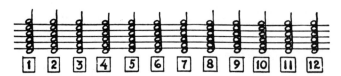

When a full quick chord is desired, it is written as above; if it is to be played in running style away from the player it is written  ;

if desired in running style toward the player, ![music] ;

and if a single tone is wanted, say the third string in the third hexad, it is written ![music]

When the four Pyrex rods or tubes are in the highest position on any Kithara, the strings are *open*, and the respective hexad numbers are used. However, when movement of the rods is required, colors substitute for the hexad number in order to avoid number-ratio confusion. Thus, on Kithara I, Hexad 1 (with sliding rod) is called *green*, Hexad 6 is *middle green*, or *MG*; Hexad 7 is *middle orange*, or *MO*; Hexad 12 is *orange*. On Kithara II Hexad 1 is *green*, 2 is *violet*, 11 is *red*, and 12 is *orange*. The notation, for example:

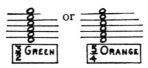

The respective colors are shown on the instruments, generally above the lists of ratios, in small colored moons. The ratios for ascending tones or chords cover approximately a 2/1 on Kithara I, and considerably more on Kithara II.

## *Surrogate Kithara*

The first Kithara parts, beginning in the early 1940's, were generally not easy, but they were not impossible either. In 1952 I wrote a dance work, *Castor and Pollux*, incorporating a Kithara part which, if played well, would have to rank as virtuosic. I very soon realized that the part would need help, and I built the Surrogate, or substitute, or assistant, Kithara at Sausalito in 1953, and divided the virtuoso part between the two.

The Surrogate Kithara consists of two resonators, or canons, fitted over tight dowels atop a lower and strengthening resonator, the whole mounted on a triangular base with a low seat at the apex for the player.[12] Pyrex rods— 1/2-inch—are used on both canons, and—in order to conform to Kithara notation, and corresponding to Kithara hexads 1 and 12—the upper (8/7–O) is called *green* and the lower (3/2–U) *orange*.

Pairs of mandolin tuning gears are used here, and each canon therefore has eight strings, rather than the Kithara's six. Boards showing the ascending ratios are attached to the front edge of each canon, and in the notation for a

---

[12] Dimensions: Each resonator is 36 inches long, 4 1/2 inches high, 5 1/2 inches deep. The Sitka-spruce soundboards are 26 1/2 inches long. The strengthening resonator beneath the canons is 36 inches long, 15 inches deep, 3 inches high beneath the first canon (orange), 5 3/8 inches high beneath the second (green). The seat on the triangular base is 14 inches high and 24 1/2 inches wide at the front; the sides of the base are 38 inches long.

SURROGATE KITHARA

particular work the desired ratio appears beneath the note or notes—5/3 (orange), 4/3 (green), and so on. The notation, showing placement of notes for the eight strings, is as follows:

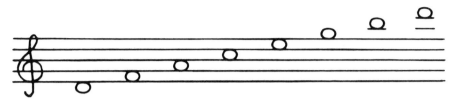

The original tuning, showing approximate pitches on five-line staves with clef signs, and the ratios below:

## GREEN

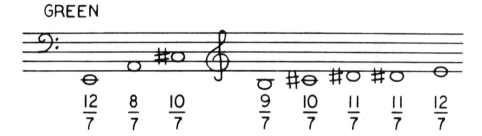

$$\frac{12}{7} \quad \frac{8}{7} \quad \frac{10}{7} \quad \frac{9}{7} \quad \frac{10}{7} \quad \frac{11}{7} \quad \frac{11}{7} \quad \frac{12}{7}$$

## ORANGE

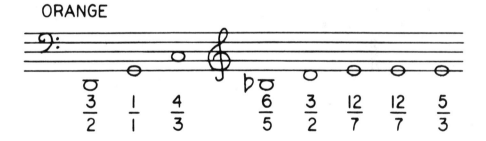

$$\frac{3}{2} \quad \frac{1}{1} \quad \frac{4}{3} \quad \frac{6}{5} \quad \frac{3}{2} \quad \frac{12}{7} \quad \frac{12}{7} \quad \frac{5}{3}$$

This tuning was used in the *Dances, The Bewitched,* and *Daphne*. In later works the tuning was almost totally different, and in order to avoid restringing and retuning, I built two more resonators for these works, and in particular for *Petals* and *Delusion*. These fit over the same dowels in the base. The later tuning:

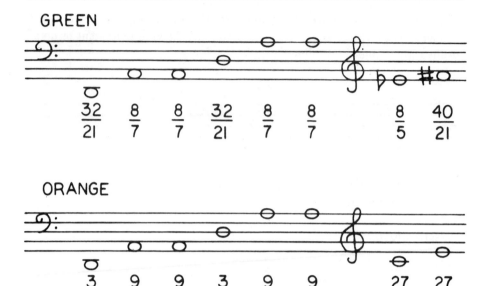

GREEN

$$\frac{32}{21} \quad \frac{8}{7} \quad \frac{8}{7} \quad \frac{32}{21} \quad \frac{8}{7} \quad \frac{8}{7} \quad\quad\quad \frac{8}{5} \quad \frac{40}{21}$$

ORANGE

$$\frac{3}{2} \quad \frac{9}{8} \quad \frac{9}{8} \quad \frac{3}{2} \quad \frac{9}{8} \quad \frac{9}{8} \quad\quad\quad \frac{27}{20} \quad \frac{27}{16}$$

It should be noted that in the first tuning of the 3/2–U resonator (orange), only the 11 Udentity is missing, while there is an inharmonic 5/3 as the highest tone. In the tuning of the 8/7–O resonator (green), only the 7 Odentity is missing. In the second tuning, the orange resonator might be considered the 3/2 Otonality with an inharmonic 27/20, or as a combination of 3/2–O and 27/20–O (both secondary). The green resonator is essentially 32/21–O with an inharmonic 8/5. The orange ratio board is valid for both tunings, but the green ratio board must be replaced for the second tuning.

    The instrument has turned out to be both more versatile and more musical than could have been anticipated. This is at least partly because human hands seem to be able to do more with a horizontal playing surface than with a vertical one (this was also discovered in the case of the Marimba Eroica—see page 276). The koto technique of controlling intonation with pressure by the left hand is very easy, while percussion techniques are well-suited to horizontal strings and are extensively used in *The Bewitched, Petals*, and *Delusion*. My comments in connection with Kithara I about competent use of the Pyrex rods also apply here.

The Surrogate Kithara has a brighter quality than any of the Kitharas, and especially Kithara I, which tends to be lyrical and melancholy. The sound is even brash, and the player must hold this quality in check.

In the *U.S. Highball* part, where in several passages the left fingers depress strings to the left of the rod while the right hand picks, the playing must be precisely rhythmic and vigorous, whether loud or soft. Callouses must be developed so that the fingers may truly dig in.

## Harmonic Canon I

This was originally the Harmonic Canon depicted and explained in the first edition (built at the University of Wisconsin in 1945), but that version was not used between 1953 and the summer of 1959, when it went through a major reconception and reconstruction at the University of Illinois. It is this reconceived instrument which will be explained here.

The soundbox has been shortened, a clear plastic base substituted for the former redwood base (now holding Harmonic Canon II), a 1/4-inch redwood belly substituted for the former grooved belly, and, most important, forty-four strings have been added to the original forty-four.[13]

The original set of forty-four strings—now called the A Set—is parallel to the belly, from right nut to tuning gears. The lowest eight strings of this set in the tilted instrument (see photograph) are guitar fifths, the next eight guitar fourths, and the remaining twenty-eight guitar seconds. The additional forty-four strings—called the X Set—are located exactly between the strings of the A Set, and are at a slight angle to the belly. The right nut for this set is approximately 3/8-inch higher than that of the A Set, and the X strings descend to bridges 3/16-inch high near the left nut, then through holes in the oak end to tuning gears of their own on a piece of birch 1 3/4 inches below the birch piece of the A Set. The eight X strings nearest the player are guitar firsts, and the remaining thirty-six are tenor-guitar firsts.

The all-important bridges are necessarily of two kinds. Those for the X Set are castellated so as to allow the A-Set strings (passing above) free vi-

---

[13] Dimensions: The total width of Harmonic Canon I, including tuning gears, is 35 inches, while that of the soundboard is 25 inches. The soundbox is 27 1/2 inches deep and 3 1/2 inches high. The instrument proper is removable from the base, which is 19 inches deep at the bottom and 28 inches deep across its slanting top. The base is almost 28 inches wide.

## TUNING OF HARMONIC CANON I FOR *PETALS* AND *DELUSION*

| String numbers | | String numbers | |
|---|---|---|---|
| **A SET** | | **X SET** (with the rod at its highest point) | |
| 44—10/9 | (above 1/1–196) | 44—16/9 | (below 1/1–1568, or—third "F" above "middle C") |
| 43 | | 43— 5/3 | |
| 42 | | 42— 4/3 | |
| 41 | | 41—10/9 | |
| 40 | | 40— 1/1–784 | |
| 39 | | 39—16/9 | |
| 38 | | 38— 8/5 | |
| 37 | | 37— 4/3 | |
| 36— 7/6 | | 36—14/9 | |
| 35 | | 35—32/21 | |
| 34 | | 34— 3/2 | |
| 33 | | 33—40/27 | |
| 32 | | 32—16/11 | |
| 31 | | 31—10/7 | |
| 30 | | 30— 7/5 | |
| 29 | | 29—11/8 | |
| 28— 9/8 | | 28—27/20 | |
| 27 | | 27 | |
| 26 | | 26 | |
| 25 | | 25 | |
| 24 | | 24 | |
| 23 | | 23 | |
| 22—21/20 | | 22—21/16 | |
| 21 | | 21 | |
| 20 | | 20 | |
| 19 | | 19 | |
| 18 | | 18 | |
| 17 | | 17 | |

HARMONIC CANON I

HARMONIC CANON I (PLAYING AREA)

(Beginning of the Pyrex rod area)

| 16— 4/3 (above 1/1–98) | 16— 4/3 (above 1/1–392) |
|---|---|
| 15 | 15 |
| 14 | 14 |
| 13 | 13 |
| 12 | 12 |
| 11 | 11 |
| 10 | 10 |
| 9 | 9 |

| 8—16/9 (below 1/1–98) | 8—16/15 (just above 1/1–392—"A♭") |
|---|---|
| 7 | 7 |
| 6 | 6 |
| 5 | 5 |
| 4 | 4 |
| 3 | 3 |
| 2 | 2 |
| 1 | 1 |

bration, while those for the A Set resemble miniature Roman aqueducts, thus allowing free vibration for the X-Set strings (passing beneath).

Two slanting vertical-grain redwood boards, or ramps, are glued to the belly under the lowest sixteen strings, and a 14-inch length of 1/2-inch Pyrex rod is inserted between the X strings and the slanting boards. A row of ratios is on the left front of the belly, indicating descending tones, with the use of the rod, from the top position, as shown in the photograph.[13]

Because the two sets of strings are on different planes, one may play the X Set only, near the right nut; the A Set only, toward the left part of the instrument; or both sets simultaneously at the point of intersection. This point is constant except for the lowest sixteen strings of each set. When the rod is high on the ramps, to the right, the point of intersection is close by the rod, but when the rod is far to the left, the point of intersection moves to the right. Tuning, because of the musical potentialities of the intersecting strings, becomes an intriguing problem.

The transformed instrument was first used in *Revelation*, where the tuning was radically different from the second tuning used until recently in both *Petals* and *Delusion*. Since the second tuning is shown in the photograph, that one will be explained.

The lowest sixteen strings of the A Set function as a drone on a 3/2 interval. Although the 16/9 (just below 1/1–98) and 4/3 is the basic tuning, the drone bridge may be moved toward the right to achieve a 40/21–10/7 drone, for example, or a 1/1–3/2 drone.

This plan does not involve significantly harmonious intersecting strings for the eight highest strings of the two sets. But, moving downward, from strings 36 through 29, there is a microtonally descending series of tones in the X Set against a lower 7/6 in the A Set; next (strings 28 through 23), a 27/20—X Set—which is a 12/5 interval higher than 9/8—A Set (an "octave" and a "minor third"); then (strings 22 through 17), a 21/16—X Set—which is a 5/2 interval above 21/20—A Set (an "octave" and a "major third"). Finally, this resolves by the small interval 64/63 (about a fourth of a semitone) upward to the 4/3 Utonality if all sixteen strings of the drone are sounded.

A totally different musical effect was obtained in the first sixteen strings of the two sets in the tuning for *Revelation*. The drone strings were tuned slightly higher—the 3/2 interval from 40/21 upward to 10/7, and the first eight of the X strings were also tuned to 10/7 (two 2/1's higher), while the next eight strings were tuned to 16/11, higher than 10/7 by the small interval 56/55 (less than a third of a semitone). No matter where the bar was moved, this parallel small-interval dissonance appeared and bestowed a strange and exciting quality to melodic phrases.

Before leaving Harmonic Canon I, three subjects need to be touched upon briefly—notation, playing techniques, and the care of strings. Notation: string numbers are indicated on strips of paper pasted to strips of thin plywood mounted above the belly so that they do not interfere with the vibrations of the strings (see photograph), the A Set of numbers to the left, the X Set to the right. Notation is entirely a matter of string numbers, with the appropriate stems indicating rhythm. The notation is only very slightly graphic, and staves are used only because they are convenient in a full score. When the playing of both sets becomes sufficiently complex, two staves, united by a bracket, are used, with the X Set on the upper staff and the A Set on the lower one. The following example, from Verse 9 of *Petals*, shows the X set played by the right hand and the A Set played by the left hand. (The other part of the duet, not shown, is Kithara I.)

The playing techniques are different from any of the common techniques on current instruments. Picks are used nearly always, fingers only occasionally. It seems almost automatic for a musician new to the instrument to whip a pick daintily in the air. This is totally wrong; the pick must generally be used in a strong, digging manner (indeed this injunction could be applied to the playing of all of my instruments, excepting only the Chromelodeons). The manner can sometimes be in the nature of a caress, but more often it should be an assault.

The tone is much better when the pick is held as flat against the string as possible, whether proceeding down or up. The flip from down to up or up to down must be accomplished with lightning speed, and the pick should never be held in the air. After a string or series of strings, is plucked, the pick rests firmly on the succeeding string, down or up, ready to plunge onward or to reverse. This results in maximum control.

A diagram showing both the vibration of a string plucked in a downward manner with a flat pick and that of a string plucked with the sideward motion of a straight vertical pick, would demonstrate clearly that the flat pick is critical for good tone. The initial attack *downward* causes a vibration pattern *away* from the grooves of the bridges and nuts, not *in* them.

As to the area to be played, strings picked close to the nut, either right or left, give a sharp, nasal tone, while those plucked halfway between nut and movable bridges give a full tone; in nearly all fast-running passages, playing should be center, between bridges and nut. Accompanying chords, generally by the left hand, should always be center, and should be soft. When vibrato by the left hand in the left portions of the strings is called for, the left fingers dig down *near* the bridge, and the forearm vibrates *down and up*, not forward and back.

The care of strings: until rust-resistant steel strings become commonplace, removal of rust with a small piece of emory cloth is an ever-recurrent chore. This is especially important where the Pyrex rods are used under strings. The moving of the rod under rusty strings causes a diabolically irritating sound. (This is true for the Kitharas, for Surrogate Kithara, and for Harmonic Canons I and II and New Harmonic Canon I, whenever rods are used.) A little paraffin on the rod (very little!) often helps. The wound strings are less of a problem, but even they are improved when refurbished and jiggled in curves to remove dirt.

## New Harmonic Canon I

In the discussion of New Kithara I (see above), five reasons were given for making duplicates, or seeming "duplicates." In the case of New Harmonic Canon I, completed at Encinitas in 1972, the first, second, and fourth reasons apply—the fourth in particular. The large amount of time-consuming work involved in shifting from one tuning to another almost necessitates a different instrument for a new tuning. New Harmonic Canon I is tuned to the requirements of *Petals* and *Delusion*, while the first Harmonic Canon I now reverts to its 1959 tuning for *Revelation*.

The immediate visual differences in the new instrument are the alternating redwood and Sitka-spruce soundboards, the partially circular music rack, and the blue-tinted (but transparent) structure that holds the canon, in contrast to the clear Plexiglas of the 1959 instrument.

The measurements of New Harmonic Canon I are almost identical with those of the first instrument. Exceptions: the two oak pieces to which the strings are attached are thicker, increasing the width across the front about one inch (excluding tuning gears); and the lower tuning gear board (to the left in the photograph) extends about one inch further to permit easier access.

## Harmonic Canon II

This instrument was built in Sausalito in 1953 to replace the original Harmonic Canon I. It consists of two identical boxes, or canons (see photograph), which are distinguished in all scores by the names of the classical astral twins, Castor and Pollux. Castor is on the left and Pollux is on the right. The stringing is not identical. All forty-four strings of Pollux are guitar seconds,

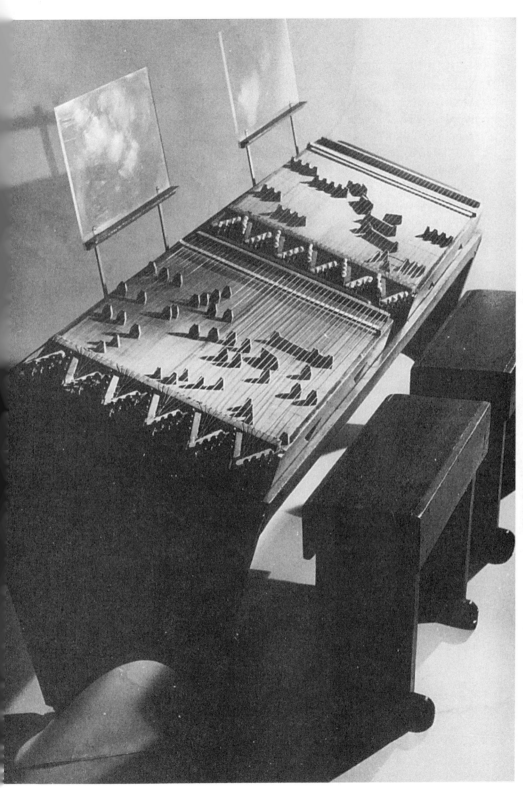

HARMONIC CANON II (CASTOR AND POLLUX)

while only the top twenty-two of Castor are guitar seconds; the twenty-two at the bottom are guitar fifths. The two boxes rest in a large tray and are removable. The two endpieces of the structure are the thick redwood sections from the original Canon I.[14]

The harmonic canon idea (harmonic law) is that of a glorified multiple monochord, and once the design and placement of bridges and the tuning of strings is decided, at least half of the creative concept is established. And this half may be just as imaginative as the writing of actual notes. Furthermore, slight readjustment of the same bridges also can result in a totally different musical effect. The bridges on Pollux, as shown in the photograph, are for the dance work *Castor and Pollux*, and the part is somewhat brash, even strident; but the same bridges, placed differently, were also used in *The Bewitched*, and the effect, much of the time, was moody and melancholy. The settings shown on Castor are those for *Two Studies on Ancient Greek Scales*: 1. Study on Olympos' Pentatonic; and 2. Study on Archytas' Enharmonic. These settings will be outlined.

*Castor*: Tuning of the higher twenty-two strings for the pentatonic scale. Those ratios representing tones within the second 2/1 of this part of the instrument are shown with lines above and below.

| String number | Chord | String number | Scale | String number | Chord |
|---|---|---|---|---|---|
| 44 | $\overline{6/5}$ | 37 | 1/1 | 28 | 2/1 |
| 43 | 8/5 | 36 | 9/8 | 27 | 3/2 |
| 42 | 6/5 | 35 | 6/5 | 26 | 1/1 |
| 41 | $\overline{6/5}$ | 34 | 3/2 | 25 | 2/1 |
| 40 | 8/5 | 33 | 8/5 | 24 | 3/2 |
| 39 | 6/5 | 32 | 2/1 | 23 | 1/1 |
| 38 | $\overline{6/5}$ | 31 | $\overline{9/8}$ | | |
| | | 30 | $\overline{6/5}$ | | |
| | | 29 | $\overline{3/2}$ | | |

Note that the five-tone scale is partially repeated in the next higher 2/1, and that the two chords are essentially duads taken from tones of the scale.

[14] Dimensions: Each canon is 30 1/2 inches broad, with an extra 5 3/8 inches for the tuning gears; each is 22 3/4 inches deep and 5 1/2 inches high to the top of the Sitka-spruce belly, or soundboard. The angled base is 73 3/4 inches long across the broad front, 26 inches high at the front, 33 inches high at the back, 25 inches deep across the top, and 19 1/2 inches deep at the bottom.

*Castor:* Tuning of the lower twenty-two strings for the enharmonic scale. These strings are all within one 2/1.

| String number | Chord | String number | Scale | String number | Chord |
|---|---|---|---|---|---|
| 22 | 16/15 | 15 | 2/1 | 7 | 2/1 |
| 21 | 8/5 | 14 | 8/5 | 6 | 8/5 |
| 20 | 4/3 | 13 | 14/9 | 5 | 4/3 |
| 19 | 16/15 | 12 | 3/2 | 4 | 2/1 |
| 18 | 8/5 | 11 | 4/3 | 3 | 8/5 |
| 17 | 4/3 | 10 | 16/15 | 2 | 4/3 |
| 16 | 16/15 | 9 | 28/27 | 1 | 1/1 |
|  |  | 8 | 1/1 |  |  |

Note that the accompanying chords are triads taken from the tones of the scale.

| Left | String number | Right | Left | String number | Right | String number | Right | Left | String number | Right |
|---|---|---|---|---|---|---|---|---|---|---|
| 14/9 | 44 | $\overline{4/3}$ | $\overline{7/4}$ | 33 | 9/8 | 22 | 11/6 | $\overline{64/33}$ | 12 | 10/9 |
| $\overline{16/9}$ | 43 | 4/3 | 7/4 | 32 | $\overline{9/8}$ | 21 | 16/9 | $\overline{16/11}$ | 11 | 7/6 |
| 14/9 | 42 | $\overline{4/3}$ | $\overline{7/4}$ | 31 | 9/8 | 20 | 8/5 |  | 10 | 4/3 |
| $\overline{16/9}$ | 41 | 4/3 | 7/4 | 30 | $\overline{9/8}$ | 19 | 16/11 |  | 9 | 21/20 |
| 14/9 | 40 | $\overline{4/3}$ |  | 29 | $\overline{9/7}$ | 18 | 10/7 |  | 8 | 1/1 |
| $\overline{16/9}$ | 39 | 4/3 |  | 28 | $\overline{11/10}$ | 17 | 7/5 | 40/21 | 7 | 2/1 |
| 14/9 | 38 | $\overline{4/3}$ |  | 27 | $\overline{11/8}$ | 16 | 7/4 | $\overline{40/27}$ | 6 | 7/6 |
| $\overline{7/4}$ | 37 | 9/8 |  | 26 | $\overline{11/7}$ | 15 | 15/8 | 40/21 | 5 | 2/1 |
| 7/4 | 36 | $\overline{9/8}$ |  | 25 | $\overline{7/5}$ | 14 | 2/1 | $\overline{40/27}$ | 4 | 7/6 |
| $\overline{7/4}$ | 35 | 9/8 |  | 24 | $\overline{7/6}$ | 13 | 14/9 | 40/21 | 3 | 2/1 |
| 7/4 | 34 | $\overline{9/8}$ |  | 23 | $\overline{9/8}$ |  |  | $\overline{40/27}$ | 2 | 7/6 |
|  |  |  |  |  |  |  |  | 40/21 | 1 | 2/1 |

*Pollux*: Bridge settings for *Castor and Pollux*. In this setting the tones to the left of the bridges are also important in more than half of the strings; the bridges must be placed to obtain the correct tones both to the right and to the left. As before, ratios intended to sound in the second 2/1 of the instrument are shown with lines above and below.

With no bridges whatever on the canons, the open guitar second strings should be tuned to approximately the 16/9 below 1/1–196 and the guitar fifths (lower half of Castor) to about the 16/9 below 1/1–98. (This is true for Harmonic Canons II and III in general, whatever the particular work to be performed.) The strings are lax, with or without bridges, and I find them preferable. One can do so much more with a lax string provided the tension is great enough to give a true tone.

The very different conception and tuning of Harmonic Canon II for *Revelation* did not, in fact, use bridges. Instead, redwood ramps (somewhat like those of Harmonic Canon I), extending one-half to three-quarters or more across each canon, were attached to the soundboard of each with impermanent rubber cement, and Pyrex rods, 3/4 inch in diameter, were inserted between the ramps and strings. With these large rods moving under twenty-two strings, powerful gliding tones were possible. Both picks and sticks (for percussive striking) were used. The sticks were 3/8-inch dowels, felted or unfelted, with handles designed so that a section of the dowel equal to the extent of twenty-two strings could strike flat.

Notation: the following example of Harmonic Canon notation is from *Oedipus*. *Cas* means the Left Canon of Harmonic Canon II (Castor and Pollux). The example shows the melody played by the right hand, right of bridges, and sweeps by the left hand, left of bridges, on bracketed staves. (One staff is all that is necessary much of the time.)

## Harmonic Canon III

The joy of the Harmonic Canon lies in its challenge to the imagination. Although it is susceptible to an infinite variety of concepts in bridge placement

HARMONIC CANON III (BLUE RAINBOW)

and design, its limitation rests in the difficulty of making changes once a setting has been determined. With a return to earlier settings or tunings, it was almost inevitable that other canons would become necessary. Harmonic Canon III, built in Venice, California, in 1965, was the result. It actually has three canons, although only two are shown in the photograph. The height from belly, or soundboard, to string level without bridges is the same in all five canons of Harmonic Canons II and III; therefore, the bridges designed for a particular work will fit on any of the five.

Because of the blue-painted arch that supports the tray for the canons (as before, they are removable), the instrument is generally notated as the Blue Rainbow. The arch is made from two sections of 1/4-inch plywood scored and glued together; and although the top of the arch is firmly glued and screwed to the center of the tray, that point acts nevertheless as a fulcrum, so that in vigorous playing with sticks, as in *Delusion*, the canons sway lightly up and down in rhythm with the action of the sticks, thus adding a visually dynamic element to the music. The sticks are 3/8-inch dowels angled so that either end will strike flat against eleven strings; one end is felted for softer playing, the other is unfelted.[15]

Since the photograph shows the setting for *Petals* and *Delusion*, this tuning will be explained. Both picks, in running passages, and sticks, in percussive passages, are used. There are four bridges on each canon, one beneath each set of eleven strings (that is, under a fourth of the forty-four-string total). Since tones on both sides of the bridges are employed, the result is eight tones on each canon, or sixteen in all. In the notation, two staves are generally used, the upper for the right hand, the lower for the left.

As in Harmonic Canon II, the lower twenty-two strings of the left canon are guitar fifths; all others are guitar seconds, and the guitar fifths are tuned (without bridges) a 2/1 below all the others. As before, ratios which occur in the second 2/1 of a particular set of strings are indicated by lines above and below. Here, there are two ratios in the left canon which are in the third 2/1 of a particular section of strings: 9/7, left, in the guitar seconds section, which is two 2/1's above the 9/7 to the right; and 8/7, left, in the guitar fifths

---

[15] Dimensions: The bellies have the same breadth and depth as those used in Harmonic Canon II, but they are now 1/4-inch vertical-grain redwood, and the height of the boxes to the tops of the soundboards is less—4 inches rather than 5 1/2. The tuning-gear sections follow the pattern of Harmonic Canon I—birch pieces 6 3/4 inches by 1/2 inch before prongs were cut. The tray, or cradle, is 66 inches by 22 3/4 inches. Two separated lengths of ponderosa pine, each 59 inches by 11 1/2 inches, hold the base of the arch together.

section, which is two 2/1's above the 8/7 to the right. These two ratios are distinguished by double lines, above and below. All the strings between the string numbers are included in the tuning—that is, 1–11 (reading up) includes all strings from 1 through 11. Tuning of Harmonic Canon III for *Petals* and *Delusion*:

| | LEFT CANON | | | | RIGHT CANON | | |
|---|---|---|---|---|---|---|---|
| String number | Ratio | Bridge | Ratio | String number | Ratio | Bridge | Ratio |
| 44 | $\overline{9/7}$ | | 9/7 | 44 | $\overline{11/10}$ | | 2/1 |
| 34 | | | | 34 | | | |
| 33 | $\overline{9/7}$ | | 12/7 | 33 | $\overline{9/8}$ | | 9/5 |
| 23 | | | | 23 | | | |
| 22 | $\overline{8/7}$ | | 12/7 | 22 | $\overline{9/7}$ | | 12/7 |
| 12 | | | | 12 | | | |
| 11 | $\overline{8/7}$ | | 8/7 | 11 | $\overline{11/8}$ | | 11/7 |
| 1 | | | | 1 | | | |

## *Bloboy, Koto, Crychord*

The technique employed on the Bloboy consists in placing one foot at about the center of the mouth of the mask (see photograph) and throwing the body's weight upon it, but even this comparatively simple exercise calls for musical control. The Bloboy is a bellows, with powerful organ-bellows springs inside, attached to the four tones of an ancient exhaust auto horn and three small organ pipes. Stamped upon the tops of the four horn pipes are the words: "PAT'D JAN. 23, 1912." An African mask is painted on the top of the bellows fairly faithfully except that the nostrils are multiple so as to provide for a quick intake of air (expulsion of air is through the horn and organ pipes).[16]

---

[16] Dimensions: The Bloboy is 29 inches deep, 19 inches wide and 17 1/2 inches high at the front (flat) end, 11 1/4 inches wide at the back (oval) end. The largest organ pipe is 22 inches high, the smallest 16 inches high.

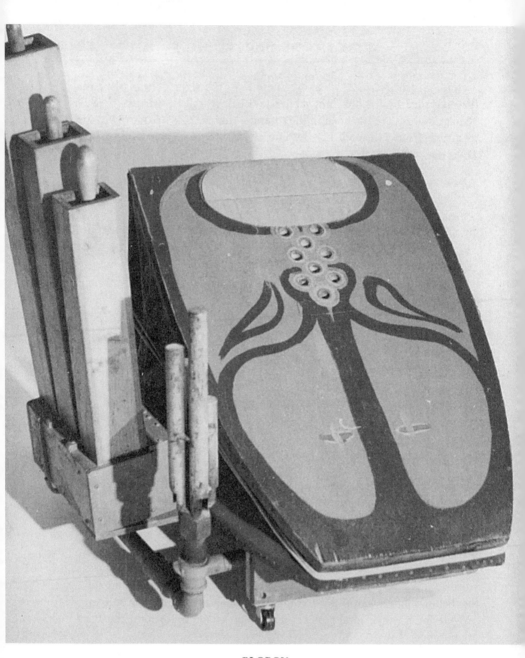

BLOBOY

The contraption (hesitation in calling it an instrument is automatic) was built for the projected recording of *U.S. Highball* in Evanston in 1958. The sound, in conjunction with a smearing technique on Chromelodeon I with the 6/5 stop out (the "octave" coupler), renders a fairly realistic impression, even to the echo in the distant foothills, of a Southern Pacific freight train crawling through the steep pass sixty miles away, then racing down the near side. (Unless bits of masking tape are used to cover, or partially cover, the lower organ pipes, the sound is more like that of a steamboat.)

The Bloyboy has twice been used as sound unrelated to freight trains. The first time was in *Revelation*, in a pseudo "pop" number, *Deep Inside, 'Way 'Way Down I Am!* and the second was in *Delusion,* at the height of the delusive battle between the pilgrim and the ghost of the man he killed.

The highest horn tone is the 14/9 above 1/1–392, the lowest the 14/9 below 1/1–392, while the lowest organ pipe is tuned (by a plunger, seen in the photograph) to the 14/9 below 1/1–196, which gives an idea of comparative register. The three organ pipes are a 2/1 below the corresponding tones of the horn.

Tuning

```
Auto horn—highest................14/9
            second highest.......... 8/7
            third highest...........40/21
            lowest................14/9

Organ pipes—highest............... 8/7
            second highest..........40/21
            lowest................14/9
```

The Koto, or Psaltery (see photograph), was given to me by Lou Harrison in the spring of 1966 for use in the projected performance of *Petals.*[17] (Although Harrison calls it a psaltery, I continue to call it a koto because I had written for this instrument previously and I use the same number of strings as before—thirteen.)[18] My only contributions are the base, a concession to Occi-

[17] It was made by Harrison's cabinet-maker friend, Morris Reynolds, in Santa Cruz, California. Dimensions: The Koto is 72 inches long—77 inches including the tuning gears. The depth across the open bottom is 13 inches, around the arched top 14 1/4 inches. For added resonance, the instrument rests on a 1/4-inch plywood "floor," 57 1/4 inches long. The player sits at the end of a triangular section placed toward the right, his legs straddling two 2 x 4's, the one to the left measuring 36 3/4 inches, that to the right 29 inches. The height of the base to the seat is 14 inches.

[18] I was given a koto by Gordon and Jacqueline Onslow-Ford before I left Sausalito for Illinois in 1956, and I used it in *The Bewitched* and much later in *Petals.* I turned to the new instrument because of its superior resonance.

dental leg muscles, which find it difficult to endure the hours called for in playing the Koto in the Japanese position, and the music rack.

My acquaintance with Japanese stringing, tuning, notation, and technique is very casual, and I make no pretense that the instrument is used in a Japanese manner, although this implies no lack of respect. The strings are monofilament nylon of various guages. In the tuning for *Petals* and *Delusion*, the ratios and the approximate pitches are as follows:

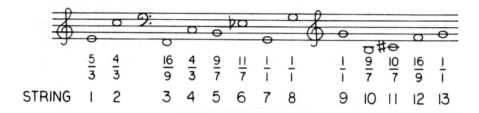

Koto notation, like that of the Harmonic Canons, is based on string numbers. In the following example, from Verse 4 of *Petals*, the stems in parentheses indicate that the pressure by the left hand, left of bridges, is released. The check marks over certain numbers indicate a left-hand pressure on the string, left of bridges, thus increasing tension. In the third bar, a 9–8–7 stroke, the check shows that the 9 is depressed, and the ratio below, 16/15, indicates that the pressure should raise the 9 string from 1/1, its tuning, to 16/15. The capital R indicates *release*—that the pressure is to be released on exactly the beat specified.

The Crychord is the name I bestowed on the instrument, although I had little to do with its construction. The resonating box was built by a student in the Industrial Design Department of the University of Illinois in the fall of 1959, as part of a project in imaginative musical instruments. The same student also conceived and built the tractile tension mechanism. At my suggestion, and in order to make the instrument more practical, the department created the standard at the back to hold the resonating box in a tilted position.

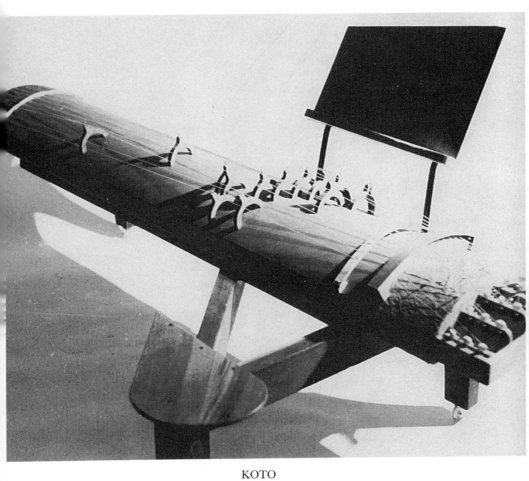

KOTO

CRYCHORD

My only contributions are the plastic strip and the index at the front (so that the player may make marks with a grease pencil for the tones he wants), and the music rack.

The instrument uses a monochord idea, but an extraordinarily flexible one. In playing, the musician moves the handle (which rests on the standard in the photograph) forward or backward, thus increasing or decreasing tension. The range of the single string depends on the gauge used. The present one is music wire diameter .020, which gives about a 2/1 and a 4/3. Because the string is subjected to so many varying tensions, breakage is rather frequent. The bridge above the resonator hole is bamboo, and its placement can be very significant, since the string may be played both below and above the bridge, even simultaneously. In the photograph it is set above the bridge for a tone two 2/1's higher than for the section below. And this relationship is fairly stable throughout the total range. However, the bridge could be set to give parallel relationships 12/5 or 5/2 or 8/3, or several others.

Technique generally involves a stick, such as a piece of dowel, in the hand, but both picks and fingers are effective. Where I have asked for precise intonation, I have used a bass clef with approximate notes and exact ratios underneath. To date, the best use of the instrument has been in a kind of improvisation, one in which the improviser is familiar with the accompanying part or parts and adjusts his intonation accordingly.[19]

## Voice Notations

In conventional practice, the voice part of a song is generally supported in 2/1's, or in unisons, or in various of the implied 5-limit ratios, by the chords of the accompanying instruments. Similarly, in my music the voice is supported in easy-to-hear intervals by the accompaniment; there is no demand for unaided vocal rendition of very small or very unusual intervals.

Voice parts have been written in several ways. At first I used ratios only, as in the Adapted Viola parts, teaching singers by rote while playing the voice part on the Viola, and my very first experience, in Oakland in 1932 with Rudolphine Radil, was a revelation: I learned that the voice is extraordinarily

---

[19] An excellent example is Emil Richards' playing of Verse One of *Petals* (see Appendix V). Dimensions: The resonator is 47 1/2 inches high, not including the 17-inch structure beneath it. It is 12 inches wide and 2 1/2 inches deep. The standard is 61 inches high at its back, 17 3/4 inches deep and 1 1/2 inches wide at the top, 21 1/2 inches deep and 10 1/2 inches wide at the bottom. The bottom 2 x 4 (not all visible in photograph) is 42 inches. The clear plastic index arm is 1/4 x 1 1/2 x 32 1/2 inches.

susceptible to alteration provided that the ear hears. Next, I wrote voice parts in Chromelodeon notation so that in rehearsal the chromelodeonist could aid in obtaining precise tones. Here the voice scores are in the usual notation, with the usual pitch values (as close as these can be figured to the actual ratios); and these scores are then used simply as guides to movement, or direction, very much as neumes were used in the days of plainsong.

The voice, having an unfixed gamut, is trained, when it sees the interval to sing the 2/1 "D"–"D" and, unlike the chromelodeonist, in

whom the mental image unconsciously evokes the corresponding physical reaction, must consciously work for the intonation intended. Hence, in the separate score, if the sequence 5/4–7/6–6/5 is required of the voice, it might be written which notes do not represent the ratios above, but do

indicate in a general way the movement of the voice part and the approximate pitches of the ratios above.

A third voice notation, used very briefly, employed the color analogy explained above on page 214. But this proved unnecessary. In more than thirty-five years of work with singers—singers far above average, to be sure, but highly diverse personalities nevertheless—I have obtained satisfactory if not phenomenal results even when the vocal requirements were most exacting. And these results were based entirely on the fact that the singers *heard*.

I have frequently limited the voice parts to "steps" and "half-steps" which correspond to Monophonic intervals in the Ptolemaic Sequence. Since the voice is very easily inclined to sing true intervals anyway, rectification from the notes of the separate score to the actual ratios is comparatively easy. When the voice is required for other than Ptolemaic-Sequence degrees, the process of rectification demands a longer period of rehearsal, but it is by no means impossible.

## Our Lack of Candor—Why Blame Singers?

Much of the oft-heard railing against the intonation of singers is scandalously lacking in candor. As composers and educators, we give them an accompanying instrument—the piano—which is continually at odds with their instincts. After they have mastered this incongruity, we pose them in an *a cap-*

*pella* choir or before an orchestra, where they are at the mercy of each intonational whim of concertmasters and conductors (who are by no means agreed on intonational rectitude). And we then proceed to criticize them for their "bad" intonation. As musicians we have no intonational norm, and we vent our annoyance over this situation upon innocent singers, who have no norm simply because we have none.

Many musicians regard as inconsequential the seventh of a semitone falsity of the "thirds" and "sixths" (ratios of 5) on the piano to which singers are trained; but we will see how so "inconsequential" a falsity as 1/50 of a semitone—2 cents—creates out-of-tuneness (page 434). The great need for a better instrument than the piano for the training of singers and the accompaniment of songs is too self-evident to be labored.

## Rhythmic Notation

In Chapter Five, on Basic Monophonic Concepts, it was observed that the human race has advanced through the number 5 in its harmonic music, and is now hovering somewhere between that eminence and the number 7. With respect to the element of rhythm, however, we modern Westerners are primitives; as compared with the subtle speech rhythms of the Middle Ages, ancient Greece, and classical China and Japan, and with the dance rhythms of the American Indians, our rhythms are aboriginal.

In the thirteenth and fourteenth centuries, shortly after the introduction of mensural music, the number 3 became endowed with the same magic as in the Pythagorean intonational system. Hawkins quotes an unnamed author of the thirteenth century to the effect that in rhythm, 3 (the Trinity) is "perfect," and therefore 243 is "five times perfect" because 3 is involved five times in arriving at 243 by the factor of 3.[20] Fortunately our forebears abandoned 3-ism in rhythm more readily than 3-ism in intonation.

From the standpoint of the intriguing metric forms which are attained within the rhythms of 2, 3, and 4—the basis of virtually all Western music—much can be said in extenuation of our present "aboriginal" condition, especially as regards the dance rhythms of the Latin Americans or Negroid Latin Americans.

[20] *History of the Science and Practice of Music*, 1:248.

Although Westerners have used basic rhythms of 5 and 7 to good effect, the field for exploration in the more complex forms of 5 and 7, the simple impulses of 11 and 13, and the rhythm of speech, is fabulously extensive. An example of a simple 13 rhythm—a strong impulse followed by twelve weaker pulsations, or an alternate 6–7 or 7–6 rhythm—is found in an old Edison cylinder record of the "Stick Game Song" from the Hoopa (or Hupa) Indians of the far north coast of California. This, and other such records which I examined at the Southwest Museum in Los Angeles in 1933, showed a wealth of rhythms more complex than anything Westerners have thus far attempted.

I have used the present orthodox rhythm notation almost without modification except as follows: 0, enclosed in a diamond, indicates the natural, easy rhythm of speech, and the notes following it are generally written without stems, at least in the voice parts; a hollow note without stem is used to represent a tone that covers two or more syllables, a solid one when a single syllable is sung to it. Duple rhythms are indicated by a 2 or 4 enclosed in a diamond, an eighth or a quarternote being the unit; the usual signs 4/4, 2/4, and 3/4 are not used because they might lead to confusion in a score in which ratios are common. The other rhythms—triple, quintuple, septuple, undecimal—are indicated on the same unit basis, the number being enclosed in a diamond.

With the introduction of percussion instruments of rather large variety, the evolution of complex rhythms becomes almost automatic. In Asia and, more notably, in Africa, with similar large varieties of percussion instruments, this tendency is manifest. And I can testify myself that with the advent of percussion in my life the development of more complex rhythms was most normal and natural. These instruments are now to be introduced.

# CHAPTER THIRTEEN

# Percussion Instruments and Their Notations

These particular instruments may be grouped into four rough categories. The first four are of the marimba type, with the traditional rectangular blocks:

Diamond Marimba
Quadrangularis Reversum
Bass Marimba
Marimba Eroica

Three of the four instruments in the second category involve bamboo; three (not exactly the same ones) are based on the tongue-with-resonator acoustical idea:

Boo I
Boo II
Mbira Bass Dyad
Eucal Blossom

The first of the five instruments in the third group employs metal bowls or bells. The sounds of the remaining four come from glass (two) and from glass and metal and wood (two).

Gourd Tree and Cone Gongs
Cloud-Chamber Bowls
Spoils of War
Zymo-Xyl
Mazda Marimba

The final group consists of a number of small hand instruments used only in *Delusion*.

## The Diamond Marimba

This instrument is the theoretical Tonality Diamond (page 159) brought to practical tonal life,[1] although the arrangement of identities is very different.

DIAMOND MARIMBA

Otonalities (ascending) are found in the six lines of blocks from lower left to upper right, Utonalities (descending) in the six lines of blocks from upper left to lower right (see photograph and Diagram 17). It may be seen and heard immediately that each tone represents at least a dual identity; 5/3, for example, may be considered either the 5 Odentity of the 4/3 Otonality or the 3 Udentity of the 5/4 Utonality.

The total range is nearly three 2/1's, the identities of one tonality being spread over about a 2/1 and a half. The relationship of identities is always 4:5:6:7:9:11 in Otonalities, and 1/4:1/5:1/6:1/7:1/9:1/11 in Utonalities; consequently, the sequence of Odentities or Udentities is 1–5–3–7–9–11, rather than the 1–9–5–11–3–7 of the Tonality Diamond. In specific range, the low 16/11 makes about 285 cycles (just above "middle C"), the middle 1/1 makes 784 cycles, and the high 11/8 makes 2156 cycles.

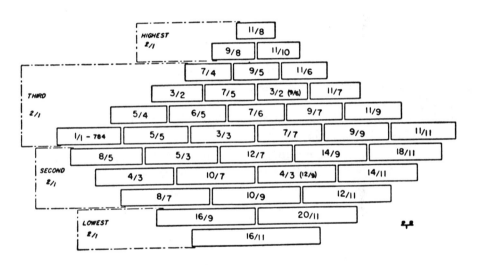

DIAGRAM 17.—BLOCK PLAN OF THE DIAMOND MARIMBA

[1] I built the Diamond Marimba in 1946 in Warren E. Gilson's shop in Madison, Wisconsin, with Gilson's advice and assistance. The height from the floor at the lowest block is 34 inches, at the highest 41 1/2 inches. The center row of 1/1's is 48 1/2 inches long, the terraced top is 27 inches deep from the front edge of the 16/11 block to the back edge of the 11/8 block. Each of the ten steps rises 3/4 inch. The white-pine crosspieces of the base are 33 x 20 1/4 inches; width—5 inches. Four 3/4-inch bronze posts support the instrument on the base.

More than half of the blocks are Pernambuco, or Brazilwood (which has the strongly resilient character required for fine violin bows), and the balance are Brazilian rosewood.[2] The tones of the blocks are amplified by large Brazilian bamboo, whose natural partitions, or knots, make the closed ends at the bottom.

The process of determining the length of block for a given tone is largely empirical, but one fact known from experiment can be of great help; when two blocks from one strip of wood of uniform width and thickness are in the ratio of two parts long to three parts long, they will give tones approximating the ratio two vibrations to one vibration, or the interval 2/1. From this rough formula it is fairly easy to determine approximately each length in a desired scale. Thus, by experiment, a block 8 inches long, 2 inches wide, and 3/4 inch thick beyond the nodes (see below) was chosen for 1/1-784. Key ratios— lowest, highest, and various others between within the range of the Diamond Marimba—were then inserted in Diagram 18, and a curve inscribed between the five 1/1's. The horizontal lines of the diagram indicate the cycles of tones as they would be determined on a given length of string making an open tone of 196 cycles, and the vertical lines indicate block lengths in inches. Thus, starting with a block 8 inches long giving a tone of 784 cycles, the ratio 16/11 at 285 cycles will be obtained from a block 14 3/8 inches long, the ratio 11/8 at 2156 cycles from a block 4 3/8 inches long, and all the others as their horizontal lines in the range of cycles (most of which are not shown) are cut by the curve along the scale of inches.

This is a formula and a theory: in practice a better tone is produced by making the blocks for low tones shorter and those for high tones longer than the formula indicates. On the Diamond Marimba, for instance, the lowest tone, 16/11, is actually 13 1/2 inches long, and the highest tone, 11/8, is 6 1/4 inches long. Furthermore, the length of block also varies from the formula because of the wood that is milled away from the underside to conserve on length and to produce a more sustained sound.[3]

[2] At the time of my 1946 visit to the J. C. Deagan Company of Chicago, builders of percussion instruments, the firm was using hormigo, or quira, from Central America for its marimbas. I am indebted to Clair O. Musser, marimbist, and Paul J. Fialkowski, technician, both of the Deagan Company at that time, for some of my observations on marimba making or their corroboration.

[3] Although the terms marimba and xylophone mean substantially the same thing when traced to their sources, in present-day usage marimba has come to signify a comparatively low tone with a comparatively long resonance period (or ring-time), and xylophone a higher tone and a shorter resonance period. The blocks for an "F" on the two instruments could be exactly the same in length and width; however, the xylophone block will be thicker between the nodes and will be a 2/1 higher.

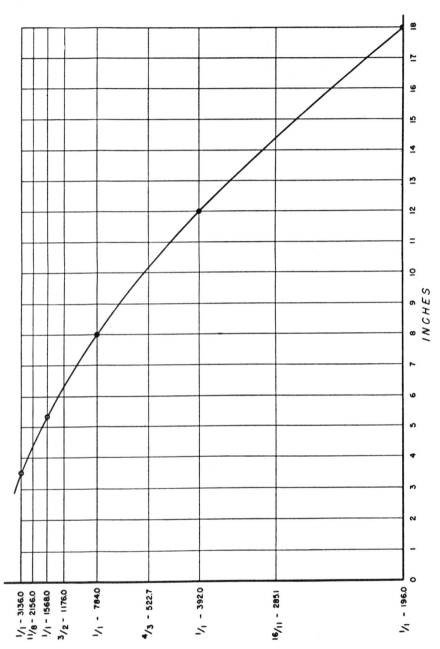

DIAGRAM 18—GRAPHIC METHOD OF DETERMINING THE LENGTHS OF BLOCKS ON THE DIAMOND MARIMBA

A block of wood vibrates when it is struck, and unless it is tightly held, it generally makes a tone of determinate pitch. In vibrating, it creates nodes— points of least or no vibration, two balancing points of seesaws, as it were—on either side of which the wood moves up and down contrarily. Striking a hexa- hedral piece of wood of the type used for marimbas produces two well-defined nodes at right angles to the length if the grain is straight and runs parallel to the length of the block. To determine the location of these nodes exactly, rest the block on a piece of polyfoam or other resilient material, shake salt on the top, and tap the wood in the center. The salt will collect in two distinct lines which indicate the nodes. In a milled piece of wood, hexahedral and of consistent width and thickness, these will be at about a fourth of the length from each end; if an arch is cut underneath to about half the thickness of the wood, the nodes will almost invariably be a fifth of the length from each end.

This arch is milled out or sawed out on a bandsaw, *between nodes*, to about half the thickness in the longer pieces and considerably less in the shorter ones. It lowers the pitch markedly—a 2/1 or more in the longer blocks and from approximately a 3/2 to a 6/5 in the shorter blocks. Thus it follows that blocks are *finely* tuned either by rasping wood away from the underside, between nodes, to flat them, or by rasping or sawing wood from the two ends to sharp them—that is, by making the center of the block thinner or by making the entire block shorter.

The blocks of the Diamond Marimba are supported at the nodes by nar- row strips of polyfoam, 1/4 to 3/8 inch thick, and are attached with rubber cement, which is non-hardening. Thus they are loosely held, allowing maximal vibration.

In determining the lengths of the bamboo resonators under the blocks, we have recourse to the formula for a stopped organ pipe. The air in a pipe closed at one end, when set in vibration, performs in such a way that approximately four lengths of the pipe are required for a complete cycle, or wave length. To determine the length of pipe that will produce a given tone, the speed of sound at an average room temperature—about 1130 feet per second[4]—is first divided by the number of cycles of the tone, thus establishing the wave length of that tone. This quotient is then divided by 4, since four lengths of pipe are needed

---

[4] About 1129 feet per second in dry air at 70 degrees Fahrenheit; the speed of sound increases or decreases by 1.1 feet per second with each degree of temperature change. Jeans, *Science and Music*, 119–120.

for one wave length. Finally, what is known as "open end correction" is applied—about 0.29 of the pipe's inside diameter is subtracted from the second quotient. The complete sound wave exceeds the open end of the pipe by about this amount, and the resulting tone will therefore be lower than that desired unless "open end correction" is made.[5] For example, the length of resonator for the degree 16/11 at 285 cycles: 1130 is divided by 285, and the quotient, 3.965, is divided by 4. Converted, this second quotient is about 11 7/8 inches, and from this about 5/8 inch (0.29 of 2 1/8 inches—the inside diameter) is subtracted for open end correction. The resonator for 16/11 at 285 cycles is thus determined to be 11 1/4 inches.

Again, this is theory, and in practical application it is well to cut the resonators a little long, especially when using the irregular shapes of bamboo, as in the Diamond Marimba. By blowing on the edge of the resonator, it is easy to determine its natural vibration, and if the tone is too low, a little should be cut off.

The effects of weather, and especially of temperature changes, on a musical instrument of coupled resonances such as the marimba are most unhappy. To be at their best, a block and its resonator should be fairly in unison (actually, the resonator can be a shade flat and make a perfect coupling [6]), but with marked changes in temperature and humidity, the two elements go out of tune in different degrees.[7]

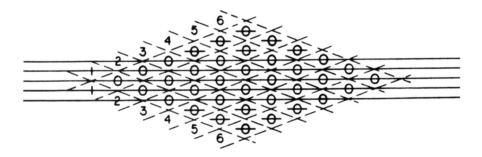

[5] *Ibid.*, 139.

[6] When encountering the much lower tones of the Bass Marimba and the Marimba Eroica, it will be observed that the interval of the resonator tone *below* the block tone seems to widen progressively in the effort to achieve a good coupling.

[7] To correct this problem, at least partially, the Deagan Company builds its marimbas so that the distance between the open ends of the resonators and the bottoms of the blocks may be adjusted.

Notation: the placement and arrangement of blocks on the Diamond Marimba determines its notation, just as the arrangement of strings on the Kitharas determines their notation. No spaces are used, only the five lines of the staff and three ledger lines above and below.

Each block has its exact placement in relation to the staff, and the only other identification needed is the number of the hexad in which it occurs. As stated before, Otonalities run from lower left to upper right and Utonalities from upper left to lower right. If the 14/11 tone is desired, it is the fourth note up in the Otonality hexad that is numbered 6, on the first line of the staff, and this number is shown *below* the note. (It could also be shown on the first line of the staff with the number 4, for that Utonality hexad, *above* it). If the 7/6 tone is desired, it is the third note down in Utonality hexad 4, on the fourth line of the staff, and this number is shown *above* the note. (It could also be shown in exactly the same position with the number 3, for that Otonality hexad, *below* it). Full arpeggio-like chords are written, either Otonality or Utonality, with the appropriate number below or above.

Since the instrument was conceived, basically, as a chordal marimba, control of this capability must be mastered immediately. The full strokes of the mallet over the hexads are slightly unnatural, in that they must curve *inward*, while the arm, in a sweep, naturally curves *outward* (quite unlike the Reversum—see below). However, a small amount of practice and concentration will make this *inward* curve second nature in either partial or complete sweeps of the hexads.[8] It is important to concentrate on the *centers of the blocks*. If the mallets strike blocks at the nodes or beyond the nodes, the instrument is not being played competently.

In running passages, the technique of playing varies little from that of the usual marimba except for the somewhat wider movements frequently necessary between strokes. Again, *concentrate on the centers*. Where the convenience of a particular tonality is not involved, as it very often is not, either the numbers below or the numbers above are used, whichever seems easier to the musician. There is a difference in notation between duads or triads to be played simultaneously with two hands and those to be played by a single stroke of one hand. The latter are written with successive notes and are indicated by slurs.

---

[8] This chordal Diamond-Marimba technique is beautifully demonstrated in the duet with Cloud-Chamber Bowls in Verse 6 of *Petals* (see Appendix V).

Mallets should never be waved in the air, daintily or otherwise. There is a tremendous loss of efficiency in the unnecessary waving of mallets.

## The Quadrangularis Reversum

The inevitable and automatic downward arpeggios, or sweeps, of the Diamond Marimba caused me to wish for a twin instrument, one in which the arpeggios would inevitably and automatically sound upward. I also longed for the same qualities of timbre in tones of the alto register. (Although the highest tone of the Bass Marimba [see below] is only about a "minor third" below the lowest tone of the Diamond Marimba, the resources of the Bass Marimba in its upper register are slight, and its timbre is vastly different.) These wishes were realized in the Quadrangularis Reversum, with the Reversum fulfilling the first wish and the alto flanks the second. The upward (Reversum) and downward (Diamond Marimba) sweeps, sometimes alternating, are prominent in the Exordium (the "overture") to *Delusion*. In fact, the duet of these two instruments, with accompanying instruments, determines a large part of the structure of the Exordium.

The center section of the instrument (see photograph) is actually a mirror reverse of the Diamond Marimba—this may be observed easily if Diagram 17, showing the Diamond Marimba, is held upside down in front of a mirror and compared with Diagram 19, showing the Quadrangularis Reversum.[9] The reversal resulted from my desire to keep both the 1/1 Otonality and the 1/1 Utonality to the left of the block arrangement, as they are in the Diamond Marimba. The instrument should truly be called Quadrangularis Mirror Reversum.

Since the tones of the Reversum are an upside-down mirror of the Diamond Marimba, there is nothing more to be said about the tuning of this section of the instrument. The only problem is notation, since the lowest tone of the Reversum is now on the third ledger line *above* the staff and the highest on the third ledger line *below* the staff. This means that notes which appear to go upward in pitch are actually going downward, while those appearing to go downward are actually going upward. I had only two choices here, either this notation or one in which the blocks of the instrument that are *low*—those close

---

[9] This mirror effect was called to my attention by Ervin Wilson, who is responsible for the new illustrations and diagrams in this edition.

QUADRANGULARIS REVERSUM

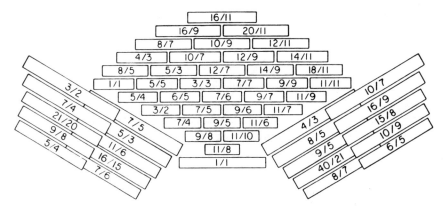

Diagram 19.—Block Plan of the Quadrangularis Reversum

to the player in a spatial sense—would be shown *high* on the staff, while spatially *high* blocks, farther away from the player, would be *low* on the staff; and I decided that the latter solution would be less tolerable. Hence, the notation illustration for the Diamond Marimba (page 265) applies here almost exactly, the only difference being that the 1–2–3–4–5–6 *above* the diagonal lines of notes now represent Otonalities (rather than Utonalities), and the 1–2–3–4–5–6 *below* the diagonal lines of notes now represent Utonalities (rather than Otonalities). This becomes important in the choice of tones for the flanking alto sections, and in order not to confuse the player thoroughly, the same type of reverse notation has been used for these sections.

The word *Quadrangularis* calls for an explanation. I had seen a piece of beautiful bamboo, not the usual round variety but *square*, or nearly so. At first I was told that the clever Japanese used forms to force the bamboo to *grow* square against its instincts. Later, I learned that there is a variety of bamboo, among perhaps hundreds of varieties, that *grows* square, *bamboo* (or *bambusa*) *quadrangularis*—taking nothing away from the cleverness of the Japanese, of course.[10] I had intended to use this almost incredible bamboo for the alto section resonators, but when I discovered that its price was roughly

[10] For anyone who doubts, a Chinese restaurant on Sunset Boulevard in Hollywood offers a startling example of the use of giant bamboo quadrangularis. It is used both at the main doorway and in much of the interior railing and paneling.

four times that of the usual round bamboo, I decided to retain the name while
staying with materials that I could afford.

The choice of ratios, as between the left and right flanks, was determined
by the fact that right-hand hexadal sweeps on the Reversum are Utonalities
and left-hand sweeps Otonalities. Therefore, ratios for the left hand on the left
alto flank are important in Utonalities, with the right hand playing on the Reversum, while ratios for the right hand on the right alto flank are important in
Otonalities, with the left hand playing on the Reversum. The illustration
shows, from top to bottom, first, the notation; second, the ratios; third, the approximate pitches, using the bass clef. The range is from the 4/3 exactly a 2/1
above the lowest Bass Marimba tone (see below) to the 5/4 above—less than a
2/1.

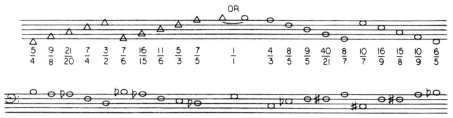

APPROXIMATE PITCHES

Since this is a marimba and therefore has limited ring-time, the use of
open notes to indicate time values is of no importance. The left-flank notes are
triangular, the right-flank notes round. The 1/1 block (1/1–196), which lies
just below the highest tone of the Reversum (11/8), is of course available in
twelve senses—six Otonality and six Utonality. The potentialities of the other
blocks of the two flanks are shown below in symbols only as high as the 7
Identity. This is similar to the explanation above of the thirteen sub-bass tones
of Chromelodeon I (see page 209). The order of ratios conforms to the illustration above, not to any sequence of pitch. Their availability is shown in
Primary Tonalities at the top of each column, and then in Secondary
Tonalities at the bottom.

Examples: left flank—5/4 may be a 1 Udentity (of 5/4–U), a 5 Odentity
(of 1/1–O), or a 3 Udentity (of 15/8–U); right flank—8/5 may be a 1
Odentity (of 8/5–O), a 5 Udentity (of 1/1–U), or a 3 Odentity (of 16/15–O).

The length of blocks for the two flanks could be determined if the curve of
Diagram 18 (page 263) were extended downward. (The block for 1/1–196

## Left Flank

| 5/4 | 9/8 | 21/20 | 7/4 | 3/2 | 7/6 | 16/15 | 11/6 | 5/3 | 7/5 |
|-----|-----|-------|-----|-----|-----|-------|------|-----|-----|
| 1–U | 1–U | 5–U | 1–U | 1–U | 3–U | 5–U | 3–U | 3–U | 5–U |
| 5–O | 3–O | 3–O | 7–O | 3–O | 7–O | 1–O |     | 5–O | 7–O |
| 3–U |     | 7–O | 3–U | 3–U |     |     |     | 1–U | 1–O |
|     |     |     | 5–O | 1–O |     |     |     |     |     |
|     |     |     |     | 5–O |     |     |     |     |     |
|     |     |     |     | 7–U |     |     |     |     |     |

## Right Flank

| 4/3 | 8/5 | 9/5 | 40/21 | 8/7 | 10/7 | 16/9 | 15/8 | 10/9 | 6/5 |
|-----|-----|-----|-------|-----|------|------|------|------|-----|
| 1–O | 1–O | 5–O | 5–O | 1–O | 5–O | 1–O | 5–O | 5–O | 3–O |
| 3–U | 5–U | 1–O | 3–U | 7–U | 7–U | 3–U | 1–U | 1–U | 5–U |
| 3–O | 3–O | 3–O | 7–U | 3–O | 1–U |     |     | 3–U | 1–O |
| 1–U |     |     |     | 5–U |     |     |     |     |     |
| 5–U |     |     |     |     |     |     |     |     |     |
| 7–O |     |     |     |     |     |     |     |     |     |

[just below the high 11/8 in the photograph] is shown on this diagram as 18 inches; it is actually 17 1/8 inches.) The lengths of the bamboo resonators follow the formula for an organ pipe closed at one end as explained above (page 264).

The blocks of the Quadrangularis are African padouk, a very resonant wood that is hard and very dark red. As I originally conceived the instrument, it was intended to float, or seem to float, as much as possible. I found two acceptable branches of eucalyptus (there are few trees that grow in so many fantastic shapes as some varieties of eucalyptus), united them at the top with a Japanese-style *tori* bar, and thus produced the effect of suspending the entire instrument. The result was about as close to a vision of flotation as I could devise.[11]

---

[11] I built this instrument in Van Nuys, California, in the spring of 1965. The height from the floor of the highest block (spatially)—the 16/11 block—is 41 1/2 inches, that of the 1/1–196 block (below 11/8) 33 3/4 inches. The height of the spatially highest rows of the alto flanks, at their back outside edges, is 37 1/2 inches, and that of the lowest rows, toward the middle of the instrument, is 31 inches. The stock for all fifty-seven blocks is 3/4 inch thick. In the Reversum, widths vary progressively from 1 3/4 inches in the tonally higher blocks to 2 inches in the lower ones; in the alto flanks, they vary from 2 to 2 1/2 inches. The tori bar is 103 inches long and 79 inches from the floor at both ends. The double redwood 2 x 4 base is 100 inches long, the base crosspieces 29 inches deep. The 5/8- x 2 1/4-inch aluminum extrusion (not visible in photograph) attached to the two branches of eucalyptus and supporting the Reversum and the alto flanks measures 82 inches.

A minor acoustical phenomenon that appeared with this instrument must be touched on briefly. A marimba block is not a string and does not function like a string—witness the fact that one-half of a block does not give the tone a 2/1 above the whole block; the ratio is more like 3/2, and, unlike the string, there are no geometric overtones. However, for many years, I had heard about or read about one strong inharmonic overtone created by this type of vibrating body. After building the Diamond Marimba, Bass Marimba, and Marimba Eroica, I still could not say that I had ever heard this overtone. Finally, with the Quadrangularis, I do hear it, in the alto flanks. By tapping lightly on the tip ends of these blocks, not the centers, I hear an inharmonic overtone that sounds very near an 11/7 ratio above, a small "minor sixth." Theory finally becomes fact.

## The Bass Marimba

Starting with the highest tones of the Diamond Marimba (duplicated in the Reversum), the discussion of this particular marimba family proceeds downward. With the Quadrangularis the lowest tone is the 4/3 below 1/1–196 (first "C" below "middle C"), and with the Bass Marimba we continue downward to the 4/3 below 1/1–98 (the cello "C"). With the Marimba Eroica, discussed below, the range is extended to a tone of 22 cycles (the "F" below the piano's lowest tone). Beyond this I do not care to experiment because the threshold of feeling has already been passed and is mixed with the sense of hearing.

The Bass Marimba (see photograph) consists of eleven vertical-grain, Sitka-spruce blocks,[12] ranging in pitch from the 4/3 below 1/1–98 to the 7/6 above 1/1–196. The longest block is 53 inches, the shortest 27 inches. The stock is called 2 x 6, but it is actually more like 1 3/4 x 5 1/2, finished. As with the other marimbas, the centers, underneath, are milled out between the nodes (about a fifth of the length from each end) to a thickness about half the original—7/8 inch. The procedure in tuning is not difficult. In testing, the block is held by one hand at one of the nodes while the other hand strikes in

---

[12] Because of its elasticity, Sitka spruce is a superb wood for musical purposes. I have used it both for soundboards and for Bass Marimba and Marimba Eroica blocks. A special advantage is that vertical-grain pieces are not difficult to obtain—the tree is often very large and very straight. I doubt that Sitka spruce is very different from the Norway spruce and Alpine spruce used for soundboards and violin bellies in Europe. Vertical-grain redwood is also excellent for soundboards, but not as good for marimba blocks.

BASS MARIMBA

the center, with a fist or a mallet, and the tone produced is then compared with the tones of the Chromelodeon.

All things fatigue, and the blocks of the Bass Marimba are no exception. Sitka spruce, although one of the harder soft woods, is still not a hard wood. After some twelve years (1950–1962) of the beatings upon it that I myself stipulated, the two ends of each block, where small mallets are sometimes used, resembled shredded wheat more than pieces of wood. In 1963, I planed off the top of each about 1/8 inch. Since this operation made the blocks thinner, it also made them flatter, and the long process of sharping had to begin. Some four hundred saw cuts and five weeks of constant testing later, the original pitches were finally restored. In 1971, after many additional beatings, the blocks were all replaced (vertical-grain Sitka spruce again being used), and the instrument has regained its earlier pristine resonance.[13]

When I first built the instrument at Gualala, California, in 1950,[14] the resonators were made of 3/4-inch redwood stock with closed ends. Ten years later, I substituted lower ends of organ pipes,[15] with plungers at the closed ends to allow adjustments in the volume of air. For maximum coupling, the natural resonances of these pipes should be slightly below those of the blocks. With smaller pipes, one can test resonance by getting an edge tone—blowing on the edge of the open end. But human lungs do not have the power to excite an edge tone in larger pipes. For these, a very good test is to tap the closed end on a solid floor, preferably concrete; the natural resonance creates a *boom* sound, which may be determined immediately on one of the Chromelodeons.

In the middle and upper registers (the six highest tones), the original redwood resonators provided good couplings. However, the five lowest couplings were less effective, and I discovered subsequently that if the diameter of the open end (converted from a square or a rectangle) is less than a tenth the

---

[13] The blocks are mounted on a 2 x 4 redwood frame (or block rack) which is supported by three 4 x 4 redwood standards—two at the bass end. The standards are mortised at the bottom into another redwood frame of 2 x 4's and 4 x 4's. Blocks are mounted on polyfoam with rubber cement. As insurance, light rubber bands (*heavy bands destroy resonance!*) are looped through holes at the nodes and attached to hooks on the block rack. The height from the floor to the top edges of the blocks is 60 inches. The 2 x 4 block rack is 76 1/2 inches long, 35 1/2 inches wide at the bass end, and 17 inches wide at the high end. The frame at the bottom is 79 3/4 inches long, with 4 x 4 crosspieces 36 inches long. The redwood riser—covered with a reddish linoleum—is 72 inches long, 18 1/2 inches wide, and 25 inches high. The music rack is 48 inches long.

[14] I received very substantial help from L. C. Marshall, then director of the Microwave Laboratory at the University of California, Berkeley.

[15] These were obtained when the Twin Cities Church of the Bible, Urbana, Illinois, was demolished in 1960. They are hooked into a horizontal supporting bar.

length of the resonator, the resonance is inferior. When I replaced the redwood resonators with the organ pipes, all resonances were very good, but I was faced with a totally unexpected problem: with the blocks tuned correctly and the resonators slightly lower, the *heard* tones were always flat in the lowest couplings. It was three years before I had the time to concentrate on this difficulty. Deliberately, then, I tuned the five lowest blocks sharp. After days of diligent sharping and testing, I finally *heard* the tones I wanted to hear. I could conclude only that both blocks and resonators are so powerful that they must compromise. Here are the data for the five lowest tones, from low to high, as of March, 1963:

| Tone to be heard | Block tuned to | Boom tone of resonator |
|---|---|---|
| 4/3 | Above 27/20 | About 21/16 |
| 3/2 | About 32/21 | About 40/27 |
| 5/3 | About 27/16 | About 18/11 |
| 1/1 | About 81/80 | About 64/33 |
| 8/7 | Above 8/7 | About 9/8 |

The notation for the Bass Marimba is probably the easiest for any of my instruments. Large red circles are painted in the exact centers of the blocks whose notes fall on the five lines of the staff: 3/2–1/1–16/11–16/9–9/8. With this aid, the player may come close to reading at sight.

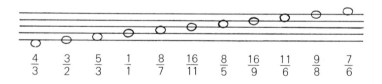

$$\frac{4}{3} \quad \frac{3}{2} \quad \frac{5}{3} \quad \frac{1}{1} \quad \frac{8}{7} \quad \frac{16}{11} \quad \frac{8}{5} \quad \frac{16}{9} \quad \frac{11}{6} \quad \frac{9}{8} \quad \frac{7}{6}$$

Playing techniques: four kinds of mallets are used, as well as the tips of fingers. For music that is not too fast, large sheepskin-covered mallets are played in the centers, directly over the resonators, for maximum resonance. Lighter large mallets are used for fast passages, again in the centers. Felted sticks (3/8-inch dowels) are struck at the ends, diagonally so that a maximum tone is achieved. Small, semihard marimba mallets are used near the ends of the blocks. Finally, finger flips, with a loose but controlled wrist, are employed in the centers. The tips of the hands are literally thrown on the blocks, in bullet-like strikes, and bounced off; the result is a bongo-sounding tone.[16] All five of these techniques are used in *The Bewitched*. (See Appendix V.)

Sound has never liked corners. If one listens to the sound of wind in the trees and then goes around a corner of a house away from the trees, the sound is greatly diminished. Every Bass Marimba that I have seen has its long resonators doubled back on themselves for the very low tones (all of these instruments descend to the cello "C") so that the player may stand on the floor. I declined to make this compromise. Like the player of Kithara II, the Bass Marimba player must stand on a high riser, and since he is always on stage, he is visually very conspicuous. His footwork over the length of the six-foot riser is therefore of considerable consequence. In fast music, the combination of hands, feet, and attitude results in a functional dance. To rate as a competent Bass Marimbist, the player must be a good musician and, in addition, both agile and graceful.

## The Marimba Eroica

My experiments with tones lower than those of the Bass Marimba covered a period of almost twelve years—1951–1963. Except for the hollowed logs used in Africa at one time (perhaps even at present), which produced a somewhat similar effect of feeling-hearing, these very low sounds were and still are, acoustically, a kind of *terra incognita*. The years of experimenting swallowed up many disappointments and were also rewarded with many happy excitements. Because of the large timbers and resonators I was obliged to use, they also involved a great deal of hard physical work.

The first Marimba Eroica (1951) had three redwood timbers, fashioned in the usual marimba style, suspended vertically in front of large and long horizontal resonators—the equivalent of organ pipes (see photograph). The narrowest of the blocks had the same tone as the highest of the four present Eroica blocks. The other two were lower, but neither went as low as the two lowest tones of the present instrument. Furthermore, redwood proved inferior to Sitka spruce in the matter of ring-time, or prolonged resonance.

---

[16] Although some of my Bass Marimba scores are marked "slap," the intention is not a whole-hand slap, which does not generally produce the sound desired, but rather a balls-of-the-fingers slap.

MARIMBA EROICA (FIRST VERSION)

MARIMBA EROICA (CURRENT VERSION)

The playing of this instrument, with its suspended vertical blocks, turned out to be very awkward, but the obvious remedy, placing the closed ends of the pipes on the floor, was thoroughly impractical. A pipe for the lowest tone of the present instrument, 22 cycles, would need to be some twelve feet high, for instance, and the player would have to stand on a riser nine feet high and use a ladder to get there. Nor could the instrument, which had to be movable, be positioned permanently, with holes dug into the ground under the centers of the blocks and lined with reinforced concrete (probably the most efficient kind of resonator).

I have often dreamed of a private home with a stairway which is in reality a Marimba Eroica, with the longest block at the bottom and the shortest at the top, and with the type of resonator described above. The owner could stipulate his favorite scale, then could bounce up to bed at night hearing it and paddle down in the morning for breakfast hearing it. He would need to be athletic, since simple walking would dampen resonance. If he were *very* athletic, he could take two or three steps at a time and produce an arpeggio.

The present Marimba Eroica (see photograph) comes in four separate parts (five, counting the player's riser)—four vertical-grain, Sitka-spruce blocks mounted at the nodes on thick polyfoam, and over holes in what I call cave-type resonators. Spatially these resonators are very inefficient; I have estimated that in the case of the lowest tone, the cave type requires more than thirty cubic feet in order to attain a good coupling, while an organ pipe would require only about twelve. But they do the job.

To facilitate discussion, the largest block and resonator pairing is here called No. 1, the second largest is No. 2, the third largest No. 3, and the smallest No. 4.

No. 1 is about the "F" below the lowest "A" on the piano; No. 2 is approximately the lowest "C" on the piano, No. 3 is the lowest "E," and No. 4 is the "A" above the piano's lowest tone. It must be remembered, however, that unlike the piano or any string tone, these blocks produce no geometric overtones. Therefore, what one hears (or feels) is the frequency of the fundamental; he does not hear overtones that build up the fundamental, as with strings, and each Eroica tone *sounds* lower than any piano tone. Here are the four ratios, their individual cycles, and the very arbitrary and very simple notation for each:

| 1 | 2 | 3 | 4 |
|---|---|---|---|
| $\dfrac{9}{5}$ | $\dfrac{27}{20}$ | $\dfrac{12}{7}$ | $\dfrac{8}{7}$ |
| 22 CPS | 33 CPS | 42 CPS | 56 CP |

As shown, the two lower tones are separated by a 3/2 and the two higher tones by a 4/3; and the two pairs are separated by a dissonant ratio which is approximately a "major third."

The tuning of the blocks is not a difficult problem except for the hard work. In this case I followed the occasional Mexican custom of milling out the wood from both top and bottom between nodes, which, as usual, are about a fifth of the length from each end. Each block is deposited on sections of polyfoam on the floor or on a table and is tapped with a large, heavy, soft mallet. (High marimba tones require comparatively light and hard mallets; as the tones descend the mallets must become heavier and softer if the resonator is to be excited.) The appropriate tone—or a tone a 2/1 or two 2/1's higher—is found on the Chromelodeon, a piece of lead is placed on the key, the instrument is pumped (the tone continues to sound), and the tones of the two sounding bodies are compared.

The cave-type resonators involve difficult problems. Unless the sides are rigidly reinforced (which suggests why concrete might be best), the tones lose power and ring-time because the sides vibrate so wildly. The sides of the two smaller resonators are tied together by steel rods, and those of the two larger ones both by steel rods and by two diagonal lengths of 2 x 4 redwood bolted to the sides. In order to make the playing area approximately level, the smaller resonators have structures that hold them high, and all four are tilted at the back, the idea being that the sounds would be more easily projected into the room. (Whether this is true or not, the slanting blocks are visually more pleasing.) The ends of large organ pipes, with plungers, are inserted in the front of each resonator. This allows some slight control over the size of the air body in each and helps in finding a good coupling.[17]

If one has an assistant for even a brief period, it is fairly easy to ascertain the boom tones of the resonators, especially the two smaller ones. The end of a resonator is picked up a few inches and dropped sharply on a concrete floor—the tone will boom forth. A second person will listen at the resonator hole, then sing that tone two or three 2/1's higher, then go to the Chromelodeon and find it.

At the time I originally built the instrument, I intended to achieve exact pitches in the Eroica tones, because for decades I had been exploring consonance in general and new consonances in particular. About 1954, with the reconception and rebuilding of the instrument, I realized that my concern was pointless. Only with the two higher tones does one begin to *hear*, with any sense of pitch in mind, and even in these the pitch is not of great consequence. With the two lower tones, even though—listening closely—precise tones are heard, in actual music there is literally no time for the ear to engender any feeling of consonance with whatever else may be going on, particularly with what is happening five or six 2/1's above in the treble range. The longest ring-time (in the two lower tones) is only about six seconds at most.

It can, however, be important for these low tones to achieve some consonance or near-consonance with each other (in powerful beats, for example). Nos. 1 and 2 are very effective together, and Nos. 3 and 4 are very effective together. In conjunction with some of the low tones of the Bass Marimba, all are effective.

The necessity of having a resonator with a natural frequency *below* its block, mentioned in the preceding marimba discussion, also applies here—and even more strikingly:

|  | Block tone | Boom tone of resonator |
|---|---|---|
| No. 1 | 9/5 | About 5/3 |
| No. 2 | 27/20 | About 14/11 |
| No. 3 | 12/7 | About 8/5 |
| No. 4 | 8/7 | About 11/10 |

---

[17] The dimensions were calculated and the resonators designed by William Loughborough in Sausalito in 1954, and both he and Gerd Stern assisted in building the resonators. All gave somewhat lower tones than I had asked for, but, as noted above, this is *terra incognita*. Dimensions of the blocks: No. 1—90 1/2 inches long, 9 7/8 inches wide, 1 7/8 inches thick; No. 2—77 inches long, 10 inches wide, 1 3/4 inches thick; No. 3—65 inches long, 8 7/8 inches wide, 2 1/8 inches thick; No. 4—55 1/4 inches long, 8 3/4 inches wide, 2 inches thick. Dimensions of the four resonators: No. 1—96 inches long, 13 3/4 inches wide, 48 inches high; No. 2—77 inches long, 12 1/2 inches wide, 44 inches high; No. 3—48 inches long, 12 1/2 inches wide, 40 inches high; No. 4—44 inches long, 12 1/2 inches wide, 30 inches high. The small triangular riser (not visible in the photograph) is 31 1/2 inches long on the sides paralleling the resonators, 18 1/2 inches wide at the base of the triangle, and 18 inches high.

In the case of the Bass-Marimba low tones, the sounds one hears in the air of the room are a compromise between the natural frequencies of the blocks and of the pipes. One does not hear, in any sustained way, the natural frequencies of the blocks, which are deliberately tuned high in order to activate the resonators to the desired *heard* tone. However, the Eroica resonators *do* throw the natural frequencies of the blocks into the air of the room, not their own frequencies.

The wave length (one complete cycle) of No. 1 is more than fifty feet, that of No. 2 about thirty-four feet. Very seldom have both of these tones sounded resonantly in the same room. In my studio in Petaluma, No. 2's resonance sometimes seemed almost overwhelming; the length of the studio turned out to be almost exactly its wave length. In the present studio No. 2 is the weakest. One is forced to conclude that the room in which these tones are heard is, in a sense, an important part of the instrument. Nos. 3 and 4 sound well in almost any room.

Playing techniques: heavy mallets are used, centers. The largest of these, made especially for No. 1, weighs four pounds; the next smallest weighs about two pounds. Lighter mallets are used as well, for fast playing, and also hands, or gloved hands (used in both the Exit Oedipus section of *Oedipus* and in the *Exordium* of *Delusion*).

The instrument requires a player with robust shoulders, back, and arms. If he possesses this equipment, and is also something of a percussionist, the playing of the instrument is not difficult, but there is more to this role than mere playing. It is his *visual* aspect that the Eroica player must cultivate. He must be a hero of the Trojan War. In exciting and furious passages he must convey the vision of Ben Hur in his chariot, charging around the last curve of the final lap.

## The Boos (Bamboo Marimbas)

*Boo I*: Sixty-four sections of bamboo with tuned tongues in the open ends are mounted in six rows, with one small piece of a seventh row at the top (see photograph). The sections are firmly held at the backs—the closed ends—by heavy rubber bands running over each section and through hooks attached to the supporting racks, or by lengths of nylon cord tied and hooked; the front ends are cushioned on polyfoam. Unlike the wood-block marimbas, which

BOO I

BOO II

retain their tunings fairly well, this instrument does not; it is very susceptible to alterations due to playing, temperature, humidity.

Most of the sequence of tones duplicates the forty-three degrees of the Chromelodeon as it was originally tuned. Beginning with the third piece of bamboo from the left in the fifth row, there are many omissions, as can be seen in the illustration on page 288.

The instrument would be more beautiful from the rear (the view that an audience generally has) if the natural knots of the bamboo could, in every case, make the closed ends. This is not always possible because of the scarcity of large bamboo in this country. Where the knot is missing, a piece of 1/4-inch plywood is glued to the end. Had the natural knots been available throughout, I would probably have left the natural off-white ends of the bamboo untouched. In the circumstances, the ends had to be painted, and I used a deep coral-pink lacquer.

The end sections of the lower two rows, being rather long, are tilted upward, somewhat like the roofline of a Chinese temple. These tilts make the end blocks easier to aim at and to strike, and—to me—more esthetically satisfying.

The fundamental requirement in tuning the bamboo is cutting a tongue to the exact desired frequency which will then couple with a blow tone—determined by blowing into one of the two saw cracks (an edge tone)—that is slightly lower. (If it *is* slightly lower, the maximum coupling will be achieved.) Once an approximate length of bamboo is determined, by experiment, for a given tone, a tongue is tentatively cut. At the critical point where a coupling begins to manifest itself, even 1/16 or 1/8 inch of further sawing of the tongue is enough—and in the higher tones more than enough. If the blow tone is good but the tongue is too flat, the end of the tongue is rasped away very slightly underneath, sharping the tone; if the tongue is too sharp, the bamboo is rasped on top at the back of the tongue, flatting the tone. (This tuning principle is exactly the same as that for the reed tongues of the Chromelodeons.) However, if the coupling is good but the tone is much too low, the whole bamboo section must be shortened, tongue and all.[18]

---

[18] As the job turned out, the tongue cuts for the lowest tones were about a third, or slightly more, of the inside lengths, those for the middle tones slightly less than half, those for the highest tones about one-half. The proportions of cuts to lengths in Boo II were considerably less (see below).

It is most important that each piece of bamboo be tuned in relation to the sequence in which it appears, not as though it were isolated in a vacuum. The harmonic content of the individual pieces varies tremendously, and one piece, which may seem to be in good tune in a vacuum, as it were, will stand out incongruously if its harmonic content differs radically from the others.

None of the bamboo would stay in tune, even temporarily, without the galvanized metal straps (sometimes called plumbers' tape) that hold each section firm by means of a bolt. Flatting can be achieved by a gentle release of the bolt, sharping by tightening it strongly. If this does not accomplish correct tuning, the band can be moved slightly to the rear for flatting, slightly forward, toward the ends of the saw cuts of the tongues, for sharping. But the band must always be firm, never loose.

When I built the instrument, in Sausalito in 1955,[19] most of the bamboo was from the Philippines, and none of it was more than 3 3/4 inches inside diameter. But good natural bass in any instrument means a particular kind of resonant power, and power in simple acoustics means *large size*. I obtained truly giant Japanese bamboo, finally, and I used it in 1963 to replace all of the lowest row and the left half of the second row. The balance of the second row and most of the third, fourth, and fifth rows are from the Philippines; the sixth row is mostly from California.[20]

By most elementary acoustical principles, a pipe or string tone that is a 2/1 lower than another tone calls for a doubling of dimensions, if either similar power or similar harmonic content is desirable. For example, if 7/6 (in the fourth row) turns out to be a good tone with a 3-inch open end (inside diameter) and a 7-inch length, the 2/1 below (the first tone of the first row) would call for a 6-inch diameter and a 14-inch length. But 6-inch diameter

---

[19] I received much good advice from William Loughborough, who had built an instrument of similar type, although in a twelve-tone equally-tempered scale—representing the usual 7-White–5-Black sequence. Most of the original bamboo was given to me by David Wheat, who worked with the orchestra on one of the President liners and brought the bamboo back under his bunk.

[20] The largest section of bamboo is 16 inches long and has an outside diameter of 5 3/4 inches. The smallest is 4 1/2 inches long, with an outside diameter of 2 1/8 inches. The lengths of the rows at the open ends: lowest, 70 1/2 inches; second, 59 1/2 inches; third, 51 1/4; fourth, 42 1/2; fifth, 37 1/2; sixth, 32 1/2. The structure holding the bamboo was completely redesigned and rebuilt in the summer of 1957. At each end, six sections of 5/8-inch brass tubing, pressure fitted into six lengths of pine at the bottom, support six racks into which pins are inserted to hold the bamboo pieces at the rear. These racks come apart for purposes of repair. The heights from the floor of the racks: lowest, 22 1/4 inches; second, 29 inches; third, 33 1/2; fourth, 38; fifth, 42 1/2; sixth, 47.

bamboo on the lowest row would make the instrument virtually unplayable—
the stretches would become far too great for the kinds of playing required.

Bamboo is infinitely capricious and unpredictable. If one part of a pole
produces a good tone, all parts will usually produce good tones. However, a
pole exactly similar to the eye may not produce any good tones. Because of
some exasperation in working with bamboo, I experimented a few years ago
with plastic tubing, which comes in many sizes. The tubing is always
predictable, and it produces a similar tone, but it lacks the beautiful and warm
quality of bamboo.

Starting with the right half of the second row, where the Philippine
bamboo begins, the blocks produce a very distinctive inharmonic overtone,
roughly a 6/5 above the fundamental. I cannot guess whether this results from
the relation of the open end to the length or from inherent qualities of
particular kinds of bamboo. As will be seen below, in the discussion of Boo II,
where each piece of bamboo has two open ends, a rationale for the 6/5
overtone becomes immediately apparent. Since there is no bamboo lumbering
industry in the American hinterland, experiments with bamboo are both difficult and costly.

*Boo II*: This instrument was completed at Encinitas in March, 1971. It is
not an exact copy of the first Boo because the bamboo sections follow a different acoustical principle. Now, each section is open at both ends and
therefore roughly double the length of each section of the first Boo (the law of
organ pipes—the cycle of a pipe open at both ends is complete after traveling
two lengths rather than four). The second important difference is the strong
inharmonic overtone, 6/5 above the fundamental, in all tones. This is
achieved by cutting the tongue to about a sixth of the total length of each pipe.
Thus, the lowest tone, 7/6, is produced by a pipe that is 28 inches long, and
the tongue is one-sixth of 28, or 4 2/3 inches, creating a 7/5 in the balance.
The 6/5 is a personal preference; other inharmonic overtones could have been
chosen.

The new Boo has two positive advantages: the sounds are projected
toward both audience and player, rather than only toward the player; and the
bamboo is all of one kind—giant, mottled Japanese Mozo—thus lending more
predictability to the sounds. Still, because of variations in the inside contours
and in the thickness of walls, formulas must remain flexible. (I had wanted

## THE RATIOS AND THE NOTATION OF THE BOOS

21/20
0

| 11/7 | 8/5 | 18/11 | 5/3 | 27/16 | 12/7 | 7/4 | 11/6 |
|---|---|---|---|---|---|---|---|
| 4 | 3 | 2 | 1 | 1 | 2 | 3 | 4 |

| 11/9 | 5/4 | 9/7 | 4/3 | 11/8 | 7/5 | 10/7 | 16/11 | 3/2 |
|---|---|---|---|---|---|---|---|---|
| 4 | 3 | 2 | 1 | 0 | 1 | 2 | 3 | 4 |

| 21/20 | 16/15 | 12/11 | 11/10 | 10/9 | 9/8 | 8/7 | 7/6 | 32/27 | 6/5 |
|---|---|---|---|---|---|---|---|---|---|
| 5 | 4 | 3 | 2 | 1 | 1 | 2 | 3 | 4 | 5 |

| 16/9 | 9/5 | 20/11 | 11/6 | 15/8 | 40/21 | 64/33 | 160/81 | 1/1 | 81/80 | 33/32 |
|---|---|---|---|---|---|---|---|---|---|---|
| 5 | 4 | 3 | 2 | 1 | 0 | 1 | 2 | 3 | 4 | 5 |

| 16/11 | 40/27 | 3/2 | 32/21 | 14/9 | 11/7 | 8/5 | 18/11 | 5/3 | 27/16 | 12/7 | 7/4 |
|---|---|---|---|---|---|---|---|---|---|---|---|
| 6 | 5 | 4 | 3 | 2 | 1 | 1 | 2 | 3 | 4 | 5 | 6 |

| 7/6 | 32/27 | 6/5 | 11/9 | 5/4 | 14/11 | 9/7 | 21/16 | 4/3 | 27/20 | 11/8 | 7/5 | 10/7 |
|---|---|---|---|---|---|---|---|---|---|---|---|---|
| 6 | 5 | 4 | 3 | 2 | 1 | 0 | 1 | 2 | 3 | 4 | 5 | 6 |

bamboo of larger diameters, particularly in the lower tones, but I was obliged to use what was available.)

At least to the ear, Boo II is a different instrument, even though a Boo part in any of my music may be played on either Boo—same notation, same sequence of tones. I assume that the different impact on the ear is caused by having the bamboo sections of Boo II open at both ends rather than closed at one end as in Boo I.

Both Boos give "dry" sounds, sharp in character and short in duration. It is impossible for me to say that one or the other has better ring-time or better resonance. In the perpetually crowded conditions of my quarters, I have not been able to have both of them in the same room at the same time. I can say only that they are different.[21]

Notation: there are thirteen pieces of bamboo in the lowest row, twelve in the second, eleven in the third, ten in the fourth, nine in the fifth, and eight in the sixth. The center piece of those rows with odd numbers of pieces is represented by 0, and the numbers 1–2–3–4–5–6 (in the lowest row) extend outward from the 0. Rows with an even number of pieces have two 1's in the center, and continue outward, 2–3–4–5–6 (in the second row); and so forth. The numbers are painted on the tops toward the ends of the tongues. On the staff, those pieces to the left of the 0's (or 1's) are on spaces, and those to the right are on lines. The range is from the 7/6 above 1/1–196 to the 21/20 above 1/1–784 (the "B♭" below "middle C" to the second "A♭" above).

Playing techniques: the blocks are always struck on the ends of the tongues. Mallets are very occasionally used, but only in very soft passages. Generally, felted dowels are employed, usually 3/8-inch dowels, but sometimes 1/2- or 1/4-inch ones (the latter only in passages limited to high tones).

---

[21] Dimensions: The largest bamboo section is 28 inches long and has an outside diameter of 4 inches. The smallest is 7 1/4 inches long, with an outside diameter of 2 1/2 inches. Lengths of the rows: lowest, 56 inches; second, 48 inches; third, 42 3/4; fourth, 37; fifth, 31 1/2; sixth, 27 1/2. Heights of the rows (to the tips of the tongues): lowest, 31 inches; second, 33 1/2 inches; third, 38; fourth, 41; fifth, 46; sixth, 51. The overall height of the instrument (including the casters) to the top of the music rack is 65 1/2 inches; its width across the front, from one redwood endpiece to the other, is 68 1/2 inches; and its depth, from the tips of the lowest bamboo sections to the back edges of the endpieces, is 30 inches. The support structure, 1 3/4 inch thick, is redwood with a core of 1/4-inch fir ply. The endpieces are 49 inches high (including casters), 25 inches deep at the bottom, 5 3/4 inches deep at the top. The height from the floor to the lowest birch rack is 24 1/4 inches.

The dowels must always be held diagonally to the ends of the tongues, so that a clear, sharp sound is obtained. If the tongues of any one row are at a consistent level, glissandi are very easy and very effective. Again, the best glissandi are achieved with dowels employed diagonally (good examples on Boo I may be found in both Verse 5 and Verse 22 of *Petals*—see Appendix V).

The player has virtually a six-foot range to cover in the lowest row, and must move rapidly and easily. When he is playing on this row in particular, even if he is a man of average height, he must bend in order to achieve the necessary diagonal of the felted dowels, but he must bend *at the knees*, not at the waist as though making a final bow to the world.

## Mbira Bass Dyad

This instrument, built at Encinitas in 1972, is an extension, in the direction of much lower tones, of the tongue-with-resonator idea implicit in the Boos, although in this case, unlike the Boos, the tongue extends over the tops of the resonators (see photograph). I have experimented with a tongue cut into an organ pipe (as with sections of bamboo) to the point that a coupling is achieved. The result is not bad, but the present solution is better.

Mbira (I am told) is an African word implying tongues—of metal, such as those of the thumb piano (see below), or of wood—extending over individual resonators or over a common resonator for all tones. The tongues are plucked or struck.

The two tones of this dyad are approximately the second "G" below "middle C" (1/1) and the "A♭" above that "G" (21/20). These tones, like those of the Boos, are "dry" sounds; but here a coupling with the resonators is all-important, especially because the sounds are "dry."

The tongues are struck on the ends with heavy bamboo mallets, about 2 inches in diameter and 12 inches long, held diagonally to the blocks. Both tongues are clamped firmly at the back ends and pass over tiny metal bridges about 2 1/2 inches from those ends, so that they vibrate freely only from the bridges to the front ends. The bridges are movable within a small range, permitting slightly lower or higher tones. If they are moved back, the vibrating lengths are increased and the tones lowered. If they are moved forward, the vibrating lengths decrease and the tones become higher.

MBIRA BASS DYAD

The blocks are osage orange, a highly resilient American wood much favored by boy scouts for bows and arrows. The front ends are weighted by additional blocks of osage orange, glued to the longer blocks, to force them to vibrate more slowly, thus producing bass tones with comparatively short pieces of wood. The wood should be vertical grain, which is difficult to find in osage orange, and it might be preferable to cut the blocks in their present form, from single pieces of wood.

The additional resonators lying on the floor are identical in dimension to those directly under the tongues and are bolted to their respective vertical resonators. These auxiliary resonators amplify the tones surprisingly. They are closed at the front but open at the back, pointing toward a hypothetical audience.[22]

## *The Eucal Blossom*

This instrument also uses bamboo, but it is based on a much simpler principle. The sections are treated much like wood blocks of the marimbas, and are mounted at about the nodes (although here the nodes seem less important). The sound is even shorter and sharper than that of the Boos, and it records very well. Since there are so many lush sounds in this family of instruments, I am happy to have these bright, dry sounds of very short duration.

The bamboo is all from San Diego. It has very thick walls, which is an important consideration for this kind of instrument. (I don't know whether this is a variety of bamboo that always has thick walls, or whether it grows more slowly because it gets no rainfall in the growing season—the summer—in California, as opposed to the large amount of summer rainfall in the Orient.)

The blocks are in three rows of eleven each (see photograph) and are mounted on polyfoam, with elastic bands attached to hooks toward the left

---

[22] Dimensions: The height to the playing level is 37 1/2 inches; the width across the bottom is 29 1/4 inches; the depth (length of the longest auxiliary resonator) is 33 3/4 inches. *Inside* measurements of the resonators: 1/1—32 3/4 inches long, 5 1/4 inches wide, 8 inches deep; 21/20—31 inches long, 4 3/4 inches wide, 7 3/4 inches deep. The blocks: 1/1—13 1/2 inches long overall, 11 1/4 inches long from bridge to end of tongue, 5 1/4 inches wide, 2 1/2 inches thick at the front end; 21/20—13 inches long overall, 10 3/4 inches long from the bridge to the end of the tongue, 4 3/4 inches wide, 2 1/2 inches thick at the front end. The vertical structure at the back (only partially seen in the photograph), mostly of 2 x 12 redwood stock, is 11 inches deep at the bottom and tapers to a 6-inch depth at the top. Height from floor: 33 inches.

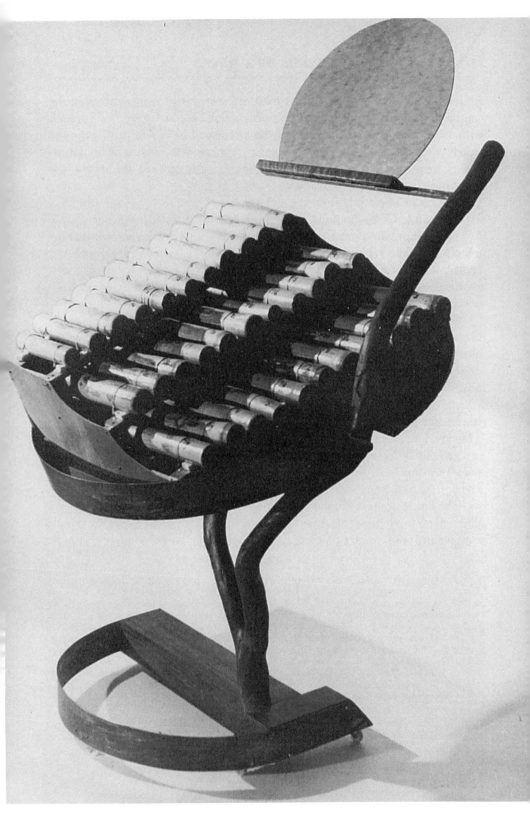

EUCAL BLOSSOM

ends to hold each in place. This is the third instrument in which I used the contorted boughs of eucalyptus as part of the base structure.[23] A branch with an appropriate crotch extends from a redwood base; one arm above the crotch is cut at the top at the angle desired for the disk holding the bamboo, and is there bolted to the disk; the other extends upward through a slot in the disk and holds the music rack.

The range of pitch is from the 4/3 above 1/1–392 to 1/1–1568 (the "C" above "middle C" to the third "G"above). It follows the Chromelodeon scale 4/3 to 4/3, but with twelve ratios excluded and with a 3/2 leap upward at the top of the scale—4/3 to 1/1. The lengths of the blocks, which vary from 8 1/2 to 16 inches, are determined experimentally. If a block is too flat, it is shortened; if it is too sharp, a piece of 1/4-inch plywood is glued to one end, which lengthens and therefore flats it.

Notation: originally, I thought that the instrument would be more easily playable if it followed the plan of the Quadrangularis Reversum, with the notation reversed—that is, with notes that seem to ascend in pitch actually descending, and vice versa. This turned out not to be the case, but since I had already written the Eucal Blossom part for *Delusion* (the only work to date in which it has been used), it seemed unprofitable to rebuild the instrument and rewrite the part for the usual concept of ascents and descents. As with the Bass Marimba, all spaces and lines of the staff and the spaces above and below are utilized. In order to distinguish between the three rows, hollow triangular note-heads are used for the highest, hollow square note-heads for the middle, and hollow round note-heads for the lowest.

The five sections of bamboo in the highest row that are notated on lines are painted, on top in the centers, with red lacquer triangles; the five of the middle row notated on lines are painted, centers, with blue lacquer squares; and the

---

[23] Eucalyptus was first used in this manner for the Gourd Tree (1964) and then for the Quadrangularis Reversum (1965). Construction of the Eucal Blossom was begun, very tentatively, in Del Mar, California, in 1964, but I did not really finish it until 1967, in San Diego. The disk, made of 1/2-inch fir plywood, is 38 inches in diameter; a rich red brocade (not visible in the photograph) is glued to the underside, toward the audience. A half-circle of 3 1/2-inch-wide aluminum stripping edges the lower part of the tilted disk, and another half-circle helps to stabilize the base, a redwood 4 x 4, 28 inches long, mortised to a 16 inch crosspiece at the right. Both aluminum strips are painted blue-green. The disk (without the aluminum stripping) is 26 inches above the floor at the front edge, 41 inches at the back edge. The arm of eucalyptus holding the music rack ends 56 1/2 inches straight above the floor. The structure holding the bamboo on the disk is 30 3/4 inches deep, 22 inches wide at the front of the instrument, 25 inches wide at the back. The rows of bamboo are stepped up (or down) by 3 1/2 inches.

five of the lowest row notated on lines are painted, centers, with violet lacquer circles. (This again follows the Bass Marimba procedure, where five of the blocks have red moons to distinguish notes on lines.)

Playing techniques: mallets with oak heads at least 1 1/2 inches in diameter are generally used. Lighter wood-head mallets and even mallets with yarn-wound heads are occasionally used for softer playing. As with the Boos, glissandi are very effective. To a player with a good percussion technique, the instrument is not at all difficult.

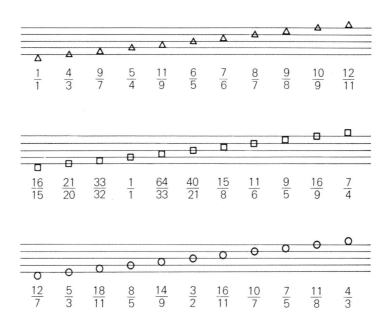

## The Gourd Tree and Cone Gongs

Twelve Chinese temple bells of various sizes are bolted to twelve gourds cut and tuned to the pitches of the bells and attached with lengths of 1/4- and

3/16-inch threaded rods to the eucalyptus bough (see photograph). This bough—the first eucalyptus I used as an essential part of one of my instruments—is held firmly upright by a redwood base of 2 x 4's and 4 x 4's. The rods are rather flexible and can be bent in order to position the bells for easy playing, as well as to give the impression of ripe fruit growing at various angles on stems, somewhat like a papaya tree, with the smallest fruit at the top.[24]

The metal of the bells is soft, and a slight amount of tuning can be accomplished easily. Metal is filed away inside the edge to flat, and the edge is filed, with the file at a right angle, to sharp. Each gourd is tested by blowing on the edge of the open hole. If it is too flat a smaller gourd is used; if too sharp a larger one is used. Flatting can also be accomplished through a partial closing of the hole. The bells are struck diagonally on the edges with light bamboo sticks padded somewhat with masking tape. Mallets are sometimes used on the lower tones.

The notation follows the Bass Marimba idea—lines and spaces of the staff, with red circles painted on the gourds of the bells that fall on lines. The twelfth bell, 5/4, which was added later, is notated by a square note on the same line as the 6/5's round note.

The two aluminum Cone Gongs form a separate unit but are generally played by the musician on the Gourd Tree. These cones were originally the

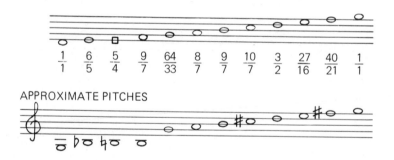

APPROXIMATE PITCHES

[24] The bells were given to me by Emil Richards in 1964, and I built the instrument that summer in Del Mar, California. The vertical height to the right angle of the bough is 72 inches; the outward extension from the angle is 39 inches. The diameter of the largest bell is 8 3/8 inches, that of the smallest 3 1/2 inches.

GOURD TREE AND CONE GONGS

nose cones of airplane gas tanks.[25] They are painted a greenish yellow, and the "stems" that support them are green—a mounting that suggests a strange variety of giant mushroom. Some 5 1/2 inches was sawed off the edge of one cone to achieve a higher fundamental. It seems inevitable that any sounding body of this type will produce a variety of inharmonic overtones, and these cones are no exception. At least two types of tones are available: edge tones with a long ring-time, and short, sharp, center tones (about halfway up). Despite the plethora of strange overtones, the edge tones give a strong fundamental sound, the larger cone giving the 16/9 below 1/1–98, and the smaller one the 6/5 above. The short center tones are not so clear, but they seem to emit, in the larger, the 12/11 that is more than a 2/1 above 16/9; in the smaller, the 4/3 that is more than a 2/1 above 6/5. The notation:

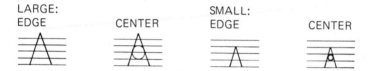

## The Cloud-Chamber Bowls

Fourteen sections of twelve-gallon Pyrex carboys—five tops and nine bottoms—are suspended from a 4 x 4 redwood frame in seven vertical lines (two carboys to a line) by means of 1/4-inch Manila rope and S hooks (see photograph). The carboys are 16 inches in diameter. Holes are bored in the center of the bottom sections and the Manila rope is knotted below each to hold it in place. Funnels hanging from the rope are used to suspend the tops of the carboys. The rope supporting each separate section is looped over an S hook in order to facilitate assembly and disassembly.[26]

[25] These were obtained from the salvage department of the Douglas Aircraft Company (at forty cents a pound), and were mounted in Venice, California, in 1965. The larger cone is 30 inches high and has a bottom diameter of 17 inches. The smaller is 24 1/2 inches high, with a bottom diameter of 16 inches. The redwood base is 35 1/2 inches long by 7 1/8 inches wide. The 2 x 4 crosspieces at the bottom of the base are 18 inches long.

[26] The length of the tori bar is 96 inches, that of the base 85 1/2 inches. The two 4 x 4 crosspieces of the base are 36 inches long, and are reinforced by two 2 x 4's 23 inches apart outside to outside. The two 4 x 4 standards, including the two mortises, top and bottom, are 73 inches high (including the casters), measured on the outside planes. All is redwood. The seven ropes are separated by 9 3/4 inches.

CLOUD-CHAMBER BOWLS

The name Cloud-Chamber Bowls arose from the fact that I found tops and bottoms—not necessarily the present ones—at the Radiation Laboratory glass shop at the University of California, Berkeley (in 1950). There, the center sections were cut out for so-called cloud chambers, designed to determine the paths of nuclear particles. I discovered that a very beautiful but complex sound could be produced if the center of a section was suspended by one hand, so that the edge was free, while the other hand struck with fingertips on the edge. As long as my experiments went on, I undoubtedly deprived various faculty wives of many punch and fish bowls.

Because of breakage, which has been a recurrent problem, few of the originals remain. Actually, short of an earthquake or other Acts of God, breakage should be no problem at all. If players are properly trained *before they look at a sheet of music,* so that their response is automatic *when they see a sheet of music,* there will be no breakage. In the case either of unusual techniques, as with the Harmonic Canons and Kitharas, or of unusual materials for percussion, as in this instrument and the three to be explained next, learning the technique before the notation will lead to less anguish all around. A bowls player staring at a piece of music and swinging wildly without looking, will produce bad sounds at the very least, but at the worst he will bring on splintered disaster. However, if he first develops an intuitive sense as to exactly how loud the bowls can be played, he will stop short, and everyone will be happier.

As with all sounding bodies of this variety, the best resonant sound is achieved by striking the side of the bowl very close to the edge with a fairly soft mallet; a soft tone at the edge is stronger and more musical than a crashing stroke five or six inches above the edge. The section with short vertical sides (the top two rows) have very clear fundamentals; those with long vertical sides (most of the bottom two rows) are far more complex.

A very different sound is achieved by striking the circular flat surface of the bottoms of the carboys (turned upside down and called *tops* in the illustration below). Unlike the long ring-time of the edge tones, these are very short and sharp, and are notated differently. Even though at least one of the bowls has since been broken, the illustration shows the ratios, notation, and approximate pitches given in the full score of *Delusion.*

Most of the bowls have been broken in rehearsals, very few in transportation, but only one in a way so unusual that it is worth recounting. In my studio in Sausalito the bowls just happened to be positioned close to the 22-cycle tone of the Marimba Eroica. At that moment of revelation, the bowls were not being played, but the 22-cycle tone *was*, and one of the top bowls simply disintegrated—trying, presumably, to vibrate sympathetically with that low frequency.

In cutting new bowls, a point on the side of the carboy is selected, largely by chance, and a line around the entire circumference is scored with a sharp three-cornered file. An appropriate electrical wire—the kind that becomes red-hot in a hot plate—is then wrapped tightly around the carboy at that point. This is connected to a resister and is plugged into an electrical circuit. After the wire has glowed red-hot for a few minutes, it is removed, a bucket of cold water is poured over the carboy, and—to date—the glass cracks at the desired point.

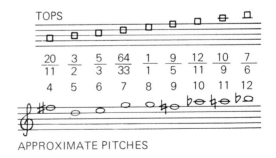

It has been impossible for me to tune the bowls—I must accept what I get, short of establishing a grinding laboratory with the technicians to run it. Therefore, in repeat performances of a particular work, and after some breakage, it is necessary to rewrite the bowls part. I did this for the work *Castor and Pollux* for a performance in 1965 (twelve years after it was first performed), and I managed to write a part that at least retained the spirit of the original. However, in 1967, while rewriting the full score of *Oedipus* (first performed in 1952), I felt that the only wise course was to leave the line for the bowls blank, to be filled in later if and when another performance is scheduled.

Techniques have been discussed, but something must be said regarding the player's physical and mental attitude. He has some seven feet of floor space to cover with athletic grace, and his footwork is very important. He must play the edges of the bowls toward the bottom of the rack, as well as those above, and he must never *bow to the bowls*, but rather bend at the knees in order to strike these correctly. He must extract and reveal—in both body and spirit—only that which is handsome.

## The Spoils of War

This instrument (see photograph), an aggregation of six percussive sounds or effects, was built at Gualala in 1950, and various sounds were added at various places in the years 1951–1965.[27] No. 1 provides a low wood-block tone, the 9/8 above 1/1–49, which is slightly below the pitch of the highest tone of the Marimba Eroica (8/7). Both tones are "A's," but the Pernambuco block on the Spoils of War is not as powerful as the comparable Eroica block, at least partly because it is narrower, and possibly because the arch underneath is cut too deeply. It is notated:

$$\downarrow$$

No. 2 consists of seven brass shell casings, with definite pitches and long ring-times, suspended just below the Pernambuco block. (The small cymbal, seen in the photograph, was used only once, in *Petals*.) These shell casings are

[27] An excellent short example of most of the sounds of the Spoils of War is to be heard in its duet with the Koto, Verse 12 of *Petals* (see Appendix V).

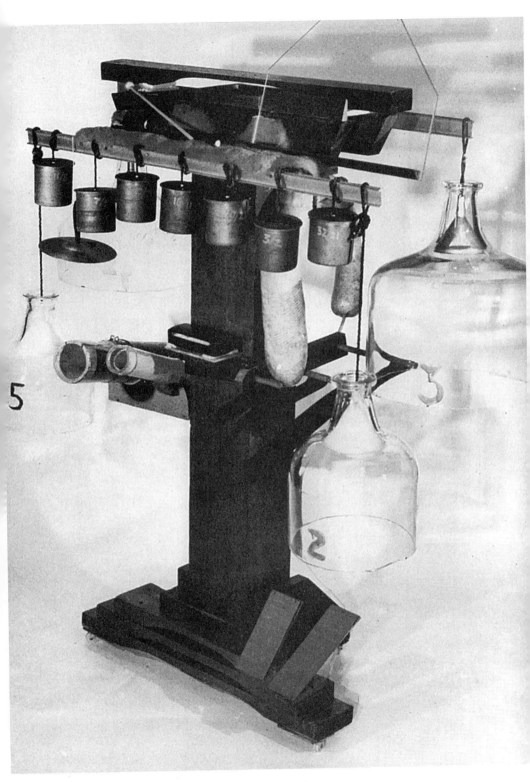

SPOILS OF WAR

tuned in the same manner as the temple bells of the Gourd Tree; the metal is
fairly soft, and the shells are thinned at the lower edge to flat and filed *on* the
edge to sharp. The ratios, the notation, and the range:

$$\frac{11}{8} \quad \frac{7}{5} \quad \frac{10}{7} \quad \frac{16}{11} \quad \frac{40}{27} \quad \frac{3}{2} \quad \frac{32}{21}$$

No. 3 has four Cloud-Chamber Bowls (all tops)—two with 16-inch
diameters (like the bowls discussed above) at the rear, and two with 11 1/2-
inch diameters at the front. Large numbers (—2–3–4–5—) are used in the
notation, 2 and 5 being the smaller bowls at the front. The approximate
pitches:

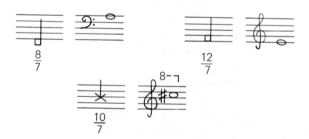

No. 4 consists of two tongued pieces of bamboo open at both ends, and of a
Chinese wood block. The bamboo sections are to the left in the photograph,
and the wood block is attached to the resonator of the Pernambuco block,
center. The ratios, the notation, and the approximate pitches:

$$\frac{8}{7} \qquad\qquad \frac{12}{7}$$

$$\frac{10}{7}$$

No. 5 consists of three Whang Guns—strips of spring steel of different
lengths, with fairly sharp bends in opposite directions at the two ends. Controlled by pedals (to the right of the base in the photograph), these steel strips
function something like musical saws. The name arises from the sound—

striking a steel strip with a wooden mallet while using a pedal produces a *whang* sound, generally with an upward inflection, but with a downward inflection also possible. The ratios, with the ranges upward, the notation, and the approximate pitches, from largest to smallest:

$$\frac{16}{15} \quad \frac{6}{5} \qquad \frac{3}{2} \quad \frac{9}{5} \qquad \frac{8}{5} \quad \frac{6}{5}$$

No. 6 is a gourd guiro (to the right in the photograph, above the Whang Guns) with the usual grooved side. It gives a rasping sound when scraped with a stick and is notated:

Because of the many and very different percussive bodies, many and very different mallets must be used. The player must learn to keep more than one mallet in each hand, if necessary—and it generally is. The Pernambuco block is effective only with a large soft mallet. The casings are brilliant under a wood-head mallet, soft and tinkly under softer mallets. They must always be struck at the edges. The bowls are played always with soft mallets, at the edges, and everything said about the Cloud-Chamber Bowls above applies here, including the necessity of learning technique before notation. The Whang Guns are usually most effective with a wood-head mallet, especially the two that are shorter. Like the Kithara glides, the glides of the Whang Guns are meaningful only if the pedal grabs the tone *at the time the steel is struck*.[28]

Much of the music for this instrument is difficult, and it cannot be played well if the musician's gaze is fixed on a piece of music paper. Rather often he

[28] The Pernambuco block is 37 1/2 inches long, 3 inches wide. Its resonator (of 3/4-inch redwood) is 59 3/4 inches high (not including the casters), 8 1/2 inches wide, 6 1/2 inches deep. The aluminum extrusions holding the bowls and casings are each 45 inches long. The length of the doubled guiro gourd is 45 inches. The larger bamboo section is 29 3/4 inches long and 4 1/4 inches outside diameter; the smaller bamboo is 19 1/8 inches long, with a diameter of 2 7/8 inches. Whang Guns: longest—24 x 3 inches; next longest— 13 x 2 1/2 inches; shortest—8 3/4 x 2 1/2 inches.

must memorize, so that he may watch his hands and mallets. The situation is no different from that faced by all musicians when great skill is called for. The player memorizes, and the notation does no more than remind him of the problem ahead.

## The Zymo-Xyl

Zymo-Xyl (zi-mock-sil, with the accent on the first syllable), built at Petaluma in 1963, is a word composed of two Greek syllables, the first denoting fermentation, the second wood. If there were a Greek syllable denoting hubcaps, it probably would have been added. Two rows of empty liquor and wine bottles are stacked upside down above a row of wood blocks (see photograph). Like the bowls, these bottles sometimes break under the excitement of playing, but, unlike the bowls, no anguish is involved. It is a curious fact that the tones of the bottles used for any particular brand generally have a range of very small latitude. Hence, one simply buys another bottle. And if the Bristol Cream Sherry bottle is not exactly a 1/1, for example, he buys another bottle and hopes for better luck. Here are the ratios and the brand names used at present, from low to high:

1. 6/5 .. Old Heaven Hill Bourbon
2. 11/9 ..Old Heaven Hill Bourbon
3. 5/4 ...... Heaven Hill (not old)
4. 4/3 ...........Gallo's Sherry
5. 7/5 ............ Gordon's Gin
6. 10/7 .......... Gordon's Gin
7. 3/2 ............. Brugal Rum
8. 11/7 ...........Bacardi Rum
9. 8/5 ....Jameson's Irish Whisky
10. 5/3 ........ Barclay's Whisky
11. 27/16 ...... Barclay's Whisky
12. 12/7 ........ Canada Dry Gin
13. 16/9 ..... Cabin Still Bourbon
14. 20/11 ....... Canada Dry Gin
15. 11/6 ......... Taylor's Sherry
16. 40/21 ........ Vat 69 Scotch
17. 1/1 ..... Bristol Cream Sherry

The notation for both bottles and wood blocks generally follows the Bass Marimba idea. Red circles are painted on those bottles and blocks that fall on lines of the staff, and straight vertical red strokes on those that fall on ledger lines above or below. The range is a 5/3, as shown in the illustration:

RANGE

ZYMO-XYL

The fourteen blocks are vertical-grain white oak cut from the old top of Chromelodeon I. The oak became available when I recased the two Chromelodeons.[29] It turned out to be a very durable and resonant wood. The blocks are held in place by cords passing through holes at the nodes and pulled tightly into slots on the edges of the single triangular resonator.[30] The scale tones are very arbitrary, even haphazard. The ratios, the notation, and the approximate pitches:

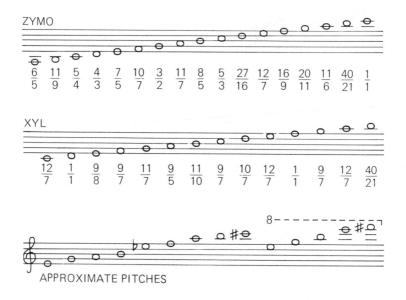

APPROXIMATE PITCHES

The parts for the Zymo-Xyl are generally written on two bracketed staves, the upper marked *Zymo* and the lower marked *Xyl.*

---

[29] The reed organs of sixty and more years ago seemed very harmonious with the other furnishings of American parlors at that time, but in their original shapes and decorations, they seemed very incongruous with my other instruments. In 1963 I remade the cases, using Philippine mahogany plywood, wrapping—in a sense—1/4-inch plywood around the four ends.

[30] The single triangular resonator box was made by a student in industrial design at the University of Illinois and proved to be effective. The length of the resonator box is 40 inches. At the bass end, the top of the triangle is 23 inches and the sides 24 inches each. At the treble end, the top is 6 inches and each side 5 3/4 inches. The longest oak block is 18 inches, the shortest 5 3/4 inches. The height from the floor of the front edge of the resonator varies from 32 1/2 to 34 1/2 inches. The height of the instrument at the back, to the top of the bottle rack, is 37 inches. The bottle rack is 47 inches long, 8 1/2 inches wide, and 12 1/4 inches high.

Three additional percussion bodies are mounted at the ends of large dowels above rubberized material. These are, from bottom to top, a 1953 Ford hubcap, called Chi; a 1952 Ford hubcap, called Zeta; and an aluminum kettle top, called Omega. They are notated by the appropriate Greek letters, and if centers—rather than edges—are to be struck, the letters are circled. The edge tone of Chi is the 11/7 below 1/1–784, and the center tone is the 32/21 below; the edge tone of Zeta is the 9/5 below 1/1–784, and the center tone is the 10/7 below; the edge tone of Omega is the 33/32 above 1/1–784, and the center tone is the 6/5 above.

Because the tones of the instrument are generally high in pitch (the Xyl section has the character of a xylophone), with clear, sharp sounds, they record very well. A good example is to be found in the trio, Zymo-Xyl, Blue Rainbow, Gourd Tree—Verse 23 of *Petals* (see Appendix V). Wood-head mallets of various weights give the best sound.

## *The Mazda Marimba*

Twenty-four light globes with their viscera removed are arranged in four ascending rows, somewhat like the bamboo of the Boo (see photograph).[31] The word Mazda was a brand name for certain light bulbs when I was young, and although it may seem ironic to invoke the name of the Persian god of light after the means of *making light* are removed, the word still seems appropriate.

The light mechanism is taken out by delicately incising a circle around the bulb's metal threads, about halfway down, with a hacksaw, and then, while holding the bulb with a piece of towel in case of breakage (I have never experienced any), snapping off the threaded portion and pulling out the connected viscera.

The range of pitch is from the 4/3 below 1/1–196 to the 5/4 above 1/1–784, almost three 2/1's. As with the Boo notation, rows with an odd number of bulbs have a central 0, with 1–2 or 1–2–3 extending from it in both directions, while rows with an even number of pieces have two 1's in the center and continue outward 1–2 in both directions. Center tones (the 0's) and

---

[31] From large to small, the six sizes of globes used measure the following (in inches): 6; 4 3/4; 3 1/2; 3; 2 1/2; 2 1/4; 1 3/4. The lowest rack is 28 1/2 inches above the floor, the highest 36 inches. The lengths of the four racks, from lowest to highest, in inches: 33; 27; 21; 21. The two supporting sides are made of 3/4-inch fir plywood, painted a royal blue on the outside and veneered with mahogany on the inside. The height at the front edge (to the lowest rack) is 22 1/4 inches; 30 inches at the rear. Both are mortised into curved blocks of cherrywood 20 inches long, 5 1/8 inches high, and 1 1/2 inches thick.

MAZDA MARIMBA

those to the left of center are on spaces; tones to the right of center are on lines of the staff. The ratios and the notation:

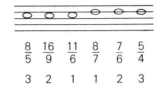

| $\frac{8}{5}$ | $\frac{16}{9}$ | $\frac{11}{6}$ | $\frac{8}{7}$ | $\frac{7}{6}$ | $\frac{5}{4}$ |
|---|---|---|---|---|---|
| 3 | 2 | 1 | 1 | 2 | 3 |

| $\frac{4}{3}$ | $\frac{11}{8}$ | $\frac{7}{5}$ | $\frac{3}{2}$ | $\frac{14}{9}$ | $\frac{11}{7}$ |
|---|---|---|---|---|---|
| 3 | 2 | 1 | 1 | 2 | 3 |

| $\frac{5}{4}$ | $\frac{21}{16}$ | $\frac{4}{3}$ | $\frac{11}{8}$ | $\frac{14}{9}$ | $\frac{11}{7}$ | $\frac{5}{3}$ |
|---|---|---|---|---|---|---|
| 3 | 2 | 1 | 0 | 1 | 2 | 3 |

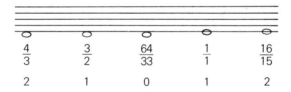

| $\frac{4}{3}$ | $\frac{3}{2}$ | $\frac{64}{33}$ | $\frac{1}{1}$ | $\frac{16}{15}$ |
|---|---|---|---|---|
| 2 | 1 | 0 | 1 | 2 |

Tuning is very easy. If a sound is too flat for a desired tone, break small pieces off the shaft end with a pair of pliers, in order to sharp. If a sound is too sharp, plastic tape may be wound around the shaft end, increasing the length, ergo flatting the sound.

This marimba must be played with very light mallets. These are 1/4-inch dowels with small rubber heads, the kind that are fitted over the legs of small objects in order to avoid marring a polished surface. (They are generally available in a variety store.) With these, there is seldom any breakage.

The delightful sounds of the instrument resemble, more than anything else, the bubbling of a coffee percolator. The instrument *must* be amplified, miked, and heard through a speaker because of its delicate resonance. An excellent example of both good amplification and good playing is found in Verse 5 of *Petals* (see Appendix V).[32]

## The Small Hand Instruments

These small instruments (see photographs) were made specifically for *Delusion of the Fury* and have so far been used only in that work. There are twenty-one, and all but two or three are percussive. They are used here and there throughout Acts I and II of *Delusion*, but most significantly in Scene 3 of Act II, *Time of Fun Together*. Most of them can be played high in the air, at head level or above, and this vision, added to the painted chests and arms of the players, gives—I am sure—more dramatic and theatrical dynamism to the scene. With four exceptions,[33] all were made by me between 1965 and 1967.

The top instrument, left, of the first photograph is my version of a Zulu instrument called an Ugumbo. It consists of a string, struck with a stick, extending over a curved branch of eucalyptus attached to a gourd resonator. I have heard the Zulu instrument on records, but I have seen only two rather poor depictions of it. I find that my version is serviceable, but I have failed to recreate the strangely beautiful sounds of the Zulu one.

The instrument adjoining the Ugumbo at the top is what I call a Waving Drum. It is struck stongly at the edge by possibly two fingers of one hand while the forearm of the hand holding the eucalyptus handle rotates as fast as

[32] I was introduced to the idea of this type of instrument in 1959 by a student in industrial design at the University of Illinois. The instrument took its present form in Petaluma in 1963.

[33] The Bolivian double flute was given to me by Ervin Wilson. Lou Harrison gave me the Mbira, or thumb piano. The first of the Waving Drums was presented by Emil Richards. The Fiji Rhythm Boat was given me by Kurt vonMeier.

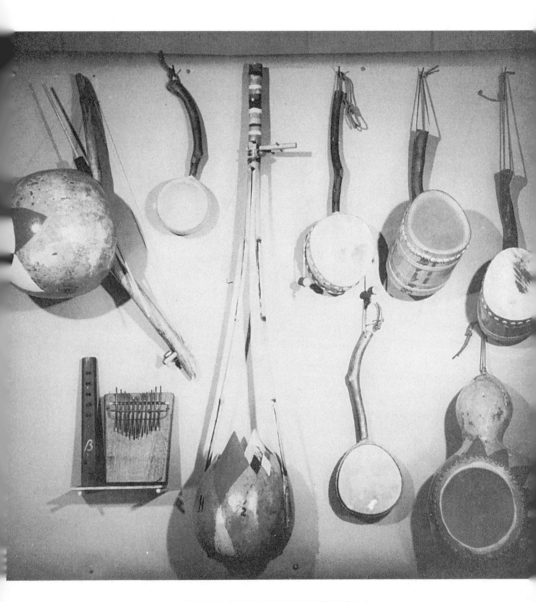

SMALL HAND INSTRUMENTS (1)

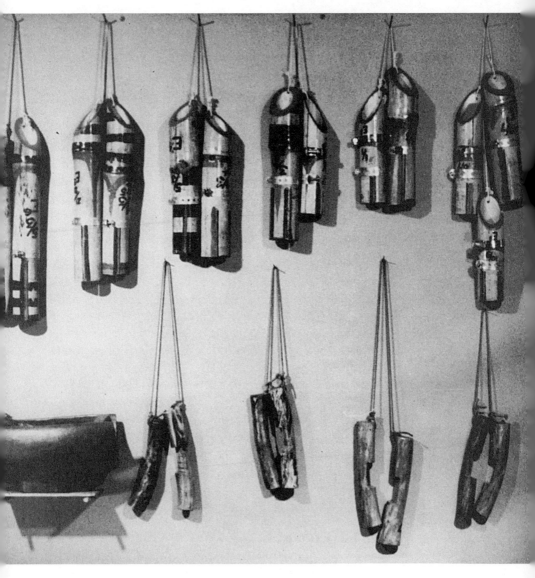

SMALL HAND INSTRUMENTS (2)

possible; because of phase differences created by this procedure, the ear perceives alternating changes in pitch, a kind of vibrato. This is similar to the effects of a Japanese percussion instrument called a "pancake drum"; there is also an East Indian equivalent.

Below the Ugumbo are a Bolivian double flute and an Mbira, or thumb piano. The shorter bore of the flute gives tones that are roughly a 6/5–5/4 above the tones of the longer bore. The range is from the 5/4 above 1/1–196 up to 1/1–784, including four overblown tones.[34] The Mbira has been used only once, in *Delusion*, to simulate fast female speech; its tuning is fairly irrational.

Proceeding toward the right, the next instrument is an Ektara, consisting of a gourd with a skin head over an opening at the bottom. A string is attached to the head and ends with the tuning gear inserted into the knot of bamboo at the top. The two flanks of bamboo bolted to the gourd are very flexible. One hand plucks or strikes the string while the other changes the intonation by either compressing the bamboo flanks (flatting the tone) or widening the flanks (sharping the tone).[35]

Next, to the right, is a Rotating Drum with knockers—small pieces of eucalyptus on the ends of cord. Something of a tonal racket is created if two hands are used rotating the handle. (Incidentally, crooked handles are much easier to wave and to rotate.) This instrument has heads covering both ends of a small section of 6 1/2-inch bamboo—it must have two heads to be effective.

Below the Rotating Drum is another Waving Drum, larger and with a lower pitch than the one described previously. Like the Rotating Drum, this instrument has heads on both ends of a 6 1/2-inch bamboo section.

The two drums at the upper right are what I call Belly Drums. Heads cover only one end of larger sections of the same 6 1/2-inch-diameter bamboo and are struck with mallets. The other ends are open. One hand strikes while

[34] Many persons who have been totally innocent of even one experiment in their entire lives have asked me why I never built any wind instruments to conform to my system of music. Heaven deliver us! I have tackled quite enough for this one life of mine without assuming the excruciating job of even *one* wind instrument. Witness Kathleen Schlesinger's work of thirty years or more with the Greek aulos and Boehm's years of work with the flute. Perhaps I have been extraordinarily lucky, but I have found both clarinet and trumpet players who could give me almost any intonation I wanted on those particular instruments.

[35] The Ektara shown in the photograph is 47 inches high, with a gourd at the bottom 8 inches in diameter at its widest. A larger Ektara, not illustrated, is 71 inches high with a bottom gourd 12 inches in diameter. It has two pairs of bamboo flanks, one for each of its two strings; these end in tuning pegs near the knots of bamboo at the top.

the other moves the drum from a position close to the bare belly (not on it) to a position a few inches away. The belly is bare because clothes dampen resonance, and it should also be fairly hairless—a mat of hair is as dampening as a shirt. It is a simple acoustical fact that when the opening of a resonant body is partly closed (moving toward the belly), the tone goes downward in pitch; when it is opened even slightly (moving away from the belly), the tone goes upward in pitch. (This idea applies as well to the Ugumbo, discussed above; the open end of the gourd should be positioned near a naked and hairless belly or chest.)

The last instrument in this photograph, lower right, is a Gourd Drum; the neck of the gourd rests in the crook of the forearm, while the other hand uses mallets on various parts of the head, for various sounds. The Gourd Drum and all instruments with skin heads will sound crisper, stronger, if they are held above an electric heater, or even a low gas flame, for a few seconds before playing.

The second photograph shows two types of claves and one other small percussion instrument. At the top are six sets of Bamboo Claves. These are all heard as duads, even though the sixth, at the right, has three sections of bamboo; the player simply has two choices in his duads. The idea here is very similar to that of the Boos, but, unlike the Boos, the tuned tongues are not struck. The two pieces are struck together on the top ends of the backs, opposite to the tongues, and at something of a right angle to each other. The bamboo sections must be thick-walled in order to survive the rather violent strikings they receive, but when tuned and played correctly they produce a very powerful effect. Like the Boos, these sections must have bands of plumbers' tape tightly bolted just below the tongue cuts.

The range of pitch is from the 5/3 below 1/1–392 to the 8/7 above 1/1–784. Starting with the lowest duad the ratios are (the lower tone is given first): 5/3–1/1; 21/20–4/3; 4/3–5/3; 3/2–1/1; 5/3–1/1; 10/7–10/9–8/7. In the last instance either the 10/9 or the 8/7 is played against the 10/7. (In the photograph, the pitches of the claves, left to right, generally progress from low to high.)

Below the Bamboo Claves are four sets of Eucalyptus Claves. A central section of one of the pieces is cut out, the hand is cupped over this opening, thus forming a resonator, and the top of the piece is struck with the other piece of eucalyptus. If the sound is too sharp, some of the central cut is rasped away to make the center thinner, therefore flatter; if the sound is too flat, a thin piece of wood is glued to the flat surface of the cut to make the center thicker, therefore sharper. In two of the pairs, those to the far right in the photograph, two choices are available: either one of each pair may be cupped and become the resonating body, being struck by the other of the pair. Six tones are thus available from the four sets. The tones are high, clear and precise if properly tuned. The range of pitch is from the 5/3 below 1/1–784 to the 8/7 above. From low to high, the tones are: 5/3, 7/4–16/9, 1/1, 10/9–8/7.

The remaining instrument, at the lower left in the second photograph, is a Fiji Rhythm Boat (this must be my name for it—it does not sound Fijian), a hollowed-out chunk of a very dark hardwood. It is struck with sticks on the edges of the two sides, either in single strokes or in tremolo (in which case it creates still another tonal racket).

## Primitive Means in a Scientific Theocracy

As is evident by now, the instruments here depicted are an anomaly—primitive means to an expanding musical idea—and this in an age of universal admiration for mechanical miracles and universal acceptance of scientific authority. Not only are the small instruments just described primitive, nearly all the others are also primitive in concept, though considerably more elaborate. The only sophisticated instruments I have are the old-fashioned reed organs (Chromelodeons); I say *sophisticated* because I do not have the competence or the sophisticated equipment needed to reproduce one, which is not true of any of the others.

I am quite aware that the seemingly endless lists of ratios and the acoustical speculations present an enormous obstacle to almost anyone wishing to understand this book. But to those who have reached this point, it should now be evident that in my large theater works I am offering—if they are seen, heard, experienced—*a visual and corporeal music and theater*—in other words, a truly integrated theater.

Perhaps I have been moved in the direction of the primitive unconsciously and intuitively, throughout almost my entire life, in order to preserve my inner health—as a kind of spiritual restorative in the face of musical establishments clinging to habitual ways and philosophies. One must also find strength to face banks of computers—the irruption of electronic artifice which, among the intellectually and musically young, is also becoming both an establishment and a habit. The appurtenances of music cannot be regarded, like vegetable-peelers and electric irons, as labor-saving devices that will immediately sell themselves if given a chance to operate. Yes, it is indeed easy to "write" music by clipping and joining sections of recorded tape, even under the harassments of technical and administrative overseers; the tape idea is indeed a labor-saving device. But does it fulfill the deep human need for creative meaning in one's existence?

As for the commercial electronic instruments, their facture has been dedicated to virtually a single purpose: *substitution*—substitution for the instruments we now have, new vehicles for exactly the same music we now have, hence designed for exactly the same limited scale we now have. Their aim might at least be higher than the production of electrical threnodies for the funeral parlors and electrical nursemaids for the televised "soaps."

## Music's Determinants—the Ear, the Hand

Although many recent musical notations have become largely diagrammatic, they have in no way reduced the inelasticity of our present musical theory, which is at least partially responsible for the misdirection of many intonational ideas that have been proposed—it is so "easy" for the notation of "quartertones," for example. But historically, in the establishment of current musical habits, there was little if any causal relation. Significant developments in notation, naturally enough, followed the development of musical artifices. The Middle Ages made two notable advances over the awkward alphabetical notation of the Greeks—both in line with harmonic innovations. Graphic notation was probably the direct result of organum; it was a translation onto paper of the pitch separation of two voice parts. Again, the rhythmic division of music was probably the direct result of part-singing; it filled the need for an indication of a steady accent, so that the several voices would keep together.

Viewed from an acoustic standpoint these developments have little or no relation to the long, sometimes agonizing, evolution of musical theory and the science of intonation. They were—and notation is—a clumsy prescript and a clumsy record; just how clumsy we can appreciate if we analyze our own translation of notes into actions, and perceive how many of those actions are not indicated in any absolute way, and often not at all. Hence the latitude of "interpretation." The present-day diagrammatic notations are an even more clumsy prescript and no record at all, nor do they address themselves to the heart of such a problem as the decadent concert idea and industry.

A musical system does not evolve as it does because it lends itself to being translated into notation. It evolves, basically, from the capacity of the ear, and is formulated and articulated by scientific and intuitive insight and creative speculation. In the modern procedure the criterion of the ear—its basic capacity, uninfluenced by conditioning factors or education—is partially disregarded in the interest of recently acquired desires, such as facility in modulation. And, finally, it is disregarded in application to instruments; the nature of the human anatomy, particularly the hand, has been allowed to pass as an argument for adulteration, especially in keyboards.[36] Hence, three factors mold our current theory: the primal criterion of the ear; the conditioned desires of the ear; the tyranny of the hand.

Does man maintain that in practice he cannot reconcile the last two of these factors with the first, the criterion of the ear? The history of the men who have undertaken to do this, extending back through hundreds of years B.C., offers a good deal of encouragement. (See Chapters 15 to 18.)

---

[36] It could perhaps be argued that the criterion of the ear is also disregarded in the formulation of a musical theory in order that it may be simple enough to be comprehensible to the least intelligent of its potential devotees. This is frequently the attitude of present-day music teachers: "But how can we expect students to learn ratios when we have so much difficulty teaching them the A-B-C's of music?" What is overlooked is that simple superficialities are more difficult both to teach and to learn than complex fundamentals. It is not surprising that they do not differentiate—today's teachers were yesterday's students, and yesterday's curriculum was simply a segment of the vicious circle. But I am sure that the more influential theorists of the formative period of the sixteenth and seventeenth centuries did not advise the course of temperament because of its superficial simplicity (see Chapter Fifteen). The persistent searches of Zarlino, Mersenne, Rameau, and many others indicate that they had a zeal for the truth, whatever the cost to a fallaciously simple concept.

# CHAPTER FOURTEEN

# The Backgrounds of Six Major Works

IT SEEMS APPROPRIATE, after describing the construction and tuning of many new instruments in the preceding two chapters, to introduce works of a more compelling creative character in which these instruments were used. This is what they are all about—why they were built; and it may be of some comfort and relief to the reader, having been so audacious as to struggle through eleven chapters that are replete with ratios, to learn that in this chapter he will encounter *not one* ratio.

Because these works have consumed such a large part of my creative energies for more than thirty years, information is here given regarding their background and motivation—information for which record jackets do not have the space. The six works are: *U.S. Highball, Plectra and Percussion Dances, Oedipus, The Bewitched, Revelation in the Courthouse Park,* and *Petals* and *Delusion of the Fury* (*Petals* was written in preparation for *Delusion*).

## U.S. Highball—A Musical Account of a Transcontinental Hobo Trip

Scored for:

| | |
|---|---|
| Subjective Voice (tenor-baritone) | Diamond Marimba |
| Several Objective Voices (mostly baritone) | Boo |
| | Spoils of War |
| Kithara II | Cloud-Chamber Bowls |
| Surrogate Kithara | Bass Marimba |
| Harmonic Canon II | |
| Chromelodeon I | |

Performance time: about twenty-five minutes.

The word *highball,* in this context, is an old railroad term. I have no idea whether it is still used by railroaders, but I am sure that it is still used by hobos. If a ball, on an arm, came down in front of an advancing train, it was a signal to stop, to slow down, to beware. This was a *low* ball. But if the train could safely proceed, the signal was a *high* ball. In time, the latter term became a verb, and any hobo knows that "Let'er highball, engineer!" means "Let's get going."

*U.S. Highball* is a hobo's account of a trip from San Francisco to Chicago and falls naturally into three parts, which might be called—whimsically—a hobo allegro form. The first part is a long and jerky passage by drags (slow freights) to Little America, Wyoming. The second is an adagio dishwashing movement at Little America. The third is a rhythmic allegro, mostly by highway (hitchhiking), to Chicago. The one word, *Chicago,* is the end of the text. Instrumentally, what follows implies a tremendous letdown from the obstinately compulsive exhilaration of *getting* to Chicago. It implies bewilderment and that ever-dominant question in the life of the wanderer—what next?

The Subjective Voice is the protagonist in the true sense of the dramatic term. Implicitly, he is always present. He does not speak, he thinks, and because this is music, he thinks in tone. His is virtually the only voice that truly sings. As he thinks, without speaking, the names of stations go through his head. And as thoughts, "Winnemucca, Nevaducca," and "North Platte, Nebras-ass-katte" are not so ludicrous. The child-fantasy amuses him, and helps to pass the long hours.

Not all of the protagonist's subjective words come from his own throat. A few of them, such as "Back to the freights for you, boy" (following upon "Going east, mister?"), are spoken in tones by one of the hobo-instrumentalists, as though the phrases were coming from some unseen supernatural commentator—as though the protagonist were projecting himself as that commentator.

The protagonist celebrates *leaving* a place, not *arriving,* and almost any hobo would know why. A new town is an unknown; when the train stops, much can happen, including his arrest. But there is immediate exhilaration upon leaving a town—one more hurdle has been passed safely.

The several Objective Voices, in my original conception, are the instrumentalists—that is, the other hobos on the trip. Their words consist of fragments of conversations, writings on the sides of boxcars, signs in havens for derelicts, hitchhikers' inscriptions. As a hobo I always carried a small notebook for many purposes—to write letters, to remind myself of something, to record addresses. The texts described above were put into such a notebook, which I still have. I really did not do any editing of them, as such. I simply got weary of the constantly repetitive obscenities and left them out.

Since I was fourteen, I had aimed at doing dramatic work in music, but I had had no wish to write *opera,* and until the moment of *U.S. Highball,* I had never felt ready. Even this was only a first tentative step. I had intended the various hobos to speak up in turn and to be spotlighted theatrically as they spoke. This has never been done, at least in part because voice microphones are necessary for all of them if they are to be heard above the accompanying music. (Although they intone rather than sing, they must maintain the range and speed of the natural speaking voice. Their intonations are always integrated, both harmonically and rhythmically. The instruments always support their speech—the music is not simply background.)

*U.S. Highball* is not epic in either an ancient or a modern sense. Its protagonist is the exact opposite of a hero as the word is used in literature or in folklore. He does not at any time yank himself by his own bootstraps from the jaws of death, or resist some predatory siren, or suffer for the sake of family and country. And yet, in the *aloneness* of his experience, and in his psychological striving for success, for achievement in the face of small difficulties—more or less constant hunger, loss of sleep, filth, and a good deal of petty apprehension and danger—he is the focus of a work that suggests epic feelings. And the concept of the work does have some slight affinity with epic chant. (It is not the value of an object gained that creates significance. It is the intensity of the effort generated, and if the intensity is meaningful, the value of the goal judged by popular standards is of no consequence.)

Nor is *U.S. Highball* essentially a piece of Americana, a documentary, although if it were only this, I would not minimize it. But it rises beyond the documentary to other levels of consciousness. It is art, in an art form, but it is an art that surges up and out of the strictly literal, the experienced narrative, even out of the abysmal. And because it is art, the strictly literal time and place of its concept form merely the flight deck for what follows.

Certain extremes of feeling were peculiarly characteristic of those times of economic depression, due in part to the continuing endeavors of many of us to cling to hope, to be something virtually impossible. My endeavor was to continue my work while thinking always of my experiences and my philosophies in music-theater terms. Such inner thoughts were certainly not typical of my fellow hobos, yet my non-heroic, non-epic experiences were very typical of those times and endow the concept of the work with a tie to other men.

I have called *U.S. Highball* the most creative piece of work I have ever done, and in the sense that it is less influenced by the forms and attitudes that I had grown up with as a child and experienced in adult life, there can be no doubt of it. The intensity of the experiences preceding it and the intensity of my feelings at the time forced me into a different welter of thought—one that I had to mold in a new way, and for this one work alone.

The opening of World War II in September, 1939, may mark the end of the Great Depression for historians, but my own personal Great Depression rolled merrily along, oblivious to world events, for three and a half years more. I found it easy, during those particular years, to get just one kind of job—dishwasher and flunky. And if my personal history between 1935 and 1943 were to be frozen in space, it would appear as a finely detailed mosaic made up of an incredible number of dirty dishes, nameless faces in WPA jobs, and almost nameless faces in hobo jungles and fruit harvests.

The experience was all the more traumatic in 1935 because I had just returned from the British Museum, Dublin, Italy, and Malta under a grant-in-aid from the Carnegie Corporation of New York. My return was to a jobless America, and I took my blankets out under the stars beside the American River (the river of gold!), carried my notebook, kept a journal, and made sketches. I called the journal *Bitter Music* (it is not included in the list of my work in Appendix III), and I even had a contract for its publication. During the Depression, it might have had a chance, but with war in Europe, the contract was cancelled and I destroyed the effort. I did so without regret, because it had given me a large and already faintly delineated canvas for the collection of ideas that I later called *The Wayward,* of which *U.S. Highball* is a part.

In the summer of 1941, quite casually, I met a man, a divinity student, who became interested in my work and described it to a friend in Chicago. The friend wrote to me almost immediately, invited me to Chicago if I could get there on my own, and ended his letter: "May God's richest blessings be upon you." Having been through more than six years of California depression, I jumped at the chance to see some midwest depression (somewhat like a prisoner in the county jail eagerly looking forward to a transfer to the county farm, or vice versa).

*U.S. Highball* begins with a very brief overture, introducing, one at a time, the sounds of the nine instruments of the ensemble in snatches of music taken from the score. Almost immediately after the protagonist's sung words, "Leaving San Francisco, Cal-i-for-ni-o—," the hymn-like setting of "May God's richest blessings be upon you" follows. This is repeated (it must not be forgotten!) more than halfway through, after the dishwashing adagio. And in the approach to success—that is, Chicago—it rises to a sonorous chorus. The inevitable instrumental anticlimax—in the dingy, pre-dawn smogginess of industrial Chicago, and with just one pocketed dime—has already been mentioned.

All of this ended, finally, in Ithaca, New York, in April, 1943, when I received notice of my first Guggenheim Fellowship. The first order of business was to put my little notebook before me and write *U.S. Highball;* and a few months later, in gratitude, I inscribed on the front cover: "To the John Simon Guggenheim Memorial Foundation and Henry Allen Moe."

The work was performed with three instruments, Guitar I, Kithara, and Chromelodeon, in the Carnegie Chamber Music Hall in 1944 (see Appendix III). I played the guitar and sang all the voice parts. Later, in Madison, Wisconsin, it was recorded with the same three instruments and, in addition, with the Harmonic Canon, which had been built in the meantime, and with another voice, the singing protagonist's. Upon studying this recording, I realized a most urgent need—percussion built for this system of music, for these theories. By 1955 I had plenty of percussion instruments and I rewrote the work, putting it in its present form.

## Plectra and Percussion Dances

This work, written for dance, is in three sections: *Castor and Pollux, Ring Around the Moon, Even Wild Horses.* Performance time, with slight intermissions: about sixty minutes.

*Castor and Pollux—A Dance for the Twin Rhythms of Gemini*
Scored for:

| | |
|---|---|
| Kithara II | Low Bass Marimba |
| Surrogate Kithara[1] | Diamond Marimba |
| Cloud-Chamber Bowls | High Bass Marimba[2] |
| Harmonic Canon II (right canon) | |

In their drama festivals the ancient Greeks, at one time at least, performed a raucous, farcical, and often obscene (by our standards) satyr play following a tragedy. After having spent many years thinking about Oedipus—who was inevitably destined for greatness and then humiliation and exile, after writing the music for Oedipus, spending six months in rehearsals, and finally doing public performances and a recording, I saw with great clarity the need for some kind of release from this truly awful and awesome story of entrapment, from, literally, too much catharsis. The story of Castor and Pollux, replete with good luck, seemed a perfect follow-up. It begins with one of the most delightful seductions in mythology, that of the beautiful Leda by Zeus in the form of a swan (frequently depicted in Greek art), and ends with the birth of twins, presumably hatched from eggs. And the good luck continues—the twins ascend to the heavens to become the auguries of favorable voyages by ancient mariners.

Here, the idea is concerned only with the processes of procreation. The twin eggs are treated separately, first Castor, then Pollux, but there is no pause in the music. Three pairs of instruments (in duets) and three pairs of dancers represent, in sequence, the Seduction, the Conception, the Incubation. Finally, all six instrumental parts and dancing movements are repeated simultaneously as a "Chorus of Delivery from the Egg."

Castor:
1. Kithara (and Surrogate Kithara) and Cloud-Chamber
   Bowls
2. Harmonic Canon and High Bass Marimba

---

[1]The Kithara and Surrogate Kithara are considered as one instrument. Soon after writing the part for the Kithara, I realized that it was certainly *possible* for one person to perform it, but only with extreme difficulty, and in 1953 I built the Surrogate Kithara in order to lessen the strain. Thus, in effect, there are really only six instrumental parts.

[2]In several works I have used two players standing on the long riser behind the Bass Marimba. Thus, two parts are written for the instrument, one of which is confined to lower tones, the other to higher tones.

3. Diamond Marimba and Low Bass Marimba
4. All of the foregoing simultaneously (the Chorus of Delivery)

Pollux:

5. Kithara (and Surrogate Kithara) and Low Bass Marimba
6. Harmonic Canon and Cloud-Chamber Bowls
7. Diamond Marimba and High Bass Marimba
8. All of the foregoing simultaneously (the Chorus of Delivery)

The piece is dithyrambic in character. The quarternote has the same value throughout, and each process requires exactly 234 beats; there is ,rubato nowhere. The performance should take no more than fifteen minutes.

I felt that 468 beats without retard or acceleration was bearable only if sufficiently varied and interesting subsidiary rhythms and beats (it is in alternate measures of 4 and 5 beats and 3 and 4 beats) were present. In order to effect the kind of unity of the parts that I envisioned, it was necessary to repeat phrases frequently. Yet this helps in gaining familiarity with the themes, and on second hearing, with melodic and harmonic elaboration and contrapuntal accumulation (in the Choruses of Delivery), the juxtapositions cause each individual repetition to be heard under entirely different musical conditions. In a sense, the work is a series of calculated "coincidences," of musical "double exposures," of climaxes to series of "single exposures."

*Ring Around the Moon—A Dance Fantasm for Here and Now*

Scored for:

| | |
|---|---|
| Baritone (speaking on tones) | Cloud-Chamber Bowls |
| Adapted Guitar I | Pernambuco Block (Spoils of |
| Adapted Guitar II | War) |
| Harmonic Canon II | Diamond Marimba |
| Chromelodeon I | Bass Marimba |

I have called this a satire on singers and singing, on concerts and concert audiences, on music in forty-three tones to the octave, on grand flourishes that lead to nothing. I wrote it at Gualala, far up on the northern California coast, in 1949–1950, before the first and third sections of the work, and called it *Sonata Dementia*. The nonsense phrases by the singer-speaker—"Well, bless my soul!"; "Shake hands now boys, and at the sound of the bell come out fighting"; "Look out! He's got a gun!"—all suggest the satire and the title.

*Even Wild Horses—Dance Music for an Absent Drama*

Scored for:

| | |
|---|---|
| Baritone | Chromelodeon I |
| Adapted Viola | Diamond Marimba |
| Adapted Guitar I | Bass Marimba |
| Kithara II | Cloud-Chamber Bowls |
| Harmonic Canon II | Spoils of War |
| (four bridge settings) | Japanese Temple Bell |

The concept entails three acts, each introduced by the same Cloud-Chamber Bowls passage, and eight scenes separated by a gong sound. Actually, there is almost no cessation of sound from beginning to end.

### Act I

Scene 1. A Decent and Honorable Mistake—Samba

Scene 2. Rhythm of the Womb, Melody of the Grave—Heartbeat rhythm

Scene 3. Happy Birthday to You!—Afro-Chinese Minuet

### Act II

Scene 1. "Ni cette bouche sur tes yeux"—Rumba

Scene 2. "Faim, soif, cris, danse, danse!"—Nañiga

Scene 3. "Patrie de l'ombre et des tourbillons"—Slow, Fast, Wild!

### Act III

Scene 1. "Neus 'je pas une fois une jeunesse aimable"—Conga

Scene 2. "Apprécions sans vertige l'étendue de mon innocence"—Tahitian Dance

An individual's life begins as a "decent and honorable mistake" (perhaps); he goes through the double heartbeat of mother and enwombed child, he is born, he suffers, and long before his day is done, he begins to "contemplate undazed the endless reaches of his innocence" (Act III, Scene 2).

The source of the title of the first scene evades me—I read it somewhere in a preface. The titles of the scenes in Acts II and III, and also the text, are from Rimbaud's *A Season in Hell*.[3] The text is in French, which I am inclined to regret, since I feel far more at home in setting English words; but at the time (1952), I had just been through the frustration of an agent denying me the use of a version of *Oedipus* and wanted no repetition of the experience.

In reading and rereading *A Season in Hell*, certain almost frenzied phrases jumped out of the book and hit me with tremendous force. The savage honesty, the primitive innocence, the acceptance of a naked humanness, the child, primordial man—values lost? Not wholly. (This succession of words perhaps suggests a motivation for a musical wedding of Rimbaud with an extension of Afro-Latin and other rhythms.)

Only two of the five sequences from *A Season in Hell* are sentence-by-sentence copies as Rimbaud wrote them. The others are structured from various sentences throughout the book in an association that seemed right for *this* musical idea. Perhaps the Rimbaud exegete cannot forgive me, but I daresay that Rimbaud the imaginative, the irreverent, would have.

My elaborations on the percussive patterns are mostly too complex for bearable verbalizations. It is enough to say that these are rhythms of here and now, and that they are not maintained throughout (the rumba excepted). The samba, the ñañiga, the conga, are metamorphosed, developed into something different from their starting moods. The Afro-Chinese minuet and the ñañiga in particular become different, and all become infused with an altered character as they move toward the child-like and explosive words of Rimbaud.

The three sections of the *Plectra and Percussion Dances* have no obvious integrating tie, although I feel that in the matter of inherent quality they belong together. They do not have the coherence, or the compelling dramatic direction, of *U.S. Highball*. Actually, in 1953, they were put to-

[3]Arthur Rimbaud, *A Season in Hell*, Louise Varese, trans. (New Directions, New York, 1945).

A SCENE FROM *DELUSION OF THE FURY*

PERFORMANCE AT THE UNIVERSITY OF CALIFORNIA, LOS ANGELES, 1969

A SCENE FROM *DELUSION OF THE FURY*

PERFORMANCE AT THE UNIVERSITY OF CALIFORNIA, LOS ANGELES, 1969

gether to constitute a new record, the first of the Gate 5 issues (see Appendix V). The total time duration of the three sections is about sixty minutes, which, at that time, was too much, and *Ring Around the Moon*, already the shortest of the three, was badly excerpted to get the music on two sides of one record.

## *Oedipus—A Music-Dance Drama*

Scored for:

*Voices:*

| | |
|---|---|
| Bass | Oedipus |
| Tenor-Baritone | Chorus Spokesman |
| Bass | Tiresias and the Herdsman |
| Low Soprano | Jocasta |
| Six Sopranos (including one High Soprano in section 17 only) | Chorus Complement |

*Instruments:*

| | |
|---|---|
| Clarinet | Chromelodeon I |
| Bass Clarinet | Chromelodeon I Sub-Bass |
| Adapted Viola | Chromelodeon II |
| Adapted Cello | Cloud-Chamber Bowls |
| Adapted Guitar I | Gourd Tree and Cone Gongs |
| Adapted Guitar II | Diamond Marimba |
| String Bass | Bass Marimba |
| Kithara II | Marimba Eroica |
| Harmonic Canon II (two players) | |

Performance time: seventy-five to eighty minutes—no intermission.

This work falls naturally into eighteen musical sections, and although segments of free dialogue occur, there is at no time a real cessation of sound. The sections:

| | |
|---|---|
| 1. Introduction | 4. Tiresias Scene |
| 2. Opening Scene | 5. Second Chorus |
| 3. First Chorus | 6. Creon Scene |

The last part of my *statement of intention* in the program for the first performance in 1952 follows:

I have not consciously linked the ancient Greece of Sophocles and this conception of his drama—twenty-four hundred years later. The work is presented as a human value, necessarily pinned to a time and place, necessarily involving the oracular gods and Greek proper and place names, but, nevertheless, not necessarily Greek. So viewed, the question as to whether the present work is consonant with what is generally taken to be the "Greek spirit" is somewhat irrelevant. Yet, from the standpoint of dramatic technique, it is a historical fact that the Greeks used some kind of "tone declamation" in their dramatic works, and that it was common practice among them to present language, music, and dance as a dramatic unity. In this conception I am striving for such a synthesis, not because it might lead me to the "Greek spirit," but because I believe in it.

The music is conceived as [the] emotional saturation, or transcendence, that it is the particular province of dramatic music to achieve. My idea has been to present the drama expressed by language, not to obscure it either by operatic aria or symphonic instrumentation. Hence, in critical dialogue, music enters almost insidiously, as tensions enter. The words of the players continue as before, spoken, not sung, but are a *harmonic part* of the music. In these settings the inflected words are little or no different from ordinary speech, except as emotional tensions make them different. Assertive words and assertive music do not collide. Tone of spoken word and tone of instrument are intended to combine in a compact emotional or dramatic expression, each providing its singular ingredient. My intention is to bring human drama, made of words, movement, and music, to a level that a mind with average capacity for sensitivity and logic can understand and therefore evaluate.

When I met with W.B. Yeats in Dublin in the fall of 1934, I had with me a musical outline of my proposed setting of his version of the ancient drama.[4] There was not yet a single musical note written down, but the outline presented a rather clear idea of what I proposed to do. The most drastic suggestion was the deletion of all of the self-analyzing and oracular expatiations in the dialogue after Oedipus' realization that, in the irrefragable pursuit of his destiny, he has fulfilled the oracle's prophecy. All that was left after his "O! O! All come to pass!" was the Fifth Chorus,

[4]W. B. Yeats, *Sophocles' King Oedipus, A Version for the Modern Stage* (Macmillan, New York, 1928).

his reentrance, blind (much reduced), and the Final Chorus. This removed perhaps an eighth of the drama's total dialogue.

In the final sections, music becomes dominant. After the Fifth Chorus,
there is the Instrumental Commentary. It begins with the announcement
that Jocasta has hanged herself, and the instruments and the chorus begin
to comment (in meaningless syllables). The section ends with what I call
a recreation of the palace madness entirely by instruments, except for the
chorus shouting "O!-O!-O!-O!" at the very end. The Antiphony begins
with the reappearance of Oedipus, and here the female chorus offers a
responsive chant to each line of his misery.

The Oedipus Scene is the Recognition Scene, and constitutes the climax
of all the dialogue that preceded it. But in Exit Oedipus: Dance-
Pantomime, the music comes to its own climax as a philosophical and
spiritual compendium of the drama (also with solo and chorus voices in
meaningless syllables). The Final Chorus and Coda bring the work to
a close.

I had been drawn to Yeats because of that marvelous experience of
seeing eye to eye with him through his writings over a period of years—
writings in which he expounded, and hoped for, a union of words and
music in which "no word shall have an intonation or an accentuation it
could not have in passionate speech." I do not recall that he objected in
any way to my proposed treatment.

In 1951, seventeen years after these consultations and twelve years after
the poet's death, I began to work out the music. But following performances and a recording, I was refused permission by the agent in charge to
use the Yeats version on records. I then prepared a text of my own from
public domain sources, mostly from the translation by Richard C. Jebb
(on which, I discovered at that time, Yeats had also relied heavily) and
rewrote the music where it joined the dialogue. This version was performed and recorded in 1954.

The new text was prepared for a modern American audience, not for
those steeped in the Greek language and Greek mythology. I therefore
omitted Greek names that would not be meaningful dramatically. My
friend Jordan Churchill, at that time a professor of philosophy at San
Francisco State College, and a Greek scholar, objected to parts of my text
and made a translation of his own. Where music was not involved, I used
some of his suggestions.

Bass Clarinet and Adapted Viola were added to the second version, and in the rewriting of 1967, I changed the Chromelodeon II part to conform to its present tuning and added the Gourd Tree and Cone Gongs. These, which are not particularly breakable, were included because of my somewhat desperate feeling that some of the Cloud-Chamber Bowls might be broken before another performance was possible. (The Cloud-Chamber Bowls part was left blank. See Chapter 13.)

A final point of explanation: I wanted Tiresias, the blind prophet, and the Herdsman, who finally reveals Oedipus' identity, to be the same voice. Tiresias is accusatory, even arrogant, and he is all-knowing; the Herdsman is reluctant, humble, and all-knowing—in this case at least. It is the *all-knowing* element that they have in common. Together, they personify Oedipus' fate.

## The Bewitched—A Dance Satire

Scored for:

| | |
|---|---|
| Solo Soprano—the Witch | Surrogate Kithara |
| Piccolo | Chromelodeon I |
| Clarinet | Cloud-Chamber Bowls |
| Bass Clarinet | Spoils of War |
| Cello | Diamond Marimba |
| Kithara II (players on both sides) | Boo |
| Harmonic Canon II (two players) | Bass Marimba |
| Koto | Marimba Eroica |

Performance time: seventy-five to eighty minutes—no intermission.

In the summer of 1952, a man visited my studio and suggested that if I would write a series of "backgrounds" for television—for airplane crashes, drownings, and murders in the park, I suppose—I might make a lot of money. But all I could really become interested in were such items as *Background Music for Filibusters in the United States Senate,* for which I saw little prospect of performance. However, this idea, plus the fact that in the ensuing years literally dozens of what I could only call *lost musicians* visited me at my studio in Sausalito, plus an old interest in the ancient idea of the *benevolent, all-knowing* witch, led to the present work.

In this and the work following *(Revelation),* I had definite ideas about a set. Some of the large instruments, on risers, dominate the stage. They are connected with the other instruments by a stairway, or rather a nexus of stairways which finally matures into one stairway making its ascent to one of the far corners at the rear (and perhaps continued with paint on canvas to give the impression of hazy endlessness).

The Witch must have virtually a three "octave" range, from the "F♯" below "middle C" to the third "E" above. She must also be an actress. She moves about the stage freely and at critical moments takes command as ostensible conductor. The male instrumentalists constitute the Singing Chorus; there must be no confusion between the sounds of the *female* Witch and her *male* Chorus. Both the Witch and Chorus express themselves only in meaningless syllables.

My notes (here much abbreviated) for the two-record set of *The Bewitched* put out under the Gate 5 label in 1957 tell the story:

*Argument*

We are all bewitched, and mostly by accident: the accident of form, color, and sex; of prejudices conditioned from the cradle on up. Those in a long-tenanted rut enjoy larger comforts of mind and body, and as compensation it is more frequently given to others who are not so easily domesticated to become mediums for the transmission of perception. Among these are the lost musicians, and their perceptions may germinate, evolve, and mature in concert, through a developing "at-one-ness," through their beat.

*Prologue. The Lost Musicians Mix Magic*

The forms of strange instruments are seen dimly on stage. How did they get here? They came on in a dark celestial silence, doing tumbles and handsprings, and for no other purpose than to be discovered by *these* musicians in *this* theater before *this* audience.

One of the musicians turns on his music light and gives a low beat, and others enter and swing in, one at a time. They are neolithic primitives in their unspoken acceptance of magic as real, unconsciously reclaiming an all-but-lost value—lost only about a minute ago in relation to that ancient time when the first single cell moved itself in such autoerotic agitation that it split in two.

In the enveloping ensemble the lost musicians have momentarily found a direction. Their direction becomes a power, and their power a vision: an ancient Witch, a prehistoric seer untouched by either gossip or popular malevolence. She corresponds to the Greek oracle, while the Chorus (the orchestra) —like the chorus of ancient. tragedy—is a moral instrument under the power of perceptive suggestion.

The Witch surveys the world, immediately becomes sad and moody, then takes command: "Everybody wants background music," the Witch-like sounds seem to murmur, and the conspiratorial tone is clear even in gibberish.

### Scene 1. Three Undergrads Become Transfigured in a Hong Kong Music Hall

The bewitched enter, and the analogy with lyric tragedy is complete: the Chorus, the Perceptive Voice, the Actors. These actors dance their parts, and although they seem always to ignore the person of the Witch and her Chorus, they are nevertheless terribly aware.

The job taken on by the Chorus is, briefly, to divest the undergrads of the confirmed xenophobia that once blanketed them so lovingly in their cradles. The comeuppance is a broad one, far beyond their young years and experience. The exotic—East or West—does not hold more mystery than it ought.

### Scene 2. Exercises in Harmony and Counterpoint Are Tried in a Court of Ancient Ritual

Like the Mindanao Deep of the Pacific, the bewitchment in musical conditioning is profound and mysterious. It is indeed so deep that a term such as *the scale* is accorded a silent and mysterious Mindanaon acceptance as obvious as *the robin* in spring.

The bewitched exercises in harmony and counterpoint are cast into a sea of ancient rules and ritual. Now the immediate colors are strong and violent, while the distant pastels of the eighteenth century are barely perceptible in the dim, dim future. The unwitched exercises suddenly gaze upon an inspired and apocalyptic new day.

### Scene 3. The Romancing of a Pathological Liar Comes to an Inspired End

The scene focuses on the sad life story of a boy and man, a pathological liar for one reason: he is pursued by the magic of his fancies just as relentlessly and in the same way that he pursues the object of his fancies. These fancies are his weapon, and he proliferates them before him, only to die many little deaths as they breathe down his neck from behind.

In the jet-stream magic of this night, the Chorus and their Witch find a poetic way out. In a flash the boy's bewitchment abandons him to light momentarily in the temple of his lady-love. Too late, the boy sees himself; out of the corner of his vision he sees a woman with lust in the shaft of her eye. Pursued, he races up the stairway and leaps. A dull thud.

*Scene 4. A Soul Tormented by Contemporary Music Finds a Humanizing Alchemy*

Of all the sad tales sung by the poets of old, some are sadder than this, some more poignant, many more tragic, but none more pathetic, for this is a scene of conflict that arises out of an absorbing regret over the passage of time—that is, the injustice of having been born at such a miserable time in history as the present. This soul has become so immersed in the bewitchment of some preceding century that he can function only in that century. Even the growing child falls somewhat behind the surge of the modern world because of the shelter of his home, and he must catch up—on his own.

The Chorus whistles dolefully, while the slow beats toll off the neuroses —one by one. The amplitude of the shocks increases. Now utter silence. Breathing loudly in a crescendo of emotion the Chorus brings the climax. The other-century soul has returned to the world of the living through a whole-souled abandonment to slapstick comedy.

*Scene 5. Visions Fill the Eyes of a Defeated Basketball Team in the Shower Room*

It seems perversely characteristic of the human male to think of his moments of weakness and failure in a female context. He may say: "Today I'm a sick woman," but he does not mean that he has changed his sex. For the sake of a moment of magic perception, however, let us impose this idea on the defeated side after a game of basketball.

With the incorrigible optimism of healthy young women dominant, the conclusion comes easily that one defeat in a basketball game is of exceedingly trivial consequence. Immediately thereafter, with the help of a capricious Witch and a conniving Chorus, the women fling themselves into something really important—a wild dance in adulation of a vision of the nude god Hermes, most knavish of the Olympian knaves.

The basketball team, now unwitched, has fallen completely under the charming belief that reality contains a compound of both experience and imagination.

### Scene 6. *Euphoria Descends a Sausalito Stairway*

The scene is one of the landings of a stairway on the steep hills that rise from San Francisco Bay at Sausalito. Adolescent love can make do with whatever it's got, of course, but there is something of poetic justice in placing it among suburban homes where baroque leaps, swoons, and pirouettes, where trunks revolving around necks and other devices of adolescent love in ballet form might attract hardly even second notice.

Anyone can *dream* of bringing control to a Sausalito love affair, but the Witch actually accomplishes it. Facing each other, the boy and girl now move backward and forward on the stairway—with quiet dignity and tenderness—in a way that suggests eternity.

### Scene 7. *Two Detectives on the Tail of a Tricky Culprit Turn in Their Badges*

Obsession makes this both a melancholy scene and a slapstick love affair. Let cities decay, but never allow even one minor culprit to believe that he does not need those conspicuous gentlemen whose lives are dedicated to the single purpose of complementing his ego!

This culprit is a recidivist. His automatic "Who, me?" response to interrogation leads to a third, a fourth, and even a fifth degree, each progressively more delightful. With a whistle and a stamp he takes off on a spontaneous angle of his own, and is stopped only when the detectives plead with him to honor the memory of his dead mother.

This is too much for the Witch and Chorus, who waste no time precipitating a crisis. At the scene's end, the unwitched trio tenderly pledge eternal cooperation, to the end that each may achieve the ultimate of fulfillment.

### Scene 8. *A Court in Its Own Contempt Rises to a Motherly Apotheosis*

The scene's gist: the heroes of a matriarchy are the sons who gain public attention in futile rebellion against it, thus making their mothers proud. It begins as a double exposure. Underneath is the quality of the very ancient matriarchy, on top the personalities of a modern trial—judge, attorneys, witness (the accused—the human male—is ambient).

The lady witness tells a sad story, but as things proceed she becomes flippant, even indignant. She is obviously in contempt, and suddenly the Witch wonders about the court itself: hasn't even one court ever become so disgusted with itself as to be in its *own* contempt?

From the single stroke of a double-bladed axe two events transpire. First, the court—unwitched—exclaims: "Why, this *is* a matriarchy!" and *is* in contempt. Second, the lady witness—unwitched—exclaims: "Why, this *is* a matriarchy!" and administers the citation. His-former-honor moves alone now, with shining eyes, to his lonely apotheosis. Her honor gazes down proudly.

*Scene 9. A Lost Political Soul Finds Himself Among the Voteless Women of Paradise*

The mood in paradise is static, suspended somewhere between exquisite joy and melancholy. Gyrating fitfully between the layers of his conscious and unconscious, the lost political soul dreams. (He sees the dreadful vision of a confession forced under torture before the League of Women Voters.) In vast relief he clutches at this paradise—final refuge of patriarchal entrenchment! And yet, at the same time, how melancholy that there is no electorate to sway.

This conflict gives him the countenance of death. The beautiful houris of paradise are only an inanimate stage set, but even now Transfiguration is moving beside him. The houris, who have very slowly emerged from paradisian refrigeration, have fallen into the houriest of all houri dances. Purged, the lost political soul finds himself functioning contentedly among constituents who played no part in his election.

*Scene 10. The Cognoscenti Are Plunged Into a Demonic Descent While at Cocktails*

It is soon evident that cognoscenti as subjects for unwitching are by all odds the most difficult, not a heel of Achilles in a drawing-room load. Now, the power of magic seems an unfair advantage, but we must remember that the lost musicians have had encounters with the cognoscenti before, and with humiliating results. Not so tonight. The power they have generated is a bit frightening, even to the cognoscenti.

"Bah!" says the Chorus, and that one word makes up in violent delivery what it lacks in intellectual sparkle. "How extraordinary!" say the cognoscenti, propelled by a chorus of dragons in backward somersaults into the middle of limbo.

Not a bad night's work. "Rrrrrrr——ee——eh!" sings the Witch, and as everyone knows this may be rendered: "I really don't give a raspberry about all this nonsense. Furthermore, it's time you children were in bed."

*Epilogue*

"Later!" says the Witch, and vanishes. But the lost musicians cannot unwind so fast, and a few of them linger with their beat, as a kind of final refuge. Then, one by one, they wander away, and finally the last turns off his music light and hurries after them.

Like their Witch, the musicians vanish, again to become almost, if not wholly, as bewitched as everyone else. The moment is gone, because perception is a sand flea. It can light only for a moment. Another moment must provide its own sand flea.

## Revelation in the Courthouse Park— *After* The Bacchae *of Euripides*

In endeavoring to attain the heights of Olympus, according to the old Greek myth, it is futile to pile Pelion on Ossa, as the Giants had sought to do. Long before Shakespeare, the drama of Western Europe (and therefore America) took its present form as a specialized theater of dialogue. It is futile, in my view, to pile device upon device in this specialized theater and still expect to attain anything remotely resembling the heights of Greek drama. Yet both the professional companies and college groups that I have heard are guilty of doing so. The present practice of choruses reciting in unison (choral speech) in every variety of range and intonation—from low bass to high soprano—is non-Greek in spirit and also absurd beyond belief. Greek drama was far more than a theater of dialogue, although how much more we cannot know. Music, which was so essential, is a fragile art, and perhaps we will never know the full impact of its use in their drama.

I had tried a much different approach in using the Sophocles *Oedipus,* and however well the audiences responded who had actually *seen* one of

DETAIL OF STAGING FOR *DELUSION OF THE FURY*

Performance at the University of California, Los Angeles, 1969

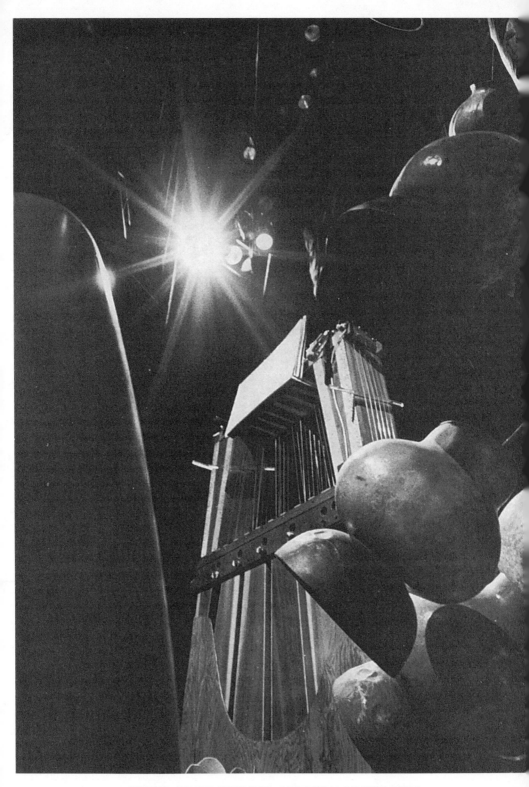

DETAIL OF STAGING FOR *DELUSION OF THE FURY*

the productions, as opposed to those who know only the record, the results somehow troubled me. It seemed that the drama of Oedipus, however compelling, was deposited by the mind in an ancient category called *classical*—that it was not brought home to the audience as a here-and-now work. Because of this insight, I first decided that I would bodily transfer Euripides' *The Bacchae* to an American setting. But in the end, the better solution seemed to be to alternate scenes between an American courthouse park and the area before the palace of ancient Thebes; and the physical courthouse itself (see below) reinforced this decision. I was determined to make this an American here-and-now drama, which, tragically, it truly is. Consequently, there are four alternations between the Courthouse Park and the area before the Theban palace. The Coda, which, in effect, is the ninth scene, brings the work to a close.

Many years ago I was struck by a strong and strange similarity between the basic situation in the Euripides play and at least two phenomena of present-day America. Religious rituals with a strong sexual element are not unknown to our culture, nor are sex rituals with a strong religious element. (I assume that the mobbing of young male singers by semi-hysterical women is recognizable as a sex ritual for a godhead.) And these separate phenomena, after years of observing them, have become synthesized as a single kind of ritual, with religion and sex in equal parts, and with deep roots in an earlier period of human evolution—all of which sounds delightfully innocent.

However, a menace may easily be hidden within them. The frenzied women in the Euripides play threaten both degradation and annihilation for anyone unwilling to praise or at least respect their particular pattern of mediocrity and conformity, and it is apparent that similar pressures toward the same end are implicit in this country. With this in mind, I have treated the Greek Choruses (much shortened and otherwise altered) as American revival meetings, even though the words I have chosen were suggested by Euripides and of course reinforced by my own experiences.

The Euripidean scenes are my version of *The Bacchae,* so abbreviated as to leave only the skeleton of the story. The rituals of the American Choruses, in theatrical detail and music, are entirely my own conception. In *The Bacchae,* revels are described but are *not* seen or heard. In the First and Third American Choruses, they *are* seen and heard, with the use of nonsense phrases, clichés, gibberish—the cult of Ishbu Kubu, "Deep inside, 'way 'way down, I am!" for example.[5] In *The Bacchae,* physical doom is implied, but it is *never* foretold, as it *was* foretold by the prophet Tiresias in a powerful scene with Oedipus. In the Second and Fourth American Choruses, a particular variety of psychological doom *is* foretold, in night-time, sleep-walking, dream-nightmare sequences—the first with Sonny, the second with Mom. Both play their roles before a mocking off-stage chorus, and both sequences end with a high male voice off stage: "Mother! Mother! No! No!"

There is thus a Greek influence operating in the American Choruses, and an American influence operating in the Greek Scenes (the revival meetings). The American Choruses are symbolic and psychological, the Euripidean Scenes mythological and realistic. Dion, the Hollywood idol, is a symbol of dominant mediocrity, Mom is a symbol of blind matriarchal power, and Sonny is a symbol of nothing so much as a lost soul, one who does not or cannot conform to the world he was born to. The fact that *mother* is a belonger and doer, and *son* is a non-belonger and voyeur, involves a bitter irony—one that is not only appropriate, but also neces-sary dramatically, in either the ancient or the modern sense.

As in the case of *Oedipus,* the anguished analyses and explanations at the end of the work are omitted, beginning with the mother's realization of what she has done, because they seem unnecessary, even tedious. This involves about an eighth of the total dialogue. I sometimes feel that Sophocles in *Oedipus the King,* Euripides in *The Bacchae,* and Aeschylus in *The Furies* all were fearful of a grand aposeopesis. But this may be a superficial judgment. It may be that the Greek audience, the Greek mind, demanded that every last drop of meaning be wrung from every action and reaction of both men and gods. (These Greek theater epilogues remind me of a time many years ago when I was reading the dialogues of Plato and came across the line. "I do not quite understand you, Socrates."

---

[5]The climax of the revels in Chorus Three, *Tumble On,* was attained with mat tumblers and with one gymnast on a trampoline. This had been rolled onstage unknown to the audience, at the rear, and with a certain beat of the Marimba Eroica, the trampolinist rose high above those on stage, his feet striking the net with each beat of the Eroica. Knowing of this scene, the gymnasts' coach at the University of Illinois asked me to perform this, with added music, at the N.C.A.A. meet, which happened to occur that year (1961) at Illinois. I wrote the script and titled it *Rotate the Body in All Its Planes.* A film was made of the exhibition (see Appendix V) .

I laughed and threw the book down. "That ought to be the title," I mused. Very frequently, I do not quite understand you either, Socrates!)

At any rate, the end of the Recognition Scene in this work is very quiet. Cadmus, the father, is gently persuading his daughter, Agave, to look at what she is carrying—her son's heroic mask, which represents his head. The music is exiguous and soft—a slow, steady Eroica beat and a muted cello. With complete realization she emits a low, whispered "No!" and drops the mask to the ground. A tremendous crash of percussion comes simultaneously, and as it diminishes, the mother removes her own mask and drops it on top of the first, with another crash of percussion. She then moves slowly backward (back to audience), downstage, and remains motionless until the Coda has run its inevitably structured course.

I feel impelled to say that whatever perception may emerge in a creative art form based on this idea must be a highly individual one. It is revealable more effectively through the abstractions of music and staging, in this case, than through verbal explanations.

*The Set:* Many, if not most, small American courthouses are pseudo-Greek or quasi-Greco-Roman in architectural concept. It is therefore very easy for the courthouse to proxy for the palace at Thebes, or vice versa. I conceived of three or four Greek-style pillars, and a few steps leading up to them; of *realistic* trees with overhanging boughs—if they are not realistic, they cannot possibly convey the feeling of a courthouse park (the instruments are distributed in the shade below); and of a small, *totally realistic* fountain on casters showing a small boy holding an umbrella over a small girl, both brightly colored, with the water going up the umbrella handle and dripping over the edges. (I saw such a fountain in the small town of Ludington, Michigan, in 1945. Victorian it certainly was, and it charmed me immensely. In the context of *The Bacchae,* it injects an inescapable visual irony.)

*Costumes:* The men are in tunics falling just to the hipline with belts around the waist. In the American sequences they wear pants, but not in the Greek ones. The women's costumes are the same in both sequences. Heroic masks are worn by all principals in the Greek scenes. Thus, the American sequences are characterized by the fountain and pants, the Greek ones by heroic masks and male legs (the fountain is rolled off stage).

*The Cast:*

Baritone: Dion, Hollywood king of Ishbu Kubu
                Dionysos, ancient god of the Bacchae—the same person
Tenor-Baritone: Sonny, young man in the Courthouse Park
                        Pentheus, young king of ancient Thebes—the same person
Soprano: Mom, devotee of Ishbu Kubu and mother of Sonny
                Agave, leader of the Theban Bacchae and mother of Pentheus—the same person
Contralto: Korypheus, leader of the Chorus of the Bacchae
Chorus of Eight Women (including Korypheus), who follow Dion and Dionysos
Chorus of Four Men
Cadmus, Tiresias, the Herdsman, the Guard, who must speak rhythmically but not on set tones

*The Entertainers* (in the Courthouse Park):

Band: two piccolos, three trumpets, two trombones, tuba, and snare and bass drum
Two guitarists, four twirlers and majorettes, eight clog dancers (four women, four men), four tumblers

*Other Instrumental Parts:*

| | |
|---|---|
| Kithara I | Chromelodeon II |
| Kithara II | Bloboy |
| Harmonic Canon I | Spoils of War |
| Harmonic Canon II (Castor & | Diamond Marimba |
| Pollux) | Boo (two players) |
| String Bass | Marimba Eroica (two players) |
| Crychord | Cloud-Chamber Bowls and |
| Adapted Guitar I | Cone Gongs (two players) |
| Adapted Guitar II | Bass Marimba (two players) |
| Adapted Viola (or Cello) | Drone Devils (jaw harps) |
| Chromelodeon I | Pre-Recorded Tape |

*The Program:*

CHORUS ONE. Late afternoon in the Courthouse Park. Ritual of welcome for Dion, Hollywood king of Ishbu Kubu.

> Park Prologue.
> Fanfare and March.
> *Forever Ummorra.* To the happy way, right or wrong, dead or alive, forevermore. First ritual.
> *Save My Soul and Bless My Heart.* Ritual for strings and clogs.
> *Wunnantu Anda.* Primitive percussion ritual.
> *Heavenly Daze and a Million Years.* Climax of welcome.

SCENE ONE. Late afternoon at the entrance to the Palace of Thebes. King Pentheus denounces the Bacchae.

> Hymn to Dionysos: *Holy Joy and Get Religion.*

CHORUS TWO. Early evening of the same day in the Courthouse Park. Sonny, ghost-walking, sees himself in a dream vision, offered up as a sacrificial victim.

SCENE TWO. Early evening of the same ancient day, at the entrance to the Palace of Thebes. Dionysos goes to jail, then escapes.

> Hymns to Dionysos: *What the Majority Believes; Glory to the Male Womb*

CHORUS THREE. Later that night in the Courthouse Park. In celebration of Dion, Hollywood king of Ishbu Kubu.

> *These Good Old-Fashioned Thrills.* Fireworks ritual.
> *Not So Young.* Ritual for Adolescent girls and brass.
> *Ishbu Kubu, Revelation of the Mystic Power.* Theme ritual.
> *Tumble On.* Climax of celebration.

SCENE THREE. Later in the ancient night, at the entrance to the palace of Thebes. Pentheus is tricked into transvestism.

> Hymn to Dionysos: *O To Be Free Where No Man Is.*

CHORUS FOUR. Midnight of the same evening in the Courthouse Park. Mom, ghost-walking, witnesses an attack upon her son, in a nightmare vision.

SCENE FOUR. Early dawn of the next ancient day, at the entrance to the palace of Thebes. Agave comes out of the night with a trophy of her power.

Hymns to Dionysos: *Hell-Hounds of Madness; Dance to the Death*

CODA. Rays of the early morning sun strike horizontally across the Courthouse Park.

Performance time: seventy-five to eighty minutes—no intermission.

## And on the Seventh Day Petals Fell in Petaluma

The instrumental scoring may be seen in the list of Verses below; no common current instrument, such as cello or clarinet, is involved. Although the work constitutes studies in preparation for *Delusion of the Fury*, it must be treated separately for reasons that will become apparent.

Regarding the title: for many years I have looked upon California as my home, and, more specifically, the San Francisco Bay area for the forty years from the mid-1920's to the mid-1960's. On two occasions during those years, I was away for six-year periods (1941–1947 and 1956–1962). Finding a studio large enough for all my instruments that I could afford was always a problem, but in 1962, I did find part of a vacated chick hatchery in Petaluma, about thirty-five miles north of the Golden Gate Bridge, that was suitable in both respects. On the day I looked the place over, I walked down the lane that led to the hatchery, and the way was strewn with petals—roses, camellias, and many others. Since I had had these studies in mind for some time, and considering my strange absence, twice, for exactly *six* years, the title came to me almost immediately.

Aside from the preparatory idea, I had two important reasons for choosing the format below. First, during my entire professional life through 1958, I had learned every instrumental part that I had written (excepting winds, which I do not play) and had sung all the voice parts (excepting those with ranges beyond me). In *Revelation*, partly because of the short time between the completed composition and the researsals, I could not do this, and I cannot feel that I am truly on top of a work unless I do know all the parts; therefore, I was determined to return to that pattern. Second, for several years some musicians had complained about the difficulties of the instrumental parts.

This time, I would not abide such nonsense. I would exploit the instrumental resources to the full, exploring new techniques and also exploring, with a minimum of players, untried rhythms and polyrhythms. Although I began the work in 1963, it took three years, using exactly six players, before I was satisfied with both performances and recordings.

Each of the first twenty-three verses is exactly one minute long, not counting the final beat. These are duets and trios. Then, by electronic synthesizing,[6] pairs of verses are combined in numbers twenty-four through thirty-three; and finally a trio of verses is combined, bringing the studies to an end with the thirty-fourth verse. The electronic syntheses result in quartets and quintets starting with number twenty-four, and with a septet at the end; all are indicated.

| Quartets and Quintets | Duets and Trios | Quartets and Quintets | Duets and Trios |
|---|---|---|---|
| Verse 24 | Verse 1—Zymo-Xyl Crychord<br>Verse 2—Surrogate Kithara Bass Marimba | Verse 30 | Verse 13—Harmonic Canon I Cloud-Chamber Bowls<br>Verse 14—Surrogate Kithara Diamond Marimba |
| Verse 25 | Verse 3—Harmonic Canon I Harmonic Canon III<br>Verse 4—Chromelodeon II Koto | Verse 31 | Verse 15—Chromelodeon I Kithara I<br>Verse 16—Koto Harmonic Canon II |
| Verse 26 | Verse 5—Mazda Marimba Boo<br>Verse 6—Cloud-Chamber Bowls Diamond Marimba | Verse 32 | Verse 17—Adapted Guitar II Mazda Marimba<br>Verse 18—Harmonic Canon I Marimba Eroica |
| Verse 27 | Verse 7—Chromelodeon II Bloboy Kithara II<br>Verse 8—Zymo-Xyl Spoils of War | Verse 33 | Verse 19—Drone Devils Gubagubi Harmonic Canon II<br>Verse 20—Koto Crychord |
| Verse 28 | Verse 9—Harmonic Canon I Kithara I<br>Verse 10—Diamond Marimba Boo | Verse 34 (Septet) | Verse 21—Spoils of War Bass Marimba<br>Verse 22—Chromelodeon I Boo<br>Verse 23—Zymo-Xyl Harmonic Canon III Gourd Tree and Cone Gongs |
| Verse 29 | Verse 11—Kithara II Marimba Eroica<br>Verse 12—Koto Spoils of War | | |

[6]Executed in Santa Monica by Cecil Charles Spiller, who spent many hours, including wee small hours, with three Magnecords and some other equipment that he designed specially for this job. A detailed analysis of *Petals*, including an analysis and discussion of its rhythms, is given in Paul Earls, "Harry Partch: Verses in Preparation for 'Delusion of the Fury,'" *Annuario —Yearbook 3* (Inter-American Institute for Musical Research, Tulane University, 1967), 1–32.

As the composition of *Delusion of the Fury* progressed, I found that I had used all but one of the duets and trios, with elaboration and added instrumentation, and—in addition—two or three of the polyrhythmic ideas.

Inasmuch as the two-act story line of *Delusion* had been on my mind for several years, the placement of these musical ideas in the larger dramatic work (see below) was constantly anticipated, although not indicated at the time. They became the structural sinews of the new work.

## Delusion of the Fury—A Ritual of Dream and Delusion

Scored for all of the instruments described in Chapters 12 and 13 (with the single exception of the Adapted Viola), and including all of the small hand instruments described in Chapter 13. The Quadrangularis Reversum and the Eucal Blossom were first used in this work. No common current instrument is involved. Performance time: seventy-five to eighty minutes— no intermission.

Although the program shows two acts, there is no cessation of sound from beginning to end. Act I, based upon a Japanese story dating from the eleventh century, and both historical and legendary, is intensely serious.[7] Act II, based upon an African tale that must be considered a folk story,[8] since no author is indicated, is highly farcical. Thus, the Greek concept of a serious play followed by a farce is encompassed in one evening of theater.

Act I, a music-theater portrayal of release from the wheel of life and death, is almost entirely depicted through the arts of mime and dance. In simplest terms, it is a final enlightenment, a reconciliation, with a total departure from the arena of mortal cravings and passions. A princely warrior has fallen in battle at the hands of a young rival, and the act begins with the slayer's remorseful pilgrimage to the scene and to the shrine. The murdered man appears as a spirit, and his son,[9] born after his death, then

---

[7]Arthur Waley, *The Noh Plays of Japan* (Grove Press, New York, n.d.) . The basis is largely *Atsumori* by *Seami* (pp. 64–73), but one character, the son, is from *Ikuta* by Zembo Motoyasu (pp. 74–80) .

[8]Peggy Rutherford, comp. and ed., *African Voices* (Grosset & Dunlap, New York, 1958) . The story is called *Justice*, "An Ethiopian Tale, Told to Wolf Leslau by a student at the Teachers' Training School in Addis Ababa" (pp. 67–68). This volume indicates that *Justice* was first published in Harold Courlander and Wolf Leslau, *The Fire on the Mountain and Other Ethiopian Stories* (Henry Holt & Co., New York, 1950) .

[9]It would be preferable for the part of the son to be played by a boy soprano, ten to twelve years old (his voice part is very slight) . But if this is not possible, the part should be given to a female soprano with a boyish figure.

enters, seeking the same shrine in the belief that he may see his father's face, as though in a dream. Spurred to resentment by the presence of his son, the ghost-father lives again through the ordeal of battle, but finally realizing his error, he seeks total reconciliation.

Act II is, in a sense, a reconciliation with life rather than death. It is a story of people caught by chance turns of fate, often ironic, always farcical and hilarious. This act is also depicted very largely by mime and dance. A young vagabond is preparing to cook a meal over twigs when an old woman who tends a goat herd approaches, searching for a lost kid. She eventually finds the kid, but due to a misunderstanding caused by the hobo's deafness, a dispute arises. Villagers gather, and after a violent dance around the quarrelling couple, they are forced to appear before the justice of the peace.

*The Cast* (the three principals):

Tenor-Baritone: The Slayer, in Act I
               The Young Vagabond, in Act II—the same person

Soprano: The Son, in Act I
             The Old Goat Woman, in Act II—the same person

Bass: The Slain as a Ghost, in Act I
             The Justice of the Peace, in Act II—the same person

Ideally, the singers would be skilled also in the arts of dancing, acting, miming, as they are in Noh and Kabuki. But in our specialist culture, singers are generally only singers, actors only actors, and dancers only dancers. Just one solution seems possible: put the singers in the pit, while the actor-dancers on stage mouth the words, the gibberish, or whatever.

The instrumentalists *are* the Chorus. As in *The Bewitched,* the choral voice sounds do not come from a separate body of persons appearing just occasionally, but from among the instruments, from musicians who are deeply involved throughout. In the present work, I wanted to progress even beyond this concept. There are many musicians on stage, but almost never do all of them play simultaneously. In fairly long periods only a small ensemble is employed, and the tacit musicians may thus become actors and dancers, moving from instruments to acting areas as the impetus of the drama requires. This must certainly be a move toward a sealing of the bond between the theater arts.

The scenes of the two acts fall naturally into segments, each with its inherent dramatic integrity.

| Act I | Act II |
|---|---|
| Scene 1. Chorus of Shadows | Scene 1. The Quiet Hobo Meal |
| Scene 2. The Pilgrimage | Scene 2. The Lost Kid |
| Scene 3. Emergence of the Spirit | Scene 3. Time of Fun Together |
| Scene 4. A Son in Search of His Father's Face | Scene 4. The Misunderstanding |
| Scene 5. Cry from Another Darkness | Scene 5. Arrest, Trial, and Judgment |
| Scene 6. Pray for Me | Scene 6. Pray for Me Again |

Singing by the Chorus is rather general. But this singing might better be described as sounds from the throat, meaningless in English verbal communication but not meaningless here. This is especially true in Act I, Scene 1 (Chorus of Shadows), and in Act II, Scene 3 (Time of Fun Together).

Preceding Act I is the Exordium, about eleven minutes in duration, which in more familiar terms might be called an overture. But the word *exordium* carries far more significance for this idea. In a philosophical sense it is an invocation—it implies the beginning of a ritualistic web, the spinning of a web, which inevitably entangles the participants in almost predictable complexities. The Exordium is totally instrumental.

Following Act I is an entr'acte, the Sanctus, about seven minutes in duration. The word may seem strange here because of its Christian (Roman Catholic) usage. However, in this case, it is polytheistic, and in its beginnings it is replete with pagan gong and bell-like tones (Cone Gongs, Gourd Tree, Hubcaps, Spoils of War, Cloud-Chamber Bowls). It is characteristic of the Roman Church to appropriate from other cultures whatever it feels it may use effectively, and I claim the same privilege. Act I, following the reconciliation (and the *pray for me* sequence), ends very softly, and it was my idea so to fill the theater with sound as to glue the audience to its seats.

Both acts might be described as occurring in an earlier time, but both certainly have present-day over- or undertones. And despite the descriptive words *Japanese* and *African,* they represent neither a precise time nor a precise place. In Act I, I am certainly not trying to write a Noh play. Noh

A Page from the Full Score of *DELUSION OF THE FURY*

A Page from the Full Score of *DELUSION OF THE FURY*

has been for centuries a fine art, one of the most sophisticated that the world has known, and it would have been senseless for me to follow a path of superficial duplication. The instrumental sounds (excepting the Koto) are not Japanese, the scales are not Japanese, the voice usage is totally different, costumes are different. Act I is actually a development of my own style in dramatic music, as previously revealed in both *Oedipus* and *Revelation*. If for no other reason than its music, its *daimon* is American.

Again, in Act II there is no attempt to depict African ritual, although this ritual, as I have heard it on records and seen it on film, has obviously influenced my writing and my concepts in this and several other works. I have made changes in the basic folk story (cited above), and I have added to it. There is nowhere dialogue as such. The mysterious, perverse qualities of these story ideas are better conveyed through music, miming, lights—and with more certain impact than through spoken or sung lines, or spoken or sung lines in response.

The words or sentences that I have used in Act II are entirely my own, and they are all American colloquial. In Act I the total of recognizable English words is ten, and in Act II forty-four (not counting repetitions in either case). Despite (or because of) the use of much percussion, the quality is American. The furious irony is deeply and certainly American.

*Synopsis of Act I:* The Chorus of Shadows (Scene 1) might be considered as a group of pilgrims or of ghosts, or perhaps both. It is dream-like. The Pilgrim (the slayer) enters (Scene 2), dancing and singing of his remorse. He ends the scene far downstage, kneeling, with his head to the ground, and during the next two scenes, he becomes a huddled, motionless, dark silhouette. The Ghost then enters (Scene 3) and sings and moves in a dream-like manner, with occasional responses from the Chorus. He exits. The Son enters (Scene 4), searching for a vision of his father. The Ghost reappears, and the two do a tender dance-duet. They finally become aware of the figure of the kneeling Pilgrim, who, during forty beats of the music, very slowly rises. In Cry from Another Darkness (Scene 5), the slayer and the slain recreate their battle of many years before. At the end of the scene, the ghost-father drops his stick (surrogate for a sword) and exclaims: "You are not my enemy!" He falls to his knees (Scene 6) and sings: "Pray for me! O pray for me again!" The Chorus softly repeats these lines.

*Synopsis of Act II:* The Young Vagabond enters (Scene 1), with a pack and with a few sticks to build a fire. He has hardly gotten settled when the Old Goat Woman enters (Scene 2) and tries to question him about her lost kid. Being deaf, the Hobo wants nothing so much as to get rid of her, and his plaintive, "Why doesn't she just go away?" spoken to the audience, is echoed by the Chorus. He points frantically, and the Old Goat Woman disappears in that direction.

Time of Fun Together (Scene 3) serves a double theater purpose: it allows time for the woman to find her kid, and it introduces the villagers, in the midst of one of their revels, to the audience. The scene features a singing and dancing female soloist, an antiphonal and polyphonic male chorus, and the most intensive use of the small hand instruments in the entire work.

The Old Goat Woman returns (Scene 4), cradling the lost kid in her arms as though it were a human baby, and almost immediately a misunderstanding arises, again because of the Hobo's deafness. The villagers return due to the commotion, arrest the quarrelling couple, and march them off to face the Justice of the Peace. When they reenter (Scene 5), the Justice, deaf and near-sighted, follows them and is seated on a kind of throne. At the end of the hearing, he demands silence and utters his pronouncement: "Young man, take your beautiful young wife and your charming child and go home! And never let me see you in this court again!" The Chorus, laughing and jubilant, launch into their song, *O How Did We Ever Get By Without Justice?*

I now quote from the full score (Scene 6): "The pantheistic deities of pre-colonial Africa, Asia, America, and Australia come to life—smile divinely, and decide that human delusion must be countered by heavenly riot. They invoke thunder and lightning, and instill—A STRANGE FEAR." The terrified revelers crouch in corners, and finally a voice is heard off-stage: "Pray for me!, O pray for me again!" The Chorus repeats the line, very softly. Then with a crash of percussion, the last section of the Sanctus is repeated, the play is over, and during the remaining music the various groups take their bows.

*The Stage:* The instruments, placed on the stage floor and on ascending risers, before a sound-reflecting cyclorama, *are* the set. Together with an effective play of lights, nothing more is called for.

*Costumes:* The musicians are in costume and are made up, as actors. In Act I they wear dark trousers and a poncho-like garment, allowing bare arms, painted in various designs. At the end of the *Sanctus* they remove these ponchos to expose both chests and arms pained in designs, in bright colors. As for the principals and the dancing chorus, the range of costume is wide, but they should not suggest a specific time or a specific place.

*In retrospect:* I pondered this idea for some five years before I ever put down a note of it on paper (not counting the work on *Petals*). It is an adventurous work, but I cannot call it experimental. I recall some famous painter (his name eludes me), exasperated because his work was called "experimental," saying, in effect, "You never see my experiments." (Hear! Hear!) Looking back on all the antecedents of *Delusion* of a theater nature, most of them outlined in this chapter, it is a very logical development. I am sure—in this unreal world—that I knew what I was doing.[10]

A synopsis cannot in any way proxy for an actual production. Only theater will bring the concept to life. And I must emphasize the fact that these verbal descriptions are intended merely as a small intimation of the art that I envision.

---

[10]Performance of *Delusion* was in charge of Danlee Mitchell throughout—in conducting the rehearsals over a period of months and in conducting both the performances on stage and the recording (see Appendices III and V) . Here and now it seems appropriate to state that without his belief in my work and his unfailing friendship, very little creative work, including this second edition of *Genesis,* would have emanated from me during the years 1966–1972.

PART IV

*Intonations: Historic, Implied, Proposed*

# CHAPTER FIFTEEN

# A Thumbnail Sketch of the History of Intonation

In essence the very earliest divinations of the nature of musical sounds were Monophonic concepts. A length of bamboo pipe and the *mono* chord of the ancient *kanon*, or monochord, were in each case a Monophonic starting point—that is, a column of air which in its vibration, or length, represented 1, and a section of chord which in its vibration, or length, also represented 1.

The development of the science of music from these concepts is a story about men, and the various ways in which men reacted to it. For the most part it is a story of the advancement of basic theories and of their reception —their acceptance and/or their rejection; but occasionally a theory appears that might be called, not in the least invidiously, "comedy relief," such as that of Sarangdev of Kashmir, who starts from the "lowest possible tone." There have undoubtedly been contributors, possibly significant ones, other than those here considered, but the basic ancient theories—which have been pretty thoroughly explored and have long been common knowledge among musical scholars—are all represented.

## The Chinese Priority

Because it is the records of the Greek arts which have been preserved for us, via the Romans and the Arabs, we are very likely to ascribe to the ancient Greeks discoveries, arts, and divinations which probably had a more remote origin. At least three great civilizations antedate the age of Greece, the Assyrian-Babylonian, the Egyptian, and the Chinese, and it is highly improbable that none of the mathematicians and scientists (or harp and bamboo-pipe players) which they produced contemplated music as a science. Records of such knowledge in Egypt and Babylon disappeared millenniums ago, but China is another story.

Sze Ma-chi'en, historian for ancient China and contemporary of Ptolemy in a culture isolated from the Greek world, ascribes the mathematical formula for the pentatonic scale to *Ling Lun*, minister or court musician under Emperor Huang-Ti, of the twenty-seventh century B.C.[1] This, the first recorded date in the history of musical theory, is one of those legendary Chinese ages whose antiquity some scholars believe to be exaggerated.[2]

The formula starts with a length of bamboo pipe arbitrarily called 81 parts. A third of these parts is then subtracted and a third of the remaining parts added, alternately, through four computations. The result is five pipes of 81, 54, 72, 48, and 64 parts.[3] The pipe of 81 parts is of course 1/1, to use the Monophonic symbol, and the others are 3/2, 9/8, 27/16, and 81/64, respectively. Arranged in order of pitch, they are:

$$1/1 \quad 9/8 \quad 81/64 \quad 3/2 \quad 27/16 \quad 2/1$$
$$\quad\ \ 9/8 \quad 9/8 \quad 32/27 \quad 9/8 \quad 32/27$$

This is a scale of so-called Pythagorean intonation which was probably never used by voices except when accompanied by instruments so tuned, which Ling Lun produced; it is possible in the Monophonic fabric starting on 16/9, thus:

$$16/9 \quad 1/1 \quad 9/8 \quad 4/3 \quad 3/2 \quad 16/9$$
$$\quad\ \ 9/8 \quad 9/8 \quad 32/27 \quad 9/8 \quad 32/27$$

But Ling Lun was not satisfied; he proceeded to continue the formula until he had two sets of six "lü," or bamboo pipes, one a Pythagorean semitone above the second, thus giving one version of a Pythagorean twelve-tone scale[4] (see the next chapter). Hence in recorded theory (though not in musical application), the twelve-tone scale is exactly as old as the five-tone scale.

## *Pythagoras—Two Millenniums Later*

Gliding down the long historic haul from the twenty-seventh to the sixth century B.C., and halfway round the world, we come to *Pythagoras of*

---

[1]Yasser, *Theory of Evolving Tonality*, 26n.

[2]*Ibid.*, 25n; Barbour, "Equal Temperament," 135. K.C. Hsaio declares that Chinese music was relatively well developed as early as 2852 B.C. See "Chinese Scale Theories," in Meyer, *Musician's Arithmetic*, 105. Somehow, the fact that the month of the year 2852 B.C. was omitted from this observation is the source of a singular kind of satisfaction.

[3]Richard, "Chinese Music," in *East of Asia Magazine*, 1:307.

[4]Yasser, *Theory of Evolving Tonality*, 27; K. C. Hsaio, "Chinese Scale Theories," in Meyer, *Musician's Arithmetic*, 107, 108.

*Samos* (fl. 540–510 B.C.), that musical Saint Paul of the early Greek world. Pythagoras, because his name is attached to them, is famous for many institutions, all of them legendary or very nearly legendary: (1) the brotherhood which dedicated itself to a pure life and pure "perfect fifths" (3/2's) and which spread to many Greek cities; (2) the demonstration of the ratios of 3 (3/2 and 4/3) on his monochord, thus allegedly proposing the generating and limiting number 3 as the symbol of universal (including musical) order; (3) his particular "comma"—531441/524288 (23.5 cents), or approximately the ratio 74/73, derived from (4) the "circle of fifths" (see the next chapter)—thereby making "Pythagorean" any scale of tones transposed from a succession of 3/2's into one 2/1; (5) the division of the monochord into twelve equal parts, thus tending to establish the first historic record of the Arithmetical Proportion;[5] (6) the increase of the number of lyre strings from seven to eight, evolved from the Pythagorean trademark, 3/2 (see Chapter 10), thus giving the Western world the heptatonic scale.[6]

As for Pythagoras the peripatetic, though the legends do not include a wholesale conversion of an island's population to the Harmonical Proportion after a shipwreck, they ignore few places in the known world of his day; he went to Egypt soon after the land was opened to Greek "exploration" and "immigration" (in the seventh century B.C.), and he also saw Chaldea and Babylon, the latter place as a captive.[7] I even recall seeing a Hindu book on musical theory which stated that Pythagoras visited India, bringing the Harmonical Proportion to its presumably benighted musicians. An account of the Pythagorean legendary journeys has point only as a symptom of the spreading Greek influence, of the fascination that this beginning of the divination of sound held for speculative men, and of the extent of the symbolism and limitations of 3, to be encountered again and again—both in time and in geography.

As the first revelation of the nature of tone among a restless and curious people, Pythagoras' 3/2 was a brilliant omen. However, the advocate of

[5]Schlesinger attributes this information to Gaudentius, pre-Ptolemaic theorist. *The Greek Aulos*, 23. The division into twelve parts is implied in Ptolemy's Equable Diatonic, presented in Chapter 10.

[6]Hawkins, *History of the Science and Practice of Music*, 1:14.

[7]Hope, *Medieval Music*, 23, 25; Farmer, *Arabian Musical Influence*, 125, 126. Farmer also quotes Iamblichos, a neo-Platonic philosopher of the fourth century A.D. and a lover of Eastern culture: "They say that it (the Harmonical Proportion) was a discovery of the Babylonians, and that it was by Pythagoras first introduced among the Greeks." *Ibid.*, 123.

this ratio seemed to reason that if one 3/2 was good, twelve were twelve times good, and after 2500 years we are still trying to correct the excesses of his judgment.

## Sparta—the Humiliation of Timotheus

The person who bore the name *Timotheus* (446–357 B.C.) is even more obscure to us than Pythagoras, but to his compatriots he was an infinitely greater trial because of his musical excesses and depredations. For he dared to expand the scale on the kithara by adding four tones to the eight established by Pythagoras. In a scene from the comic poet Pherecrates the personification of music bemoans her outrage at the hands of Timotheus' twelve strings: "But now comes Timotheus, who has most shamelessly ruined and massacred me. Who is this Timotheus? asks Justice, one of the other persons of the play. A red-haired Milesian, is the answer. He has exceeded all the others in wickedness. He has introduced weird music like the crawlings of an ant-heap, unharmonic with most unholy high notes and pipings. He has filled me full of maggots like a cabbage. And once, when by chance he met me walking alone, he disrobed me and tied me up in pieces with twelve strings."

And for the crime of twelve strings (one account reduces the offense to eleven strings) the Spartans drove the immoral Timotheus from their city.[8] Timotheus seemingly had failed to realize that to dream of desirable changes is one thing, to act upon those dreams quite another, that his fellow man's basic credo was (and is): down with action! But like all the "immorally" inclined, Timotheus wasn't satisfied with dreams (nor has history revealed the possible culpability in the naked fact of a "red-haired Milesian"), and as a perfectly natural result he found himself catapulted onto a Spartan hillside by a Spartan bouncer.[9]

## Reform by Archytas—and China

Returning to the less spectacular but much more far-reaching and more basic Pythagorean excesses, we find in *Archytas* (*c.* 400 B.C.), a native of Tarentum, Italy—philosopher, mathematician, general, statesman, and

[8]Kinkeldey, "The Harmonic Sense," in *Papers of the Music Teachers' National Association,* 18:10, 11.

[9]The later history of Timotheus shows that he was encouraged by the tragic dramatist Euripides and that the Athenians "ate up" all his twelve strings could offer—thus making another Peloponnesian War fairly inevitable.

friend of Plato—one of if not the first to decide that reform was in order. Archytas substituted the pure 5/4 for the unsingable Pythagorean 81/64 in the tetrachord of the enharmonic genus, and by implication substituted all the ratios of 5 in between-degree relationships of the heptatonic scale. He also replaced the 9/8 with an 8/7 in the diatonic tetrachord, and impliedly recognized all ratios of 7 (in the complete enharmonic and diatonic scales) as scale degrees (see Chapter 10).

And what had China done in the twenty-three centuries since Ling Lun to break from the tyranny of its own brand of Pythagoreanism? In theory apparently nothing, in practice at least something. E. M. von Hornbostel gives the ratios for a sculptured bronze kin, the "scholar's lute," dating from before the third century B.C. This involves ratios of both 5 and 7 (see page 178), which von Hornbostel, with his predilection for Pythagoreanism, relegates to what he calls "cosmological considerations"[10]—or acoustic accuracy.

## *The Harmonists versus the Aristoxeneans*

Sometime between Pythagoras and Archytas a school of philosophers and mathematical theorists known as the Harmonists developed, of which Archytas was obviously a prominent member.[11] The inevitable reaction against what seemed to be ratio-happy rampancy among the Harmonists found its first voice in *Aristoxenus* (*c.* 330 B.C.), a native of Tarentum and a pupil of Aristotle, and resulted in the establishment of an opposing school, known as the Aristoxeneans. The war was on. But Aristoxenus, too, was guilty of excesses. His thesis, that the ear, not mathematical calculation, is the judge of musical materials (the results by ear and by small-number ratios are of course identical) would have proved more substantial and more consistent had he not (1) substituted a system of approximation, and then (2) proceeded to use, like all temperers, a simple mathematical ratio, 2/1, as his first measure.

Aristoxenus' *Elements of Harmony*, which is said to be the earliest treatise on Greek music extant, includes the following passage: "A tone is the difference in compass between the first two concords, and may be divided by three lowest denominators, as melody admits of half-tones, thirds of tones

---

[10]"Musikalische Tonsysteme," in *Handbuch der Physik*, 8:436.

[11]Both Aristotle and Aristoxenus thought enough of Archytas to write biographies of him, mentioned by ancient writers but never found. Smith, *Dictionary of Greek and Roman Biography*, 1:274.

and quartertones, while undeniably rejecting any interval less than these. Let us designate the smallest of these intervals as the Enharmonic diesis, the next smallest Chromatic diesis, and the greatest a semitone."[12] The prototypes of all scales engendered by a partitioning of the "tone" into "semitones," "third tones," and "quartertones" had therefore been formulated as early as the fourth century B.C. It is thus evident that from the beginning of controversy over the relationship of sounds the conflict was between that which was natural, reasonable, and inherently pleasing, and that which was easy, convenient, and without logical aural causation—a conflict that has had no end.

## Euclid the Deflater

The prolix Aristoxenean writings on intonational approximation (numbering 453 separate works, according to one authority[13]) have been combed and lauded by modern history-conscious theorists defending Equal Temperament. They were also combed, and meticulously deflated, by the father of geometry, *Euclid*, who flourished at Alexandria under Ptolemy I (ruled 323–283 B.C.), and who made the first "essay towards a determination of the ratios by the supposed division of the chord"[14] (division of the monochord in the two-2/1 "Immutable System"; see frontispiece). In a series of point-by-point theorems in his *Section of the Canon*, which he figuratively flung in the face of the Aristoxeneans, he showed, among other things, in Theorem 9 that six 9/8's are greater than a 2/1 by the Pythagorean "comma," and—just in case anyone still had any doubts—in Theorem 14 that 2/1 is less than six 9/8's by the same interval; in Theorem 15 that 4/3 is less than two and a half 9/8's, and that 3/2 is less than three and a half 9/8's. He then caps this particular sequence with Theorem 16, which proves that it is fallacious to speak of "half a tone" or "half 9/8," since 9/8 cannot be divided in half (in allusion to the Aristoxenean halving, thirding, and quartering of "tones").[15] Ptolemy acidly adds, in effect, "If the Aristoxen-

---

[12]Schlesinger, "Further Notes on Aristoxenus and Musical Intervals," in *Classical Quarterly*, 27:88. Funk and Wagnalls' *New Standard Dictionary* calls a diesis one of several intervals varying from a semitone to a quartertone in width. Schlesinger speaks of the diesis as an "introduction" to another genus. *The Greek Aulos*, 205.

[13]Smith, *Dictionary of Greek and Roman Biography*, 1:344.

[14]Hawkins, *History of the Science and Practice of Music*, 1:20.

[15]Davy, *Letters*, 2:276–277, 282–284; Johnson, *Musical Pitch*, 50–51. But in his *Elements*, in the "ninth of the sixth," Euclid provides a formula that can be adapted to the division of 9/8 or any other interval into halves—geometrically (see Chapter 6). The proof of Theorem 16

eans cannot find something better let them use what mathematics provide."[16] Euclid also called the intervals of 1 and 3 (2/1, 3/2, 4/3) consonant, the first clear statement of this idea.[17]

## Eratosthenes, and Further Reforms

Whereas Euclid's contributions to musical science were mostly defensive, although aggressively so, those of *Eratosthenes* (276–196 B.C.), a native of Cyrene (Africa), were definitely creative. Eratosthenes, who was director of the famous library at Alexandria, was not only a musical philosopher, but an astronomer, geographer, cartographer, and inventor of astronomical instruments.[18] In music he is generally credited with substituting the good-to-the-ear 6/5 for the more difficult Pythagorean 32/27 in his chromatic genus tetrachord, although this interval was implied by Archytas in his enharmonic scale. Also, Eratosthenes emerges as the first notable proponent of the Arithmetical Proportion, determining both his enharmonic and chromatic tetrachords on the basis of aliquot divisions of a string (see Chapter 10). All of Eratosthenes' writings are lost; it is only from the pages of Ptolemy that we derive what we know of his musical work.

## King Fang Anticipates Mercator—Didymus

To preserve chronology a geographic break must be made, back to that isolated but fructiferous civilization China, and a contemporary of Era-

amounts to the proposition that 9/8, being a superparticular ratio, cannot be divided by a "mean proportional," that is, cannot be divided into equal aural parts by ratios of rational numbers. The geometric division demonstrated in the "ninth of the sixth" is a surd. The only ratios that can be divided into equal aural parts by ratios of rational numbers are of course those in which both numbers are multiples—for example, 9/4 (3/2 × 3/2), 16/9 (4/3 × 4/3), 81/64 (9/8 × 9/8).

[16]Torr, "Greek Music," in *Oxford History of Music*, Introductory Volume, 5.

[17]A. J. Ellis in Helmholtz, *Sensations of Tone*, 226n; Johnson, *Musical Pitch*, 50–51. Pythagoras may have expressed the idea of consonance (see Hawkins, *Science and Practice of Music*, 1:10), but none of his writings has come down to us, our information regarding his theories being derived from the writings of the group loosely termed Pythagoreans, of whom Euclid was one. Euclid defined consonance as "the blending of a higher with a lower tone," and dissonance as "incapacity to mix, when two tones cannot blend, but appear rough to the ear." Johnson calls Euclid's "the earliest statement in which the ratios are explicit given for the musical consonances." Whether Euclid and the Greeks in general went beyond the ratios of 3 in recognizing *symphoniai*, or consonances, is much debated. Schlesinger (*Is European Musical Theory Indebted to the Arabs?* 10) states flatly that certain ratios of 5 ("thirds") were called *symphoniai*, but with a consecutive, not a simultaneous connotation, which is not at all the modern sense and therefore valid only in an evolutionary perspective—as a step along the way.

[18]Smith, *Dictionary of Greek and Roman Biography*, 2:44–47.

tosthenes, *King Fang* (royalty not implied), who anticipated by some eighteen centuries the discovery of the fifty-three "cycle" of 3/2's in the West.[19] King Fang calculated exactly the proportional numbers for lü that would give a scale based on a succession of sixty 3/2's and observed that the fifty-fourth lü was practically identical with the first (3.6 cents above).[20] This very early discovery by King Fang is particularly noteworthy when we consider that the fifty-three "cycle" has been the subject of much conjecture in recent decades and has been the theoretic basis for at least three new harmoniums. Leaving this brief excursion into China we return to the now Roman-engulfed Greeks and *Didymus*, academic philosopher of Nero's time (ruled 54–68 A.D.), who gave his name to another "comma," 81/80 (21.5 cents), the difference between two between-degree relationships— 9/8 and 10/9—in his diatonic tetrachord. Besides introducing the logical 9/8–10/9 combination in the diatonic scale, Didymus substituted the easier-to-hear 16/15 for 28/27 in the diatonic genus,[21] and in so doing anticipated *Claudius Ptolemaeus*, or *Ptolemy* (139 A.D.–?).

## Ptolemy the Investigator

Ptolemy (not to be confused with the Ptolemy Dynasty, terminating with Cleopatra), a native of Alexandria, was a mathematician, astronomer, geographer, and—most important for us—a repository of musical theory and a ratio thinker of no mean pretensions.[22] In his *Harmonics*[23] he condemned both Pythagorean and Aristoxenean intonations, the first as improper reasoning and the second as something even worse.[24]

[19]Yasser, *Theory of Evolving Tonality*, 31.

[20]Barbour, "Equal Temperament," 137–138.

[21]Hawkins, *History of the Science and Practice of Music*, 1:32.

[22]In addition to reforming the Greek modes, Ptolemy also gave the positions of 1,022 stars in the constellations, devised a set of parallels and meridians, and (as though this were not enough for one lifetime), made maps of the world which were the final authority for some twelve hundred years after his death. These involved a wide underestimation of the earth's circumference, thus persuading Columbus that a western passage to India was feasible and leading inevitably to the discovery of America. Smith, *Dictionary of Greek and Roman Biography*, 3:577, 579.

[23]The *Harmonics* is represented by a 1652 edition edited by the German philologist Meibomius, a 1682 edition by the Englishman Dr. John Wallis, prepared from a manuscript in the original Greek in the Bodleian Library (Hawkins, *Science and Practice of Music*, 1:86), and a later edition by Wallis which includes Porphyry's commentary (Smith, *Dictionary of Greek and Roman Biography*, 3:573). All three editions are in Latin. Throughout the *Harmonics* Ptolemy gives full credit to his predecessors, about whose musical theories, and particularly those of Archytas, Eratosthenes, and Didymus, we would otherwise know little or nothing.

[24]Hawkins, *History of the Science and Practice of Music*, 1:83–85.

Specifically, Ptolemy tended to translate Greek musical scales into ratios of the smallest numbers compatible with the nature and esthetic purpose of each; he defined the scale that was to become the basis of harmonic music in later Europe (the Ptolemaic Sequence), and he stipulated or implied the whole body of ratios based on the 11 limit in his interpretations of scales (see Chapter 10). Thus he anticipated, though in a manner much less specific, the 11 limit of Monophony.

The number of outstanding men famous for other work who undertook to influence musical thinking is a notable feature of this age in the West; astronomers, geometers, geographers, philosophers, statesmen, expressed themselves in no quibbling terms on current musical philosophies. It is difficult to escape a feeling of depression in contrasting the present-day attitude. Even when modern writers in fields other than music are impelled to discuss it, or are obliged to skirt it because it impinges upon their subject, one reads between their lines: ". . . but of course I am not a musician, and current usage in the art of music is not for me to debate." Plato, Aristotle, Euclid, and Ptolemy stood in no such awe.

## Semitones and Asses—Back to China

From the century following Ptolemy one more Greek name may be cited, the last in practically a thousand years of contributions to the science of music. *Porphyry* (c. 233–304), a native of Syria and philosopher of the neo-Platonic school, was a prolific writer on many subjects.[25] A single quotation from his work on music will serve. In his commentary on Ptolemy, where he is discussing the Aristoxenean constituents of 4/3, he says (here paraphrased): "What is left after taking two whole tones from 4/3 is no more a semitone than a mule is a semi-ass."[26]

Porphyry was the last of the Greek contributors to the controversy over the science of intonation, but he is far from representing the end of the Greek influence, for the repercussions of the chords struck by Pythagoras, Aristoxenus, Ptolemy, and many others of their culture have never ceased.

Leaving Ptolemy and the Greek world for the time being, we turn to the Chinese *Ho Tcheng-Tien* (c. 370–447), who anticipated twelve-tone Equal

[25]He wrote a fifteen-book treatise against the Christian religion which led to Emperor Theodosius' order, in 388, for the burning of his books. Smith, *Dictionary of Greek and Roman Biography*, 3:500; Hawkins, *op. cit.*, 1:89.
[26]Perrett, *Questions of Musical Theory*, 55.

Temperament in Europe by about thirteen centuries. Ho gave string lengths for such a scale, in which the maximum deviation from equally tempered degrees was 9 cents.[27] Ho's scale, however, seems to have been achieved more by Ho's ear than by formula. In arriving at the mathematical formula China and Europe were virtually simultaneous, but, as one might expect, China arrived with greater exactitude (see below).

## China and Greece—Loci of Impetus

It is interesting to see how the geographic setting of these men of musical science swings about the earth, resting transiently only where a civilization is vital, imbued with the spirit of investigation and controversy. On the basis of available records priority goes to the Chinese; imagination and insight to the Greeks. The Greek influence was borne eastward directly and via the Byzantine Empire into Arabia, Persia, and India, and westward via the Arabs and the Roman Church into modern Europe. The Chinese influence is both more limited and more conjectural, but probably extended eastward to Korea and Japan, and southward to the peninsulas and islands of the Far East. The two early cultures of Greece and China to a large extent delineated the musical acoustical thought of the entire civilized world.[28]

## The Arab Link

The thousand years' blackout during which Europe lapsed into automatic cant derived from (and automatic *can't* because of) Aristotle and Ptolemy was not an entirely sterile millennium as regards the science of music. Shortly before the Arabic conquest of the Mediterranean region *Zalzal the Lutist* (d. 720), a performer and composer, and only incidentally a theorist, reformed the largely Pythagorean intonation of the ancient and Persian "fretting" of the instrument.[29] He retied some of the lute ligatures, moving them closer to the natural intervals most gracious to the ear. Among these were several ratios of 11, namely 12/11, 16/11, 18/11.[30]

In changing the ancient tuning, Zalzal played the role that Archytas had filled in relation to Pythagoras, but he was followed by no Euclid, Era-

---

[27]Barbour, "Equal Temperament," 138.

[28]The extent of Greek influence is clearly shown in Schlesinger's "The Greek Foundations of the Theory of Music," in *Musical Standard*, volumes 27 and 28 (1926).

[29]Ellis, "Musical Scales of Various Nations," in *Journal of the Society of Arts*, 33:493; Ellis in Helmholtz, *Sensations of Tone*, 281n.

[30]*Ibid.*, 516.

tosthenes, or Ptolemy, and despite the fact that the science of music was a course of study in Arabic institutions (Western schools of music note well!) Arabic theory fell into a groove of Pythagoreanism from which it has seemingly never extricated itself.

Still one more theorist of the early Mohammedan world must be heard, *Alfarabi* (870–950). In his *Kitab al Musiqi* he writes: "The aim of a writer in every theoretical art should be determined by three axioms: the first, a complete statement of fundamental principles. The second, the ability to elucidate what follows from these principles. Third, the ability to combat errors which meet him in that science, and strength to restrict the opinions of others, to discriminate between the right and the wrong, and to rectify the imperfections of those whose opinions are obscure."[31]

Unfortunately the record as yet reveals no significant musical contribution springing from these words of wisdom, and the work of Alfarabi and subsequent Arabic theorists seems to be of value simply as a repository of Greek learning and a source of information. The fretting of the Southern Tambour of Bagdad, one bit of such information provided by Alfarabi which greatly excited the nineteenth-century Riemann, was theoretically divided into forty equal parts, with five frets at the nut.[32] Whether or not there is a historical connection, this is an expansion of the first three degrees of Eratosthenes' enharmonic tetrachord (see Chapter 10), derived from the same Arithmetical Proportion.

Thus up to this point the Harmonical Proportion, the Arithmetical Proportion, Pythagoreanism, and the approximations of Aristoxenus are the chief ideas that figure in the story of the science of music. From here on the names of the ideas will begin to change and there will be greater precision in details. Nevertheless the same four ideas are to be the bones of contention for a thousand years more, for they are very much gnawed over by theorists even today.

## The Medieval World Catches On

In the frocked men of the Roman Church medieval Europe found the first agents of a vitality that was to rouse it from its intellectual lethargy. *Franco of Cologne* (a person of obscure identity, placed uncertainly from the

[31]H. G. Farmer, *Historical Facts for the Arabian Musical Influence*, 67–68 (quoted by permission of William Reeves, Ltd.). Schlesinger shows that this is in part at least a "rewrite" of Aristoxenus. "Greek Foundations of the Theory of Music," in *Musical Standard*, 27:63.

[32]Ellis in Helmholtz, *Sensations of Tone*, 517, 521; Farmer, *Arabian Musical Influence*, 232–234.

eleventh to the thirteenth century) and the English monk *Walter Odington*
(*c.* 1240–1280) examined the common practice of singing in closer harmony than 2/1's and 3/2's, and decided that the intervals of this new popular art (*faux bourdon*), or some of them, were "imperfect consonances."[33]
That it is not entirely clear just what Odington stood for is at least partly
the fault of Odington. In classifying his "concords of discords," some of
which, he observes, "are smoother than others," he remarks insouciantly,
"but which comes first is no care of mine."[34]

Odington stated that consonant "thirds" had the ratios 5/4 and 6/5 and
that singers used them intuitively rather than the Pythagorean ratios 81/64
and 32/27, as measured on the monochord.[35] The popular harmonies of
*faux bourdon*, then already at least a century old,[36] forced an academic re-
examination of the Euclidean dictum that consonance was limited to the
number 3. Sensing the phenomenon of tonality, Odington also mentions the
"major" chord, possibly for the first time in the history of music theory. But
he gives it as 64:81(for 80):96:128, in Pythagorean form, which—considering that the Pythagorean ratios are a travesty of the small-number ratios
they are intended to represent—may be aptly termed "imperfect."[37]

In a catalogue of English learned men of the order of Saint Benedict
appears the following paragraph: "Walter, monk of Evesham, a man of fa-
cetious wit, who applying himself to literature . . . used at spare hours to
divert himself with the decent and commendable diversion of musick, to
render himself the more chearful for other duties; whether at length this
drew him off from other studies I know not, but there appears no other work
of his than a piece intitled Of the Speculation of Musick."[38]

## Indian Voice Off-Stage

For another delightful quotation and a bit of relief from the men of ratios we cross to far-away India. A contemporary of Odington, the renowned

[33]Helmholtz, *Sensations of Tone*, 190, 196; Hughes, in the *Oxford History of Music*, Introductory
Volume, 129. Kinkeldey reveals that the term "imperfect consonances" as applied to "thirds"
is derived from a music treatise of about 1180. "The Harmonic Sense," in *Papers of the Music
Teachers' National Association*, 18:13.

[34]*Ibid.*, 14.

[35]Barbour, "Equal Temperament," 12.

[36]Van den Borren, "Mystery of Faux-Bourdon Solved," in *Musical Times*, 70:317; Schlesinger,
"Greek Foundations," in *Musical Standard*, 27:209.

[37]Kinkeldey, "The Harmonic Sense," in *Papers of the Music Teachers' National Association*,
18:14–15; Combarieu, *Music—Its Laws and Evolution*, 116.

[38]Hawkins, *History of the Science and Practice of Music*, 1:184.

theorist *Sarangdev of Kashmir* (thirteenth century), in his work on music, *Sangit Ratnakar*, gives the following directions for tuning the vina: "Verse 12: Take two vinas with 22 wires each and tune as follows: Let the first wire give the lowest possible tone, the next a little higher, and so on, so that between the tones given by any two adjacent wires a third tone is impossible."[39]

## Zalzal Survives, in Name Only

On the way back to Europe, stopping to inquire what transpired in the Arabic world after Zalzal and Alfarabi, we find two theorists, *Mahmoud* (*d.* 1315) and *Abdulqadir* (fourteenth century), who were obviously deeply troubled. In fact, they were appalled—in contemplating the six hundred years of practical use of Zalzal's fretting of the lute—by so many centuries of unrelieved Pythagoreanless Zalzalia (Zalzal had substituted smaller-number ratios for the Pythagorean ratios of the ancient tuning).

Thought Mahmoud and Abdulqadir, "My, my—this will never do!" as they added three consecutive 3/2's below the nine consecutive 3/2's below 1/1 which they already had in the ancient tuning of the lute.[40] Thus they could preserve at least a suggestion of Zalzal's tones at the same time that they gave them a Pythagorean motif, which Zalzal had partially abandoned, with a nice string of sixteen 3/2's. Just what they intended to do with them, having got them, history has not told, but as a fitting cap to their dark deed Mahmoud and Abdulqadir affixed the label "Zalzal" on some of their ratios; Zalzal's tones were thus reconciled with the theorists' Pythagorean predilections. Such is the evolution of the Arabic seventeen-tone scale (see the next chapter).

## Fatal Day in Halberstadt

Back in western Europe, in the cathedral of the Saxon city of Halberstadt, on February 23 of the year 1361, an organ-builder by the name of Nicholas Faber completed the construction of an organ with three man-

---

[39]Clements, *Indian Music*, 53. Ellis observes (*Journal of the Society of Arts*, 33:489, 490) that Indian treatises "ostentatiously eschew arithmetic," and adds that "some musicians, like the Indian, repudiate all measurement and all arithmetic from the first, and leave everything to the judgment of the ear." Up to a certain point, of course, arithmetic and an acute ear accomplish exactly the same results.

[40]Helmholtz, *Sensations of Tone*, 282. Ellis calls the procedure "fourths" upward (*Journal of the Society of Arts*, 33:495), which as a source of scale degrees is synonymous with "fifths" downward.

uals,[41] the third of which was selected by some inscrutable destiny to send its descendants over the face of the earth and to make them the procreators of virtually all musical thought. This instrument—commonly known as the Halberstadt Organ—had as its third manual a series of nine front keys

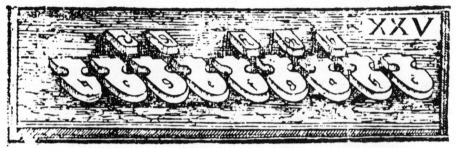

DIAGRAM 20.—THIRD MANUAL OF THE HALBERSTADT ORGAN
(Reproduced from Praetorius' *Syntagma Musicum*, 1619)

(the two highest were "octaves") and five raised rear keys in groups of twos and threes, as shown in Diagram 20. Here is the proto 7-White-5-Black!

The front keys were three inches wide and were probably played with the whole hand; the raised rear keys ("blacks") were two and a half inches above the lower keys ("whites"). Apparently they were not different in color.[42]

## *The Keyboard—Apple in Eden*

At the time of its creation the Halberstadt manual of destiny was no more than a crude physical thing. The tones which were to conceive its soul had not yet appeared, although the seeds of approximation—fated to be the agent of conception—, which had been blowing about on sterile soil ever since Aristoxenus, found a niche in the next century, the fifteenth, and began to germinate.

The Spaniard *Bartolomeus Ramis de Pareja*, who published his *Musica Practica* in 1482, is widely credited (or discredited) as the first temperer. "We have made all our divisions very easy," wrote Ramis of his division

---

[41]*Grove's Dictionary*, 7:741, 742.

[42]*Ibid*. The term "proto" applies to the physical arrangement of the seven in succession with the five in groups of three and two; it does not refer to color. The first instance of the use of black

of the monochord. These "easy" divisions were actually certain just ratios—5/4 and 10/9, for example—substituted for the accepted Pythagorean tuning, which was "tiresome for singers and irksome to the mind."[43] This hardly constitutes temperament, either in fact or in attitude, but the break with Pythagoreanism had been made, and by the close of the next century there is hardly a *musica practica* that does not present theories tooled by the "practical" hand of adulteration. Theorists were pretty generally aware of the felicity of just intervals on their monochords but nevertheless were impelled to remember the *musica practica*.

To the blind German organist *Arnold Schlick* and the astronomer *Henricus Grammateus* seem to be due whatever honors are reserved for the first articulation of temperament. Early in the sixteenth century both gave tuning rules or formulas, Schlick an analysis of a current tuning practice for organs which was a precursor of Meantone Temperament, and Grammateus a proposal for rendering the tones of the black keys into equal aural parts, by Euclid's "ninth of the sixth."[44]

Without the help of weighty academic theory musicians were thus demanding and getting solutions for the already pressing problem of keyboards, which Europe's musicians were determined to have. It was the European people's love of the simultaneous sounding of the intervals of 3 and 5 that created harmonic music and showed Just Intonation in its most beautiful application, and it was harmonic music, through its seemingly essential keyboards, that relegated these same intervals to the ash-heap as a conscious practice and a science.

In the sustained tones of the organ the human consciousness heard the simple consonances as it possibly had never heard them before, at the same time that it began to realize how tremendous was the problem of applying them to keyboards with anything like the freedom of intonation which inheres in the voice. Theorists and builders of organs undoubtedly wanted

and white to distinguish the seven from the five seems to have been the organ of the Barefooted Friars' Church at Nuremberg, built in 1475, in which present convention was reversed—the lower seven being black and the upper five white, a practice that prevailed for some three hundred years, to the end of the eighteenth century. *Ibid.*, 3:745.

[43]James Murray Barbour, "Equal Temperament: Its History from Ramis (1482) to Rameau (1737)" (ms. thesis), 28a. A word must be said in appreciation of this work, source of much of the material in this chapter. The detailed accounts of musical theories in the period defined by the title, and the many delightful quotations, are a significant service to scholarship. That Barbour's attitude is strongly in favor of temperament and opposed to Just Intonation is beside the point. It is highly gratifying that a work so deserving brought its author the degree of Ph.D.

[44]*Ibid.*, 32, 41, 42.

to apply the Just Intonation of the Ptolemaic Sequence (although they never called it that, and possibly by no name at all), but they were prevented from doing so by the limitations of (1) comprehension; (2) the mechanics of instrument construction; (3) the hand; and (4) the familiar notation (which had been in the course of evolution ever since the days of the Greek-letter symbols).

### Salinas—and the Enharmonic (on Paper)

Probably the first theorist of this early period to examine the problem of keyboards with any profundity was the blind organist, writer, and professor, *Francisco de Salinas* (1513–1590), a Spaniard who spent most of his life in Italy. It is interesting to note that from this time until the close of the nineteenth century nearly every important theorist considered temperament in keyboards inevitable (with the potentiality of parallel modulations as a sop to the ear), whatever his general acoustical attitude. And it is also interesting to observe how captivated the Renaissance theorists were with the enharmonic genus of the ancient Greeks, with its "microtonal" scale degrees—not quite comprehensible, not quite attainable in the everyday musical world, and—thoroughly fascinating.

In his voluminous *De Musica* Salinas considered the Greek theoretical works in the utmost detail, diagrammed the three genera (considered the enharmonic the most perfect[45]), described several temperaments, some in use in organs of his time, and invented at least one temperament of nineteen tones.[46] Regarding Meantone Temperament, which Salinas is widely credited with devising,[47] a contemporary wrote: "For in order that the four consonances ['thirds' and 'sixths'] may be made sweeter, it was necessary that one, namely the fifth, should be altered."[48] The current temperaments varied, then (for the most part), according to how much the "fifths" were altered to make the "thirds" sweeter. To obtain a "sweet" 5/4 two "mean tones" were employed, the mean being computed between 10/9 and 9/8, since $10/9 \times 9/8 = 5/4$.[49]

[45]Hawkins, *History of the Science and Practice of Music*, 1:414.

[46]Barbour, "Equal Temperament," 97, 98.

[47]The germ of this tuning idea was enunciated by Schlick some decades previously, as we have seen, and Barbour tells us that the system was adequately represented for practical musicians by Pietro Aron in 1523. *Ibid.*, 47–48.

[48]*Ibid.*, 112.

[49]This was the practice in the so-called "quarter comma" tuning; that is, most of the "fifths" were a "quarter comma" (5.4 cents) flat. This temperament became general for organ tuning

Since, unlike Equal Temperament, Meantone intonation was not a "closed" system, but one in which the "3/2's" were 5.4 cents flat at best and the "6/5's" were 5.3 cents flat at best, its triads fell naturally into two groups: "good" and "bad" (see Chapter 17). And although the sixteen "good" triads (eight "major" and eight "minor") were on the whole acoustically superior to the triads of Equal Temperament, the eight "bad" triads irked keyboard musicians. And, as is well known, they eventually threw Meantone's virtues out the window for triads without contrast—all equally "bad" and equally "good."

## *Vicentino Gets Beyond Paper*

Despite (or because of) Salinas' erudition, and his preoccupation with the Greek genera, compromise was his only tack. Unlike many theorists, he had abundant excuse for leaving his enlightening analyses on paper, for he was blind, but he chose to condemn those who did not. The "Archicembalo" of *Don Nicola Vicentino* (*c.* 1550), a harpsichord type of instrument with thirty-one tones to the 2/1 in six banks of keys, built with the avowed purpose of reviving the ancient Greek genera, had few or no friends among the erudite.[50] Although Vicentino's instrument was said to have been played with "wonderful skill" by the organist of a duke, and although two organs after this model were later built, one at Rome under orders from the Cardinal of Ferrara,[51] Vicentino found the learned musicians of his time massed in a phalanx against him. Wrote one of them, "I have often wondered at the confidence of Vicentino, who although he could not but be sensible that he had but slender, or rather no learning and knowledge

throughout Europe and persisted in England as late as 1850. Ellis in Helmholtz, *Sensations of Tone,* 549.

[50]Hawkins, *History of the Science and Practice of Music,* 1:395, 415–416. According to Barbour, Vicentino's theory and the tuning of his instrument were somewhat at odds. According to his theory he used ratios with numbers through 22, excluding 17 and 19, and including, of course, such ratios as 11/9, 9/7, 8/7, 14/13, and 13/12. But the tuning was specified as that of "common practice," which would indicate a meantone intonation with "fifths" flatted by varying amounts. The Archicembalo's digitals were in six "orders." The first order had seven white keys, the second order five black keys, and the third seven "sharped" or "flatted" keys. To this point it was no different from the nineteen-tone instruments described by Salinas and Zarlino (see below). However, the fourth and fifth orders were called "enharmonic," and had seven and five keys respectively. The sixth order, of seven keys, was a duplication of the first. Barbour, "Equal Temperament," 63, 65, 67.

[51]Hawkins, *History of the Science and Practice of Music,* 1:446. Kinkeldey says the instrument was relegated "to the Duke of Ferrara's museum of curious musical instruments." *Papers of the Music Teachers' National Association,* 18:24.

of antiquity, nevertheless did not hesitate to undertake so great a work. But I cease to wonder when I reflect on that Greek sentence: 'Ignorance makes men bold, but learning timid and slow.' " Two hundred years later Hawkins remarks that "it seems hardly yet determined whether his [Vicentino's] ingenuity or his absurdity be the greater."[52] All of which inevitably recalls the sharp humor of Rousseau: "Whatever he does, he is bound to be wrong for two reasons, the one because he is an inventor; the other, because he has to do with musicians."[53]

## *Zarlino—the Forthright Monophonist*

Another of Vicentino's disparagers[54] was *Gioseffe Zarlino* (1517–1590), the Venetian monk and canon of Chioggia, Saint Mark's, astronomer and mathematician. Despite his criticism of Vicentino, Zarlino ranks as the first forthright Monophonist and the first, moreover, to maintain that the Harmonical and Arithmetical Proportions are inherent in the same musical schema.[55]

In view of the new feeling of tonality in music some statement of the Monophonic idea was inevitable; its first formula was Zarlino's "senario," the consecutive numbers 1–2–3–4–5–6. These, in successive-number ratios (2/1–3/2–4/3–5/4–6/5) were the simplest consonances, said Zarlino; "composites" within 6, as, for example, $5/3(4/3 \times 5/4 = 5/3)$, were next simplest; and "composites" involving an even number higher than 6—for example, $8/5 (4/3 \times 6/5 = 8/5)$—were next simplest. He held that the Harmonical Proportion—expressed as a string and fractional parts thereof (1–1/2–1/3–1/4–1/5–1/6)—is the source of "major," and that the Arithmetical Proportion—expressed as equal parts of a string (1–2–3–4–5–6)— is the source of "minor" tonality; the "minor" scale, he stated, naturally descends (the harmony of the "minor" triad is 6–5–4), whereas the "major" naturally ascends. He called prime numbers higher than 6 irrational, comparing the integers 1 to 6 to the six sides of a cube; as there is no seventh side to the cube there is none in music.[56]

[52]Hawkins, *op. cit.*, 1:219, 396.

[53]Perrett, *Questions of Musical Theory*, v. Rousseau was speaking of a composer who had claimed discovery of a new mode.

[54]Hawkins, *op. cit.*, 1:415n.

[55]Shirlaw, *Theory of Harmony*, 35, 38.

[56]*Ibid.*, 35, 39–41, 46; Meyer, *Musician's Arithmetic*, 81.

Although Zarlino considered the Ptolemaic Sequence the "natural" scale, although he decried Aristoxenean irrationality,[57] and although his extensive theoretical works[58] give diagrams of two keyboards, one of seventeen and the other of nineteen tones to the 2/1,[59] obviously looking toward greater resources, he himself subscribed to approximation for keyboards and lutes, and joined the company which is forever ready to greet each new nonplussed theorist. Zarlino's attitude toward temperament was nevertheless essentially negative. In correcting Galilei's oversimplified formula for a fretting of the lute in twelve equal tones (see below) Zarlino protected his flank from Galilei's attack and showed himself a skilled mathematician at the same time. He gave, by means of a diagram, a "temperamentally" correct solution to the lute's fretting.[60]

## The Frets of Galilei

Zarlino's championing of the Ptolemaic Sequence reveals clearly both a fact and a delusion regarding music theory of the Middle Ages. The fact is that theoretical intervals were based, not on the Ptolemaic Sequence, but on the Pythagorean Sequence;[61] the delusion is that singers of the Middle Ages ever used such a sequence except when forced to do so by instruments so tuned.

The extensive attachment to Pythagorean theory reveals itself in many ways, among others in the attack on Zarlino by a former pupil, *Vincenzo Galilei* (died *c.* 1600), on the grounds that another theorist, Lodovico Fogliano (*c.* 1530), not Zarlino, was the first to "introduce" Ptolemy's "Intense"

[57]Hawkins, *History of the Science and Practice of Music*, 1:399.

[58]*Tutte l'opera del R. M. Gioseffe Zarlino da Chioggia*, complete edition, published at Venice in 1589.

[59]The illustration of a nineteen-tone instrument in *Le Istitutione Harmoniche* (Venice, 1562), pp. 140–141, shows a two–2/1 range, the "blacks" being doubled and one of each pair actually white, and in addition a single raised white key between "B—C" and "E—F." Zarlino designed the instrument to show that "anyone can make in the future an instrument similar to the one which I have demonstrated . . . because I have one such instrument made in Venice in . . . 1548 in order to see in what way the chromatic and enharmonic harmonies would result. It was a clavichord . . . in which not only the major semitones but also all the minor ones are divided into two parts." *Ibid.*

[60]Barbour, "Equal Temperament," 89–90; Shirlaw, *Theory of Harmony*, 33; Miller, *Anecdotal History of Sound*, 33, 34.

[61]Schlesinger attributes the theoretically "high imprimatur" of this scale in the Middle Age mind to a "mistaken origin in *The Creation of the Soul*, by the Pythagorean philosopher Timaeus." *Is European Musical Theory Indebted to the Arabs?* 4.

into Italy.[62] All seemed to overlook the reiteration of the basic intervals of the Ptolemaic Sequence in the form

$$\begin{array}{ccccc} 1/1 & & 10/9 & & 5/4 & & 4/3 \\ & 10/9 & & 9/8 & & 16/15 \end{array}$$

centuries before by Hucbald (840–930).[63] That it required fourteen centuries for the Western musical world to discover Ptolemy for its practical musical purposes, when his scales had never ceased to be part of our direct heritage,[64] is comment enough on the dark ages.

But the Ptolemaic Sequence, even when rediscovered, seemed to fit the construction and playing of the lute no more felicitously than it did the keyboard. Galilei, a practical lutenist and the father of Florentine monody (see Chapter 1), believed that he had solved the puzzle of a constant numerical ratio for his frets. "I divide then the whole line AB into 18 parts," he wrote in 1581, "and . . . at the end of the first part, I place the first fret. I divide anew the remainder of the string into the same number of parts and at the same band below the first I place the second fret: and in the same way the entire line remaining below the frets is to be divided, even to the 12th fret. This brings me to the midpoint of the whole string; the first and lower octave thereof I find I have divided into twelve equal semitones and six tones, as said by Aristoxenus."[65]

Galilei's statement about his "midpoint" is of course wrong—the twelfth fret would be slightly more than 12 cents below the midpoint, the 2/1—but considering the degradation of the consonances in the successive intervals 18/17–18/17–18/17, etc., there seems to be something of a quibble in the concern of Galilei's critics over his degradation of the "octave," the "2/1," his "midpoint." At any rate, here is the best successive-number ratio that can represent the "semitone," or 1/12 of a 2/1; its exposition by Galilei is a milestone in the evolution of fretted instruments.

## China Wins the 12th Root of 2 by a Nose

Meanwhile China, which had hardly anything to compare with Europe's surge of harmonic music, nevertheless could still pace Europe on

---

[62]Shirlaw, *Theory of Harmony*, 208.
[63]Schlesinger, "Greek Foundations of the Theory of Music," in *Musical Standard*, 27:177.
[64]Schlesinger shows the extent of consciousness of the Greek heritage. *Ibid.*, 27:109.
[65]Barbour, "Equal Temperament," 106–108; this and other passages from this dissertation are quoted by permission of the author.

the score of theory. In 1596 *Prince Chu Tsai-yü* published a work in which he gave string lengths for twelve-tone Equal Temperament "with absolute correctness to nine places." Of the prince's accomplishment a contemporary modern theorist reminds us that "the computation would have to begin, for certain tones, with numbers containing 108 zeros, of which the 12th root would have to be extracted, as Mersenne did, by taking the square root twice and then the cube root. This lengthy and laborious procedure was followed without error."[66]

Prince Chu was puzzled by the discrepancy between the traditional just tuning of the kin, the "scholar's lute" (see Chapter 10), and the millenniums-old series of twelve lü, of Pythagorean genesis. "I reflected day and night upon that difficulty," he said, "and one morning I suddenly saw the light." Deciding that the lü were intended by the ancient theorists to give only approximate sounds, the prince determined to make them less approximate. The "light"—filtering through no less than 108 zeros—was in effect the formula $\sqrt[12]{2}$, and the ratio 1:1.0594631 for the equal semitone.[67]

Any practical Western musician might wonder what good a formula is if it offers no practical help in tuning a piano, but in China such a question would have been academic, since Chinese scholars solved theoretical problems by the score at the same time that the Chinese people went right on playing what they had always played before, and what their emperors by edict permitted them to play,[68] which was not a piano.

## Mersenne's Break-through to 7

The Prince Chu of Europe was the French monk, mathematician, and physicist *Marin Mersenne* (1588–1648), who was both less and more. He discovered the overtone series in the natural sounds of the trumpet, observed that these produced the "major" chord but that the series did not stop there, and saw no reason why tonality and consonance should end at

[66]*Ibid.*, 135, 143. The title of Prince Chu's work was *Lü Lü Ching I* (translated: "a clear explanation of that which concerns the lü").

[67]*Ibid.*, 140–142; Yasser, *Theory of Evolving Tonality*, 32. The prince intended his ratios of Equal Temperament for a set of lü, in the ancient manner. He also determined the size of the fundamental lü in an ancient manner, as one that would hold 1200 grains of millet. Barbour points out that this gives the Chinese another priority in musical science, since each succeeding pipe—in theory—would hold 100 fewer grains, thus anticipating Ellis' measure of cents. A European constructed a set of pipes after Chu Tsai-yü's directions (which included computations for pipe "correction") and found them "exactly in tune." Barbour, *op. cit.*, 143–145.

[68]Meyer, *Musician's Arithmetic*, 113–114.

Zarlino's arbitrary 6. Thus, to Mersenne, the overtone series explained at least one part of the dual phenomenon of tonality. Seeing the series go beyond the "major" triad, he proposed the inclusion of 7 as an integral musical resource, calling 7/6 consonant[69]—the first such pronouncement regarding a ratio of 7—and designed many keyboards[70] with greater resources than the already common 7-White–5-Black.

The contributions Mersenne made to the subject of temperament were less penetrating and less original, although he is widely known as the first Westerner to give the correct mathematical solution for Equal Temperament. It appears that he was undertaking little more than a compendium of information on this subject; he meticulously credits his tables of proportional numbers for equal divisions to his contemporaries, the geometer de Beaugrand and one Gallé, neither of whom quite reached the "light" of Prince Chu Tsai-yü and his 108 zeros.[71] But what is more to the point in a world in which music is something more than an occult contemplation, in speaking of this division he tells of "certain people" who tune their instruments by the "number of tremblings"—beats—made by the "consonances."[72]

We are now confronted with the complete change in terminology, from ancient to modern: the Harmonical Proportion is now the overtone series (Mersenne); the Arithmetical Proportion is now a limited "minor" tonality (Zarlino); Aristoxenean approximations are now any of various temperaments (Ho Tcheng-tien, Schlick, Salinas, Galilei, and Mersenne), and Pythagoreanism is now more often one of the "cycles of perfect fifths" (King Fang and Mercator—see below).

## Doni—Europe Matches King Fang

The proponents of the Just Intonation of the ancient Greek philosophers were surely losing ground in the face of expedience and of Zarlino's and Mersenne's partial capitulation, but there were still voices to protest against temperament's "incantable" tones. The Florentine student of Greek culture *Giovanni Battista Doni* (1593–1642), who coincided with the monodic resurgence, was one of these, and one who was not content to

---

[69]Shirlaw, *Theory of Harmony*, 32.

[70]In *Harmonie Universelle*, published at Paris in 1636.

[71]Barbour writes that Mersenne shows clearly, as Beaugrand did not, that each tone is to be the 12th root of some power of 2. "Equal Temperament," 171, 172, 174.

[72]*Ibid.*, 184.

voice his dissatisfaction only verbally.[73] He built a "Lyra Barberina," a double lyre in imitation of ancient models and with a multiplicity of strings, and a three-manual keyboard instrument with twenty tones on each manual (but only thirty-eight different pitches). The first manual gave the Dorian mode, the second the Phrygian, and the third the Lydian, each apparently capable of all three genera. Doni commends the enharmonic of Archytas (compare the recommendation on page 170), but used the Arithmetical Proportion of Didymus for "convenience."[74]

It is thus evident that so long as no solution for the keyboard problem had crystallized, there was much serious consideration of multiple-toned manuals. Appearing frequently in these verbal-mathematical investigations was the idea of "cycles," implying those scales generated from a succession of 3/2's where an $n$th 3/2 nearly coincides with an $n$th 2/1, and the favorite "cycle" was the fifty-three, offered to China by King Fang far back in the third century B.C. Its advocacy in the West is generally attributed to *Nicholas Mercator* (1640?–1694), who, according to an eighteenth-century writer, "deduced an ingenious Invention of finding and applying a least Common Measure to all Harmonic Intervals."[75] This would indicate that an actual scale of fifty-three tones was the farthest thing from Mercator's mind; at any rate, in 1640 a keyboard in this temperament, or something very close to it, had already been constructed, by Nicolaus Ramarinus,[76] and at least three others designed for the same tuning have been built in the past hundred years (see Chapter 18).

The computation of fifty-three 3/2's above 1/1, which would give a tone 3.615 cents higher than the thirty-first 2/1 above 1/1, and the subsequent subtraction of one-fifty-third of 3.615 cents from each of the fifty-three 3/2's in order to temper the "cycle," was apparently too much for

[73]*Ibid.*, 93. Barbour seems to believe that thinking in equal divisions of sound is "modern," and, as an implied corollary, that any thinking that is not modern is underdeveloped. Regarding Doni's keyboard, he writes: "The result, like those of General Perronet Thompson and others in the nineteenth century, was foredoomed to failure, for it is never possible to get enough keys in just intonation to provide for all the demands made by composers." *Ibid.*, 134, 196. What demands? Also, what composers? Does any single system of music encompass all possible demands? Unfortunately few composers give any thought whatever to the intonation they have or would like to have, but the assumption that those who do concern themselves with intonation are unanimously agreed is disproved by the present work.

[74]*Ibid.*, 190–196.

[75]*Ibid.*, 247. Barbour says that both Mersenne and Kircher (1602–1680) referred to the fifty-three "cycle" before Mercator did so, and that before Mersenne it was "in the mind of almost every writer who said that the tone is divided into 9 commas." *Ibid.*, 248.

[76]Hawkins, *History of the Science and Practice of Music*, 1:396.

seventeenth-century musicians; the result would have given them 5/4's and 6/5's with only 1.4 cents falsity and 3/2's with less than .07 cent falsity (see the next chapter).

## *Halberstadt Gains Its Soul (via Hamburg)*

Forty years after the death of Mersenne, in 1688, the first organ was tuned in accordance with his formula for Equal Temperament by *Art Schnitger* at Hamburg,[77] thus setting the clavier stool for three-year-old Johann S. (for *Sempervirens!*) Bach, the Western stage for nearly three hundred years of music's "golden age," the classroom for the complete divorcement of the science of music from music theory, the concert hall for the benevolent fraud of equally-tempered modulation, the radios of *x* million American homes for a twenty-five-year siege by the industrialized harmony-armies of mediocrity, and else we know not what.

It is perhaps inevitable that anything of real cultural significance to the Western world must somehow be dragged through the house of Hebraic theology. *Andreas Werckmeister* (1645–1706), who is popularly regarded as the first champion of Equal Temperament, mentions his acquaintance with the idea as follows: "A certain theologian has quoted this [equal tuning by beats] in a strange treatise, revealing some secrets of the Holy Scriptures, in which he not only derived all musical consonances from Solomon's temple, but also in particular has quoted a mathematical description of the molten sea that stood upon twelve oxen."[78] Passing over any "divine" connections of the consonances, the rest of the theologian's picture is a pretty good prototype for our modern "molten sea" of atonality that has poured over to submerge our "twelve [all-too-equal] oxen."

No one, when he enters the precisely restricted profession of "serious" music, is handed a list of the assets and liabilities of the scale he is obliged to use. Perhaps he does not expect a mundane appraisal, a warning and a reminder—music is so "mysterious." But the really serious student might wish for some sort of epigrammatic substitute. I suggest the words of *Johann*

[77]Jeans, *Science and Music*, 175; Ellis in Helmholtz, *Sensations of Tone*, 548. Barbour believes that Equal Temperament was used in keyboard instruments to some extent early in the seventeenth century (*op. cit.*, 317), and since practice generally preceded the mathematical rationalizations of it, he is probably right. As the first well-known application of the idea the occasion at Hamburg is nevertheless symbolical, and may serve as such until further research proves that an equally dark day preceded it.

[78]Barbour, *op. cit.*, 234.

*Niedhardt* (1685–1739), chapel-master to the Prussian court at Königsberg: "Equal Temperament carries with itself its comfort and its discomfort, like the Holy estate of matrimony."[79]

## Descartes the Retrencher

In following the story of Equal Temperament to its first important consummation we have left twenty-two-year-old *René Descartes* (1596–1650) far behind. Descartes, who wrote his one work on music theory, *Compendium Musicae*, while soldiering in a garrison, takes us back once more to the musical philosophy of Zarlino and Mersenne and something more meaty than music's "Holy estate of matrimony." Descartes agreed with Zarlino on the whole, abjuring 7, and finding 5/4 and 3/2 the only "original" intervals (the only intervals within the 5 limit which create tonality above 1/1). René was also a Monophonist in a limited way; he liked the idea of unity, but he was apparently overawed by the newly perceived overtone series. Said he, in regard to Zarlino's reverse "senario": "Sound is to sound as string to string; but each string contains in itself all others which are less than it, and not those which are greater: consequently, every sound contains in itself those sounds which are higher but not those which are lower."[80]

## Rameau the Inconstant

This dictum seemed to carry weight with *Jean Philippe Rameau* (1683–1784), who could agree with everyone now about "major" tonality— Zarlino, Mersenne, Descartes—since everyone agreed. "Minor" tonality, however, was still a puzzle; later it became a war. Persisting in contention over the "minor" bone and ignoring the fact that Descartes had already tried to bury it, Rameau decries Zarlino's reversion of "the beautiful order of harmony which presents itself at once in the division of the string. . . . In the descending progression 6–5–4–3–2–1 the number 6 cannot represent unity, nor serve as the source of the foundation of the harmony."[81] Strangely, Rameau does not wonder why 1 cannot represent unity, nor does he consider the building of harmony upward as simply a custom.

[79]*Ibid.*, 265. Inscribed over the entrance to the "harmony" classroom, and with the always-sobering phrase *"until death do us part"* appended, this quotation might well result in a consequential repulsion of males from the classroom and quite possibly a renascence of music in the West.

[80]Matthew Shirlaw, *The Theory of Harmony*, 59–62; this and other passages from *The Theory of Harmony* are quoted by permission of Novello and Company, Ltd.

[81]*Ibid.*, 80.

As a positive retort he offered at different times two explanations for "minor": first, 1/1 generates 5/4, but 5/4 is generated also by 5/3 (the relationship 3/2); therefore the triad 5/3–1/1–5/4 (ascending) is the unity of 1/1.[82] In this analysis he anticipates Helmholtz (see below) and hands Hindemith a key on a platter to every door in the equally tempered house (see page 420). Rameau's second explanation: the "minor" triad is 10:12:15 in the overtone series.[83]

Rameau also was a Monophonist at heart, but he too was intimidated by the new plaything of theorists, the overtone series, and it taxed his ingenuity to the utmost to explain Monophony in terms of the new plaything. His "tonic-dominant-subdominant" all sprang from unity in this manner: 1/1–5/4–3/2 is the "subdominant" of 3/2–15/8–9/8, and 9/8–45/32–27/16 is the "dominant" of 3/2–15/8–9/8, making 1 the Numerary Nexus (Monophonic terminology) throughout. This is of course perfectly true as regards musical practice, but his 3/2, not 1/1, is unity, which can hardly be reconciled with simple arithmetic, and Rameau could have obtained exactly the same result had he ignored his new plaything to the extent of constructing triads downward as well as upward and accepting the inherent "minor." He also forgot his role as revelator of the natural basis of harmony when he said that 7, 11, and 13 are "false" or "out of tune."[84] Nevertheless, Rameau's ratios show a degree of perception and a very apparent groping for the truth—the stressing of the "subdominant" or "other dominant" genesis, for example. This same groping, perceiving yet not wholly perceiving, also permeates the theories of *Giuseppe Tartini* (1692–1770), violinist and composer.

## Tartini and Serre—with the Ghost Enharmonic

Like Descartes, Tartini turned to music to forget other things. With Tartini it was not the boredom of garrison duty, but a flight for his life after marrying the niece of a cardinal against that dignitary's wishes. He obtained refuge at the monastery of Assisi, where he begot "Tartini tones," or difference tones[85] (which in turn have begot a whole race of "difference tone" theorists), and eventually two works on theory. The crux of these was an altogether original explanation of "minor," deduced from his newly

[82]*Ibid.*, 233–236.          [84]*Ibid.*, 138, 163.
[83]*Ibid.*, 83.              [85]*Grove's Dictionary*, 5:268.

perceived difference tones, and a fundamental truth regarding consonance and the expansion of musical resources.

The successive-number *intervals* 2/1–3/2–4/3–5/4–6/5, sounded in the order given, said Tartini, generate difference tones as follows:

| Highest 2/1 . . . . . . . . . . . . . . .2/1 | 3/2 | 4/3 | 5/4 | 6/5 |
|---|---|---|---|---|
| Fourth 2/1 . . . . . . . . . . . . . . . .1/1 | | | | |
| Third 2/1 . . . . . . . . . . . . . . . . . . . . . .1/1 | | | | |
| Second 2/1 . . . . . . . . . . . . . . . . . . . . . . . . . . . . .4/3 | | 1/1 | | |
| Lowest 2/1 . . . . . . . . . . . . . . . . . . . . . . . . . . . . . . . . . . . . . . . . . . . . .8/5 | | | | |

thus achieving the "minor" triad (descending and "inverted"—4/3–1/1–8/5).[86] Although this has only a superficial resemblance to Zarlino's genesis of "minor"—the reverse "senario"—it is nevertheless a conception downward in nature, and actually creates an "undertone series."

The two-thousand-year-old ghost of the enharmonic walks again in Tartini, for the passage from diatonic to enharmonic is accomplished, he declares, in going beyond the first six terms of the overtone series, that is, to the seventh.[87] *Jean Adam Serre*, whose *Essais sur les Principes de l'Harmonie* appeared in 1753, a year or so before Tartini's *Trattato di Musica*, supplies an example: if "C" is to "E" as 4 to 5, and "C" to "G" as 2 to 3, and "G" to "E♯" as 4 to 7, then "E" is to "E♯" as 5/4 is to 3/2 × 7/4 (21/16), or 21/20.[88] The passage from the 5 Odentity of "C" to the 7 Odentity of "G" is thus an entry into the enharmonic, via the ratio 21/20, according to Serre.

The advocacy of Equal Temperament by his better-known contemporary, Rameau, and Rameau's prejudice regarding 7, Serre ties into a single invidious reference: "It is not surprising that the theory which, so to speak, drowns the commas and the quartertones in the modern temperament, and moreover banishes from harmony, without any modification, without any reservation, the sound . . . expressed by the ratio 4:7, as a false and non-harmonic sound—it is not surprising, I say, that this theory gives us no enlightenment as to the origin and the possibility of the enharmonic of the Ancients."[89]

[86]Shirlaw, *Theory of Harmony*, 295. The triad would be expressed acoustically—4/3–1/1–4/5.
[87]Wilfrid Perrett, *Some Questions of Musical Theory*, 62.   [88]*Ibid.*, 60.
[89]*Ibid.*, 61; this and the subsequent passage from *Some Questions of Musical Theory* are quoted by permission of W. Heffer and Sons, Ltd.

And Tartini, in further consideration of the number 7, achieves a kind of final perception, declaring that "this harmonic 7th is not dissonant but consonant. . . . it has no need either of preparation or of resolution: it may equally well ascend or descend, provided that its intonation be true."[90]

"Provided that its intonation be true" is a phrase that is implicit in every page of this volume, and the whole of Tartini's assertion applies equally well to every one of the identities of Monophony, including 9 and 11 (with the reservations made in Chapter 11), and should bring pause to those who are so willing to tamper with any acoustic interval more complex than a 2/1.

## Euler—Further Support for 7

Affirmation of the number 7 by Serre and Tartini was not left to wither. Their insight was emphasized by an impressive line of musical thinkers, beginning with the contemporary *Leonard Euler* (1707–1783), the Swiss mathematician and physicist whose theories on consonance and dissonance were cited earlier (Chapter 9). The Belgian music historian F. J. Fétis speaks of Euler as a "great man" to whom music theory owes "a truth as irrefragable as it is new. He has been the first to see that the character of modern music resides in the chord of the Dominant Seventh, and that its determining ratio is that of the number 7."[91] This is part of the historic background for the debate over the immanence of 7 in modern harmony, however badly portrayed by Equal Temperament, to which the present volume makes repeated reference.

## Recapitulation of Pre-Modern Developments

It may be well, before pursuing the more recent contributions to musical science, to recapitulate briefly and to point out other backgrounds—the salient historic taproots of Monophony. Pythagoras, or Ling Lun, is significant as the first recorded diviner of musical relationships, Ptolemy as the one who reduced relationships to the simplest terms compatible with their esthetic purpose, Zarlino as the forthright exponent of expansion from unity, above and below; Mersenne and Tartini as the perceivers of the true nature of "major" tonality and of the value of resources beyond the custom-made limit of their times.

The chief burdens of theoretical controversy from here on are the source

[90]*Ibid.*, 62.     [91]Shirlaw, *Theory of Harmony*, 348.

of "minor" tonality, new suggestions for the employment of purer intervals on keyboards, various new analyses of temperaments, and the in- or exclusion of 7.

## Helmholtz, Öttingen, Herzogenberg—the "Minor" Triad

As a gate to further musical resources 7 was more or less ignored by *Hermann Helmholtz* (1821–1894), surgeon, physiologist, and physicist,[92] although he declared that it is used—"probably often"—by singers in the "dominant seventh" chord.[93] It perhaps has been the tendency in recent years to overstate Helmholtz's contribution to music theory, or at least to emphasize the wrong "contributions." His analysis of beats is of course important, since it throws light on the determination of relative consonance (see Chapter 9), but his impatience with temperament was, in my opinion, more important—a salutary and long-overdue influence. "I do not know that it was so necessary to sacrifice correctness of intonation to the convenience of musical instruments," he wrote, and called the mixture stops on the equally tempered organ a "hellish row" and the difference tones of Equal Temperament a "horrible bass."[94]

In other respects Helmholtz was inclined toward musical conservatism.[95] Downward building of chords he rejected. In place of it he enlarged on Rameau's first explanation of "minor": in the chord 1/1–6/5–3/2, he said, 3/2 is in the overtone series of both 1/1 and 6/5, but neither 1/1 nor 6/5 occurs in the other's series, ergo, 1/1–6/5–3/2 may be regarded as a "compound tone" of 1/1 with an added 6/5 or as a "compound tone" of 6/5 with an added 1/1.[96] Such an explanation was far too equivocal for *Arthur J. von Öttingen* (1836–1920), who declared that a triad so analyzed was left without any origin at all.[97]

Öttingen showed that the clash of upper partials was as great in the "major" as in the "minor" triad (sometimes actually less in the "minor," given similar harmonic contents), and he held that unity for the "minor" triad was found in the first partial common to all three tones.[98] This is of course the second 2/1 above the highest tone in the triad: 3/2 in the triad 1/1–6/5–3/2 (ascending), or 1/1 in the triad 4/3–8/5–2/1 (ascending). However, Öttingen failed to consider difference tones of the "minor," which, if they are loud enough to deserve consideration, introduce equivo-

[92]*Sensations of Tone*, 195 and *passim*.     [93]*Ibid.*, 347.     [94]*Ibid.*, 314, 323, 327.
[95]See, for example, Meyer, *Musician's Arithmetic*, 83, for another theorist's appraisal.
[96]*Sensations of Tone*, 294.     [97]Shirlaw, *Theory of Harmony*, 385.     [98]*Ibid.*, 386.

cations or "muddiness" not produced by difference tones in the "major" triad. Öttingen's explanation is certainly more fundamental than that of Helmholtz, but it still parried the essential question, namely, where is 1, or unity, *in* the "minor" triad—not unity two 2/1's above it?

The composer *Heinrich von Herzogenberg* (1843–1900) also disagreed with Helmholtz, trying to make "minor" rational through 1/1–7/6–3/2,[99] which is certainly not an unpleasant triad on the Chromelodeon; it is, in fact, one of the qualities in the variety of tonality outlined previously (Chapter 10), though it certainly is not as consonant as 1/1–6/5–3/2.

## Riemann the "Reverser"—with Limitations

For a truly Zarlinean conception of "minor" in the nineteenth century we come to *Hugo Riemann* (1849–1919), prolific producer of "harmonies," dictionaries, and histories, who accepted the concept of reverse order without equivocation, though his explanations sometimes become involved. Riemann was deeply affected by the Arabic Arithmetical Proportion, calling it the "Measure-theory of the Arabic-Persian Theorists which demonstrates the theory of intervals from a string divided into twelve equal parts."[1] He saw no need for justifying the descending manifestation of the Arithmetical Proportion beyond this division and declared that the "minor correlatives have a subjective existence," that even though the "major proportions measured downwards" were not phenomenal (referring to "major's" overtone series), they were nevertheless a "fact of experience" and formed "as good a foundation on which to build as acoustical phenomena."[2] (Monophony's explanation of unity in Utonality has been given in the Tonality Diamond and the inherence of ratios; see Chapter 10).

The "fifth of the chord" is unity, said Riemann, and what is ordinarily considered its "root" is its "dominant"[3]—which certainly goes the whole hog in reverse thinking. Riemann's surprising musi-schizophrenia suddenly comes to the fore, however, in his rejection of the number 7 as a legitimate musical resource,[4] an attitude that for practical purposes is irreconcilable with acceptance of the principle of Arithmetical Proportion, which involves the 7 Identity if it implies a division into only seven equal parts (see page 175).

[99]Meyer, *Musician's Arithmetic*, 87.

[1]*Nature of Harmony*, 6. Riemann dates the procedure from the end of the thirteenth century, but of course it goes back to Eratosthenes in the third century B.C., if not earlier.

[2]Shirlaw, *Theory of Harmony*, 172, 389, 390.     [3]*Ibid.*, 390–391.

[4]*Nature of Harmony*, 17; Shirlaw, *Theory of Harmony*, 391.

## *To Realize the "Visions of Guido and Mersenne"*

The next contributors to the science of intonation require a brief introduction, in which it is necessary to backtrack a bit. The ebbing spirit of the Renaissance in the hundred years between Tartini and Helmholtz was paralleled by the ebbing and cessation of attempts to establish new intonations and new keyboards or to stem the widening and unthinking acceptance of Equal Temperament. For a time after Tartini there were no new intonational proposals. Even those more modern theorists thus far considered— Helmholtz, Öttingen, Riemann—were simply commentators, analyzing existing or implied materials, neither proposing nor experimenting with new intonations and new musical instruments.

Quite a different spirit began to manifest itself in a few individuals during the last half of the nineteenth century, a spirit which still lives and which has been growing stronger in recent years. Realizing the absolute interdependence of keyboards and Equal Temperament, a number of learned and ingenious men, working independently, set themselves the task of ameliorating the ills of temperament by forcing keyboards to the will and desire of the ear, that is, to the end of Just Intonation or something more nearly approaching Just Intonation.

It has been said that keyboards do not spring to life like Athena from the head of Zeus, but slowly evolve from those scale-vehicles that happen to exist at the moment. The present 7-White–5-Black keyboard evolved with the early development of harmonic music, reaching its present form with the highest manual of the Halberstadt organ in 1361 (see above). Since that time, nearly six hundred years, its "evolution" (it could hardly be called spectacular) has consisted in such refinements of whatever "happens to exist at the moment" as plastic whites to replace ivory whites.

To our nineteenth-century experimenters the pertinent question was (as it still is): can the 7-White–5-Black keyboard be adapted to the end of better intonation? *Perronet Thompson*, British general, editor, and member of Parliament, gives in his book[5] the following naively confident dedication to the blind organist who played his instrument (see photograph facing page 213): "To Miss E. S. Northcote . . . In commemoration of the talent by which, after six lessons, she was able to perform in public on the enharmonic organ with 40 sounds to the octave; thereby settling the question of the practicability of just intonation on keyed instruments, and realising the

---

[5]*On the Principles and Practice of Just Intonation*, 9th edition, 1866.

visions of Guido and Mersenne, and the harmonists of classical antiquity."[6] Alas, the "practicability" of Just Intonation on keyed instruments is far from settled nearly a century after the general's touching dedication!

In the nineteenth century Boston was the scene of two experiments with departures from twelve-tone temperament and the 7-White–5-Black pattern. About 1850 *Henry Ward Poole* (1826–1890) built a pipe organ in just intonation, and some years later constructed a cardboard model of a keyboard with 100 digitals to the 2/1, with true 1–3–5–7 Identities in nineteen tonalities (Utonalities built upward). And in the decade 1877–87 *James Paul White* built four harmoniums, three of which had keyboards designed for the fifty-three "cycle"[7] (see Chapter 17).

## Name Your "Octave" and Take It Away

The man who has answered as well as anyone our question whether the 7-White–5-Black keyboard is capable of expansion is *R. H. M. Bosanquet* (1841–1912), and the instrument he offered as his answer is his Enharmonic Harmonium (see photograph––opposite page). Bosanquet's organ is based on the fifty-three "cycle" expressed in fifty-three equally tempered degrees (see Chapter 17; also the diagram in Helmholtz's *Sensations of Tone*, 429).

That intonational curiosity was running high in the England of those days is evident from an advertisement at the end of Bosanquet's book:[8]

T. A. Jennings, builder of
Bosanquet Enharmonic Organ
Harmonium with one reed to
each key—compass 4½ octaves:
I. 24 keys per octave   36 £
II. 36 keys per octave   52 £
III. 48 keys per octave   70 £
IV. 60 keys per octave   90 £
V. 72 keys per octave  108 £
VI. 84 keys per octave  126 £

---

[6]Helmholtz, *Sensations of Tone*, 423n. Thompson's organ has a keyboard of the evolved type with three manuals of variously colored keys and with a range of five 2/1's. It was designed to play fifteen "major" and fifteen "minor" scales justly. Three such instruments were built, one of which I examined in the South Kensington Museum in London in 1935.

[7]Tipple and Frye, *Introduction to the Harmon*, frontispiece, 9–13. Poole pays tribute to the "acuteness of the common ear. From many experiments, I have been led to believe that among a thousand persons taken at random, not more than one could be found who, when he had the opportunity for comparison, would not perceive the difference between perfect and tempered octaves, fifths, thirds or sevenths."

[8]*Elementary Treatise on Musical Intervals and Temperament.*

*Top:* BOSANQUET'S ENHARMONIC HARMONIUM
*Center:* COLIN BROWN'S VOICE HARMONIUM
*Bottom:* GENERAL THOMPSON'S ENHARMONIC ORGAN
British Crown Copyright, Photographs by the Science Museum, London.

Aside from Bosanquet's Enharmonic Harmonium, I have seen no reference to any other experimental instrument built by Name-Your-Octave-Pay-Your-Pounds-and-Take-It-Away Jennings.

## Further Evidence of the English Resurgence

Colin Brown, lecturer on music in Andersonian University, Glasgow, produced an entirely different and non-Pythagorean solution. His Voice Harmonium (photograph facing page 392), with more than forty tones to the 2/1 and a range of five 2/1's, was devised to play fifteen "major" scales and triads and fifteen "minor" scales and triads in perfect intonation. Brown's system—designed less as a basis for a future music than as a pure-interval vehicle for existing musical literature—might be called a "polyphonic" system, since it had no exact "mono" point, or unity. The keyboard has few familiar aspects, except that the 2/1 distance is the same as on the piano.[9] Three instruments were built, one of which I examined in a home near London. I found it easy to play and its intervals and triads a delight to the ear. (For a more detailed discussion of Brown's harmonium see Chapter 18.)

Brown also felt impelled to show musical genesis in the overtone series, finding the "major" scale from the 24th to the 48th overtones: 24:27:30: 32:36:40:45:48, or the ratios 24/24–27/24–30/24–32/24–36/24–40/24–45/24–48/24,[10] which, reduced, are of course the ratios of the Ptolemaic Sequence: 1/1–9/8–5/4–4/3–3/2–5/3–15/8–2/1. The rub in this is that 24 is not the 1 Identity, but the 3 Identity of the overtone series which starts on 1. This puts Brown's scale on the same level with Rameau's genesis of triads (making the "dominant" unity—see above), and also on the level of Schönberg's triad explanation (see Chapter 17). There is a good deal of natural "scenery" before arriving at the 24th overtone—also, a good many natural "wonders" between 24 and 48, over which Brown blissfully slides. One of these—one of the "common things" to which the title of Brown's book alludes—is the Identity 7, of which he pleasantly remarks that though it is "very pleasant to the ear," it is "foreign to the scale."[11] The one scale of divine sanction, no doubt?

A third new instrument of this period was the Indian Harmonium, suggested or ordered by one K. B. Deval but planned and built by *H.*

[9]Diagram in Helmholtz, *Sensations of Tone*, 471.
[10]*Music in Common Things*, 15.
[11]*Ibid.*, 9, 14, 24n.

*Keatley Moore*, in London, as an example of what might be done to save India from complete 7-White–5-Black corruption. This had the usual white and black keys but in addition eleven brass pegs, or studs, on the black keys and at the backs of the white keys, giving the twenty-two just "srutis" to the 2/1 of the Indian intonational system, and one alternate key. The instrument gives at least five tonalities capable of all identities through 9 (Otonality).[12]

The result of this effort we already know (see Fox-Strangways' letter, Chapter 11), but it need not be too discouraging. Our own potentiality for exotic music is very satisfying, and with that knowledge we can gaze with equanimity on the pump organs in the community halls of India (and on the pianos in the Buddhist temples of California).

One of the most important British figures of this period was *Alexander J. Ellis* (1814–1890), philologist, mathematician, musician, inventor of the ratio-navigation instrument of cents, and translator and copious annotator of Helmholtz's *On the Sensations of Tone*. Ellis was also greatly preoccupied with historic and comparative intonations, made many experiments in intonation and with contemporary scales from remote parts, and proposed his "Unequally Just Intonation" as a basis for the attainment of purer intervals. This involved fifty-three tones to the 2/1, derived almost if not wholly by Pythagorean processes. Ellis was a strong advocate of 7 in harmony, calling the numbers 4:5:6:7 the "justification" of the "dominant seventh."[13]

## Introduction to Current Theories

With Ellis ends our discussion of those who were chiefly preoccupied with the music of their own time. The following chapters deal in some detail with the theories of seven living persons who, whatever their attitudes toward the theories of the immediate past, are intent on evolving a basis for a future music. This creative attitude is in itself a tremendous forward step.

Three of the seven theorists are satisfied to apply their intonational ideas to the instruments now in use. One expounds a just intonation idea but applies it to tempered instruments, another a nineteen-tone equal temperament, and the remaining two propose Just Intonations.

[12]Clements, *Introduction to Indian Music*, 8n, 9, 90 (diagram of keyboard), 93.
[13]Ellis in Helmholtz, *Sensations of Tone*, 346, 465.

*Arnold Schönberg* (b. 1874) proposes, in his *Problems of Harmony*, a twelve-tone basis for musical structure to replace the classical seven-tone basis. For this purpose he goes as high as the thirteenth partial but tacitly applies the idea to present instruments. *Paul Hindemith* (b. 1895), author of *The Craft of Musical Composition*, works toward the same end but is partial-shy, refusing to admit even the seventh. *Henry Cowell* (b. 1897), author of *New Musical Resources*, believes in a chordal music that legitimizes "seconds," which, he considers, represent partials through the fourteenth.

*Max F. Meyer* (b. 1873), psychologist, takes the trouble, in *The Musician's Arithmetic*, to state the case for ratios as a nomenclature for musical materials, these being the only terms "safe from ambiguity."[14] Meyer uses what Monophony would call identities through 9 (including 7), disavows both overtones and undertones as constituting the source of tonality, and, somewhat disappointingly, applies his ideas to a "quartertone" harmonium (see Chapter 17).

*Wilfrid Perrett* (b. 1873), author of *Some Questions of Musical Theory*, also stops at the 9 Identity, basing his scale on tones related by the number 7 in a "polyphonic" just system—and, like Meyer, rejects the "undertone" idea as the source of "minor" tonality. He applies his system in a harmonium of perfect tuning in nineteen tones to the 2/1, the keyboard of which deviates slightly from the familiar 7-White–5-Black (see Chapter 18).

*Joseph Yasser* (b. 1893) is an outright advocate of a new equal temperament, which he presents with broad historical perspective in *A Theory of Evolving Tonality*. Yasser has made one experiment, on a piano, with nineteen equal divisions of tone in the 2/1 (see Chapter 17).

*Kathleen Schlesinger* has deduced from the ancient Arithmetical Proportion the plan of the ancient Greek harmoniai, going beyond the 11 limit expounded here to use ratios of 13 in the diatonic genus, and still larger prime numbers in the chromatic and enharmonic genera. Her concepts are presented in *The Greek Aulos*. Schlesinger's is a Monophonic system, since it includes all ratios within the 13 limit; it is presented as a plan for the future, and has been tested and ·examined in detail in aulos relics, reproductions of ancient kitharae, and in a piano tuned in the ratios Schlesinger gives (see Chapter 18).

If the reader has found long and tedious this panorama of the men and women of musical science as seen through Monophony's distinctively

[14]*Musician's Arithmetic*, 104.

colored glasses, he may comfort himself with the knowledge that much material of relative importance was omitted to reduce it even to its present compass. The world of musical science is rich in stimulating ideas, and the individuals who populate it are as human and diverse and idiosyncratic as the persons in our daily lives. As the ideas clarify, and as the personalities emerge—through this and similar works—the review will slip to the level which it is meant to occupy—an introduction.

# CHAPTER SIXTEEN

# Pythagoreanism

## *The 3-Idea Paralysis*

BY PLUCKING a string of a given tension and then plucking it while it is stopped at the exact midpoint, we produce the interval 2 parts to 1 part, or 1 vibration to 2 vibrations, the ratio 2/1. It is clear, then, that stopping the string at the halfway point creates a tone a 2/1 higher. But it is not easy to say just what this mysterious likeness is. From any standpoint of psychological reaction except pitch it is the same tone, and only by its pitch do we know that it is not the same tone. But so closely does it simulate the lower tone that we do not even accord it an identity in music; we call it by whatever name we have given its generating 1. We could go on dividing the string, the half in half, the quarter in half, the eighth in half, and so on, and in so doing would produce a series of such likenesses, ascending in pitch.

Obviously such a series of tones serves as little more than a skeleton in theories and actual tonal structures, and when man discovered the number 2 in music, and this series of likenesses, however intrigued he may have been, he was not satisfied to stop.

He next discovered the relationship 2 to 3, and here he found a tone which was definitely not a likeness of 1, but a tone which presented a new and powerful relationship to 1. Having found the number 3, by dividing the string, or pipe, into three parts, he hit upon the idea of dividing the third of the string into three parts, the ninth into three parts, and so on, just as he might have divided each half into two parts, each quarter into two parts, and each eighth into two parts. One of the results of this procedure, he discovered, gave him a series of successive 3/2 ratios, ascending in pitch, and producing, with each new ratio, an entirely new tone, quite unlike the result of successive divisions by the number 2. And this process was intellectually satisfying to him, and it has been intellectually satisfying ever since to both learned individuals and whole peoples, as evinced in their body of theoretical knowledge. But strangely, having advanced from the number 2 to the number 3, they have been quite content to stop, indeed have aggressively resisted all attempts to show how the string can also be divided into five parts.

The 3 idea, which has come to be known as Pythagorean intonation, was the first intonational pattern in both the early musical cultures which became prototypes, the Chinese and the Greek.[1] It prevailed in China and Arabia almost to the exclusion of anything else, was for many centuries the only system in ecclesiastical Roman and Byzantine music, and today is still being presented in American and European classrooms thinly disguised as the twelve "cycle," or the "circle of fifths."

## Chronic 3-ism—the Various "Cycles"

Ling Lun's formula for the Chinese pentatonic, which was the first recorded expression of the Pythagorean intonation, though not predicated on string lengths, was nevertheless a 3-pattern (see previous chapter), and Ling Lun continued this pattern to achieve a set of twelve tones of fixed pitch for the transposition of pentatonic melodies. His lü, or bamboo pipes, are supposed to have been in series of six each, the starting tones of the two series separated by a Pythagorean "semitone." And each series was a succession of 9/8's, with one exception, which is noted below. Thus Ling Lun is reputed to have achieved the twelve "cycle" minus the Pythagorean "comma."[2]

In the twelve "cycle"—if "C" is called 1/1, the tone which is twelve 3/2's above, or "B♯," would be higher than the tone seven 2/1's above 1/1 by the ratio 531441/524288 (see Diagram 21—4096 is multiplied by 2 seven times, that is, transposed up seven 2/1's), which is 23.5 cents or approximately one-eighth of a "tone" or one-quarter of a semitone. The subtraction of this comma, distributed over twelve 3/2's of 702 cents each, gives "fifths" of 700 cents and twelve equal degrees. In Diagram 23 the spiral showing deviation of the true from the tempered is overdrawn about sixfold.

In superposing 3/2's above a given tone some approximation of one of the 2/1's of this tone is of course reached periodically, which periodic point is considered the end of the various "cycles."[3] In the past two millenniums

---

[1]Kathleen Schlesinger gives a somewhat different picture for Greece. See Chapter 18.

[2]Yasser, *Theory of Evolving Tonality*, 27; K. C. Hsiao, in Meyer, *Musician's Arithmetic*, 108.

[3]Joseph Sauveur (1654–1716), geometer and acoustician, listed twenty-five "cyclic" systems, including those of twelve, seventeen, nineteen, thirty-one, forty-three, fifty, fifty-three, fifty-five, sixty-seven, and two hundred and fifty-six degrees. He himself favored the forty-three "cycle" (any resemblance to the main subject matter of the book in hand is entirely accidental). Barbour, "Equal Temperament," 241, 247.

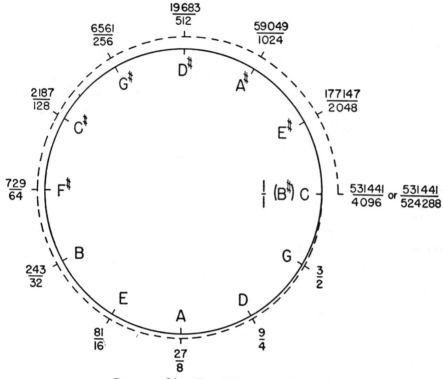

DIAGRAM 21.—THE "CIRCLE OF FIFTHS"

the nine "cycles" given below have been seriously analyzed or proposed as a basis of temperament. They are given in order of tonal multiplicity, along with the amount of the all-important approximation, or the discrepancy between the beginning and end of each "cycle," in cents:

1. Five "cycle"—90.2 cents below the third 2/1.
2. Seven "cycle"—113.7 cents above the fourth 2/1.
3. Twelve "cycle"—23.5 cents above the seventh 2/1.
4. Nineteen "cycle"—137.1 cents above the eleventh 2/1.
5. Thirty-one "cycle"—160.6 cents above the eighteenth 2/1.
6. Forty-one "cycle"—19.8 cents below the twenty-fourth 2/1.
7. Fifty-three "cycle"—3.6 cents above the thirty-first 2/1.
8. 306 "cycle"—1.8 cents below the 179th 2/1.
9. 347 "cycle"—21.6 cents below the 203rd 2/1.

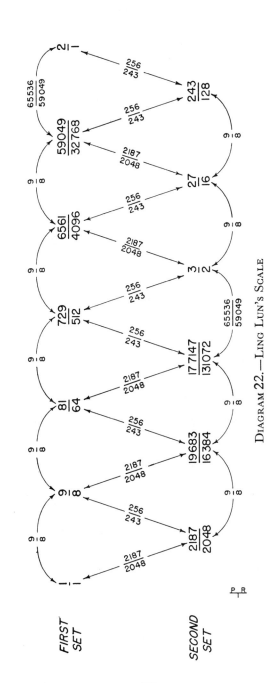

DIAGRAM 22.—LING LUN'S SCALE

No. 9 has been recommended by both Paul von Janko and E. M. von Hornbostel as the step that music must take to improve the fifty-three "cycle."[4]

## Ling Lun's Bamboo Pipes

The tones—expressed by ratios—that appear in the twelve "cycle" also appear in Ling Lun's lü, except that the lü show the tones transposed within one 2/1 rather than in extended position (see the previous page). Also, the thirteenth degree, 2/1, is added in the diagram. Were the final interval shown as 9/8 (instead of 65536/59049), it would reach a tone higher than 2/1 by the Pythagorean "comma."

As is seen in the second set of lü, the sequence of 9/8's (203.9 cents) between degrees is interrupted by the much smaller 65536/59049 (180.4 cents), but the Chinese confounded these intervals and actually considered each of the twelve degrees of the two sets as being an equal "semitone" apart, that is, 1/12 of 2/1,[5] even though two widths of Pythagorean semitone are involved—2187/2048 (113.7 cents) and 256/243 (90.2 cents).[6]

The practical theorist may wonder why the ancient Chinese went to the trouble of so much mathematical computation when the results were equivocal anyway, and when the same end could have been achieved more

[4]Hornbostel, "Musikalische Tonsysteme," in *Handbuch der Physik*, 8:446; Barbour, "Equal Temperament," 250. Should anyone be tempted to take that step, he perhaps ought to be warned as to what tradition will expect of him—a *sui generis* work involving a prelude and fugue in each of 347 "major" and 347 "minor" tonalities, and atonality for the modernists, or the use of a grand total of 120,409 senses!

China, which invariably produces a "Paul Bunyan" tale to make the storyteller wish he had kept still, produced a theorist, Chien Loh-tze by name (*c*. 430 A.D.), who tried to establish a degree of the scale for every day in the year, along with a mandamus to force the music of a given day to stick to its "key." Hsiao in Meyer, *Musician's Arithmetic*, 113.

[5]*Ibid.*, 108. A somewhat more rational procedure—one that would at least involve smaller numbers—would appropriate five 3/2's below 1/1 and six 3/2's above, which would give the ratios of a twelve-tone scale, in one 2/1:

| 1/1 | | 256/243 | | 9/8 | | 32/27 | | 81/64 | | 4/3 | | 729/512 |
|-----|-----|-----|-----|-----|-----|-----|-----|-----|-----|-----|-----|-----|
| | 256/243 | | 2187/2048 | | 256/243 | | 2187/2048 | | 256/243 | | 2187/2048 | |

| (729/512) | | 3/2 | | 128/81 | | 27/16 | | 16/9 | | 243/128 | | 2/1 |
|-----|-----|-----|-----|-----|-----|-----|-----|-----|-----|-----|-----|-----|
| | 256/243 | | 256/243 | | 2187/2048 | | 256/243 | | 2187/2048 | | 256/243 | |

Changing the expression of a succession of 3/2's does not change their inherent relationships—it only changes their relationships in what is implied as the 2/1. The above scale, with the same successive intervals between degrees, is found in Ling Lun's scale starting on 243/128, the twelfth degree, and proceeding thereafter with 1/1.

[6]A distinctive nomenclature has developed with Pythagoreanism. The ratio 256/243 is called the "limma," the difference between the compass of two 9/8's and 4/3. The ratio 2187/2048 is called the "apotome"—what is left after taking the limma from 9/8.

forthrightly by ear. Apparently Ho Tcheng-Tien, three millenniums later, did wonder (see previous chapter). Before we adjust our hatbands along with Ho, however, we should remember that we go through exactly the same confounding and the same confounded process every time we present the "circle of fifths."

If the Chinese had practised their Pythagorean theory of the pentatonic, they would have been obliged to use 81/64 instead of 5/4, 32/27 instead of 6/5, 27/16 instead of 5/3, and 128/81 instead of 8/5, as a square of the Ling Lun pentatonic, produced below, reveals; the interval relationships are upward in pitch from the column at the left to the horizontal line at the top:

|        | 1/1    | 9/8   | 81/64 | 3/2   | 27/16 |
|--------|--------|-------|-------|-------|-------|
| 1/1    |        | 9/8   | 81/64 | 3/2   | 27/16 |
| 9/8    | 16/9   |       | 9/8   | 4/3   | 3/2   |
| 81/64  | 128/81 | 16/9  |       | 32/27 | 4/3   |
| 3/2    | 4/3    | 3/2   | 27/16 |       | 9/8   |
| 27/16  | 32/27  | 4/3   | 3/2   | 16/9  |       |

Actual tests show that the large-number Pythagorean intervals are impossible to sing without the aid of instrumental accompaniment, and Helmholtz frequently uses the ratios of 5 in analyzing the pentatonic[7]; for example (ascending):

$$1/1 \quad 9/8 \quad 5/4 \quad 3/2 \quad 5/3 \quad 2/1$$
$$\quad 9/8 \quad 10/9 \quad 6/5 \quad 10/9 \quad 6/5$$

## Pythagoras and His Arab Acolytes

In pursuing the story of Pythagoreanism we cross an apocryphal twenty-one centuries (Ling Lun's antiquity is probably exaggerated) and come to Pythagoras himself, who, rightfully or not, is the Western symbol of 3-determined intonations. Pythagoras the individual and his reputed theories have been amply discussed (Chapters 10 and 15). The Pythagorean heptatonic scale (see Chapter 10), beginning on any one of its degrees, was considered the theoretical basis of music throughout the Middle Ages, as we have seen, and is also, according to Schlesinger, the scale which the Arabs translated and studied, then bore "along their victorious path through

[7]*Sensations of Tone*, 259.

Persia, India, North Africa, Spain and Sicily."[8] Thus the Pythagorean scale from the Greek source via the Roman ecclesiastical and the Arabic worlds met in southern Europe, especially in Spain.

The scale is easy to tune, but it does not necessarily follow that it is easy on the ear, as Archytas and Ptolemy and numerous others discovered. And as each new degree in a Pythagorean-inspired scale is added, the number of intervals ungratifying to the ear is disproportionately increased, as a square of any such scale would show. The Arabic seventeen-tone scale is a case in point. Both the intonational systems antedating the seventh-century Zalzal (see previous chapter) involved large-number ratios, but only the "ancient" was purely Pythagorean.[9] On a five-stringed lute the ancient fretting, with its fourteen-degree scale, can be deduced easily from a succession of thirteen 3/2's (expressed acoustically in relation to a single 1/1): 512/19683— 256/6561—128/2187—64/729—32/243—16/81—8/27—4/9—2/3—1/1— 3/2—9/4—27/8—81/64.

In the seventh century Zalzal, following the Greek pattern of reform, moved two of the four frets or ligatures (which had already been moved in the so-called Persian tuning some time before) onto ratios with much smaller numbers. But, as we have seen, in the fourteenth century a pair of 3/2 recessionists, Mahmoud and Abdulqadir, restored the ancient tuning and added three 3/2's below the first ratio given above, or (ascending): 4096/531441—2048/177147—1024/59049—(512/19683), which they apparently thought would be close enough to Zalzal's tones to preserve their musical effect and at the same time give them Pythagorean legitimacy.[10] Expressed in cents and transposed into one 2/1 the consecutive scale degrees are:

| Scale degrees. | 1 | 2 | 3 | 4 | 5 | 6 | 7 | 8 | 9 |
|---|---|---|---|---|---|---|---|---|---|
| Cents...... | 0 | 90.2 | 180.4 | 203.9 | 294.1 | 384.4 | 407.8 | 498.0 | 588.3 |

| Scale Degrees... | 10 | 11 | 12 | 13 | 14 | 15 | 16 | 17 | (1) |
|---|---|---|---|---|---|---|---|---|---|
| Cents......... | 678.5 | 702.0 | 792.2 | 882.4 | 905.9 | 996.1 | 1086.3 | 1176.5 | 1200 |

---

[8]"Further Notes on Arixtoxenus," in *Classical Quarterly*, 27:93.

[9]Ellis, *Journal of the Society of Arts*, 33:493–494.

[10]Ellis in Helmholtz, *Sensations of Tone*, 281n, 454–456, 516, 520. Zalzal's fretting, which can be reconstructed easily from the tables of Ellis (who attributes his information to the Arabist J. P. N. Land), was far from a consistent small-number intonation. The tuning of the five open strings in successive 4/3's (1/1–4/3–16/9–32/27–128/81 or 9/8–3/2–1/1–4/3–16/9) would alone have insured some large-number relationships, and his scale was therefore partially Pythagorean. If Zalzal's lowest string, which we will call 1/1, was fretted in these ratios: 1/1 (open string)–

With knowledge of the cent values of the simpler acoustic intervals it is obvious that this scale has little virtue.[11] To the Monophonist as psychologist it is interesting and worth analyzing only as evidence of the extremes to which a man and a people and an age will carry a single idea. It impresses upon us the pointlessness from an esthetic standpoint, and the unhappiness from the standpoint of the simplicity-loving ear, of successions of 3/2's as the basis of a scale. Helmholtz, who, despite his musical conservatism, generally thought clearly on fundamental issues, saw no hope for intonational catharsis in Pythagoreanism, which he characterized as devoid of "any right principle."[12]

## "Chaos"—the Heritage of Centuries

Immoderate Pythagoreanism verges on acoustical chaos for the very simple reason that the ear can bring no judgment to its large-number ratios. Viewed simply as a basis of modulation, as Brown uses it in his "polyphonic" just system (see Chapter 18), there can be little or no objection to it, but as a series of relationships to 1/1 it is irrational; even a ratio as close as 27/16—just three 3/2's higher—is beyond the ear's capacity to determine accurately. Many of the intervals found in successions of 3/2's occur in the Monophonic fabric, but the implication is entirely different. In the Chinese pentatonic and Greek heptatonic the ratio 32/27, for example, is implied in the tonality of 1/1. In the Monophonic fabric 32/27 is not implied in the tonalities of 1/1 but in the Otonality 32/27 and the Uto-

54/49–9/8–27/22–81/64, the fretting of the four higher strings—in successive 4/3's—could be deduced, since the four frets went straight across the fingerboard. In practical terms, Mahmoud and Abdulqadir simply added two new frets to the four frets of the ancient Pythagorean tuning, the 1/1 string of which was fretted as follows: 1/1 (open string)–256/243–9/8–32/27–81/64. The two new frets corresponded to Zalzal's two frets 54/49 and 27/22. Aside from the many ratios of 3, 9, and 11 in Zalzal's scale, and the absence of those of 5 and 7, the only notable characteristic are the small intervals 54/49 to 9/8, i.e., 49/48 (35.7 cents), and 27/22 to 81/64, i.e., 33/32 (53.2 cents), which Abdulqadir made even smaller (65536/59049 to 9/8 and 8192/6561 to 81/64—both the Pythagorean "comma," 23.5 cents).

[11]Ellis proposes a Pythagorean scale of twenty-seven degrees, which, he says, "this temperament would require for ordinary modulations" (*ibid.*, 433); and S. G. Hatherley, obviously under the influence of Byzantine 3-ism, proposes a Pythagorean scale of thirty-one tones to play "Oriental" music correctly, fifteen successive 3/2's below 1/1 and fifteen successive 3/2's above. "It will be a question of pleasant pastime," he writes, "for the reader to work out for himself a series of thirty-one such proportions." Having indulged himself in this "pastime," Hatherley then constructs 289 heptatonic scales from the thirty-one ratios, and gives many examples of Byzantine and Near-Eastern folk music "demanding" them. *Treatise on Byzantine Music*, 1, 3, 6, 46.

[12]*Sensations of Tone*, 322.

nalities 4/3 and 40/27, with all three of which it necessarily has small-number relationships.

With a 3 limit in music the inclusion of small-number multiples, such as 9/8 and 16/9, is not irrational, and with each raising of the limit—to 5, 7, or 11—more of the 3-generated ratios can be admitted with logic, that is, when they involve the smallest multiples that would fill a particular musical requirement. This is not immoderate Pythagoreanism.

Thinking in successions of "dominants" around a "circle," which is immoderate, is an old and hallowed habit, and in its tempered expression it is virtually the foundation of our musical theory, and does not represent chaos to the average musician. To him chaos or order is dependent on the forms those tones—whatever their genesis—take after a composer discovers them and transforms them into music. Thus when a person is heard to remark, after listening to a half hour of serious contemporary music followed by a half hour of the latest swing on the radio, that music is in a state of chaos, he completely ignores the basic ingredient, namely, the scale.

We have had the Pythagorean-generated twelve-tone scale for nearly three hundred years, and with slight deviations for nearly six hundred years; the same keyboard for nearly six hundred years, and its application to the pianoforte for over two hundred years; the violin in exactly its present form for four hundred years; the same vocal techniques for a thousand years or more; and the same compositional forms for one hundred to four hundred years. True, in recent decades we have occasionally heard compositions or a few phrases of an excessively dissonant nature, but the fact is that they depend on the same source scale, the same instruments, the same forms, and the same manner of presentation that we have had for centuries. Let us examine the basic ingredient of this "chaos."

# CHAPTER SEVENTEEN

# Equal Temperaments

## *The Intonational Crossroads*

JUST ONE interpretation seems to be clearly deducible from the somewhat obscure story of intonational crystallization in Europe's sixteenth to eighteenth century—that our present scale developed as it did through a combination of two antithetical bodies: a body of intuitive desire and adventurous searching—spurred by a few perceptive or at least daring individuals—and an opposite body of inertia. For many centuries ecclesiastical music and music theory were singularly representative of non-action; the popular movements, which literally conceived and propagated harmonic music, were exclusively representative of intuitive desire. In time the charm and fascination of the popular harmonies forced a re-examination of the theocratic teachings of Pythagoreanism, for didactic tradition could not possibly be reconciled with the acoustic advances unconsciously made in the popular forms. And, having made the break from Pythagoreanism—euchred into the action, as it were—certain of the clerics went further; indeed, they did more toward divining acoustical potentialities than at any time in the history of the Church. So it came about that the new harmonic music was explained in the only terms that made acoustic—that is, aural—sense; namely, the terms of the Ptolemaic Sequence.

From this point on the roles were at least partially reversed. That body of intuitive desire which had created harmonic music fell into the easiest method of perpetuating it, whereas the force that had represented reaction produced interpreters who saw clearly the path that might be taken to present it in its best and most significant form.

The first temperings, back in the fifteenth century, were not adulterations of Ptolemaic, but of Pythagorean intonations. And by the time the musical rectitude of the Ptolemaic was generally recognized—in the Italy of the sixteenth century—the form of the keyboard, the chief reason for temperament, was already a habit, and therefore tempering was a habit; the notation born and bred with that keyboard was a habit, and therefore the mental reaction of musicians was a habit. In short, inertia had the day.

Considering the whole situation it is not remarkable that the new instruments of Vicentino, Doni, Ramarinus, and, in a later day, of Thompson, Brown, and Bosanquet, all of whom worked toward better intonations, ended in museums, untouched except by musicologists come to patronize. Without composers to insufflate them, and especially without musicians to operate the complementary bellows, they were actually foredoomed. But this is hardly synonymous with "failure."

These men lived in a day that required a regimentation of theoretical knowledge and a standardization of product, simply for the purpose of perpetuation. The keyboard, king instrument of harmonic music, had become an essential, and limitations in the building and use of keyboards, both inherent and conditioned, led to a standard solution. Limited comprehension of acoustical potentialities, the five-fingered hand, the mechanics of instrument building, and the familiar notation forced the establishment of a level, the level of the body of musicians on whom devolved the task of perpetuating music. For most composers and theorists it was a case of determining on or accepting a realizable or realized system, understandable and available to all who might be attracted to it.

The means of perpetuating music on some other than this common level did not exist. It was not a matter of painting a picture—painting it once and letting it stand as an intrinsic value. It was a matter of repainting, again and again, and the means of this repainting had to be common practice among musicians. A man could not be inspired to devise a theory, build instruments, write music, play it once or twice, and call that the end. He had to feel that he was bestowing something more enduring than himself; and to have any assurance that he was doing this, any assurance at all, he was obliged to articulate his work on the level dictated by the habits and training of the body which was capable of perpetuating it. That this knowledge frequently operated as an incubus, and was no small determinant in molding the work and the attitudes of musical thinkers, is certainly not a farfetched conclusion.

To the experimenters of the sixteenth century there were obviously only three possible courses, of varying degrees of advisability: (1) to force key-boards into the pattern of the Ptolemaic Sequence, and carry on a parallel program of education for the perpetuating body of musicians; (2) to adulterate the Ptolemaic Sequence by tempering it in the least harmful or least obnoxious way, in order to bring it to the level of current patterns and capacity; (3) to dispense with keyboards altogether—if they proved in-tractable—as an essential element in music.

The first solution was tried by a number of men who have already been named (see Chapter 15), and probably by others; the second was advo-cated by Salinas, Zarlino, and Mersenne, the most authoritative voices of their times (that they accepted temperament reluctantly is nevertheless indicated by the theoretical and practical lengths to which they went to mitigate it); the third was never considered at so late a date, though the introduction of keyboards had met with considerable opposition earlier, and for a reason other than music itself. Far back in the seventh century, when organs were brought from Byzantium, their use was actually con-sidered sacrilegious by many; for example, by the Magdeburg commen-tators, who "invidiously insinuate that it was in the year 666 that organs were first used in churches, from whence they infer the unlawfulness of this innovation, as commencing from an era that corresponds with the number of the beast in the Apocalypse."[1]

By the seventeenth century the beast had become the family pet, too beloved to relegate to the beast-house, and since the mechanical ingenuity and/or comprehension of musicians was apparently unequal to the prob-lem of the Ptolemaic Sequence justly represented in every desired tonality in keyboards, there remained but one course: temperament, and in the seventeenth century Meantone Temperament.

## *The Meantone—Consequence of Its Virtues*

The name of this temperament reveals what its initial purpose was—namely, to preserve the true character of 5/4 (which is so essential in the Otonality 1–5–3 triad) by appropriating two "mean tones." Inasmuch as 5/4 is the compass of 9/8 and 10/9 the mean would be 193.2 cents—be-

---

[1]Hawkins, *History of the Science and Practice of Music*, 1:147. Hawkins adds that "the wit of this sarcasm is founded on a supposition that, upon enquiry, will appear to be false in fact." The introduction of the organ was even earlier, dating from the time of Saint Ambrose in the fourth century.

tween 9/8 (203.9 cents) and 10/9 (182.4 cents). Organs were tuned from "Eb" to "G#," with eight true 5/4's,[2] as indicated below:

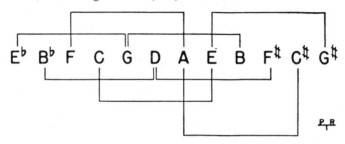

The small and large "semitones" in Meantone—76.1 and 117.1 cents— show up clearly in the Table of Comparisons given later in this chapter, four of the seven large "semitones" appearing in pairs. Obviously not all triads in such a plan would be "good." Both the "good" and "bad" triads reveal themselves in the table below, the column under 6/5 containing the distinctive ingredient of the "minor" triad, the column under 5/4 containing the distinctive ingredient of the "major" triad, and the column under 3/2 containing the ingredient required in both triads (note that the best "3/2" in Meantone—696.6 cents—is 5.4 cents too flat, or 3.4 cents flatter than the same interval in Equal Temperament):

| Key of: | 6/5 (315.6 cents) | 5/4 (386.3 cents) | 3/2 (702.0 cents) |
|---|---|---|---|
| Eb | 269.2 | 386.3 | 696.6 |
| E | 310.3 | 386.3 | 696.6 |
| F | 269.2 | 386.3 | 696.6 |
| F# | 310.3 | 427.4 | 696.6 |
| G | 310.3 | 386.3 | 696.6 |
| G# | 310.3 | 427.4 | 737.6 |
| A | 310.3 | 386.3 | 696.6 |
| Bb | 269.2 | 386.3 | 696.6 |
| B | 310.3 | 427.4 | 696..6 |
| C | 310.3 | 386.3 | 696.6 |
| C# | 310.3 | 427.4 | 696.6 |
| D | 310.3 | 386.3 | 696.6 |

Those Utonalities involving the approximation to 6/5 of 310.3 cents and the approximation to 3/2 of 696.6 cents, and those Otonalities involv-

[2]Ellis in Helmholtz, *Sensations of Tone*, 434.

ing the exact 5/4 of 386.3 cents and the approximation to 3/2 of 696.6 cents, are the "good" triads; these number sixteen.

The "bad" triads? European musicians had great fun modulating a ring-around-the-rosy from one "key" to another until they had used every one of the twelve tones of the temperament as a "tonic," and got back to where they started, but the four "major" triads and the four "minor" triads that were not "in tune" and were not intended to be—with their bruited "howling of wolves"—soured the rosy. Thereupon, one or a group of gentlemen, whose pictures hang above the pianos of nearly every music studio in America, came along and showed how, by using a new system of tuning, musicians could have triads without the obnoxious contrast, all equally bad and equally good. And one in particular demonstrated, in a way that has since become known as a classic of success, that with this tuning the musician could rosy around all day long with completely satisfying, undeviating monotony—from the standpoint of intonation.

## Expansion of the Meantone Idea

Before this new tuning had become a *fait accompli*, however, there were several attempts to obviate the "bad" triads through expansion of the Meantone principle. The organ of Georg Friedrich Handel was tuned in Meantone Temperament from "D♭" to "A♯," with twelve true 5/4's, thus:[3]

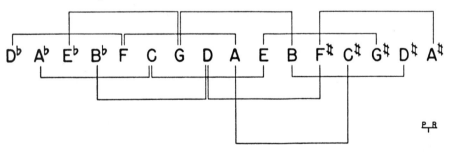

It had sixteen tones to the 2/1, with pairs of keys for "C♯–D♭, G♯–A♭, D♯–E♭, A♯–B♭," and gave Handel twelve "good" triads in "major," each with its characteristic "3/2" of 696.6 cents and exact 5/4 of 386.3 cents, and twelve "good" triads in "minor," each with its characteristic "3/2" of 696.6 cents and "6/5" of 310.3 cents. The "sharp" of one tone and the "flat" of the next higher—expressions of a concept which grew up with

[3]*Ibid.*

temperament and which have no meaning outside temperament—are not confounded in Handel's organ. The "good" triads of this organ are these[4]:

| "MAJOR" | | "MINOR" | |
|---------|---------|---------|---------|
| C–E–G | F♯–A♯–C♯ | C–E♭–G | F♯–A–C♯ |
| D♭–F–A♭ | G–B–D | C♯–E–G♯ | G–B♭–D |
| D–F♯–A | A♭–C–E♭ | D–F–A | G♯–B–D♯ |
| E♭–G–B♭ | A–C♯–E | D♯–F♯–A♯ | A–C–E |
| E–G♯–B | B♭–D–F | E–G–B | B♭–D♭–F |
| F–A–C | B–D♯–F♯ | F–A♭–C | B–D–F♯ |

An earlier instrument, having an even more extensive Meantone application, was the Clavicymbalum Universale, described by Praetorius, writer and composer of the late sixteenth century, who saw it in Prague[5] (this instrument was mentioned in Chapter 12 in connection with Chromelodeon II). It had nineteen tones to the 2/1 over a compass of four 2/1's. Each of the ordinary five black keys was doubled, and in addition there was a black key between "E" and "F" and between "B" and "C." This would of course increase the number of "good" triads.

But even such slight modifications as Handel's organ and the Clavicymbalum Universale, looking toward better intonation, were apparently too complicated for Europe's musicians, who refused to abandon the 7-White–5-Black, dating back to 1361.[6] And since the bad Wolf Meantone was annoying them, and they had already plunged into the sea of compromise, it was the most natural thing in the world to sink.

## Another Act—Equal Temperament at the Dénouement

By the late nineteenth century, when individuals in England and Germany and this country began to work aggressively for better intonation,

---

[4]Note the impossibility of using small-number ratios in examining temperament. One must either fall back on logarithms or cents (which express a value only indirectly and comparatively) or surds (which are exactly what the word implies, irrational) or invoke those equivocal symbols of surds—"A-B-C," etc., which imply too much and therefore nothing specific. The term "A," for example, can mean any intonation from the limits of "G♯" to the limits of "B♭." Only the student who has become exasperated in endeavoring to learn the true intention of theorists using this nomenclature will really understand the description of it as all-meaning and therefore no-meaning. Perhaps the factor which more than any other renders pointless and meaningless much otherwise conscientious work on the part of accousticians and theorists is their adherence to it. I venture to suggest that it is long past time for the "A–B–C's" of music to be liquidated in favor of the 1–2–3's of music.

[5]Helmholtz, *Sensations of Tone*, 320.

[6]Unequal temperaments, of which Meantone is one, were proposed in many forms and for a variety of keyboards in the sixteenth and seventeenth centuries. Actual applications to instru-

a huge literature of significant music based upon the instruments of compromise had come into being. Since music is written for specific vehicles, with all their faults and virtues woven into its woof, this literature proved to be too great a handicap to those who were essentially theorists, however empirical, rather than creative persons with a will to begin the work that might one day at least counterbalance the handicap.

It is pointless to argue that music would not have reached the pinnacle of the eighteenth and nineteenth centuries had earlier Europeans been more perceptive and more successful in preserving the Ptolemaic Sequence in keyboards.[7] The world is not ending on any predictable date, and there is still time to show what can be done in another climate, under other auspices. That other climate is actually with us, and it is an anomaly that we, a mechanically talented modern people, should insist on accuracy to the millionth part of an inch in certain precision instruments, while we nonchalantly accept at least a seventh of an equal "semitone" as an "inconsequential" error in music and dismiss mathematical computations as having "nothing to do with music"[8] because our mechanical and scientific talents remain uncorrelated with our musical talents. Were this immoderate tendency toward artificial divorcement of different branches of learning to go even slightly into eclipse the benefits to the music of the future would be fabulous.

Moreover, with our highly developed reproducing media, there can be no conceivable objection to the coexistence of different intonational philosophies, allowing the individual composer the choice of anything current or anything he can concoct. His work can be preserved in records, just as the diverse materials and techniques of literature and the visual

ments varied a good deal, but probably not to the extent of the theories. Aside from the usual twelve-degree Meantone Temperament and the nineteen-degree Clavicymbalum Universale, there were proposals for twenty (Doni), twenty-three (Niedhardt), thirty-one (Vicentino), fifty, and fifty-five degrees. Barbour, "Equal Temperament," 61, 195, 245, 253, 285, and *passim*. More recently Ellis proposed a twenty-seven-degree Meantone intonation which "would have been nothing to offend the ears of Handel and Mozart." In Helmholtz, *Sensations of Tone*, 434.

[7]The statement in the *Harvard Dictionary of Music* that the "advantages of the system [Equal Temperament] far outweigh its flaws" (page 735) is made with such authority as almost to convince me that the *Dictionary* got it from Bach, and that Bach got it from God.

[8]Combarieu, one-time professor of music history at the Collège de France and a fervent defender of Equal Temperament, nevertheless speaks of its "constitutional viciousness," and says that "its triumph is due to what . . . the sociologist might call the tyrannic influence of collectivity." But these faults he sweeps away because "it is immensely convenient—eliminating all the complex peculiarities of things . . . and it places before the eyes of the theorist symbols which save him from loss of time." *Music—Its Laws and Evolution*, 120, 292. If the musical theorist can get the mathematician to eat his breakfast cereal for him he can save even more time.

arts are preserved in print and paint. The tendency in music has long been against diversity, both economically and educationally. That the economic world should encourage uniformity is at least understandable, for a pattern that has proved economically successful is attractive, but that education should dedicate itself to uniformity and at the same time loudly proclaim its noble fulfillment of the ideal of education is the compounding of a felony. Let us examine some of the erudite reasoning behind the excuse for branding the entire world with twelve semitones.

## Character Witnesses Take the Stand

The claim is frequently made that the musicians playing the tonally unfettered instruments of the orchestra unconsciously make the necessary adjustments to correct the falsities of Equal Temperament, and this is certainly true in some string quartet work. But it is infinitely more difficult in the complex symphonic body, where the ablest intoners must conform to the poorest—the winds of fixed pitch, for example.[9] It is commonly maintained also that, properly considered, Equal Temperament is not a rigid scale in itself but a just scale in any "key," that is, twelve theoretical starting points, susceptible of an infinite number of adjustments. Theorists are by no means agreed as to what these adjustments should be; they have occasionally designed "experiments" conducted with "observers" and have presented the results in tables which "prove" that the ear accepts deviations from true ratios, becomes habituated to them, and sometimes actually prefers them—all designed to show that the adjustments are not particularly important in any case. An example:[10]

| Interval mistuned | Acceptable often enough with, say: |
|---|---|
| 3/2 | about 3 cents deviation |
| 4/3 | about 4 cents deviation |
| 5/4 | about 5 cents deviation |
| 5/3 | about 6 cents deviation |

[9]Ogden's is an example of that happy delusion so characteristic of our intonational attitudes. He optimistically informs us that "the musician knows the difference between harmonic and equal intervals, and makes imaginative allowances for the discrepancies he hears. With an instrument self-tuned like the voice or, to some extent, the violin, the artist will, of course, make his intervals what he desires them to be—harmonic or equal, according to his needs. Thus no discrepancies are felt, and both harmonic and equal intervals may be woven into a single complex pattern." *Hearing*, 173 (quoted by permission of Harcourt, Brace and Company, Inc.). "Complex" is a good word, but I can think of others.

[10]Meyer, *Musician's Arithmetic*, 142. Meyer quotes this table, and does not concur in the interpretation of results presented by the original author, whom he does not identify.

Note that 5/4 and 5/3, given in Equal Temperament with respective falsities of 13.7 and 15.6 cents, are here considered of doubtful acceptability if they deviate more than 5 and 6 cents, respectively. Except for this interesting feature the table is not significant, since, like all attempts to justify temperament in acoustical psychology, it fails to differentiate between what the ear will accept and what the ear prefers, if given a choice. The question is, what does the ear prefer for a particular musical concept? Even more to the point, can it tell the difference between, say, 5/4 and 503/400? My ear might "prefer" both, but it would most certainly resent the substitution of one for the other.

A more subtle bid for acceptance of Equal Temperament and its nomenclature is made by Glen Haydon. In summing up his approach, Haydon says that "the fundamental musical intervals may be mistuned, but still maintain their identity as fifths, sixths, seconds, and so forth. In other words, the amount of change in frequency necessary to produce a noticeable difference in pitch is very much less than that necessary to produce a change in interval classification."[11]

Before someone tartly asks, "*Whose* interval classification?" let us hear what W. Van Dyke Bingham has to say of one of his psychological experiments. Bingham writes that "with each of twelve observers . . . the characteristic feeling of 'relationship' [pure interval] was nearly always still present when the interval had been increased (or diminished) 32 cents (a third of an equally tempered semitone)." Citing a specific interval, Bingham declares: "Since the ratio 3:4 has no monopoly upon the characteristic 'relational' qualities of the fourth, but is rather only a modal ratio about which cluster an immense number of larger and smaller ratios manifesting in some measure identically the same psychological qualities, the use, without qualification, of the symbol 3:4 to represent that particular kind of 'relationship' is misleading."[12]

Bingham is considering melody, that is, tones sounded in succession, not simultaneously. It would be natural enough for an acoustician hearing 497/373, for example, in a succession of tones, to say casually, "It's a 4/3." His ear knows 4/3 as a precise experience; his ear does not know slight deviations as precise experiences. I risk the suggestion that no one who has

---

[11]*Introduction to Musicology*, 84, citing Pratt, *The Meaning of Music*; the passage from *Introduction to Musicology* is quoted by permission of Prentice-Hall, Inc.

[12]"Studies in Melody," in *Psychological Review Monograph Supplements*, vol. 12, no. 3, p. 22.

ever tuned intervals to small-number ratios would maintain that in the more important matter of a *simultaneous* sounding one of the recognizably dissonant ratios clustering around 4/3 manifests the identical psychological quality of 4/3.

It is easy to overestimate the reactions of "observers." They are not necessarily a revelation of anything but a flippant attitude or a response conditioned by unconscious absorption of tradition; Bingham himself does not entirely overlook the "effect of habituation."[13] But what does the psychologist himself hear? Does he not consider himself a competent "observer"? Does he think that his "controlled" group can possibly be as interested in results as he is?[14] Unlike the creator, who is disposed to affect a self-sufficient competence, the psychologist is apt to affect an all-discerning abstraction, and to appear to base his findings on the reactions of any and every mind except the *one* mind most interested.[15]

Helmholtz expresses his own opinion when he observes that "it is usual to say that the thirds [*ratios of 5*] are much less perfect consonances than the fifth [*ratio of 3–3/2*] and consequently also less sensitive to errors of intonation," but he adds: "In a consonant triad every tone is equally sensitive to false intonation."[16] Because the ear is less sensitive to errors of intonation in the ratios of 5 it hardly follows that it is therefore proper to render these ratios out of tune. So long as the ear is capable of hearing an identity as a comparative consonance, that identity should certainly be given a fighting chance as a comparative consonance. At that point where the ear can no longer make the distinction between the identity and any deviation from it the importance of both vanishes. Just where this point is has not been de-

---

[13]*Ibid.*, 39.

[14]Both "observer" reactions and psychological musical tests boil down to the same purpose, since the reaction of the "observer" is eventually turned into an index of his "musical ability." It is difficult to escape the conclusion that these tests and analyses become, actually, measures of a type of musical mimicry and memory recall—the ability to perceive sound patterns quickly and to express reactions to them facilely. This is certainly not valueless, but whatever agreement the music psychologist may attain between test-result and proved "talent," the question of "measuring" the probabilities with regard to a potential music creator is entirely different.

[15]Apropos of such detachment Philip Guedalla finds the same fault in historians, who "write as if they took no interest in the [their] subject. Since it is not considered good form for a graduate of less than sixty years' standing to write upon any period that is either familiar or interesting, this feeling is easily acquired . . . a modern historian, when he is really detached, writes like someone talking in the next room, and few writers have equalled the chilly precision of Coxe's observation that the Turks 'sawed the Archbishop and the Commandant in half, and committed other grave violations of international law.'" *Supers & Supermen*, 14; quoted by permission of G. P. Putnam's Sons and Hodder & Stoughton, Ltd.

[16]*Sensations of Tone*, 320.

termined, but 11 is definitely within it, as is proved in the tuning of the Chromelodeon (see Chapter 9).

It is also frequently argued that in music a pentatonic scale is not heard in only five senses, nor the heptatonic in seven,[17] nor the twelve-tone scale in twelve; that the five, seven, or twelve tones can give the impression of, let us say, ten, or fourteen, or twenty-four tones.[18] Also true, because of the amazing versatility of the ear, but this is true of any scale, tempered or otherwise, and the ear does not budge for an instant from its demand for a modicum of consonance in harmonic music nor enjoy being bilked by near-consonances which it is told to hear as consonances. The ear accepts substitutes against its will.

Fundamentally, equal temperaments are based upon and deduced from Pythagorean "cycles," in whole or part. This procedure is followed for just two reasons: (1) by compressing a "cycle" of 3/2's into a certain number of 2/1's the system is "closed"; any tone of the scale can be used as a "dominant," with a small degree of falsity, and consequently, (2) any of the scale intervals smaller or larger than 3/2 will also go into 2/1 or an $n$th power of 2/1 an exact number of times (see page 135 for the acoustical facts). Thus any degree of the scale is available in "any" sense (for example, "mediant," "supertonic," etc.), the assumptive capacity of the ear decreasing as the falsity of the sense increases. The falsity of any 5 Identity in Equal Temperament, for example, is not so great as to lie outside this assumptive capacity, but it is possible if not probable that any 7 Identity will lie outside, because of its excessive falsity.

## *How the Moderns Explain It—Schönberg*

At least three modern composers have predicated geneses, or musical fabrics, on the assumption of more than the usually accepted senses of Equal Temperament. One of these is Arnold Schönberg. The "major" scale, he says, "is to be explained as nothing else than the addition of the tones of the three main triads" ("tonic, dominant, and subdominant"); he declares that "we actually to some extent hear and to some extent feel this relationship in every sounding tone," which is a reflection both of Rameau and Colin

[17]Meyer, *Musician's Arithmetic*, 40.

[18]Compare Ellis: "The object of temperament is to render possible the expression of an indefinite number of intervals by means of a limited number of tones without distressing the ear too much by the imperfections of the consonances." In Helmholtz, *Sensations of Tone*, 431; quoted by permission of Longmans, Green and Company, Ltd.

Brown (see Chapter 15). Continuing, and of course implying the usual twelve-tone scale, "if we note the more distant overtones (up to the 13th) of these same fundamental tones, F, C, G [4/3, 1/1, 3/2] . . . we find the chromatic scale. Thus there appear

"Bb as the 7th overtone of C

"F♯ as the 11th overtone of C

"Eb as the 7th overtone of F and the 13th of G

"Db as the 13th overtone of F and the 11th of G

"Ab as the 13th overtone of C."[19]

If this statement is analyzed in cents, "C" = 0 cents, "F" = 500 cents, "G" = 700 cents; the 7th, 11th, and 13th partials are not expressible in straight alphabetical symbols, but within a single 2/1 from any unity, 7 = 968.8 cents, 11 = 551.3 cents, 13 = 840.5 cents. Schönberg's statement, analyzed in cents, is as follows:

|  | Schönberg's "Overtones" | Cents in Schönberg's "Overtones" | Cents in Overtones |
|---|---|---|---|
| 1. | 7th of C (Bb) | 1000 | 968.8 |
| 2. | 11th of C (F♯) | 600 | 551.3 |
| 3. | 7th of F (Eb) | 300 | 268.8 (500+968.8—1200 = 268.8) |
| 4. | 13th of G (Eb) | 300 | 340.5 (700+840.5—1200 = 340.5) |
| 5. | 13th of F (Db) | 100 | 140.5 (500+840.5—1200 = 140.5) |
| 6. | 11th of G (Db) | 100 | 51.3 (700+551.3—1200 = 51.3) |
| 7. | 13th of C (Ab) | 800 | 840.5 |

Schönberg's No. 1 and No. 3 are 31.2 cents false. His No. 2 and No. 6 are 48.7 cents false, very nearly a "quartertone": it would seem almost as logical to call No. 2 "F" as "F♯," and No. 6 "C" as "Db," as is obvious from this analysis:

"F"................500.0 cents          "C"................0.0 cents
11th overtone.........551.3 cents        11th overtone.........51.3 cents
"F♯"..............600.0 cents          "Db"..............100.0 cents

His Nos. 4, 5, and 7 are all 40.5 cents false. As though this were not enough, 268.8 cents (7th of "F"), and 340.5 cents (13th of "G"), separated by 71.7 cents, or about seven-tenths of a "semitone," are presumed to be the same tone, "Eb." And 140.5 cents (13th of "F") and 51.3 cents (11th of "G"), separated by 99.2 cents, or virtually a whole "semitone," are presumed to be the same tone, "Db."

[19]"Problems of Harmony," in *Modern Music*, 11:170.

Schönberg observes that "the more perceptible overtones sound more familiar to the ear than those it hears but faintly; these last therefore remain strange to it."[20] Strange indeed!

## Demands beyond Our Instruments—Cowell

It is refreshing, in view of the above equivocations, to find Henry Cowell observing that the 7th, 11th, 13th, and 14th overtones do not "exactly coincide" with tones on the piano. These overtones, however, are theoretical constituents of the Cowell chords built on "seconds," which he declares have a "sound acoustical foundation." By "seconds" Cowell means two intervals, the ratio 55/49 (approximately; every tempered-scale interval is a surd, not an exact ratio; see the footnote on page 101) for the "major second," and the ratio 89/84 (approximately) for the "minor second," the only "seconds" found in Equal Temperament. What relation the intervals 8/7, 9/8, 10/9, 11/10, 12/11, 13/12, 14/13, etc., etc. (which are found in the range of the overtone series Cowell refers to), have to the ratios 55/49 and 89/85 is thoroughly obscure until we remember the aforementioned affable assumption that the ear actually hears 8/7, 9/8, 10/9, 11/10, 12/11, 13/12, 14/13 when all it gets is 55/49 and 89/84. However, Cowell goes some distance to acquit himself when he says:

"Since we have seen the development of the use of chords from the simplest ones in ancient times, through somewhat more complex ones later, and still more complex ones in present-day music, all following the overtone series on upwards, it seems inevitable that the system of building up chords must eventually include the next overtones after those related in 3rds [*in this range the "thirds" are 5/4, 6/5, 7/6*], namely, from the seventh overtone upwards. There seems to be need of such a system to further the understanding of contemporary material, which has had no adequate theoretical coordination, in spite of being in everyday use in composition."[21]

It has long been evident that composers have been taxing both the system and its instruments far beyond their capacities, and that the continued tyranny of Equal Temperament is leading to the degeneration of tonality. A tone that is a "quartertone" too sharp is called a true identity of tonality for no reason except a lack of the proper instrument and rational nomen-

[20] *Ibid.*, 171.
[21] *New Musical Resources*, especially pp. 11, 113, 114; quoted by permission of Alfred A. Knopf, Inc.

clature. It would be healthy for us to realize fully that our instruments are exactly as poor as the system and habits of thought with which they evolved.

## Explanation by Multi-Genesis—Hindemith

Paul Hindemith goes to inordinate lengths to justify a twelve-tone scale as an entity, not merely as a vehicle for transposition of essentially heptatonic music. The justification is, again, the overtone series, appropriated through the device of considering a generated tone in two or more senses, for instance, as the third partial of one series and the fifth of another, the fundamentals of which are then assumed as degrees in the equal twelve-tone scale. Hindemith gives his partials in frequencies, or cycles, but the frequencies reduce to exact ratios, and since the ratios are mostly small-number, and have all been introduced previously, they will be used here. The boxed ratios in Diagram 23 are the "generating" (high) tones, the ratios in the first or lowest 2/1 (at the bottom) the final scale tones, and each column of ratios is some part of an overtone series. Diagram 23 is deduced from the schema appearing between pages 48 and 49 of Hindemith's *Craft of Musical Composition*, Volume 1.

What Hindemith accomplishes in this plan, by a process of partials, plus partials of partials, plus partials of partials of partials, is accomplished in Monophony by the one-act application of the 5 limit. In other words, Hindemith's elaborately conceived twelve-tone scale (minus 10/9 and 9/5) is exactly the just scale of the 5 limit (minus 45/32 and 64/45) given in Chapter 7.

Here is the Hindemith scale arranged in the order of pitch (ascending):

| C | D♭ | | D | E♭ | E | F | ⎡——F♯——⎤ | |
|---|---|---|---|---|---|---|---|---|
| 1/1 | 16/15 | | 9/8 | 6/5 | 5/4 | 4/3 | 45/32 | 64/45 |
| | 16/15 | 135/128 | | 16/15 | 25/24 | 16/15 | 135/128 | 20 |
| | | | | | | | | cents |

| | G | A♭ | A | B♭ | | B | C |
|---|---|---|---|---|---|---|---|
| (64/45) | | 3/2 | 8/5 | 5/3 | 16/9 | 15/8 | 2/1 |
| | 135/128 | 16/15 | 25/24 | 16/15 | 135/128 | 16/15 | |

In another part of his book (page 42) Hindemith implies that the relationships between

| C | ——D♭ | ——D | ——E♭ | ——E |
|---|---|---|---|---|
| | 16/15 | 17/16 | 18/17 | 19/18 |

are as shown, whereas, in the multi-partial provenance of his diagram they are the exact ratios 16/15–135/128–16/15–25/24 (see above). Again, the composer-theorist expects the ear to hear something it fails to get, and even the composer himself cannot make up his mind what it is he wants it to hear. But what the ear actually gets between these degrees is exactly what it has always got in Equal Temperament: 89/84–89/84–89/84–89/84, the equally-tempered "semitone," or generally something close to it.

Partials are exact mathematical ratios. Ratios are precise magnitudes. After going to all the trouble of showing the genesis of his scale in frequencies which are exact small-number ratios, Hindemith destroys their integrity, as in the five-degree example on the preceding page, by accepting

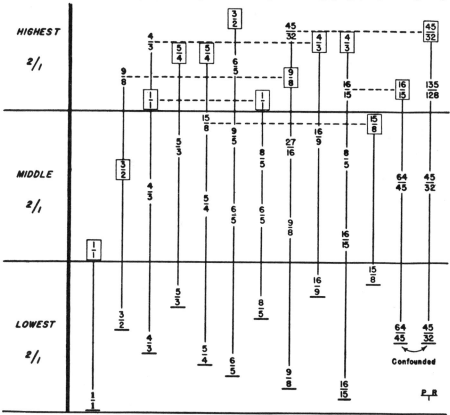

DIAGRAM 23.—HINDEMITH'S SCHEMA

varying amounts of temperament in practical music, and in asserting that "we can dispense with the decimal points."[22] It would be a doloriferous world indeed in which a tuner would fix a tone at 55 cycles, then remark that in tuning the 2/1 below he could "dispense with the decimal points"— in other words, tune his lower 2/1 to 27 or 28 cycles, not 27.5! Hindemith describes temperament as "a compromise which is presented to us by the keyboard as an aid in mastering the tonal world, and then pretends to be that world itself."[23] Quite so, confusing even to those who perceive its tyranny.

### Explanation through the Occult—Křenek

Ernst Křenek, who is genuinely sympathetic toward all musical experimentation, provided it does not tamper with tonal materials on an acoustical basis, calls the "diatonic" scales a "marvelous intuition," and declares that "it was a mistake to suppose that by hearing overtones directly they [the theorists] could range them in the form of a major or a minor scale. Even if the theorists had heard them, this kind of disposition would have been arbitrary . . . in all the history of tonality there is not the slightest indication of acoustical observations or experiments which might have led to the establishment of tonal scales."

As a positive explanation Křenek finds that most happy, if not most fecund, of answers: "Would it not be simpler to say that the major-minor system was produced by creative minds because it was better suited than any other to the expression of their thoughts? It would not only be simpler but also more correct."[24]

### At 11:55 by the Clock—A Transfusion of Overtones

What impresses one most in these endeavors within Equal Temperament is that a strenuous effort is being made to find more and ever more in the present resources, more than there can really be any hope of getting. It is indeed wishful thinking to believe that we can give expression to theoreti-

---

[22]*Craft of Musical Composition*, 1:42.    [23]*Ibid.*, 1:155.

[24]*Music Here and Now*, 197, 198; quoted by permission of W. W. Norton & Company, Inc. (copyright 1939 by the publishers). Contrast Křenek's attitude with that of the German philosopher Herbart: "There are allegations whose authority is due to audacity alone; for instance, it is claimed that numbers and their ratios (which give the sole and unique means of distinguishing consonance from dissonance) are not the true elements of the *Beautiful* in music!" Combarieu, *Music—Its Laws and Evolution*, 285.

cal complexities in an inflexible and irrational system. Let us first have instruments which give true 7th, 11th, and 13th overtones, and true ratios of 8/7–9/8–10/9–11/10–12/11–13/12–14/13, and the true ratios 16/15–135/128–16/15–25/24, before writing music for them; in other words, let us relieve our long-suffering ears of some of its burdens.

In this brief examination of contemporaries we are also very conscious of their repeated use of the word overtone, their evident desire to tie our everyday scale to something a little beyond us, to one of the phenomena of nature. For centuries, ever since Mersenne, a procession of exegetes has been polishing the ritualistic platters with overtones, in dozens of theoretical disquisitions. (Křenek, too, objects to this, but in getting away he bolts through the first open door he sees, one labeled "Occult.")

Let us look at the facts: the genesis of twelve-tone Equal Temperament had nothing to do with overtones. It evolved from three prime factors: (1) the ecclesiastical modes and the desire, largely unconscious, for small-number ratios; (2) the growth of *faux bourdon* and other popular forms, and of keyboards (which grew together); (3) the tyranny of the five-fingered hand.

Now let us look at the vehicle: it is a "cycle" of twelve 3/2's compressed into seven 2/1's, with the result of twelve equal "semitones," in the framework of which, fortuitously, the all-important 5/4's and 6/5's are only so out-of-tune as to be not quite insufferable.

In drawing this forthright picture I have no intention of belittling the total result. Even in the light of the long years and great labor that man has expended in striving for beauty in intonation, we must say, when we consider the treasure which has been produced on the tempered basis, that twelve-tone Equal Temperament was an unfoldment of genius. We also know that it was attended by an evil genius, but the treasure nevertheless survives. And now, at 11:55 by the clock, would-be resuscitators are rushing to the bedside with transfusions of overtones, apparently assuming that a critical illness exists.

For nearly three hundred years Equal Temperament has acquitted well the creative aspect of its work, and it will probably continue to do so for some time to come, at least for those who like it, and who come by that liking through honest analytic labor, and not because they found it in their stockings at Christmas. The popular forms of music especially seem to be sliding hither and thither among the equal degrees with youthful vitality, without theoretical overtones, and it is quite conceivable that if they do not beat their heads too dizzily against the 1–2–3–4 walls of their duple-rhythm cubicle, they will one day slide onto the basic relations of Just Intonation.

## Sixty Miles above the Earth—a Mosaic Revelation

Progress toward better intonation could certainly be facilitated by laboratory and classroom work with the acoustical actualities (the scale Hindemith desires but does not get, for example). As things now stand the intonation which the individual composer desires (Schönberg, Cowell, Hindemith, or anyone else) is left to the fingers of the violinist, the lips of the flautist, and the laps of the gods—all tender mercies, we hope—simply because of the iniquitous determination of musical education to withhold from students any adequate comprehension of the problems of intonation.

A certain radio class which had been studying the so-called ionosphere, a layer of ionized air some sixty miles above the earth's surface, was asked in an examination to define it. The answer of one student was: "It is a theory which exists sixty miles above the earth."

It would be hard to find any few words in the English language that would be more applicable than these— "a theory which exists sixty miles above the earth"—to the musical scheme conceived in Just Intonation, which goes through the processes of evolvement, vegetation, validation in the popular mind by publication, and eventual application to the same familiar tempered-scale instruments. Why are all theories—however Mosaic in the ionosphere—perennially reduced to these same instruments *on* the earth?

An acoustician writes in his book that Just Intonation is impossible of attainment in a practical system of music, a psychologist repeats this in his book, authors of harmony repeat it in their books, and finally a veritable army of theorists, composers, and instrumentalists repeats it verbally—of whom not one in a hundred thousand can speak from personal experience.[25] Meanwhile, the individual composer goes right on imagining tones

---

[25]Whether or not he is one in a hundred thousand, a recent example is Carlos Chavez, who writes: "If we were to try to achieve purity in the intervals proceeding from the 5th, 7th, 11th, 13th, etc., harmonics, the complications would become fantastic." A strong word, that "fantastic." But Chavez also speaks of "permitting progress in the conquest of pure intervals," and remarks that "the tendency is unquestionably in that direction." *Toward a New Music*, 151–152.

he seldom gets, implying his tones in a system that does not encompass them, and knowing that they will be played by musicians who do not comprehend them.

It is the individual composer's privilege to choose his tonal materials, and the possibility that a composer might actually prefer twelve-tone Equal Temperament—even if given a choice—is always conceivable. But, I repeat, the privilege of choice carries with it an obligation—the obligation to make both acoustic examination and self-examination. That obligation is not fulfilled by merely accepting a legacy.

## First Result of Expansion—"Quartertones"

Proposals and instruments looking toward expanded resources within the framework of some temperament fall naturally into two classes. The first comprises those which divide the already equal "tone" (1/6 of a 2/1— six "tones" to the 2/1) into further equal parts, such as "quartertones" (twenty-four-tone temperament), or "sixth tones" (thirty-six-tone temperament). These procedures might be called a tempered expression of "Polypythagoreanism," since they are based on a small-interval juxtaposition of two or more Pythagorean twelve "cycles," in exactly the manner the Chinese created a twelve-tone scale by juxtaposing two sets of six lü (see previous chapter). The second class includes those which compress one of the Pythagorean "cycles" into the 2/1 to obtain such divisions as nineteen equal degrees and fifty-three equal degrees.

Composers and theorists in the first category assume, for reasons best known to themselves, that the interval compass of the "tone" is Mosaic law, a fundamental error. The most that can be said for the series of secondary errors resulting from division of the "tone" into four, six, eight, and even sixteen, equal parts is that "musical" resources are thus increased with a minimum of disturbance to the status quo, but such divisions are always lazy theory and fallacious aural psychology.

Michael Meshaqah, nineteenth-century Syrian theorist, proposed a division of the 2/1 into twenty-four equal parts and collected Arabic folk melodies which, he said, demanded this scale.[26] Prominent in Zalzal's fretting of the lute were several ratios of 11 (see Chapters 15 and 16); his scale was used for seven centuries before the fourteenth, and has probably

[26]Helmholtz, *Sensations of Tone*, 264.

also been used since, despite the "reforms" of Mahmoud and Abdulqa-dir.[27] In view of the fact that the division into "quartertones" gives two of the ten ratios of 11 with a falsity of only 0.6 cent, two with a falsity of only 1.3 cents, and two with a falsity of 2.6 cents, the probabilities are that Meshaqah's claims for Arabic folk melodies are valid.[28] But the fate of the other ratios of 11, and of the 5 and 7 Identities in "quartertones," is another story (see below).

A "quartertone" is of course 50 cents. Below are given the number of cents in each of the six ratios mentioned above and in the corresponding "quartertone":

| Cents in "quartertone" | 150 | 350 | 550 | 650 | 850 | 1050 |
|---|---|---|---|---|---|---|
| Ratios | 12/11 | 11/9 | 11/8 | 16/11 | 18/11 | 11/6 |
| Cents in ratios | 150.6 | 347.4 | 551.3 | 648.7 | 852.6 | 1049.4 |

About 1895 Julian Carillo began to work with scale degrees of 50 cents, also with degrees of 25 cents, and even of 12.5 cents (the latter "eighth" and "sixteenth tones"), using them in his own compositions and employing instruments of his own devising.[29] At least one record of these compositions was made, which seems to have achieved a wide distribution.[30] Carillo's theories were publicized under the maladroit caption of "Trece Sonido," that is, the "thirteenth sound" beyond the twelve we now have on the piano. A guitarra (a large guitar) was used for "quartertones," an "octavina" (a type of contrabass guitar) for "eighth tones," and a large harp-zither for "sixteenth tones."[31]

The fact that Carillo also appropriated everything from the "thirteenth" to the "ninety-sixth sound" ("sixteenth tones") is not revealed in his title, which seems to suggest a monotone achieved somehow on the number 13, whatever that would be. That the title was a conscious linking of a "tone" whacked into four and more equal parts with the "spell" of the number 13

[27]Ellis remarks that Zalzal's tones were "evidently too deeply rooted in popular feeling to be really lost." *Journal of the Society of Arts*, 33:496.

[28]Seventeenth-century theorists familiar with the Aristoxenean approximations occasionally discussed "quartertones," and one—Lemme Rossi (1601–1673)—gave numbers for the string lengths of equal "quartertones," possibly for the first time. Barbour, "Equal Temperament," 201, 220.

[29]Meyer, *Musician's Arithmetic*, 70–71, 122.

[30]The title of the composition was *Preludio á Cristobal Colon*, for harp-zither, octavina, cello, trumpet, soprano; it was played by the "13th Sound Ensemble" of Habana.

[31]Overmyer, "Quarter-Tones—and Less," *American Mercury*, 12:208.

can hardly be doubted. It should also be obvious that this "thirteenth sound" has not the remotest connection with the 13 Identity as used in the present work (and in Schlesinger's analyses) or with the 13th partial.

## Meyer's "Quartertones"

One of the most interesting of contemporary theories, which finally wound up in twenty-four-tone temperament, is that of Max F. Meyer. The very title of Meyer's book on theory, *The Musician's Arithmetic*, reveals that its author is cognizant of music's mathematical basis. He has taken the trouble, for example, to state the case for ratios as common musical terms with a clarity which is probably unsurpassed. His hydraulic model of the cochlea and his book on the nature of tonal impact on the inner ear[32] indicate that his observations were well considered. Of ratios he says: "No other terms are safe from ambiguity"; therefore, "the musician who abhors numbers . . . abhors the way leading toward an understanding of musicianship, an understanding of the psychology of music." In surveying musical theory, "our whole endeavor is directed toward deriving the history of music from the 'preference,' so to speak, for smaller number symbols, other conditions permitting a choice."

The highest identity number Meyer uses is 9, and he criticizes Ptolemy for his prodigal use of prime numbers such as 31.[33] "Even 11 is probably already outside our sphere of interest," he writes; he calls this identity an "intellectual chastisement," though he adds that it "should not be dogmatically excluded." He scoffs at the idea that the ear can like any unusual interval merely through habituation, and gibes at the "mythology" of overtones[34] and the "hallucinations" of undertones as sources of tonality, calling the ordinarily considered "dominant" in the Utonality 1–5–3 triad the "worst chosen keynote."

And, when all is said but not yet done, Meyer applies his theories on a harmonium of twenty-four-tone temperament.[35] He holds that "quarter-

[32]*Mechanics of the Inner Ear.*

[33]The number 31 occurs in the enharmonic tetrachord attributed by Ptolemy to Didymus. Hawkins, *History of the Science and Practice of Music*, 1:32.

[34]Acknowledgement is here made of the salutary effect of Meyer's argument on the presentation of material in this book.

[35]*Musician's Arithmetic*, especially pp. 8, 19–20, 25, 39, 76, 80, 89, 104, 141–142. Meyer's harmonium (1902) was probably the first "quartertone" keyboard and is even today one of the few with a novel keyboard (illustration p. 57). The loose usage of the word "quartertones" (encountered in Meyer's book also) to mean any small division of the scale is exceedingly un-

tones" are necessary for such monogenetic intervals as 8/7 and 7/6, yet 8/7 is 18.8 cents below an equal "quartertone," and 7/6 is 16.9 cents above (see below); these are greater deviations from true ratios than any deviations from the ratios of 5 in twelve-tone temperament. Regarding simultaneity he writes: "Tone relations can be *more easily observed* in succession, when the peculiar roughness often resulting from simultaneity does not *distract the listener's attention.*"[36] "Roughness" is a characteristic of intervals out of tune. Except for certain of the ratios of 3, 9, and 11, "quartertones" are all badly out of tune. The nature of a simultaneity represented by "quartertone" surds could only be rough.

## Resources of "Quartertones"

"Quartertones" are obtained by a simple duplication of the twelve-tone tempered scale a "quartertone" higher. The original, since it is the usual scale, has good 3 Identities and two fairly good 9 Identities, but poor 5 Identities (13.7 and 15.6 cents false). The doubling, a "quartertone" higher, gives six of the ten 11 Identities almost perfectly, but fails to represent the other four at all; it comes closer to the 7 Identities than the original, but not close enough, since they show a maximum falsity of 18.8 cents; it improves the 5's not at all.

## Table of Comparisons

On page 430 is a table of the number of cents in various systems of intonation as compared with most of the small-number ratios which theorists consciously or unconsciously reach for in proposing solutions to the problems of tuning, the Monophonic ratios in other words. The important historical and contemporary propositions are included.

The cents value of each degree is shown on the same line as the Monophonic ratio to which it is closest; in both the thirty-six-tone and fifty-three-tone scale two scale degrees are sometimes close to a single Monophonic degree; for example, on the line of the Monophonic degree 33/32 in the fifty-three-tone scale are the degrees "45.3 & 67.9" (cents). The rules under certain just ratios indicate their correspondence to the degrees of

---

fortunate. As for the terms tempered "quartertones" and just "quartertones"—both of which are encountered—the first has a redundant adjective and the second is a confusion of concepts. The word "quartertones" defines itself—twenty-four equal degrees, and therefore tempered.

[36]*Ibid.*, 55.

the twelve-tone chromatic scale. In the column under Meantone the four extra degrees which gave Handel's organ sixteen degrees to the 2/1 are indicated by an "H." Here also zero cents equals "C."

In the column under Pythagorean twelve-tone scale thirteen degrees are shown, since both tritones are given (588.3 and 611.7 cents), between which is the Pythagorean "comma" (23.5 cents). This scale is deduced from the following succession of 3/2's (ascending), each expressed within its 2/1:1024/729–256/243–128/81–32/27–16/9–4/3–1/1–3/2–9/8–27/16–81/64–243/128–729/512. The difference between 1024/729 and 729/512, in the same 2/1, is 531441/524288 (the Pythagorean "comma"), and the total compass of the 3/2 succession, from lowest to highest, is seven 2/1's and the "comma."

It is obvious from this table that the validity of the twelve-tone scale is impaired by tempering and that a twenty-four-tone scale has little validity to impair. As a temporary expedient, as an immediately feasible method of creating new musical resources, "quartertones" are valuable. That they are comparatively easy to obtain is evidenced in the many composers and performers who have used them: Alois Haba, with three piano manuals, the first and third of which played identical tones and the second a "quartertone" higher;[37] Hans Barth, with two piano manuals, the second tuned a "quartertone" higher than the other; and Mildred Couper, with two pianos, the second tuned a "quartertone" above the first. These of course involve the usual pattern of keyboard. The "quartertone" instruments of both Meyer and Moellendorf, however, were deviations from the 7-White–5-Black.[38]

## "Sixth Tones" and Busoni

The division of the "tone" into six equal parts (thirty-six-tone equal temperament) is, acoustically, another Polypythagoreanism in tempered expression, being an original twelve-tone equally tempered scale with two duplicates, each juxtaposed a sixth of a "tone," or 33.3 cents, higher. Ferruccio Busoni became enamored of this temperament and incorporated it in a harmonium with a novel keyboard (before the war in the Berlin Hochschule für Musik). The instrument has two manuals, black and white keys alternating throughout each. Both manuals play "third tones" (eighteen to the 2/1), with the second tuned a "sixth tone" higher.

[37]Overmyer, *American Mercury*, 12:208.  [38]Meyer, *Musician's Arithmetic*, 57–58.

| Monophonic Ratio | Monophonic Cents | 12-Tone Equal | 12-Tone Pythagorean | 16-Tone Meantone | 17-Tone Arabic | 19-Tone Equal | 24-Tone Equal | 31-Tone Equal | 36-Tone Equal | 53-Tone Equal |
|---|---|---|---|---|---|---|---|---|---|---|
| 1/1 | 0 | 0 | 0 | 0 | 0 | 0 | 0 | 0 | 0 | 0 |
| 81/80 | 21.5 | | | | | | | | 33.3 | 22.6 |
| 33/32 | 53.2 | | | | | 63.2 | 50 | 38.7 | 66.7 | 45.3 & 67.9 |
| 21/20 | 84.5 | | 90.2 | 76.1 | 90.2 | | | 77.4 | | 90.6 |
| 16/15 | 111.7 | 100 | | 117.1H | 126.3 | | 100 | 116.1 | 100 | 113.2 |
| 12/11 | 150.6 | | | | | | 150 | 154.8 | 133.3 | 135.8 |
| 11/10 | 165.0 | | | | | | | | 166.7 | 158.5 |
| 10/9 | 182.4 | | | | 180.4 | 189.5 | | | | 181.1 |
| 9/8 | 203.9 | 200 | 203.9 | 193.2 | 203.9 | | 200 | 193.6 | 200 | 203.8 |
| 8/7 | 231.2 | | | | | | | 232.3 | 233.3 | 226.4 |
| 7/6 | 266.9 | | | 269.2H | | 252.6 | 250 | 271.0 | 266.7 | 249.1 & 271.7 |
| 32/27 | 294.1 | 300 | 294.1 | | 294.1 | | 300 | | 300 | 294.3 |
| 6/5 | 315.6 | | | 310.3 | | 315.8 | | 309.7 | | 317.0 |
| 11/9 | 347.4 | | | | | | 350 | 348.4 | 333.3 & 366.7 | 339.6 & 362.3 |
| 5/4 | 386.3 | 400 | | 386.3 | 384.4 | 378.9 | 400 | 387.1 | 400 | 384.9 |
| 14/11 | 417.5 | | 407.8 | | 407.8 | | | 425.8 | | 407.5 |
| 9/7 | 435.1 | | | | | 442.1 | 450 | | 433.3 | 430.2 & 452.8 |
| 21/16 | 470.8 | | | | | | | 464.5 | 466.7 | 475.5 |
| 4/3 | 498.0 | 500 | 498.0 | 503.4 | 498.0 | 505.3 | 500 | 503.2 | 500 | 498.1 |
| 27/20 | 519.5 | | | | | | | | 533.3 | 520.8 |
| 11/8 | 551.3 | | | | | | 550 | 541.9 | 566.7 | 543.4 & 566.0 |
| 7/5 | 582.5 | 600 | 588.3 | 579.5 | 588.3 | 568.4 | 600 | 580.6 | 600 | 588.7 |
| 10/7 | 617.5 | | 611.7 | | | 631.6 | | 619.4 | 633.3 | 611.3 |
| 16/11 | 648.7 | | | | | | 650 | 658.1 | | 634.0 & 656.6 |
| 40/27 | 680.5 | | | | 678.5 | | | | 666.7 | 679.2 |
| 3/2 | 702.0 | 700 | 702.0 | 696.6 | 702.0 | 694.7 | 700 | 696.8 | 700 | 701.9 |
| 32/21 | 729.2 | | | | | | | 735.5 | 733.3 | 724.5 & 747.2 |
| 14/9 | 764.9 | | | 772.6 | | 757.9 | 750 | 774.2 | 766.7 | 769.8 |
| 11/7 | 782.5 | | 792.2 | | 792.2 | | | | | 792.5 |
| 8/5 | 813.7 | 800 | | 813.7H | | 821.1 | 800 | 812.9 | 800 | 815.1 |
| 18/11 | 852.6 | | | | | | 850 | 851.6 | 833.3 & 866.7 | 837.7 & 860.4 |
| 5/3 | 884.4 | | | 889.7 | 882.4 | 884.2 | | 890.3 | | 883.0 |
| 27/16 | 905.9 | 900 | 905.9 | | 905.9 | | 900 | | 900 | 905.7 |
| 12/7 | 933.1 | | | | | 947.4 | 950 | 929.0 | 933.3 | 928.3 & 950.9 |
| 7/4 | 968.8 | | | 965.8H | | | | 967.7 | 966.7 | 973.6 |
| 16/9 | 996.1 | 1000 | 996.1 | 1006.8 | 996.1 | | 1000 | 1006.5 | 1000 | 996.2 |
| 9/5 | 1017.6 | | | | | 1010.5 | | | | 1018.9 |
| 20/11 | 1035.0 | | | | | | | | 1033.3 | 1041.5 |
| 11/6 | 1049.4 | | | | | | 1050 | 1045.2 | 1066.7 | 1064.2 |
| 15/8 | 1088.3 | 1100 | | 1082.9 | 1086.3 | 1073.7 | 1100 | 1083.9 | 1100 | 1086.8 |
| 40/21 | 1115.5 | | 1109.8 | | | | | 1122.6 | | 1109.4 |
| 64/33 | 1146.8 | | | | | 1136.8 | 1150 | 1161.3 | 1133.3 | 1132.1 & 1154.7 |
| 160/81 | 1178.5 | | | | 1176.5 | | | | 1166.7 | 1177.4 |
| 2/1 | 1200 | 1200 | 1200 | 1200 | 1200 | 1200 | 1200 | 1200 | 1200 | 1200 |

This temperament, in which Busoni strives to draw "a little nearer to infinitude,"[39] is included in the table above and forces the same conclusions as "quartertones." Most of the 7 ratios are present with very little falsity, but the 5 ratios are still in the same situation as in twelve-tone temperament—13.7 and 15.6 cents false, and the 11's are not represented at all. Neither this scale nor the "quartertone" scale can be theorized as an expanded prime-number limit, growing from the 5 limit generally implied in twelve-tone temperament, without involving falsities so great as to destroy the assumptive ability of the ear. If a temperament is changed to favor one identity, two or three others will suffer; it is forever a case of robbing the brothers Peter to pay Paul. In Just Intonation the Peters and Paul and all their kin would each get his exact due.

### Nineteen-Tone Temperament—Yasser

The division of the 2/1 into nineteen equal parts has been periodically suggested as a better intonational vehicle than twelve equal parts—among others by the builder of the nineteen-tone harmonium now in the Stockholm Museum (constructed in 1845),[40] and much more recently by Joseph Yasser.

This also is one of the Pythagorean "cycles" (see previous chapter), the nineteenth 3/2 above a given tone being higher than the eleventh 2/1 above that tone by an interval of 137.145 cents, which, from this standpoint, stamps it immediately as inferior to the twelve "cycle," which has only an interval of 23.5 cents to be apportioned in the tempering of its twelve 3/2's.

The "3/2" resulting from nineteen equal divisions is of course 694.7 cents ($137.145 \div 19 = 7.218$—this is then subtracted from the true 3/2, 701.955 cents); virtually the same interval is found in the Monophonic fabric in several places, for example, from 18/11 upward to 11/9, the interval 121/81, or 694.8 cents, and also on Perrett's Olympion (see the next chapter). After hearing this interval on the Chromelodeon it somehow

[39]*Sketch of a New Esthetic of Music*, 30–31 (quoted by permission of G. Schirmer, Inc.). Wrote Busoni (p. 24): "We have divided the octave into twelve equidistant degrees, because we had to manage somehow, and have constructed our instruments in such a way that we can never get in or above or below or between them. Keyboard instruments, in particular, have so thoroughly schooled our ears that we are no longer capable of hearing anything else—incapable of hearing except through this impure medium. Yet nature created an *infinite gradation—infinite!*"

[40]Yasser, *Theory of Evolving Tonality*, 281n.

borders on the absurd to be asked to consider it as the strongest consonance in music next to 2/1.

On the side of assets, nineteen-tone temperament gives 6/5's and 5/3's almost exactly, and 5/4's and 8/5's with a falsity of 7.4 cents, which is certainly an improvement over the falsities of these intervals inherent in twelve equal divisions—15.6 cents for 6/5 and 5/3, and 13.7 cents for 5/4 and 8/5. The ratios of 7 are somewhat better also, but still with a maximum falsity of 21.4 cents (33.1 cents in twelve-tone temperament). The ratios of 11 are not represented at all.

Yasser is an outright exponent of temperament, his interest being not the betterment of intonation but the formulation of a theory for the growth of musical resources. He delves into the relatively primitive contemporary musical cultures of Java and Siam to show his evolutionary plan, which extends into the future also, and is nothing if not broad. The Javese scale is explained as consisting of two regular and three auxiliary degrees ("sub-infra-diatonic"; this scale was listed as one of the "cycles" in the previous chapter), the Siamese scale as five regular and two auxiliary degrees ("infra-diatonic," also listed as a "cycle"), the current Western scale as seven regular and five auxiliary degrees ("diatonic"). The total of any one scale thus becomes the number of regular degrees in the next scale, and the number of auxiliary degrees in the next following scale; for example, the total of five degrees for the "sub-infra-diatonic" becomes the number of regular degrees of the "infra-diatonic," and in turn the number of auxiliary degrees associated with the "diatonic."

Having established this formula, Yasser suggests as the scale for the immediate future twelve regular and seven auxiliary degrees ("supra-diatonic," nineteen equal steps), and for the more distant future $19+12=31$, and $31+19=50$, the "ultra-diatonics." The entire evolution is thus: $2+3=5; 5+2=7; 7+5=12; 12+7=19; 19+12=31; 31+19=50$ (all the numbers representing the number of scale degrees). [41]

## Fox-Strangways on Yasser

The historic substantiation of this thesis, which must be omitted here, is quite convincing in Yasser's scholarly presentation, to anyone who is not a Monophonist. The plan has won the approval of many theorists, especially

[41]*Ibid.*, especially pp. 7, 114, 136, 153.

A. H. Fox-Strangways, who observes: "The point to be clear about is that our present scale is worn down flat, and that it is a new scale, a new set of conventions, that is wanted, for us to explore."[42]

Those "new conventions" which are not legitimate descendants of the Holy Trinity of Equal Temperament, John Sebastian Bach, and Seven White and Five Black Keys are not to be considered by those who agree with Fox-Strangways, for he believes that "such alterations as may come will come gradually, as it did with clavichord, harpsichord and piano-forte."

It is regrettable that Fox-Strangways or someone else with equally strong convictions does not begin the exploration he recommends. Ambitious and highly individualistic composers have, in Yasser's book, a plan that has been widely approved, and it can be had for the asking. From the standpoint of slow evolution of existing materials, ideas, and thought habits, Yasser's proposal is much more credible and adaptable than the one presented in this book. It is no explosive and rebellious counter-action, and Yasser does not attempt to set up an independent pendulum of his own.

To a Monophonist, of course, Yasser's proposal is unacceptable, despite its breadth, because of the false 3/2's it involves and because the Monophonist regards as equivocal the expansion of tonality on any basis except the small-number identities. These, aside from 5, are either not represented at all in his scheme or are represented badly.

## Further Expansion—the Fifty-Three "Cycle"

The Pythagorean fifty-three "cycle" gives the closest approximation to the *n*th 2/1 of the starting tone of any thus far considered, the fifty-third successive 3/2 being only 3.615 cents higher than the thirty-first 2/1 above 1/1. In its tempered expression, therefore, each of the fifty-three 3/2's is flatted by 1/53 of 3.615, or .068 of a cent, giving a degree of falsity that might really be called—and for the first time I use the word without quotation marks—inconsequential. The effect on the integrity of some of the tonality identities other than 3, however, is something else.

As is seen in the table on page 303, this temperament is a nearly perfect solution for the composer who insists on any-tone-in-any-sense up to the 5 limit, and who is therefore satisfied with the present triad basis ("major"

---

[42]"Whence? Whither?" *The Observer* (London), March 11, 1934, p. 16.

and "minor") of tonality. All of the thirteen just degrees within the 5 limit (see Chapter 7), and in addition the 45/32 and 64/45 of Hindemith's scale (see above), are given with a falsity of only 0.1 to 1.5 cents.

But from the standpoint of tonality expansion there are serious defects: all six of the 7 Identities (based on a 7 limit) are 4.8 to 6.2 cents false; both the 9 Identities involving 7 are 4.9 cents false; all the 11 Identities are from 6.5 to 10.0 cents false. From a general standpoint none of these falsities is really bad, but remembering the caution regarding careful intonation of the weaker identities of tonality (see Chapter 11), we must take care that the integrity of 11 is not jeopardized, as it would be by a falsity of 10 cents, just as 7 is jeopardized in twelve-tone temperament by a falsity of 33.1 cents. Further, the "consonance" of the hexad basis of tonality most acceptable to the ear—the hexad of the small-number Identities 1–3–5–7–9–11—would become equivocal. Tests of some of these small falsities are discussed below.

If we were to combine the predilection of fifty-three-tone temperament for the 3's, 5's, and 9's with the predilection of thirty-six-tone temperament for the 7's and the predilection of twenty-four-tone temperament for the 11's, we would have a tonal system capable of all identities within this limit, numbering 113 tones to the 2/1! Many of these degrees would of course be acoustically meaningless, except in modulations seven to fifty 3/2's removed, and if we tossed out the degrees required by distant modulations we would have left about forty-three just ratios, the number of degrees in the Monophonic fabric.

## On the Matter of Hearing a 2-Cents Falsity

Given perfect tuning in twelve-tone Equal Temperament, the very least falsity that is involved in its representation of small-number ratios is the discrepant 2 cents in "3/2" and "4/3," which is considered even by most advocates of just tuning as "inconsequential." Also, in fifty-three-tone equal temperament, the four ratios of 5 involve a discrepant 1.4 cents (see table above). That mistuning ratios by an interval of somewhat less than 2 cents does not make an insensible difference in simultaneous soundings is easily demonstrated on the Chromelodeon—thanks to Helmholtz, who shows how to find the "skhisma," of 1.954 cents,[43] which is virtually identical with the difference between 3/2 and the tempered "fifth" (1.955 cents). Eight 3/2's

---

[43]*Sensations of Tone*, 280, 316.

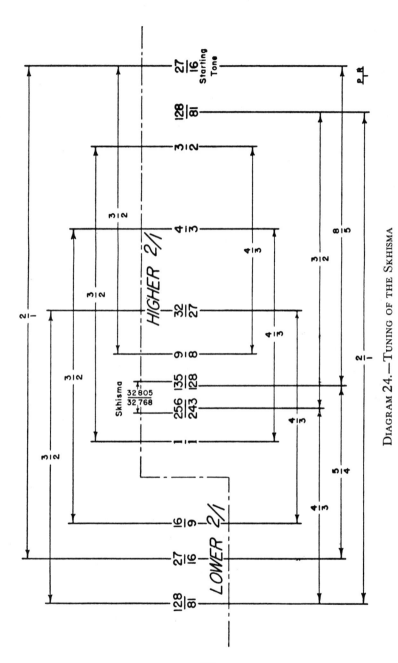

DIAGRAM 24.—TUNING OF THE SKHISMA

downward from a given tone will produce a tone lower than 5/4 above five 2/1's below the given tone by the interval 32805/32768. A convenient ratio to start from on the Chromelodeon is 27/16; the first part of the procedure is expressed: $27/16 \times (2/3)^8 = 16/243$, which, transposed up four 2/1's, is 256/243. For convenience we then use the 2/1 below the original 27/16 to which to add a 5/4: $27/32 \times 5/4 = 135/128$. Then, 135/128 is to 256/243 as 32805 is to 32768—1.954 cents.

The Chromelodeon already has a succession of six 3/2's downward from 27/16 (see page 167), and if we take a 3/2 down to 9/8, a 4/3 up to 3/2, a 3/2 down to 1/1, a 4/3 up to 4/3, a 3/2 down to 8/9 (16/9), a 4/3 up to 32/27, a 3/2 down to 64/81 (128/81), and a 4/3 up to 256/243, the procedure is the same—so far as tonal ingredients are concerned—as eight 3/2's downward, and the necessity of transposing the result up four 2/1's is avoided. The final procedure is to determine the 5/4 above the 27/16 a 2/1 below the starting 27/16. In making the experiment on the Chromelodeon it is only necessary to tune three extra reeds: 128/81 and 256/243 in the alternate 3/2–4/3 succession, and 135/128, which can of course be done perfectly by ear, since only the ratios 3/2, 4/3, and 5/4 are involved. A schema of these ratios (reading downward in pitch from *right* to *left*) is shown in Diagram 24.

If another reed is tuned to the 2/1 above 128/81 (first ratio at the left in the diagram), we will have four of the strongest consonances—3/2, 4/3, 5/4, and 8/5—to test in deliberate small mistunings: (1) the true 3/2 downward from 128/81 to 256/243, and the "3/2" downward from 128/81 to 135/128, which is diminished by 32805/32768, or 1.954 cents, making it virtually a tempered "fifth"; (2) the true 4/3 upward from 128/81 to 256/243, and the "4/3" upward from 128/81 to 135/128, which is augmented by the same 1.954 cents, making it virtually a tempered "fourth"; (3) a true 5/4 upward from 27/16 to 135/128 and a "5/4" upward from 27/16 to 256/243, which is diminished by 1.954 cents (the "5/4" in fifty-three-tone temperament is diminished 1.4 cents—see table above); (4) the true 8/5 downward from 27/16 to 135/128 and an "8/5" downward from 27/16 to 256/243, which is augmented by 1.954 cents (the "8/5" in fifty-three-tone temperament is augmented by 1.4 cents).

The number of beats created per second by these mistunings depends of course on the range of pitch chosen, but it can be determined comparatively by a simple example. Assuming that two reeds which make 600 and

801 cycles (about the second "D♯" to the second "G♯" above "middle C") are sounded together, approximately in the ratio 4/3 (800/600), beats numbering three per second would be produced, the third partial of 801 (2403) beating with the fourth partial of 600 (2400). The amount of mistuning (augmentation, as in Equal Temperament) is the ratio 801/800, or 2.1 cents.[44] In the same range of pitch, mistuning by 1.954 cents would of course produce beats slightly less frequent.

The point of this examination is that a *heard* 2-cents discrepancy is a sensible difference in simultaneous soundings. This immediately brings up a subject dear to the hearts of those who advocate tempered scales, that this sensible difference is something very valuable in music, that they like the continuous beating effect of the "consonances"; the "shimmering tone of massed violins not quite in unison" is a remark I happen to recall. The Monophonic fabric has many intervals some 3 or 4 cents removed from consonance, each of which is valued for its particular dissonance and type of beating, but the fact still remains that they do create beats and are dissonant, as is perceived once the nearest consonance is offered the ear as a comparison.

Somewhat the same effect as this dissonance is produced by the Vox Humana stop on some organs and harmoniums, two pipes or reeds not quite in unison being sounded for each key depressed. Unfortunately the Western world pulled out the Vox Humana stop on the organ at least three centuries ago, and the instrument has been Vox Humana-ing ever since. We have in effect installed a prop on it to insure that it will never be closed. This "shimmering tone" is no longer a device for contrast, to be used as the composer wishes, but a ubiquity, in which contrast is lost. It is something

[44]Relating this small interval to average pitch discrimination, Seashore's graph shows the line of "just noticeable differences" dipping onto or very close to the abscissa of "1/100ths of a tone" (*Psychology of Music*, 60)—that is, 2 cents. In the simultaneous sounding of two tones the resulting beats extend this perceptibility over a far greater range. Ellis corroborates this statement, saying that the falsity of 2 cents makes "a distinct difference in consonances" (*Journal of the Society of Arts*, 33:487). I made the test of a "skhisma" at a lecture at the University of Wisconsin, playing a "3/2" mistuned by this interval in a median register, and opening the Chromelodeon damper. The beats were apparent to all, about one and a half per second. As for perception of successive soundings of two tones separated by about two cents—which would theoretically imply the ability to hear some six hundred separate tones in the 2/1 chosen—I attach no great importance to it. Not only have I thus far been able to pick the higher and the lower of the two tones without difficulty when others tested me, but others too, whose ears were not experienced, generally distinguished between the tones correctly. The only point to be made is the one emphasized throughout this book—that the ability of the human ear is vastly underestimated.

that the composer inevitably gets. And he would continue to get it in fifty-three-tone temperament—although in slower, more "vibrato-like" pattern —as anyone who has had experience in tuning reeds knows.

## Fifty-Three-Tone Keyboards

At least three keyboard instruments have been constructed for fifty-three-tone equal temperament. In 1640 Nicolaus Ramarinus produced a keyboard on which the "tone" (9/8) was divided into nine "commas," according to Hawkins.[45] The fifty-third part of 2/1 is approximately the width of the "comma" of Didymus, 81/80 (21.5 cents; see table above), and since six 9/8's are larger than a 2/1 by approximately this interval (the "comma" of Pythagoras, 23.5 cents), this procedure would result in a fifty-three-tone scale.

R.H.M. Bosanquet's Generalized Fingerboard on his Enharmonic Organ (see the illustration facing page 392) is the most interesting of the present fifty-three-tone adaptations, because it seems eminently practicable.[46] Here is another theory for the composer of the future to investigate, along with Yasser's proposal. As an added advantage, it already has a practical instrument as a springboard, which Yasser's scale does not have.

Another harmonium in this temperament bears the name plate, "Harmon No. 3, Jas. Paul White, Inventor & Maker, 1883." Still another, with more than fifty degrees to the 2/1 (probably based on the fifty-three "cycle"), is the Eitz Harmonium, which was in the Hochschule für Musik in Berlin before the war.

White's harmonium is now in the New England Conservatory of Music in Boston. I examined it there in 1943 and found the tones of its very impractical keyboard[47] to conform fairly well to fifty-three-tone temperament; so far as I could learn, it had not been tuned in many years. Although it represents one of the historic intonational ideas actually brought to life, it stands isolated in a practice room, ignored by both faculty and students. It will one day be "discovered," no doubt, along with King Fang. A few decades ago, in this country at least, the history of music began with Bach. As time went on Purcell, Palestrina, and Monteverdi were "dis-

[45]*History of the Science and Practice of Music*, 1:396.
[46]See the keyboard diagram in Helmholtz, *Sensations of Tone*, 429.
[47]See *ibid.*, 482, for an indication of its form by number arrangement. Also see Tipple and Frye, *Introduction to the Harmon*, for a history and analysis of this instrument.

covered," and today there is even examination of plain-song and the music of the Gregorian and Ambrosian periods. Farther than that we have not gone.

But the trend can give us faith that eventually our processes of education will encompass the earlier divinations—the monochord of Pythagoras and Euclid, the kithara of Terpander, the auloi of Olympos, and the bamboo pipes of Ling Lun. True, these are sometimes mentioned in music histories, but for all practical purposes are never comprehended by students, since all questions of musical theory arise from, and are solved on, the piano keyboard.

# CHAPTER EIGHTEEN

# Just Intonations

## Colin Brown's "Polyphonic" Demonstration

ALTHOUGH it gained no usage among musicians, Colin Brown's Voice Harmonium (see the illustration facing page 392) was successful as a solution of the problem of just tuning on a keyboard instrument, so far as it went. It was designed to provide perfect intonation for music based on a 5 limit, and since the implication of 7 is difficult to escape, even in music of the classic period, this very elementary limit is the harmonium's weakness— a weakness, however, that is susceptible of correction.

The Voice Harmonium's cleverly devised "polyphonic" Just Intonation is predicated on a series of unities, or fundamentals, in a Pythagorean succession of fourteen 3/2's from 1024/729 below 1/1 to 6561/4096 above 1/1 (each expressed within its 2/1 here), arranged on the keyboard in diagonal series of degrees, each degree being separated from the succeeding diagonal degree by a 9/8.[1]

At this point the Pythagoreanism of the plan ends. The diagonals of fundamentals are given white keys, which are alternated with diagonal series of shorter black keys, each three-fourths as long as the white. "The arrangement of the keyboard is highly ingenious," writes Ellis. "Observing that in the major scale there are four notes [tones] in the column of Fifths, and three in the column of Thirds, it became evident that each note [tone] of the first would last during four successive modulations into the dominant, whereas each of the latter would last only through three modulations. Hence the digitals containing the former were made four parts long, and those containing the latter three parts long."[2]

In each black key is a red peg, making diagonal series of pegs within the blacks. The ingenuity of the plan and the Just Intonation which is possible

---

[1]Brown, *Music in Common Things*, 39.
[2]Ellis in Helmholtz, *Sensations of Tone*, 472; quoted by permission of Longmans, Green and Company, Ltd.

on the basis of each fundamental, or "keynote," lie in the relation of the whites to pegs and whites to blacks and pegs to blacks,[3] which may be deduced from Diagrams 27 and 28. The plan involves more than forty degrees to the 2/1, but since it is not conceived as a Monophonic system, there is no particular point in showing it in its entirety in Monophonic ratios. Brown does not use ratios in his analyses, but since his hypothesis and his subsequent procedure are both obvious, his plan is presented in ratios in order to relate it to previous material.

## The Result on Brown's Harmonium

The result of the keyboard plan is a perfect Ptolemaic Sequence on every white key, and a series of inherent triads, Otonality and Utonality, in perfect tune (see Diagram 25). Fingering is exactly the same in every Ptolemaic

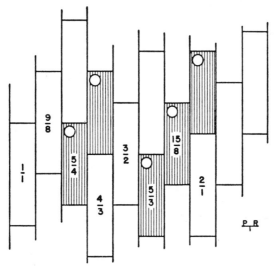

DIAGRAM 25.—A SECTION OF THE KEYBOARD OF
COLIN BROWN'S VOICE HARMONIUM

Sequence (each key of a diagonal row is on a separate plane, the planes ascending as the tones ascend in pitch), the player using one or two keys in five series of diagonals.

All the "minor" tonalities related to the scale above also have scales in perfect intonation, and in every one of the three types—"natural," "melod-

[3]Brown, *Music in Common Things*, 39, 40, 41.

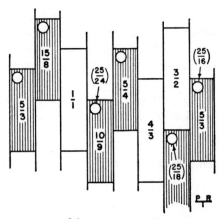

DIAGRAM 26.—ANOTHER SECTION OF
THE KEYBOARD OF BROWN'S HARMONIUM

ic," and "harmonic." These types, upward from 5/3 ("relative minor"),
are shown in Diagram 26. The second tetrachord in the "natural":

$$5/4 \qquad 4/3 \quad 3/2 \qquad 5/3$$
$$16/15 \quad 9/8 \quad 10/9$$

in the "melodic":

$$5/4 \qquad 25/18 \quad 25/16 \qquad 5/3$$
$$10/9 \qquad 9/8 \qquad 16/15$$

and in the "harmonic":

$$5/4 \qquad 4/3 \qquad 25/16 \qquad 5/3$$
$$16/15 \quad 75/64 \qquad 16/15$$

It is not possible to have the true 6/5 (and consequently a true "minor"
scale) above each white key, which Brown considers as a fundamental for
"major," but it is quite possible to build perfect Ptolemaic Sequences in
"major" starting on twelve of the black keys; this is accomplished by using
the "melodic minor" above, substituting the red peg 25/24 for 1/1, for instance. Consequently, although only fifteen Otonalities and the same number of Utonalities were originally stipulated, the harmonium actually has
twenty-seven Otonalities.[4] All Pythagorean heptatonic scales are possible,
but they are not easy to play and in any case are interesting only historically
and comparatively.

A computation of the number of cents in each of Brown's harmonium
tones reveals that several pairs of tones are separated by the skhisma,

[4]*Ibid.*, 43.

1.954 cents (see previous chapter); the black key 135/128, for example, is higher than the red peg 256/243 by the skhisma. The deliberate use of the key 1.954 cents flat in a consonance such as 6/5, which requires the higher tone, causes an immediate and serious deterioration in the consonance, and a very perceptible beating.

The number of keys in the 2/1, on the edge of the harmonium facing the player, is the same as on the piano; that is, the octave keyboard distance is the same, and encompasses eight keys, which is an advantage because familiar.[5] Three of these harmoniums were built by Brown, and I had the good fortune to examine one of them at the home of a relative of his near London. It was delightfully easy to play, besides presenting an intriguing intonational arrangement, altogether a gracious experience in absolute and relative consonance.

Here is a third idea which future composers might profitably investigate (those previously recommended for study and development being Yasser's "supra-diatonic" nineteen-tone temperament and Bosanquet's fifty-three-tone Enharmonic Organ). It would be interesting to see how susceptible of expansion Brown's idea might be—that is, to a "polyphonic" just system capable of the Identities of 7 also, and perhaps even of the 11's and 13's. Some thirty years before Brown, Henry Ward Poole, working in Boston, produced a cardboard model of a keyboard that anticipated Brown's, in which he provided for the 7 Identities. Neither of these experimenters had knowledge of the other's work.[6]

## *Perrett Finds 7 through Olympos*

The intonational system that Wilfrid Perrett uses on his evolved-keyboard harmonium, which he calls the Olympion, is a "polyphonic" Just Intonation with a 9 limit, although Perrett does not explain it in these terms. It results from disparate conjectures regarding the famous auloi player Olympos in ancient Greece, the phenomenon of difference tones, and the Greek notation; however tenuous this hypothesis may appear in so brief a summation, when it leads to a just system with identities intact through 9 its remote inspiration is of small importance.

The designer of the Olympion is a plain-spoken retriever of basic values, denying the necessity of an unbroken chain of "perfect fifths" and rejecting

---

[5]See the plan of the keyboard in Brown, *op. cit.*, 38, and Helmholtz, *op. cit.*, 471.
[6]*Ibid.*, 474–479. See also Tipple and Frye, *Introduction to the Harmon*, 9–13.

atonality as a course for the future. As for twelve-tone temperament, the composer has no choice, declares Perrett, but to modulate into "other keys no better than the first, seeking rest and finding none, all his twelve keys being equally imperfect . . . and with the natural dissonances and the natural consonances compromised into the same dead level of uniformity everywhere." Replying to the oft-heard observation that only the hyper-sensitive ear can take offense at temperament, he retorts: "The art of the musician who is not hypersensitive is not a fine art, *voila-tout*."

A twelve-year search, "consisting almost entirely of interruptions," for the key to the enharmonic, ended in the following conclusion: Olympos (*c.* 660–620 B.C.), the father of the enharmonic, according to Plutarch, had perhaps discovered the beauty of the ratios of 7 by sounding the auloi (double pipes) in the ratio 7/5; he may thus have heard the primary difference tone 2 (7–5) and the secondary difference tones 3 (5–2) and 4 (7–3) and 1 (5–4). Among these tones he found the quadrad 2:3:5:7, or, in Monophonic ratios, 1/1–3/2–5/2–7/2 (the four identities represented being 1–3–5–7).

In at least partial substantiation Perrett writes that by holding a tuning fork of 256 cycles, "C," to his ear, and singing a falsetto "F♯," he produced clear difference tones of 2 (102.4 cycles) and 3 (153.6 cycles), showing that his "F♯" was to "C" as 7 is to 5.

Olympos, then, might have built a new Dorian scale having exactly the same sequence of intervals as in the old Dorian—the Greek "national mode"—and "enharmonically" related to the old Dorian by the ratios of 7. This is a partial echo of Tartini's thesis that the move into the ratios of 7 invoked the ancient genus enharmonic. But Perrett, unlike Tartini, uses the idea as the germ of an intonational system, being led into the project at least partly from a desire for a new chromatic scale, one which would not only replace the dissonant 45/32 with the consonant 7/5, but include other intervals of 7. This led naturally enough to the conjecture regarding the circumstances of the birth of the enharmonic in Olympos' ear.[7]

## *Perrett's Systemic Procedure*

Perrett proceeds to do just this, getting a fourteen-degree scale, in the ratios given below, deduced from his "Tablature." Here, to achieve ratios of smaller numbers, "C" rather than "E" is represented by 1/1. Perrett,

[7]Perrett, *Some Questions of Musical Theory*, especially pp. 2, 25, 29, 90.

like Brown, uses variations of alphabetical nomenclature to represent his ratios, but since he consistently gives the number of cents in his intervals, the ratios are easily deducible. The old Dorian (descending):

| Perrett's symbols | E | | D | | C | | B | | A | | G | | F | | E |
|---|---|---|---|---|---|---|---|---|---|---|---|---|---|---|
| Old Dorian | 5/4 | | 9/8 | | 1/1 | | 15/8 | | 5/3 | | 3/2 | | 4/3 | | 5/4 |
| | | 10/9 | | 9/8 | | 16/15 | | 9/8 | | 10/9 | | 9/8 | | 16/15 | |

The new Dorian is a duplicate of the old a 21/20 above; thus all but one degree of the new scale is in a 7/5 ratio to some degree of the old; for example, 5/4 upward to 7/4 is the relationship 7/5. The new Dorian (descending):

| Perrett's symbols | $^7$F | | $^7$E♭ | | $^7$D♭ | | $^7$C | | $^7$B♭ | | $^7$A♭ | | $^7$G♭ | | $^7$F |
|---|---|---|---|---|---|---|---|---|---|---|---|---|---|---|
| New Dorian | 21/16 | | 7/6 | | 21/20 | | 63/32 | | 7/4 | | 63/40 | | 7/5 | | 21/16 |
| | | 9/8 | | 10/9 | | 16/15 | | 9/8 | | 10/9 | | 9/8 | | 16/15 | |

In developing his scale Perrett adds five more degrees to the fourteen given above, apparently to make maximal use of his keyboard (see below), and achieves the following nineteen-degree sequence:

| Perrett's symbols | C | | $^7$D♭ | | $^7$D | | D | | $^7$E♭ | | E♭ |
|---|---|---|---|---|---|---|---|---|---|---|---|
| Cents | 0 | | 84.5 | | 155.2 | | 203.9 | | 266.9 | | 315.6 |
| Degrees | 1/1 | | 21/20 | | 35/32 | | 9/8 | | 7/6 | | 6/5 |
| | | 21/20 | | 25/24 | | 36/35 | | 28/27 | | 36/35 | | 25/24 |

| Perrett's symbols | E | | $^7$F | | F | | $^7$G♭ | | $^7$G | | G |
|---|---|---|---|---|---|---|---|---|---|---|---|
| Cents | 386.3 | | 470.8 | | 498.0 | | 582.5 | | 653.0 | | 702.0 |
| Degrees | 5/4 | | 21/16 | | 4/3 | | 7/5 | | 35/24 | | 3/2 |
| | | 21/20 | | 64/63 | | 21/20 | | 25/24 | | 36/35 | | 21/20 |

| Perrett's symbols | $^7$A♭ | | A♭ | | A | | $^7$B♭ | | B♭ | | B |
|---|---|---|---|---|---|---|---|---|---|---|---|
| Cents | 786.4 | | 813.7 | | 884.4 | | 968.8 | | 1017.6 | | 1088.3 |
| Degrees | 63/40 | | 8/5 | | 5/3 | | 7/4 | | 9/5 | | 15/8 |
| | | 64/63 | | 25/24 | | 21/20 | | 36/35 | | 25/24 | | 21/20 |

| Perrett's symbols | $^7$C | | C |
|---|---|---|---|
| Cents | 1172.7 | | 1200 |
| Degrees | 63/32 | | 2/1 |
| | | 64/63 | |

This sequence is presented by Perrett not as a Monophonic system but as a development of the ancient Dorian in an enharmonic sense, which sense he regards as necessarily involving the 7 Identity. For a true appreciation of Perrett's deductions and for sheer literary enjoyment *Some Questions of Musical Theory* should be examined.

With respect to tonality potential the scale given above shows the following: three Otonalities complete through the 9 Odentity (on 1/1, 4/3, 8/5); two other Otonalities complete through the 7 Odentity (on 6/5 and 3/2), and four other Otonalities complete through the 5 Odentity, that is, "major" triads (on 21/20, 7/6, 7/5, 7/4); two Utonalities complete through the 9 Udentity (downward from 21/16 and 63/32); two other Utonalities complete through the 7 Udentity (downward from 35/32 and 7/4), and five other Utonalities complete through the 5 Udentity, that is, "minor" triads (downward from 1/1, 9/8, 5/4, 3/2, 15/8). Possible 6:7:8 triads, for example, 1/1–7/6–4/3, are pointed out by the author, also possible 6:7:9 triads, for example, 1/1–7/6–3/2, both of which he claims to be consonant. These triads are included in the tables which were given to show variety in the quality of tonality (Chapter 8) and occur in nearly all of Monophony's twenty-eight tonalities.

Like Helmholtz (the cracks in whose theoretical armor he delights to spotlight), Perrett eschews the "downward thinking" concept, yet in timidly or tacitly accepting Serre's decision that the ear "finds pleasure" in hearing the "inverse order" of intervals in the "minor" triad, Perrett,[8] like Rameau and a good many others, has already taken the first fatal step downward, the path of reversion. *Facilis descensus Averni*—and the fact of "Averni" is, in this case, not nearly as "infernal" as the anticipation! Preoccupation with the upward manifestation of overtones has too long misled theorists into rigid conceptions of the "natural."

## *The Olympion*

The Olympion keyboard is a plain evolution of the 7-White–5-Black, having two levels of "black" keys; the second of these levels, colored brown, is immediately to the right of, and higher and more recessed than, the first level of blacks; in addition, there is a black key between "E" and "F" and between "B" and "C," making the total of nineteen keys. I have also seen

[8]*Ibid.*, 12–13, 86, 95, 96.

and played this instrument, at the kind invitation of its originator; the remarks made anent Brown's harmonium apply here also, with the added interest of a true 7 Identity.

Perrett's ideas offer the fourth stimulus to the adventurous composer, in positing the 7 and 9 ratios for every tonality (the three previously recommended are Yasser's, Bosanquet's, and Brown's). In a sense he has continued the refining process begun long ago by Archytas—the recognition of small-number ratios and their substitution for the large-number and dissonant ratios of Pythagorean and tempered systems. The Perrett ideas might be combined with a development of the Brown keyboard, or, as Perrett himself has desired, with the Bosanquet keyboard.

## *Kathleen Schlesinger Hazards 13*

In halting at the 9 Identity Perrett calls the next logical step, the number 11, "this distressing string."[9] Kathleen Schlesinger, on the other hand, in long and sedulous work in the field of Just Intonation, has exceeded the 11 limit and has appropriated all the ratios of 13 in her deductions concerning the ancient Greek harmoniai, or modes, in the diatonic genus.

Schlesinger's thesis is Monophonic from every standpoint, even though each harmonia is based on a different Arithmetical Proportion, because *Mese*, the tonal pole of a melody to the Greeks, is always one of the Otonality identities on 1/1, from 1 to 13. For a real appreciation of the breadth of Schlesinger's deductions *The Greek Aulos* itself should of course be studied. For our purpose here, the seven Arithmetical Proportions, to which she ascribes the genesis of the seven ancient harmoniai,[10] will be referred to the familiar monochord, or harmonic canon, rather than to the more complex aulos, which she considers the instrumental agent, or law, of the Greek musical development.

For the seven harmoniai, seven harmonic canon strings are divided successively into fourteen, thirteen, twelve, eleven, ten, nine, and eight equal parts. Since we are interested in determining the scale for one 2/1, only half

---

[9]*Ibid.*, 76. Perrett refers to the "isolated undecimal interval" of the "trumpet eleventh"— 11/8.

[10]Ogden speaks constantly of the "law of equal intervals," as though the surds of temperament satisfied a hunger in the human animal and were not merely an expedient to overcome the handicap that the human animal developed no more than ten fingers. *Hearing*, 151, 157, 158, and *passim*. The Schlesinger thesis, that the equally spaced holes on the aulos satisfied a visual desire and, providentially, also satisfied an aural desire in the just ratios of the Arithmetical Proportions, puts the matter of human desires on an entirely different and more credible plane.

the string will be used in each case, and six of the Arithmetical Proportions will theoretically be doubled—thirteen, for example, will become twenty-six—to make certain scale degrees available. As the plan emerges this doubling does not in any case involve prime numbers above 13, at least in the diatonic genus.

The Mixolydian harmonia, based on the division of the string into fourteen equal parts, requires no doubling; the scale is made up of the first seven marks from the nut, counting the open string, which is 14/14 or, in Monophony's ratio usage, 1/1, the eighth mark (counting the nut) being exactly the halfway point, 2/1, or, as seven parts to fourteen parts, 7/14. The Lydian harmonia uses the first seven marks of the division into thirteen equal parts (counting the nut, 1/1, or 13/13), but the eighth mark calls for the division into twenty-six parts, 6½/13, or 13/26, or, in Monophonic usage, 2/1. The Phrygian uses the first six marks of the division into twelve equal parts (counting the nut, 1/1, or 12/12), the seventh mark calling for the doubling into twenty-four parts, or 13/24, or, in Monophonic usage, 24/13. The Arithmetical Proportions of the string by the seven divisions are shown in Diagram 27,[11] with Schlesinger's ratios above and the Monophonic interpretation below the representation of each string.

There is of course no acoustic difference between the Schlesinger ratios, which better reveal the Arithmetical Proportion genesis of each scale, and the Monophonic interpretation, which better reveals the Schlesinger scales in relation to the scales, tonalities, and concepts presented previously. In this volume all interval relationships not otherwise qualified are impliedly expressed in terms of vibrations—the upper number of each ratio representing the higher tone and the under number the lower tone—rather than in parts of a sounding body, the Schlesinger usage.

## Incidence of Her Ratios in the Monophonic Fabric

By arranging all the ratios given in the diagram above in their order of pitch we find that they number forty. Nearly every ratio in this scale has its complement in the corresponding position in the other half of the scale (7/5–10/7 as the center). There are three exceptions: 14/9, 7/4, and 16/15, the complements of which are 9/7, 8/7, and 15/8. If these ratios are included, the result is a forty-three-degree scale (expressed below in Monophonic ratios) which contains all the ratios of a 13 limit, and in addition the multiple-number ratios 16/15 and 15/8. The symbols over each scale

[11] *The Greek Aulos*, 7–29.

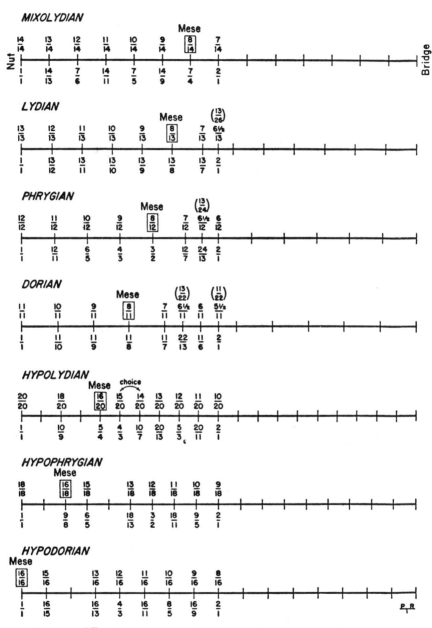

DIAGRAM 27.—THE ANCIENT HARMONIAI ACCORDING TO SCHLESINGER

degree signify the harmonia in which it appears and what degree it represents; for instance, "D-2" means that this ratio—11/10—is the second degree (ascending) in the Dorian harmonia. (M = Mixolydian; L = Lydian; P = Phrygian; D = Dorian; HL = Hypolydian; HP = Hypophrygian; HD = Hypodorian)

| | All harmonia-1 | HD-2 | M-2 | L-2 | P-2 | |
|---|---|---|---|---|---|---|
| Cents...... | 0 | 111.7 | 128.3 | 138.6 | 150.6 | |
| Degrees..... | 1/1 | 16/15 | 14/13 | 13/12 | 12/11 | |
| | 16/15 | 105/104 | 169/168 | 144/143 | 121/120 | |
| Cents........ | 111.7 | 16.6 | 10.3 | 12.0 | 14.4 | |

| | D-2 | HL-2 | HP-2 | | M-3 | L-3 |
|---|---|---|---|---|---|---|
| Cents...... | 165.0 | 182.4 | 203.9 | 231.2 | 266.9 | 289.2 |
| Degrees..... | 11/10 | 10/9 | 9/8 | 8/7 | 7/6 | 13/11 |
| | 100/99 | 81/80 | 64/63 | 49/48 | 78/77 | 66/65 |
| Cents........ | 17.4 | 21.5 | 27.3 | 35.7 | 22.3 | 26.4 |

| | P-3<br>HP-3 | D-3 | HD-3 | HL-3 | M-4 | |
|---|---|---|---|---|---|---|
| Cents...... | 315.6 | 347.4 | 359.5 | 386.3 | 417.5 | 435.1 |
| Degrees..... | 6/5 | 11/9 | 16/13 | 5/4 | 14/11 | 9/7 |
| | 55/54 | 144/143 | 65/64 | 56/55 | 99/98 | 91/90 |
| Cents........ | 31.8 | 12.0 | 26.8 | 31.2 | 17.6 | 19.1 |

| | P-4<br>HL-4<br>L-4 | HD-4 | D-4 | HP-4 | M-5 | |
|---|---|---|---|---|---|---|
| Cents...... | 454.2 | 498.0 | 551.3 | 563.4 | 582.5 | |
| Degrees..... | 13/10 | 4/3 | 11/8 | 18/13 | 7/5 | |
| | 40/39 | 33/32 | 144/143 | 91/90 | 50/49 | |
| Cents........ | 43.8 | 53.2 | 12.0 | 19.1 | 35.0 | |

| | HL-4 | L-5 | HD-5 | P-5<br>HP-5 | HL-5 | M-6 |
|---|---|---|---|---|---|---|
| Cents...... | 617.5 | 636.6 | 648.7 | 702.0 | 745.8 | 764.9 |
| Degrees..... | 10/7 | 13/9 | 16/11 | 3/2 | 20/13 | 14/9 |
| | 91/90 | 144/143 | 33/32 | 40/39 | 91/90 | 99/98 |
| Cents........ | 19.1 | 12.0 | 53.2 | 43.8 | 19.1 | 17.6 |

| | D-5 | HD-6 | L-6 | HP-6 | HL-6 | |
|---|---|---|---|---|---|---|
| Cents...... | 782.5 | 813.7 | 840.5 | 852.6 | 884.4 | |
| Degrees..... | 11/7 | 8/5 | 13/8 | 18/11 | 5/3 | |
| | 56/55 | 65/64 | 144/143 | 55/54 | 66/65 | |
| | 31.2 | 26.8 | 12.0 | 31.8 | 26.4 | |

|  | D–6 | P–6 | M–7 | HD–7 | HP–7 | HL–7 |
|---|---|---|---|---|---|---|
| Cents | 910.8 | 933.1 | 968.8 | 996.1 | 1017.6 | 1035.0 |
| Degrees | 22/13 | 12/7 | 7/4 | 16/9 | 9/5 | 20/11 |
|  | 78/77 | 49/48 | 64/63 | 81/80 | 100/99 | 121/120 |
| Cents | 22.3 | 35.7 | 27.3 | 21.5 | 17.4 | 14.4 |

|  | D–7 | P–7 | L–7 |  | All har-monia–8 |
|---|---|---|---|---|---|
| Cents | 1049.4 | 1061.4 | 1071.7 | 1088.3 | 1200 |
| Degrees | 11/6 | 24/13 | 13/7 | 15/8 | 2/1 |
|  | 144/143 | 169/168 | 105/104 | 16/15 |  |
| Cents | 12.0 | 10.3 | 16.6 | 111.7 |  |

Two "HL-4" symbols appear, indicating a choice of ratios for the fourth degree in the Hypolydian. Although numbering forty-three degrees on a 13-limit basis, this scale does not include secondary ratios, aside from 16/15 and 15/8. Fourteen of such secondary ratios, with the twenty-nine ratios of the 11 limit, make the forty-three-degree total of the Monophonic fabric (see Chapter 8). Inclusion of secondary, or multiple-number, ratios on the 13 basis would bring the number of degrees to fifty or sixty to the 2/1, if the method of Chapters 7 and 8 were followed. However, instruments designed for the forty-three-tone 11-limit scale could fairly easily be adapted to the forty-three-tone 13-limit source scale of Schlesinger's ancient harmoniai; for instance, the Chromelodeon would require only twelve extra reeds in each 2/1 (for the ratios of 13).

## Schlesinger on "Undertones"

Schlesinger poses an especially interesting question regarding the alleged reinforcement of *Mese* in one of its higher 2/1's when any of the aforementioned Arithmetical Proportions is played on the aulos. If true, this would redound indirectly to the enhancement of the long-debated "undertone series" as a legitimate acoustical phenomenon (see Riemann, page 264). She gives a diagram of the form of the air space inside the aulos, with fingerholes spaced at equal distances (the Arithmetical Proportion), and observes: "The indentations represent the centers of the covered fingerholes in the interior of the aulos, and denote the position and nature of the stimulus provided, with the effect that the column of air is induced to vibrate in segments in response to the breath of the piper propelled through the mouthpiece and the resonator."[12]

[12]*Ibid.*, 99; quoted by permission of Methuen and Company, Ltd.

On a monochord divided into fourteen equal parts (Mixolydian) the part nearest the bridge would give the tone three 2/1's above *Mese*, the unity of the "undertone series" produced by stopping the string at each successive mark from the bridge down (see Diagram 27).

Considering the ratios at each mark as parts of a string length from *right* to *left* they are: one part to fourteen parts, two to fourteen, three to fourteen, and so on. Schlesinger is suggesting that, since the fingers of the piper do not fill each aulos hole like a plug, the air is forced to vibrate in segments by the edges of the series of holes. The pitch of the subsidiary vibrations—those of the equal segments—is fixed, then, by the first segment from the bridge (or mouthpiece), 1/14 in the example above. Consequently, regardless of what tone is played on the aulos, the tone of this first segment (the unity, three 2/1's above *Mese*) is continually being reinforced.

In the example, assume that the open string makes 100 cycles; by touching it at the 1/14 node we get a tone of 1400 cycles. Now place the movable bridge at 13/14, and touch the string at the same point, which is now 1/13 of the string length from bridge to movable bridge, and the tone is still 1400 cycles. This is fairly parallel to what happens in playing the aulos, since uncovering the first hole (13/14) has the effect of shortening the sounding body 1/14, and the edges of the equally spaced holes are the agent which cause the nodes to operate—that is, to divide the vibrating air body into segments. Thus, according to Schlesinger's deductions, whatever the degree of the "undertone series" played on an aulos of a given number of equal parts, it is continually reinforcing its unity, or *Mese*. Those who might assert that—even if these conclusions are substantiated—this is an artificial situation in the aulos will be reminded that the tensing of a string over two bridges for the purpose of touching nodes and thereby demonstrating partials is another artificial situation.

## On the Enharmonic; on the Ethos

The Schlesinger analysis applied to the chromatic and enharmonic genera involves increases in the various Arithmetical Proportions by the factor of 2, and, like Eratosthenes' chromatic and enharmonic (see Chapter 10), produces very large prime numbers. Whether such ratios as 52/51, involving the prime number 51, deduced from an equal division into fifty-two equal parts for the Lydian enharmonic ($2 \times 2 \times$ Lydian diatonic's 13), and Eratosthenes' 40/39 for his enharmonic tetrachord, on a basis of forty equal parts,[13] can possess even a fractional part of the strength of their small-number fellows in the descending series seems doubtful. Multiple-number ratios of approximately the same magnitudes are more versatile, since they increase tonality resources, and for the purposes of the enharmonic genus they are the ratios of smallest numbers compatible with the musical purpose.

The *ethos* of each harmonia, so much discussed by the ancients, is determined through the identity of the partial in the overtone series which fixes the particular arithmetical division; the fourteenth partial, for example, determines the division into fourteen parts and also the *ethos* of the Mixolydian, according to Schlesinger.[14] This would be true regardless of overtone association; any system based upon equal divisions of strings tuned in unison, of any numbers of parts, would inevitably produce from the single part nearest the bridge one of the odd-number Odentities of the open string. If the strings are 1/1, the part nearest the bridge in the Mixolydian is 1/14 of the whole, or the point which represents 7/4 (expressed as a Monophonic symbol) in the fourth 2/1 above the open string, the 7 Odentity of 1/1 Otonality; in the Lydian the corresponding part is 1/13 of the whole, or 13/8 (in the fourth 2/1 above the open string), the 13 Odentity of 1/1 Otonality, and so on.

## Resources of Schlesinger's Tonalities

Compared with the Monophonic tonality schema Schlesinger's Arithmetical Proportions are simply the Utonalities through a 13 limit. The complete Otonalities and Utonalities inherent in her plan, if complements 8/7 and 9/7 are added for the ratios 7/4 and 14/9, would number fourteen, seven of each, without invoking what Monophony calls the secondary ratios, and each would be complete through its 13 Identity, with a septad basis of tonality: 1–3–5–7–9–11–13. These are easily seen in a Tonality Diamond with a 13 limit (Diagram 28). As before, Otonalities are shown between solid lines, and Utonalities between dotted lines.

The 7/4 Utonality, used as an example, has the Numerary Nexus 7 over the Identities 1(4), 9, 5, 11, 3(6), 13, and 7, in the order given, all expressed within a 2/1. Compare this with the Mixolydian scale shown above, which is in exactly the same order. The other harmoniai, in the Tonality Diamond through the 13 limit, all begin on the *Mese* of the Schlesinger scales (the first

[13]*Ibid.*, 214.    [14]*Ibid.*, 7.

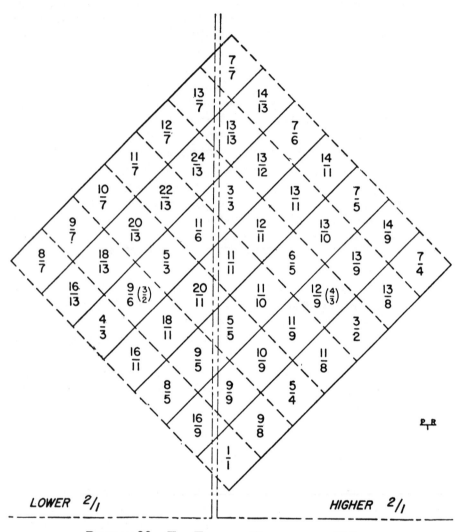

DIAGRAM 28.—THE TONALITY DIAMOND ON A 13 LIMIT

454

row of ratios between solid lines on the right), rather than on 1/1, as Schlesinger shows them. The ratios 8/7 and 9/7, in the diamond, are absent from Diagram 27; consequently the scales of the diamond in which they occur do not exactly correspond.

One Otonality will be traced: in 8/5 Otonality the upper 8 indicates the unity, or 1 Odentity, of an Otonality, and the Odentities 9, 5, 11, 3(6), 13, and 7 follow in that order (expressed within a 2/1), over the Numerary Nexus 5.

Schlesinger exploits to the full the Utonalities inherent in her ratios, but mentions only one Otonality, the source of which she gives as the overtone series on "F," each overtone within the determined limit being a *Mese*, thus fixing the scale's *ethos* (see below). Compare this idea with the Monophonic Tonality Diamond; the Odentities on 1/1 are unities of Utonalities (or Arithmetical Proportions), but the Udentities on 1/1 are also unities, of Otonalities (or Harmonical Proportions), both Otonalities and Utonalities being implicit in the odd numbers (actual or achieved by the divisor 2) of ratios (see Chapter 5).

In the Greek sense the *ethos* centered around *Mese*,[15] and the highness or lowness of the *tessitura* (the range in which the music hovers) was consequently definitely linked to the harmonia—a high *tessitura* in the Mixolydian, since *Mese* is high, and a low *tessitura* in the Hypodorian, corresponding to a low *Mese*. This is also true to some extent in the Monophonic system, since each tonality—Otonality or Utonality—has its own distinctive character, arising always from its ratio to 1/1, and because each unity is a precise related pitch.

## Schlesinger as Empirical Theorist

To Schlesinger as a historian the presupposition of her schema as the actual theoretical system of the ancient harmonists is very important. To a composer weighing possibilities for the future her historical antecedents, whether substantiated or not, are of minor importance. The marked similarity of the Schlesinger and Monophonic theories, the one born of a historian's digging in the ancient past for relics, and the other from a composer's digging in today's back yard for musical resources at about the same time, is a striking coincidence, although the manner of pre:entation and the values implied are sometimes about as divergent as could be imagined.

[15]*Ibid*. 135.

Schlesinger is nothing if not an empirical theorist. At my one brief interview with her in London in 1935 I saw several kitharas[16] (Monophony's Kithara was inspired by them) built after the lines of kitharas depicted on ancient vases, a piano tuned modally, and historic or facsimile flutes and auloi beyond my power to appreciate immediately. Needless to say, all her theories have been and are being demonstrated.

## *The Consciousness of Capacity*

Schlesinger's, then, is the sixth of the intonational systems recommended as a possibility for investigation and development, the five previously examined being my own (expounded in Parts II and III), Yasser's, Bosanquet's, Brown's, and Perrett's. Music is a *physical* art; it is not a mathematical abstraction, and I shall risk another repetition of the assertion that an investigation which is not physical is all but wasted, to the individual himself and to the culture of which he is a part.

This brief presentation of comparative intonations may suggest that the world is exceeding rich in tonal plans and resources, and so it is. Yet the ordinary citizen would never know it. In our familiar world the single plan that is current acquires the force of censorship, nipping the individualistic approach in the bud long before it can become operative as a creative force; it not only envelops us but seeps into and supplants what we call the exotic (note Fox-Strangways' jeremiad, Chapter 11). And, as if this were not bad enough, it has reached the stage of deterioration that all cultural forms do when they devote the burden of their practice to the minutiae of "interpretation."

With this "censorship" as the fundamentally determining factor to the builders of musical instruments, the publishers of music, the record companies, the bands and symphony orchestras, and the concert system, "interpretation" is virtually the only margin of esthetic "value" left, and what we have in the twelve-tone tempered scale is actually a High Czar for Musical Economics, protecting all the aforesaid investments. If one of the substantial instrument or record companies were to follow the example of electronics, chemistry, and telephony concerns and make an investment in musical research looking toward the evolution of a system, or systems, and instruments really capable of utilizing historic materials and of expansion

[16]A photograph of one of the Schlesinger kitharas, reproduced from the lines of a vase of about 500 B.C., is shown in the *Oxford History of Music*, Introductory Volume, opposite page 95.

in the future, music as an art might become imbued with the spirit of curiosity and investigation which characterizes our sciences.

A composer who wants the system that was used to such admirable advantage by Bach, Beethoven, *et al.* should most certainly have it—though the handicap of a vehicle which has become only a fashion-horse for "interpretive" *décor* is even greater than the economic handicap of the pioneer —but he should also have freedom of choice. Each expression would then reach its own niche in the reactions of the human mind, and in that niche would find its own particular appreciation and possible posterity.

If nearly two decades of presenting a work far off the beaten path has demonstrated nothing else, it has shown me that human responses are unpredictable; one does not need the testimony of history to realize that they are perpetually kinetic. But where advance reputation does not operate, where responses spring from an intrinsic hunger, they are likely to be pretty dependable, and—obviously—a very real hunger for stimulation and beauty exists, in isolated individuals everywhere.

One of the comforting features of life in this world is that whatever a man has to offer he will somewhere and sometime find a hunger that will be satisfied by his offering—if he lives long enough. But even if he doesn't, the means of recording his testimony and demonstration in behalf of a new liberality are still available—manuscripts and records; he then has the satisfaction of having endeavored to exert some small influence. Now and then one meets an individual with so intense a desire for knowledge of the tonal verities and the whole breadth of their philosophic connotations as to bring one round to the belief that the ills of music are not quite irremediable. And whether he is a "representative" individual is not particularly pertinent—the fact that he is a human animal is enough.

*Appendices*

# Cents Values of Intervals

### Including the 340 Intervals Narrower than a 2/1
### Found in the Monophonic Fabric

| Interval | Cents | Interval | Cents | Interval | Cents |
|---|---|---|---|---|---|
| 1/1 | 0 | 35/33 | 101.9 | 729/640 | 225.4 |
| 32805/32768 | 1.954 | 297/280 | 102.0 | 8/7 | 231.2 |
| 169/168 | 10.3 | 17/16 | 105.0 | 63/55 | 235.1 |
| 144/143 | 12.0 | 1701/1600 | 106.0 | 55/48 | 235.7 |
| 121/120 | 14.4 | 1089/1024 | 106.6 | 147/128 | 239.6 |
| 105/104 | 16.6 | 16/15 | 111.7 | 1024/891 | 240.9 |
| 100/99 | 17.4 | 2187/2048 | 113.7 | 280/243 | 245.4 |
| 99/98 | 17.6 | 77/72 | 116.2 | 231/200 | 249.5 |
| 91/90 | 19.1 | 15/14 | 119.4 | 140/121 | 252.5 |
| 81/80 | 21.5 | 189/176 | 123.4 | 81/70 | 252.7 |
| 78/77 | 22.3 | 14/13 | 128.3 | 297/256 | 257.2 |
| 531441/524288 | 23.5 | 320/297 | 129.1 | 512/441 | 258.4 |
| 74/73 | 23.6 | 27/25 | 133.2 | 64/55 | 262.4 |
| 66/65 | 26.4 | 121/112 | 133.8 | 220/189 | 263.0 |
| 65/64 | 26.8 | 693/640 | 137.7 | 7/6 | 266.9 |
| 64/63 | 27.3 | 13/12 | 138.6 | 90/77 | 270.1 |
| 56/55 | 31.2 | 243/224 | 141.0 | 2560/2187 | 272.6 |
| 55/54 | 31.8 | 88/81 | 143.5 | 75/64 | 274.6 |
| 50/49 | 35.0 | 160/147 | 146.7 | 88/75 | 276.7 |
| 49/48 | 35.7 | 49/45 | 147.4 | 33/28 | 284.4 |
| 45/44 | 38.9 | 12/11 | 150.6 | 189/160 | 288.4 |
| 6561/6400 | 43.0 | 35/32 | 155.2 | 13/11 | 289.2 |
| 40/39 | 43.8 | 800/729 | 160.9 | 32/27 | 294.1 |
| 36/35 | 48.7 | 11/10 | 165.0 | 44/37 | 300.0 |
| 33/32 | 53.2 | 54/49 | 168.2 | 144/121 | 301.2 |
| 512/495 | 58.4 | 441/400 | 168.9 | 25/21 | 301.8 |
| 648/625 | 62.6 | 243/220 | 172.2 | 105/88 | 305.8 |
| 28/27 | 63.0 | 567/512 | 176.6 | 176/147 | 311.7 |
| 80/77 | 66.2 | 256/231 | 177.9 | 6/5 | 315.6 |
| 126/121 | 70.1 | 65536/59049 | 180.4 | 19683/16384 | 317.6 |
| 25/24 | 70.7 | 10/9 | 182.4 | 77/64 | 320.1 |
| 2673/2560 | 74.8 | 49/44 | 186.4 | 135/112 | 323.3 |
| 22/21 | 80.5 | 891/800 | 186.5 | 880/729 | 325.9 |
| 21/20 | 84.5 | 28/25 | 196.2 | 98/81 | 329.8 |
| 81/77 | 88.3 | 121/108 | 196.8 | 121/100 | 330.0 |
| 256/243 | 90.2 | 55/49 | 200.0 | 40/33 | 333.0 |
| 135/128 | 92.2 | 9/8 | 203.9 | 243/200 | 337.2 |
| 128/121 | 97.3 | 640/567 | 209.7 | 128/105 | 342.9 |
| 200/189 | 97.9 | 112/99 | 213.6 | 11/9 | 347.4 |
| 18/17 | 99.0 | 363/320 | 218.3 | 60/49 | 350.6 |
| 196/185 | 100.0 | 25/22 | 221.3 | 49/40 | 351.4 |
| 89/84 | 100.1 | 256/225 | 223.5 | 27/22 | 354.5 |

| Interval | Cents | Interval | Cents | Interval | Cents |
|----------|-------|----------|-------|----------|-------|
| 315/256 | 359.0 | 200/147 | 533.0 | 180/121 | 687.6 |
| 16/13 | 359.5 | 49/36 | 533.8 | 112/75 | 694.3 |
| 448/363 | 364.2 | 15/11 | 537.0 | 121/81 | 694.8 |
| 100/81 | 364.8 | 2187/1600 | 541.0 | 220/147 | 698.0 |
| 121/98 | 365.0 | 48/35 | 547.0 | 433/289 | 700.0 |
| 99/80 | 368.9 | 11/8 | 551.3 | 3/2 | 701.955 |
| 56/45 | 378.6 | 441/320 | 555.2 | | (702.0) |
| 96/77 | 381.8 | 243/176 | 558.5 | 2560/1701 | 707.7 |
| 8192/6561 | 384.4 | 112/81 | 561.0 | 448/297 | 711.6 |
| 5/4 | 386.3 | 18/13 | 563.4 | 121/80 | 716.3 |
| 1120/891 | 396.0 | 320/231 | 564.2 | 50/33 | 719.4 |
| 44/35 | 396.2 | 168/121 | 568.1 | 243/160 | 723.5 |
| 63/50 | 400.1 | 25/18 | 568.7 | 32/21 | 729.2 |
| 121/96 | 400.7 | 891/640 | 572.8 | 84/55 | 733.2 |
| 512/405 | 405.9 | 88/63 | 578.6 | 55/36 | 733.7 |
| 81/64 | 407.8 | 7/5 | 582.5 | 49/32 | 737.7 |
| 80/63 | 413.6 | 108/77 | 585.7 | 135/88 | 740.9 |
| 14/11 | 417.5 | 1024/729 | 588.3 | 1120/729 | 743.4 |
| 32/25 | 427.4 | 45/32 | 590.2 | 20/13 | 745.8 |
| 77/60 | 431.9 | 512/363 | 595.4 | 77/50 | 747.5 |
| 9/7 | 435.1 | 800/567 | 596.0 | 54/35 | 750.7 |
| 567/440 | 439.0 | 140/99 | 599.9 | 99/64 | 755.2 |
| 165/128 | 439.6 | 99/70 | 600.1 | 256/165 | 760.4 |
| 128/99 | 444.8 | 567/400 | 604.0 | 880/567 | 761.0 |
| 35/27 | 449.3 | 363/256 | 604.6 | 14/9 | 764.9 |
| 100/77 | 452.5 | 64/45 | 609.8 | 120/77 | 768.1 |
| 13/10 | 454.2 | 729/512 | 611.7 | 25/16 | 772.6 |
| 729/560 | 456.6 | 77/54 | 614.3 | 11/7 | 782.5 |
| 176/135 | 459.1 | 10/7 | 617.5 | 63/40 | 786.4 |
| 64/49 | 462.3 | 63/44 | 621.4 | 128/81 | 792.2 |
| 72/55 | 466.3 | 1280/891 | 627.2 | 405/256 | 794.1 |
| 55/42 | 466.8 | 36/25 | 631.3 | 192/121 | 799.3 |
| 21/16 | 470.8 | 121/84 | 631.9 | 100/63 | 799.9 |
| 320/243 | 476.5 | 231/160 | 635.8 | 35/22 | 803.8 |
| 33/25 | 480.6 | 13/9 | 636.6 | 891/560 | 804.0 |
| 160/121 | 483.7 | 81/56 | 639.0 | 8/5 | 813.7 |
| 297/224 | 488.4 | 352/243 | 641.5 | 6561/4096 | 815.6 |
| 1701/1280 | 492.3 | 640/441 | 644.8 | 77/48 | 818.2 |
| 4/3 | 498.0 | 16/11 | 648.7 | 45/28 | 821.4 |
| 578/433 | 500.0 | 35/24 | 653.0 | 160/99 | 831.1 |
| 147/110 | 502.0 | 3200/2187 | 659.0 | 196/121 | 835.0 |
| 162/121 | 505.2 | 22/15 | 663.0 | 81/50 | 835.2 |
| 75/56 | 505.7 | 72/49 | 666.2 | 363/224 | 835.8 |
| 121/90 | 512.4 | 147/100 | 667.0 | 13/8 | 840.5 |
| 400/297 | 515.4 | 81/55 | 670.2 | 512/315 | 841.0 |
| 66/49 | 515.6 | 165/112 | 670.8 | 44/27 | 845.5 |
| 27/20 | 519.5 | 189/128 | 674.7 | 80/49 | 848.6 |
| 177147/131072 | 521.5 | 1024/693 | 676.0 | 49/30 | 849.4 |
| 693/512 | 524.0 | 262144/177147 | 678.5 | 18/11 | 852.6 |
| 256/189 | 525.3 | 40/27 | 680.5 | 105/64 | 857.1 |
| 224/165 | 529.2 | 49/35 | 684.4 | 400/243 | 862.8 |
| 110/81 | 529.8 | 297/200 | 684.6 | 33/20 | 867.0 |

| Interval | Cents | Interval | Cents | Interval | Cents |
|---|---|---|---|---|---|
| 200/121 | 870.0 | 16/9 | 996.1 | 189/100 | 1102.1 |
| 81/49 | 870.2 | 98/55 | 1000.0 | 121/64 | 1102.7 |
| 729/440 | 874.1 | 216/121 | 1003.2 | 256/135 | 1107.8 |
| 224/135 | 876.7 | 25/14 | 1003.8 | 243/128 | 1109.8 |
| 128/77 | 879.9 | 1600/891 | 1013.5 | 154/81 | 1111.7 |
| 32768/19683 | 882.4 | 88/49 | 1013.6 | 40/21 | 1115.5 |
| 5/3 | 884.4 | 9/5 | 1017.6 | 21/11 | 1119.5 |
| 147/88 | 888.3 | 59049/32768 | 1019.6 | 5120/2673 | 1125.2 |
| 176/105 | 894.2 | 231/128 | 1022.1 | 48/25 | 1129.3 |
| 42/25 | 898.2 | 1024/567 | 1023.4 | 121/63 | 1129.9 |
| 121/72 | 898.8 | 440/243 | 1027.8 | 77/40 | 1133.8 |
| 37/22 | 900.0 | 800/441 | 1031.1 | 27/14 | 1137.0 |
| 27/16 | 905.9 | 49/27 | 1031.8 | 625/324 | 1137.4 |
| 22/13 | 910.8 | 20/11 | 1035.0 | 495/256 | 1141.6 |
| 320/189 | 911.6 | 729/400 | 1039.1 | 64/33 | 1146.8 |
| 56/33 | 915.6 | 64/35 | 1044.8 | 35/18 | 1151.3 |
| 75/44 | 923.3 | 11/6 | 1049.4 | 39/20 | 1156.2 |
| 128/75 | 925.4 | 90/49 | 1052.6 | 12800/6561 | 1157.0 |
| 2187/1280 | 927.4 | 147/80 | 1053.3 | 88/45 | 1161.1 |
| 77/45 | 929.9 | 81/44 | 1056.5 | 96/49 | 1164.3 |
| 12/7 | 933.1 | 448/243 | 1059.0 | 49/25 | 1165.0 |
| 189/110 | 937.0 | 24/13 | 1061.4 | 108/55 | 1168.2 |
| 55/32 | 937.6 | 1280/693 | 1062.3 | 55/28 | 1168.8 |
| 441/256 | 941.6 | 224/121 | 1066.2 | 63/32 | 1172.7 |
| 512/297 | 942.8 | 50/27 | 1066.8 | 128/65 | 1173.2 |
| 140/81 | 947.3 | 297/160 | 1070.9 | 65/33 | 1173.6 |
| 121/70 | 947.5 | 13/7 | 1071.7 | 73/37 | 1176.4 |
| 400/231 | 950.5 | 352/189 | 1076.6 | 1048576/531441 | 1176.5 |
| 243/140 | 954.6 | 28/15 | 1080.6 | 77/39 | 1177.7 |
| 891/512 | 959.1 | 144/77 | 1083.8 | 160/81 | 1178.5 |
| 256/147 | 960.4 | 4096/2187 | 1086.3 | 180/91 | 1180.9 |
| 96/55 | 964.3 | 15/8 | 1088.3 | 196/99 | 1182.4 |
| 110/63 | 964.9 | 2048/1089 | 1093.4 | 99/50 | 1182.6 |
| 7/4 | 968.8 | 3200/1701 | 1094.0 | 208/105 | 1183.4 |
| 1280/729 | 974.6 | 32/17 | 1095.0 | 240/121 | 1185.6 |
| 225/128 | 976.5 | 560/297 | 1098.0 | 143/72 | 1188.0 |
| 44/25 | 978.7 | 66/35 | 1098.1 | 336/169 | 1189.7 |
| 640/363 | 981.7 | 168/89 | 1099.9 | 65536/32805 | 1198.046 |
| 99/56 | 986.4 | 185/98 | 1100.0 | 2/1 | 1200 |
| 567/320 | 991.3 | 17/9 | 1101.0 | | |

# Tonality Relationships and Common Tones

In Table 1 on the next page Otonalities are indicated by the letter *O* and Utonalities by *U*. For the benefit of music students it should be explained that the names of degrees for "minor" are the reverse of "major," and all relationships for "minor" are downward; that is, the "dominant" of "minor" is found five scale "steps" below the "tonic," and the "subdominant" is found four scale "steps" below. Also, the "dominants" and "subdominants" of Otonalities are Otonalities, and the "mediants" and "relatives" of Otonalities are Utonalities; the "dominants" and "subdominants" of Utonalities are Utonalities, and the "mediants" and "relatives" of Utonalities are Otonalities. The relationships given in Table 1 are confined to those involving the smallest numbers.

In Table 2 the Monophonic tonalities are listed according to the place of their 1–5–3 triads (upward for Otonality and downward for Utonality) in the 2/1. The lowest tones of these triads are the 1 Odentities of Otonalities and the 3 Udentities of Utonalities. The 3 Udentities, ordinarily considered the "tonic" degree in "minor," are shown in parentheses, and the 1 Udentities, which Monophony considers the true unities in Utonality, are shown on the same lines, without parentheses.

In the chart on pages 338 and 339 the unities of the Monophonic tonalities are given at right and left, and the forty-three Monophonic ratios horizontally at top and bottom. Converging points show the identity of each ratio in a tonality, and the number of senses in which a ratio may be taken is simply the total number of identities in its vertical column.

TABLE I

| Tonalities | Their 3/2 Tonalities ("Dominant") | Their 4/3 Tonalities ("Subdominant") | Their 5/4 Tonalities ("Relative") | Their 15/8 Tonalities ("Mediant") |
|---|---|---|---|---|
| 1. 1/1–O | 3/2–O | 4/3–O | 5/4–U | 15/8–U |
| 2. 1/1–U | 4/3–U | 3/2–U | 8/5–O | 16/15–O |
| 3. 16/15–O | 8/5–O | . . . . . | 4/3–U | 1/1–U |
| 4. 10/9–U | 40/27–U | 5/3–U | 16/9–O | 32/27–O |
| 5. 9/8–U | 3/2–U | 27/16–U | 9/5–O | 6/5–O |
| 6. 8/7–O | . . . . . | 32/21–O | 10/7–U | . . . . . |
| 7. 32/27–O | 16/9–O | . . . . . | 40/27–U | 10/9–U |
| 8. 6/5–O | 9/5–O | 8/5–O | 3/2–U | 9/8–U |
| 9. 5/4–U | 5/3–U | 15/8–U | 1/1–O | 4/3–O |
| 10. 21/16–U | 7/4–U | . . . . . | . . . . . | 7/5–O |
| 11. 4/3–O | 1/1–O | 16/9–O | 5/3–U | 5/4–U |
| 12. 4/3–U | . . . . . | 1/1–U | 16/15–O | . . . . . |
| 13. 27/20–O | . . . . . | 9/5–O | . . . . . | . . . . . |
| 14. 11/8–U | . . . . . | . . . . . | . . . . . | . . . . . |
| 15. 7/5–O | . . . . . | . . . . . | 7/4–U | 21/16–U |
| 16. 10/7–U | . . . . . | . . . . . | 8/7–O | 32/21–O |
| 17. 16/11–O | . . . . . | . . . . . | . . . . . | . . . . . |
| 18. 40/27–U | . . . . . | 10/9–U | . . . . . | . . . . . |
| 19. 3/2–O | . . . . . | 1/1–O | 15/8–U | . . . . . |
| 20. 3/2–U | 1/1–U | 9/8–U | 6/5–O | 8/5–O |
| 21. 32/21–O | 8/7–O | . . . . . | . . . . . | 10/7–U |
| 22. 8/5–O | 6/5–O | 16/15–O | 1/1–U | 3/2–U |
| 23. 5/3–U | 10/9–U | 5/4–U | 4/3–O | 16/9–O |
| 24. 27/16–U | 9/8–U | . . . . . | 27/20–O | 9/5–O |
| 25. 7/4–U | . . . . . | 21/16–U | 7/5–O | . . . . . |
| 26. 16/9–O | 4/3–O | 32/27–O | 10/9–U | 5/3–U |
| 27. 9/5–O | 27/20–O | 6/5–O | 9/8–U | 27/16–U |
| 28. 15/8–U | 5/4–U | . . . . . | 3/2–O | 1/1–O |

TABLE 2

| | | | |
|---|---|---|---|
| 1. 1/1–O | 8. 32/27–O | 15. 16/11–O | 22. (7/4)21/16–U |
| 2. (1/1)3/2–U | 9. 6/5–O | 16. (40/27)10/9–U | 23. 16/9–O |
| 3. 16/15–O | 10. (5/4)15/8–U | 17. 3/2–O | 24. (16/9)4/3–U |
| 4. (10/9)5/3–U | 11. 4/3–O | 18. (3/2)9/8–U | 25. 9/5–O |
| 5. (9/8)27/16–U | 12. (4/3)1/1–U | 19. 32/21–O | 26. (11/6)11/8–U |
| 6. 8/7–O | 13. 27/20–O | 20. 8/5–O | 27. (40/21)10/7–U |
| 7. (7/6)7/4–U | 14. 7/5–O | 21. (5/3)5/4–U | 28. (160/81)40/27–**U** |

# Chart of

| | 10/7 | 16/11 | 40/27 | 3/2 | 32/21 | 14/9 | 11/7 | 8/5 | 18/11 | 5/3 | 27/16 | 12/7 | 7/4 | 16/9 | 9/5 | 20/11 | 11/6 | 15/8 | 40/21 | 64/33 | 160/81 | 1/1 |
|---|---|---|---|---|---|---|---|---|---|---|---|---|---|---|---|---|---|---|---|---|---|---|
| 1/1-O | | | | 3 | | | | | | | | | 7 | | | | | | | | | 1 |
| 1/1-U | | 11 | | | | | | 5 | | | | | | 9 | | | | | | | | 1 |
| 16/15-O | | | | | | | | 3 | | | | | | | | | | | | | | |
| 10/9-U | | | 3 | | | | | | | | | | | | 5 | | | | | 9 | | |
| 9/8-U | | | | 3 | | | | | 11 | | | | | | | 5 | | | | | | 9 |
| 8/7-O | 5 | | | | | | 11 | | | | | 3 | | | | | | | | | | 7 |
| 32/27-O | | 5 | | | | | | | | | | | | 3 | | | | | | | | |
| 6/5-O | | | | 5 | | | | | | | | | | | 3 | | | | | | | |
| 5/4-U | 7 | | | | | | | | 3 | | | | | | | 11 | | | | | | 5 |
| 21/16-U | | | 7 | | | | | | | | 3 | | | | | | | | | | | 3 |
| 4/3-O | | | 9 | | | | | | 5 | | | | | | | | 11 | | | | | 3 |
| 4/3-U | | | | 7 | | | | | | | | | | 3 | | | | | | | 11 | |
| 27/20-O | | | | | | | | | | 5 | | | | | | | | | | | | 11 |
| 11/8-U | | | | | | 7 | | | | | | | | | | | 3 | | | | | 11 |
| 7/5-O | | | | | | | | | | | | 5 | | | | | | | | | | |
| 10/7-U | 1 | | | | | | | | | | | | | | | 3 | | | | | | |
| 16/11-O | | 1 | | | | | | | 9 | | | | | | | 5 | | | | | | 11 |
| 40/27-U | | | 1 | | | | | | | | | | | | | | | | | | 3 | |
| 3/2-O | | | | 1 | | | | | | 9 | | | | | | | | 5 | | | | |
| 3/2-U | | | | 1 | | | | | | | | 7 | | | | | | | | | | 3 |
| 32/21-O | | | | | 1 | | | | | | | 9 | | | | | | 5 | | | | 5 |
| 8/5-O | | | | | | | | 1 | | | | | | | 9 | | | | | | | 5 |
| 5/3-U | | 9 | | | | | | | | 1 | | | | | | | | 7 | | | | |
| 27/16-U | | | 9 | | | | | | | | 1 | | | | | | | | | | | |
| 7/4-U | | | | | 9 | | | | | | | | 1 | | | | | | | | | 7 |
| 16/9-O | | | | | 7 | | | | | | | | | 1 | | | | | | | | 9 |
| 9/5-O | | | | | | | | | | | | | | | 1 | | | | | | | |
| 15/8-U | | | 5 | | | | | | | 9 | | | | | | | | 1 | | | | |
| | 10/7 | 16/11 | 40/27 | 3/2 | 32/21 | 14/9 | 11/7 | 8/5 | 18/11 | 5/3 | 27/16 | 12/7 | 7/4 | 16/9 | 9/5 | 20/11 | 11/6 | 15/8 | 40/21 | 64/33 | 160/81 | 1/1 |

# Common Tones

| 81/80 | 33/32 | 21/20 | 16/15 | 12/11 | 11/10 | 10/9 | 9/8 | 8/7 | 7/6 | 32/27 | 6/5 | 11/9 | 5/4 | 14/11 | 9/7 | 21/16 | 4/3 | 27/20 | 11/8 | 7/5 | |
|---|---|---|---|---|---|---|---|---|---|---|---|---|---|---|---|---|---|---|---|---|---|
|  |  |  |  |  |  |  | 9 |  |  |  | 5 |  |  |  |  |  |  |  | 11 |  | 1/1-O |
|  |  |  |  |  |  |  |  | 7 |  |  |  |  |  |  |  | 3 |  |  |  |  | 1/1-U |
|  |  |  | 1 |  |  |  |  |  |  | 9 |  |  |  |  |  | 5 |  |  |  |  | 16/15-O |
|  |  |  |  |  |  | 1 |  |  |  |  |  |  |  |  |  |  |  |  |  |  | 10/9-U |
|  |  |  |  | 1 |  |  |  |  |  |  |  |  |  |  | 7 |  |  |  |  |  | 9/8-U |
|  |  |  |  |  |  | 1 |  |  |  |  |  |  |  |  | 9 |  |  |  |  |  | 8/7-O |
|  |  |  |  |  |  |  |  | 1 |  |  |  |  |  |  |  | 9 |  |  |  |  | 32/27-O |
|  | 7 |  |  |  |  |  |  |  |  | 1 |  |  |  |  |  |  | 9 |  |  |  | 6/5-O |
|  |  |  |  |  |  |  | 9 |  |  |  | 1 |  | 1 |  |  |  |  |  |  |  | 5/4-U |
|  | 5 |  |  |  |  |  |  |  | 9 |  |  |  |  |  |  | 1 |  |  |  |  | 21/16-U |
|  |  |  |  |  |  |  |  |  | 7 |  |  |  |  |  |  |  | 1 |  |  |  | 4/3-O |
|  |  | 5 |  |  |  |  |  |  |  | 9 |  |  |  |  |  |  | 1 |  |  |  | 4/3-U |
| 3 |  |  |  |  |  |  |  |  |  |  |  |  |  |  |  |  |  | 1 |  |  | 27/20-O |
|  | 3 |  |  |  | 5 |  |  |  |  |  | 9 |  |  |  |  |  |  |  | 1 |  | 11/8-U |
|  |  |  |  |  |  |  | 5 |  |  |  |  |  |  |  |  |  |  |  |  | 1 | 7/5-O |
|  |  |  |  |  |  |  |  |  |  |  |  |  |  |  |  |  |  |  |  |  | 10/7-U |
|  |  |  | 3 |  |  |  | 5 |  |  |  |  |  |  | 7 |  |  |  |  |  |  | 16/11-O |
|  |  |  |  |  |  |  |  | 5 |  |  |  |  |  |  | 7 |  |  |  |  |  | 40/27-U |
|  | 11 |  |  |  |  |  | 3 |  |  |  |  |  |  |  |  |  |  |  |  |  | 3/2-O |
|  |  | 11 |  |  |  |  |  |  |  |  | 5 |  |  |  |  |  | 9 |  |  |  | 3/2-U |
|  |  |  |  |  |  |  | 3 |  |  |  |  |  |  |  |  | 7 |  |  |  |  | 32/21-O |
|  |  |  |  |  | 11 |  |  | 3 |  |  | 3 |  |  |  |  |  |  |  |  | 7 | 8/5-O |
|  |  |  |  |  |  |  |  | 3 |  |  |  |  |  |  |  | 5 |  |  |  |  | 5/3-U |
|  |  |  |  |  |  |  |  |  |  |  |  |  |  |  |  |  | 5 |  |  |  | 27/16-U |
|  |  |  |  |  |  |  |  | 3 |  |  |  |  |  | 11 |  |  |  |  |  | 5 | 7/4-U |
|  |  |  |  |  | 5 |  |  |  |  |  |  | 11 |  |  |  | 3 |  |  |  |  | 16/9-O |
| 9 |  |  |  |  |  |  | 5 |  |  |  |  |  |  |  |  |  | 3 |  |  |  | 9/5-O |
|  |  |  |  |  |  |  |  |  |  |  |  | 3 |  |  |  |  |  |  |  |  | 15/8-U |

| 81/80 | 33/32 | 21/20 | 16/15 | 12/11 | 11/10 | 10/9 | 9/8 | 8/7 | 7/6 | 32/27 | 6/5 | 11/9 | 5/4 | 14/11 | 9/7 | 21/16 | 4/3 | 27/20 | 11/8 | 7/5 |

# Music — Theater Works — Major Performances

*Seventeen Lyrics by Li Po*[1] (1930–1933) [2]

For Adapted Viola and Intoning Voice

*Two Psalms* (1931)

*The Lord is My Shepherd* (No. 23; based on the spoken inflections of a cantor)

*By the Rivers of Babylon* (No. 137)

Both for Adapted Viola and Intoning Voice; *Babylon* was rewritten in 1941 with Chromelodeon and Kithara added.

*The Potion Scene* (from Shakespeare's *Romeo and Juliet*) (1931)

Originally Adapted Viola and Voice. Rewritten in 1955 with Chromelodeon, Kithara, Bass Marimba, Marimba Eroica, and two high female voices (heard toward the end) added.

*Some of these early works were performed for the first time for the New Music Society, San Francisco, on February 9, 1932. They were also performed for many small groups and clubs in and around San Francisco, Los Angeles, and New York between 1932 and 1934.*

*The Wayward* (1941–1943)

1. *Barstow—Eight Hitchhiker Inscriptions from a Highway Railing at Barstow, California* (1941)

---

[1]**From** Shigeyoshi Obata, *The Works of Li Po, the Chinese Poet* (E. P. Dutton and Company, New York, 1922) .

[2]**The** dates of composition are given in parentheses.

Originally Adapted Guitar I and Voice. Rewritten several times, last in 1954 with another Voice, Surrogate Kithara, Chromelodeon, Diamond Marimba, and Boo added.

2. *U. S. Highball—A Musical Account of a Transcontinental Hobo Trip* (1943)

See Chapter 14.

3. *San Francisco—A Setting of the Cries of Two Newsboys on a Foggy Night in the 'Twenties* (1943)

For two Baritone Voices, Adapted Viola, Kithara, Chromelodeon.

4. *The Letter—A Depression Message from a Hobo Friend* (1943)

For Intoning Voice, Kithara, Harmonic Canon, Surrogate Kithara, Diamond Marimba, Bass Marimba. The instrumentation of the recording (see Appendix V) is an earlier version, now lost.

*Yankee Doodle Fantasy* (1944)

For Soprano, Tin Flutes, Tin Oboe, Flex-a-tones, and Chromelodeon.

*The five pieces immediately above were performed for the League of Composers as* A Program of Compositions on Americana Texts, *in Carnegie Chamber Music Hall on April 22, 1944, and for Columbia University soon thereafter.*

*Dark Brother* (1942–1943)

A setting of two paragraphs from Thomas Wolfe's essay, *God's Lonely Man.*[3] For Intoning Voice, Chromelodeon, Adapted Viola, Kithara (Bass Marimba added later).

*Two Settings from Joyce's Finnegan's Wake*[4] (1944)

1. *Isobel*
2. *Annah the Allmaziful*

Both for Soprano, Kithara, and two Flutes.

[3]Thomas Wolfe, *The Hills Beyond* (Harper and Brothers, New York, 1935), 196–197.
[4]James Joyce, *Finnegan's Wake* (Viking Press, New York, 1939): "Isobel," 556; "Annah," 104.

*"I'm very happy to be able to tell you about this . . ."* (1945)

A setting of a broadcast transcription by glider pilot Warren Ward. Now lost. For Soprano, Baritone, Kithara, and Indian Drum.

> *Nearly all of the compositions above (excepting especially the Li Po settings) were performed in three programs at the University of Wisconsin, February 28, March 7, and May 3, 1945.*

*Two Studies on Ancient Greek Scales* (1946)

1. *Olympos' Pentatonic*
2. *Archytas' Enharmonic*

Both originally for Harmonic Canon; Bass Marimba added later.

*Eleven Intrusions*[5] (1949–1950)

Nos. 1 and 2 are the two Greek studies above.

| | |
|---|---|
| 3. *The Rose* | 8. *Lover* |
| 4. *The Crane* | 9. *Soldiers—War—Another War* |
| 5. *The Waterfall* | 10. *Vanity* |
| 6. *The Wind* | 11. *Cloud-Chamber Music* |
| 7. *The Street* | |

Together these studies used all of the instruments of that period (see Appendix VI).

*Ring Around the Moon* (1949–1950)

The middle section of *Plectra and Percussion Dances;* see Chapter 14.

*Oedipus—Dance-Drama* (1951; rewritten 1952–1954)

See Chapter 14.

---

[5]Nos. 3 and 5, and the first part of No. 6, are from Ella Young, *Marzilian and Other Poems* (Harbison & Harbison, Oceano, California, 1938), 24, 37, 61. The last half of No. 6 is a quotation from Lao-Tse. No. 4 is from Arthur Waley, *Japanese Poetry, the "Uta"* (Lund Humphries & Co., Ltd., London, 1946), 98; No. 7 from Willard Motley's novel *Knock on Any Door* (Appleton-Century-Crofts, Inc., New York, 1947), 504. No. 8, by George Leite, is from the magazine *Circle* (Berkeley, California), vol. 1, no. 3 (n.d.), p. 57; and Nos. 9 and 10, by Giuseppe Ungaretti (translated by William Fense Weaver), are from *Circle*, vol. 1, no. 10 (Summer 1948), pp. 25–27. No. 11 is instrumental and involves a Zuñi melody from New Mexico.

*Performed at Mills College, Oakland, California, March 14, 15, 16, 1952, using the W. B. Yeats version. Conductor: Marjorie Sweazey. Director: Arch Lauterer. Oedipus: Allan Louw. The rewritten version was performed on Shell Beach, Sausalito, September 11 and 12, 1954, in connection with the Sausalito Arts Fair. Conductor: Jack Hohensee. Oedipus: Allan Louw.*

*Castor and Pollux* (1952)
*Even Wild Horses* (1952)

The first and third sections of *Plectra and Percussion Dances;* see Chapter 14.

*The complete* Plectra and Percussion Dances *was first performed at the International House, Berkeley, on November 19, 1953, under the auspices of radio station KPFA. Three performances in the Sausalito studio followed soon afterward.*

*Two Settings from Lewis Carroll* (1954)[6]

1. *The Mock Turtle Song*

For Singing-Intoning Voice, Surrogate Kithara, Spoils of War.

2. *O Frabjous Day!* (The Jabberwock)

For Intoning Voice, Harmonic Canon, Bass Marimba.

O Frabjous Day! *was written for and included in a program of the Young People's Concert Series of the Mill Valley (California) Outdoor Art Club, February 13, 1954.*

*Ulysses at the Edge* (implicit: *of the World*) (1955)

Written for Alto Saxophone (E♭) or Trumpet (B♭), Baritone Saxophone (E♭), Diamond Marimba, Boo, Cloud-Chamber Bowls, and Rhythmic Voice at the end: "So you say that your name is Ulysses, that you're wandering around the world. Tell me, sir, have you ever been arrested before?" This became the fifth item in the collection entitled *The Wayward* (see above).

[6]No. 1 is from Lewis Carroll, *Alice's Adventures in Wonderland* (Modern Library, New York, 1946), 119; and No. 2 from Carroll, *Through the Looking Glass* (Modern Library, New York, 1946), 18.

*The Bewitched—A Dance Satire* (1955)

See Chapter 14.

> *First performed at the University of Illinois, March 26, 1957, and again the following day for Washington University, St. Louis. Conductor: John Garvey. The Witch: Freda Pierce. Choreographer: Alwyn Nikolais. Also performed for Columbia University, New York, April 10 and 11, 1959, and at the University of Illinois, April 24, 1959. Conductor: John Garvey. The Witch: Freda Pierce. Choreographer: Joyce Trisler.*

*Windsong* (1958)

The soundtrack for a film by Madeline Tourtelot (see Appendix V) based on the myth of Daphne and Apollo. Scored for most of the instruments in use at that time (see Appendix VI). Rewritten in 1967, without substantial change, as music for dance, retitled *Daphne of the Dunes,* and performed twice (see below).

*Revelation in the Courthouse Park—After* The Bacchae *of Euripides* (1960)

See Chapter 14.

> *Performed at the University of Illinois, April 11, 1961 (afternoon and evening performances). Conductor: John Garvey. Director: Barnard Hewitt. Choreographer: Jean Cutler. Set and costume designer: George Talbot.*

*Rotate the Body in All Its Planes* (1961)

Music for an exhibition of gymnasts. Scored for most of the instruments used in *Revelation.* A film was made of the exhibition (see Appendix V).

> *Performed at the Huff Gymnasium, University of Illinois, during the NCAA national gymnasts' meet, April 8, 1961.*

*Bless This Home* (1961)

Setting of an unpublished poem by Vincenzo Prockelo. For Intoning Voice, Oboe, Adapted Viola, Kithara, Harmonic Canon II, Mazda Marimba.

*Water! Water!—An Intermission with Prologues and Epilogues* (1961)

Commissioned by the Illini Union Student Activities, University of Illinois. This is a farce (although my preferred title was *Like Tears*), but it is not a finished work. The two or many more years really needed to ponder and develop such an idea were not available, nor was there time to evolve, through long rehearsals, the techniques of farce, which in some ways are infinitely more exacting than straight drama or tragedy. Only ten months elapsed between the beginning of composition and the performance.

*Performed March 9 and 10, 1962, at the University of Illinois, and March 17, 1962, at the Studebaker Theater, Chicago.*

*And on the Seventh Day Petals Fell in Petaluma* (1963–1966)

See Chapter 14.

*Performed at the University of California at Los Angeles, May 8, 1966. Also on the program were* Two Studies on Ancient Greek Scales *and* Castor and Pollux *(with dance, choreographed by Storie Crawford).*

*Delusion of the Fury—a Ritual of Dream and Delusion* (1965–1966)

See Chapter 14.

*Performed at the University of California at Los Angeles, January 9 through 12, 1969. Conductor: Danlee Mitchell. Choreographer: Storie Crawford. Set designer: John Crawford.*

*The Dreamer That Remains—A Study in Loving* (1972)

Part of the soundtrack for the film *The Dreamer That Remains: A Portrait of Harry Partch,* commissioned by the producer, Betty Freeman. Directed by Stephen Pouliot. Conducted by Jack Logan. Scored for Narrating/Intoning Voice, Chorus, and fifteen instruments, including the four built since 1971 (see Appendix VI).

\* \* \* \* \* \*

Four performances of mixed works during the 1960's are perhaps notable for either location or sponsorship. These are the following:

1. Demonstration program presented in connection with the Eighteenth National Convention of the American Symphony Orchestra League, Sheraton-Palace Hotel, San Francisco, June 20, 1963. Short excerpts from many works were performed.

2. August 29, 1965, at the Deepest Valley Theater, in the so-called Alabama Hills, near Lone Pine, California. The program included *U. S. Highball* and *Castor and Pollux*.

3. University of California at San Diego Art Gallery, May 11 and 12, 1968. Included in the program were *Two Studies on Ancient Greek Scales,* excerpts from *Petals, Daphne of the Dunes, Castor and Pollux,* and, from Act II of *Delusion,* Time of Fun Together (Judith Mullen, soloist), anticipating the performance of the complete work in Los Angeles. Conductor: Thomas Nee. Choreographer: Susan Long.

4. Whitney Museum of American Art, New York, September, 1968; a program in connection with the International Music Congress, consisting of excerpts from *Petals,* the *Two Studies on Ancient Greek Scales, Barstow, Castor and Pollux, Daphne of the Dunes,* and the Exordium from *Delusion,* again anticipating the Los Angeles performance. Conductor: Danlee Mitchell.

# Bibliography on Harry Partch

A. *Writings About Harry Partch's Work*

1. Selby Noel Mayfield. *New Orleans Times-Picayune,* November 16, 1930. Illus.

2. Alexander Fried. *San Francisco Chronicle,* February 10, 1932. Review.

3. Marjorie M. Fisher. *The San Francisco News,* February 10, 1932. Review.

4. Bertha McCord Knisely. *Saturday Night* (Los Angeles weekly), May 14, 1930; February 25, 1933; December 30, 1933.

5. Noel Heath-Taylor. "Artist in the Wilderness." *California Art & Architecture,* July, 1939. Illus.

6. Noel Heath-Taylor. "Monophony: Looking into the Future." *Pacific Coast Musician,* August 19, 1939.

7. Paul Bowles. *New York Herald Tribune,* April 23, 1944. Review of Americana program.

8. R. L. *The New York Times,* April 23, 1944. Review of Americana program.

9. Henry Simon. "A Theorist with a Heart." *PM* (New York), April 24, 1944.

10. "Kitharist." *The New Yorker,* May 27, 1944. pp. 21–22.

11. Ars Longa (Noel Heath-Taylor). "Some Observations on Speech Song." *Frontier* (Los Angeles), September 1, 1950.

12. R. H. Hagan. "The Mills College Production of 'King Oedipus.'" *This World (San Francisco Chronicle),* March 9, 1952. Illus.

13. Alfred Frankenstein. *San Francisco Chronicle,* March 16, 1952. Review of *Oedipus* performance.

14. Clifford Gessler. *Oakland Tribune,* March 17, 1952. Review of *Oedipus* performance.

15. Marjorie M. Fisher. *The San Francisco News,* March 17, 1952. Review of *Oedipus* performance.

16. Joseph Biskind. "Sophocles, Yeats, and Harry Partch." *The Argonaut* (San Francisco), March 21, 1952.

17. Jack Foisie. "Atomic-Age 'Oedipus.'" *New York Herald Tribune,* March 22, 1952. Illus.

18. "Goblin Music?" *Time,* March 24, 1952. Illus.

19. Margaret Schubart. "Bay Area Diary. Partched Sound." *Counterpoint,* April, 1952, p. 30.

20. Wilford Leach. "Music for Words Perhaps." *Theatre Arts,* vol. 37, no. 1 (January, 1953), p 65. Illus.

21. Peter Yates. *Arts & Architecture,* July, 1953, p. 33. Review of *Oedipus* tapes.

22. R. H. Hagan. *San Francisco Chronicle,* October 4, 1953. Review of *Dances* record. Illus.

23. Clifford Gessler. *Oakland Tribune,* October 11, 1953. Review of *Dances* record. Illus.

24. Harold Rogers. *The Christian Science Monitor,* December 1, 1953. Review of *Dances* record. Illus.

25. *Good Listening,* December, 1953, pp. 7, 30. Review of *Dances* record.

26. *High Fidelity,* March, 1954, p 65. Review of *Dances* record. Illus.

27. "Tonal Ingenuity." *Audio Engineering,* March, 1954. Review of *Dances* record.

28. *Etc: A Review of General Semantics,* Summer, 1954. Review of *Dances* record.

29. Alan Tory. "Unique Play, Unique Instrument." *Fortnight* (Los Angeles), October 6, 1954. Illus.

30. Harold Rogers. *The Christian Science Monitor,* October 19, 1954. Review of *Oedipus* records. Illus.

31. R. H. Hagan. *San Francisco Chronicle,* October 24, 1954. Review of *Oedipus* records.

32. Peter Yates. *Arts & Architecture,* December, 1954, p. 33. Review of *Oedipus* records.

33. Jacques Barzun. *Music in American Life.* Indiana University Press, Bloomington, 1955.

34. Oliver Daniel. "Harry Partch." *Music at Home,* January-February, 1955. Illus.

35. "The Music of Harry Partch." *The American Record Guide,* January, 1955, pp. 149–151. Review of *Oedipus* records.

36. Thomas B. Sherman. *St. Louis Post-Dispatch,* January 13, 1955. Review of *Oedipus* records.

37. Ray E. Ellsworth. "Americans on Microgroove." *High Fidelity,* August, 1956, pp. 63–64.

38. Charles Menees. *St. Louis Post-Dispatch,* March 28, 1957. Review of *The Bewitched* performance.

39. Francis A. Klein. *St. Louis Globe-Democrat,* March 28, 1957. Review of *The Bewitched* performance.

40. Wilson Krebs. *The Daily Illini* (University of Illinois), April 3, 1957. Editorial, under *Piano e Forte,* regarding the propriety of a choreographer changing totally the creator's concept.

41. "Tunes from Tumblers." *Newsweek,* April 8, 1957, p. 75. Illus.

42. Irving Sablosky. "Festival at Urbana." *The New York Times,* April 21, 1957, sec. 2, p. 11.

43. Irving Sablosky. "43 to the Octave." *The New York Times,* July 21, 1957, sec. 2, p. 7. Illus.

44. Scott Goldthwaite. "Urbana, Illinois." *Musical Quarterly,* July, 1957.

45. Harold Rogers. "Exotically Weird Music from Harry Partch." *The Christian Science Monitor,* July 6, 1957.

46. "World of Harry Partch." *The Dayton* (Ohio) *Daily News,* August 17, 1957. Editorial.

47. Peter Yates. "Schubert, Berg, Partch, Tremblay." *Arts & Architecture,* January, 1958.

48. Walter Terry and Jay S. Harrison. *New York Herald Tribune,* April 11, 1959. Reviews of *The Bewitched* performance.

49. John Martin. *The New York Times,* April 11, 1959. Review of *The Bewitched* performance.

50. Suzanne Block and Peggy Glanville-Hicks. "From the Mail Pouch: Pro Partch." *The New York Times,* April 26, 1959.

51. Robert Evett. *The New Republic,* May 25, 1959. Review of *The Bewitched* performance.

52. *Dance News,* May, 1959. Review of *The Bewitched* performance. Illus.

53. Robert Sabin. *Musical America,* June, 1959. Review of *The Bewitched* performance.

54. Walter Sorell. *Ballet Today,* June, 1959. Review of *The Bewitched* performance.

55. S. J. C. *Dance Magazine,* June 1959. Review of *The Bewitched* performance. Illus.

56. Peter Yates. Introductory Essay to *Some Twentieth Century American Composers.* The New York Public Library, New York, 1959. Illus.

57. Murray Schafer. "New Records." *Canadian Music Journal,* Winter, 1959, pp. 55–58. Review of *U.S. Highball* record.

58. Muriel Lederer. "Mathematics Makes a New Music." *Science and Mechanics,* December, 1960, pp. 74–77. Illus.

59. Joseph Machlis. *Introduction to Contemporary Music.* W. W. Norton & Co., New York, 1961, pp. 631–632.

60. J. David Bowen. "Music Between the Keys." *Hi Fi/Stereo Review,* February, 1961, pp. 50–53. Illus.

61. Lynn Ludlow. *Champaign-Urbana Courier,* April 10, 1961. Review of *Rotate the Body* performance.

62. Nicholas Temperley. "An Orgy of the Arts." *Champaign-Urbana Courier,* April 12, 1961. Review of *Revelation* performance.

63. David Ward-Steinman. *The Daily Illini* (University of Illinois), April 12, 1961. Review of *Revelation* performance.

64. Lynn Ludlow. *Champaign-Urbana Spectator,* April 17, 1961. Review of *Revelation* performance.

65. Peter Yates. "Revelation in Illinois." *Arts & Architecture,* August, 1961, p. 4. Review of *Revelation* performance.

66. Alfred Frankenstein. "Partch's Instruments." *San Francisco Chronicle,* June 22, 1963. Review of program for Symphony League. Illus.

67. Wilfrid Mellers. "An American Aboriginal." *Tempo: A Quarterly Review of Modern Music,* Spring, 1963, pp. 2–6.

68. "Harry Isn't Kidding." *Time,* July 5, 1963, p. 50. Illus.

69. Peter Yates. "Genesis of a Music." *High Fidelity,* July, 1963, pp. 35–38, 85. Illus.

70. Oscar Thompson, ed. *The International Cyclopedia of Music and Musicians.* 9th ed., Dodd, Mead & Co., New York, 1964. p. 1589.

71. Mary Fuller. "Harry Partch, Musician-Sculptor." *Art in America,* December, 1964, pp. 47–49.

72. John Tasker Howard. *Our American Music.* Thomas Y. Crowell, Co., New York, 1965.

73. Wilfrid Mellers. *Music in a New Found Land.* Alfred A. Knopf, New York, 1965, pp. 169–177.

74. Ray Ellsworth. "CRI Explores the Universe of Harry Partch." *The American Record Guide,* March, 1965, pp. 606–608. Illus.

75. Peter Yates. *Arts & Architecture,* July, 1966. Review of *Petals* performance.

76. William W. Austin. *Music in the Twentieth Century.* W. W. Norton & Co., New York, 1966.

77. Gilbert Chase. *America's Music.* McGraw-Hill Co., New York, 1966, pp. 585–587.

78. Peter Yates. *Twentieth Century Music.* Pantheon Books, New York, 1967, pp. 297–300, 347–348.

79. Wilfrid Mellers. *Caliban Reborn.* Harper & Row, New York, 1967, pp. 133–135.

80. Paul Earls. "Harry Partch: Verses in Preparation for 'Delusion of the Fury.'" *Anuario—Yearbook,* Inter-American Institute for Musical Research, Tulane University, vol. 3 (1967), pp. 1–32. Illus.

81. Arthur Woodbury. "Harry Partch: Corporeality and Monophony." *Source, Music of the Avant Garde,* July, 1967, pp. 91-113. Accompanied by Partch's first published score. Illus.

82. Theodore Strongin. "Have You Ever Heard a Gubagubi?" *The New York Times,* February 25, 1968. Illus.

83. Heuwell Tircuit. *San Francisco Examiner & Chronicle,* May 19, 1968, p. 34. Review of *Petals* record. Illus.

84. Martin Bernheimer. "Partch: A Latter-Day Don Quixote." *The New York Times,* September 8, 1968. Illus.

85. Theodore Strongin. *The New York Times,* September 9, 1968, p. 58. Review of Whitney Museum program.

86. Carmen Moore. *The Village Voice* (New York), September 12, 1968. Review of Whitney Museum program. Illus.

87. Winthrop Sargent. "Musical Events." *The New Yorker,* September 21, 1968, pp. 137–138. Review of Whitney Museum program.

88. Paul D. Zimmerman. "A Prophet Honored." *Newsweek,* September 23, 1968, p. 109. Illus.

89. Martin Bernheimer. "A Philosopher Seduced into Carpentry." *Los Angeles Times Calendar,* January 5, 1969, p. 28. Illus.

90. Camilla Snyder. "Harry Partch an Innovator." *Los Angeles Herald-Examiner,* January 5, 1969, p. E-1. Illus.

91. Martin Bernheimer. *Los Angeles Times,* January 11, 1969. Review of *Delusion* performance.

92. Winfred Blevins. "Partch's 'Delusion' Ritualistic Primitivism." *Los Angeles Herald-Examiner,* January 14, 1969. Illus.

93. Carl LaFong. "Notes from the Underground." *Record World,* January 25, 1969.

94. Lou Harrison. "Partch's Glorious New 'Delusion.'" *San Francisco Examiner & Chronicle,* January 26, 1969. Review of *Delusion* performance. Illus.

95. Peter G. Davis. "Composer Harry Partch—With Boo and Eucal Blossom." *High Fidelity,* January, 1969, pp. 30, 36.

96. Camilla Snyder. "Tempo." *Los Angeles Herald-Examiner,* March 2, 1969. Article on *Delusion* film.

97. Albert Goldberg. *Opera News,* March 8, 1969. Review of *Delusion* performance.

98. Irving Kolodin. "The Sound of Harry Partch." *Saturday Review,* May 31, 1969. Review of Columbia record. Illus.

99. "Sight and Sound." *McCall's,* June, 1969, p. 12. Review of Columbia record.

100. Gilbert Chase. "Toward a Total Musical Theatre." *Arts in Society,* Spring-Summer 1969, pp. 25–37. Illus.

101. William Flanagan. *Stereo Review,* July 1969, p. 90. Review of Columbia record. Illus.

102. Karen Monson. "Harry Partch: California's Musical Maverick." *Coast FM & Fine Arts,* August, 1969, pp. 12–17. Illus.

103. Paul Hertelendy. "Harry Partch—Rebel Composer." Oakland Tribune, November 23, 1969. Illus.

104. Anthony Hiss. "Hobo Concerto." *The New Yorker,* February 7, 1970. 1970.

105. Dean Drummond. "Ear Liberation—the Music of Harry Partch." *Protos* (Los Angeles), November, 1970. Illus.

106. *Baker's Biographical Dictionary of Musicians.* 5th edition with 1971 supplement. Nicolas Slonimsky, ed. G. Schirmer, New York, 1971.

107. Ken Spiker. "Harry Partch." *Earth* (San Francisco) March, 1971.

108. Larry Stempel. *Saturday Review,* November 27, 1971. Review of *Delusion* records. Illus.

109. John Rockwell. *Los Angeles Times,* December 5, 1971. Review of *Delusion* records. Illus.

110. Don Heckman. *The New York Times,* December 12, 1971. Review of *Delusion* records. Illus.

111. Alfred Frankenstein. *High Fidelity,* January, 1972. Review of *Delusion* records.

112. "Harry Partch, Rebel." *BMI: The Many Worlds of Music* (monthly), February, 1972, pp. 16–17.

113. Eric Salzman. "A Visit With Harry Partch." *Stereo Review,* March, 1972. Illus.

114. Heuwell Tircuit. "A Flawless 'Delusion' of 20th Century Music." *This World (San Francisco Chronicle),* March 12, 1972.

115. David W. Moore. "Delusion of the Fury." *American Record Guide,* July, 1972, pp. 544–547. Review of *Delusion* records. Illus.

116. Edward Tatnall Canby. *Audio,* August, 1972, pp. 55-56. Review of *Delusion* records.

117. Bruce Parsons. "Former Madisonian Harry Partch Does Strange Things With Music." University of Wisconsin *Daily Cardinal,* Sec. 2, December 8, 1972. Interview with Harry Partch.

118. Darrell E. Flugg. *Film News,* Vol. 30, No. 1, February, 1973, p. 15. Review of film *Delusion of the Fury.*

B. *Reviews of the First Edition of* Genesis of a Music

119. *Musical Courier,* May 15, 1949, p. 27.

120. *Etude,* August, 1949, p. 467 .

121. Keith McGary. "Music as Challenge." *Antioch Review,* Fall, 1949, pp. 421–423.

122. *Musical America,* vol. 69, no. 1 (1949), p. 31.

123. Charles W. Hughes. *Journal of Aesthetics and Art Criticism,* vol. 8 (1949), pp. 273–274.

124. James M. Barbour. *Musical Quarterly,* January, 1950, pp. 131–135.

125. *The Book Exchange* (London), January, 1950, p. 11.

126. *Saturday Review,* January 7, 1950.

127. *Violins,* May-June, 1950, p. 181.

128. Charles Warren Fox. *Music Library Association Notes,* June, 1950, pp. 432–433.

129. "Musicology." *Times Literary Supplement* (London), September 29, 1950.

130. William K. Archer. "Microtonality Revisited." *Etc: A Review of General Semantics,* Winter, 1951, pp. 146–150.

131. Jacques Barzun. *"Genesis of a Music* by Harry Partch." In *American Panorama,* Eric Larrabee, ed. New York University Press, New York, 1957, p. 262.

C. *Writings by Harry Partch*

132. "A New Instrument." *Musical Opinion* (London), June, 1935, pp. 764–765. Illus.

133. "Bach and Temperament." *The Carmel* (California) *Pine Cone,* July 18, 1941.

134. "The Kithara." *The Carmel Pine Cone,* September 19, 1941. Illus.

135. "Barstow." *The Carmel Pine Cone,* September 26, 1941. Illus.

136. "W. B. Yeats." *The Carmel Pine Cone,* October 17, 1941. Illus.

137. "Show Horses in the Concert Ring." *Circle* (Berkeley), Summer, 1948, pp. 43–51. Illus.

138. "No Barriers." *Impulse* (San Francisco) , Summer, 1952, pp. 9–10.

139. "The Ancient Magic." *Music Journal,* June-July, 1959, pp. 16, 45–47. Illus.

140. "Symposium." *Arts in Society,* vol. 2, no. 3 (1963), pp. 22–23. Illus.

D. *Published Scores of Harry Partch*

141. "A Somewhat Spoof." *Soundings,* April 1972. (Peter Garland, 15102 Polk St., Sylmar, Ca. 91342)

142. *And on the Seventh Day Petals Fell in Petaluma. Source,* vol. 1, no. 2 (July, 1967). (*Source,* 2101 22nd St., Sacramento, Ca. 95818)

143. *Barstow. Soundings,* April 1972. (Peter Garland, 15102 Polk St., Sylmar, Ca. 91342)

# Recordings and Films

---

*Recordings*

Although a number of acetate records of my music were made during the years 1942–1945, and although most of the masters remain in fairly good condition, these are not listed. The pressed recordings fall into three categories—private, GATE 5, commercial. The private recordings are at 78 rpm, while the others are long-playing records. All except No. 7 are twelve-inch records. Only the last three commercial recordings are stereo.

*Private Recordings*

1. *U.S. Highball* (1946). GME Recording (Warren E. Gilson), Madison, Wisconsin. Three records, six sides. Out of print.

2. *Ten Settings of Lyrics by Li Po* (1947). GME Recording (Warren E. Gilson), Madison, Wisconsin. Two records, four sides. Out of print.

3. *Partch Compositions* (1951). Issued by Lauriston C. Marshall, Berkeley, California. Includes a discourse and sample passages, *The Letter, Dark Brother,* and eight of the *Eleven Intrusions.* Five records, ten sides. Out of print.

*GATE 5 Recordings*

In a sense, these were also private recordings. The first two were initiated as subscription records—they were paid for even before rehearsals had started, and indeed had to be if the project was to succeed. None of the GATE 5 records were listed in catalogs, but they were widely reviewed and continued to sell by mail order for over nineteen years. The back page of the photo supplement that accompanied the records beginning in 1957 follows:

## IN EXPLANATION OF "GATE 5"

There has been some misapprehension regarding the source of this term. GATE 5 was not picked out of a hatful of the most unlikely names, although there are probably worse ways. During the recent war Sausalito—on San Francisco Bay—became the site of one of those feverishly built shipyards and upon termination of the war the property went into private hands. The shipyard had five gates, and the sign: GATE 5, was still to be seen when Harry Partch moved his instruments into a building previously used by the Army at the entrance to it. After the war, a number of people took over converted ferries, barges, and houses on stilts in this area, which is known locally as GATE 5. There is also a GATE 5 bus stop. Beyond the prosaic fact that Partch lived, wrote music, built instruments, organized and rehearsed ensembles, and manufactured records here, there is the more intriguing circumstance that GATE 5 carries an occult meaning in sundry ancient mythologies. In ancient pictographs the city, the center of culture, has four pedestrian gates. These are tangible; they can be seen; physical entrances can be shown. But the city also has a fifth gate, which cannot be shown because it is not tangible, and can be entered only in a metaphysical way. This is the gate to illusion.

The last edition of the Gate 5 records was brought out in 1962, with the six records labeled Issues A-B-C-D-E-F. All are out of print.

4. *Plectra and Percussion Dances* (1953). Sausalito ensemble. Reissued 1957, 1962 (Issue C).

5. *Oedipus* (1954). Sausalito ensemble. Originally a two-record set. Excerpted for one record and reissued in 1957 and again in 1962 (Issue D).

6. *The Bewitched* (1957). University of Illinois ensemble. Originally a two-record set. Excerpted for one record and reissued in 1962 (Issue E).

7. *U.S. Highball* (1958). Ensemble in Evanston, Illinois. Originally one ten-inch record, this recording was reissued in 1962 as a part of *The Wayward* (see below).

8. *Revelation in the Courthouse Park* (1961). University of Illinois ensemble. Excerpted for one record and issued in 1962 (Issue F).

9. *The Wayward* (1962; Issue B) Consists of *U. S. Highball* (recorded 1958), *The Letter* (recorded 1950), and *Ulysses at the Edge* (recorded 1958).

10. *Thirty Years of Lyrical and Dramatic Music* (1962; Issue A). Con-

sists of one excerpt and various short pieces composed between 1931 and 1961 and recorded at various times and places.

*Commercial Recordings*

11. *From the Music of Harry Partch* (1964). Composers Recordings, Inc. (CRI 193). Compiled from GATE 5 Issues A, B, C, and E (see above). Consists of *Castor and Pollux, The Letter, Windsong* (excerpted), and Scene 10 and the Epilogue of *The Bewitched.*

12. *And on the Seventh Day Petals Fell in Petaluma* (1967). Composers Recordings, Inc. (CRI 213 USD). Stereo. Performed by a Los Angeles ensemble.

13. *The World of Harry Partch* (1969). Columbia Stereo MS 7207. Consists of *Daphne of the Dunes, Barstow,* and *Castor and Pollux.* This was recorded following the Whitney Museum program in September of 1968 (see Appendix III).

14. *Delusion of the Fury—A Ritual of Dream and Delusion* (1971). Columbia Stereo M2–30576 (three records). Two records of the complete work plus one discussion-demonstration record. Performed by a Los Angeles ensemble and conducted by Danlee Mitchell.

15. *New Music For Trumpet* (1972). Orion Stereo ORS 7294. Included on this recording is a new performance of *Ulysses at the Edge,* by a San Diego ensemble. Jack Logan, Trumpet Soloist.

*Films*

Six of the eight films listed below were produced by Madeline Tourtelot and four are distributed by Grove Press, New York. The exceptions are the TV film (No. 6), and the Whitelight-Tantalus film (No. 8).

1. The soundtrack for *Windsong* (1958), the story of Daphne and Apollo in the sand dunes on the eastern shore of Lake Michigan. Black and white. 25 minutes.

  *Brussels International Experimental Festival, 1958*

2. *Music Studio—Harry Partch* (1958). Shows the making of the soundtrack for *Windsong*—the instruments, the player (Partch), with audio overdubs. Color. 18 minutes.

  *Contemporary Arts Festival, University of Illinois, 1959*
  *American Festival, New York, 1959*
  *Edinburgh Festival, 1959*

3. *Rotate the Body* (1961) . Filming of an exhibition of gymnasts at the University of Illinois. Script and music by Partch (see footnote 5, Chapter 14, and Appendix III). Color. 14 minutes.

    *Edinburgh International Festival, 1961*
    *American Festival, New York, 1962*
    *Karlovy Vary, Czechoslovakia, 1962*

4. *Revelation in the Courthouse Park* (1961). Produced by Madeline Tourtelot for WILL-TV, University of Illinois. A totally inadequate film representation of my concept of integrated theater. Not released. Black and white. About one hour.

5. *U.S. Highball* (1968). The filming began with shots of the ensemble in action in Evanston, Illinois, in 1958, and was completed later along the route of that trip. Color and black and white. 30 minutes.

    *Belgium International Experimental Festival, 1963*

6. *The Music of Harry Partch* (1968). KPBS-TV (NET), Channel 15, San Diego. Producer: Peter Kaye. A filming of *Daphne of the Dunes* on the lawn in front of the Art Gallery at the University of California at San Diego. Interview included. Shown by fifteen NET stations in the western states and Hawaii, July 22, 1969. Color. 28 minutes.

7. *Delusion of the Fury* (1969) . Filmed after performances at the University of California at Los Angeles (see Appendix III) . Color. About one hour.

8. *The Dreamer That Remains: A Portrait of Harry Partch* (1972-73). Produced by Whitelight-Tantalus Productions; 1040 N. Las Palmas Ave., Los Angeles. Directed by Stephen Pouliot. Music written especially for this film—*The Dreamer That Remains, A Study in Loving* (see Appendix III) . Color. 28 minutes.

# Chronology of Instruments

Most of the instruments were built, initiated in some way, or rebuilt, in California, in places from the fairly far north to the far south. In chronological order, these are:

| | |
|---|---|
| San Francisco | Sausalito |
| Santa Rosa | Petaluma |
| Pasadena | Del Mar |
| Santa Barbara | Van Nuys |
| Los Angeles | Venice |
| Carmel | San Diego |
| Gualala | Encinitas |
| Oakland | |

The only other places significantly related to this work are, chronologically:

| | |
|---|---|
| New Orleans | Madison, Wisconsin |
| London | Yellow Springs, Ohio |
| Chicago | Evanston, Illinois |
| Ithaca, New York | Champaign-Urbana, Illinois |

1925– Experiments begun in San Francisco with paper coverings for finger-
1926 boards of a violin and a viola. Markings for Just Intonation, mathematically determined, were on the coverings. A string quartet based on this idea followed, but was destroyed in 1930.

1928 *Adapted Viola.* A new and lengthened fingerboard completed in Santa Rosa. Attached to my viola by a violin-maker in New Orleans, 1930.

1933    Model of an experimental keyboard made in Pasadena. Later named *The Ptolemy* (see below).

1934    *Adapted Guitar,* now called *Adapted Guitar I.* Its fingerboard fitted with frets in Just Intonation. Rebuilt many times, most significantly at Carmel, 1941.

1934–   *The Ptolemy.* Reed organ with the keyboard designed in 1933 built
1935    in London and shipped to Santa Barbara, where it was soon abandoned in a garage. Fate unknown. (The abandonment was not intended; eight more years of hoboing lay ahead.)

1938    *Kithara,* later called *Kithara I.* Built in an adult education woodshop in a Los Angeles high school. Major rebuildings: Carmel (1941), Ithaca (1943), Madison (1945), Urbana (1959). The last, when the tuning was changed totally, was the most important.

1940    A new model of *The Ptolemy,* with a complete case, built in Los Angeles, but abandoned a year later in Carmel. Fate unknown.

1941    *Chromelodeon.* The first, adapted and tuned in Chicago, using the reeds from *The Ptolemy.* This was the basis for all subsequent Chromelodeons, and the only practical solution for a composer without huge financing. It employed the usual 7-White-5-Black keyboard (really quite impractical for the system of music expounded herein), but with all reeds retuned.

1945    *New Chromelodeon,* now called *Chromelodeon I,* adapted and tuned at Madison. Rebuilt and retuned at Gualala, 1949.

1945    *Harmonic Canon,* now called *Harmonic Canon I.* Built at Madison with 44 strings; totally reconceived and rebuilt at Urbana, 1959.

1945    *Guitar I.* Smooth fingerboard and electronic amplification. Used in several recordings. Tuning of the earlier Guitar (as rebuilt in Carmel, 1941) employed. Given to someone in Sausalito in 1956 to hold for me. Fate unknown.

1945    *Guitar II.* Adapted in Madison with ten strings. Still called *Guitar II.*

1946    *Diamond Marimba.* Built in Madison. Most of the blocks replaced with Pernambuco wood, Gualala, 1949–1950.

1946   *Old Chromelodeon II.* A chapel organ adapted and retuned in Madison. Given an unusual keyboard (see Diagram 15, p. 000). The solid walnut case was abandoned in Gualala in 1951. The keyboard was saved but was loaned to someone in Venice in 1966. Fate of both unknown.

1949–   *Bass Marimba.* Built at Gualala. Rebuilt at Oakland, 1951, and all
1950   Sitka-spruce blocks replaced at Encinitas, 1971.

1950   *Cloud-Chamber Bowls.* Built at Gualala. Rebuilt at Oakland, 1951. Bowls replaced many times following breakage.

1950   *Spoils of War.* Built at Gualala. Various sounds added many times—Oakland, Urbana, Petaluma, Van Nuys, 1951–1965.

1950   *New Chromelodeon II.* Rebuilt and retuned in Sausalito, 1954 with unsatisfactory results. Satisfactory adaptation and tuning accomplished at Urbana, 1959.

1951   *Marimba Eroica.* Built in Oakland, with vertical redwood blocks. Reconceived in Sausalito, 1954, using horizontal Sitka-spruce blocks and new resonators. Improved at Champaign-Urbana, 1960, and again at Petaluma, 1963.

1953   *Surrogate Kithara.* Built at Sausalito.

1953   *Harmonic Canon II (Castor and Pollux).* Built at Sausalito, using the base of *Harmonic Canon I* (which was given a new Plexiglas base in Champaign-Urbana, 1959).

1954   *Kithara II.* Built at Sausalito. Improved at Urbana, 1959.

1955   *Boo I.* Built at Sausalito. Rebuilt at Yellow Springs, 1957, and—more importantly—at Petaluma, 1963.

1958   *Bloboy.* Built at Evanston.

1959–   *Crychord.* Built at Champaign-Urbana. Standard added in 1961.
1960

1963   *Zymo-Xyl.* Built at Petaluma.

1963   *Mazda Marimba.* Built at Petaluma.

1964   *Gourd Tree.* Built at Del Mar. The first instrument employing eucalyptus boughs as important structural elements.

1964   *Eucal Blossom.* Begun in Del Mar, although not completed until 1967 at San Diego. Another instrument with a structural eucalyptus bough.

1965   *Quadrangularis Reversum.* Built at Van Nuys, using eucalyptus boughs for the two standards. The original hormigo wood of the blocks, from Guatemala, was replaced with padouk, from Africa, in 1971 at Encinitas, and gives a much-increased ring-time.

1965   *Cone Gongs.* Added to the *Gourd Tree* at Venice.

1965   *Harmonic Canon III (Blue Rainbow).* Built at Venice.

1966   *Surrogate Kithara.* Two new canons, with the tuning required in *Petals* and *Delusion,* made at Venice.

1966   *Koto.* Received as a gift at Venice. (An earlier koto, also a gift, was received at Sausalito in 1956 and used in *The Bewitched.*)

1966– *Ektaras.* Two built at San Diego.
  1967

1967   *Small Hand Instruments.* Nearly all of those not given to me were made at San Diego.

1971   *Boo II.* Built at Encinitas.

1972   *New Harmonic Canon I.* Built at Encinitas with blue-tinted Plexiglas base.

1972   *New Kithara I.* Built at Encinitas.

1972   *Mbira Bass Dyad.* Built at Encinitas. An experiment that is far from complete.

*Works Cited and Index*

# Works Cited

APEL, WILLI. *Harvard Dictionary of Music.* Harvard University Press, Cambridge, 1944.

ARISTOTLE. *Politica,* translated by Benjamin Jowett (*The Works of Aristotle,* Ross ed., vol. 10: *Politica, Oeconomica, Atheniensium Respublica*). Oxford, Clarendon Press, 1921.

Aristotelian *Problemata,* translated by E. S. Forster (*The Works of Aristotle,* Ross ed., vol. 7). Oxford, Clarendon Press, 1927.

BARBOUR, JAMES MURRAY. "Equal Temperament: Its History from Ramis (1482) to Rameau (1737)." Manuscript thesis in library of Cornell University, Ithaca. 1932.

BARZUN, JACQUES. *Darwin, Marx, Wagner.* Little, Brown and Co., Boston, 1941.

———— *Teacher in America.* Little, Brown and Co., Boston, 1945.

BERLIOZ, HECTOR. *Memoirs.* Alfred A. Knopf, New York, 1932.

———— *Selections from His Letters, and Aesthetic, Humorous, and Satirical Writings.* Henry Holt and Co., New York, 1879.

BINGHAM, W. VAN DYKE. "Studies in Melody." *The Psychological Review Monograph Supplements,* vol. 12, no. 3 (January, 1910).

BLITZSTEIN, MARC. "Music in the Theatre." John Gassner, *Producing the Play,* 470–475. Dryden Press, New York, 1941.

BOSANQUET, R. H. M. *Elementary Treatise on Musical Intervals and Temperament.* 1876.

BROWN, COLIN. *Music in a Sound* and *Music in Figures* (*Music in Common Things,* Parts I and II, respectively, paged consecutively). Wm. Collins Sons, Ltd., London, 1885.

BUCK, PERCY C. *Acoustics for Musicians.* Oxford, Clarendon Press, 1918.

BURNEY, CHARLES. *A General History of Music.* Harcourt, Brace and Co., New York, 1935.

BUSONI, FERRUCCIO. *Sketch of a New Esthetic of Music.* Schirmer, New York, 1911.

CHAVEZ, CARLOS. *Toward a New Music.* W. W. Norton and Co., Inc., New York, 1937.

CLEMENTS, E. *Introduction to the Study of Indian Music.* Longmans, Green and Co., London, 1913.

COMBARIEU, JULES. *Music—Its Laws and Evolution.* D. Appleton and Co., New York, 1910.

COWELL, HENRY. *New Musical Resources.* Alfred A. Knopf, New York, 1930.

DAVY, CHARLES. *Letters, Addressed Chiefly to a Young Gentleman . . . Including a Translation of Euclid's Section of the Canon,* vol. 2. Printed for the author by J. Rackham, Bury St. Edmond's, 1787.

DURANT, WILL. *The Life of Greece.* Simon and Schuster, New York, 1939.

ELLIS, ALEXANDER J. "On the Musical Scales of Various Nations." *Journal of the Society of Arts*, 33: 485–527 (March 27, 1885.).

FARMER, H. G. *Historical Facts for the Arabian Musical Influence.* Wm. Reeves, London, 1930.

FLETCHER, HARVEY. *Speech and Hearing.* D. Van Nostrand Co., Inc., New York, 1929.

FOX-STRANGWAYS, A. H. "Whence? Whither?" *The Observer* (London), March 11, 1934.

GILMAN, LAWRENCE. *Debussy's Pelléas et Mélisande.* G. Schirmer, New York, 1907.

*Grove's Dictionary of Music and Musicians.* Macmillan, New York, 1935.

GUEDALLA, PHILIP. *Supers & Supermen.* G. P. Putnam's Sons, New York, 1924.

HATHERLEY, S. G. *A Treatise on Byzantine Music.* Wm. Reeves, London, 1892.

HAWKINS, SIR JOHN. *A General History of the Science and Practice of Music,* 2 vols., paged consecutively. Novello, Ewer and Co., London, 1875.

HAYDON, GLEN. *Introduction to Musicology.* Prentice Hall, Inc., New York, 1941.

HELMHOLTZ, HERMANN L. F. VON. *On the Sensations of Tone as a Physiological Basis for the Theory of Music,* translated by Alexander J. Ellis. Longmans, Green and Co., London, 1885.

HENDERSON, W. J. *Some Forerunners of Italian Opera.* Henry Holt and Co., New York, 1911.

HERZOG, GEORGE. "Speech-Melody and Primitive Music." *Musical Quarterly,* 20: 452–466 (1934).

HINDEMITH, PAUL. *The Craft of Musical Composition,* vol. 1. Associated Music Publishers, Inc., New York, 1942.

HOPE, ROBERT CHARLES. *Medieval Music: An Historical Sketch.* Elliot Stock, London, 1894.

HORNBOSTEL, E. M. VON. "Musikalische Tonsysteme." *Handbuch der Physik,* vol. 8, *Akustik,* 425–449. Julius Springer, Berlin, 1927.

HUGHES, DOM ANSELM. "Theoretical Writers on Music up to 1400." *Oxford History of Music,* Introductory Volume. 1929.

JEANS, SIR JAMES. *Science and Music.* Macmillan, New York, 1937.

JOHNSON, C. W. L. *Musical Pitch—the Measurement of Intervals among the Ancient Greeks.* Johns Hopkins University, 1896.

KINKELDEY, OTTO. "The Harmonic Sense: Its Evolution and Its Destiny." *Papers and Proceedings of the Music Teachers' National Association,* 18: 9–26 (1923). Hartford, 1924.

KREHBIEL, H. E. "Chinese Music." *Century Magazine,* 41(N.S.19): 449–457 (January, 1891).

KŘENEK, ERNST. *Music Here and Now.* W. W. Norton and Co., Inc., New York, 1939.

LAWRENCE, D. H. *Phoenix: the Posthumous Papers of D. H. Lawrence.* Viking, New York, 1936.

LEUBA, JAMES H. *God or Man?* Henry Holt and Co., New York, 1933.

LI PO. *The Works of Li Po, the Chinese Poet*, translated by Shigeyoshi Obata. Dutton, New York, 1928.

LLOYD, LLEWELLYN S. *Music and Sound*. Oxford, 1937.

——— *A Musical Slide Rule*. Oxford, 1938.

LOCKSPEISER, EDWARD. *Debussy*. J. M. Dent and Sons, Ltd., London, 1936.

LOMBARD, F. A. *An Outline History of the Japanese Drama*. G. Allen and Unwin, Ltd., London, 1928.

McNAUGHT, W. *Modern Music and Musicians*. Novello and Co., Ltd., London, 1937.

MEKEEL, H. SCUDDER. "Race Relations." *Mental Hygiene*, 29: 177–189 (April, 1945.)

MEYER, MAX F. *An Introduction to the Mechanics of the Inner Ear* (*University of Missouri Studies*, vol. 2, no. 1). 1907.

——— *The Musician's Arithmetic* (*University of Missouri Studies*, vol. 4, no. 1). 1929. Appendix 6, pp. 105–117, is an exposition of "Chinese Scale Theories," by K. C. Hsiao.

——— "Unscientific Methods in Musical Esthetics." *Journal of Philosophy, Psychology, and Scientific Methods*, 1(1904): 705–715.

MILLER, DAYTON C. *Anecdotal History of the Science of Sound*. Macmillan, New York, 1935.

——— *The Science of Musical Sounds*. Macmillan, New York, 1922.

——— *Sound Waves: Their Shape and Speed*. Macmillan, New York, 1937.

MOORE, HENRY T. "The Genetic Aspect of Consonance and Dissonance." *Psychological Monographs*, vol. 17, no. 2 (September, 1914).

MYERS, ROLLO H. *Modern Music, Its Aims and Tendencies*. Kegan Paul, Trench, Trübner and Co., Ltd., London, [1923?].

NAUMANN, EMIL. *History of Music*, translated by F. Praeger, vol. 1. Cassell and Co., Ltd., London, 1886.

NEWMAN, ERNEST. *Hugo Wolf*. John Lane Company, New York, 1909.

NIETZSCHE, FRIEDRICH. *Ecce Homo and the Birth of Tragedy*. Modern Library, New York, 1927.

OBATA, SHIGEYOSHI, translator, see LI PO.

OGDEN, ROBERT MORRIS. *Hearing*. Harcourt, Brace and Co., New York, 1924.

OVERMYER, GRACE. "Quarter-Tones—and Less." *The American Mercury*, 12: 207–210 (October, 1927).

PERRETT, WILFRID. *Some Questions of Musical Theory*. W. Heffer and Sons, Ltd., Cambridge, 1926.

PLATO. *The Dialogues of Plato*, B. Jowett ed., vol. 3 [*Republic, Timaeus, Critias*]. Oxford, 1924.

——— *The Dialogues of Plato*, B. Jowett ed., vol. 5 [*Laws*]. Oxford, 1924.

REHDER, HELMUT. *Nietzsche and His Place in German Literature, 1844–1944*. Reprinted from *Monatshefte für Deutschen Unterricht* (Madison, Wisconsin), vol. 26 (December, 1944).

RICH, GILBERT J. "A Study of Tonal Attributes." *American Journal of Psychology*, 30: 121–164 (1919).

RICHARD, MRS. TIMOTHY. "Chinese Music." *East of Asia Magazine* (Shanghai), vol. 1, part 4: 301–314 (December, 1902).

RIEMANN, HUGO. *The Nature of Harmony*, translated by J. C. Fillmore. Theo. Presser, Philadelphia, 1887.

RIESEMANN, OSKAR V. *Moussorgsky*. Tudor, New York, 1935.

SCHLESINGER, KATHLEEN. "Further Notes on Aristoxenus and Musical Intervals." *The Classical Quarterly*, 27: 88–96 (April, 1933).

———— *The Greek Aulos*. Methuen and Co., Ltd., London, 1939.

———— "The Greek Foundations of the Theory of Music." *The Musical Standard*, 27: 23–24, 44–46, 62–63, 96–98, 109–110, 134–136, 162–164, 177–178, 197–198, 208–209; 28: 31–32, 44–45 (1926).

———— *Is European Musical Theory Indebted to the Arabs?* Harold Reeves, London, 1925.

SCHOLES, PERCY A. *Oxford Companion to Music*. Oxford, 1938.

SCHÖNBERG, ARNOLD. "Problems of Harmony." *Modern Music*, 11:167–187 (May-June, 1934).

SEASHORE, CARL E. *Psychology of Music*. McGraw-Hill Book Co., Inc., New York, 1938.

SHIRLAW, MATTHEW. *The Theory of Harmony* (Handbooks for Musicians, edited by Ernest Newman). Novello and Co., Ltd., London, and the H. W. Gray Co., New York. First published in 1917.

SMITH, SIR WILLIAM. *Dictionary of Greek and Roman Biography and Mythology*. Chas. C. Little and James Brown, Boston, 1849.

SPENGLER, OSWALD. *The Decline of the West: Form and Actuality*, translated by Charles Francis Atkinson. Alfred A. Knopf, New York, 1945.

THOMSON, VIRGIL. *The Musical Scene*. Alfred A. Knopf, New York, 1945.

———— *The State of Music*. Wm. Morrow and Co., New York, 1939.

TIPPLE, ESTHER WATSON, and FRYE, ROYAL MERRILL. *A Graphic Introduction to the Harmon*. Privately printed, 1942.

TORR, CECIL. "Greek Music." *Oxford History of Music*, Introductory Volume. 1929.

VAN DEN BORREN, CHARLES. "The Mystery of Faux-Bourdon Solved." *The Musical Times* (London), April 1, 1929.

WAGNER, RICHARD. *Prose Works*, translated by William A. Ellis, vol. 2. Kegan Paul, Trench, Trübner and Co., Ltd., 1907.

WALTER, BRUNO. *Gustav Mahler*, translated by James Galston, with biographical sketch by Ernst Křenek. Greystone Press, New York, 1941.

WELLESZ, EGON. *Arnold Schönberg*. J. M. Dent and Sons, Ltd., London, 1925.

YASSER, JOSEPH. *A Theory of Evolving Tonality*. American Library of Musicology. New York, 1932.

YEATS, WILLIAM BUTLER. *Plays and Controversies*. Macmillan, London, 1923.

ZARLINO, GIOSEFFE. *Le Istitutione Harmoniche*. Venice, 1562.

# Additional Works Cited
## Second Edition

*African Voices,* Peggy Rutherford comp. and ed. Grosset & Dunlap, New York, 1958.

CARROLL, LEWIS. *Alice's Adventures in Wonderland* and *Through the Looking Glass.* Modern Library, New York, 1946.

EARLS, PAUL. "Harry Partch: Verses in Preparation for 'Delusion of the Fury.'" *Annuario—Yearbook,* Inter-American Institute for Musical Research, Tulane University, 3 (1967), 1–32.

JOYCE, JAMES. *Finnegan's Wake.* Viking Press, New York, 1939

MOTLEY, WILLARD. *Knock on Any Door.* Appleton-Century-Crofts, Inc., New York, 1947.

RIMBAUD, ARTHUR. *A Season in Hell.* Louise Varese, trans. New Directions, New York, 1945.

WALEY, ARTHUR. *The Noh Plays of Japan.* Grove Press, New York, n.d.

————. *Japanese Poetry, the "Uta."* Lund Humphries & Co., Ltd., London, 1946.

WOLFE, THOMAS. *Beyond the Hills.* Harper and Brothers, New York, 1935.

YEATS, W. B. *Sophocles' King Oedipus, A Version for the Modern Stage.* The Macmillan Co., New York, 1928.

YOUNG, ELLA. *Marzilian and Other Poems.* Harbison & Harbison, Oceano, California, 1938.

*Index*

# Index

Abbey Theater, needs of, 38–39
Abdulqadir, 373, 404, 426. *See also* Arabic theory
Abstract music, assumed nobility of, 5; defined, 8–9; language and, 12n, 15n; in China and Greece, 13; in Christian era, 15–17; Germanic expression, 16n, 17, 18n, 24n; "thinking" in, 17; in opera, 23, 24; in Moussorgsky's time, 33; result of concert music, 43, 44; in Wagner's works, 46; reign of, 48–49; and technicians, 49–50; current fate, 50; words translated by, 51; in concert halls, 53–54, 215; and interpreters, 55. *See also* Corporeal music
Abstraction, synonym for music, 18n; and paintings, 49, 54. *See also* Abstract music
*a Cappella* singing, *see* Singers
Acousticians, Fox-Strangways on, 192, 193; ambiguous usage by, 412n
Acoustics, *see* Science of musical sound
Adapted Guitars, confusion regarding their roman numeral designations, 203; description and tunings, 205–206
Adapted Viola, fingerboard and tuning, 200–201; manner of playing, 201–202; computations for, 201; notation for, 202
Alfarabi, on aims of theorist, 371
*And on the Seventh Day Petals Fell in Petaluma,* 348–350
Antiphony, non-Corporeal pattern, 14. *See also* Ecclesiastical chant
Approximation, Aristoxenus' theory of, 365–366; long disputed, 371; germination of, 374; decried by Zarlino, 379; in modern theory, 382. *See also* Temperament
Arabic theory, link to Europe, 370–371, 403–404; Arithmetical Proportion of, 390; seventeen-tone scale, 247, 404, 428–429, 430; "quarter-tones" in, 425–426
Archicembalo, *see* Vicentino
Archytas, ratios of 5, 7, and 9 used by, 91, 92, 172 (*see also* Enharmonic genus); diatonic genus of, 174; use of small-number ratios by, 364–365

Aristotelian *Problems,* recitation, 10
Aristotle, and "concert" music, 10, 56; on food consumed at drama, 54n; digital facility and "artists," 57
Aristoxenus, approximations of, 365–366; cited by Galilei, 380
Arithmetical Proportion, defined, 69; in modern theory, 90, 382; in division of interval, 103; in genera, 171, 173; in Ptolemaic scale, 174–176; in Terpander's scale, 178; ascribed to Pythagoras, 363; of Eratosthenes, 367, 371; long disputed, 371; and Harmonical Proportion, 378; advocated by Riemann, 390; in Greek harmoniai, 447–448. *See also* "Undertone series"; Utonality
Aron, Pietro, 376n. *See also* Meantone Temperament
"Artists," dexterity the criterion of, 4; and press agents, 55; and personality deterioration, 57
Atonality, and twelve-tone scale, 154n
"Augmented fourth," *see* "Tritone"
Aulos, Schlesinger's work with, 315n; harmoniai on, 447; "undertone series" on, 451–452

Babylon, records of theory lacking, 361; and Pythagoras, 363
Bach, J. S., symbol of Abstract music, 18n, 23, 24, 50; and Equal Temperament, 384, 413n, 433; and music history, 438
Bamboo pipe, Monophonic nature of, 361 *See also* Lü
Bamboo resonators, *see* Resonators
Barbour, James M., history of Equal Temperament, 375n, 384n; on Chinese "cents," 381n; on "modern" tunings, 383n
Bardi, Count, and Florentine coterie, 21–22
Barth, Hans, "quartertone" piano of, 429
Barzun, Jacques, on Wagner, 28, 30–31; on transmutation of words, 51; on music educators, 51, 97

*503*

Organ, introduction of, 409. *See also* Keyboard, 7-White-5-Black

Oriental music, Berlioz on, 28–29; small intervals in, 122

Otonality, defined, 72; coexistent with Utonality, 88–89, 110, 455; in Tonality Diamonds, 110–111; 159, 160, 453–455; in 5 limit, 116; in 11 limit, 158–161; Ptolemaic Sequence in, 165; in guitars, 206; in color analogy, 214–215; in Kithara-Diamond Marimba hexads, 261, and *ethos*, 455. *See also* Tonality; Utonality

Öttingen, A. J. von, 389, 390. *See also* "Minor" triad

Overtone series, perceived by Mersenne, 71, 381–382; and Harmonical Proportion, 382; "minor" tonality in, 386; and enharmonic genus, 387; "major" scale in, 394; applied by Schönberg, Cowell, and Hindemith, 418–421; current theory and, 423, 424n, 427; Schlesinger's usage, 453, 455. *See also* "Major" tonality; Otonality

Painter, independence of, 193

Partials, and Arithmetical Proportion, 69; defined, 72; and ear, 87; and identities, 89. *See also* Overtone series

*Pelléas and Mélisande, see* Debussy, Claude

Pentatonic scale, just and Pythagorean, 103, 362, 403; of Olympos, 177–178, 214; on koto, 178; more than five senses, 417

"Perfect fifth," and "perfect fourth," 77, 82–83; tempered, 101, 135. *See also* Ratios: 3/2

"Perfect fourth," *see* Ratios: 4/3

Perpetual Tonal Descent and Ascent, 128, 129–131; placing ratios from, 131–132

Peri, Jacopo, opera "prototype" by, 22; singer defeats, 23; *Daphne* and Schütz, 35n

Perrett, Wilfrid, on 7 Identity, 93n, 120, 153–154, 163; summation tones, 161n; harmonizes enharmonic, 170–171, *Some Questions of Musical Theory*, 396, 446; "polyphonic" Just Intonation, 443–447; recommended, 456

Phase, like and opposite, 142–143; and consonance, 143; change of, 153

Phonodeik records, *see* Miller, Dayton C.

Phrygian *harmonia, see* Greek harmoniai

Piano, and ratios, 82–84; evolution and, 95; interval "equations" on, 135–136; tuning of, 179n. *See also* Keyboard, 7-White-5-Black

*Pierrot Lunaire, see* Schönberg, Arnold

Pioneer instruments, 137; "menance" of, 193

Pitch, 1/1–392 interpreted, 69

Pitch discrimination, test of, 121–122, 437n

"Plagal cadence," in ratios, 188

Plain-song, Greek music in, 15n. *See also* Ecclesiastical chant

Plato, words and music, 10–11, 33, 56; and cerebral reactions, 54; on "enharmonic" measurers, 171

*Plectra and Percussion Dances,* 324–331

Poetry, for Corporeal music, 8, 9; and print, 20. *See also* Spoken words

Poliziano, secular music-drama, 21

"Polyphonic" Just Intonation, on Brown's harmonium, 440–441; on Poole's and Perrett's keyboards, 443

Polyphony, and opera degeneration, 25

Polypythagoreanism, defined, 72, 425

Poole, H. W., and 7 Identities, 392, 443

Popular movements, intuitive desire in, 20, 52, 60, 407; and ecclesiastical chant, 49

Popular music, often Corporeal, 9, not colloquial, 58; and temperament, 423–424

Porphyry, Ptolemy's *Harmonics,* 368n; on tetrachord, 369

"Powerful Coterie," and Florentine, 32

Praetorius, *see* Clavicymbalum Universale

Primary ratios, 127, 155, 157, 158–159

Primary tonalities, in Tonality Diamond, 159; in color analogy, 215

Prime unity, defined, 72; under and over, 81; senses of, 113, 163. *See also* Unity

Primitive music, Abstract origin, 8

Program music, often Corporeal, 9

Progress, misconceptions regarding, 5–6, 383n

Proportion, axiom of, 80, 99. *See also* Small-number ratios

Prosody, and Abstract music, 50–51

Psaltery, *see* Koto

Psychologists, tests by, 121–122, 414, 415–416; terms of, 154n. *See also* Consonance

Ptolemaic Sequence, defined, 72–73; in Monophonic Fabric, 164–167; in voice parts, 256; groping for, 375–376; "natural" scale, 379; and lute fretting, 380; in overtones, 394; keyboard problems of, 409

Ptolemy, intervals recognized by, 92; ratios of 11 used by, 126–127, 369; genera of, 167, 169–170, 173–174; Arithmetical Proportion of, 174–176; Burney on, 176–177; on Aristoxeneans and Pythagoreans, 366–367, 368; and harmonic music, 369 (*see also* Ptolemaic Sequence); antecedent of Monophony, 388

Ptolemy keyboard, description of, 219

Pythagoras, as Monophonist, 71, 388; twelve "cycle" of, 73; "missionary" work of, 89; inter-

# Picture Credits

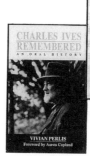